the AVOCADO PLANTATION

BOOM AND BUST IN THE AUSTRALIAN FILM INDUSTRY

DAVID STRATTON

M

First published 1990 by Pan Macmillan Publishers Australia
A division of Pan Books (Australia) Pty Limited
63–71 Balfour Street, Chippendale, Sydney

Stratton, David.
The avocado plantation: boom and bust in the
Australian film industry.

Includes index.
ISBN 0 7329 0250 9.

1. Motion pictures, Australian. 2. Motion picture
industry—Australia. I. Title.

791.43750994

Set in Bodoni and Berkeley Old Style
by Midland Typesetters
Printed in Hong Kong

Book design by Kate Slingo

• CONTENTS •

• ABBREVIATIONS •

ABC   Australian Broadcasting Corporation
AFC   Australian Film Commission
AFFDA   Australian Feature Film Directors Association
AFI   Australian Film Institute
AFTRS   Australian Film Television and Radio School (previously
         Australian Film and Television School)
ASDA   Australian Screen Directors Association
ATAEA   Australian Theatrical and Amusement Employees
         Association
CDB   Creative Development Branch of AFC
CFU   Commonwealth Film Unit (later known as Film Australia)
FGH   Film and General Holdings
FFC   Film Finance Corporation
FV   Film Victoria
GU   Greater Union
IFM   International Film Management
NIDA   National Institute of Dramatic Art
NSWFC   New South Wales Film Corporation
SAFC   South Australian Film Corporation
SPAA   Screen Producers Association of Australia
VFC   Victorian Film Corporation (later known as Film Victoria)

This book is for Susie
also for my father, Jim, and Mary, Giles and Nathan,
and in memory of Arch Nicholson (1941–1990).

• FOREWORD •

■
■

T he title of this book was suggested to me during a conversation
with writer-producer-director John Dingwall who, on more than
one occasion, referred to 'the avocado plantation' as a metaphor for
the Australian film industry in the 1980s, a period during which people
with taxable income to 'lose' in legitimate investments could choose
between various approved options—films and avocados among them.
It is, perhaps, a cynical title for a book about filmmaking in Australia
during the last decade, but, then, there is a profound air of cynicism
among many of the filmmakers.

The Avocado Plantation is intended to be a companion to my earlier
book, *The Last New Wave—The Australian Film Revival*, published
by Angus and Robertson in 1980. Like that book, this one is constructed
chiefly around interviews—a great many interviews with people from
different areas of the film industry.

Direct quotes used in the book are derived from these interviews.
Much of the material which is not subjective discussion of the films
themselves also comes from interviews. Most of these interviews were
conducted specifically for this book: a few others were originally
conducted for inclusion in *The Movie Show* on SBS-TV, and, in a few
cases, my colleague Margaret Pomeranz conducted the interview.

Wherever the date of a film is listed, this is the copyright date
as it appears on the film itself: Australian producers are sometimes
sloppy about this, so that, although, for example, *Dead Calm* was released
in the middle of 1989, the date, as it appears on the film's credits,
is 1988; so, for the purposes of this book, the film is a 1988 production.

There are a great many exclusions. This book attempts to deal with
every feature film made during the 80s, and a list (complete I hope)
of these films, with principal cast, credits and a brief synopsis, can

be found in the appendix: I hope this will be valuable for future reference. Films are included even if they did not get theatrical release, but films *made as* telemovies are not listed (unless they received some kind of theatrical or film festival exposure), and nor are mini-series, feature documentaries (*Vincent* is a special case), animated films or films running under an hour.

I realise that these omissions leave out a good deal of interesting and important material, but it has not been possible to include in these pages the categories mentioned above.

In an attempt to clarify the inevitable confusion between the two George Millers working as directors in the industry, I have described them in this way: George Miller (1) is the director of the *Mad Max* films and the founder (with Byron Kennedy) of Kennedy-Miller; George Miller (2) is the director of *The Man from Snowy River* and other, lesser, films. There are also two Paul Hogans in the industry, but it seems doubtful if the star of the *Crocodile Dundee* films would ever be confused with the director of *The Humpty Dumpty Man*. Similarly, it is unlikely that writer David Williamson would ever be confused with his camera operator namesake.

I would like to thank the following, whose time and memories have been invaluable: Gillian Armstrong, Antonia Barnard, Paul Barron, Bill Bennett, Bruce Beresford, Richard Brennan, Michael Brindley, Anne Britton, Bryan Brown, Anthony Buckley, Graham Burke, Geoff Burrowes, Geoff Burton, Ken Cameron, Jane Campion, Peter Carey, Jonathan Chissick, Graeme Clifford, Rosa Colosimo, Peter Corris, Paul Cox, Gary Day, Rolf De Heer, John Dingwall, Gosia Dobrowolska, John Duigan, David Elfick, Bob Ellis, Margaret Fink, Richard Franklin, Antony I. Ginnane, Brian Hannant, David Hannay, Chris Haywood, Paul Hogan, Paul Hogan, Frank Howson, Barry Humphries, Steve Jodrell, Gary L. Keady, Graham Kennedy, Craig Lahiff, Verity Lambert, Ray Lawrence, Genevieve Lemon, Ben Lewin, Joan Long, Patricia Lovell, Richard Lowenstein, Ross Matthews, George Miller (1), Vincent Monton, Philippe Mora, Scott Murray, Sue Murray, Leo McKern, Don McLennan, Sam Neill, Arch Nicholson, Phillip Noyce, George Ogilvie, Julia Overton, Irene Papas, David Parker, Michael Pattinson, Barry Peak, James Ricketson, Brian Rosen, Mark Rosenberg, Peter Sainsbury, Keith Salvat, Fred Schepisi, Roger Scholes, Carl Schultz, Yahoo Serious, Errol Sullivan, Nadia Tass, John Tatoulis, Sophia Turkiewicz, Deborah Unger, Stephen Wallace, Peter Weir, Bob Weis, David Williams, Kim Williams, David Williamson, Karl Zwicky.

In addition, I would like to acknowledge the advice and support of Mike Harris and also Jan Bunny, Lindsay Cullens, Steve Elliott, Tina Kaufman (and the *Filmnews* archives), Blake Murdoch, Scott Murray and *Cinema Papers*, Teresa Pitt, Margaret Pomeranz and Giles Stratton; and special thanks to Margarita Goodluck.

David Stratton
Sydney, January 1990

LA

DECADE

PRODIGIEUSE

■
■

*The taxation incentives were created for all the right reasons and used
in all the wrong ways. The quality of our films gradually deteriorated
during the 80's. Budgets went from $1 million to $6, 7, 8 or 9 million.
Accountants and lawyers became executive producers, and they only
cared about what money they'd get from the project. I haven't a common
language with people like that. I want to talk about the quality of
the film, but I'm dealing with people who see my project as another
avocado plantation.*

John Dingwall, *writer-producer-director*

*Nobody ever went into a movie theatre because the deal was right.
They went in because the emotion was right.*

Jeff Dowd, *Los Angeles-based producer and marketing authority*

T he 70s were a period of direct government involvement in the
Australian film industry; in the 80s, that involvement became
indirect. Tax concessions were used to encourage private investment
in Australian films, with the federal government's film body, the
Australian Film Commission (AFC), and sometimes the state film
corporations, used to 'top up'. They supported culturally worthy
projects, plus a variety of vital fringe film activities: film festivals,
the Australian Film Institute (AFI), publications, like the magazines
Cinema Papers and *Filmnews*, and script development.

There had been private investors before the tax concessions were
introduced, of course. Usually they were distributors. Hoyts, Roadshow
and, particularly, Greater Union (GU), under the enlightened
stewardship of David Williams, backed a great many Australian films
during the 70s. It is instructive to look at the financial structure of
two key films made in 1979: *My Brilliant Career* and *Breaker Morant*.

My Brilliant Career was produced by Margaret Fink on a budget
of $890,000. Mysteriously, the AFC repeatedly rejected the project:
funding came from the New South Wales Film Corporation (NSWFC),
which put in $450,000, and from GU, which put in $200,000; the
balance of $240,000 was raised from private investors.

Breaker Morant was made for around $800,000. The principal investor
was the South Australian Film Corporation (SAFC), with money also
coming from the AFC and pre-sales to Roadshow and the Seven television
network.

It seems amazing, now, that both these films—period pieces with
large casts—could be made for less than $900,000: but, it must be

remembered, that creative people—producers, directors, actors—were not well paid in the 70s. Gillian Armstrong was paid only $15,000 to direct *My Brilliant Career*, which occupied two years of her life; Phillip Noyce was paid the same amount to direct *Newsfront* (1978).

All that was to change very soon. The direct funding policy had, by the end of the 70s, been attacked by a great many people in the industry, for a number of reasons. Some producers felt that the whole thing smacked of a closed shop: if you were 'in' with the AFC or one of the State funding bodies, fine: if not, you had no chance. There was really nowhere to go if a project had been rejected by those organisations. The AFC was accused of backing a certain type of film: the historical drama was seen as a typical AFC picture (though, as we have seen, the AFC refused to back one of the key historical films, *My Brilliant Career*).

The other argument came from the AFC itself: there was a fear that the government (at the time a Liberal Party one under Malcolm Fraser) would tire of funding the AFC, despite the growing success of Australian films at home and abroad. It was felt that tax concessions would be a cheaper option for Treasury, and thus make the industry more secure in the long term.

And so the industry was in general agreement when the tax concession regulations, which became known as 10BA, were introduced on 1 1 October 1980. The concessions involved were extraordinarily generous: investors could claim 150 per cent tax concessions on their investment at risk, and a further 50 per cent concession on any profit up to the amount actually invested. Thus, not surprisingly, the industry as a whole was elated: a total of $50 million was raised in the first full year for which 10BA operated. Fifteen features were produced in 1980; there were twenty-two in 1981 and thirty-three in 1982 (note that, as explained in the foreword, these dates are the copyright dates printed on the films: a film carrying a 1982 date may have been actually produced in 1981).

The changes brought about by this largesse were swift and dramatic. Setting up a film became infinitely more complicated. Provisional certification had to be received from the Department of Home Affairs to show that the film's Australian content was sufficient to warrant the tax exemptions: at the beginning of 10BA, films had to be publicly exhibited before the end of the financial year in which they were produced. Once a film was completed, final certification had to be issued to confirm that the Australian content had been maintained during production. As we shall see in the case of one film, *The Return of Captain Invincible*, this was not always entirely straightforward.

All of this led to incredible problems including the notorious 'bunching'—so many films were in production at the same time that crews and actors were in short supply. It was the old story of a famine which became a feast. Crash courses were held to train production managers and assistant directors: some were imported from overseas.

Almost immediately, production costs began to soar. Not only were crews demanding a lot more money, but the raising of tax investment money became a growth industry all its own. Brokers and lawyers and underwriters entered the industry in droves, all charging high fees. Some producers quickly adapted to the new conditions: others never really did. One of the tragedies of the 80s is the fate that befell some of the most promising producers of the 70s—the Patricia Lovells and the Margaret Finks.

By the time he produced his first 10BA film, *Undercover*, in 1983, David Elfick's films had all been commercially successful. They included two feature documentaries, *Crystal Voyager* and *Morning of the Earth* and the feature films *Newsfront*, *The Chain Reaction* and *Starstruck*. As a producer, Elfick had been involved in every aspect of production and distribution. He had overseen the ad campaigns, the press previews and promotions. 'Although I was consulted about the promotion of *Undercover*, I no longer had any power,' he says. 'Previously, they were my films. I dealt with the distributor. The worst aspect of 10BA was to remove the entrepreneurial role of the producer. That's why I resigned from SPAA [Screen Producers Association of Australia]: in the early days, I'd be at SPAA meetings with the McElroys and Matt Carroll and others, and we could really help and support each other. But with 10BA all those so-called executive producers joined SPAA, and I didn't want to sit in a lot of meetings with people who weren't really producers at all.'

Another key producer of the 80s, Bob Weis, disagrees: 'I think 10BA was an absolutely crucial period,' he says. 'It was always designed as a short-term way of changing the industry from being an old boys' club led by the AFC into a wider-based industry that developed new talents and infrastructures. Under 10BA, people who weren't able to play the bureaucratic game, or weren't favoured by a small group of arts administrators, could make films. And the resulting explosion was an enormous development of the industry.'

Graham Burke, Managing Director of Village–Roadshow, is not a fan of 10BA: '10BA was like someone who needed micro-surgery being attacked by a meat-axe,' he says. 'Talent was spread too thin, and people made pictures they weren't passionate about.'

Kim Williams, Chief Executive of the AFC during most of the 80s and subsequently Chairman of the Film Finance Corporation, looks back on the 10BA films with mixed thoughts: '10BA was a double-edged sword,' he says. 'Tax concessions gave the film industry rapid growth which was way beyond the industry's or the government's expectations. A great many people had opportunities to make films, some of which should never have been made. 10BA insulated and isolated Australian filmmakers from the harsh realities of dealing with the international film community. There were also cost pressures, caused by competition for film crews and by "bunching". The scheme was also subject to massive manipulation. Not all offer documents were manipulated, of course, but those that were were manipulated very severely, bringing the industry as a whole disrepute in the eyes of the government.'

Within a short space of time after the introduction of 10BA, investment companies were formed by people with only tenuous knowledge of the film industry: packages (that dreadful word!) were put together to siphon off all the tax millions flooding in. One of the most blatant of these companies was Filmco, which was established late in 1980 by Peter Fox and Bob Sanders (who merged his Pact Productions into the larger company). John Fitzpatrick, a former lawyer at the SAFC, joined Filmco to executive-produce the films.

The Filmco slate consisted of some of the most dismal films ever produced in Australia. *Early Frost*, *A Dangerous Summer*, *The Dark Room*, *Midnite Spares*, *Double Deal*—these were films that could never have been made under the old system. Indeed, of that particular bunch, only one—*Midnite Spares*—was actually shown in cinemas: and it did not last very long. The fact that, at the very end of its existence, Filmco produced two reasonably good films, *Far East* and *Undercover*, does not diminish the scandalous waste of money the Filmco productions represented.

Other film investment companies came up with better product, though UAA, a Perth-based company operated by John Picton-Warlow and David Thomas, was criticised for raising Australian tax money and then investing it in overseas productions. UAA also made a number of Australian films, including *Emoh Ruo*, *Razorback* and *The Right Hand Man*. Producer Phillip Adams formed another such company in partnership with media mogul Kerry Packer: Adams–Packer was also short-lived, producing only four films: *We of the Never Never*, *Kitty and the Bagman*, *Lonely Hearts* and *Fighting Back*. After the company dissolved, in 1983, Adams was appointed Chairman of the AFC, a position he held until the end of the decade. Other companies which formed included the Burrowes Film Group, managed by Geoff Burrowes, producer of *The Man from Snowy River*.

When the Hawke Labor government came to power in March 1983, things started to change. In the budget that year the Treasurer, Paul Keating, reduced the 10BA tax concessions from 150 and 50 per cent to 133 and 33 per cent. There was gloom and doom in the industry as a result but, by the end of the next financial year, it was clear that the reduced benefits had not slowed investment at all: in 1983–4, a massive $145 million was invested under 10BA, which was topped the following year with an incredible $185.7 million. Treasury was clearly appalled at this level of foregone revenue, and in 1985 the benefits were further reduced to 120 and 20 per cent: although the result was a slightly smaller rate of investment ($159 million in 1985–6) it was still obviously far too high. A country with a population the size of Australia cannot possibly support the production of thirty-five or forty feature films a year; moreover, 10BA tax money was also going into television programmes and documentaries.

One side-effect of this tax-based industry involved attempts to Americanise Australian films. This had already been a controversial factor during the 70s, especially with the films produced by Antony I. Ginnane, for which he increasingly imported foreign actors. Ginnane's first production of the 80s, *Harlequin*, starred Robert Powell, David Hemmings and Broderick Crawford, and his second, *The Survivor*, was directed by Hemmings and starred Powell again, together with Joseph Cotten and Jenny Agutter.

By this time, Actors Equity was getting understandably concerned. The destruction of the English-speaking Canadian film industry during the early 70s by just such a policy of tax concessions and an open go for foreign actors, had been well documented: Canada still has not recovered from that dreadful period. Free marketeers may say, with some justification, that directors or producers should be allowed to hire any actor they like if such casting will help the film attain commercial success. But what was this casting doing to the Australian film industry?

As Bob Ellis suggested at the time, if Fred Schepisi were to have made *The Chant of Jimmie Blacksmith* in the environment of the early 80s, he might have been pressured into casting Richard Pryor in the lead. And who would take a risk on an expensive film like *My Brilliant Career* with two unknowns like Judy Davis and Sam Neill? True, Sam Neill is a New Zealand actor: the argument seems mainly directed against the miscasting of Americans in Australian roles, of which the most obvious, and destructive example, is probably Charlie Schlatter in *The Delinquents* at the end of the decade. Interestingly, Equity did not stand in the way of this particular piece of casting, nor of Meryl Streep as Lindy Chamberlain in *Evil Angels*, though there was a part for an Australian actress if ever there was one. Indeed, Streep won the Best Actress prize at the 1989 AFI Awards for her performance.

Equity's new, tougher guidelines, issued in the middle of 1980, had some immediate results. Tony Ginnane announced that he would shift production of his large-budget *Race for the 'Yankee Zephyr'*, from Queensland to New Zealand: this was because Ginnane had wanted four foreign actors (plus a foreign director) involved in the film. Ginnane further stated that he would shift all his activities to New Zealand and, indeed, he made five features across the Tasman before returning to executive produce and raise money for a series of films in the second half of the decade. Also linked with Equity's stand was an announcement

1986. Minister for the Arts Barry Cohen poses with Australian Film Commissioners. (left to right) William Gurry, the author, Sophia Turkiewicz, Kim Williams, Barry Cohen, Matt Carroll, Gill Appleton, Ray Beattie, Phillip Adams.

by the SAFC that it would abandon feature production in favour of television.

The issue of imported actors is still hotly contested, and will doubtless continue to be. It could be argued that Equity's stand limited foreign casting and thus enabled the Australian film industry to keep some semblance of national character. It could equally be argued that Equity should have been tougher: that Meryl Streep and Charlie Schlatter should simply not have been allowed in. And, again, it could be (and is) said that Equity is unwarranted in its interference with the rights of producers and directors to decide for themselves, and thus potentially jeopardise international sales.

Matters actually got worse when the tax concession rates were reduced to 120 per cent on investment and 20 per cent on profits. Because the concession rate was lower (and personal income-tax rates were also lowered) a way had to be found to increase return to the investor. This increased return was generally found in the form of a pre-sale, and quite large pre-sales (over 50 per cent) became the norm from 1987 onwards. A pre-sale means selling your film *before* it is made, instead of making it first and then offering it to local and overseas distributors. Pre-sales changed the dynamics of the industry: distribution companies demanded some control and creative input over films they were, in effect, financing. They wanted a say in casting, even in content. In some cases, Australian dialogue was actually 'neutralised' so that the simplest American could understand it (and some of the companies with which pre-sales were arranged were staffed by some pretty simple Americans). On the other hand, some Australian producers, like Tony Ginnane and Tom Broadbridge, knew exactly what they were doing and played the market accordingly.

Pre-sales gave overseas distributors the chance to buy quality productions at the lowest possible rates. Producers desperate to get their films off the ground would eagerly go for that pre-sale, only to regret it later. To quote an article in *Variety* (datelined Los Angeles): '[To] the endless flow of packagers, pre-sale experts, bankers and other folk . . . film is simply a product, something wrapped in black paper in a can, to be transacted with no interest in whether any human being will ever watch it, let alone enjoy it or be edified by it.'

Another significant factor of the decade was the video revolution, which drastically affected the film production market: here was a whole new way of seeing films. Before long, certain types of films were made with video release primarily in mind—horror films, for example. If a film failed in the cinema, it might still be a success on video.

With the advent of pre-sales, Australian filmmakers started losing control of their own films. Insidiously, those film-destroying compromises started to become the norm; even the Film Finance Corporation, when it was established in 1988, seemed to have accepted them.

Another factor of the late 80s was the short-lived establishment of foreign production companies in Australia: in 1987, New World and Dino De Laurentiis both set up production offices in Sydney. De Laurentiis floated an Australian subsidiary, Dino De Laurentiis Entertainment Ltd (DEL) on the Australian stockmarket early that year, attaining capital of $55 million (47 per cent owned by the company's American branch, DEG). The Italian-born producer built a large film studio on the Queensland Gold Coast, but after only ten months announced a book loss of $22.7 million. When DEG itself got into financial difficulties, De Laurentiis quickly backed out of his Australian plans, sold his studio to Warners and Village–Roadshow, and cancelled a high-budget sci-fi project, *Total Recall*, which was to have been directed by Bruce Beresford.

New World Pictures (Australia) was also floated on the Australian stockmarket in 1987, with capital of $52.5 million: the announced intention was to produce four feature films a year in Australia. In the event, NWA produced just one feature, *The Punisher*, during 1989: by early 1990, it was still unseen. Typically, this 'Australian' production, directed by American Mark Goldblatt, starred Dolph Lundgren (the Russian boxer in *Rocky IV*), Lou Gossett and Jeroen Krabbe in the leads: Australians like Barry Otto and Todd Boyce were allowed to fill supporting roles. At least the crew, led by cinematographer Ian Baker, was Australian. In September, 1989, NWA was liquidated by its American parent. Meanwhile, Kings Road Entertainment produced *The Salute of the Jugger* in 1989, also directed by an American, David Webb Peoples, and starring Rutger Hauer, Vincent D'Onofrio and Joan Chen. David Eggby shot the film which again used an Australian crew and Australian supporting actors: but, adding insult to injury, the opening credits do not even spell actor Hugh Keays-Byrne's name correctly.

Presumably the Australians who worked on these pictures were not terribly proud of what they were doing: they needed the money. These pictures, like various American television series shot here (notably *Mission Impossible*) not only, to quote Joan Long, 'reap the benefit of our low costs, and of our unique locations; they are reaping the benefits which years of government support have made possible, such as highly-trained production crews, experienced actors, flourishing support industries such as laboratories and sound studios, and many other specialist skills. Years of taxpayer-subsidised films have resulted in a big increase in trained crews who have to keep on eating and paying their mortagages: so, they take jobs with the American productions, if they're the only productions around. If you ignore the cultural arguments all this may seem okay. But is this why we fought to establish a film industry of our own—to become an off-shore branch of the American film industry? Aren't our locations just as much our precious natural resources as are oil and minerals? Why should their coinage be debased by frequent use by overseas productions?'

D uring the 80s, the AFC found its role changing dramatically. Ken Watts, the first Chief Executive, retired in 1981 to head production at Adams-Packer, and was succeeded by Joseph Skrzynski, a former merchant banker who had been Financial Advisor to the NSWFC before joining the AFC as General Manager in 1980. Affable and popular in the industry, Skrzynski oversaw the transition period to 10BA and then resigned, after a three-year term, to be replaced, in 1984, by Kim Williams. Williams, son of GU's David Williams, was a brilliant administrator; before his appointment to the AFC he had been Chief Executive of Musica Viva, a publicly-funded music body. Hard-working and dedicated, he nonetheless oversaw a period during which the AFC's reputation in the industry suffered a decline. After he left, he was appointed the first Chairman of the Film Finance Corporation. His replacement at the AFC, Daniel Rowland, lasted a surprisingly short time, during which period the Commission underwent a lengthy government review: the final Chief Executive of the decade was Cathy Robinson, who was backed by a new and exceptionally dynamic General Manager, Peter Sainsbury.

During the decade, the AFC's role changed on many fronts. Its documentary division, Film Australia (which had been almost completely moribund for years) was incorporated as a government-owned company operating on commercial guidelines, and allowed to compete for business in the marketplace. A Special Projects Fund was instituted by the AFC to enable the 'topping up' of worthy projects which were having difficulty raising money in the marketplace, and its cultural activities were maintained and expanded, with such initiatives as the Women's Film Fund.

The role of the AFC in marketing also changed crucially. During the 70s, the Commission established offices in London and Los Angeles to help promote and sell films in which the AFC had invested. But, increasingly during the 80s, the Commission found that producers were appointing international sales agents to handle their films. Sometimes these agents did a better sales job than the AFC might have done: often, they did not. But the AFC found more and more that its two overseas marketing offices were simply providing bases for Australian film people in Britain or America, and that, instead of sales, the marketing division was involved in cultural events such as film festivals and film weeks around the world.

At the same time, the AFC was working with the government on ideas for the inevitable post-10BA period. Treasury was impatient with the amount of money going into the film industry, especially since rumours were growing of excessive above-the-line fees, and rorts of all kinds. Its solution was the establishment of the Film Finance Corporation (FFC), which was announced by Treasurer Paul Keating in May 1988. The FFC, it was hoped, would end the abuses of 10BA and set the film industry on a sound commercial footing. Projects would be assessed according to their commercial viability: in the words of Kim Williams, its role is 'the entrepreneurial application of subsidy'. The Treasurer committed $205.8 million to the new Corporation, to be drawn over three years and, in addition, provided $63 million for 1991–2. The $70 million pegged for the FFC's first year of operation was intended to be augmented by $30 million from the public sector to produce $100 million worth of film; at the same time, 10BA was reduced to a flat 100 per cent write-off from the beginning of the 1988–9 financial year.

Kim Williams as Chairman of the FFC was joined by David Pollard, a former New South Wales public servant who had also worked for the Catholic Commission for Justice and Peace, as the FFC's first Chief Executive. They talked a lot about the 'deal-related', 'market-driven' nature of the Corporation: it all sounded very impressive, but what about the quality? Was it not possible, as Joan Long has suggested, for the FFC to fund 'a load of market-driven rubbish'? Pollard announced (at an Arts Law Centre of Australia conference in December 1988) that the FFC would not base its judgements 'on the aesthetic qualities of the script'. Thus, commercial viability is apparently the watchword.

The first film to bear the FFC logo is *The Delinquents*, a crass attempt to 'internationalise' a very Australian story. It is to be hoped that this fiasco represents just an error of judgement, and that films like *The Delinquents* will not become the future of the Australian film industry. Kim Williams is quick to point out: 'You can't blame the funding mechanism for the talents [or, presumably, lack of talent] of filmmakers. The FFC provides a framework—a formula which is modestly responsible on the marketing level. The film industry has to confront the harsh issue of quality.'

Pollard and his board committed $83.45 million to fifty-one projects with a total value of $149 million by the end of its first financial year (1988-9) year of operation. But the drawbacks of the new system quickly became clear. How could the FFC determine what was commercial and what was not? In addition, the FFC has sometimes proved dictatorial. One filmmaker was told that his project would be backed only if he got rid of the producer he had been working with and replaced him with a producer designated by the FFC. The new situation is a throwback to the days before 10BA: if the FFC turns you down, there is nowhere else to go.

Tony Ginnane, one of the most active and controversial producers of the 10BA period, feels that the legal and fundraising costs which boosted budgets so dramatically during the 80s (outlined above) have not diminished with the arrival of the FFC. 'I find it amusing', he says, 'that the proponents of the FFC, who argued so strongly against 10BA, and criticised the cost of legal fees and the deal-oriented approach to projects, have now embraced all those things themselves.' The early FFC-backed films, like *The Delinquents* and *Blood Oath*, have certainly been made on extremely large budgets, but both were based at the Gold Coast studios, which are costly for a variety of reasons, not least because cast and crew have to be accommodated near the studio.

Filmmakers with modest projects (which are not necessarily uncommercial) did have another source of funding at the beginning of the 90s: this was a leaner, more innovative AFC. During 1989, Peter Sainsbury, dubbed by some 'the Mikhail Gorbachev of the Australian film industry', announced innovative plans for funding low-budget (under $1 million) features of artistic merit: one such was Paul Cox's *Golden Braid* (1990), budgeted at around $900,000. There is a possibility, thanks to Sainsbury's innovation, that the kind of modest feature Australia should be making will continue, perhaps at the rate of about ten films a year: new directors, so vital to any industry, can also be encouraged by such means.

Says Sainsbury: 'Australian filmmakers seem to think in the following terms: We want to make medium-budget films, because they usually turn out best. But they're not commercially viable, so do we make tiny films to nullify the risk, or huge films to get profit? Once you think in those terms, you have a huge problem. The name of the game isn't financial viability, total recoupment or making a profit. Probably only in India do you have a self-sustaining film industry, because of the massive population, tiny labour costs, and small TV penetration. Many Australian filmmakers lock themselves into the notion that you have to run an industry that's viable in commercial terms, but more attention needs to be paid to the *marketable* film rather than the *commercial* film: the film with an international profile but not necessarily the one that's going to make everyone rich.'

This implied criticism of the entire basis on which the FFC was established is significant. The monolithic source of film funding for the 90s is not sufficiently flexible or varied to allow for the kind of Australian film which really will work internationally: the high quality art-house film. It is true that there have been some extraordinary successes on a far more commercial level: the *Crocodile Dundee* films are the most obvious and spectacular examples of this. But you cannot build a film industry on Paul Hogan, or even Mad Max; and *The Delinquents* certainly isn't the answer.

In the light of all this, the official Liberal Party policy to abolish the AFC could, if implemented, be the death knell for the kind of indigenous Australian film industry we really need.

S outh Australia was, in 1973, the first State to establish its own film corporation. It was followed in 1977 by New South Wales and, by the end of the decade, every other State except Western Australia. During the 80s, however, the fortunes of these State operations shifted dramatically.

The SAFC, headed by John Morris, switched to television production as noted above: but not before the organisation which produced some of the finest Australian films (*Sunday Too Far Away*, *Picnic at Hanging Rock*, *The Last Wave* and *Breaker Morant*) had attempted to find a commercial formula by means of as woeful a series of misguided failures as was produced anywhere: *Pacific Banana*, *Run, Chrissie, Run!* and the botched *Robbery Under Arms* among them.

The NSWFC, under Paul Riomfalvy, produced consistently more

interesting and ambitious films during the 80s, among them *Bliss*, *Careful He Might Hear You* and *Short Changed*. But the Corporation was forever making controversial decisions, not least the establishment, at colossal expense, of its own marketing office in Los Angeles. Since the AFC already had an effective marketing office in LA, it might have been thought that the NSWFC could have saved a considerable amount of taxpayers' money by sharing the AFC facilities, as the other State corporations did. But the marketing department of the NSWFC, run first by David Roe and later by Danny Collins, appeared imbued with an astonishing arrogance about its product and its destiny. Ultimately, an American called Bob Lewis (one of those Americans who wears so many gold chains around his neck that he seems in danger of curvature of the spine) was hired to head the NSWFC operation in the US: his salary was more than that of Premier Neville Wran, a fact much remarked on at the time.

Some NSWFC productions sold well overseas, among them *My Brilliant Career*, *Newsfront* and *Careful He Might Hear You*. Others, hardly less interesting, were more difficult to place: *Stir*, *The More Things Change . . .* and *Short Changed* are films of undoubted quality, but less easy to sell abroad. It was only at the end of 1989, after the NSWFC had been disbanded by the Liberal Government which won office in 1988, that the story broke about the NSWFC's methods of selling. Since 1983, the Corporation's productions had been sold, one by one, to a company called Pepper Distribution Corp, registered in Panama, but based at a lawyer's office in Los Angeles. The films were sold for seventy-five years (an extraordinarily long period) and all rights were involved (video as well as television and cinema) for the whole world (including Australia). Rights in films like *My Brilliant*

Paul Riomfalvy, chief executive of the New South Wales Film Corporation.

Career, which were already in distribution with other companies, would revert to Pepper once the original distribution deals expired.

It seems that the producers of these films were ill-informed about the details of these unprecedented deals. And the income derived from Pepper was not large, given the length of the time and the rights and territories involved. And just who was Pepper Distribution, anyway? Nobody seemed to know for certain, although Danny Collins went to work for Pepper after the NSWFC was shuttered. At the time of writing, the Independent Commission Against Corruption was investigating the whole shoddy affair.

When the incoming Greiner Government closed down the NSWFC, they replaced it with the New South Wales Film Office, and appointed John Morris (ex-SAFC) as its head. One of the most visible activities of the new organisation was to take advertisements in the international trade press indicating that New South Wales was a great location to shoot action films and that Sydney could stand in for any North American city. It was hardly encouraging for the production of quality Australian cinema.

The Tasmanian Film Corporation produced only two features before it folded, and the Queensland Film Corporation, after backing a handful of pictures (including the incredibly sleazy *Final Cut*) shut down under a cloud when its Chief Executive, Alan Callaghan, was convicted for financial misdealings.

Of all the state bodies, only Film Victoria (FV) seems to have maintained high standards and integrity. FV has consistently backed the most interesting and innovative Victorian filmmakers: Paul Cox, Ian Pringle and others.

A mong the rorts said to have taken place during the 10BA years are those involving excessive fees taken off the top. Presumably the stockbrokers and the lawyers and the underwriters and the completion guarantors and the executive producers (and 'associate producers' and all the rest) have to be paid something, but when, time and again, you hear of a situation in which almost half the budget— often more than $1 million—went in such fees, then clearly something is wrong.

Tony Ginnane, whose International Film Management (IFM) raised the finance for a great many films in the late 80s, had good contacts with small distributors in the US and so was able to arrange essential pre-sales for his projects. Producers would come to Ginnane with a project: he would assess them and decide on viability, taking into account a wide number of factors. He would then arrange a pre-sale and take responsibility for raising the finance.

'One of the myths of 10BA', says Ginnane, 'is that lots of people made millions of dollars. The brokerage and underwriting fees might indeed have been 8 per cent or 9 per cent [of the budget], but it was a bit like a pyramid: somebody would get 1 per cent of that and the next layer down people would get a couple of points, and so on. People naively or ingenuously took twenty prospectuses and added up all the brokerage fees and figured that one person made millions of dollars in a year. But the reality was that on a typical 9 per cent raise fee, you'd be lucky to be left with 2 per cent by the time you paid underwriters, sub-underwriters, retailers, mailing costs, advertising costs—there were a lot of costs in those 10BA movies.'

A ustralian films were screened widely around the world during the 80s, not only in festivals and film weeks, but in cinemas, on television and on video. The success of *Crocodile Dundee* (see Chapter 10) is phenomenal by any standard, but long before that Australian cinema was 'flavour of the month' in America: the international edition of *Time* for 28 September 1981 carried a cover story headed: 'Movie Boom from Down Under', and used the (modest) success of *Gallipoli* in New York as a starting point to discuss developments in Australian cinema. Australian films competed regularly at the prestigious Cannes Film Festival, and other international events.

One result of this was that our best directors and actors were tempted away from the always-struggling local industry, and made a name for themselves overseas. Peter Weir is the prime example: he made only two Australian films in the 80s, *Gallipoli* and *The Year of Living Dangerously*: both were financed only after terrible struggles. At the end of the decade, he had become a world-class director, with three acclaimed and successful American films behind him *(Witness, The Mosquito Coast* and *Dead Poets Society)* and another in production *(Green Card)*.

During most of the 80s Weir has been able to observe at a remove the industry to which he contributed so much. He says: 'We went through a bad period when there was a lot of pressure on filmmakers from writers, academics, critics. We were told that films should be contemporary and relevant. But creativity doesn't work that way. I don't know why I was impelled to make *Gallipoli*: it was something from the unconscious. Now, spurred on by that pressure, a lot of films were made about social issues. Unfortunately, those relevant, but contemporary films were also being made in Berlin and London and Chicago: and our films didn't have a lot that was new to say. In other words, filmmakers should be encouraged to dare to do any kind of film—anything they like. That's why I like Jane Campion [director of *Sweetie*]—she dares to be different.'

Weir sees the 10BA period as 'disastrous'. 'It was a horrible period—so wrong. There were instances where a project was announced: the producer was named and even the cast, but not the director. And all those lawyers who got into it for the glamour and the tax relief.' For Weir, there are two major requirements for a filmmaker: energy and recklessness.

Peter Weir is not the only major Australian director to work successfully abroad. Fred Schepisi made only one film (*Evil Angels*) in Australia in the 80s. Other Australian directors to have worked overseas represent almost a roll-call of our brightest and best: George Miller (1), Carl Schultz, Gillian Armstrong, Bruce Beresford and Phillip Noyce.

Actors, too, have found success abroad. Mel Gibson became a superstar after the *Mad Max* movies; Sam Neill, Bryan Brown and Judy Davis are in constant demand (Davis was cast in the first Woody Allen film of the 90s). These three return frequently to Australia to make films, and many of our filmmakers still prefer to live here. Cinematographers like Russell Boyd, Dean Semler, Don McAlpine, and John Seale work regularly in the US: Ian Baker has shot all Fred Schepisi's films, wherever they were made. Australian production designers, editors, grips, gaffers and assistant directors have frequently followed Australian directors to work overseas. Early in 1990, Geoffrey Simpson shot *Green Card* for Peter Weir in New York and David Gribble shot Gillian Armstrong's *Fires Within* in Florida.

There's nothing wrong with this, of course. It is a natural evolution for talents to migrate to the centre of the world film industry: America. It has been like that since the beginning. Their departure, regrettable as it may be, makes way for the newcomers. Certainly their exodus is no reason to support the point of view that, because Judy Davis can work for Woody Allen, so Charlie Schlatter can play an Aussie. The Australian film industry is so small it can easily be swamped by the mindless American casting which some producers seem to favour in their quest for a quick buck.

The departure, temporary or permanent, of some of our creative people has been offset during the 80s by the remarkable contributions made to the industry by a multicultural group of directors, producers and actors who came to this country, some in the distant past, some quite recently, to work in cinema.

For example, four of our most interesting and challenging directors are, by birth, non-Australians. Paul Cox was born in 1940 in Venlo in the Netherlands; he came to Australia in 1963, and several of his films touch on the loneliness he experienced when he first arrived in Melbourne. The films he made in the 70s (*Illuminations, Inside Looking Out* and *Kostas*), interesting as they were, give little indication of the vitality and importance of his 80s films, especially *Lonely Hearts, Man of Flowers, My First Wife, Cactus, Vincent* and *Golden Braid* (which will actually be distributed in 1990).

Carl Schultz was born in Zalaszentgrot, Hungary, in 1939, and fled the country, at the age of seventeen, during the anti-communist revolution of 1956. He came to Australia by way of England, worked in drama for the ABC, and, in the 80s, made a number of superb films: *Goodbye Paradise, Careful He Might Hear You*, the underrated *Bullseye* and *Travelling North*. He made an American film, *The Seventh Sign*, in 1988, and then returned to work on the *Cassidy* mini-series.

Nadia Tass, whose first film, *Malcolm*, astonished and charmed audiences, comes from Macedonia, where she was born in 1956. Like Paul Cox, she came to Australia in 1963 and she worked as an actress before turning to direction, ably assisted by her husband, cinematographer-screenwriter David Parker. Though the film Tass made after *Malcolm, Rikky and Pete*, was a disappointment, high hopes are held for her third feature, *Mark Clark Van Ark* (1990).

Jane Campion is a New Zealander, born in 1955, who came to Australia in 1977. Her father was a theatre director, her mother an actress. Campion studied painting and sculpture and obtained a diploma in anthropology before winning a place at the Australian Film Television and Radio School (AFTRS) with a Super-8mm short film, *Tissues*. She made a series of wholly original short films at the AFTRS, and then, with the ABC telemovie *Two Friends* and her extraordinary first feature, *Sweetie*, proved a remarkable new vision was at large in Australian cinema. Though she returned to New Zealand for her next project, *An Angel at My Table*, Campion is expected to make more Australian films in the 90s.

Some of the best, and busiest, actors of the 80s, including Sam

Neill, Bruno Lawrence and Chris Haywood, are also originally non-Australian: Neill and Lawrence, like Campion, are from New Zealand and Haywood comes from Britain. Neill has worked in many different countries, but has regularly returned to Australia to film, most notably in *Dead Calm* and in *Evil Angels*, for which he won an AFI award playing Michael Chamberlain. He is also willing to work in low-budget films, and early in 1990 he was in Melbourne for the leading role in John Ruane's *Death in Brunswick*. Lawrence's gruff but kindly persona has enhanced many a film (he was one of the few bearable elements in *The Delinquents*). Chris Haywood seems to be in just about every other Australian film of the 80s: his first film role was in Peter Weir's debut, *The Cars That Ate Paris* (1974) and since then he has hardly looked back. He won an AFI award for playing a dying victim of Agent Orange in Bill Bennett's *A Street to Die*, and people who work with him constantly refer to his energy, dedication and enthusiasm. Like Sam Neill, he is willing to appear in low-budget films.

The 80s were a period during which significant roles for women were comparatively rare; early in the 80s, Wendy Hughes (in *Lonely Hearts*, *My First Wife* and *Careful He Might Hear You*) and Noni Hazlehurst (in *Monkey Grip* and *Fran*) gave memorable performances but, by the end of the decade, they were either saddled with poor

Three of the most individualistic talents of the 80s: director Paul Cox with actors Gosia Dobrowolska and Chris Haywood on the set of Golden Braid.

material or working in other media. On the other hand, Gosia Dobrowolska, who arrived in Sydney in 1982 unable to speak English, managed, through hard work and talent, to acquire leading roles in a wide range of films, bringing to them a style unique in Australian cinema. Born in Wroclaw, Poland, she trained in the acting school there and appeared in Polish plays and one or two films before migrating. Her first Australian role, as the Polish migrant in *Silver City*, established her. Her later parts confirmed her talent; they included the comedy *Around the World in 80 Ways*, the thriller *The Surfer*, the excellent but little-seen drama *Phobia*, and Paul Cox's sensual comedy *Golden Braid* (opposite Chris Haywood).

The actress in most demand at the end of the 80s is Deborah Unger, who came to Australia from Vancouver, Canada, because she wanted to learn acting in Australia. She was accepted into the National Institute of Dramatic Art (NIDA) after some hair-raising problems involving her visa. At the end of her three-year course, she was immediately cast in three feature films: *Breakaway*, *Blood Oath* and *Till There Was You*. It was quite an achievement for this newcomer. Also hailing from Canada, incidentally, is the Perth-based producer, Paul Barron.

In the following pages, the contributions to the film industry of these people, and countless others from all over Australia, will be discussed as we explore the vast variety and range of tax-funded Australian feature films of the 80s.

A pproximately 270 feature films were made in the 80s (compared to 110 during the 70s). The AFC estimates that the budgets of films financed under 10BA between 1980 and 1989 total almost $985 million. It is not recorded how many of those films wound up in profit— under 10BA, they did not really need to. A significant number of them were, as we shall see, never released in cinemas in Australia.

What were they like, these films of the Avocado Plantation? Did Australian taxpayers get value for their money during the 10BA period? We tend to look back on the 70s as the glorious era of Australian cinema, but we will discover in the ensuing pages that a significant number of fine films was produced in the 80s, films as varied as *Gallipoli* (the first film discussed in this book) and *Sweetie* (the last). In fact, probably as many good films was made in the 80s as were made in the 70s; it is just that a very great many bad films were made as well.

We shall explore them all in the following chapters.

• C H A P T E R •
2

TRUE

STORIES

■
■

D uring the 80s, it became fashionable in some quarters to denigrate the historical Australian film. Some commentators referred, derisively, to the 'AFC films'—whatever that meant—to attack films dealing with the country's past. Some filmmakers, funding bodies, even critics were intimidated by this misplaced aversion to the historical subject, and yet some of the best, and most successful, films of the decade were stories based on historical events.

Foremost among them is certainly *GALLIPOLI* (1981) which remains, for many, *the* Australian film. It was a subject Peter Weir had been trying to make for several years. Weir (b. 1944 in Sydney) had emerged from the 70s as the country's leading director with such trail-blazing films as *The Cars That Ate Paris* (1974), *Picnic at Hanging Rock* (1975)—the first non-comedy to be a major box-office success—*The Last Wave* (1977) and the telemovie *The Plumber* (1978). (For a full coverage of Weir's entry into films and his 70s work, see *The Last New Wave*.)

In 1976, returning from Europe after the London opening of *Picnic at Hanging Rock*, Weir had stopped over in Turkey to visit the beach and the cliffs where so many Australians and New Zealanders had died fighting Turkish forces in 1915. On that beach, which is preserved as a war memorial, he found an empty Eno's bottle embedded in the sand. At once the thought came to him of an Australian mother sending her son off to war with a remedy for upset stomach—and from that moment, he became determined to make a film about Gallipoli (when he finally did, he used the very same Eno's bottle in one key scene).

At the time, Weir was based in Adelaide where he was working with the South Australian Film Corporation, which had backed *Picnic* and also the project he was about to shoot, *The Last Wave*. He wrote a rough storyline of *Gallipoli* and gave it to David Williamson to turn into a screenplay. Williamson (b. 1942) was then Australia's most popular playwright and several of his plays had been made into successful films (*Stork, The Removalists, Don's Party*); he had also written the screenplay for Tim Burstall's adventure-comedy *Eliza Fraser*. He recalls: 'When Peter and I started on the script, it was the whole Gallipoli canvas with a cast of thousands; we worked on it off and on for four years. It was a long evolutionary process.' Weir recalls that one draft even included a potted history of Australia's labour movement, and there was a period when the screenplay was titled *There and Back*.

There was a devastating moment when Weir, who had assumed he had the full support and backing of the SAFC, was told that Corporation decision-makers did not like the script and did not think the project was commercial. Admittedly, at the time the script was far less simple than it eventually became; and a costing suggested a budget of the then unheard-of sum of $4.5 million. But it was still a bitter blow for Weir, who had counted on the SAFC's support. It was May 1979, and his friend Patricia Lovell, who had co-produced *Picnic at Hanging Rock*, was in Cannes. Weir called her and told her the news. 'He asked me if I'd take it over,' says Lovell. 'And I immediately said "Yes", even though I hadn't read the script.' When she did read the script, she was a little dismayed: it was obviously a hugely expensive project; however, she acquired the property from the SAFC. The filmmakers were then faced with a choice: to go with the existing script and make a mini-series, or to simplify the story and make a feature film on a much smaller budget.

Some time later, Lovell recalls, Weir phoned her: 'I've got it,' he said. 'They're runners. They run in competition, they run to the pyramids. One of them runs to his death.' With a $9000 loan from the AFC, a new treatment was prepared, and Lovell started trying to raise money. 'It still looked like a $2 million film,' says Lovell. 'And the most I could raise in Australia was $850,000, which included an interest from GU, whose Managing Director, David Williams, was extremely keen on the project. But he could only put up $300,000; I found a private consortium of businessmen to put up $500,000, but I couldn't get past that. We couldn't raise enough money.'

During 1979–80, Weir divided his time between *Gallipoli* and another project, *The Year of Living Dangerously* (see Chapter 6), but neither

Peter Weir on the Gallipoli *location.*

had been financed when an American producer, Edward Lewis, offered him *The Thorn Birds*, a feature-film version of the Colleen McCullough novel to be produced by the American company Warner Bros (see Chapter 6). This came to nothing, and Weir returned to Australia at the beginning of 1980 and decided to proceed with *Gallipoli*.

Fortunately, at about this time two internationally famous expatriate Australians, Robert Stigwood and Rupert Murdoch, decided to join forces and form a film company which they called Associated R & R Films. On 1 May 1980, they held a press conference at the Sydney Hilton to announce their plans: after the conference, Weir and Gillian Armstrong were invited to join them for dinner. Both Stigwood and Murdoch liked the *Gallipoli* script, and agreed to make the film as the company's first (and, as it turned out, last) production. Lovell, who was again in Cannes, flew from France to Bermuda to meet Stigwood: they made a deal, on the beach in front of his house, to make the film on a budget of no more than $3 million (Australian). 'At the time,' says Lovell, 'the budget was $2.4 million; we eventually went to $2.8—any other costs involved fees for those extraneous people Associated R & R felt should be attached to the film as associate producer, executive producer or whatever.'

Meanwhile, Williamson completed a final draft and Weir set about casting; he had seen and liked Mel Gibson in *Mad Max* and cast him as Frank. First assistant director Mark Egerton flew around the Australian coastline looking for a beach that could stand in for Gallipoli: ironically, he found just the right place in South Australia near the fishing town of Port Lincoln. Consequently, the production was based in the State whose film arm had walked away from it. Interiors, including an Egyptian street, were built inside the Safcol fish company warehouse (the film was shot out of the tuna-fishing season) and crew members to this day recall the smell of fish that permeated the set.

Though Stigwood gets the producer billing, Lovell says: 'He left me entirely alone. He said to me, "Pat, I trust you and Peter Weir." He came to Egypt when we were there and actually makes an appearance in the film as an Arab. When I could deal directly with him, there were no problems. It was dealing with some of the people assigned to the picture by Associated R & R that was more difficult; none of them had worked on a film before, they had a brief to oversee production, and unfortunately they came on location a lot of the time.' Lovell did, however, have a positive relationship with Ben Gannon who, together with Martin Cooper, gets associate producer credit;

Francis O'Brien is billed as executive producer.

During the shoot, there was, for a short time, a difference of opinion between Weir and Williamson which took place after the latter had viewed some rushes. Weir had encouraged the actors to improvise their dialogue at times, and Williamson felt his script was being diminished. However, the dispute—though it raised the old question of conflict between the director and the writer on a film—was soon over.

Another hiccough was the behaviour of David Argue, the actor cast in the role of Snowy, a virginal Presbyterian youth. Argue, used to improvising and never easy to control (see the making of *Backlash* in Chapter 7) unsettled some of the other actors, and Weir, though delighted with his wildness, had to remind him he was part of an ensemble. Meanwhile, one of what Lovell refers to as 'the extraneous people' on the set reported details of the brief row between Weir and Williamson back to Stigwood. Says Lovell: 'One of the excesses on the budget was $5000 worth of the executive producer's phone calls to New York.'

Despite these minor problems, shooting at Port Lincoln went

Gallipoli. *Robert Grubb, Mel Gibson, David Argue, Tim McKenzie.*

relatively smoothly, though the savage winds (which nobody had been warned about) blew dust into the eyes of actors and technicians alike during the scenes on the beach and the cliffs. Weir, however, decided that the film badly needed an extra scene, a scene not written or budgeted for. This would be a farewell ball, a scene to provide welcome light relief (and the introduction of some female characters) before the fighting. He came to Lovell with the idea on a Monday morning: and she agreed, though the cost (an extra $60,000) had to be approved by Associated R & R. Williamson was asked to write the ball sequence and he came up with 'a lovely scene'; the relationship between writer and director ended on such an amicable note that Weir asked Williamson if he would tackle *The Year of Living Dangerously* for him. Williamson also came to Egypt, and can be seen in the film as a lanky member of the Australian forces, playing an impromptu game of football.

Looking back, Weir's only regret about the film is that, in condensing the events in the attack on The Nek there is an implication that the British soldiers were cowards. 'We got some flak in the British press,' he says, 'and it's simply a misunderstanding. The soldier who sent those men to their deaths was an Australian officer, but the actor speaks with a British accent (and there was an earlier reference to the fact that the British had landed and were having breakfast, which was true but not the fault of the men, but of the British leadership at Suvla). So, the implication was that we were Pom bashing, whereas they'd fought valiantly, and suffered terribly, alongside us. Apart from that, the events were portrayed pretty accurately.'

When the film was completed, a fine cut was sent to Stigwood, who called Lovell: 'How can I thank you?' he said. Stigwood did a deal with Paramount for world-wide release (outside Australia)—the first instance of an Australian feature film being distributed in the US by an American major. There was a lively contest between the three main distribution companies for the Australian rights to the film. Jonathan Chissick, of Hoyts, recalls: 'Everyone was asked to bid for the picture. We knew Roadshow had in a good bid, but we badly wanted it so we really worked on our bid. We thought we made a very, very expensive offer, and we were devastated when we were told Roadshow had the picture.'

The film was a major success in Australia, not surprisingly, and won nine Australian Film Institute Awards that year including Best Film, Director and Screenplay. In hindsight, Weir feels the film should have been retitled for the US, where many people had trouble even pronouncing the name, let alone knowing what it meant (it was even mistaken for a biography about actor David Gulpilil). Paramount advertised it with the tag-line: 'From a place you never heard of . . . a story you'll never forget', but it did less business than expected. Although the film made a profit worldwide, it remains the only production of Associated R & R Films. In London, the film had a Royal Premiere, attended by the Prince and Princess of Wales; Weir was unable to attend, and Pat Lovell represented the film.

In the end, all the time and effort and money that went into *Gallipoli* was worth it. The characters of Archy and Frank (see the synopsis of the film in the appendix), who left their Western Australian home in a spirit of adventure and found camaraderie, fear and, in Archy's case, death in a foreign war, became Australian archetypes. The sweep of Weir's vision, the humour, the tension, the painstaking recreation of the Gallipoli beach and cliffs, all make for a film of astonishing power. The impact is significantly reduced on video, where Russell Boyd's Panavision photography suffers very badly.

G allipoli is a story of a noble defeat; *THE LIGHTHORSEMEN* (1987), another true story from World War I, concerns an epic victory— the charge of the Australian Light Horse on Turkish-occupied Beersheba in 1917, which was not only one of the world's last great cavalry charges, but which also changed the political face of the Middle East. The charge was used as the climax of Charles Chauvel's flag-waving *Forty Thousand Horsemen* in 1941, but somehow has never captured the imagination of the Australian public the way the defeat at Gallipoli has; it is not surprising, then, that Simon Wincer's film lacked the impact, and box-office appeal, of Peter Weir's.

Like *Gallipoli*, *The Lighthorsemen* was long in the planning stages. The story of the Light Horse was originally announced as a Hoyts-Edgley project in the middle of the decade, with Gil Brealey involved as producer (on the finished film, Brealey gets a credit as 'Production Consultant'); but a decision was made by Terry Jackman of Hoyts-Edgley to produce *Burke and Wills* instead of *The Lighthorsemen*, and the project went into turnaround. However, Simon Wincer eventually managed to secure a $6 million pre-sale to the American distributors RKO; Antony Ginnane's Film and General Holdings company helped to raise the rest of the money and oversee the financial side of the production.

The screenplay was written by Ian Jones, who had scripted the

The Lighthorsemen. *The final charge.*

television series *Homicide, The Sullivans* and *Against the Wind* for Crawfords, and who had become obsessed with the story of the Australian Light Horse when he was writing an episode of *Matlock Police* in 1971. 'I wanted to look at how people in a small town handled a controversial issue like war,' he says, 'particularly the war in which Australia was involved at the time—Vietnam. To get a greater perspective on it, I made one of the characters a veteran of the Light Horse. While researching for that episode, I talked to many Light Horse veterans, then in their 70s and 80s.' As a result, Jones wrote two books about the Light Horse. He visited Beersheba in 1979, studied British and Australian official histories of the attack as well as Turkish and German accounts and was fascinated at the discrepancies he found: 'History isn't inviolate,' he says.

Wincer (b. 1943 in Sydney), a former executive at Hoyts-Edgley, made his reputation as a television director (*The Sullivans, Homicide*) before directing a couple of Ginnane thrillers (*Snapshot*, 1979, and *Harlequin*, 1980). He was co-executive producer (with Michael Edgley) on *The Man from Snowy River* (1982), and then directed *Phar Lap* (1983) for the newly-formed Hoyts–Edgley. In 1985, he made the science-fiction film *D.A.R.Y.L.*, which was set in America though filmed in Britain.

Wincer's skills as a director are indisputable, but he is no Peter Weir and Ian Jones is no David Williamson. The crucial problem with *The Lighthorsemen* is the screenplay, which is pedestrian and uninvolving and which includes an extraneous love affair between the hero, Dave (Peter Phelps) and a nurse played by Sigrid Thornton. Despite this attempt to engage audience sympathy, the central characters in the film never come alive the way Archy and Frank did in *Gallipoli*.

The film was shot not far from Port Lincoln, mostly at Hawker, a township north of Adelaide. Indicative of the way budgets leaped during the 10BA period is the fact that *Gallipoli* was made for $3 million, including the Egyptian shoot, while six years later the budget for *The Lighthorsemen* was a whopping $10.5 million. The production was dogged by bad weather, unseasonable rain that led to the loss of shooting time.

The film is extremely disappointing except for the 14-minute charge that forms its climax (after an interminable 104-minute build-up). It is reminiscent of the climax to the Michael Curtiz epic *The Charge of the Light Brigade* (1935). Wincer and his formidable stunt team created a sequence of breathtaking excitement as the horsemen charge towards the Turkish guns. The film is worth seeing (in Panavision on the cinema screen) for this sequence alone; otherwise it is best to forget the routine plotting and dialogue, the embarrassing performances of Ralph Cotterill as a German officer, Gerard Kennedy as a villainous Turk, and even the unnecessarily imported Anthony Andrews as an engimatic aide to Allenby. Comparisons with *Gallipoli* are reinforced by the presence of Tim McKenzie and Bill Kerr in both films; acting honours in Wincer's picture go to Peter Phelps as the dogged hero who, in the best soapie tradition, does not want to kill.

A sad postscript to the film occurred the day after shooting was completed in December 1986; actor Jon Blake, aged twenty-eight, left Hawker to drive home, but 40 kilometres from Port Augusta was involved in a serious accident. He was in a coma for many months, and at the end of 1989 (three years after the accident) was still undergoing constant therapy.

The Lighthorsemen was not a commercial success, even in Britain (where it was thirteen minutes shorter than it had been in Australia). Possibly the public had already tired of this kind of historical subject as many would have us believe; more likely, the film was doomed because not enough trouble was taken to write convincing characters or situations. The powerful emotional charge that Weir and Williamson brought to their film was completely lacking in *The Lighthorsemen*; Wincer and Jones had made a handsome, but uncompelling, epic.

A t one point in *Gallipoli*, there is a specific reference to another famous Australian failure, one that had occurred fifty-seven years before the Anzac defeat. Every Australian schoolchild learned about the explorers who, in 1860, crossed the continent from Melbourne to the Gulf of Carpentaria, and died on the way back. *BURKE AND*

WILLS (1985) was the brainchild of Graeme Clifford, an Australian expatriate who had become one of the world's most significant film editors.

Clifford was born in Sydney in 1942 and, after completing his education, studied medicine. But he was always interested in films, and abandoned his medical studies in 1962 for a job at Artransa, where he became a studio trainee, working in every department of the studio. The aspect of filmmaking that fascinated him most was editing. 'It seemed to me that the film was virtually rewritten in the editing room,' he says. 'It's in editing that films are finally made to work.' At the end of 1964, he went to London and, somewhat to his surprise, immediately found a job at the BBC in the editing department. After a period there, he moved on to Canada, worked for CBC as an editor, and was making television commercials and documentaries in Vancouver in 1968 when he met Robert Altman, who at the time was making a film called *That Cold Day in the Park*. 'I applied for a job on the film,' he says. 'I hadn't worked on a feature before, and I worked as assistant editor and also as 2nd assistant director—Altman agreed to allow me to do both jobs as long as I only took one salary.' When the Vancouver shoot was finished, Altman suggested Clifford come to Los Angeles to work on the mixing process. 'I jumped at the opportunity,' he says.

Clifford stayed with Altman for five years, working in different capacities on seminal films such as *M*A*S*H*, *Brewster McCloud*, *McCabe and Mrs Miller* and *The Long Goodbye*. He was unable to join the film editors' union for a while, and the first film he cut for Altman, *Images*, was edited in England; but on the other films he worked as assistant director or as personal assistant and even casting director.

After his period with Altman, Clifford returned to London. He had become friendly with Julie Christie during the shooting of *McCabe and Mrs Miller*, and she suggested he read the screenplay of a film she was about to do for Nicolas Roeg, *Don't Look Now*. Clifford had seen and admired Roeg's Australian-made film *Walkabout*, and phoned the director to see if they could meet. 'We met at a little pub,' says Clifford, 'we had a few beers, he saw and liked *Images*, and the next thing I knew, I had a job.' The famous lovemaking sequence between Christie and Donald Sutherland was cut during a 36-hour non-stop session.

Clifford also edited Roeg's subsequent film, *The Man who Fell to Earth* (1974), and soon after that met Australian director Jim Sharman

who asked him to edit his film of *The Rocky Horror Picture Show* (1975);
in subsequent years he edited films for Norman Jewison (*Fist*) and
Bob Rafelson (*The Postman Always Rings Twice*). Meanwhile, in Britain,
he started directing for television: he made the last series of *The Avengers*
('It taught me to think on my feet'), and in the US, episodes of the
TV series *Barnaby Jones*.

By this time, he was eager to direct a feature film, and was attracted
to the idea of making a film about Burke and Wills in his native Australia;
on Christmas trips home to visit family, he started researching the
Burke and Wills story. In 1978, he approached the British company
EMI, because he knew they had been involved with a screenplay about
the explorers on which Terence Rattigan had been working before he
died. 'Originally, I wanted to do a film based on Rattigan's screenplay,'
says Clifford, 'though it was very theatrical. But there were all sorts
of problems associated with that, so I decided to hire my own
screenwriter and start from scratch.'

In 1980, he teamed up with another Australian expatriate, writer
Michael Thomas (who later wrote the screenplay for *Scandal*, the
Christine Keeler story) and they approached the AFC for backing. He
was also aware through his discussions with EMI that David Williams
of GU was interested in the project. With Williams' backing, and an
acceptable screenplay, it looked as if, finally, *Burke and Wills* would
be a goer.

In the event, though, Clifford's first film was not made in Australia:
in 1982 he directed *Frances*, a biography of actress Frances Farmer,
which starred Jessica Lange (whom Clifford had met during the making
of *The Postman Always Rings Twice*), which was shot in the US with
the backing of EMI and Mel Brooks' company, Brooksfilms. The
dramatic and tragic true story of an unconventional actress destroyed
by the Hollywood system was deemed 'a problem picture' by an
unenthusiastic film industry, and received mixed reviews and below
average box-office returns.

With *Frances* behind him, Clifford resumed his attempts to produce
Burke and Wills. Although he found that David Williams was very
supportive, Clifford felt that GU 'was interested in a much smaller
scale picture than I was. I quickly saw that the film I wanted to make
he wasn't going to finance.' Clifford offered his project to Hoyts–Edgley,
and Terry Jackman quickly came up with the extra money Clifford
felt he needed to make the film.

One of the reasons the film was so expensive (the budget was $8.9

million) was that, as far as possible, Clifford wanted to follow the steps of the explorers and film on authentic locations. 'It was important to me that we shot at Cooper Creek,' he says. 'We investigated more accessible rivers, which would have been cheaper—but they didn't look the same. Nothing looks like Cooper Creek. And I felt certain that being in the authentic place where Burke and Wills had been would affect the actors and the crew. It was incredibly difficult: intensely hot, terrible flies, boredom—but the experience has rubbed off on the film.'

Charlton Heston had, at one time, been interested in playing Burke but Clifford had always envisaged Jack Thompson in the role. By chance, Clifford spotted Thompson in the departure lounge at LA airport— both were on the same flight to Sydney. Clifford had the fifth draft of the screenplay with him, introduced himself to the actor, and asked him to read it on the plane. 'We shook hands and agreed to do the picture at 35,000 feet outside the business class toilet,' Clifford says. Casting Wills proved more difficult: neither of the Australian actors Clifford wanted was available, and eventually British actor Nigel Havers was cast in the role. This provoked a dispute with Actors Equity: the matter went before an Arbitration Committee, which found in Havers' favour.

Principal photography commenced in the middle of September 1984, and lasted thirteen weeks; given the difficulty of the location shoot, it is something of a miracle that shooting finished a day under schedule. Rushes were flown to the location in twin-engined aircraft and screened outdoors in a home-made cinema built at Cooper Creek, until the screen was blown away during a windstorm. Other arrangements were made, but the projector continually broke down because of dust. Several months later, in England, a further three days of material was filmed.

The finished film runs 2 hours 20 minutes and early test screenings proved positive. But when Hoyts released it, late in 1985, the results were disappointing. In hindsight, Jonathan Chissick of Hoyts thinks 'it was basically a bad concept for a movie. A heroic story, but, frankly, the audience just didn't want to see a picture about two guys schlepping through the desert and dying. It was a brilliant picture, well directed. beautifully photographed; it looked fantastic—and nobody wanted to see it.'

Maybe Chissick's assessment is correct, but there have been plenty of films about famous people who met with tragic ends (*Scott of the Antarctic, Gandhi*) which were extremely successful; the reasons for the film's commercial failure lie elsewhere. Despite the attention to detail, in terms of exact location, and despite its length, the film is muddled in vital areas; the motives of members of the Melbourne Establishment who in effect betrayed the explorers and left them to die, remain murky. Was the expedition's backer Ambrose Kyte (Hugh Keays-Byrne) jealous of Burke because he, too, loved Burke's mistress, Julia Matthews (Greta Scacchi)? The focus of attention is, rightly, on the relationship between fiery, stubborn Burke (beautifully played by Thompson) and sensitive, intelligent Wills, but there is still something lacking in this ambitious movie, despite the formidable camerawork of Russell Boyd and the immense scale of the project.

Director Graeme Clifford, with Greta Scacchi, on the set of Burke and Wills.

The best moments in the film are small ones: King (Matthew Fargher) seeming to emerge from the screen after Burke's death (an effect achieved by simultaneously tracking back and zooming in); the magical moment when, in England, Wills has a frightening experience when he is lost in a maze—a scene worthy of Nicolas Roeg himself. Clifford cheats by having the explorers actually reach the sea (in reality they reached a swamp which would have been far less dramatic): the scene in which Burke's horse gallops through the waves is genuinely exhilarating.

After the disappointing box-office in Australia, overseas sales proved difficult; the film has never opened theatrically in Britain. So, after all the time and effort and money, after the years of planning and work, relatively few people saw *Burke and Wills* as it was meant to be seen, in Panavision on the big cinema screen. Clifford returned to America and, after this apparent failure, found many doors closed to him. It was three years before he directed his next film, a skateboard thriller called *Gleaming the Cube* (1988) which was another box-office failure.

At the time, some people in Australia felt that the failure of *Burke*

Wills and Burke. *Garry McDonald, Kim Gyngell.*

and Wills was, at least in part, due to the arrival on the scene of a rival production, a parody called *WILLS AND BURKE* (1985), which was released by GU and which opened in cinemas one week before Clifford's film. It would have been quite possible to confuse the two pictures, and the damning reviews given to *Wills and Burke* may have unintentionally reflected on *Burke and Wills*.

Wills and Burke came to producer Bob Weis originally as a mini-series, but he felt it better suited to a feature film format. 'We enjoyed making it,' he says, 'and thought it worked as a black comedy.' GU backed the project. Says David Williams: 'It's almost like a *Monty Python* thing—they were a couple of idiots who got lost in the middle of the desert and I think they deserved to be sent up.' Weis decided to direct the film himself: 'I had a feeling for the subject,' he says. The budget was a little under $2 million.

Weis recalls that he spoke to Graeme Clifford on the phone in Los Angeles, unaware at the time that they were working on the same subject. 'He told me he was off to Australia to do a picture called *Burke and Wills*; I said "Me too." There was a long silence on the other end of the phone. Then I told him I was doing a comedy. That was the last time we spoke.'

Weis' casting was certainly promising: Garry McDonald as Burke, Kim Gyngell as Wills and Nicole Kidman (in her first adult role) as Julia Matthews; Chris Haywood, who also appears in Clifford's film, has a cameo as a trigger-happy policeman. But Philip Dalkin's screenplay, though apparently well researched, is short on laughs, and the running gags (aristocratic Wills wearing formal clothes throughout the trek) are worked to death. The film was savaged by critics, and died at the box-office.

'It was universally badly reviewed,' says Weis. 'I saw it as an opportunity to take an Australian genre—the theme of the Great

Australian Loser—and celebrate this character: the hero who tries valiantly, but doesn't succeed. And, historically, these guys really were wacky. Clifford's film is a very romantic version of the truth.'

T hirty years before Burke and Wills perished in Central Australia, Aborigines by the thousand were being killed in Tasmania; this was the infamous 'black line' and it forms the background to *MANGANINNIE* (1980), which was the first feature produced by the Tasmanian Film Corporation. Most of the film is a two-hander involving Manganinnie (Mawuyul Yanthalawuy), an Aboriginal woman who is the sole survivor of a massacre, and Joanna (Anna Ralph), the little white girl whom she 'adopts'. First-time director John Honey makes few concessions to the audience: Yanthalawuy speaks her own language throughout, and is occasionally translated by the child (who shows a remarkable aptitude in this regard). The film lacks the passion the subject deserved, but is ravishingly photographed by Gary Hansen. Somewhat surprisingly, it recovered its modest costs ($481,000) and made a profit.

Manganinnie. *Anna Ralph, Mawuyul Yanthalawuy.*

T he years that followed World War I seemed to spawn a new criminal class in both Sydney and Melbourne, and it turned out to be another of those coincidences that, in the same year, two films were made about the underworld of the teens and 20s, both inspired by real-life villains.

SQUIZZY TAYLOR (1982) was the first of the two to be released, and tells the story of one of Melbourne's most colourful and infamous criminals. Director Kevin Dobson (b. 1953) started out as an editor at Crawfords and graduated to direction with *Matlock Police*; his only cinema feature prior to *Squizzy Taylor* had been the visually lush but emotionally barren *The Mango Tree* (1977). Squizzy's story had been told before on screen in Nigel Buesst's 1969 documentary, *The Rise and Fall of Squizzy Taylor*, but the new film, scripted by executive producer Roger Simpson, was a much more elaborate affair which took the basic facts of the gangster's career and embroidered them with a fictional story about his romantic affairs.

Squizzy Taylor. *David Atkins.*

David Atkins, a choreographer (*Starstruck*) is 153 centimetres (5 feet 2 inches) tall; he was perfectly cast as the diminutive Squizzy. Shortly before being cast in this film he had narrowly missed out on the role of Billy Kwan in Peter Weir's film of *The Year of Living Dangerously*— see Chapter 6. The filmmakers used Melbourne locations whenever possible, shooting in Fitzroy and downtown Flinders Street, and the film is strong on atmosphere—the mean streets, dance halls, gambling dens, brothels and police stations of the era. Production designer Logan Brewer and cinematographer Dan Burstall are the stars of the film.

Though the drama sags a bit in the middle, Dobson keeps the action bubbling for most of the film's length, and has fun exploring the early days of police corruption and media manipulation through his gangster story. Local critics were harsh on the film, however, pointing out its deficiencies in areas of character development and narrative. Chosen to open the 1982 Sydney Film Festival, the film was politely, if unenthusiastically, received, and went on to do modest business. To date, Kevin Dobson has not directed another film.

The other 1982 movie to deal with gangsters of the 20s was *KITTY AND THE BAGMAN*, the last of four films produced by Tony Buckley and directed by Donald Crombie; the team had a falling out during production. Crombie (b. 1942 in Brisbane) had previously directed *Caddie* (1976), *The Irishman* (1978) and *The Killing of Angel Street* (1981) for Buckley, as well as the migrant drama *Cathy's Child* (1979); his background was principally in Film Australia documentaries.

Kitty, budgeted at $2.5 million, was one of the productions of the short-lived Adams–Packer production company. As with *Squizzy Taylor*, great effort was spent on the look of the film, which was shot in Panavision by Dean Semler. An elaborate street set was built at the Mort Bay studios in the Sydney suburb of Balmain, and much of the film was shot there.

At this time, the film industry was lobbying in favour of the retention of the 10BA tax scheme, and *Kitty* was the only film then in production. Producer James Vernon asked Buckley if he could invite Federal Treasurer John Howard on to the set; Howard came to Mort Bay on a Tuesday and appeared to be fascinated with what was going on. So fascinated, in fact, that on the Friday of the same week Buckley had an hour's notice that Prime Minister Malcolm Fraser would be paying a visit. 'Suddenly the place was crawling with security people,' says Buckley. 'Fraser arrived and spent some time looking at what was going on. We had to alert crew members to be on their best behaviour, because Fraser wasn't the most popular person at the time.'

The gangsters in *Kitty and the Bagman*, notably the notorious Big Lil, are not as well known as Squizzy, but were based on real characters from the period after World War I, and Crombie and Buckley originally planned to make a slightly exotic film peopled with Fellini-like faces. Several of the actors hailed from television soap operas (both Val Lehman, who played Lil, and Colette Mann were regularly seen in *Prisoner*) and John Stanton made an impression as The Bagman, the cop who elevates Kitty (Liddy Clark) into a gang boss to rival Lil.

The film's mood is light-hearted, but the plotting is aimless and lacks sparkle, and some of the minor characters are underdeveloped. Perhaps the tension on the set filtered down into the finished product. Nevertheless, when the film was completed in the autumn of 1982, GU, the distributors, appeared delighted with it and screenings for exhibitors were also positive. Unaccountably, GU decided to hold back the release until February 1983—almost a year—and at the same time vetoed participation in the 1982 Sydney Film Festival. By the time the film appeared in cinemas, it had to compete with big Oscar contenders, like *Gandhi* and *Tootsie*. Reviews were fair to good, but the film did dismal business: it had simply been delayed too long.

UNDERCOVER (1983) is also set in the 20s, though the theme is far removed from that of the two gangster films. The screenplay was written by Miranda Downes, who had worked on the Ian Barry thriller, *The Chain Reaction* (1980) as production secretary. On that film, she met producer David Elfick and told him about an idea she had for a screenplay about Fred Burley, pioneer manufacturer of women's underwear. Elfick thought the idea showed promise, and obtained AFC money for script development.

Elfick (b. 1944 in Sydney) was a hands-on filmmaker who brought in as director David Stevens (b. 1940 in Palestine), a former television director (*Homicide*) and screenwriter (*Breaker Morant*) who had scored a success with the mini-series of *A Town Like Alice* and with his first feature, *The Clinic* (1981), a comedy about a VD clinic (see Chapter 10). Says Elfick: 'There was plenty of innuendo and spice in the *Undercover* story.' Stevens was attracted to the glamour inherent in the subject and saw it as 'an Australian fairy story'.

The budget was fairly high at $3.5 million, and finance was raised through Filmco. This was, in fact, the last production of the company which had produced a number of tax-shelter films at the beginning of the decade. Given the level of investment, an American 'name' was required by Filmco. Stevens and Elfick decided on Dennis Quaid; Stevens visited the actor on the set of *Jaws 3D*, and he expressed immediate interest in the role. At the time Quaid had recently completed a major role in *The Right Stuff*, and was 'hot'. But Actors Equity claimed never to have heard of him (despite his Academy Award nomination for *Breaking Away*) and refused to allow him to take the role. Instead, Equity approved Michael Pare, who was much less well known. He played Max Wylde, the American publicist with whom heroine Libby (Genevieve Picot) falls in love. Pare did a competent job but, as Elfick now says, 'Casting is so important, and I often think how different the film might have been with an actor like Dennis Quaid, with all his energy, in that role.'

Casting problems were not the only difficulties on *Undercover*; the relationship between Filmco and Elfick was not always harmonious. 'I think the pressures put on us in the period leading up to making the film, sapped our energies,' says Elfick. 'Peter Fox [founder of Filmco] had been killed [in a 1982 car accident on the Pacific Highway near Taree], Richard Toltz was running the company, and right through pre-production we were getting constant demands, demands which, we were told, if we didn't meet, the finance would fall away as a result. So the production office was constantly servicing quite difficult demands from Filmco, and it put a great strain on David Stevens. On one occasion, he had to go in front of Filmco's Board and act out the whole story of the movie for them—he came back from that experience shattered, and despising the people concerned. Perhaps as a result of all that strain, the end result wasn't as good as I'd expected.'

Undercover certainly does not live up to expectations. The focus of attention shifts from country girl Libby, from whose viewpoint we enter the fashion world of the 20s, to Fred Burley (John Walton) and his lavish campaign in support of Australian manufacturing; the shift robs the film of narrative drive. Genevieve Picot is rather wan as Libby, and seems under a strain throughout. On the other hand, Dean Semler's Panavision photography is lush, and there is an acidly funny performance from Sandy Gore as Nina, Burley's chief designer ('I'm sure I represent every structural problem known to man').

Roadshow released the film, to modest returns; it was Elfick's first commercial failure. There are a couple of postscripts to the production. Miranda Downes subsequently started work on *Cane*, a drama about Italian cane-cutters in northern Queensland, but was tragically murdered on a beach north of Cairns while she was researching the subject. *Cane* eventually became the very popular mini-series, *Fields of Fire*, which had two sequels which Elfick dedicated to Downes. David Stevens found himself unable to get backing for any of his Australian projects after *Undercover*; his only other film of the 80s, *Kansas* (1988) was made for an independent Hollywood company, and received only a limited release.

A s Bob Weis has pointed out earlier in this chapter, so many mythic Australian characters are losers: the Anzacs who died at Gallipoli, Burke and Wills, Squizzy Taylor and the rest. *PHAR LAP* (1983) is a film about Australia's most famous racehorse and, in the Australian version at least, opens with the animal's death, in 1932, in America.

David Williamson wrote the screenplay for the film, and it was seen at the time as something of a departure for him: snobbishly, some commentators seemed to feel the subject was beneath him. Yet Williamson's carefully crafted screenplay is a model of its kind: 'It wasn't a story about the horse, it was about the people around the horse,' he says, 'I liked it a lot, and I thought Simon Wincer did a terrific job. He's denigrated as a director because he did a lot of television, but it was a really well-made film. The script looks deceptively simple, but it took a lot of work to get it right.' During scripting, Williamson was careful to stick as closely as possible to the facts, and Wincer relished the chance to direct 'a rattling good yarn'.

With a budget of $5 million, *Phar Lap* was an expensive film; yet it had to be made on a tight schedule because of the 10BA rules about completion within the financial year.

Phar Lap was produced by many of the same people who had made *The Man from Snowy River* a year earlier; it was a John Sexton-Michael Edgley production, and Tom Burlinson, The Man from the earlier film, plays Tommy Woodcock, the groom who cared for the famous racehorse. The real Woodcock, a sprightly 78-year-old at the time the film was made, acted as adviser on the production and is fleetingly seen in one sequence. Most importantly, *Phar Lap* was the film that elevated Simon Wincer from being a routine director of television shows and bottom-drawer thrillers to the level of a successful commercial director. His handling of the racing scenes is as powerful as anything in Australian cinema, and his characters, so well written by Williamson, all come vibrantly alive. The film was a major box-office success for Hoyts, and spurred the formation of the Hoyts–Edgley production company.

Overseas, the film was slightly shortened and re-edited so that Phar Lap's death takes place at the end, not at the beginning. In the US, the film was re-titled *A Horse Called Phar Lap* by distributor 20th Century-Fox.

Just as the real Tommy Woodcock appears on-screen in *Phar Lap*, so Wattie and Agnes Doig appear at the beginning and end of *STRIKEBOUND* (1983), a remarkable first feature from Richard Lowenstein (b. 1959 in Melbourne). The Doigs were actively involved in the Gippsland miners' strike of 1937, and it was an inspired idea to allow the audience to see them in this film version of their story.

In the film, Wattie and Agnes are played, most convincingly, by

Chris Haywood and Carol Burns. The screenplay was originally titled *The Sunbeam Shaft*, the name of the mine itself; it is based on a book, *Dead Men Don't Dig Coal*, by the director's mother, Wendy Lowenstein.

For a first film by a 23-year-old director, this was an immensely ambitious project. Lowenstein, who trained at Swinburne, first met the Doigs while researching *Evictions* (1982), a short film about the Depression. He taped interviews with them, and with other veterans of the 1937 strike at Korumburra, Victoria. He originally envisaged a 50-minute dramatised documentary, but the film finally evolved into a feature budgeted at $750,000, brilliantly shot on Super-16mm by Andrew De Groot.

Lowenstein wanted to film on the original locations, and in a real mine, not a studio set. A mine was found at Wonthaggi that had been disused for several years; it had to be drained and the ventilation shaft restructured.

Chris Haywood likes to research all his roles, and he took a crash course in mine safety. During the shooting of one scene, he complained

Strikebound. *Chris Haywood, Carol Burns.*

that working conditions within a tunnel in the mine were unsafe: 'It had a flaky roof, which is extremely dangerous,' he says. Props were placed under the roof, and the shot began, a very long tracking shot which follows the actor through the mine and ends up at a small seam, where he starts to use a pickaxe on the coalface. 'We did Take One, and I said "Shit, we've done it—I'm out of this." But they said, "Let's do Take Two." Again it went all right, and then they called for Take Three; on Take Three, when I hit the coalface, a huge slab of rock fell from the roof and hit me on the back. I managed to crawl out as more of the roof started falling. It was a near thing. And then it turned out that the local volunteer rescue service official, who we always had standing by, had just had an operation on his knee: he could stand by, but he couldn't actually do anything. I had the cuts on my back dressed, then went down and we shot some more.'

Haywood met with Wattie Doig, a long-time member of the Communist Party, drank a lot of whisky and smoked a fair number of Havana cigars with him. But, he says, 'I learned more about Wattie from the people who'd been around him. He was a self-educated man who'd travelled to Moscow and Beijing, and here he was, living in a fibro house on the edge of an old mining town.'

Though at times Lowenstein has trouble providing a coherent narrative, *Strikebound* is an impressively uncompromising film, with a documentary-style urgency. The writer-director also takes care to make the police human, not just stock villains, and does not flinch from depicting the brutal way the striking miners dealt with scabs. Distributed by Ronin Films, *Strikebound* made a positive impression wherever it was screened.

T he pioneer of the New Australian Cinema of the 70s, Tim Burstall, started the 80s with a war adventure loosely based on real events: this was *ATTACK FORCE Z* (1980). Burstall (b. 1929 in Stockton-on-Tees, England) had come to Australia with his family in 1937, and had worked in the film division of the National Library before embarking on a career making short films and documentaries. He worked for a while in Hollywood, notably as an assistant on the Martin Ritt western, *Hombre*. His first feature was the pioneering *2,000 Weeks* (1968), the film which predates the Australian film revival of the 70s, and he helped get that revival going with *Stork* (1971), an immensely popular adaptation of David Williamson's play of that title. Subsequently, Burstall's films were variable in quality, and included the simple sex farce *Alvin Purple* (1973), the very perceptive study of an Australian macho man, *Petersen* (1974), which was scripted by Williamson, the thriller *End Play* (1975), the semi-comic period adventure *Eliza Fraser* (1976), starring Susannah York, and *The Last of the Knucklemen* (1979), a film version of John Powers' play. The last five of these films were made for Hexagon, the company Burstall had formed in 1972 in collaboration with Village–Roadshow and Bilcock and Copping; but the disappointing returns for the costly *Eliza Fraser*, and the failure of *Knucklemen*, had brought Hexagon's productions to an end.

Attack Force Z, originally titled *The Z Men*, was to have been directed by Phillip Noyce soon after he made *Newsfront*. Noyce had been offered this project by producers John McCallum and Lee Robinson; it was to be a co-production with the Central Motion Picture Corporation in Taipei. Noyce had wanted to make more than just a war film: he also wanted to explore aspects of colonialism. He hired an unusually strong cast of Australian actors—Sam Neill, Mel Gibson, John Waters and Chris Haywood—but was unhappy with the producers' choice for the lead actor, a second-rate Hollywood star called John Phillip Law. The female lead was one of Asia's top actresses: Sylvia Chang.

Before production began, Noyce quarrelled with Robinson and McCallum about his attitude to the material. He was fired, and Burstall was brought in to replace him. The shoot became chaotic, not helped by almost constant rain. There were delays while Burstall worked on rewriting Noyce's script. Chris Haywood recalls: 'It became a horror show. I'd been keen to work with Phil again after *Newsfront*, particularly in the way he talked about interpreting this picture. I'd even done some training with commandos in Sydney to prepare myself. During rehearsal, we all established a good relationship with the Chinese crew members. After Phil was fired, we just sat there in Taiwan for a couple of weeks; and then Burstall arrived. And he took a very heavy-handed approach, which I thought was very bad.'

Haywood also remembers a nasty moment during the shoot. He was being prepared for his death scene. 'The special effects people were loading bullet hits on my back, which were triggered by finger contact. While the guy was loading them, one exploded and blew his eye out. Everyone thought I'd accidentally touched the trigger, which I hadn't. They started to load another, with someone holding my hands to stop me triggering it: it went off again, and they discovered there was a short in the wiring.'

Roadshow acquired the rights to *Attack Force Z*, but it did so poorly when it opened at the Forum in Melbourne in June 1982 that it was never shown in cinemas in other States. However bad it was, a film starring Gibson, Neill, Waters and Haywood would appear to have a good chance at the box-office. It is, indeed, a very poor film in which the bland and uninteresting American lead, Law, is ill-advisedly given centre stage. The five 'Australians' are simply discovered on the Japanese-held island, with no preliminary explanation for their presence, and Sam Neill's brutal act in giving the wounded John Waters the *coup de grace* in the first reel turns the audience off the so-called heroes from the very start. The film moves fast, it looks handsome, the direction is tolerable, the actors (apart from Law) are effective, and Mel Gibson gets to survive at the end. It is not the film Phillip Noyce would have made, though, so McCallum and Robinson had only themselves to blame for its failure to perform. It seems to have had a rich career on video.

Two years later, McCallum and Robinson made another co-production, this time with Japan. The film is *SOUTHERN CROSS* (1982), known in Japan as *Minami Jujisei* and in Britain as *The Highest Honour*. This time, the producers hired a director, Peter Maxwell, whose credentials presumably made him a safe bet: Maxwell has never been known for his personal projects. The 108-minute version (the film ran more than half an hour longer in Japan) was never released in cinemas in Australia. For the most part it is a routine, *Boys' Own* shoot-'em-up, filled with unexplored sub-plots. The last half hour deals with the friendship that grows between John Howard, as the officer in command of Australian POWs, survivors of a failed Z Force mission, and the Japanese prison camp interpreter, who eventually has to behead him in a ritual execution; it contains the seeds of something that, in better hands, might have made a formidable drama.

F ilms about war can be divided between those that claim to be based on real characters and real incidents, and those that are basically adventure stories. *DEATH OF A SOLDIER* (1985) comes into the former category, because Philippe Mora's film deals with Edward J. Leonski, the American soldier who strangled three Melbourne women in 1942 and was executed on the orders of General MacArthur.

Mora (b. 1949 in Paris) grew up in Melbourne; he is a film buff with a fascination for history. A co-founder of the magazine *Cinema Papers*, he made a low-budget feature, *Trouble in Molopolis* (1969) and two feature-length documentaries—*Swastika* (1973) and *Brother Can*

You Spare a Dime? (1975)—in London before returning to Australia to make *Mad Dog Morgan* (1976), a bushranger saga. Subsequently, he has alternated between low-budget American films—*The Beast Within* (1981), *A Breed Apart* (1984), *Howling II* (1984) and *Communion* (1989)—and Australian projects: *The Return of Captain Invincible* (1982), *The Marsupials: Howling III* (1987) and *Death of a Soldier*.

Philippe Mora, director of Death of a Soldier.

The idea of making a film about the ill-fated Leonski had originally come from William Nagle, who wrote the novel on which Tom Jeffrey's 1979 film *The Odd Angry Shot*, about Australian involvement in Vietnam, had been based. Not happy with the way his novel had been filmed, Nagle had written a screenplay which he wanted to produce himself, but eventually David Hannay joined him to co-produce the project. It was originally titled *The Brown-Out Murders* and, later, *War Story* and *The Leonski Incident*. Mora was not involved in the project from the beginning: American director Dick Richards (*The Culpepper Cattle Company*, *Farewell My Lovely*) worked on the project at an early stage. At one time, television personality Don Lane was reported to have been cast in the role of Major Dannenberg, the character eventually played by James Coburn.

Mora and the producers wanted to import American actors to play three key roles: that of Leonski himself; Dannenberg, who defends him; and Gallo, his best friend. During lengthy discussions, Equity baulked at three importations, and in the end there were only two: James Coburn and Reb Brown. It was preposterously suggested that Australian actors be sent to the US for six weeks to learn how to 'act American'. In the event, one of the few weaknesses in a generally strong film proved to be the unconvincing playing by Australian actors of the minor American roles, so that a case could have been made for even more importations.

The film was budgeted at $3 million, but in the event that budget seriously underestimated the cost of the production. Additional funds were raised during shooting by executive producers Richard Tanner and Oscar Scherl, and the final budget was closer to $4 million, but even to keep it at that level it was decided that cuts in the script had to be made. Mora and Hannay worked every day on pruning the screenplay to weed out inessentials. ('The original script was almost a mini-series,' says Hannay.) The result was a shorter shooting schedule. 'Crew members all had contracts which said they could be given a week's notice,' says Hannay. 'And we gave them more than a week's notice that we were going to truncate the shoot by about a week and a half, explaining that the film was costing far more than its original budget. Most crew members accepted this, but a few didn't and complained to the Australian Theatrical and Amusement Employees' Association (ATAEA).' The dispute that followed would crucially affect the fate of the film.

Mora's interest in newsreels and historical subjects stood him in good stead with *Death of a Soldier*. 'Because of my background in documentary,' he says, 'I was fascinated by the subject.' The theme is also similar, in some ways, to *Mad Dog Morgan*; in both films, an unstable protagonist breaks the law and is ruthlessly treated by the authorities. Nagle's screenplay divides neatly into two halves: the first half deals with the murders and the investigation both by American military authorities and Australian police (Bill Hunter, Maurie Fields); the second half centres on the punishment meted out to Leonski.

US-Australian relations at the time are depicted as being very bad; the film opens with a fight between the supposed allies in which several people are hurt. 'Incidents like that were going on all the time,' says Mora. 'We researched all that carefully. I found Censor reports on letters written home by Australian soldiers, and they were filled with vitriolic stuff against the Yanks—the Americans had more money, and Australian women, who'd only seen Americans in movies until then, went crazy for them. The basis of the animosity was sex.'

As Leonski, Mora cast Reb Brown, an actor with whom he had worked on *Howling II*: 'I thought he had a good all-American look, and I liked the idea of playing the psychotic realistically, not having someone who looked crazy. As we know, in real life murderers don't look crazy at all.'

Mora handles the subject with grim realism, extracting excellent performances from Brown and from James Coburn. Overall the film not only recreates wartime Melbourne effectively, but also explores the gross injustice of the legal system of the day. Says Mora: 'I find that whole issue of sanity and the law very interesting. At what point does society start killing people who are insane? The Nazis did it— it was palatable to the German people at the time to kill crazy people. But it's a very fine line, and it's a litmus test of civilisation to see the way the insane are treated.'

When the film was completed, ATAEA slapped a black ban on it. Since cinema employees are members of the same union, no distributor or exhibitor would touch it. A year went by without the film being seen (during which time it opened in the US to generally positive reviews). Eventually, Oscar Scherl distributed the film himself, in independent cinemas. But by that time it stood no chance; *Death of a Soldier*, Philippe Mora, William Nagle and the others all deserved better treatment.

Another true story involving a war trial is the powerful *BLOOD OATH* (1990), Stephen Wallace's film about the events on the island of Ambon, 650 kilometres north-west of Darwin, in the months that followed the end of the war. The film is based on the character of Judge (then Captain) John Williams, who had prosecuted Japanese officers in charge of the POW camp at Ambon during the war: 600 Australians were imprisoned there at the beginning of the war; three years later there were only 120 survivors, most of them in poor condition.

The screenplay for *Blood Oath* was written by Williams' son, Brian: as a child, he had found a trunkload of his father's papers, and had become fascinated with the grim story. Later in life he had ambitions to become a writer, and was so impressed with the television mini-series, *The Last Bastion*, that he approached its writer, Denis Whitburn. Whitburn and Williams then teamed to write and produce *Blood Oath*. They decided Bryan Brown would be perfect as the prosecutor (renamed Cooper in the film) and sent him a copy of the screenplay (he was filming *Gorillas in the Mist* in Africa at the time); and Williams approached director Stephen Wallace at the Sydney Film Festival in 1987.

Wallace (b. 1943) had been the director who 'discovered' Bryan

Brown: Brown's first film role had been in Wallace's first featurette, *Love Letters from Terabla Road* (1977), a beautifully observed drama about the life of an ordinary suburban bloke. Brown had also starred in Wallace's first feature, *Stir* (1980), about the Bathurst prison riots (see Chapter 7); subsequently, the director had made two less successful features, *The Boy Who Had Everything* (1984) and *For Love Alone* (1985), plus a couple of excellent telemovies, including the award-winning *Olive* (1987).

Says Wallace: 'I'd just made a television documentary about the army for *Willesee's Australians*. Brian Williams came up to me and said: "Really liked that army thing you did. I'm writing a film about my father: you'd be the right man to direct it." I said "Fine", and he said he'd send me a script. But then I didn't hear from him, and later I heard Geoff Murphy [the New Zealand director of *Utu* and *The Quiet Earth*] was making the film. Then I got a call from [co-producer] Charles Waterstreet to tell me Murphy was no longer involved, and asking me if I was still interested.'

After being cleared 'by seventeen different people,' Wallace started work on the $10 million production, which was filmed at the Village–Warner Film Studios on the Gold Coast. 'The studios are great to work in,' says Wallace. 'There are no distractions there.' Russell Boyd was cinematographer, and the supporting cast included Ray Barrett, Nicholas Eadie, Jason Donovan, John Clarke and Canadian-born Deborah Unger, who plays a nursing sister on the island. 'She has an easy sexuality that few Australian actresses have naturally,' says Wallace. 'The camera just loves her.'

Equally important in the film are the Japanese actors. 'Working with them was a great experience,' says Wallace. 'Most of them couldn't speak English: they had to learn by rote, but you could never tell by seeing the film.' The Japanese actors are particularly fine in the film.

But *Blood Oath* belongs to Bryan Brown, who gives one of his strongest screen performances. 'I loved working on the film,' he says. 'It's honestly Australian without being indulgently so. There are no games or gimmicks: no emotional tricks. The film isn't saying "This is right or this is wrong." It's saying: "Let's remember our humanity." '

Blood Oath is an ironic drama about justice. The film creeps up on the viewer, inexorably confounding any preconceived notions of right and wrong. At the outset, it seems clear enough: the Japanese committed atrocities and must be punished. But the film asks the

Blood Oath. *Tetsu Watanabi, Bryan Brown.*

question: *Who* should be punished? When Baron Takahashi (George Takei), the Oxford-educated aristocrat who ran the camp, is exonerated thanks to the intervention of an American security man (Takahashi is needed to help run post-war Japan), the way is cleared for underlings who only obeyed orders to be punished in his place. When Cooper witnesses the execution of Hideo Tanaka at the end of the film, we realise, as he does, that he is now also implicated in the death of an innocent man. *Blood Oath* is a very strong picture indeed, and is unquestionably Wallace's best film to date.

T he changes that have occurred in Australia since the end of World War II are in no small part attributable to the migrant programme. Two projects were filmed on this theme during the 80s. *The Dunera Boys*, about a boatload of Jewish refugees from Central Europe, was a longtime project for Melbourne filmmaker Ben Lewin and was originally announced in 1981 as a feature for the Adams–Packer company; in the event, it was made as a mini-series (with Bob Hoskins and Warren Mitchell among the cast).

The second project was *SILVER CITY* (1984), which was produced by Joan Long and directed by Sophia Turkiewicz (b. 1946). The two women originally met in 1974 in Adelaide, where Turkiewicz was living. Long had been invited by the newly formed SAFC to develop some writing talent in the state. Turkiewicz attended Long's course and remembers talking to her about what a powerful film could be made from the story of the post-war immigrants; it would be ten years before such a film was actually made. Long had, coincidentally, suggested a film on the subject, titled *A Boatload of Hope*, while she was at the Commonwealth Film Unit in 1971; this became the working title for Turkiewicz' eventual screenplay.

In the meantime, Turkiewicz attended the Australian Film and Television School in Sydney where she made, as her diploma film, *Letters from Poland*, a short drama starring future television personality Basia Bonkowski as a young Polish refugee. After leaving the school, Turkiewicz received a travel grant from the Polish Consul in Sydney (who had seen *Letters from Poland*) to further her film studies there. She spent six months in her mother's homeland in 1978, and was lucky enough to work as an observer on Andrzej Wajda's *The Maids of Wilko* and in a similar position on Krzysztof Zanussi's German-financed *Paths in the Night*.

While she was in Poland, Turkiewicz started writing what became *Silver City*; in keeping with the working title, she concentrated the action on a ship filled with Polish refugees bound for Australia. By the time she commenced a second draft, Turkiewicz realised she had started the story in the wrong place: the essential drama was not what happened on the boat, but what happened when the migrants arrived in Australia, and subsequent drafts started with the arrival of the boat. She sent an outline to Joan Long, who had admired *Letters from Poland*, and, by the time she returned to Australia, Long had obtained a script-development grant from the AFC.

Developing the screenplay proved very difficult, and the AFC rejected subsequent drafts. Early in 1982, Turkiewicz felt she had come to

Silver City. *Tim McKenzie, Debra Lawrance, Gosia Dobrowolska.*

an impasse. Long felt that part of the problem was Turkiewicz' lack of experience as writer-director, and suggested a co-writer be brought on to the project. Long had met Thomas Keneally when they both attended the Australian film festival at Sorrento, Italy, in October 1980. Keneally had just finished researching his book *Schindler's Ark*, and had spent some time in Poland, so he was a natural choice for the *Silver City* project. Turkiewicz happily agreed to this proposal and gave Keneally her latest draft, together with all her research material; he wrote the next draft. Keneally kept to the framework of the story Turkiewicz had already written; but he injected some new ideas into the story, including the political atmosphere in the camp and the lovely confessional scene, and his name on the project as co-writer proved the key that was needed to unlock further funding. Turkiewicz returned to the project with fresh inspiration, and wrote further drafts.

It was becoming obvious that *Silver City* would be a major project, and Turkiewicz had never directed a feature film before. She and Long decided that it might be wise to develop a more modest project and delay the Polish story, and so Turkiewicz started work, with Frank Moorhouse (with whom she was living at the time), on a script called *Balmain Daddy*, based on a couple of Moorhouse short stories. Eventually titled *Time's Raging*, this project, modest as it was, also failed to attract a distribution guarantee by the following 30 June: without this, Long felt the investors' money should not be put at risk. At the start of the 1982–3 financial year, a decision had to be made whether to spend another year on *Time's Raging*, or return to *Silver City*; they decided on the latter course.

Silver City was budgeted at $2.3 million, and the management company, Cinevest, working together with Long, eventually raised the finance under 10BA tax concessions of 150 and 50 per cent on 30 June 1983.

An early candidate for the central role of Nina had been Gosia Dobrowolska, who had arrived in Australia a few months earlier. She heard about the project from the Multicultural Artists Agency, and, intrigued to hear that a director with a Polish name was working on a Polish subject, phoned Turkiewicz to introduce herself. Turkiewicz met with Dobrowolska at the Villawood migrant hostel where she was living with her husband; at the time she spoke no English and was pregnant. They had a long talk, and as she was about to leave, Turkiewicz said to the actress: 'When I was writing my script, I imagined Nina would look like you.' 'She was gorgeous,' says Turkiewicz, 'but I couldn't seriously consider her.' However, Turkiewicz brought photos of Dobrowolska to show to Joan Long. 'I thought she looked exactly right,' says Long. 'The camera could never go wrong with that face. I put her photo up on my notice board convinced she was our star. I realised she couldn't speak English, but I felt that even if she learnt the English dialogue phonetically we should use her. I didn't see her lack of English as a great drawback.'

Long and Turkiewicz were keen to have Dobrowolska in the role, but shooting was due to start in September (only a month after her baby was expected). Casting agent Helen Rowland organised an audition for a number of potential actresses, including Dobrowolska, which Long did not attend. For Dobrowolska, what followed was a disaster: with her still-limited English, she thought a 'reading' meant simply a reading of the script, which is what she did, while other candidates 'acted' their roles. After the audition, Turkiewicz told Long about the various candidates. 'But what about Gosia?' asked Long. 'She was hopeless,' Turkiewicz replied. 'She didn't understand what was going on.' In the end another actress, Megan Williams (who had been in the television series *The Sullivans*), was cast as Nina. Later, Dobrowolska read a newspaper interview with Williams: 'I felt sad,' she says. 'It was a wonderful part, and I felt so right for it.'

Then came the further delays in financing described above, and, in the intervening year, Dobrowolska learnt basic English. Meanwhile, Turkiewicz had been having increasing doubts as to the ability of any Australian actors to play Polish characters authentically. As it happened, Gosia Dobrowolska had been cast in the leading role in a stage production of *The Bacchae*: she sent Turkiewicz tickets to come and see her performance. (One evening, arriving at the theatre, she saw on the notice board the *National Times* review in which the critic referred to her performance in this, her first English-speaking role, as 'outstanding'. She was not certain what the word meant and thought maybe it meant she was outstandingly bad. Too nervous to ask other cast members, she endured a painful performance before being able to go home and check the meaning of the word in the dictionary.) Turkiewicz had no such doubts about her performance. 'I was now absolutely convinced she was the one,' she says.

Joan Long was in America at the time for the launch there of her previous production, *Puberty Blues*. Although it was late to make such a crucial casting change, Long readily agreed to Dobrowolska replacing Megan Williams, provided the correct steps were taken to achieve this.

Williams was offered a cancellation fee, but took legal action against the filmmakers, and the matter was settled out of court.

With the role of Nina finally cast, the next problem was to cast Julian, her married lover. For a while it looked as if the role would go to Polish actor Andrzej Seweryn, who had appeared in several Andrzej Wajda films, including *Land of Promise* and *Rough Treatment*; but contract complications frustrated this idea. Sam Neill was another contender, but was unable to take the role because of delays in the film he was shooting in France at the time (it was *Possession* which, ironically, was being directed by another Pole, Andrzej Zulawski). Eventually, the Australian actor Ivar Kants won the role, with Steve Bisley and Anna Jemison cast in the key supporting parts. John Seale was chosen as director of photography, and Igor Nay as production designer, both of them making outstanding contributions to the look of the film. Production commenced in October 1983, and the shoot lasted seven weeks. For Turkiewicz, bearing the heavy responsibility of a feature film (with a substantial budget) for the first time, it was not an easy experience, though she received full support from the crew. For Dobrowolska, it was 'an unrepeatable experience, though very hard work. I was in every scene and often exhausted, but very happy.'

The film was completed just in time to be screened in the Market at the 1984 Cannes Film Festival: Long took Dobrowolska with her on the trip to Cannes, which resulted in favourable publicity and consequent sales and invitations to other festivals, such as Montreal and London. In Australia, the film was distributed by Filmways; it had a fairly successful cinema release and subsequently an even more successful career on video, where it is in high demand. The film received numerous nominations in the AFI awards that year, including Dobrowolska for best actress (she lost to Angela Punch McGregor in *Annie's Coming Out*); awards were received for Best Supporting Actress (Anna Jemison) and Actor (Steve Bisley) as well as Costume Design (Jan Hurley).

Silver City is one of the best films of the 80s, though it remains underrated. It tackles a theme too often ignored in Australian cinema, and deals with a painful love story most effectively. The film strongly criticises the attitude of Australian authorities towards the migrants, and scenes in the camp are powerful (the powers-that-be have decided that German be the official language in the camp, hardly a happy choice for these refugees). If there is a criticism, it is of Ivar Kants' performance as Julian; perhaps it is not entirely the fault of the actor, but he comes across as rather a weak man not worthy of the love and loyalty Nina offers him. Bisley and Jemison, on the other hand, lend powerful support; but the film belongs to Gosia Dobrowolska who gives a performance variously described as 'radiant' (Britain's *Monthly Film Bulletin*), 'vibrant' (Sally Hibbin in the London Film Festival programme) and 'luminous' (this writer in *International Film Guide*). Had she not had an accent, Dobrowolska might, after this performance, have become a major star of Australian cinema.

O ne of the most rigorous true stories told in the Australian cinema is *A STREET TO DIE* (1985), which deals with Agent Orange victim Colin Simpson, and which was the first feature directed by former journalist Bill Bennett. Bennett (b. 1953 in London, of Australian parents) was brought up in Brisbane and studied medicine—his father was a dentist—before switching to journalism. In 1972, he got a job as cadet reporter at the ABC in Brisbane and made his first film about Olympic swimmer Stephen Holland. 'From that moment, I was besotted by film,' he says.

He spent two years in Adelaide working on the ABC current-affairs programme *This Day Tonight*, and then went to Sydney to work for Mike Willesee. During this time he received a Logie award in 1978 as Reporter of the Year for two stories, one on illegal street demonstrations in Brisbane, the other on a hunt for a rogue crocodile in the Northern Territory. While working for Willesee, Bennett was involved in a serious car accident, broke his back, and was in hospital for three months: 'It turned out to be a cleansing period,' he says. 'I lay in hospital thinking about the morality of current-affairs programmes, and decided I really would prefer to make films.' At the height of his career as a television journalist, Bennett returned to the ABC to make programmes for *The Big Country*. Later, he joined Peter Luck to work on his series, *The Australians*.

It was at about this time that he read the story of Colin Simpson in *The Weekend Australian*: Simpson was a Vietnam veteran who had died while trying to claim money from the Repatriation Department, and he lived in a suburban street where a significant number of Vietnam veterans had been housed, many of them suffering from sickness of various kinds. Bennett suggested the story as a subject for *The Australians*, but Luck felt it was too dark.

So Bennett decided to try to tell the story in a dramatic feature

A Street to Die. *Chris Haywood, Jennifer Cluff.*

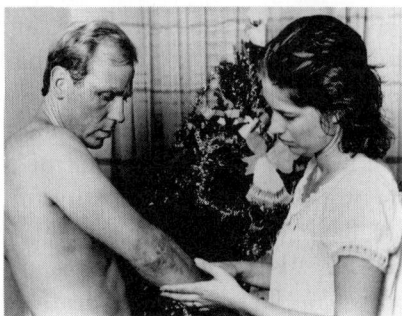

film. 'I knew it had to be made cheaply,' he says, 'so I set the budget at $325,000, printed brochures, made up a Show Reel of some of my documentaries, and headed north.' He decided that it would be better to get far away from the capital cities, where film financing under 10BA was the new growth industry, and ended up in Mackay, where he phoned every accountant and every solicitor in the phone book. 'I had no pre-sale,' he says. 'But I knew the Mackay area, I knew sugar prices had been good, and I thought maybe there were some untapped tax dollars to be invested.' After Mackay, Bennett continued travelling north, from town to town, until he reached Port Douglas, raising money in relatively small amounts along the way. 'Once, I stopped at a petrol station in a tiny little sugar town, and I saw this white Cadillac. It belonged to a local real-estate developer, and as his car was being filled I collared him: he ended up investing.'

Research indicated that Simpson (called Colin Turner in the film) was a feisty character, 'a real larrikin', and Bennett immediately thought of Chris Haywood for the role. 'It was the hardest role I ever had to play,' says Haywood. As Lorraine, Turner's wife, Bennett cast his own wife, Jennifer Cluff. He decided he wanted Geoff Burton as cinematographer, because of his documentary background. 'I delayed the shoot six months until Geoff was available,' he says. 'I knew Geoff would be a crucial element, and I needed a really experienced cinematographer because I hadn't done drama before.'

Bennett decided that, for the sake of authenticity, he wanted to film in the very street in the Sydney suburb of Whalan where Simpson had lived, and Simpson's widow gave him permission to film in her own house; shooting lasted four weeks. Burton, who had decided to film on Super-16mm, says of the experience of shooting the story exactly where it had happened: 'The reality of the street was constantly pressing down on us.' Says Bennett: 'It was a very traumatic shoot. Not only was there the subject matter, and my own inexperience, but it was quite eerie for us all to be in the house. And Lorraine, who had been invaluable during the research period, had difficulty during the filming. Chris was physically very similar to Colin, he literally wore Colin's clothes, and he'd spent a lot of time perfecting Colin's mannerisms.' Haywood had great sympathy for the subject and the character, and for Bennett's ability to get the guts of the story on-screen but, he says, 'I was always terribly aware of Lorraine's presence while I was portraying her husband's death. It was emotionally very hard to do.' Haywood won the AFI Best Actor award for this role.

Bill Bennett, director of A Street to Die.

On one occasion, Lorraine Simpson was in the house when she saw the crew filming the scene of her husband's collapse on the lawn outside. The incident, quite naturally, upset her, and she nearly called a halt to the filming; when the film was finished, however, she was very pleased with it. Despite the emotional problems involved, production was completed three days ahead of schedule.

Though, looking back, Bennett feels *Street* was more of a telemovie than a theatrical feature, he achieved considerable success with it. It was invited to several international film festivals, including Karlovy Vary, where it won the Grand Prix in 1986 (and, as a result, sold all over Eastern Europe, with a 12-print theatrical run in Czechoslovakia). The Other Cinema released the film in Britain, and Bennett was offered a US sale by Miramax (which he turned down hoping for a better offer which never came). In Australia, the film was released by a small company, Octopus, and was snapped up by the Ten Network.

A Street to Die was one of a number of very low-budget films made in the mid-80s and one of the best of them. Chris Haywood does, indeed, give a painfully tough performance as the dying Colin, and his laconic humour is a welcome aspect of the character. Jennifer Cluff brings a strength and determination to the role of Lorraine that is equally inspiring. Apart from one poorly handled sequence, involving an unsympathetic doctor, in which Bennett's inexperience with actors shows, the film grips the viewer throughout; it is a profoundly moving experience.

So, too, is *ANNIE'S COMING OUT* (1984), a film based on the true story of Ann McDonald, brain-damaged at birth, who spent fifteen years of her life in a mental institution. Her story was originally told in a best-selling book which she wrote in collaboration with Rosemary Crossley, the former social worker who worked hard and fiercely to have her released when she realised that McDonald was not mentally, but only physically, retarded.

Rights to the book were purchased by Film Australia, which at the time was the documentary arm of the AFC. Twelve years earlier, Film Australia (then the Commonwealth Film Unit) had been, for a brief while, an exciting place to make films and had attracted up and comers like Peter Weir. But in 1978 Home Affairs Minister John Ellicott stepped in to order the cancellation of what was to have been Film Australia's first feature film, *The Unknown Industrial Prisoner* (to have been produced by Richard Mason and directed by Arch Nicholson); morale at the Film Unit plummeted again. Production of *Annie's Coming Out* restored that morale, for a while at least.

Budgeted at just under $1 million, the film used mainly Film Australia personnel; direction was assigned to Gil Brealey (b. 1932 in Melbourne). It was Brealey's first effort at direction; better known as a producer, he was, for several key years, Director of the SAFC. The screenplay was written with the full collaboration of Crossley and McDonald, and originally it was intended that McDonald play herself in the film. However, by the time shooting started, she had grown physically too big (her growth rate after leaving hospital was, by all accounts, remarkable). Instead, Brealey found 9-year-old Tina Arhondis who was born with cerebral palsy and suffered the same handicaps as McDonald. Angela Punch McGregor was cast as Rosemary Crossley (the character is called Jessica Hathaway in the film).

Shooting started in September 1983 and lasted four weeks. It took place mainly at the Convent of the Good Shepherd in the Melbourne

Gil Brealey, director of Annie's Coming Out.

suburb of Abbotsford. Handicapped children from all over Melbourne were brought to Abbotsford every day for filming. Not surprisingly, there was considerable pressure on the set brought about by the short schedule and the nature of the subject but, says Brealey, 'that intensity brought a sense of emotional immediacy to the film.'

Brealey's treatment is commendably sober and unsentimental, but, inevitably, the Jessica/Rosemary character is glamorised for the film. Still, you could hardly miss with this material, and Punch McGregor underplays so well that she won the 1984 AFI Best Actress award (against stiff competition from Wendy Hughes in *My First Wife* and Gosia Dobrowolska in *Silver City*). The film is not a complete success: some of the supporting actors, playing unsympathetic hospital staff or bureaucrats, descend into caricature, and there is a glibness at times in the treatment; but Tina Arhondis is heartbreakingly effective as Annie and there are solid supporting performances from Drew Forsythe (as Jessica's boyfriend), Simon Chilvers (her lawyer) and Charles Tingwell (the judge).

Annie's Coming Out. *Tina Arhondis, Angela Punch McGregor.*

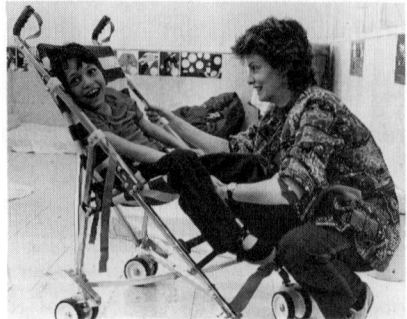

Hoyts distributed the film in Australia. 'It was a great movie,' says Jonathan Chissick, 'with great performances. But, basically, it was a depressing picture and people shied away from it. We felt it needed support, but it was a very hard film to handle.' Universal Pictures, somewhat surprisingly, bought the US rights to the film, changed the title to *A Test of Love*, and released it with the tagline, 'They were looking for a miracle—but found something more.' The film did very little business.

F ilm biographies have not been all that common in Australian cinema. One intriguing project was announced in 1982, but never came to anything: it was *The Percy Grainger Story*, to have been scripted by Thomas Keneally and produced by Tom Haydon. At the end of the 80s, producer Frank Howson and director Brian Kavanagh were working on *Flynn*, a biography of the early days of Errol, with Guy Pearce in the lead, for 1990 release. There is also the virtually unseen *Call Me Mr Brown* (1987), about the Qantas extortionist, made as a telemovie for the Ten Network with Scott Hicks as director and Chris Haywood in the leading role. This was completed, but never aired by the network (concern on the part of Qantas is rumoured to be the reason). At one stage, negotiations were completed for the film to be released theatrically, but to date this has not eventuated.

Undoubtedly the most controversial true story of the 80s is *EVIL ANGELS* (1989), Fred Schepisi's treatment of the Lindy Chamberlain case. The film, based on John Bryson's book about the events that followed the disappearance of tiny Azaria Chamberlain at Ayers Rock in 1980, marked Schepisi's return to Australia to work on a feature film for the first time since *The Chant of Jimmie Blacksmith* in 1978. Schepisi (b. 1939 in Melbourne) had been a key figure of the New Wave of the 70s, with many regarding his 1976 film, *The Devil's Playground*, as the film of the decade. Since the disappointing critical and public reaction to *Blacksmith*, Schepisi had been working abroad, where he had made *Barbarosa* (1982), a western with Willie Nelson, *Iceman* (1984), a sci-fi drama with John Lone as a prehistoric man, *Plenty* (1985), an adaptation of the David Hare play, with Meryl Streep, and *Roxanne* (1987), a popular comedy based on *Cyrano de Bergerac*, with Steve Martin and Daryl Hannah.

Schepisi had been away from Australia at the time of Azaria's disappearance, but in the following months he frequently visited Melbourne and heard about the case through dinner-party conversations. 'They were incredibly distorted,' he says, 'and I remember being fascinated at the passion with which people were having these discussions and at the absolutely irrational behaviour of normally rational people.' Bryson's book, published in 1985 while Lindy Chamberlain was in prison, came to the attention of British producer Verity Lambert, who was attracted by the theme of miscarriage of justice. She bought the rights and forced a reluctant Schepisi to read it: 'By about 150 pages, I became appalled about how little information the people who talked so much about it actually had. And when I finished, I was outraged, and angry at myself because I'd participated in this process.' Making a film of the story seemed to Schepisi at first to risk doing the Chamberlains further harm.

Lambert sent a copy of the book to Meryl Streep, whose immediate interest in the project was a crucial factor. Robert Caswell was hired to write a screenplay, and eventually Schepisi was persuaded to take on the film. Initially, the Chamberlains themselves were nervous about the prospect of a film being made about them: 'We asked them to reveal themselves to us,' says Lambert. Caswell spent time with them, and, says Schepisi, 'they realised we didn't want to sensationalise, but to present the facts as accurately as we could. They felt that we were worth trusting.'

Lambert was able to raise money from the Cannon Group with a guaranteed worldwide release through Warner Bros. Equity raised no objection to the casting of Streep, on the grounds that she was an actress of indisputable stature. It was Streep who suggested Sam Neill (with whom she had worked on *Plenty*) for the role of Michael Chamberlain.

Evil Angels became the biggest production ever undertaken in Australia. Locations, in Melbourne, Darwin and Ayers Rock, were thousands of miles apart, the speaking cast numbered 350 and there were nearly 4000 extras in all. In Central Australia, the crew filmed in temperatures up in the 50s (celsius), and dust storms plagued the unit. So did journalists anxious to interview Streep, the most famous actress to have worked in an Australian-based production since Ava Gardner in *On the Beach* thirty years earlier. Having Streep in the film was, according to Sam Neill 'a shot in the arm. The crew were on their toes, all the other actors were making bloody sure they didn't forget their lines.' Playing Michael was, for Neill, 'bloody scary. I'd never done a real-life person before, and Michael's a hard character to get a handle on.' Streep and Neill met the Chamberlains, as well as other key characters in the real-life drama. But for Neill, 'watching the newsreel footage was equally important—to see how Michael dealt with reporters. He didn't know what to say, and so he was quite revealing about himself.'

It is interesting to see how the events depicted in *Evil Angels* parallel those in Peter Weir's *Picnic at Hanging Rock*: there is the rock itself, to begin with, a rugged natural landmark. There is the picnic, the disappearance, and the way that disappearance affects the lives of so many other people. Above all there is the lack of resolution: the victim's body is never discovered, the mystery never solved. Says Schepisi: 'This case combined a whole series of elemental things that somehow threaten us and so we attack back. The message of the film is that there *are* no simple answers, there are often things that can't be explained and should just be left alone.'

The film is also an attack on the media. 'We get very little actual information from television news reports,' says Schepisi. 'We get a lot of sensational entertainment in very small quick parcels which reinforce whatever bias we first formed.' Schepisi also depicts the powerlessness of the individual to fight against the media and the Establishment: 'I wanted the world to see how two, seemingly very ordinary people, somehow survived this ordeal, but showed amazing

Evil Angels. *Meryl Streep, Sam Neill.*

strength of character and amazing faith. I think the Chamberlains are remarkable people.'

Evil Angels is also a remarkable film, and Schepisi's best to date. Whatever one's position on the Chamberlain case may be, there is no doubt that the film tackles a complex subject and makes it a model of clarity. Not only is a moving human drama brought to the screen with impeccable performances and a high degree of emotion, but a panorama of Australia in the 80s is presented through the use of ordinary people from many different walks of life who comment on the case as the drama unfolds.

The film was invited to compete in the 1989 Cannes Film Festival as an Australian entry (yet, unaccountably, was presented with its international title, the very bland *A Cry in the Dark*). Streep, Neill, Schepisi and Lambert were in attendance, and Streep won the Golden Palm for Best Actress. Later in the year, she also won the AFI award, an interesting choice given the on-going concern about Americans playing Australian roles. Sam Neill deservedly won as Best Actor, and the film also won awards for Schepisi's direction, Caswell's screenplay and for Best Film.

And yet it did not perform at the box-office as well as might have been expected, given the positive reviews and the quality of the production. It may be that, as was the case with *Jimmie Blacksmith* a decade earlier, Schepisi was confronting Australians with a subject they really did not want to know about. Whatever the reason, the film is unquestionably a contender as one of the best films of the decade.

THE

BIG

COUNTRY

■
■

T he vast expanses of the continent of Australia are ideally suited to the outdoor adventure film. Many films made during the 80s used the Australian landscape as a symbol of freedom and escape; in other films, conversely, the landscape becomes a prison.

Before *Crocodile Dundee* came along in 1986, the most successful Australian feature film was *THE MAN FROM SNOWY RIVER* (1982); audiences responded with extraordinary enthusiasm to this old-fashioned, but often thrillingly filmed, saga which was inspired by Banjo Paterson's poem. Geoff Burrowes and George Miller (2) produced and directed the film respectively; like Paul Hogan, they were no fans of the Australian film establishment. In interviews, Burrowes has referred to 'intellectual wankers' and 'Aussie bleeders' among the industry, while Miller derides film critics as 'ignorant', 'low-grade' and 'wrong'.

Burrowes (b. 1945) and Miller (b. 1943) both worked at Crawfords where they learnt the business of making fast-paced film for television (Burrowes was also, for a while, press secretary to Labor federal politician Moss Cass). Miller was born in Scotland, but moved to Melbourne with his parents when he was a child; among the many television series he directed were *Cash and Company*, *Against the Wind* and *All the Rivers Run*. Burrowes is deeply committed to the outdoor life but (judging from his subsequent film, *Cool Change*, discussed in Chapter 7) takes a conservative view about the environment.

According to Burrowes, the inspiration for *Snowy River* came during a dinner party when someone suggested the poem would make a good basis for a film. Burrowes was enthusiastic about the idea, even though the poem basically only supplies a climax and the names of three characters: Clancy of the Overflow, the legendary hero; Harrison; and 'The Man' himself, though the poem makes clear that the character is 'a lad'. Over a weekend, Miller and Burrowes devised a story outline, which they then developed over several weeks; they finally turned it over to John Dixon to write the screenplay.

At first, Burrowes and Miller got little encouragement. They were television people who had no track record in feature-film production ('which', says Burrowes sarcastically, 'I take to mean, we had not failed five times in the film business.') The men were advised by some 'senior figures in the industry' to keep the budget at about $750,000, or to make it for television. Eventually, Simon Wincer, who had at the time directed *Snapshot* and *Harlequin* for Tony Ginnane and who was working with entrepreneur Michael Edgley on possible film projects, contacted Burrowes. Edgley and Wincer joined the production as executive producers, and raised the $3 million budget.

It was decided to shoot in the Victorian High Country around Mansfield—where Burrowes' wife's family had lived for several generations—rather than in the Snowy Mountains themselves; the Mansfield region is spectacularly beautiful, and it was logistically more convenient. Miller had worked with Sigrid Thornton before, and Wincer had directed her in her first film, *Snapshot*; she was cast as Jessica, the feisty heroine. Jack Thompson was also an easy choice for Clancy, but an early decision was made not to give the character too much screen time in case he overshadowed the central character, which meant that the actor has very little to do and looks almost like an afterthought. This was Tom Burlinson's first film, and he was cast after a long period of auditions and screen tests for which Sigrid Thornton made herself available to act opposite potential co-stars.

The most controversial casting decision was that of Kirk Douglas. Initially the characters of Harrison, Jessica's landowner father, and Spur, the hermit friend of young Jim, were to have been former friends. It was decided in the end to make them long-lost brothers, and to have Douglas play them both. Burrowes and Miller appear not to have

The Man from Snowy River. *Sigrid Thornton, Tom Burlinson.*

been perturbed at the bizarre notion of casting a Hollywood veteran in such a deeply Australian project: 'We wanted to get outside the fortress mentality,' says Burrowes. Of course, having a name like Douglas in the picture, no matter how incongruous it might seem, would do no harm to box-office prospects in America.

When the film was released, there was understandable confusion between its director and the George Miller who had made the hugely successful *Mad Max* three years earlier (and who was currently shooting its sequel, *Mad Max 2*). The *Snowy River* director had, unquestionably, preceded the *Mad Max* director in the business, but only in television. It is a pity that he did not consider identifying himself with even a middle initial on the *Snowy River* credits. But he did not, and confusion has reigned ever since. The film critic of *The Australian*, Evan Williams, assumed in his review of *The Man from Snowy River* that the film had been directed by the *Mad Max* Miller. Some time later, when American actress Rosanna Arquette arrived in Yugoslavia to make the MGM film, *The Aviator*, opposite Christopher Reeve, she was amazed to find that her director, an Australian called George Miller, was not the same man who had directed *The Road Warrior* (as *Mad Max 2* was known in the US).

Most critics greeted *The Man from Snowy River* without enthusiasm, and no wonder. The screenplay is a mass of simple-minded clichés, and Kirk Douglas huffs and puffs embarrassingly in his dual roles. The young leads, Tom Burlinson and Sigrid Thornton, rise above their material, but the stars of the film are undoubtedly the horses and their riders, plus the spectacular mountain scenery, lovingly shot by Keith Wagstaff. Also deserving unstinting praise are all those responsible for staging the climactic 'ride', a breathtaking sequence in which a mob of horses and riders charge down what appears to be a hillside so alarmingly steep that it constitutes almost a sheer drop.

If the critics resisted the film, the public took to it in an unprecedented way. Hoyts distributed the film (the company already had a relationship with Michael Edgley) and the box-office results were little short of astonishing. Within a short while, the film became the biggest-grossing Australian film of all time, and would have been the most successful film ever released in Australia if not for the release the same year of Steven Spielberg's *E.T.*, which topped it. By the end of 1988, *The Man from Snowy River* was fourth in the all-time list of Australian box-office rental champs (according to *Variety*) with an accumulated gross film rental of $7,820,000. The filmmakers had to be content with money, not awards: at the 1982 AFI awards, the only prize the film received was for Bruce Rowland's rousing music score.

Overseas, the film was sold to 20th Century–Fox and did good enough business in the US for Sigrid Thornton and Tom Burlinson to be considered 'names', at least for a while.

The sequel, *THE MAN FROM SNOWY RIVER II* (1988), was not such a success story. Burrowes moved from the producer's chair to the director's (just as John Cornell, producer of *Crocodile Dundee*, would take over as director of *'Crocodile' Dundee II*), so George Miller (2) was out; out also were Simon Wincer and Michael Edgley. (In the interim the Hoyts–Edgley production company, formed in the wake of the first film, had made a number of films which had disappointing box-office returns.) John Dixon returned as screenwriter, this time sharing a credit with Burrowes; and Keith Wagstaff and Bruce Rowland repeated their vitally important roles as cinematographer and composer respectively. Gone, mercifully, was Kirk Douglas. He was replaced, in the Harrison role, by another American actor, Brian Dennehy, who proved far better in this role. Gone was Jack Thompson's Clancy; gone, indeed, was any hint of Banjo Paterson. Tom Burlinson and Sigrid Thornton, of course, returned in the leads.

'I didn't want to make directing a career move,' says Burrowes. 'I was quite happy being a producer. But the film was very important to me: the whole ethos, the whole milieu was part of me. I was living up in the high country, I farmed there. The film was my own view of the traditions, legacies and values of the people who live in that country. I felt that, even with the best director in the world, I'd be all over him criticising everything he did. It would have led to clashes, and I'd probably have to have walked away. Instead, I decided to do it myself, though I had some wonderful collaborators. I distrust and dislike the auteur theory.'

Burrowes also rejects the self-criticism of many Australian films. 'I only want to entertain, never to depress,' he says. As a result, he lays great stress on what he sees as the uplifting moral values of both the central character and the film itself. He wanted to ensure audience expectations from the first film were fulfilled, so the basic themes of the two films are identical. But, in the intervening eight years, technical advances in film stock and also better equipment (cranes, dollies) allowed more spectacular footage. 'We built a special rig so that we could film a rider's point of view while doing a flat gallop,' says Burrowes.

The second film is, if anything, a marginal improvement on the first. The script still abounds with clichés ('It's him or me!' 'Let's get outta here!') and Jim Craig's moral values are as heroic and as saintly as ever, but the action scenes are even better staged and shot, the obligatory ride down the steep hillside is even more breathtaking, and on a purely technical level the film is, quite simply, superb.

Significantly, the film lacks the usual title stating that no animals were hurt during the making of it (such a title is usually displayed in films of this kind these days). During shooting, it was reported that a wounded horse was bludgeoned to death by members of the film crew, apparently to stop its suffering. The RSPCA instituted proceedings against the Burrowes Group; these were dismissed by the court.

Although the sequel performed significantly less well than the original ($2,579,000 in gross rentals by the end of 1988), it did very respectable business, though perhaps not commensurate with its far larger budget. In the US it was released by the Walt Disney company ('In the Great Disney Tradition!' claimed the advertisements), but was mysteriously retitled *Return To Snowy River Part II*; quite what the 'Part II' is doing there is unclear, since the first film retained its original title in America. Box-office returns were disappointing.

Geoff Burrowes was also financially involved with *MINNAMURRA* (1988), which is almost *Snowy River III* in terms of plot and character. Originally titled *Outback*, this outdoors adventure was written and produced by John Sexton and directed by Ian Barry. It also centres on a feisty, independent young woman (Tushka Bergen) who lives on a country property; and it also features a mob of horses and riders galloping across country at the climax.

Barry was a film editor who had made a number of interesting short films (most notably *Waiting for Lucas* in 1973) and had previously made *The Chain Reaction* (1980) for producer David Elfick (see Chapter 8). He had not directed a feature since, though he had worked in television. It is a pity that his comeback was so bland, and, in the event, such a box-office failure. But *Minnamurra* is one of those films in which the plot is edited down to the bone (presumably to get on with the action and romance) so that it often becomes confusing, and even stalwart character actors like Sandy Gore (the heroine's free-living aunt) and Richard Moir (a scheming embezzler) are left undernourished.

The inevitable American import here is a handsome, but

uncharismatic, fellow called Jeff Fahey, but the film is stolen by Steven Vidler who gives a thoroughly professional performance as a drover inexplicably passed over by the heroine in favour of the American. Visually the film is a treat; photography is by Ross Berryman.

T he three films discussed above all take themselves very seriously: *BULLSEYE* (1986) does not take itself seriously at all, but its ribald sense of humour is so appealing that the film's almost complete disappearance is a cause for considerable regret. The original screenplay, written by Robert Wales, was called *Trailblazer*, and it was based on a real-life character: Harry Radford, the flamboyant outlaw who, not so long after Burke and Wills had perished in Central Australia, stole 1000 head of cattle in Roma, Queensland, and successfully drove them all the way to the stockyards in Adelaide. PBL Productions, at the time an offshoot of the Nine Network, acquired the screenplay and at one stage Joan Long planned to produce, with Peter Yeldham working on a new draft. At this stage, the idea was to film a straightforward, truthful, historical epic—perhaps a cross between *Burke and Wills* and *Robbery Under Arms*; but then Carl Schultz was offered the film, and he thought that it had possibilities—not as a serious, dramatic story, but as an adventure film with lots of humour. 'I thought the script was funny,' says Schultz. 'It was overstated and quite hilarious.' Schultz suggested to Brian Rosen, who at the time was working for PBL, that 'all this script needs is an angle. If you do it as a realistic piece, it'll just be guys trudging through the desert again. Let's make it a comedy.' Yeldham did not see the project the same way as Schultz, so dropped out; Bob Ellis was brought in to write additional dialogue.

PBL formed an association with a British company, Dumbarton Films, to make *Bullseye* (as it was eventually called); Dumbarton was an offshoot of Video Arts, the John Cleese company, and part of the deal was that Dumbarton had worldwide marketing rights to the film— *including* Australia.

The film was shot in the new anamorphic System 35 by Dean Semler, on a $4.5 million budget, under the working title *Birdsville*. Production was based at Bourke, where designer George Liddle built some magnificent sets, including the main street of Roma, and the homestead where the cattleman (Paul Chubb) and his argumentative wife (Lynette Curran), live in splendour. Later, the production returned to Sydney, and the sequences set in the Adelaide brothel—with Kerry Walker a formidable madam—were shot in the Mort Bay studios at Balmain.

Bullseye. *Production Designer George Liddle's magnificent outdoor set of nineteenth century Roma (built at Bourke showgrounds).*

When the film was completed, Brian Rosen showed it to Jonathan Chissick of Hoyts; Chissick was immediately interested in distribution, but Dumbarton had more ambitious plans: the company apparently wanted a Hollywood major to handle the film worldwide in much the same way as *Crocodile Dundee* (which, at the time, was breaking box-office records). By the time every American company had seen the film, and had either rejected it or made an offer Dumbarton was not prepared to accept, Dumbarton had been closed down. This put the film into limbo while lawyers determined who owned the vitally important marketing rights—and months went by. By the time it was finally sorted out, and Hoyts acquired the film for Australia, two years had passed. No-one was very enthusiastic about *Bullseye* any more; it had been hanging around too long. Hoyts opened it in Brisbane for a test booking (Schultz heard about this only after the event); when it failed to ignite the box-office there, they withdrew it altogether. Soon after, the picture was released on video, where Dean Semler's magnificent wide-screen photography looked puny indeed. 'It was very frustrating,' says Schultz. 'The director is totally powerless in that situation. All those months of work, and so few people saw the film.'

Schultz attempts something risky in *Bullseye*; he has his young romantic leads, newcomers Paul Goddard and Kathryn Walker, play their roles straight, while all around them a gallery of splendid character actors indulge in some ripe comedy. Among them are such stalwarts as John Wood, as the hero's reluctant offsider, Bruce Spence, as a treacherous cowhand, and, as already mentioned, Chubb, Curran and Walker. The late John Meillon has a wonderful cameo as a drunken judge in the climactic trial scene, which is beautifully lit by Semler; indeed, the photography (unacknowledged at the AFI awards that year) is outstanding throughout: amazing landscapes of desolate desert country contrast with the low-key filming of the beautifully designed sets. Schultz's wild comic approach to the material goes overboard a couple of times, but generally he is right on target. This is certainly no gloomy trek through the desert; the film positively zips along, and Chris Neal's music score is one of his best.

Few enough good films are made made in Australia, and fewer still that are also hugely entertaining; the neglect of *Bullseye* is one of several wasted opportunities of the 80s. And it is even more frustrating when the non-release of the Schultz film is contrasted with the wide distribution given to the thoroughly dull *ROBBERY UNDER ARMS* (1985), the laborious fifth version of Rolf Boldrewood's book (which is said to have been inspired by the exploits of the same Harry Radford whose story Schultz told in *Bullseye*).

Earlier film versions of the story were made in 1907, 1911, 1920 and 1957, the latter with Peter Finch in a British-made version directed by Jack Lee. They had been quite popular; but the decision of the SAFC to make the new version as both a television mini-series and a feature film set the seal on its failure. As most filmmakers know, cinema and television are very different, and though attempts have been made before to combine a film and a television series they have never really succeeded. At the time, producer Jock Blair explained that the idea for a mini-series came first, but it was felt to be too expensive. Separate scripts for the two formats were written, but, at 141 minutes, the feature film is ludicrously overlong.

Ken Hannam, who was responsible for the SAFC's first production, and first triumph, *Sunday Too Far Away*, was brought back from Britain to co-direct with Donald Crombie, and the combined budget for both formats of the film became $7.3 million. Hannam had been understandably bitter about the way an earlier regime at the SAFC had recut (some say ruined) *Sunday Too Far Away* (as described in *The Last New Wave*); he was initially wary about returning, but worked well with Donald Crombie, alternating the direction hour by hour.

Sam Neill, ideally cast as the charismatic Captain Starlight, recalls: 'Ken and Don are very different. Don's a great enthusiast, but I think Ken got a bit bored with it all about halfway through. I think Ken's a more natural director, though.' Neill also sees the attempt to combine cinema and television formats as a crucial problem with the film: 'You can't cut something both ways,' he says. 'You do one or the other. You shoot them differently. The film version of *Robbery Under Arms* goes on forever but doesn't make sense because there are whole areas

of the story that just don't exist in the film. So it's all over the place.'
Neill remembers the shoot with affection, however, especially the
spectacular location (the Flinders Ranges), and the chance to work
with Steven Vidler, excellent as Dick Marston, and Aboriginal actor
Tommy Lewis, as Warrigal. 'And I'll do anything on horses,' he says.

Neill's comments are very accurate; in trying to have it both ways,
Robbery Under Arms falls flat on its face. It strives to be a humorous
adventure (during production, Blair described it, most ingenuously,
as akin to *Butch Cassidy and the Sundance Kid* or *Raiders of the Lost
Ark*) but falls wide of the mark—a mark much more accurately hit
by the unfortunate *Bullseye*. The film version is disjointed, uninvolving
and almost totally lacking humour. Sam Neill makes a charming
gentleman bushranger, Ed Devereux has some good moments as the
head of the Marston clan, and Steven Vidler has a strong presence.
But one of the film's many annoyances is that it introduces an excellent
character in Mungo, the gourmet outback cook so amusingly played
by Paul Chubb, and then drops him after a brief establishing scene.

The general public was not enthralled by this fiasco. I well remember
the opening night in a Sydney cinema, which was sparsely attended.
When the 'intermission' title came up, after an almost unbearable first
half, the woman sitting behind me turned to her partner and said:
'Do we *have* to stay?' The answer was obviously no, since they did
not return. Sometimes the role of a film reviewer is a hard one: I
had to stay.

Tommy Lewis also appears to advantage in another outdoor adventure
film made the same year: this is THE NAKED COUNTRY (1985), an
adaptation of Morris West's 1957 novel. This project was initiated
by Robert Ward, managing director of the independent distribution
company, Filmways. He thought West's book would make a good film,
and brought it to the attention of Ross Dimsey who, at the time, was
Chief Executive of the Victorian Film Corporation (Ward was a member
of the VFC Board). Rights to the novel were acquired, and Tim Burstall
was brought on to the project. It was budgeted at $2.75 million, of
which about 10 per cent came from the Queensland Film Corporation,
with the proviso that the film was shot in that State. In the event,
production was based at Charters Towers, where it was very hot and
humid during production.

Burstall turns the film into an Australian western, and much of
The Naked Country is quite exciting, especially in the scenes in which
hero John Stanton struggles to survive after he has been wounded

by Aboriginal lances and left to die in the bush. Unfortunately, the sentiments of the 50s which are basic to the novel, although worked over considerably in the screenplay by Burstall and Dimsey, still come across in the 80s as patronising and insensitive towards blacks, and this impression is heightened by the embarrassing miscasting of Neela Dey, an Asian actress who had played Junie Morosi in the mini-series *The Dismissal*. To cast Ms Dey as an Aboriginal woman in the mid-80s boggles the mind; it might have been supposed that such clangers ended back in 1967, when Ed Devereux and Kamahl appeared as Aborigines in an almost-forgotten shocker called *Journey out of Darkness*.

The Naked Country suffers from another piece of miscasting: Ivar Kants as the weak, drunken outback policeman. A sequence in which he has an affair with Rebecca Gilling, playing Stanton's bored and lonely wife, was dropped after early rough-cut screenings indicated that such a relationship did not work on screen, and this was in part due to Kants' lacklustre performance. By removing that whole section of the plot, Burstall was, however, able to concentrate even more on the action elements of the drama. In the event, though, neither audiences nor critics responded to the picture.

D USTY (1982) is an outdoors film of a more modest type. Bill Kerr plays the lead, an old drover, now working as a station hand, whose beloved dog and best friend is part-dingo and like his master gets the call of the wild. John Stanton plays a dingo-hunter, out to track down the pair, but all is resolved in a more or less happy ending. This is simple family fare ably directed by John Richardson. It has a rock-solid performance from Kerr, a scene-stealing dog, and most attractive locations in the farm country of northern Victoria.

A very different approach to the landscape of Victoria's High Country is to be found in *THE PLAINS OF HEAVEN* (1982), the first feature of director Ian Pringle. Pringle had worked briefly at the ABC and made a handful of documentaries and a 50-minute mini-feature, *Wronsky* (1979) prior to this; he is a director with a very striking way of relating characters to their environment. At times his approach can be precious, even pretentious (as in his later *The Prisoner of St Petersburg*), but in *The Plains of Heaven* the technique is fresh.

The film was produced by Seon Films (the company established by Pringle, Bryce Menzies and Timothy White) on a tiny budget (basically $100,000, which, when augmented with deferrals and a marketing grant, became $160,000); most of the money came from the Creative

Development Branch of the AFC. Shooting took place at Falls Creek, in the Bogong High Plains, and the story is a two-hander involving the relationship between two men (Richard Moir, Reg Evans) working at an isolated satellite relay station.

Pringle asks his audience to explore the minds of these characters, but denies access to their backgrounds. Instead, we watch as they go about their daily routines: Moir, transfixed by television game shows, Evans pottering about the chilly-looking hills bird-watching or using his pet ferrets to catch rabbits. When both characters are driven over the edge of sanity, it is, we assume, the loneliness and isolation that is responsible (though, in Moir's case, a frightening trip to the noise and pressure of Melbourne is also to blame). The two central performances are memorable, and Pringle even allows for a fleeting appearance from that mascot of low-budget Victorian filmmakers, academic and occasional actor John Flaus.

The Plains of Heaven compares interestingly to *SPIRITS OF THE AIR, GREMLINS OF THE CLOUDS* (1988), another idiosyncratic feature in which landscape plays an important role. Writer-director Alex Proyas, a graduate of the Australian Film, Television and Radio School, made an impact with his prize-winning 1981 short film, *Groping* (which he co-directed), a film as controversial as it was brilliant. But the best thing to be said about his first feature is that it does, indeed, have a special vision.

The setting is the desert, apparently some time in the future. The situation involves a brother and sister, unable—for unspecified reasons—to leave this remote place, and the stranger who arrives to try to help them build an aircraft to fly away. Unfortunately, the actors are not up to the demands Proyas makes of them, and even while appreciating the brilliance of Sean Callinan's production design (the wooden house, the hundreds of burning candles and religious icons), the film frustrates because of its lethargy and stiltedness. The credit titles are an additional annoyance, written as they are in such a spidery hand as to be virtually illegible.

Also flawed, but overcoming its problems thanks to the purity of its vision, is *THE TALE OF RUBY ROSE* (1987), a pictorially magnificent film set in the snow-covered mountains of the Central Highlands of Tasmania. This is the work of Roger Scholes (b. 1950 in Launceston) who had attended art school in Tasmania and who, when he saw *Doctor Zhivago* at the age of eighteen, decided he wanted to be an art director. He enrolled in the film course at Swinburne Institute of Technology and worked for a while with the Melbourne production company Bilcock and Copping. In 1973, when the four-part film *Libido* was made, he had the opportunity to photograph the Fred Schepisi episode, *The Priest*, under the supervision of Ian Baker.

But, after this training and experience, Scholes became disillusioned. The only future he could see was making documentaries and commercials, so he dropped out of the film industry and left for Europe. He was away during most of the 70s, when the film revival in Australia really got going: he built chalets in Switzerland, and worked for a photographer in Oxford. Towards the end of the decade, he returned to Tasmania and worked in a farm community workshop.

He was also working on a personal project: a collection of oral histories of people living in the Central Highlands, for which he took more than 500 photographs of places and people in the remote region. This experience became the genesis for his first feature. 'I met people on whom I later based the characters in the film,' says Scholes.

Fired with enthusiasm for cinema, now, Scholes enrolled in a postgraduate course at Swinburne and made three short films. Terence McMahon and Greg Tepper (of Film Victoria) gave him encouragement and, more importantly, money to write the screenplay for the film, but this was a process he found extremely difficult: 'My beginnings were in documentary,' he says. 'I found it difficult to make the transition to drama.' In the end, he feels, he never did fully make that transition:

The Tale of Ruby Rose. *Melita Jurisic.*

the oral history genesis of *Ruby Rose* remained a very powerful aspect of the film. 'In the end, the screenplay was only three-quarters right,' he says. 'And that became hazardous when other people got involved.'

Seon Films, the same company that had produced *The Plains of Heaven*, backed Scholes, and financing was arranged through Tony Ginnane's Film and General Holdings (FGH) company. The budget was $1.2 million of which nearly $500,000 was, in Scholes' words, 'bled off', leaving $730,000 with which to make the film. Part of the problem in making the film—and a major contribution to its success— was the location itself: most of the shooting took place in a natural valley, with high cliffs on three sides, known as the Walls of Jericho. Special permission was granted by the Tasmanian authorities to fly in aluminium sheds to house the crew, and also to bring a small number of horses, goats and chickens into the area. A mess hall was built with two gas fires for drying clothes; camp stretchers were used for beds. During production, water froze at night and conditions became almost unbearable.

Scholes had seen Melita Jurisic in a production of Louis Nowra's play, *The Golden Age*; at first he thought she was too young to play Ruby, but later he was satisfied she could act older than her age. As for Chris Haywood, Scholes saw him in Bill Bennett's *A Street to Die* and knew, instantly, he had to play Henry Rose.

Says Haywood: 'It was a total adventure. We filmed in the middle of winter, and it got pretty bleak there.' Says Scholes: 'It got pretty hairy, very harsh. We had to live in terrible conditions. I'm surprised nobody rebelled against it, and I certainly wouldn't put people through that again.' Haywood was taught how to snare wallabies and other small animals by a local, and also how to survive in the rugged conditions. 'We had to eat wallaby during the shoot,' he says, 'because we ran out of supplies. We lived on our wits. I even had to cook for a while.' It had been planned to fly supplies into the valley by helicopter, but it turned out to be such a harsh winter that the 'copter was grounded for most of the shoot. Backpackers had to bring in supplies, including the film rushes.

Three weeks of the six-week shoot took place in these conditions, but at the end of those six weeks only 70 per cent of the film had been shot. During the shoot, Scholes worked every night on rewriting, and cut major sections of the original script to save time. Even so, after principal photography was finished, a depleted second unit had to return to the location for a further three weeks; cinematographer

Steve Mason was unable to spend more time on the film, so Scholes shot the remaining 30 per cent of the film himself. These scenes include the barn raising, timber gathering, and Ruby's journey down to the valley and back. Says Haywood: 'When we came back for the reshoot, conditions were even worse. Our facilities had been partially dismantled in the meantime, and we had very little support.'

The magnificent scenery frequently overshadows the human characters in *The Tale of Ruby Rose*, which, on one level, is so rich that its flaws are all the more disappointing. The gaps in the narrative are all too apparent, and Melita Jurisic is often stilted and awkward as the traumatised, isolated protagonist. On the other hand, Chris Haywood, with Welsh accent, is splendid as her unfeeling husband, and one wishes the film had concentrated on his character rather than on hers. Rod Zuanic, as their adopted son, is unable to make much of a sketchy role.

The problems seem to stem partly from the scenes that were dropped during shooting, but equally as a result of post-production recutting: twelve minutes were removed after Scholes' original cut, undoubtedly contributing to the holes in the narrative. Scholes acknowledges that 'it is a flawed film,' but feels that he learnt a lot. 'I'd do it very differently if I could do it again,' he says. But the way of life depicted in such a tactile manner in the film, and the link between the amazing setting and the people who live there, comes across strongly, and the film has a look and feel like no other Australian film. Notable, too, is Paul Schutze's award-winning music score. The film did quite good, if not spectacular, business in Australia, and screened theatrically in several other countries including the US and Canada.

The landscape of New Zealand is also a major factor in the films of Vincent Ward, *Vigil* (1984) and *THE NAVIGATOR: A MEDIEVAL ODYSSEY* (1988). The latter film rates a mention here, because it was a co-production with Australia and, as a result, was able to sweep the pool at the 1988 Australian Film Institute Awards, with prizes given to most of its Australian crew members. But the film, magnificent as it is and, like *Ruby Rose* demonstrating a genuinely original vision, deserves pride of place in a book about the New Zealand cinema; the vision is the vision of a New Zealander.

The other Australian–New Zealand co-production of the decade is *RACE FOR THE 'YANKEE ZEPHYR'* (1981), and this is interesting, not so much as a film, but for the implications of its production. Everett De Roche's screenplay was based on a true incident: the wartime disappearance of an American DC3 military aircraft carrying the payroll for the Pacific fleet. The wreck was, in fact, discovered off Cape York some years later, but De Roche and director Richard Franklin developed the idea that the plane with its valuable cargo is discovered in the present day, and that the discovery leads to a race by rival salvagers; they envisaged an adventure comedy in the style of *It's a Mad Mad Mad Mad World*.

Tony Ginnane was to be the producer, working in association with Peter Fox's Pact Productions, and this was to have been the follow-up to *Harlequin* and *The Survivor*, Ginnane projects of the early 80s which were unabashedly 'international' (see Chapter 9). But Australian unions, especially Actors Equity, were getting angry about these 'mid-Pacific' productions, and had brought in new tough regulations which would have prevented Ginnane importing the four foreign actors he wanted for *Yankee Zephyr* (George Peppard, Donald Pleasence, Lesley Ann Warren and Ken Wahl). Despite the fact that the film was supposed to be set in a rainforest in Queensland's tropical north, Ginnane threatened to relocate to New Zealand if Equity did not relent. Equity stood firm, and so Everett De Roche rewrote the screenplay and set it in South Island lake country (with the production based in Queenstown). At this point Richard Franklin dropped out of the project (not, apparently, because he objected to the imported actors, but because he was unhappy about the relocation). Seemingly undeterred by the disastrous direction of *The Survivor*, Ginnane gave Franklin's job to his co-producer, David Hemmings.

Hemdale was financially involved in the $6 million project, which was co-produced by Auckland producer John Barnett's company Endeavour Films. As a result of this deal, several New Zealand technicians and actors (Bruno Lawrence, Grant Tilly) participated in the film.

As a film, *Yankee Zephyr* is unquestionably more successful than *Harlequin* or *The Survivor*, but Hemmings' pacing is so leaden that *Crawl for the 'Yankee Zephyr'* would have been a more accurate title. The American leads are dull, and George Peppard's cod-English accent is absurd, but Donald Pleasence brings his usual professionalism to his role as the discoverer of the wrecked plane (good work here from production designer Bernard Hides). Never before have so many bullets missed their mark as in the wanly-staged action scenes, but the New Zealand locations are well utilised (and very well shot in Panavision by Vincent Monton) and the basic story is strong enough to have deserved more intelligent casting and less tentative treatment. Hemmings has not directed a film since.

So peeved was Ginnane with what he saw as Equity's denial of his right to select the cast of his choice, that he produced his next four films in New Zealand: *Dead Kids* (director Michael Laughlin, 1981); *Second Time Lucky* (Michael Anderson, 1984); *Prisoners* (Peter Werner, 1984) and *Mesmerized* (Michael Laughlin, 1986). Of these four, *Prisoners* (made for 20th Century–Fox and starring Tatum O'Neal, Colin Friels, David Hemmings and Shirley Knight) is the most elusive and least seen, while *Second Time Lucky* is a coy and juvenile sex comedy. The Michael Laughlin films, especially *Dead Kids*, are more interesting.

A year after the *Yankee Zephyr* fracas, there was another battle over the 'Australianism' of an Australian film: this was *THE RETURN OF CAPTAIN INVINCIBLE* (1982), produced by Andrew Gaty's Seven Keys company. This time the row centred on a dispute between director Philippe Mora and producer Gaty; it was claimed that, after Mora had finished the film, Gaty, acting on the advice of his American distributor, had recut it, presumably to make it more acceptable for the US market (compare *Crocodile Dundee*, Chapter 10). Mora had objected to this tampering with his film, and the matter was brought before the Minister for Home Affairs, Tom McVeigh, who took the step of refusing the final certification which was required to qualify for the 150 per cent tax deduction for investors; Gaty challenged the decision in court and, to the surprise of many, won. As a result, McVeigh announced tightening of guidelines for Australian certification.

This post-production tampering, and the resulting legal battle, delayed release of the film for a year, but when *Captain Invincible* finally emerged in mid-1983, it was, perhaps inevitably, disappointing. The film starts well: Mora's affection for old newsreels is demonstrated in the mock opening in which Alan Arkin, as a Superman-style hero of another time, is besmirched during the McCarthy era and drops out, to be discovered many years later living in the present in alcoholic anonymity in Sydney. Arkin is funny as 'Vince', there are good-humoured supporting performances (Graham Kennedy as the gutless Australian Prime Minister, Michael Pate as the US President, a former Boy Scout) and there is some very imaginative production design (David Copping). But the good humour of the early scenes gives way to some fairly feeble suspense later on, and the film loses steam and ends on an extremely tame note. Several songs are no help at all.

Rare indeed is the Australian action film which really succeeds.

Certainly *SKY PIRATES* (1985) is not among them: in its feeble attempt to emulate Spielberg and *Raiders of the Lost Ark*, this looks more like one of those Italian rip-offs than the genuine article. John Lamond wrote and produced it, but left the direction to Colin Eggleston, and it is sad to see the man who made the interesting thriller *Long Weekend* (1978) involved in such tripe.

Spielberg is not the only heavy influence on this vapid adventure: there is a major plot reference to *The Philadelphia Experiment*, knowing nods to *The Deer Hunter*, *Dirty Harry* and *Mad Max* and even a rehash of the risqué love-on-a-train sequence from Hitchcock's *North By Northwest*. But all these hand-me-down elements go for nothing, given the incoherent screenplay, sluggish direction and indifferent acting on display here. Max Phipps' villain (in jackboots and dyed blond hair) is a feeble creation when compared to the same actor's work in better films (*Dark Age* for example). As for John Hargreaves, he does his best, but the odds are firmly stacked against him. Above all, for a film which attempts to be a state-of-the-art action adventure piece, the stunts and special effects are second-rate.

T here are, happily, always the exceptions that prove the rule, and *MAD MAX 2* (1981) is certainly one of them. The original *Mad Max* (1979) had been a surprise success and had established George Miller (1) as a major director of action films. Miller (b. 1945 in Chinchilla, Queensland) was a qualified doctor who had practised for eighteen months at Sydney's St Vincent's Hospital; he was also an insatiable film buff, and, in 1971, met Byron Kennedy (1952–83) at a film workshop arranged by the Australian Union of Students at Melbourne University: among the tutors was Phillip Noyce.

The following year, over the Easter weekend, Miller and Kennedy produced a short film, *Violence in the Cinema Part 1*, which lampooned academic attitudes towards cinema violence in such then-current films as *Straw Dogs* and *A Clockwork Orange* (actor Arthur Dignam delivers a text originally written by Phillip Adams in this hilarious short). The film was rated R, shown at the 1972 Sydney Film Festival, and distributed by GU (there never was a Part 2).

Mad Max was made very cheaply, for less than $400,000. It became a huge success in Australia despite, or because of, a weird attack on the film by Phillip Adams in the *Bulletin*, who compared its moral values to those of *Mein Kampf*. It was sold to American-International for the US and Canada and Warner Bros for the rest of the world

Mad Max 2. *Mel Gibson.*

(it was banned for a while in France). Apart from Adams, reviews for the film were very supportive, with critics around the world recognising Miller's extraordinary filmmaking abilities; and the film helped to make an international star of Mel Gibson.

'*Mad Max* was such a success we had a lot of choice,' says Miller. 'I was offered several films from American companies as a result of it [among them was the original Rambo film, *First Blood*, which he turned down]. I'd met Terry Hayes when he wrote the novelisation of *Max Max*, and he came with me and Byron to LA. I'd decided I wanted Terry to work on my next screenplay, and meanwhile I did some acting classes at UCLA and Byron started learning about distribution.' Miller and Hayes wrote a screenplay, 'a real special effects horror movie, very surreal, inspired by the punk-rock era and set in America.' Warner Bros were interested in that project, but then Miller lost interest in it, started thinking about what was wrong with *Mad Max* and, almost subconsciously, started working on *Mad Max 2*.

'I got very fired by the opportunity to do the film again,' says Miller. 'Not to repeat it, but to use all the residual ideas we had.' Kennedy suggested that, instead of getting trapped in the Hollywood studio system, they should return to Australia and, using 10BA, make *Mad Max 2* there. 'We got back to Australia, and had to find an office quickly: although the first film was based in Melbourne, we decided to base in Sydney, and rented the old Metro cinema in Kings Cross. We did the film on the run, almost making it up as we went along,

George Miller, director of the Mad Max *films.*

but we shot in sequence all on one location [around Broken Hill]. Film is an act of will, and if you weaken your resolve you make bad films. So we were determined to make it work.' *Mad Max 2* was budgeted at $4.5 million.

Brian Hannant co-scripted the film with Hayes and Miller, and doubled as second unit director and assistant director. He recalls: 'Jenny Day, who was production co-ordinator on *Mad Max*, and I were partners, so I used to go down to see her in Melbourne and got to know George and Byron. I stayed in touch with them when they were in the US, and when they made the decision to come back to Australia, they called me.' At this stage, the 'script' was just a few pages of ideas. 'George asked me to co-write the film,' says Hannant. 'But at the time I hadn't met Terry Hayes, and when I did there was a certain tension in our relationship.' 'Terry and Brian didn't get on,' says Miller. 'But Brian was a great sounding board.'

Hannant says that about one-third of the script is his: the basic set-up, of a world of the future gone crazy, was already in place, but 'the screenplay itself was developed by the three of us. George and I worked on the visual things, including the stunts. For example, we spent two days working out the scene in which the Feral Kid throws the boomerang. All the stunts were scripted, of course; Terry did the actual writing.' Hannant credits Hayes with a lot of the humour in the film, such as the Gyro Captain's muttered 'Lingerie. Remember lingerie?'

The film was influenced by Miller's attraction to Japanese cinema.

The first film had been a big success in Japan, and Miller's work had even been compared to that of Akira Kurosawa (Max was seen as a kind of samurai figure). 'I'd never even heard of Kurosawa,' says Miller. 'So I made a point of looking at as many of his films as I could. They had a big influence on the way the film developed.'

There was a lot of pressure on the filmmakers, because the aim was to complete the film in time for Christmas release in Australia and Japan. Miller had been unhappy with the quality of the cinematography on the first film, and hired Dean Semler (whose work on the short film, *A Steam Train Passes*, had impressed him). Miller storyboarded the film with a series of beautifully drawn sketches, but, interestingly, disliked starting to film a sequence with a master shot, preferring to concentrate on specific bits of action.

During production, atrocious weather helped cause tension. 'I remember one awful day,' says Hannant, 'when George wouldn't do the wide shot first. He started off with a close shot, and then got himself in a terrible mess by the time he got back to the wide shot, because people were looking the wrong way—so he had to reshoot the close shots and, by the middle of the afternoon, we were back to the first set-up of the day.' Hannant, in his role as first assistant director, tried to persuade Miller to work in a more traditional way, but to no avail. 'I didn't have the authority to make George work differently,' he says. Production manager Pat Clayton took over as first assistant director after about four weeks, and Hannant directed a second unit.

After the 12-week shoot, there was a lot of pressure to have post-production completed as quickly as possible. David Stiven headed several teams of editors, who cut different reels of the film simultaneously. It was a very hectic, even frenzied, time, but the film was completed just in time for Christmas release, and Roadshow (the distributors) had cinemas booked and ready. 'We knew the film had to get an M rating as opposed to the R rating given to the first film,' says Miller. 'We had agreed to that even before we started shooting. So we were completely taken aback when the censors gave it an R. Time was short, and we asked Janet Strickland [the Chief Censor] to tell us what to cut to get an M. She told us: "It's the overall tone of the film, nothing specific." '

It was a serious situation for Kennedy–Miller, and a deeply frustrating one. Reluctantly, Miller decided to make some very minor cuts. 'We cut about fourteen seconds,' he says. 'A close-up of an arrow in a

man's arm; an incredibly brief—7-frame—shot during the final chase
of two men being hit by the truck. We went back to the censors,
and again they said no. We couldn't believe it. We saw other M-rated
films which were currently in release, like *Alien* and *Escape from New
York*. And then an incredible thing happened: I was walking in the
street when a member of the Censor Board—not Strickland—came
up to me and said: "Look, I don't want to say too much, but you're
being screwed. I want you to know that some of us think this is a
wonderful film." And he shook my hand!'

Miller went to the Censorship Board of Review, and asked them
to see footage from *Alien* and other M-rated films before making their
decision. The Board of Review gave *Mad Max 2* the crucial M rating,
with only days to spare before the release: but the fourteen seconds
of cuts then had to be removed from all the prints which had been
already struck by the lab. 'There's probably an argument for censorship
of broadcast television,' says Miller. 'But that incident made me really
cynical about the way censors work.' The negative of the film was
never cut, and the rest of the world saw the integral version.

Mad Max 2 depicts a rather grim, desolate, arid world of the future,
but allows Mel Gibson to assume a genuinely heroic role, backed by
the amusing comic performance of Bruce Spence as the lanky Gyro
Captain. The sense of humour on display here is a dark and violent
one, and the links with Hollywood westerns (with the classic plot of
Indians attacking the fort) are strong. The climactic chase has never
been equalled: the stunts are breathtaking, the speed of the staging
and the intensity of the sequence are remarkable. *This* is cinema, and
Mad Max 2 became one of the most imitated films of the 80s. Countless
Italian and low-budget American thrillers set in the future emulated
the style of Miller's picture.

Warner Bros, who had distributed the first film internationally but
not in the US, were involved in the film from the outset. They decided
to retitle it *The Road Warrior* for the US market, partly because the
original had not been as successful there as it had been in other
countries, and partly because they had not distributed it themselves.
The film was a major success around the world; in Australia alone
it took $3,700,000 in gross rentals, and a further $11,300,000 in the
US and Canada. It was also a huge success in Japan.

Kennedy–Miller could have gone almost anywhere after that success:
they chose to go into television. *The Dismissal*, which Hayes scripted
and Miller co-directed (along with George Ogilvie and Carl Schultz)

was Kennedy–Miller's first major mini-series, and this story of the overthrow of the Whitlam Government proved fertile ground for such an approach (other directors as varied as Phil Noyce and Paul Cox had earlier toyed with the subject as a feature film).

In 1983, the partnership came to a tragic end when Byron Kennedy was killed when the helicopter used in *Mad Max 2*, which he was flying, crashed. His death was a great loss to the film industry: many considered him the most visionary of all Australian producers.

Miller kept on working. Immediately after *The Dismissal*, he went to Hollywood (at the invitation of Steven Spielberg) to direct the fourth (and best) segment of the troubled *Twilight Zone*: *Nightmare at 20,000 Feet* is a small masterpiece of suspense, with John Lithgow superb as a terrified airline passenger. After this, Miller started planning Mad Max 3, which eventually became known as *MAD MAX BEYOND THUNDERDOME* (1985).

Miller had been very impressed with George Ogilvie's contribution to *The Dismissal*; Ogilvie, one of Australia's leading theatre directors, had introduced to Kennedy–Miller the concept of of a different kind of group rehearsal, involving a kind of workshopping. The procedure had been used again in subsequent Kennedy–Miller mini-series (*Bodyline*, *The Cowra Breakout*) and appealed to Miller's instinct that a filmmaker needs to be a comprehensive artist: that a director should know how to write, a writer how to direct, a director how to act, and so on.

Miller wanted Ogilvie to co-direct the third *Mad Max*, which was to be made on an even bigger budget (Mel Gibson was by now

Mad Max Beyond Thunderdome. *Mel Gibson.*

commanding a very hefty salary) and with a wider scope. 'The only reason I agreed,' says Ogilvie, 'was the chance of doing some wonderful workshops. Pre-production was very exciting, but the film was awesomely large, and I never want to do anything that big again.'

Ogilvie was in charge of the actors' workshops, but Miller took over on the set (though at times the two handled separate units.) 'George directed the film,' says Ogilvie. 'I learnt so much from watching him work: his persistence, his obstinacy. It was a great experience, but I'm happier in a smaller world. But I actually directed one of those stunts—and I'm very proud of that!'

Looking back on the film, George Miller says: 'We really had too much material. It was almost three films. We could have made a whole movie from the Bartertown sequence alone. But part of me knew this would be the last Mad Max film, so I wanted to throw everything in.' One wonders, too, if Byron Kennedy would have toned down the depiction of Max as almost a Christ in leather. Miller seems to have been most interested in the story of the lost children, survivors of a nuclear war, discovered by Max in the desert. But these are the least satisfactory elements of the film, and the children's scenes were reduced in length after disappointing test screenings in America.

The principal location for the film was the opal mining town of Coober Pedy, but Bartertown—lorded over by Tina Turner's Aunty Entity—was built at the old State brickworks in Sydney's western suburbs.

During shooting, it became apparent to close friends that George Miller very much missed the support of Byron Kennedy. 'Byron made me question everything,' he once said. Terry Hayes and Doug Mitchell co-produced with Miller, but there was a feeling that no-one was really producing him, overseeing his work. One crew member recalls: 'George [Miller] would say: "Why is this costing us so much money?" and then he'd be out on set saying: "I must have 600 more extras." Extras that weren't budgeted for, but, as director, he demanded them and, as producer, he wouldn't deny himself.'

Shooting at Coober Pedy lasted five weeks. Getting people there was complicated: chartered planes took the cast and crew to Andamooka, and buses drove them the rest of the way (about 275 kilometres). As with the earlier film, there were relatively few accidents during production, given the complex and dangerous stunts involved. One stunt car caught fire, and the driver was burnt; but the worst accident involved a caterer when a gas oven exploded.

There were other problems. The rains came early and there were floods, so that rescheduling was required. The shooting of the scenes in which Max discovers the fifty children (filmed in the Blue Mountains) were delayed because of the freezing conditions. In all, the production went over time by about six weeks. There were difficulties, too, in securing permission to film 400 pigs within the Sydney metropolitan area. The local council took Kennedy–Miller to the High Court to prevent the company using the pigs, which were being filmed on a location adjacent to Parramatta Road in Camperdown: Kennedy–Miller, which had complied with all the regulations regarding livestock in the city, won the case. Other animal problems involved the use of camels. Camels, apparently, have to follow a leader: two leaders were chosen, and trained. Two days before the animals were due to travel to the location, one of the leaders died after a fall; and the other expired during the journey to Coober Pedy. The leaderless beasts would not perform as scripted, and Miller had to change the film's opening sequence as a result.

Endless trouble was also taken to get an aerial shot of the ruined city of Sydney (constructed at North Head): bad weather and changing conditions caused problems even with this apparently simple scene.

When the film concentrates on action scenes—the gladiatorial combat in Bartertown, the thrilling chase that climaxes the picture—it is as good as its predecessor. Again, there is that malicious sense of humour, not only in the Miller–Hayes dialogue, but in Grace Walker's superb sets and in Tina Turner's amazing performance. But, all too often, the film seems to be trying to make an epic statement about the post-nuclear world and the children who survive it, and this, despite the cuts that were made after the American tests, slows down the action. The combination of message and action rarely works, and the best scenes of *Mad Max Beyond Thunderdome* are those in which the message is left firmly behind.

Nonetheless, the film is awesomely well crafted, and its very ambition deserves admiration. It may not be quite the visceral experience of its predecessors (interesting how each film in the trilogy is completely different in style from the other two), but it is still a considerable achievement. In the US it actually performed considerably better than *Mad Max 2* (nearly $18 million in gross rentals), but in Australia it lagged behind ($2.3 million). Subsequently, George Miller went to America to direct *The Witches of Eastwick* (1987), a popular (though for him troubled) production. For the rest of the decade Kennedy-

Miller produced television (*Vietnam*, *Dirtwater Dynasty*, *Bangkok Hilton*) and feature films by other directors (Phil Noyce's *Dead Calm*; John Duigan's *The Year My Voice Broke* and *Flirting*).

T he *Mad Max* films use the landscape of the Australian outback with extraordinary imagination. An adventure film made on a much more modest scale, *BUDDIES* (1983), is also located in a unique part of the country: the sapphire fields of Central Queensland. The film was written and produced by John Dingwall and directed by Arch Nicholson. Dingwall (b. 1940 in Rockhampton, Qld) was a journalist by profession who had written the superb screenplay for Ken Hannam's *Sunday Too Far Away* (1974). Nicholson (b. 1941 in Melbourne) spent his childhood in Western Australia, and trained as a teacher. He decided he wanted to make films after seeing *Last Year at Marienbad* and joined the Commonwealth Film Unit, where he spent twelve years working on documentaries. He was the man chosen to direct *The Unknown Industrial Prisoner* (which was never made), and he also directed an excellent telemovie, *A Good Thing Going*.

It was this film that persuaded Dingwall that Nicholson was the right person to direct *Buddies*. 'I love to tell stories,' says Dingwall. 'I decided to search for a good story, and I drove around Australia to find one. I found the sapphire fields and I found a story about the essence of freedom.' He wrote numerous drafts of a screenplay, and set about trying to raise money. The AFC welcomed him as a writer, but not as a producer since he had no track record in that capacity. Money was finally raised with the help of Rex Pilbeam, former mayor of Rockhampton. 'This was the 10BA period, and we went around Queensland raising money from individuals and organisations. The budget was $1.9 million.'

Dingwall and Nicholson worked on further drafts of the screenplay ('arguing fruitfully,' Nicholson says) while the money was raised. Casting was done by Alison Barrett just three weeks before production: Colin Friels and Harold Hopkins are excellent as the two friends. Shooting took place on location at Emerald, and lasted an enjoyable, if very hot, six weeks.

Buddies is an enormously entertaining film. The screenplay is packed with humour and interesting characters, including Norman Kaye as a tourist; Simon Chilvers as a salesman of light aircraft, who sheds his big-city exterior to shack up with Kris McQuade; Dennis Miller as the baddie who drives a mean bulldozer; and the gawky Bruce Spence.

Best of all, Dingwall and Nicholson constantly undermine audience expectations with skilful use of the anti-climax: the fist fight that does not take place, the love scene the characters never quite get around to. Perhaps the film's most endearing sequence has a drunken Chilvers giving a hilarious flying lesson.

But this thoroughly entertaining genre film had the greatest of difficulty finding an audience. Dingwall thinks this partly stems from a matter of perception: 'The image we created with *Buddies* was of a high-action genre piece with blood and guts and bulldozers; but the essence of the film wasn't that at all. We should have thought about that before we made it. In other words, we didn't make a film violent enough to satisfy the action audience: no-one was killed in the film. When people saw it, they loved it. It tested better than *The Man from Snowy River*, but no-one wanted to see it; the image of the film was such that we fell between two markets.'

In the end, Dingwall actually took the film with him to country cinemas in Queensland, renting them, putting up posters, taking advertisements, giving local interviews: and by this method he found some success. But the film had pitifully short runs in the capital cities, and is undeservedly forgotten.

Arch Nicholson directed three more feature films, two of which, *Fortress* and *Dark Age*, will be discussed in subsequent chapters. Late in 1988, he discovered he was terminally ill with ALS (the motor neuron disease), but continued to work on his final feature, *Weekend With Kate* (called *Depth of Feeling* during production), for producer Phillip Emanuel. This film remained unseen at the time of Nicholson's death on 24 February 1990. He was the first director of his generation to pass away.

Buddies in the wide open spaces are also featured in *BLOWING HOT AND COLD* (1988), the most ambitious production of Melbourne producer Rosa Colosimo. Colosimo (b. 1949 in Calabria, Italy) came to Australia with her family in 1951. She became involved in filmmaking by way of distribution; she bought Fellini's *Orchestra Rehearsal* and other major Italian films for Australia in the early 80s. She made an attempt to produce an Australian-made Lina Wertmuller film, titled, in the typically long-winded style of this director, *Daniel in the Lions' Den Discovers Among the Aborigines in Terra Australia Only Sons of Bitches Can Save the World*. It came to nothing, even though Colleen McCullough (author of *The Thorn Birds*) was hired to write the screenplay and Mel Gibson briefly became interested in the project.

After this expensive failure ('It was because of my complete inexperience,' says Colosimo) she tried to raise money to bring the popular actor Giancarlo Giannini to Australia to star opposite actress Arkie Whiteley in a film called *Blowing Hot and Cold*, to be directed by Brian Trenchard Smith: these plans were announced in 1984, but nothing came of them. After making two low-budget features (*The Still Point*, *Hungry Heart*), Colosimo finally produced *Blowing Hot and Cold* with Marc Gracie directing. Joe Dolce (whose recording 'Shaddap Your Face' had been a mysterious smash-hit earlier in the decade) played the role originally conceived for Giannini.

Gracie's background was in television: he had been a sound recordist who went on to become a producer-director; and he was director and co-writer of the *Wogs out of Work* stage production.

Four writers, including Colosimo herself, worked on the screenplay. The resulting film—in which a voluble Italian befriends a country garage owner (Peter Adams) whose daughter has run off with a drug-dealer—is a pretty thin experience. It lacks the requisite comedy and tension—or even a spirit of genuine camaraderie between the two actors. As a road movie, it is a fizzer.

DOUBLE DEAL (1981) is an odd little hybrid which also evolves into a road movie of sorts. It is very similar in plot to Keith Salvat's *Private Collection* (1972). *Double Deal* is about the bored wife (Angela Punch McGregor) of a wealthy man (imported Louis Jourdan) who joins her lover (perennially bare-chested Warwick Comber) to rob hubby; then, on the road, they knock over a store or two. Brian Kavanagh is one of the country's best film editors (*The Chant of Jimmie Blacksmith* et al.) but his films as director have not been distinguished to date, and this is no exception: it is neither erotic (despite Punch McGregor's attempts to be sexy), witty, comic (despite Bruce Spence in a tiny role) or suspenseful. Warwick Comber is simply too weak to make the role of the lover convincing, and the best scene involves the wife's visit to her mother, during which her working-class origins begin to show through. Even the outdoor sequences in the last part of the film are no relief from the too shimmering photography (Ross Berryman) or over-insistent music (Bruce Smeaton).

The bush takes centre-stage in *INITIATION* (1987), in which Rodney Harvey plays a young New Yorker who comes to Australia in search of his long-lost father (Bruno Lawrence) and winds up lost in the bush with him after a plane crash. The contrived casting is a bit ludicrous (the film was executive-produced by Tony Ginnane) but Michael

Pearce's film has an excellent feel for the mountainous country, which is spectacularly shot by Geoffrey Simpson. There is some sharp observation, too, in throwaway moments like the shot of a picture of the Queen on the wall of the house in which Kulu (Barry Smith), the Aboriginal who teaches the young American bush lore, lives. But the film would have been a lot more acceptable if it had not been so very determined to focus attention on all those koalas and kangaroos, as if the filmmakers were more interested in foreign audiences than local ones.

At least it is several cuts above *The Earthling* (1980), which rates a passing mention. Although it is an American film by a British director (Peter Collinson) it was partly funded and entirely shot in Australia, and stars Jack Thompson and Olivia Hamnett in minor roles alongside leads William Holden and young Ricky Schroder. Schroder, we are asked to believe, is the son of Thompson and Hamnett (his accent, needless to say, is resolutely American) orphaned when the bad-tempered Thompson drives his caravan over a cliff. He stumbles across Holden, playing an expatriate who, dying of cancer, has returned to the bush he had left forty years earlier. Once again, Australian fauna is insistently and repeatedly on display, and the script—by an American writer unburdened by a deep knowledge of Australia—beggars belief. At least Don McAlpine's cinematography is pretty.

Since films set in the Western Australian outback are few and far between, one wishes *DAISY AND SIMON* (1988) had been just a little better. This 'odd couple' movie was long in the planning: it was first announced as *Daisy* in 1983, with Richard McCarthy set to direct; later (1985) it became *The Distance* and had Michael York starring as an English schoolteacher. But in neither guise did it get off the ground, and it was finally shot in 1987 (as *Where the Outback Ends*) with Sean Scully (not as a teacher, English or otherwise, but as an absconding accountant) and Jan Adele. The director, Stasch Radwanski Jr, is based in Hong Kong.

Given that he is a man on the run, it is hard to understand why the seemingly sensible Scully would linger for any length of time with Jan Adele, who is meant to be playing a scruffy, but loveable, old derelict who pines for her dead husband and lost youth. Scully is excellent, as he usually is; but Adele is encouraged to play to the gallery and as a result overbalances the film and tips it into sentimental melodrama. The plot is pretty slight stuff to be stretched out to 106 minutes.

But the outback itself, as photographed by John McLean, looks spectacular, emphasising once again the vast range of locations available to Australian filmmakers. From the sapphire fields of Queensland to the dust of Broken Hill and Coober Pedy, to the magnificent High Country of Victoria and the Walls of Jericho in Tasmania, the country's locations have constantly provided fascinating backgrounds and, occasionally, assumed more importance than the films of which they are a part.

Daisy and Simon. *Jan Adele, Sean Scully.*

• C H A P T E R •

4

LOVERS AND OTHER STRANGERS

L ove stories have featured strongly in the Australian cinema of
the 80s, and have provided some of the most satisfying—and,
in a few cases, the most frustrating—experiences of the decade. Not
surprisingly, the filmmakers who have proved to be best at presenting
the joys and pains of relationships have been those people most willing
to reveal and even expose themselves in their work—Paul Cox and
Bob Ellis foremost among them.

Paul Cox's trilogy of love films—*Lonely Hearts*, *Cactus* and *My First
Wife*—are among the most beautiful and painful of Australian movies.
(His films in which he explores wilder, weirder relationships are to
be discussed in the following chapter.)

LONELY HEARTS (1981), his first film of the 80s, stars Wendy
Hughes, cast very much against type as a middle-aged, painfully shy
woman who falls in love with an equally isolated older man (Norman
Kaye). 'Lonely Hearts has a lot to do with my arrival in Australia,'
says Cox. 'The first six months I was here, I wandered the streets
with no-one to talk to. I was used to living in a place where people
talked to each other: in Melbourne, they didn't. I discovered just how
many lonely people there are in the world.'

Lonely Hearts. *Norman Kaye, Wendy Hughes.*

He wrote two drafts of a screenplay about two such lonely people,
but received a less than enthusiastic response from funding bodies.
'They told me: "You don't put people like these on screen; audiences
would never identify with these characters." But, of course, we're
all a little like these people.' Luckily, Phillip Adams came to the rescue,
and proposed that the film be made as one of the four productions
of the Adams-Packer company. Humourist John Clarke was brought
in to contribute to the screenplay, especially the dialogue ('He was
very good,' says Cox, 'and he contributed a lot'), and John Murray,
whom Cox had known for some years (and who had just left the troubled
production of Adams–Packer's *We of the Never Never*) was assigned
as producer. The film's budget was $690,000; Cox himself received

$30,000 ('the first payment I ever got for making a film.')

As soon as shooting started, differences of opinion between director and producer threatened the production. 'Murray wanted to have total say,' says Cox. 'He wanted to tell me what to do. He would even tell me where to put the camera. I got very angry.' The experience convinced Cox that, in future, he must produce his own films.

Despite the production problems, the film turned out so well that it won Best Film at the 1982 Australian Film Institute Awards (over such tough opposition as *We of the Never Never, Monkey Grip* and *Mad Max 2*). Backed by generally positive reviews, the film, released by GU with the tag-line 'A Funny Sort of Love Story', was a surprise success, and also sold well overseas (the Samuel Goldwyn Co. in the US; Gala in Britain). American critic Judith Crist compared it favourably to the classic *Marty*, and the film's substantial success on the US art circuit established Cox's reputation in that country.

The two central performances contribute a lot to the success of *Lonely Hearts*. Wendy Hughes, in her second Cox film, is at her best as Patricia, who, though in her thirties, still lives with and is dominated by, her conservative parents. Norman Kaye, an accomplished musician whom Cox nursed into an acting career, makes 50-year-old Peter, with his foolish toupée and passion for amateur theatricals, a very human character. Their fumbling love story is told with great tenderness and compassion, and a welcome sense of humour. Also very precise, as it is in all Cox's work, is the production design of Neil Angwin: Peter's dingy flat is contrasted with the bright, sterile, well-ordered apartment of Patricia. Almost miraculously, Cox avoids the trap of sentimentality: his film is sharp, truthful and very human.

Skipping over, for a moment, Cox's next two features, *Man of Flowers* and *My First Wife*, we find in *CACTUS* (1986) another story of lonely, dislocated people coming together. Though mysteriously it is not as highly regarded as the previous three films, *Cactus* is, in fact, one of the great achievements of Australian cinema, a deceptively simple love story filled with pain and beauty.

The inspiration for the film, as with most of Cox's films, is autobiographical; when he was a hypersensitive teenager in a small Dutch town, he returned home one day to find his mother was blind. 'I'll never forget the fear that almost paralysed me,' he says. 'Soon after I saw her in hospital, and she said to me: "Don't be afraid; I'm at peace here." ' The mother's sight gradually returned (she had been affected by a blood clot), but the memory has stayed vividly with Cox all his life. Another source was the true story of a Frenchman, blind from birth, who on one occasion bumped his head and, for a split second, could see; nobody believed him.

Over the years, Cox made several attempts to turn these powerful images into a screenplay. At one stage he planned a story in which Norman Kaye would be the father of a young (Australian) woman who suddenly starts losing her sight. Then, at the Cannes Film Festival, he had dinner with his friend Werner Herzog and met Isabelle Huppert; at first, he did not know who she was, but when he realised she was the actress from *The Lacemaker* (a film which had moved him profoundly), they started talking—and Cox became convinced that she should appear in his 'blind' project. Having discovered his actress, Cox went to work on the screenplay, most of which was written in trains and railway stations in France and Belgium. His casting decision was not without problems. Bob Ellis, who had collaborated on the dialogue of the previous two Cox films, was unhappy about the change in plot. Says Ellis, 'We had a premise where a French girl on holiday in Australia finds she's going blind and is determined to stay and see the country. If you were going blind in Afghanistan, naturally you'd stay there and see the country, rather than come home to a good hospital. I just couldn't bear the idea, but I tried to write some scenes to make it logical. Cox hated them; we had a terrible fight. I think he lost his status as a great filmmaker with *Cactus*.' 'Ellis had very little to do with the film, even though he gets co-scripting credit,' says Cox. 'I kept my agreement with him, and paid him, but actually Norman Kaye contributed more to the screenplay.'

Cox cast Robert Menzies, grandson of the former Prime Minister, as Robert, the young cactus collector who is blind from birth. He had already used Menzies as an extra at the end of *Man of Flowers*, and wanted to use him again. He also wanted an actor in the role who was new to the screen (Menzies had acted only on stage). 'Otherwise,' he says, 'you'd have said: "Here's Mel Gibson playing a blind man." I never screen-tested him. He read the script, made some very sensible comments, and I knew he was right. Putting him up against Isabelle could have been a problem, but it worked out fine.' Menzies rehearsed for two months as a blind man; he is so effective that, after the film was released, some people thought the actor really *was* blind.

The metaphor of the cactus came about because Cox recalled a documentary he had once made about blind people. He had met a

Cactus. *Isabelle Huppert, Robert Menzies.*

blind man who grew orchids: 'I watched him for a long time. He loved those flowers, and knew them all by name. But he also had a few cacti which he managed to water without pricking himself. And that gave me the idea that Robert should grow cacti. They say cactus thrives on neglect, but in fact it needs a lot of care and attention. It's the same with people: we neglect one another, but we need a lot of care, a lot of warmth, a lot of water. Also, the cactus is visually an interesting plant: it gives almost a.primeval feeling to the film.'

Actors Equity initially objected to the importation of Isabelle Huppert, and as a result Cox threatened at one stage to make the film in Canada. Fortunately, wisdom prevailed. Shortly before shooting was due to commence in Melbourne, Cox was in Canada to attend a conference of Ten Filmmakers of the Future, when he suddenly suffered an acute lack of confidence. He recovered, and, on his return to Australia, rewrote the entire screenplay.

The budget for the film was the largest Cox ever worked with: $1.5 million (of which $150,000 was paid to Huppert). Production designer Asher Bilu found the house where the film was set, spectacularly located in the Dandenongs outside the city. Says Cox, 'Asher never gets enough credit for what he does, because he does it so subtly.' Yuri Sokol, working on his fourth film with Cox, provided some extraordinarily beauuful images, probably the finest cinematography in any Australian film. The opening shot is a 360-degree pan which introduces the principal characters, establishes the house in its context, and gets the story going; it is a virtuoso achievement which clearly required the most complex focusing and re-focusing on the part of the camera operator, Nino Martinetti (who later shot Cox's feature, *Golden Braid*). Not long after there is another complex shot in which Huppert and Norman Kaye walk to the top of a lookout, talking as they survey the view, when a light plane comes into sight dead on cue. And later in the film is a transition from darkness to light (achieved entirely with lighting effects) as the lovers, Huppert and Menzies, awake in bed together. (Sokol had the great bad luck to be up against another astonishingly well-shot film, *The Right Hand Man*, photographed by Peter James, at the AFI awards that year; James won.) The film also has an exceedingly rich soundtrack in which bird cries, especially the strange sound of the whip bird, play an important part.

Cactus is the most tactile Australian film since *Picnic at Hanging Rock*. The word 'primeval' is an apt one to describe this story of a blind, virginal youth, surrounded by extraordinary foliage and living with an enigmatic Aboriginal woman companion; his senses, if not his eyes, are opened by Colo, a beautiful, though for him unseen, foreigner. There are several unforgettable moments in the film, one of them a flashback in which Robert, as a child, is able to see for a fleeting moment. (Cox tells the painfully moving story of the blind child he cast in this tiny role; when his role was explained to him, the youngster, blind from birth, innocently asked, 'And will I *really* see?') Who can forget, either, the ending of the film: Robert, who thinks Colo is reunited with her husband, is joined by her in his garden of cacti: 'I wanted to see you again,' he says, and the irony of the statement is matched only by the depth of emotion with which he speaks the line.

Being a Paul Cox film, *Cactus* makes splendid use of excerpts from classical music. There is also an amusing visit to a society of cactus collectors (Julia Blake making a brief appearance as a cranky speaker); and there is a get-together by friends and neighbours of Norman Kaye and Monica Maughan after the annual Anzac Day march which provides a sweet gallery of eccentrics to entertain Colo. At the centre is Isabelle Huppert as the young wife whose marriage has reached a crisis and who would rather stay in the peace and tranquillity of this lovely house with her close friends and reorganise her life than return to France and a past that has become impossible (her motives, *pace* Ellis, seem completely understandable).

The mystery is that this remarkable film was given such short shrift by reviewers and the public at large, as well as by Cox's peers (it won nothing in the AFI awards in 1986). The pacing is slow, but not unusually so; indeed, it could hardly have been quicker. The theme is universal and extremely affecting. The performances are beyond praise. The direction and technical work reveal inspired craftsmanship. If anything, *Cactus* improves on repeated viewings and is surely overdue for serious reassessment.

Both *Lonely Hearts* and *Cactus* deal with lonely people beginning the painful process of a relationship. One of the films Cox made between the two, *MY FIRST WIFE* (1984), is about the traumatic end of a relationship. Says Cox, 'It was inspired by the breakup of my marriage, but the only recognisable character is the husband, me.' The film was written when he was at a low ebb: his marriage had broken up bitterly, and he had been on the verge of suicide. He escaped from the pain of his life in Melbourne by working with his friend, Werner Herzog, on *Where the Green Ants Dream*, the film Herzog made in the Australian outback, but even that experience proved depressing because the two men had several disagreements over the film and its attitude to Aborigines. Cox, unable to sleep at night in the desert, started writing the screenplay of *My First Wife*. Later, he showed it to Bob Ellis, with whom he had worked on *Man of Flowers*. Says Ellis: 'I thought it was very good. We booked into the Hydro Majestic at Katoomba for eight days to work on it, but then Cox decided he wanted to write *Cactus* first, and in the end we only spent two days on *My First Wife*, between games of pool. Cox doesn't understand that, if we'd spent a month writing each film, they'd have been better. He regards films

My First Wife. *Wendy Hughes, John Hargreaves.*

as being effusions of his own tortured soul, and dialogue being mere detail, like set painting.' Later, Cox was annoyed to read in an Ellis interview that he took credit for the screenplay of *My First Wife*, all of which paved the way for the disagreements between them on *Cactus* noted earlier.

'The character of the husband, with all his weakness and bad behaviour, was based on me,' Cox says. 'But I wasn't pointing an accusing finger at anyone else, and the characters of the wife and lover aren't based on reality but are purely fictitious.' Despite this, the AFC, before it would support the project, demanded that Cox's ex-wife sign a release form in which she waived any future legal action against the film. 'How dare they?' says Cox. 'That was really disgusting of them, and it still makes me angry that those AFC people would say to me: "Go and get your ex-wife to sign a form, then you can make your film." What sort of minds are these?'

Wendy Hughes was cast as the wife who suddenly informs her husband, John Hargreaves, that their marriage is over and she no longer wants to sleep with him. The film was shot quickly, on a budget of $690,000, mostly at a house in Williamstown, in the inner suburbs of Melbourne. Cox was in an angry mood during production: 'I had to get it out of my system,' he says. When *My First Wife* begins, John appears to have it all: a good job which he enjoys, a beautiful wife, a lovely daughter, a fine house. But, as soon as Helen makes her dramatic announcement, his world falls apart, and he reacts very badly to the pain and hurt and humiliation.

This was the third film in a row Cox had made with cinematographer Yuri Sokol (*Cactus*, the fourth, would follow). 'By this time, our working relationship was excellent,' says Cox. 'On the first two we had some arguments because he came here with that Russian experience which is a bit like Hollywood in 1920, using lots of lights and so on. We had a big fight on *Lonely Hearts*, but on *My First Wife* we were very happy with each other.'

Cox rates *My First Wife* high among his work ('It doesn't piss around') and he is right to do so. The film is a lacerating, devastating experience, the more so because the viewer can understand and sympathise with both husband and wife. Hughes gives one of her finest performances as the wife who pities her husband and still loves him in a way, but who no longer wants him. Hargreaves, who deservedly won the Best Actor prize at the AFI awards that year (Hughes lost to Angela Punch McGregor for *Annie's Coming Out*) is astonishingly good as the husband who loses his grip, attempts suicide, gets violent, and even kidnaps his own daughter for a brief while. His painful attempt at reconciliation is just one of the many strong scenes in the film. Cox was awarded for best direction and best screenplay (the latter award perhaps an ironic one given co-screenwriter Bob Ellis' views of the script as noted earlier); his direction is totally assured, as he punctuates the dramatic scenes with images of trains, glistening water, trees and birds, and floods the soundtrack with classical music. He also includes his customary documentary footage, in this case a flashback showing Wendy Hughes actually giving birth to a baby (a scene taken from *For a Child Called Michael*, a dramatised documentary Cox had made in 1979 when Hughes was married to Chris Haywood). In all, another great Australian film.

*M*y *First Wife* was widely distributed by Roadshow in Australia, and was well received by critics and audiences in art houses around the world. Sadly, the only other Australian films of the 80s to deal with the break-up of a marriage which come close to the intensity of the Cox film have hardly been seen at all, yet *Phobia* and *Jilted* are almost as powerful.

PHOBIA (1988) came about because, after the sometimes frustrating experiences of *Sunday Too Far Away* and *Buddies* (see Chapter 3), John Dingwall wanted to direct a film himself. He wanted to make it as simply as he could, and devised a treatment involving only two characters, a husband and wife, and one location, their house. He decided from the beginning that he wanted the wife to be played by Gosia Dobrowolska, having very much admired her work in *Silver City*. 'I wasn't troubled about her accent,' he says. 'We're so bloody parochial here—we accept Michael Caine, with his cockney accent, playing an American in an American film, but we're so insular about casting actors with accents in our films. So I was happy to use Gosia, and I was able to use her Polish background as a further reason for her isolation in terms of the story.'

Dobrowolska was responsive to Dingwall's plans for the film and, over the next three months, became involved in mapping out ideas which would be eventually incorporated into the screenplay. Together with Paul Thompson (head of the writing workshop at the AFTRS), who was chosen to play the husband, Dingwall, Dobrowolska and producer John Mandelberg met over a series of Sunday afternoon script discussions. It was decided that the wife would suffer from agoraphobia

Phobia. *Gosia Dobrowolska.*

(fear of open spaces) and the actress and writer visited psychiatrists to research the character. It was after one such visit, an unproductive and frustrating one, that Dobrowolska started to speculate what it would be like to be married to a psychiatrist: and suggested to Dingwall that this should be the husband's profession.

After all this research and discussion, Dingwall wrote the basic screenplay in a week. Without attempting to raise money through 10BA, or the usual funding bodies, Dingwall mortgaged his Newport home (where the film was to be shot) to raise the tiny $120,000 budget for the film. The crew were all fresh from the film school, and Mandelberg was to double as producer and editor. It was decided to have a three-week shoot, preceded by a week of rehearsals with the two actors and crew. But at the last moment Paul Thompson dropped out of the project, and Dingwall had to find a replacement actor. With casting director Alison Barrett he started a frantic search; several possibilities were unavailable and on the Friday before rehearsals were due to start they still had not come up with an actor. At that point they decided to look through *Showcast*, the publication that lists all professional actors, and, under 'S', saw Sean Scully. 'We tested him, and he made us cry,' says Dingwall. Scully was introduced to Dobrowolska next day, and rehearsals started two days later.

'I had never directed anything before,' says Dingwall, 'and so the input of the actors was very important. I feel that a director is basically a mirror to the talent of the actors, but I wish I'd had more time and more money to use those actors even better.' During February and early March 1988, the tiny cast and crew worked feverishly on what become a very emotional film. 'It was very tough,' says Dobrowolska. 'But we were doing something we believed in. I was physically exhausted, but mentally invigorated.' One of the problems was to balance audience sympathy between the two characters, and Scully's emotional range was so great that Dobrowolska found herself having to fight for her character. 'It was important that Renate didn't seem to be too weak,' she says.

The film was completed with incredible speed: two weeks after the final scenes were shot, a rough cut was screened for the cast and crew, and *Phobia*, complete with music score, was finished in time to screen in the market section of the Cannes festival six weeks later: the speed of production must, in itself, constitute something of a record.

It is an astonishingly powerful film, thanks to the quality of the writing and the painfully real performances. As Renate, struggling against her phobia to leave her husband and gradually realising he will do anything to stop her leaving, Gosia Dobrowolska is extraordinarily good, and the reserves of strength she summons to stand up to her persecutor in the final reel are powerfully conveyed. Sean Scully is equally fine as the husband, a charmer on the surface, but a devious, relentless schemer with a violent temper and an awesome capacity for self-pity—this is the best work Scully has done for the screen.

The film uses video in a fascinating way. Not only do the couple divide up their tape collection prior to their separation ('You can take *Heaven's Gate*'), but David is frequently seen obsessively watching videos he had taken in happier times. One shows Renate cheerfully trying on a number of different dresses. Another shows her, naked, in bed: the first time we see this, the atmosphere is playful as she coquettishly begs David not to film her body and will allow him only the briefest glimpse. At this point, David stops the tape—only when we see it again later do we realise how sadistic he could be towards her, even at a time when their relationship seems to have been, on the whole, happier.

Given the disturbing qualities of the film, its almost total disappearance is cause for considerable regret. Amazingly, it received only one nomination at the AFI awards that year (Sean Scully for Best Actor, a category won by John Waters for *Boulevard of Broken*

Dreams); Dobrowolska was completely overlooked, as were the script and direction of Dingwall. Some kind of award recognition might have helped the film find distribution; it was clearly unsuited to a Hoyts–Village–GU style of release and, surprisingly, was rejected by Sydney's usually progressive Dendy cinema. It screened at several overseas festivals, including London, where Sean Scully introduced the film; but on the whole it has sunk without trace.

JILTED (1987), Bill Bennett's fourth feature, fared little better. Like *My First Wife*, it was inspired by the break-up of the director's first marriage. Says Bennett, 'After the marriage I shared a flat (platonically) with a girl who'd been dumped on by a lot of men, and who didn't want to commit to another relationship because she was scared of getting hurt. It occurred to me what an awful way that was to go through life.' Bennett had also wanted to make a film in which characters were placed in a limited space—the 'crucible' effect, he called it—and so instead of setting the story in a city flat, he set it on an island. 'I wanted to juxtapose dramatic emotions with the apparently easy-going, relaxing atmosphere of an island resort.'

The film was shot on a budget of $600,000 (partly funded by a 50 per cent pre-sale from J. C. Williamson) and shooting took place entirely on Fraser Island in February 1987. Bennett cast his second wife, Jennifer Cluff, as Harriet, the unhappy divorcee, and it was Cluff who suggested she play the role with her head shaved. Richard Moir, whose 'vulnerability and sense of compassion' Bennett admired, was cast as Al, the chef with whom Harry has an affair, and the excellent cast was rounded out by Tina Bursill, Steve Jacobs and Helen Mutkins.

It was not an easy shoot for Bennett. 'I had to direct my wife in two pretty torrid love scenes,' he says. 'I found it awkward, and Richard found it awkward. Jenny was the only one who seemed relaxed about

Jilted. *Tina Bursill.*

it all. I'd steered away from sex in my previous films, but I felt I had to confront it here, and I was very apprehensive about it.' Apart from that, the shoot went smoothly in conditions Bennett describes as 'idyllic'.

When the film was finished, initial screenings were positive but, both in Australia and overseas, distributors never committed themselves. 'Universal almost picked it up,' says Bennett. 'They loved the film, but in the end decided against it. Some potential distributors didn't like it all. The common complaint was that the characters were too unsympathetic.' In the end, despite a well deserved Best Supporting Actress award for Tina Bursill at the AFI awards, no distributor took the film on and, at the end of 1989, it was finally released on video. 'It's really tough to get a small, serious film released,' says Bennett. 'I seem to make films that aren't quite commercial enough to be on at Hoyts, and not quite arty enough to be on at the Academy or the Dendy. I seem to straddle that line, unfortunately. I think the only solution is for filmmakers to form their own distribution set-up.'

The fate of both *Phobia* and *Jilted* clearly indicates the flaws in Australia's distribution system. *Jilted* is a beautifully scripted, beautifully acted film whose quintet of characters interact somewhat in the style of an Alan Rudolph film. All of them have been jilted in one form or another: Harriet (named after a hurricane, she says) found her husband in bed with another woman; Paula (Bursill) was abandoned literally at the altar years earlier; Cindy (Mutkins), the waitress, has an unhappy affair behind her but is involved with Al, the resort chef, who also has a broken marriage behind him, while the hotel manager, Bob (Jacobs) is a Vietnam veteran whose barmaid wife left him.

The relationships that form, dissolve and re-form between these characters are often painful: there is no love here, only sex, which is either highly-charged and erotic (Al and Harriet) or bitterly disappointing (Bob and Paula). Amid the sexual tension and the pain, there is also a bitter sense of humour: it is a sophisticated, perceptive film, marred only by a conventional music score, but it is Bennett's finest achievement to date.

A few other films about marriage were made in the 80s, though none of them carry the impact of *My First Wife*, *Phobia* or *Jilted*. *THE MORE THINGS CHANGE* . . . (1985) comes closest, with its keenly observed screenplay by Moya Wood, based on an idea by producer

Jill Robb. The film is about a modern marriage in which the husband, Lex (Barry Otto) looks after his child at a farmhouse in the country and the wife, Connie (Judy Morris) works in the city. Robb selected actress Robyn Nevin (b. 1940) to direct this, her first film (she had already directed theatre). She was wise enough to select as cinematographer Dan Burstall, who had experience as a television director (if only Judy Morris had made a similarly sensible choice of collaborator when she attempted her first film as director, *Luigi's Ladies*, in 1989). As a result, Nevin was able to concentrate on the performances and Burstall on the look of the film.

The More Things Change. *Victoria Longley, Judy Morris, Barry Otto, Owen Johnson.*

Although his name no longer appears on the film's credits, Michael Brindley was co-screenwriter with Wood. He recalls, in early script conferences, being dismayed at Nevin's lack of knowledge about the way films are made. 'I realised that Robyn doesn't see many movies,' he says. 'She complained that the scenes were short, and didn't seem to understand the way a screenplay worked. She wanted dialogue written in which the characters explained themselves; Moya reluctantly wrote it, and it was filmed. But, of course, it was cut later because it was quite unnecessary.' At the same time, he feels that the film should have been handled in the style of a European comedy of manners, instead of which it became a weepie.

Robb budgeted for a three-week rehearsal period, but the benefits of this were almost lost when Barry Otto broke a bone in his foot on the second day of shooting; the production had to be entirely rescheduled as a result. Still, the film turned out well, though the ending, which suggests that the marriage may be at an end, is not sufficiently prepared: Connie's problems do not on the face of it seem to warrant her decision to break up the family. Apart from the excellent performances from Otto and Morris, Victoria Longley is a great asset to the film as Geraldine, the pregnant young woman brought in to help Lex; a scene in which a telephone repairman assumes Geraldine is Lex's wife and is naturally confused when Connie returns home, is situation comedy at its best.

Unlike *Phobia*, with its ultra-low budget, *The More Things Change . . .* (budgeted at around $2 million) seems, if anything, overproduced: the Panavision format is unnecessary for this kind of intimate dramatic-comedy, and the Dolby soundtrack smacks of audio overkill. Still, by any standards, it is an accomplished film and deserved a bigger success (both here and overseas) than it had.

AFRAID TO DANCE (1988) is another relationship film which failed to get a cinema release and ended up on the video shelf. Producer Andrena Finlay acquired Paul Cockburn's pleasant, mood-shifting screenplay, which was variously known as *Letters* and *Kick Start* during production, and hired Denny Lawrence to direct. Lawrence (b. 1951), an actor turned writer, had written a few screenplays, including the award-winning *Goodbye Paradise* with Bob Ellis. He directed some excellent short films as well as television soaps (*The Restless Years*) and series (*Bodyline*), the feature *Emoh Ruo* (1985) and the telemovie *Archer* (1986).

Afraid to Dance is about a loser (rather monotonously played by Nique Needles) and his relationship with a young woman (Rosey Jones) he meets while heading north. Jones' character is the most interesting one in the film: abandoned by her boyfriend after a pack rape in her office left her with syphilis, she is one of the walking wounded. Through her (somewhat unlikely) love for Needles, she finds a kind of redemption, and the film—which starts off a caper movie, turns into a love story, and ends as a tragedy—belongs to her. She was nominated for an AFI award, but failed to win. Also notable in the film is a brief appearance from Tina Bursill as a provocative woman who gives Needles a lift in her car and then robs him, pre-empting his plan to rob her.

The theme of friends who become lovers has been used in a couple of Australian films. *UNFINISHED BUSINESS* (1985) is the first film directed by Bob Ellis (b. 1942). It is as modest in its budget ($102,000) and its scope as *Phobia*: it also uses the director's house as a single-set, and is a virtual two-hander. (Another link with *Phobia*: Ellis can be briefly glimpsed in a party scene caught on video in Dingwall's film.) For Ellis the experience was 'the best—I've never been busier, and never been happier. I think cheap films are great for that reason.'

Ellis' concept was originally rather different. He wanted to make a film along the lines of Louis Malle's *My Dinner with André* which would feature his friends, humorists Patrick Cook and John Clarke. It was to have been called *Business Lunch*, and Clarke would have played an ABC executive who was about to tell Cook he had been fired; dialogue would have been largely improvised. The sum of $60,000 was raised by Patric Juillet and neophyte co-producer Rebel Penfold-Russell to make the film, and then Clarke became permanently unavailable and time starting running out. With a supreme piece of lateral thinking, Penfold-Russell suggested the money be diverted to another project with 'business' or 'lunch' in the title so that the investors would not know it was a different film.

Ellis wrote the screenplay for *Unfinished Business* in three days, tailoring his characters specifically for Michele Fawdon and John Clayton. 'But it proved impossible to find a time when they were both free. Eventually, we started shooting with only one day of pre-production and one day of rehearsal, and for much of the film we were still shooting at 2 a.m. after both of them had finished work.' The film was shot in only eleven days.

Under the circumstances, it is a miracle that the film works as well as it does. Ellis is convinced that his casting choices were all-important. 'Had it starred Wendy Hughes and John Waters, it would have been of little interest. But because we had these two warm, cuddly, marsupial people, who may not be all that good looking but who, in their own way, are very sexy, it worked very well.' He is not so happy with the ending. 'We buggered it up. We shot a scene that was much fiercer, but didn't use it. So the audience doesn't actually cry at the end, and they should. But we didn't have the time or money to improve it.'

In contrast to *Phobia* and other films about the bitterness and violence which can accompany a disintegrating relationship, *Unfinished Business* is filled with humour and optimism. Geoff agrees to help Maureen, his ex-lover whom he has not seen in fifteen years, 'engender a potential taxpayer' because her husband (a brief role for Norman Kaye) is apparently sterile. The arrangement is businesslike at first: Maureen will not allow sex until her temperature is right. But it blossoms into middle-aged passion and finally love, paving the way for a bitter-sweet ending. The dialogue and performances are bright and witty, and Ellis has learnt from his erstwhile collaborator, Paul Cox, that existing music is often the apt complement for a scene—in this case the repeated use of the Peter Dawson song 'I'll Walk Beside You' is quite perfect.

Unfinished Business. *Michele Fawdon,
John Clayton.*

Despite its obvious entertainment value, the film had the most limited exposure, reinforcing Bill Bennett's comments earlier about the uphill battle facing the modestly budgeted film.

Friends also become lovers in *THE BEST OF FRIENDS* (1981). This film is notable chiefly for its screenplay, for which Donald Macdonald won $10,000 in a competition arranged by the NSWFC for best original comedy. (The following year, a Hollywood film with a remarkably similar plot was released: Norman Jewison's *Best Friends*, with Goldie Hawn and Burt Reynolds; and there are elements of the same story in Rob Reiner's 1989 success, *When Harry Met Sally*.) At the time there was much speculation about the quality of the other scripts submitted, for this winner hardly sparkles.

The film is produced by Tom Jeffrey, who gave up directing films after three decent efforts in the 70s—*The Removalists*, *Weekend of Shadows* and *The Odd Angry Shot*. It was the directorial debut of Michael Robertson, whose forte was television commercials. Graeme Blundell, an experienced comedy player, was well cast as Tom, the practising

Cinematographer David Gribble (left) *and director Michael Robertson working on* The Best of Friends.

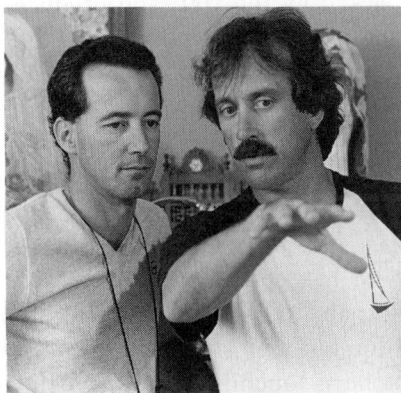

Catholic who beds Melanie (Angela Punch McGregor, less happily cast) after a drunken celebration of the twentieth anniversary of their hitherto platonic friendship.

Despite photography by David Gribble that uses Sydney locations in a genuinely creative way, and despite some unusually witty opening titles, *The Best of Friends* is a weak effort, which moves sluggishly and repetitively towards a predictable fade-out. The best scene is a disastrous dinner held for the respective parents of the couple, during which Ruth Cracknell is able to provide some welcome, if theatrical, humour.

Robertson's only other film of the decade, *GOING SANE* (1985), written and produced by John Sandford, featured John Waters in one of his several mid-life crisis roles. Possibly inspired by *Bliss* (produced the same year, also for the NSWFC), the film does not work as comedy. There is an extended and alarmingly humourless sequence involving a visit by Waters, accompanied by his sexually voracious secretary, Irene (Linda Cropper) to an outback storekeeper (Tim Robertson, with the phoniest of Welsh accents) and his generously-endowed wife (Anne Semler). Nor does it work as romantic drama. Judy Morris has the most thankless role of her career as Waters' nagging wife, and even the late introduction of Kate Raison, as a sweet-natured environmentalist, is of little help.

The theme of peace in the outback, featured in both *Bliss* and *Going Sane*, crops up again in the altogether more successful *THE SETTLEMENT* (1983), the only feature film to date directed by Howard Rubie. Rubie (b. 1938) filmed the Maitland floods when he was fifteen years old, and subsequently made scores of documentaries, telemovies and episodes of television series (such as *Spyforce*). *The Settlement*, backed by the QFC and produced by veteran television producer and actor Robert Bruning, starts off with the advantage of a very good screenplay by Ted Roberts. Set in a small Queensland town in the 50s, the film is strong on atmosphere and characterisation, with lively performances from the principals. This is probably John Jarratt's finest hour, but Bill Kerr and Lorna Lesley are equally good as the other angles of the triangle relationship. There is an unusually good supporting cast including Tony Barry as the town's frustrated policeman whose wife has opted for religion with preacher David Downer instead of sex; and Alan Cassell as the lecherous hotel owner. It is not an ambitious film, but a most attractive one, with a central love story that manages to be as touching as it is unorthodox.

Another first (and so far only) feature about relationships is ... *MAYBE THIS TIME* (1980), which Chris McGill directed from a screenplay by Bob Ellis and his wife, Anne Brooksbank. Judy Morris is excellent as a university researcher in this Whitlam-era story. Nearing the age of thirty, Fran decides that her three lovers (Ken Shorter as the boyfriend from the country, Bill Hunter as the secretary to the Labor Minister, Mike Preston as her boss) are unfulfilling. Jill Perryman won Best Supporting Actress at the AFI awards for her performance as Fran's widowed mother, and there are top supporting players (Chris Haywood as a randy travelling salesman with a nice line in dirty jokes; Michele Fawdon as Fran's married sister; Jude Kuring as the wife of the Bill Hunter character).

Cleanly shot by Russell Boyd, the film, which was produced by Brian Kavanagh, is rather stiffly directed. Unlike the best Australian films about relationships, it seems self-conscious about its approach to its subject, especially to the sex scenes. The film was originally titled *Letters from a Friend*, the friend being the unseen Jenny, who has been living overseas, and the touching ending, revealing her death, provides the best moment in a generally uneven film.

A ll the films about relationships discussed so far have been essentially Australian stories, some of them more successful than others. But a handful of films, in their quest for international audiences of differing kinds, have introduced significant foreign elements. Take, for example, *BREAKFAST IN PARIS* (1981), an inept romance. It was optimistically described (by the director) as 'a big-budget glossy production . . . a warm, sentimental, good-hearted and humorous love story in the *A Touch of Class* style' (he was referring to the film *A Touch of Class*, presumably, not the notorious Sydney brothel). The director in question is John Lamond (b. 1947) whose stint as a publicist at Village–Roadshow seemed, for a while, to guarantee distribution for his painful films; they included softcore sex items like *Felicity* (1978), crude slasher-horror like *Nightmares* (1980) and sex-comedy like *Pacific Banana* (1980).

American actress Barbara Parkins plays a Melbourne dress-designer whose man has betrayed her with another woman; she travels first-class to Paris (generous plugs for French airline UTA), meeting handsome Aussie Rod Mullinar on the plane. Romance blossoms; then they quarrel, she goes back to Melbourne, changes her mind, returns to Paris, and (without a hint of jetlag) all ends well. The banal screenplay by Morris Dalton is sub-television soap material, but the dialogue, fortunately, is often drowned out by Brian May's syrupy score. At the screening I attended, the audience applauded when Ms Parkins was hit by a car at just the wrong moment (compare Irene Dunne in *Love Affair* or Deborah Kerr in *An Affair to Remember*).

Roadshow released *Breakfast in Paris* with the tagline 'From the world's most romantic city comes a dream of a love story'. Berlin is a location with a very different ambience, and *THE PRISONER OF ST PETERSBURG* (1988), an Australian–West German co-production, is a very different kind of love story. Ian Pringle's third feature stars Noah Taylor as a mysterious youth apparently fixated with Russian literature after a visit to Leningrad. Ray Argall's evocative black-and-white photography of the chilly Berlin streets is the principal asset of this rather remote and pretentious film which, although it received some film festival exposure, is so lacking in humour and tension that it appeared to be commercially doomed from the beginning. The actors, including Solveig Dommartin who was so memorable in Wim Wenders' *Wings of Desire*, are able only to go through the motions.

A more exotic setting for a love story is to be found in *ECHOES OF PARADISE* (1987), also known as *Shadows of the Peacock* (and, at various stages of pre-production and production as *Love on a Tourist Visa* and *Promises To Keep*). Jan Sharp's screenplay was originally set in Bali, and involves a passionate love affair between a Sydney wife (Wendy Hughes) and a Balinese dancer. In the latter role, John Lone seemed like perfect casting: he had already appeared in Fred Schepisi's *Iceman* and Michael Cimino's *Year of the Dragon*, and was about to play the lead in Bernardo Bertolucci's *The Last Emperor*.

Sharp's husband, Phillip Noyce, was set to direct, and Sharp originally planned to produce the film; but conflicting schedules with *The Umbrella Woman*, which she was also producing, led her to hand over production

Echoes of Paradise. *John Lone.*

to Jane Scott. It was planned to shoot on location in Bali, and then return to film some interiors, and the film's opening and closing scenes, in Sydney. Location surveys had been carried out in Bali (which had not been used as a location for an Australian feature film before); production manager Antonia Barnard had already paid deposits on hotel accommodation and was having sets built when disaster struck. The *Sydney Morning Herald* published an article which suggested that the wife of the Indonesian President was as corrupt as Imelda Marcos. Immediately, all Indonesian visas for Australians were cancelled. Scott tried in vain to persuade the Indonesian authorities to allow the shoot to take place.

Agonising decisions had to be made. Noyce flew to Thailand to see if it would be possible to film at Phuket, and decided it would be. Meanwhile, the entire film was rescheduled so that the interiors and the Sydney scenes would be shot first. The problems faced by Barnard and the production team were enormous, since contra deals had been arranged to enable the Bali shoot to be accommodated within the budget: now, new deals had to be struck to get the cast and crew to Thailand (Thai International came to the party). Also, the script had to be rewritten (none too convincingly, as it turned out) to explain why a Balinese dancer was living in Thailand.

Since Sharp was busy with *The Umbrella Woman*, Anne Brooksbank was hired to write the additional material. When the crew left for the three-week Thai shoot, Brooksbank wrote the new dialogue and faxed it every day to the location. As a result, the actors found it difficult to get an overall grasp of their characters. It was hardly any easier for Noyce, who had many sleepless nights trying to plan the following day's shoot.

John Lone was having problems too. He had spent a month in Bali before the film was rescheduled, living with a local prince and learning how to perform Balinese dances. He felt he understood the character, and did not want to play a Thai (which would have been far more logical). It was impossible to delay the shoot, because he was going straight on to *The Last Emperor*. It was, by all accounts, a nightmare; to top it all, several crew members, including Noyce, fell ill. Yet, incredibly, at the end of production, the picture came in only $14 under budget!

It was very unfortunate that Phillip Noyce's feature film comeback (this was his first film since *Heatwave* in 1981) should be so troubled. Ironically, the sequences shot in a dismal-looking Sydney are far stronger than the location footage: Wendy Hughes gives another good performance as Maria, mother of three, who discovers that her lawyer husband (Steve Jacobs, also excellent) has been having an affair. She also faces personal tragedy with the death of her father. But once we get to Phuket, and despite the welcome presence of Peta Toppano as Maria's best friend, the film loses its conviction, and the love scenes are singularly passionless. Ambiguities abound, bits of plot are unresolved, and John Lone seems in a constant state of unease. Apart from Hughes and Jacobs, the film's chief asset is the rich cinematography by Peter James and a pleasant music score by William Motzing.

A s we have seen, Australians can travel to far-flung places in search of romance; there are, of course, also the films about foreigners, invariably Americans, who come to Australia and find the object of their dreams. Such a film is *REBEL* (1985), set in 1942, about a romance between a young GI deserter and a Sydney singer whose husband is fighting in New Guinea. This started life as a play, *No Names, No Packdrill*, by Bob Herbert, and the original Sydney production starred Mel Gibson and Noni Hazlehurst. Herbert collaborated on the screenplay with director Michael Jenkins, and the film was produced by Phillip Emanuel in close collaboration with Roadshow, very much with the American market in mind.

To this end, Matt Dillon (who had appeared, to some acclaim, in Francis Coppola's *The Outsiders* and *Rumble Fish*) was cast as Rebel. Kathy, a postal sorter in the play, was transformed into a singer in a female band, since Emanuel originally hoped to have Olivia Newton-John play the role. But Newton-John proved unavailable, and the role was given to Debbie Byrne. Byrne had been a star of the television show *Young Talent Time* when she was twelve years old, and by the time she made *Rebel* had received a fair amount of publicity for her hectic lifestyle, which included an addiction to drugs. (After completing *Rebel*, she won leading roles in the stage productions of *Cats* and *Les Misérables*.)

Jenkins (b. 1946) is a television scriptwriter (*Bellbird, Water Under The Bridge*) whose adaptation of the Sumner Locke Elliott novel *Careful He Might Hear You* was filmed in 1983 by Carl Schultz and who, in the same year, directed the provocative ABC television series, *Scales of Justice*. But the dominating influence on *Rebel* is not the director but the production designer. Brian Thomson, who had designed *The Rocky Horror Picture Show* for Jim Sharman and *Starstruck* for Gillian

Rebel. *Debbie Byrne* (centre) *with Kim Deacon* (left).

■

■

Armstrong, as well as several stage productions, created sets of staggering vulgarity which swamped the film with their overpowering use of variations on the colour red. Why Jenkins and Emanuel went along with the hideous stylisation of the film is anyone's guess, but they did. Perhaps they felt that, since Peter Best's songs, though excellent in themselves, were totally anachronistic (they are not 40s songs and they are not performed in 40s style), they might as well go the whole hog and make a fantasy.

As a result we get 80s instead of 40s dialogue, everyone looks far too affluent, there is no hint of reality, and the plot is cut to the bone in a frantic race to get to the next musical number. Matt Dillon's mannered performance is irritating (he seems to be emulating Marlon Brando and James Dean), and did nothing to further a promising career, but Debbie Byrne grabs all her chances and Bryan Brown is quite funny as the unscrupulous conman, Tiger Kelly. As members of the band, Julie Nihill and Kim Deacon have far too little screen time, as does Ray Barrett, rather touching in his few moments as the club's MC. But the suffocating use of colour swamps just about everything, and the AFI award given to Thomson for his work remains one of the many mysteries that surround this increasingly dubious annual event.

A novel by Danielle Steel was the basis for *NOW AND FOREVER* (1982), for which Cheryl Ladd was imported to play the long-suffering American wife of Sydneysider Robert Coleby, whose fling with the apparently willing Christine Amor (while the missus is away) leads to an unwarranted accusation of rape. The producers, Treisha Ghent and Carnegie Fieldhouse, obviously determined to crack the American market, were not content with Ms Ladd: they hired another American,

Richard Cassidy, to write and direct. The screenplay is a mess of clichés, with situations and dialogue that would hardly pass muster in a South American telemovie, and we will never know how talented Mr Cassidy might have been as the director because he was replaced by Adrian Carr, the film's Australian editor, during production. Despite the general woefulness of *Now and Forever*, it received the sought-after American release and presumably found favour with the Mills and Boon set.

An ugly American-Australian businessman, played by Michael Pate, lusts after Claire Binney, an Australian secretary, in *DUET FOR FOUR* (1981), which was scripted by David Williamson. Since Williamson's name is usually synonymous with quality, the few people who saw the picture might have been understandably annoyed by it, but this was a screenplay Williamson had written seven years earlier, around the time of *Petersen* (1974), which had been successful enough for Hexagon to commission the second screenplay. Says Williamson: 'Tim Burstall said to me, "Do a script on mid-life crisis." Well, I was twenty-nine at the time, so that was a bit difficult, plus I was pushed for time, so I rattled out this script in about eight days.' Roadshow did not care for the screenplay (which was originally titled *The Toy Man*) and it languished in a desk drawer until the arrival of 10BA made an unfilmed Williamson screenplay valuable (at the time, scripts were sold in perpetuity). With virtually no revision, it went into production under the title *Partners*, with Burstall directing and a cast that included Mike Preston and Gary Day as partners in a toy-manufacturing business, and Wendy Hughes as the philandering Preston's de facto wife. The cast also included Diane Cilento as his ex-wife, and Sigrid Thornton as their daughter. Pate's character is that of an expatriate Australian who works for an American toy manufacturer.

Much of the dialogue is risible, and the only actor to come out of the film with any credit is Wendy Hughes who gave a convincingly bitchy performance. The film tries to cover too much ground, and treats its subject with bland superficiality, though it can be seen (and Williamson may well have intended) as a parody of the Village–Roadshow organisation itself, as it had been structured at the time. In this light, the film contains a few amusing, but very 'in', jokes about the distribution and exhibition industry as it was in the early 70s and, perhaps, some of the personalities involved.

The three films discussed above all have American characters involved, romantically or sexually, with Australians; none is successful. *THE WINDS OF JARRAH* (1983), which is about an English woman in love with a rugged Aussie forest-worker, does not work either. Unlike the others, this is not because it *smacks* of Mills and Boon—it *is* Mills and Boon. It was adapted by Bob Ellis and Anne Brooksbank from *The House in the Timberwoods*, a Mills and Boon book by Joyce Dingwall.

Mark Egerton (b. 1947 in England) directed: he was Australia's leading first assistant director in the 70s and early 80s, having worked with Peter Weir, Gillian Armstrong and others on some of the key Australian films. In 1982, he took over direction of the troubled *Crosstalk* (see Chapter 8) from Keith Salvat, but *The Winds of Jarrah* was the first (and, as it turned out, only) film which he had directed from the beginning. He also re-jigged the screenplay, but did not omit some of the more embarrassing dialogue exchanges ('I'm sorry for the trees.' 'So am I—I was a tree way back, probably a cedar.')

Not surprisingly, given such dialogue, the actors are wooden. Susan Lyons, as the Englishwoman, towers over her co-stars, but her love interest, Terence Donovan, is uncharismatic when set beside his rivals (Harold Hopkins and Steve Bisley). The film's only asset is the way it looks. It was filmed entirely on location at Dorrigo, New South Wales, in real rainforest country, and cinematographer Geoff Burton filmed it in Panavision. The house on which the story centred was specially built for the film (spectacular work by production designer Graham Walker) and scenes of a logging competition, a dance and a near-drowning are quite spectacular. Ironically, the film was never seen in cinemas and was released direct to video. For Geoff Burton, who considers it his best wide-screen work, this was maddening: 'I was fairly shattered about that,' he says. 'I got angry at the time to think of all the work we put into it and then for it not to be seen. Now, I like to talk about elements of my work in that film to people I'm working with, and nobody's seen it.' Sadly, despite its impressive visuals, the film was just too trite and passionless to merit the cost of a cinema release.

So, too, was *BOUNDARIES OF THE HEART* (1988), which was also bypassed for cinema release despite a cast that included Wendy Hughes, John Hargreaves and Norman Kaye. This is not Mills and Boon material, though Peter Yeldham's screenplay might just as well have been with all its old-fashioned dialogue. Hughes' husband, Patric Juillet, produced for their company, Tra La La Films and Tony Ginnane executive-produced as part of the Hemdale package; the unit went to the expense of travelling to Coolgardie, a small township near Kalgoorlie in Western Australia, for location shooting.

Former actor Lex Marinos (b. 1950 in Wagga Wagga) directed, but was quite unable to make anything of Yeldham's dialogue. The actors perform well below their usual standard; Wendy Hughes plays the same kind of spinster she did in *Lonely Hearts*, but gives a strident, self-conscious performance and John Hargreaves, who adopts an ultra-slow drawl for his cowboy role, has never been less effective. Even the usually reliable Norman Kaye is all at sea with the corny dialogue and situations (not helped by an obvious and unbecoming wig), and only Julie Nihill, as the woman he decides to marry, comes out of the film with any honours. This tale of sexual frustration in the outback needed a bit of genuine passion in the direction, writing and acting, but it totally lacks pace and style and conviction. Maybe the desert heat got to them all. It is sad to reflect on the great work these same actors did earlier in the decade. It should be noted that Hughes won Best Actress award at the Seattle Film Festival for this role: one wonders about the competition.

T he last few films under discussion were made on relatively high budgets; but, as we have seen, some of the most interesting films about relationships were very modest in scope. In Melbourne, producer Rosa Colosimo made a series of low-budget films during the 80s, the best of which were love stories.

HUNGRY HEART (1987) was her second production; she had written the screenplay herself, but to direct she signed Luigi Acquisto, a graduate of Swinburne Institute of Technology, whose short film *Saventepasseri* she had seen and liked. The film, about a love affair that starts passionately but quickly goes sour, was shot in August 1987, on a budget of just under $500,000. Colosimo's own house was used as one location for the film and suffered considerable damage (for which the insurance company would not pay).

The film is uneven, but the lead actors (Nick Carrafa and Kimberley Davenport) are good and it has excellent moments such as the unexpected arrival of Katie's father—a telling cameo from John Flaus—the morning after she has spent a night with Sal.

Acquisto charts the way the love affair goes wrong with conviction (Sal's irritation at Katie's habit of walking around the apartment naked), but tries to take on too much, and a subplot involving Sal's friend Charlie occupies screen time better spent on the lovers. Dasha Blahova, the Czech-born actress, is not comfortably cast as an Italian mother, but does the best she can with the role. Norman Kaye, as an ex-priest, has only a few scenes but brings to them a resonance reminiscent of his work for Paul Cox. The film is good enough to have warranted some kind of release but, as with subsequent Colosimo productions, it was shunned by distributors and exhibitors, and received only the most limited exposure.

In 1988–9 Colosimo produced five more features, all of which suffered the same fate. The AFC and Film Victoria have consistently refused to support her with government money, saying her projects lack quality ('I think they're racist and sexist,' she says) and because she continues to raise money she faces rumours and innuendo that she is funded by the Mafia. 'I don't get money from the Mafia,' she says. 'I don't know where all of it comes from, but it was all raised via 10BA, through stockbrokers, or privately via risk finance, or investment companies like Chancom. The National Australia Bank has been a big supporter. My films may not be among the best Australian films, but they're far from being the worst.' None of her films has ever been nominated in any categories for the AFI awards, meaning that they have never been screened for the AFI membership. So they remain largely unknown.

Colosimo describes her other film about love, *CLOSER AND CLOSER APART* (1989) as 'pure soap', but this modest, well-observed, film is better than that. Inspired by *La Cavalleria Rusticana*, the story, like that of much of *Hungry Heart*, is set in Melbourne's Italian community. What fascinates is not so much the relationships between old buddies Sam and Alfio and their girls, chaste Angie and easy-going Lola, but the details of the community itself: religious icons dominate in the parents' homes, regular visits to church are the norm, and traditions die hard. The four young actors are excellent, and the filming on location, in shops, markets, cafés and on the street, adds a lot to the mood. Above all is the feeling of Italian Australians torn between two worlds and two cultures, a theme convincingly dealt with by director Steve Middleton. As a love story, Alfio's devotion to the unfaithful Lola is consistently touching.

This theme of lonely, alienated people looking for love brings us full circle back to the theme of *Lonely Hearts*, and it crops up again in *WITH LOVE TO THE PERSON NEXT TO ME* (1987), a low-budget feature from documentarist Brian McKenzie. Here again are Paul Cox references since, like the lonely protagonist of *Kostas*, the alienated Wallace, touchingly played by Kim Gyngell, drives a taxi around the Melbourne streets; he often tapes the conversations he has with his passengers and listens to them played back later. Like McKenzie's documentaries, the film is overlong and rather formless, but the characters are fascinating, especially Paul Chubb and Barry Dickins as a couple of foul-mouthed and incompetent thieves who are frequent visitors to Gail (Sally McKenzie), the woman who lives in the next apartment to Wallace. The settings are seedy and depressing, but thanks to the direction of the actors there is a welcome sense of humour among all the angst, and Ray Argall's photography is, once again, worthy of note.

SWEET DREAMERS (1981) is an oddity: a very personal film which is really too personal a story to be worth the telling. Director Tom Cowan (b. 1942) is better known as a cinematographer, though he directed three features in the 70s—*The Office Picnic* (1972), *Promised Woman* (1974) and *Journey Among Women* (1977). In *Sweet Dreamers* he attempted an autobiographical story about the relationship between a filmmaker, Will (Richard Moir) and Josephine (Sue Smithers), who comes to live with him. Through Will, Cowan expresses his feelings about the the film industry at the beginning of the 80s: Will fears the Americanisation of the Australian film industry, and swears at the 'geriatrics' in the AFC who refuse support for his latest project. But, despite attractive performances and Brian Probyn's camerawork, the film simply fails to ignite: it remains tentative and flabby and lacks impact. Maybe a more forthright depiction of the passion and pain of the relationship would have helped: but, after a disastrous unspooling at the 1981 AFI screenings, *Sweet Dreamers* sank without trace, and Cowan returned to cinematography. He has not directed a film since.

One cinematographer who made an outstanding feature film in the 80s is Ray Argall whose *RETURN HOME* (1989) is a film about many kinds of love. Argall (b. 1957 in Melbourne) started making Super-8 films when he was young and studied at the AFTRS from 1977 to 1979. While he was still a student, he photographed Ian Pringle's 50-minute featurette *Wronsky* (1979).

In 1980, Argall and John Cruthers founded a company, Musical Films, to produce music clips and music related productions; Argall directed *Pop Movie*, a series of six half-hour programmes (shown on ABC television) about the rock music industry. He also photographed a number of significant low-budget feature films: Ian Pringle's *The Plains of Heaven*, *Wrong World* and *The Prisoner of St Petersburg*; Brian McKenzie's *With Love to the Person Next to Me*; and Mary Callaghan's *Tender Hooks*.

Return Home. *Dennis Coard, Frankie J. Holden.*

For his first feature as writer-director, Argall chose a subject with autobiographical elements. Like Noel McKenzie (beautifully played by Dennis Coard), Argall had spent much of his youth in suburban Adelaide, where his father moved after his parents divorced; and, like Gary (Ben Mendelsohn), he had a love of hot cars. Funded by the AFC and FV (and with no private investment), Argall made *Return Home* on a budget of just $350,000. It was shot in six weeks by Mandy Walker on standard 16mm, but on its completion the AFC agreed to pay for a blow-up to 35mm, and the film was invited to the Panorama section of the 1990 Berlin Film Festival.

On the surface, the story is extremely simple. Noel, who has a high-pressure job in Melbourne, is divorced; evidently in mid-life crisis, he returns to his roots—the beachside Adelaide suburb where he lived with his brother, Steve (Frankie J. Holden) as a child. Steve and his hard-working wife, Jude (Micki Camilleri) still run the petrol station the family owned when the brothers were young, but the place has fallen on hard times.

Some of the film simply explores the suburb itself; the tree-lined streets, the shopping centre that has taken business away from the old part of town, the beach, the pier, the funfair. Through Noel, we also meet the locals: among them his ex-girlfriend, who now lives with a German, and a solitary guitar player who has obviously been drifting around for years.

But in the main the action concentrates on the relationships between Noel, Steve, and Gary, the mechanic, a lovesick youth whose girl (Rachel Rains) has obviously got fed up with him. The scenes around the garage are minutely observed, and Argall builds up the characters with myriad details (significantly omitting a family reunion scene in which the brothers dine with their parents).

The result is a perfect little gem, which is completely unpretentious and consequently even more effective in its loving observation of these people and of the environment where they live. Coard (relatively new to acting after spending fifteen years of his life working for Telecom) is a great discovery: his sympathetic Everyman speaks wonders with just a look or a half-smile. Though undoubtedly too 'minimal' for many tastes, this tale of brotherly love and the return of a stranger to his past is a wholly satisfying experience, and we await Argall's work in the 90s with eager anticipation.

A

WALK

ON

THE

WILD

SIDE

■
■

L oneliness, love, and the pain of parting; as we saw in the previous chapter, these themes recur again and again in Australian cinema. But there is a significant group of films which deal with wilder kinds of love: stronger emotions are in play in those films which deal primarily with sexual obsession. A sub-heading for this chapter could be Sex and Drugs and Rock 'n' Roll.

We started Chapter 4 by looking at Paul Cox's 'realist' films about love: *Lonely Hearts*, *Cactus* and *My First Wife*. The prolific director has also made significant films which fall into the area of obsession. Many think *MAN OF FLOWERS* (1983) is Cox's best film; it is certainly an extraordinary combination of pain and humour, sex and death, poetry and magic. The film came about during a period, after the success of *Lonely Hearts*, when Cox was offered various projects, none of which came to anything: among them was *The Nostradamus Kid*, scripted by Bob Ellis, which was to have been produced by Jane Ballantyne and Patric Juillet and to have starred Robert Menzies; another was *Should Auld Acquaintance Be Forgot*, scripted by Anne Brooksbank, produced by Ballantyne, to star Wendy Hughes. When these ideas came to nothing, Cox was understandably frustrated. 'I wanted to work,' he says. 'So, during a plane trip, I started to write *Man of Flowers*. I felt my life was changing, and all my childhood memories came to the fore, all the suppression I'd gone through. I was determined to make this film. I wrote the story in two days, gathered people around me—even my lawyer, who's normally very strict, put money into it. I found an office, put up a sign, connected the phone, and said I was in pre-production: but, actually, we had no money at all.'

Chris Haywood was living in Melbourne at the time and was seeing Cox socially; they had worked together before. Haywood, who had been married to Wendy Hughes, had a small part in *Kostas*, and had appeared, with Hughes, in the dramatised documentary, *For a Child Called Michael*. He recalls: 'We were chatting away about the state of the industry, and he suddenly said: "Hey, we can make a film for nothing." And I said: "There's never been a really erotic Australian film—we should make an erotic film." We started from that point, with Paul, me and Alyson Best, who was my girlfriend at the time. We planned to defer all the payments. We had a camera, we had a Steenback [editing table]. The basics were all there. Then Jane Ballantyne said she felt she could get some investment, which she did.'

Cox asked Bob Ellis to help him write the dialogue. Ellis recalls:

Man of Flowers. *Barry Dickins, Norman Kaye.*

'It was one of those periods when funding regulations changed so we couldn't get *The Nostradamus Kid* off the ground; naturally, Cox was terribly frustrated. He rang me one day and said: "We're going to make a blue movie." I was amazed, but he said: "Trust me." Then he rang and said: "I've got a storyline. We start filming on Monday week. Can you come down?" I said: "I can't be there till Saturday." He said: "That's all right, we'll write it over the weekend." I arrived on the Friday night, and we got drunk. On Saturday we started work at 8 a.m. At 12, Cox had to go off to see people and have some drinks. I decided to quit, and wrote him a letter with five pages of carefully reasoned abuse. Then I had a few drinks and put the letter away. Next day, exactly the same thing happened again.' Cox says: 'I'd give Ellis a scene, and he'd go into a little trance and then write that madness he's so good at. His contributions were great, but it all happened in a screaming hurry. Ellis had trouble with my methods, but it was a hectic time for me. What would normally have taken a year took a month; what would have taken a week took an hour.'

Cox cast his old friend Norman Kaye in the leading role of Charles Bremer, the wealthy eccentric who pays a young woman to strip for him while he listens to classical music. 'The film was a celebration of our friendship,' says Cox. 'I learnt a lot from Norman. We trust each other, and there's something that clicks between us.'

Jane Ballantyne had raised $240,000 to make *Man of Flowers*. 'We shot in three weeks,' says Cox. 'We had very little film stock. The house we used belonged to Asher Bilu, the production designer.' Chris Haywood recalls that Cox wanted some exceptionally long takes: 'There's a scene with Norman Kaye in the studio where my character lives, and that was done with a long, complex shot which travels right through the studio. That was about three pages of dialogue, and learning lines isn't my forte—I'm too lazy. But it worked very well.'

Also in the film, playing Bremer's father in the flashbacks, is German director Werner Herzog, an old friend of Cox. 'I rang him in Germany,' says Cox. 'And I told him: "It's you or me. One of us has to play the father." He said: "It's me," and he came out in no time. I shot his scenes myself on Super-8, and I remember asking him if he'd ever seen a Panavision camera. He hadn't. Neither of us knew what one looked like. So here we were, me and Werner, a very famous director, making a film with this tiny little Super-8 camera.'

The film was edited in three weeks, and the magnificent sound mix was the work of Jim Currie at Hendon Studios ('He's an unsung hero of the Australian cinema,' says Cox.) Cox had used the Donizetti aria in the film without having the music rights. 'I went to the record company and went down on my knees and said: "I'm not leaving until you give me the rights to this music." I had no money to pay for it.'

Man of Flowers is an extraordinary achievement, and shows, once again, just what can be done on a tiny budget when the people involved are both dedicated and talented. Norman Kaye (who deservedly won Best Actor at the AFI awards that year) plays the strange, obsessed Bremer who is forever writing letters to his dead mother; he makes him a gentle and kindly character, even at the end when he decides to rid the world of the odious David (Haywood) whose 'action' paintings are as ugly as his attitudes towards Lisa (Alyson Best), the young woman Bremer loves in his own, distant way. The film *is* erotic; the nude scenes are unselfconscious, but very beautiful (helped no end by Yuri Sokol's lovely photography and that soaring music); but it is also very witty. Ellis himself appears as Bremer's psychiatrist (and gives himself some very choice lines); Patrick Cook is an eccentric who proposes that, instead of being buried or cremated, the dead should be covered in copper and kept at home; Barry Dickins is the chatty postman, full of mournful quips about the state of the world. When Lisa's friend, Jane (Sarah Walker) describes lesbian sex as 'smooth and restful', Lisa responds, 'Sounds like Milo!' There are visual jokes, too, like the brief shot of the paint-spattered parrot in David's studio.

Outrageous, funny, erotic, sad, 'elegantly kinky' (as film critic Molly Haskell described it in *Vogue*): no wonder *Man of Flowers* was such a success. It enjoyed excellent art-house runs in Australia, and overseas too, and it won the Grand Prix at the Chicago Film Festival. In Britain, it was so popular that it was adapted into a play (without Cox's involvement) and performed at the Edinburgh Festival.

After this major success, Cox continued to make memorable films. *My First Wife* and *Cactus* were followed by *VINCENT: THE LIFE AND DEATH OF VINCENT VAN GOGH* (1987). This became a very personal journey for Cox, who photographed the film himself, much of it in his native Holland. His identification with Van Gogh is evident throughout: the film is a portrait of one deeply committed, sometimes misunderstood and neglected, artist by another. John Hurt's mellow voice on the soundtrack reads the remarkable letters Van Gogh wrote to his brother Theo, in which the artist describes his obsessions and struggles. 'I do not mind being eccentric,' he says. And he says that he wants people to say of him that 'he feels deeply, tenderly'. This is very much a Paul Cox film, and its success on the world's art-house circuits is heartening. In the US it was in continuous release for two years.

The inspiration for *ISLAND* (1989) goes back twenty years to an early short film Cox made about a Greek island. 'The images always haunted me,' he says. The new film centres on three women who represent different cultures: Eva (Eva Sitta) is a Czech-Australian; Marquise (Irene Papas) is from the Greek mainland; and Sahana (Anoja Weerasinghe) represents the Third World of Asia. Men are marginal in the film: Eva is pursued by a sadistic French drug-dealer (she is trying to kick her habit); Sahana waits for her husband who never returns; Marquise lives alone.

'The film represents Australia's multicultural background,' says Cox. 'It's a very Australian film, even though it was shot entirely in Greece. The crew was all-Australian. The film isn't about real women; these aren't simple characters to be explored. They represent the way one part of the world relates to another. It's about the way the East gives the West spirit. In the film, East tells West she has to find herself; the East is always giving to the West, even as the West exploits the East.'

Cox was plagued with shortage of money on the film, and the screenplay was never completed to his full satisfaction. It is a flawed work, and his least satisfying film of the decade, but it does contain some marvellous things. One of them is Irene Papas, who was cast thanks to Cox's old friend Takis Emmanuel (associate producer on *Island*). Says Papas: 'Takis told me about Paul and showed me the film they did together, *Kostas*. He said he was looking for an actress like me. I said: "Why *like* me? Why not me?" ' The character of Marquise was not fully defined in the screenplay, and, for the first

Island. *Anoja Weerasinghe, Irene Papas, Eva Sitta.*

time in her film career, Papas had to improvise: but she rises to the occasion with a stirring performance, and overshadows her co-stars. 'I was surprised to find I could work that way,' she says. 'And I thank Paul for teaching me how to use my inner self. I'm very glad to have worked with him.'

The other joy in the film is Chris Haywood, who plays Janis, a deaf-mute Greek islander (there is a large community of deaf-mutes on the island where the film was shot). 'Chris is a great actor,' says Cox. 'He can virtually do anything. This role was a marvellous challenge for him. He spent time with the real deaf-mutes, working alongside them on building sites. He gave his heart and soul to the film. He even picked up the sign language they invented themselves.' 'I had to be entirely self-sufficient,' says Haywood. 'There was no make-up, no wardrobe. I had to do my own make-up to make me look dark. On the island, I lived as much as possible as an islander. I based my performance on a real deaf-mute and I worked alongside him as a builder, even after filming started. When they needed me for a scene, I'd down tools and go in front of the camera.' 'Chris is marvellous in the film,' says Irene Papas. 'He's so very moving.'

Months later, Cox screened *Island* for the islanders themselves, on a tiny screen in the community centre. 'They were stunned by Chris' performance,' he says. 'He totally convinced them. They loved him.'

Photographed by Michael Edols, *Island* is, as might be expected, an extremely beautiful film. The pacing is slow, as befits a film set in the calm serenity of a Greek island, and scenes such as a spontaneous dance in a café are beautifully handled. But it is not as completely satisfying as Cox's best work; the underdeveloped screenplay is part of the problem, and the too-placid performance of Eva Sitta is another. It is a fascinating experiment that was well worth doing, but falls short of the very high standards Cox himself has set. Still, even a disappointing

Cox film contains a beauty and a sincerity that puts it above many other films.

The film was invited to compete in the Venice Film Festival, and was distributed around the world. It received several nominations in the 1989 AFI awards (Best Film, Director, Actor and Actress among them) but won nothing. Despite a vitriolic review by Christine Cremen in *The Australian* (in which she claimed to have found his work since *Lonely Hearts* 'little more than catalogues of the furniture of high culture, laid out for their target audience to admire . . .' and further 'suspect[s] this pretentious display of cultural credentials exists merely to give tone to an enterprise of dubious value') the film did reasonably well in art-house cinemas.

Cox was back on top form with *GOLDEN BRAID* (1990), which was shot towards the end of 1989 on a budget of about $900,000 and a tight four-week schedule (it would have been five weeks, but, during the shoot, Cox flew to Italy to attend a retrospective of his work). The idea for the film came from the director's sister; she showed him the story by Guy de Maupassant and suggested it would make a good film. He agreed, and within a few days had written the first draft, updating the original and setting in present-day Melbourne. He then invited humorist Barry Dickins (the postman in *Man of Flowers*) to help him with the dialogue: 'I needed his kind of wit.'

'We're all chasing our dreams and memories,' says Cox. 'And in this film the theme of time became very important. Why have we stopped winding our watches? There's no point in making us all

Golden Braid. *Chris Haywood, Gosia Dobrowolska.*

dependent on those little batteries—particularly as those watch batteries are such polluters—they do a lot of damage. I also wanted to show the profession of watchmaking—another dying profession. What's going to happen to those people? So the film is saying: where's the sense in that? Where's the heart?'

Funding came from Film Victoria, always a loyal supporter of Cox's films, and ('for a change,' he says) from the AFC. 'I went to see Peter Sainsbury,' he says. 'I didn't know him at the time, and I showed him the script, and I said: "I need some money; please don't give me any shit." He was great, and supported it from the start.' In fact, *Golden Braid* is one of the few features since the 70s entirely funded by government bodies.

'I had no money worries on this film,' Cox says. 'I could correct my mistakes. I had the money to shoot extra scenes after we finished principal photography. It was marvellous to have that luxury.' Almost all of the film was shot in Albert Park, the Melbourne suburb where Cox lives and works. The house owned by Bernard (Chris Haywood) is Cox's own house; the antique shop run by Monica Maughan is just a few doors up the street.

Cox had Chris Haywood in mind for the role of Bernard from the beginning. The actor says: 'Another very challenging role for me. A man obsessed by time; clocks are his life. He's also obsessed with the passing of time, with regaining past moments of time. He wants to create links between the present and the past, the living and the dead.' Cox settled on other key casting from the beginning: Norman Kaye would play a psychiatrist, and he, Cox, would play a priest. But it proved more difficult to cast the vital role of Terese, the married woman whose love, sensuality and strength pull Bernard out of his increasingly irrational obsessions. It was while he was in Venice for the screening of *Island* that he thought of Gosia Dobrowolska, and he asked Chris Haywood back in Sydney to make contact with her agent.

Intrigued by Haywood's rather vague enquiry, Dobrowolska, who had always wanted to work with Cox and who was excited to hear he was about to make a new film, determined to meet the director. She accepted a role in an episode of *Mission Impossible* merely to have the chance to go to Melbourne. A five-hour meeting with Cox sealed the deal: 'The part is yours,' he told her.

'Her part was difficult,' says Cox. 'She had to be the Earth Mother, the giver. I've never worked with an actress like her before. She's totally giving. She was marvellous to work with. She gives a very original performance.'

The first week of the shoot was not entirely straightforward. Haywood seemed ill-at-ease, and Cox had difficulty getting hold of his character. But suddenly everything clicked into place and some of the early scenes were reshot as a result. 'Working with Paul doesn't compare with working with anyone else,' says Dobrowolska. 'I felt he could see inside me, tap my feelings. He's not just a director: he's absolute creator. And he opens a door and lets you into his world and though it's *his* world he allows you to create as well, to be a part of the film. The people around him are like a family who love him; everyone trusts and supports him. He's not always easy, but he's very rewarding. His crew is kept to a minimum; but we worked easy hours, fewer hours on any other film I've done—no overtime. Yet we achieved more; we just worked faster and better. He didn't let me wear make-up at all; and that was a clue to the character. I thought Terese should be absolutely pure.'

During production, the script changed in emphasis. 'Paul called us together,' says Dobrowolska. 'He asked us how we felt about those changes. He sought our suggestions. Sometimes he accepted them, sometimes he didn't. I suggested my opening line in the film: even though we discover Terese and Bernard are in the middle of an affair, I knock at the door and say "Good evening, sir, can I come in?" That wasn't in the script. But without Paul's inspiration I wouldn't have been able to make such a suggestion.'

Golden Braid returns Cox to the high level of achievement of *Man of Flowers*. Indeed, the films have elements in common: the eccentricity of the central character, the house that reflects his obsessions (in this case, the passing of time); the mother complex; the obsession with death (inevitable scenes in a cemetery); the dreams; the eroticism of the love scenes; the unexpected shafts of humour. But the new film has something more: a beautiful central love story. It says much for Gosia Dobrowolska's sensational performance that she does not allow Chris Haywood to overshadow her: Terese may come on in the beginning as a woman simply enjoying the thrill of a secret love affair, finding herself a different world from that of her stuffy, abstracted husband (Paul Chubb); but, by the end, she dominates the film, just as she gradually intrudes on Bernard's dreams. Her need for love, her passion and her warmth become tangible, and overcome her lover's strange obsession for the hank of hair he finds in a piece of antique furniture.

The scenes of Bernard's obsession with the hair are strange and funny. He talks to it ('I love all of you—every single hair'). He even makes love to it. After a tense scene in a restaurant with Terese and Joseph, Bernard says to the hair: 'Sorry to put you through all that.' One eerie scene opens with an image of golden hair on Bernard's pillow; it turns out to belong to Terese, lying beside him; he turns to her and she to him; they kiss and start to make love—and she disappears from beneath him: he is left with only the hair. Also notable are the scenes with Norman Kaye's sympathetic, but not overly perceptive, psychiatrist, who, on being told about the affair with Terese, tactlessly asks his patient: 'What do you think attracts her to you?' 'She's a social worker,' is Bernard's reply.

*M**an of Flowers* and *Golden Braid* are two films about erotic and obsessive behaviour which stand alone. But a surprisingly large number of films in the 80s deal with other examples of the 'wild side' of love and passion. One of the most striking is *IN TOO DEEP* (1989), a moody erotic thriller by newcomers John Tatoulis and Colin South, who were both born in Melbourne in 1954. They both worked in the television industry, Tatoulis at SBS, South at Channel 10, and met when both were using the same facility house, VideoVision.

In 1981, Tatoulis and South formed a company, Media World. They were philosophically opposed to making television commercials, but produced a variety of TV specials—concerts, sports events—before moving into drama with the successful children's series, *Adventures on Kythera*. They then decided to make a feature, the original idea being to capture the mood of Melbourne on summer nights, especially the city's jazz scene. Deborah Parsons, who had scripted the *Kythera* series, wrote a screenplay based on ideas furnished by Tatoulis and Smith.

The filmmakers decided to raise money without seeking government funding, and they put a lot of their own money into the $800,000 budget, securing the rest through private investment: there was a nasty moment when a major investor pulled out two weeks into the five-week shoot.

Hugo Race, a Melbourne rock singer ('and kind of anti-hero', says Tatoulis), plays Mack, the young, knife-wielding bank robber. 'I met him when I did a special on his group, Wreckery, for the SBS programme, *The Noise*,' Tatoulis says. Santha Press, the sultry jazz singer with whom Mack becomes involved, was cast as a result of lengthy auditions, and Rebekah Elmalogou, who plays her younger sister, had worked with Tatoulis and South on the *Kythera* series. 'I wanted John Flaus for the role of the cop,' says Tatoulis. 'I'd always admired John, and he'd only had bit parts until this.' Flaus gives a definitive performance as the world-weary cop who, as he says, just wants respect.

In Too Deep. *Santha Press, Hugo Race.*

Tatoulis and South planned the details of the film together, but, on set, Tatoulis did most of the direction. There are also two credited cameramen, one of whom, Mark Gilfedder, concentrated on the lighting while the other, Peter Zakharov, operated. The result is a significant achievement for these two newcomers, though there were major problems during production. The film started shooting in February 1989, and after two weeks it was discovered that the camera was faulty. The production shut down, and resumed several months later, in June, when it was bitterly cold and hard to recreate the summer heat essential to the film's mood. Nevertheless, the finished product looks seamless, and convincingly hot and humid.

In Too Deep is an Australian film in the French style. It is light on plot and very strong on atmosphere. It is another rare example of a successful erotic film being made in this country: scenes between Santha Press and Hugo Race are uninhibited and steamy, while the disturbing effect the lovers have on the 15-year-old sister is vividly portrayed by Rebekah Elmalogou. The film is a genre movie with a distinctive look and style.

Before seeking out an Australian distributor for *In Too Deep*, Tatoulis and South decided to try to sell it overseas, and they were very successful. Skouras Pictures took world distribution rights (except for Australia) and sold it to a large number of countries. Clearly the film, though obviously not a picture for everyone, was destined to recover its costs and allow its talented creators to move on to their next project.

In addition to these films about passion and obsession, there are the films about prostitutes, of which Bob Ellis' *WARM NIGHTS ON A SLOW MOVING TRAIN* (1987) is probably the best (and has to win the prize for the best title of the decade). Ellis remembers: 'Denny Lawrence and I were on a train and he said: "I wonder if there's a hooker that works this train?" Within about twenty-five seconds we'd arrived at the idea and the title. The idea was that each client would be some part of the Australian male: the crippled athlete, the tired commercial traveller who's lost his wife and found God, the failed nightclub satirist, the politician, the ASIO man, and so on. Patric Juillet liked the idea, so we wrote a screenplay.'

This would be a film made on a much larger budget than Ellis' debut, *Unfinished Business* (see previous chapter). And with the budget came compromises. 'I always felt that if you had the right script and the right cast, you couldn't go wrong,' he says. 'There are so many people on set to help and advise a director. But if you don't have the script, or don't have the right cast, you're in trouble. I didn't want Wendy [Hughes] for the leading role, but I was told by the producer: "I can get the money tomorrow if it's Wendy." So I broke my own rule; and I paid for it. Everybody else in the cast was exactly right. Wendy was astonishingly better than I'd expected, and she was a joy to work with, but she wasn't right for the role.'

Ellis made another mistake on the picture. 'We shot most of it in Melbourne. Melbourne's a place of total misery and bitterness. It's a terrible town; everyone there is interested mainly in revenge.' Problems arose with co-producer Ross Dimsey. 'He kept provoking me, saying "We need more sex." I wouldn't let him prevail, but it was pretty wearying. I spent a lot of the time writing him memos. In addition, Yuri Sokol, who is a genius, had no clear distinction as to the difference between a director of photography [which he was] and a director. He'd yell at me: "No, no, no, Bob. You're an idiot! We'll do it *this* way. Believe me, you're a cretin." It was hell, and meanwhile there was Wendy with her clothes off and different men climbing all over her. We were confined to a very small set most of the time, and at one point it fell down and we were nearly all killed . . .'

When the film was completed, the director's cut ran for approximately

Warm Nights on a Slow Moving Train.
Wendy Hughes, John Clayton.

130 minutes (though Ellis also cut a 118-minute version). I was fortunate enough to see the longer version, which, although about ten minutes too long, was full of wit and humour, fascinating characters and cameos, and graced by Wendy Hughes' best performance since *My First Wife*. But Dimsey's version, running 91 minutes, was the version that was released. It is very inferior to the longer version; true, it moves along at a spanking pace, but that was not the point. No longer is there time to breathe, to savour the Ellis humour, to prepare ourselves for the shift in emphasis from the sexual comedy of the first half to the assassination plot of the second half.

'What happened to *Warm Nights* was the worst experience of my life,' says Ellis. 'I didn't even get paid what I should have. It was just dreadful. The moral is: Never go to Melbourne.' It is, indeed, a shame, because if the director had been left to himself he might have turned out a quite remarkable film. There are still enough great scenes to indicate what it might have been; those involving John Clayton and Norman Kaye as the broken-down sports-writer and the travelling salesman respectively are especially fine.

An interesting footnote: attempts by Ellis late in 1989 to interest the FFC in backing his long-planned *The Nostradamus Kid* were met without enthusiasm, and Ellis suspects that, as a result of the events surrounding *Warm Nights*, he may now be on somebody's blacklist for future projects as a director. It is hard to believe such could be the case, but there are some very shortsighted and vengeful people in this industry, so anything is possible.

A very different kind of film about a prostitute is *CANDY REGENTAG* (1987), also known as *Kiss the Night*, which was directed by James Ricketson. Ricketson (b. 1949) was in that famous first intake of Australian Film and Television School students, along with Gillian Armstrong and Phillip Noyce, and he had made a number of interesting short films and featurettes before his first feature, *Third Person Plural* (1978), which starred, among others, Bryan Brown. The film was never released, and it was nine years before Ricketson had the chance to make another feature: in the interim, he made a great many documentaries, directed the first episode of the television series *Women of the Sun*, and wrote unproduced feature-film screenplays.

The budget for *Candy Regentag* was $750,000, a very low one by the prevailing standards of the end of the 80s; it was fully funded by the AFC. The script was written by executive producer Don Catchlove, and deals with a young woman, played by Patsy Stephens, who works in a Kings Cross brothel, Bambi's. At the time of the film's belated release, some publicity was given to the fact that, in researching the film, Ricketson had visited such a brothel and spent time with a prostitute. 'It is basically a love story, but set in a very unusual context,' says Ricketson. 'I knew nothing about brothels before I started on this picture, and I discovered that there are an awful lot of them. And an enormous number of people frequent them—far more than I ever would have thought.'

Michael Edols photographed in Super-16mm on locations in the Cross during August and September 1986; much of the film was shot in a brothel constructed for the film on one floor of a building in which there had once been a real brothel on another floor.

The film compares interestingly to Lizzie Borden's *Working Girls*; it is a bleak, but quite gripping, study of a rather romantic young hooker, but Ricketson's documentary background shows in the detailed attention given to the routine of the brothel (the compulsory penis inspection, shower and so on). The grim little love affair is not presented in a predictable way, and there is a painfully strong performance from Patsy Stephens in the leading role. The intrinsic boredom of work in the brothel is neatly established.

After its completion, the film waited a long time for some kind of cinema release, and was ignored in preselections for the AFI Awards. As a result, it was two years before it had a brief, but quite honourable, cinema run. The AFC, which backed the picture, might have been expected to take swifter action in getting its investment out into the marketplace.

One of the two female characters in Terry Bourke's *BROTHERS* (1982) is a prostitute (played by Margaret Laurence) who commits suicide when abandoned by her lover (Chard Hayward) in favour of 'nice girl' Jennifer Cluff. Bourke (b. 1940) is a journalist and filmmaker whose first feature, *Sampan* (1968), was made in Hong Kong, and who has specialised in cheap (and sometimes not so cheap) thrillers like *Night of Fear* (1972), *Inn of the Damned* (1975), and *Lady, Stay Dead* (1982); he has also made the comedy *Plugg* (1976) and an adventure film, *Little Boy Lost* (1978). He is a second-rate director, and *Brothers* is a second-rate film, in which the 'hero', as played by Hayward, is so boorish and unsympathetic that the audience quickly loses any sympathy for him. Brother Ivar Kants is equally uninteresting, and though Bourke can handle the action scenes (the opening massacre of newspapermen in East Timor, the coach crash that kills the Cluff character) his big dramatic scenes are poorly written and awkwardly acted.

CENTRESPREAD (1981) is not about prostitutes, but about women who pose naked for sex magazines, and Tony Paterson (who directed and edited) packs in as many photographic sessions as possible. The film actually begins with one such scene, and includes lingering close-ups of the nipples, bottom and genitals of a model who has shaved her pubic hair.

Paterson (b. 1948) is a film editor who worked on other sex films (*Fantasm, Fantasm Comes Again, Final Cut*) as well as more reputable films like John Duigan's *Dimboola* and *Mouth to Mouth*; this is the only film he has directed, and it is quite simply atrocious, with a pitifully thin story to accompany all the gratuitous sex. The acting is as woeful as the script and direction.

Equally prurient is *LEONORA* (1985), a sex film written, directed and photographed by Derek Strahan and starring Mandi Miller as the fun-loving wife of a car salesman. Here, too, the script is feeble and the acting non-existent; but there is lots of soft-core sex, including female masturbation, lesbian lovemaking and a rape. All the ingredients, in fact, for a success on the soft-core video circuit which, presumably, is where these films end up.

On an entirely different level, the sad world of a Kings Cross hooker was sensitively and seriously explored in John Duigan's *WINTER OF OUR DREAMS* (1981); the young woman's lifestyle is contrasted with that of a 60s radical who now lives in a yuppie world of lapsed idealism. This character had originally featured in a completely different screenplay called *Someone Left the Cake Out in the Rain*, written by Duigan in the late 70s; he was unable to find finance for this story about a European woman, with a background of militant opposition to nuclear weapons, who comes to Australia.

Duigan (b. 1949 in Hartney Whitney, Hampshire, England) had come to Geelong with his family in 1961 (his father was Australian) and, after obtaining a master's degree in philosophy at Melbourne University, became interested in theatre, especially the radical political theatre centred in Carlton in the 60s. He acted in a couple of low-budget featurettes (Brian Davies' *Brake Fluid* and Nigel Buesst's *Bonjour Balwyn*) before directing his first feature, *The Firm Man*, in 1974. This was followed by *The Trespassers* (1976), the excellent *Mouth to Mouth* (1978) and the very disappointing *Dimboola* (1979). After this, Duigan moved to Sydney, and *Winter of Our Dreams* was the first film he made there.

'This screenplay had a different dynamic from *Someone Left the Cake . . .,*' says Duigan, 'and it was much more marketable. I was able to get Bryan Brown and Judy Davis to play the leads, and their involvement helped get the film financed.' Duigan asked Richard Brennan to produce the film, but Brennan was involved with another project and suggested Richard Mason, who had been for many years at Film Australia, but who had resigned after the cancellation of *The Unknown Industrial Prisoner*, which he was to have produced. 'We were both interested in political and ethical themes,' says Duigan. 'He liked this script and we went into production very quickly, because it was a small [$320,000] budget.'

The shoot, preceded by three weeks of rehearsals, lasted five weeks, on locations around Kings Cross and Balmain; Duigan was able to explore Sydney locations for the first time. Davis prepared for her role by talking to so many addicts that, she said at the time, she felt almost like part of the community. This was the only occasion so far on which Duigan has worked with the actress, who won an AFI award for her role. 'She's very intense and places great demands on herself,' he says. 'She expects a corresponding level of commitment from the people around her. I've got the greatest respect for her. Bryan's a very different kind of actor, but they worked well together.'

Brown gives a very restrained and interesting performance as the comfortably trendy ex-radical who lives in an 'open' marriage with wife Cathy Downes and who has an affair with the young prostitute played by Davis: the latter has to play a scene in which she goes 'cold turkey' to end a heroin addiction—sure-fire material for any actor, but Davis brings it that extra edge. It is a subdued, intelligent, thoughtful film which says a lot about Australia's urban lifestyles at the beginning of the decade, and Tom Cowan's cinematography is a considerable asset.

Winter of Our Dreams. *Judy Davis, Bryan Brown.*

The film was a major success, and enjoyed a five-month run in Sydney. In commercial terms, it is probably still the most successful 'serious', low-budget film made in Australia; it is also a very notable achievement.

W hen discussing films about sex and drugs and rock 'n' roll, you cannot go past *MONKEY GRIP* (1981), which has all three in generous proportions. This was the first feature film directed by Ken Cameron (b. 1946 in Tenterfield), a former high-school teacher (1970–2) who during the 70s made a trio of excellent medium-length films: *Sailing to Brooklyn*, *Out of It* and *Temperament Unsuited*. Cameron had read Helen Garner's semi-autobiographical book and wanted very much to make a film of it. He sought help from producer Patricia Lovell, whom he met at an AFC assessment panel; she encouraged him to write a screenplay.

Raising money was painfully difficult. At the beginning, in early 1979, the budget was $553,000 but no distributor was interested in the project. David Williams of GU told Lovell it would never make a cent; the AFC—apart from John Daniell—disliked it ('Perhaps they saw it as pornographic,' says Lovell); the NSWFC likewise shied away from it. 'The film fell over for lack of $150,000,' says Lovell.

Shooting had to be postponed, and Lovell produced *Gallipoli* instead.

When the 10BA tax deductions were announced, Lovell decided to try again: but in the meantime costs had risen so far that a revised budget came to $1 million. 'The above-the-lines were the same as before,' says Lovell. 'Ken was paid only $45,000 to write and direct: I shared a $40,000 producer's fee with the executive producer. It was crew costs that went up.' Danny Collins offered to help Lovell raise the money, and became executive producer, but it was an unhappy relationship. Just before production began, it looked as though a last-minute hitch in funding would delay the shoot by two weeks. Suffering from nervous exhaustion, Lovell was hospitalised and sedated for forty-eight hours.

During the first week of shooting there were anxious moments because an investor, secured by Bankers Trust, who had agreed to put up the entire budget, had not signed the contract. Lovell discovered that the investor was a client of Filmco, and was told by Filmco's John Fitzpatrick that the only way the money would be forthcoming would be if Filmco became executive producers (and charged accordingly) and were given a hold on Lovell's next project. She declined, and, thanks to Bankers Trust, was able to get enough money to keep the production afloat; eventually, she took out a personal overdraft and borrowed money from friends to keep the movie going. 'It was a nightmare,' she says. 'And I worried so much about the money, I couldn't always give Ken the support he needed.'

Meanwhile, Ken Cameron had been struggling with the problem of casting the crucial role of Nora. He considered various actresses before he met Noni Hazlehurst, whom he first interviewed for the supporting role of Angela, the singer in the film. 'I was impressed by her warmth and vitality,' he says. But it was not easy to persuade Lovell, or the investors, that the relatively unknown actress should play the leading

Monkey Grip. *Colin Friels, Noni Hazlehurst.*

role. Colin Friels was also virtually unknown when he was cast as Javo. 'I'd bypassed him at first,' says Cameron. 'He came in for an interview wearing a beard, and I didn't know who he was. I cast someone else, a rock singer; but lost him three weeks before the shoot when he had to go on tour. Then I saw Colin play Hamlet at the Opera House, and decided he'd be right for Javo.'

Monkey Grip was one of those films made in the first half of 1981 when 'bunching' reached ludicrous proportions. Says Lovell: 'So many people on that film had never worked on a feature before. David Gribble's camera crew turned out to be marvellous, and so were the grip and lighting crews. But the art department was another matter; the production designer, Clark Munro, developed glandular fever during production and a lot of people in that department just didn't know what was involved in making a feature film.'

One crucial element in the film is the passion and frankness of the lovemaking scenes. Says Cameron: 'I had no problem with the actors during the filming of those scenes. I felt it was worth going all the way with them, and I was young enough not to have hang-ups. The atmosphere on the set was a bit funny: in the end, I had the entire crew, myself included, rehearse naked. Everyone was terrific, but it probably wouldn't be possible to shoot those scenes today. There's a repressiveness and a prudishness today we didn't have then. But we all believed in the novel and the film, so we felt those scenes had to be done that way.' Later, Lovell heard that the Cannes Film Festival director, Gilles Jacob, had been advised 'by someone in authority' that 'the Australian government would not be pleased if *Monkey Grip* competed in Cannes.' 'I found this utterly amazing,' she says. 'It's a film about a woman's sensuality. Why be ashamed of that?'

Hazlehurst gives an extraordinary performance in the film, and richly deserved her Best Actress award. The film compares interestingly with *Winter of Our Dreams*, which was made the same year. Both films seem an accurate representation of inner-city lifestyle in the early 80s (*Monkey Grip*, though set in the Melbourne suburb of Carlton, was filmed in Sydney): feminism, sexuality, sensuality, single parenthood, anguished doubts, close and warm friendships—all are lovingly depicted. Scenes between Hazlehurst and her daughter, beautifully played by writer Helen Garner's daughter, Alice, are among the best and most moving in *Monkey Grip* which, above all, is distinguished for its total honesty, in script and performance.

While Lovell was in London for the Royal Premiere of *Gallipoli*, Danny Collins screened *Monkey Grip* for the three main distributors, all of whom turned it down. One even claimed not to understand it. Another told Lovell later: 'I loathed it.' For the first week of the film's Melbourne release, at a Village cinema, Lovell distributed it herself, with the support and advice of Village's Marketing Director, Alan Finney, who loved it. When the first weekend's takings were a formidable $40,000, Roadshow picked up the film. 'They admitted they were wrong,' says Lovell, 'and later opened it in two cinemas in Sydney. It made half its budget back in Australia, a huge amount for this sort of movie. But it didn't fare so well overseas. American and British distributors acquired it for no upfront money, and I made nothing from it.'

DOGS IN SPACE (1986) evokes an inner-city world similar to that of *Monkey Grip*. This was Richard Lowenstein's second film, after *Strikebound*, and it is set in 1978 in a house inhabited by a floating population of young people involved in the music and drug culture. Lowenstein had originally planned to turn his personal experiences (he had lived in such a house in the Melbourne suburb of Richmond) into a low-budget feature, but, in the planning stages, *Dogs in Space* became a lot bigger than that.

Lowenstein says: 'I worked on the screenplay in much the same way as I'd worked on *Strikebound*, using oral histories, getting people to tell me about their experiences. About 40 per cent of it is autobiographical: I borrowed from real life a lot, and there are some things in the film I personally experienced. I encapsulated the experiences of a three-year period into a three-week period for the film. Potential investors told me: "This is too bizarre to be real." But I hadn't made any of it up. I steal from real life, which is so much weirder than fiction.'

The $2 million film was produced by Glenys Rowe, who had handled publicity on Lowenstein's first film; the money was raised through the Burrowes group and Entertainment Media. Michael Hutchence, popular lead singer of the rock group INXS, was persuaded to play the leading role of Sam, whose attitude towards drugs inadvertently causes the death of Anna (Saskia Post), his girlfriend. 'I wrote the script with Michael in mind,' says Lowenstein. 'He was physically similar to the character on which I based Sam. Some people had hesitations about casting him, but I thought he was very good.' As for music, 'there are actually seven different bands in the film, and the vocals and music were recorded on location and mixed into the backing track.'

Dogs in Space. *Michael Hutchence* (left), *Nique Needles* (right).

In connection with the drug scenes in the film, Lowenstein recalls the death of a friend from a drug overdose: 'It wasn't at all like the image we have of someone becoming emaciated and covered in pimples and ending up dying after a few years. This happened quite suddenly, without warning, after only a few intakes of the drug. And I was aware that a lot of people were getting involved with drugs without knowing the consequences. I made *Dogs in Space* to show that there are reasons to get involved with drugs, but then I wanted to hit audiences in the stomach and show them just what can happen. It has a very strong anti-drug message.'

Hoyts, as part of the company's arrangement with Burrowes, had agreed to release the film at Christmas but, as had happened with *Mad Max 2* five years earlier, the Film Censorship Board threw a spanner in the works by giving the film an R rating, on the basis that the film 'glamourised the lifestyle [depicted] sufficiently to make it appear not only acceptable but also "trendy" and attractive.' Since the film ends with Anna's death as a direct result of a drug overdose, it is impossible to support the Board's contention that Lowenstein showed drugs to be 'a pleasant adjunct to daily life', but on this occasion even the normally more rational Board of Review members voted to retain the R. As a result, a film made with a teenage audience in mind was crippled with a rating that excluded that very audience, and *Dogs in Space* suffered very badly as a result. 'It was absolutely ridiculous,' says Lowenstein. 'I never dreamed we'd get an R rating. The audience I made the film for couldn't see it, and many TV programmes couldn't even show clips from it. I was very angry.'

Ironically, although the Film Censorship Board maintains a tight control over the way films are handled in cinema, there is virtually no control over videos. As a result, R-rated videotapes of *Dogs in Space* (and other far less suitable films) have probably been screened by eager young teenagers all over the country.

Lowenstein's sincerity in making the film is never in doubt. *Dogs in Space* seems an accurate depiction of a lifestyle, but the director is in no way endorsing that lifestyle. Early scenes are cheerful enough. To start with, these seem like good times, golden days: it is exciting, there is a youthful ebullience, there are new ideas, new music, political discussions and so on. But the mood darkens as characters start to use hard drugs, and the consequences of those actions are grim indeed, foreshadowing the decline in popular culture of the early 80s. The film has a very moral message. There is little conventional plot: just a series of comings and goings (including a marvellous cameo from Chris Haywood as a manic character deeply devoted to chainsaws, and Fiona Latham as a young radical who seems able to communicate only in slogans). Lowenstein directs with ferocious confidence, and great good humour, and Andrew De Groot's exceptional camerawork, with its fluid tracking shots through the narrow rooms and passages of the house, is a major asset. Hutchence gives a convincing performance as Sam, and Nique Needles has one of his better screen roles as Tim, an oddball who winds up with a wide-eyed girl (Deanna Bond) who just drifts into the house one day and stays on. With its deafening music score and unpatronising exploration of its characters and their world, *Dogs in Space* is almost as good, but never as likeable, as *Monkey Grip*.

GOING DOWN (1982) also centres on the inhabitants of an inner-suburban house, this time in Sydney. This *is* a low-budget film, the first from director Haydn Keenan (b. 1951), former partner of Esben Storm; Keenan had won acclaim with some award-winning short films, and had produced Storm's first feature, *27A* (1974).

Keenan attempts the difficult task of combining a dramatic and realistic story about young people, with scenes of comedy bordering on farce. On one level, there is a serious look at the lifestyles of four young women (with Tracy Mann giving the best performance), but, on another, David Argue is encouraged to play his nerd character, Greg, up to and beyond the hilt (moreover, he scores a second, unconnected, role as a drug-addicted transvestite).

Perhaps not entirely surprisingly, Keenan found difficulty getting distribution for his film, which omits any scenes of sexual activity, but which contains plenty of chundering and talk of drugs and death, and the obligatory soundtrack of rock music. Sadly, Vera Plevnik, who plays Jane, one of the four central characters, was accidentally killed before post-production was completed.

Mary Callaghan's *TENDER HOOKS* (1988) is, in many ways, very similar to *Going Down*. It is also about life in the inner suburbs, but it lacks even the manic humour that Keenan gave to his film. Much had been expected of Callaghan, whose medium-length *Greetings from Wollongong* had been acclaimed; but in her first feature she goes the drab, kitchen-sink route, but without any element of poetry which might have made the drama bearable.

Jo Kennedy has the thankless role of Mitch in this chronicle of Kings Cross drifters, petty crooks, druggies, prostitutes and no-hopers; she gives a creditable performance, but is let down by co-stars Nique Needles (getting more indulgent with each screen appearance) and Robert Menzies (a depressing appearance in a very marginal role for this gifted actor).

Callaghan seems to be striving to make a love story set against a particularly grim milieu, but she brings no illumination to these frankly boring characters, and the irritatingly ambiguous freeze-frame that ends the film is no substitute for enlightenment. The inevitably grainy photography and all-over-the-place editing are not much help.

In complete contrast, *PUBERTY BLUES* (1981) deals with wild teenage behaviour in a way that is probably no less insightful, but a lot more accessible. Margaret Kelly, a successful television writer, had approached Joan Long to see if they could work together on a project so that Kelly could learn about producing. Kelly had been teaching at a writing workshop at a small suburban theatre and there she had met Kathy Lette and Gabrielle Carey who had written a number of (at the time unpublished) short stories about their experiences on the surfing beaches south of Sydney. 'The stories were much more raw than they eventually became,' says Long. 'But the magic was there. And, what I especially liked about them was that they dealt, with humour and authenticity, about young *women* growing up; I felt we'd seen enough films about teenage boys.' Kelly befriended the young women, who were in their late teens, and helped them with their writing. The stories were unconnected episodes, and Kelly, with Long's help, fashioned a screenplay which integrated the anecdotes, and added some new ones, which were specially written, into a storyline. (Lette and Carey, who became known as The Salami Sisters, wrote a weekly column in the *Sun-Herald* for a while; and their stories eventually found a publisher.)

Bruce Beresford was always first choice for director. 'We never

thought he'd have time to make a film as modest as ours,' says Long.
'So we didn't even approach him at first. Gillian Armstrong turned
it down. In the end, Bruce wrote to me and said he'd like to do the
film. It was very good news, because you can only do so much as
a producer. I felt you could trust Bruce with all aspects of a film,
because his judgement is so good. He's good at casting, script assessment,
editing, everything: he's a film person—he didn't come up from
television—and he's a director after my own heart. He's a good
communicator, a bit of a larrikin, and a joy to work with.'

Beresford tested a number of youngsters for the leading roles. It
was Margaret Kelly who suggested he should consider Nell Schofield
(daughter of food critic Leo Schofield) for the role of Debbie, while
Jad Capelja was found by casting director Alison Barrett. Beresford

Puberty Blues. *Nell Schofield, Jad
Capelja.* (Photo: *Michael Roll.*)

brought his regular collaborators onto the picture: cinematographer
Don McAlpine, editor William Anderson, production designer David
Copping and sound recordist Gary Wilkins among them.

The budget was $800,000, and the film was shot, over seven weeks,
in the area around Cronulla, south of Sydney, where it was set.
Roadshow distributed. The film proved a success, but one feels that
it could, and should, have been more successful.

Any doubts one may have had about a 40-year-old man directing
a film about the lifestyles of 15-year-old schoolgirls are quickly dispelled
by Beresford's handling of the material; this is one of his best, most
relaxed films. He covers similar territory to that dealt with in Michael
Thornhill's *The F.J. Holden*, but with more humour and style. The
film could easily have been a catalogue of horrors: the joyless sex
scenes, the death by drug overdose, the incomprehension of the parents.
Instead, it is a life-affirming picture, filled with humour. For instance,
there is the scene in which Danny, Debbie's first boyfriend, a bricklayer,
drinks tea with her appalled parents, while her mother gazes, horrified,
through her curtained windows at his suspicious-looking Kombi parked

outside. The acting is naturalistic and, in the case of Schofield, particularly fine, and the ending—in which the girls defy tradition and take to the surf—is laudably upbeat. *Puberty Blues* sold well overseas: Universal released it in the US, and 20th Century-Fox in Britain.

T he youngsters in *Puberty Blues* just want to have fun: in *STARSTRUCK* (1982), Jackie Mullens (Jo Kennedy) wants to have fun, too, but she also wants to be famous. This was the second feature for Gillian Armstrong, whose debut, *My Brilliant Career* (1979) had already made her worldwide reputation. Armstrong was born in 1950 in Melbourne, and her original ambition was to be a costume designer. She changed direction when she developed a fascination for film while at Swinburne Institute of Technology, and was in the first year's intake at the Australian Film and Television School where she made an exceptionally fine short film, *100 A Day*. After more success with a medium-length film, *The Singer and the Dancer*, Armstrong was given the chance, by producer Margaret Fink, to make her first feature, and the rest is history. But how to follow *My Brilliant Career*?

'I didn't want to make another period picture about a woman fighting for her identity,' she says. 'I wanted to do something completely different.' That 'something different' came in a screenplay written by Stephen Maclean, who had grown up in a Melbourne pub, worked as a child actor, and had been in the props department at Crawfords; he had also worked with David Elfick on the music magazine *Go-Set* in the late 60s. 'Stephen was always a very witty and amusing fellow,' says Elfick. 'He'd been living in London, and when I was there for the launch of *Newsfront* we got together and he told me his idea for a musical. I thought it would be great to do an Australian musical, and I coined the title, *Starstruck*. I gave him all my spare travellers' cheques and said: "Write a script!".'

Elfick's first choice for director was expatriate Graeme Clifford: 'He was very interested, but pulled out to make *Frances*. Who needs an Australian musical when you've got Jessica Lange?' Meanwhile, Armstrong had heard about the project (from Jim Sharman), and, when she met Maclean at a party, told him she was interested in it. 'It was a critical career move for her,' says Elfick. 'But she likes a challenge.'

The film was one of the first financed under 10BA, with 150 and 50 per cent write-off. The budget was $2.5 million ('and it went a couple of hundred thousand over,' says Elfick.) The sheer task of staging a musical was complex: there were differences of opinion between Armstrong, Elfick and Maclean on the songs to be included. Despite the expertise and background Elfick and Maclean had in the music business, Armstrong was not happy with the 'chaotic' way the music was assembled for the film. 'We had a battle, and Gillian won,' says Elfick. 'It's fair enough that she won. At the time, I felt my music background should have scored me a few more points in the decision making: but only one person can direct a film. The deal was that she had control, and that was it. She made a highly original film.'

Armstrong wanted to cast newcomers in the roles of 18-year-old Jackie and her 14-year-old cousin, Angus; they were supposed to be slightly off-the-wall characters. At a casting session in Melbourne, where dozens of hopefuls were being auditioned, Armstrong was startled when a couple burst into the room carrying a fire hose and yelling: 'There's a fire!' For a moment, Armstrong believed there really was one, but the couple were Jo Kennedy and Ross O'Donovan who had got together and decided to do their audition the same way Jackie and Angus acted in the script. Despite the fact that both of them had very limited acting experience, Armstrong loved their approach, and they got the parts.

The production of *Starstruck* was not always easy: there were tensions on the set, the inexperience of the lead actors called for enormous patience on the part of Armstrong and her crew; and the original musical director resigned during production over a disagreement with Armstrong. 'We'd started shooting,' she says, 'and I'd say to him: "Where are the songs?" I had a choreographer waiting, and I couldn't start planning shots until I had the songs. And the songs being submitted just didn't suit the script. We had some great rock composers writing songs for us, but they couldn't write for a drama. Stephen would give a detailed brief: for example, the finale had to have a happy, upbeat song. And then we'd get this song and I'd say: "This person thinks this is a *happy* song?" It was more like a funeral march. The most difficult thing about a musical is that it doesn't come alive until you have the music. It was a great education for me, but it took a lot of time.'

Armstrong worked closely with her choreographer, David Atkins, and cinematographer, Russell Boyd, to stage the musical numbers. But, in the end, the choreography is the weakest element in *Starstruck*, perhaps because of limited time available to devise and stage the routines.

Starstruck. *Jo Kennedy*.

Visually, the film, with an imposing team in the art department, is magnificent.

Starstruck was another Australian film to encounter annoying censorship problems. Says Elfick: 'A lot of the success of the film depended on getting the music before the young audience. Mushroom Records produced the soundtrack album, and we were set to go on *Countdown* [the television programme which set the trend for music in Australia at the time] with clips promoting the film.' The Censorship

Gillian Armstrong, director of Starstruck.

Board gave the film an NRC (not recommended for children) rating; when the film clips of the musical numbers needed for *Countdown* were presented by Mushroom Records to the Censor, they were informed that the clips came from an NRC film and therefore should not be shown on *Countdown*, which was a programme aimed at young people. It was a ludicrous policy, because clips from American films (such as *Grease* and *Saturday Night Fever*, also rated NRC) were regularly featured on the programme. 'It was totally discriminatory against an Australian product,' says Elfick. 'As a result, no part of *Starstruck* was ever shown on *Countdown*: Jo and Ross hosted the programme one week without being able to show any of their footage from the film. The Censor took a key piece of our promotion away from us.'

Starstruck is certainly a courageous attempt at an Australian musical, but it is not entirely successful. There is an awkward opening reel which was much improved by further cutting for the American release of the picture. The abundance of musical numbers tends to overwhelm the slight plot; a nude love scene is totally unnecessary; and a ghastly scene of gay men in a swimming pool with plastic sharks represents a low point in Australian cinema. On the plus side, Jo Kennedy and Ross O'Donovan are, despite initial awkwardness, energetic and lively as the young entrepreneurs, there are some superb visual effects, and the script contains a number of witty lines. Scenes set in the family pub under the Sydney Harbour Bridge are the most enjoyable in this uneven, but ultimately endearing, film.

Two years later, another film about a teenager with musical ambitions was produced: this was *STREET HERO* (1984), the second feature from director Michael Pattinson who had previously scored a modest success with *Moving Out* (see Chapter 12). Pattinson (b. 1957 in Melbourne) studied film at Swinburne (1975–7) as soon as he finished high school. 'My father was a very keen amateur photographer,' he says. 'And I always had an interest in photography and film.' After graduating, he worked as assistant editor on a number of commercials and documentaries, and eventually started directing commercials. He directed some soap operas for Grundy's, and then made *Moving Out* in 1982.

The idea for *Street Hero* came while making the earlier film. 'A couple of kids with small parts in that film came from an area of high-rise flats and very underprivileged families: some teachers at their school had encouraged them to become involved in music. It was an inspiring story. So Jan Sardi and I decided to construct a screenplay around that.'

Vince Colosimo, the teenage actor whom Pattinson had discovered for *Moving Out*, was cast in the leading role as Vinnie, a kid from a violent background who tries to rise above his environment. In hindsight, Pattinson feels that 'the film suffers from not pursuing its dramatic line, and from dwelling too much on music. I relied too much on montage to tell the story.'

Pattinson took his screenplay to Bonnie Harris, an American who, at the time, was working for Roadshow on the development of Australian projects. Roadshow was interested in the film, and, in order to secure the best possible music, Paul Dainty was approached, and became executive producer. Dainty, a music producer and showman, was anxious to get into films, possibly inspired by Michael Edgley's success in this area. Music by Leo Sayer, Dragon and Sharon O'Neil was included in the film ('Maybe a bit too middle-of-the-road,' says Pattinson.) The budget was $2.5 million and the film was shot in nine weeks, mostly on studio sets built in Melbourne.

The film was not a great success: it opened in a blaze of publicity (ads of Colosimo's torso), but did less than average business. It appealed to teenage girls, but did not cross over to a wider audience. Critics complained about the overburdened plotline, and the simplistic treatment given to some of the characters. Later, it sold handsomely to television, and is in demand on video.

Street Hero has an overabundance of energy, and Colosimo is charismatic as the eponymous hero: but a plot that includes gangsters, corrupt cops, a brutal de facto stepfather, a childhood trauma, boxing and music—as well as teenage romance—is altogether too busy, and so is Brian Thomson's typically garish production design, which calls attention to itself throughout. Sigrid Thornton is charming, but rather too old to be playing a high school teenager, while Peta Toppano is much too young to be playing the hero's battered mother; and Sandy Gore is her usual acidic self as the encouraging educator. The best thing to be said about the film is that the pace is so fast that the audience has little time to wonder what on earth is going on.

Vincent Monton (b. 1944) was cinematographer on *Street Hero*, as he had been on numerous other films including *Newsfront*, *Road Games*, *Heatwave*, *Hostage* and *Moving Out*; two years later, he turned director himself for *WINDRIDER* (1986), which is another film about sex and

Windrider. *Tom Burlinson.*

rock 'n' roll. The film was produced by Paul Barron, and the original screenplay, by Everett De Roche and Bonnie Harris, was basically a comedy. 'I went on a search for The Great Australian Comedy Director,' says Barron. 'There weren't too many possibilities, so I started looking at candidates nobody would have thought of.' Bonnie Harris had left Roadshow, and was working on the project not only as co-writer but as associate producer. She suggested Barron should talk to Monton; the two men met and Barron decided to take a chance on new talent: he offered Monton the chance to direct his first feature. 'It was a great transition for me,' says Monton. 'I was lucky to get the film. But it wasn't the sort of film I'd have chosen for myself. I wasn't really plugged into it.'

When Monton came on to the film, it was still just an outline. 'I never saw it as a comedy,' he says. 'I saw it as something like *Risky Business*: a youth film with comedic episodes. The hero has lost confidence in life, lost direction. In the original outline, he'd even suffered an accident which is why he couldn't compete in the surf carnival. It wasn't basically comedy material.'

Not surprisingly, the final film is not so much a comedy as a youth romance with rock music. 'We should have gone more for comedy,' says Barron. 'We couldn't really decide where the emphasis should be placed.' Says Monton: 'It was a problem with people of one age group making a film for another age group. We decided at the beginning we wanted an M-rated film, which was probably a mistake, since our most likely audience was 12-year-olds.'

Nicole Kidman had played her first feature role in Barron's production of *Bush Christmas*; she appears in her first nude scenes in *Windrider*. She is Jade, the rock star in love with P.C., the rich young surfie, played by Tom Burlinson, and some of their love scenes together are startlingly frank, perhaps unnecessarily so, given the overall slightness of the material. In production, the film was called *Making Waves*, which might have been a better title for this basically rather bland picture which—apart from a sequence of a shark attack and the aforementioned love scenes—leaves little impression apart from the charms of high living in Perth.

The music scene forms the background to *HEAVEN TONIGHT* (1989),

Heaven Tonight. *John Waters, Kim Gyngell.* (Photo: *Greg Noakes.*)

the third production of Boulevard Films (for details of Boulevard Films and producer-screenwriter Frank Howson, see the next chapter). Howson co-scripted with Alister Webb this story of an ageing rock star trying to make a comeback and jealous of the success of his son. John Waters plays Johnny Dysart, and fears that the film would descend into the bathos that ruined the first Boulevard production, *Boulevard of Broken Dreams*, are eventually dispelled by Waters' much tougher performance (though director Pino Amenta still seems not to know when enough is enough).

'I knew the characters in that film very well,' says Howson, who formerly worked in the music business. Kim Gyngell appears in his third Boulevard film as Dysart's former buddy, who is trying to break a drug habit, and Rebecca Gilling is sympathetic as Dysart's long-suffering wife; but the best performance in the film comes from Sean Scully, who underplays his role of record producer and, as a result, makes him all the more powerful than similar characters overplayed by Kevin Miles and Max Phipps in the other Boulevard films. 'It was great to watch John and Sean working together,' says Howson.

The rock music is even wilder in *SONS OF STEEL* (1988), which was the brainchild of rock clip director Gary L. Keady. Keady had co-directed (with Yahoo Serious) a 12-minute music film called *Knightmare* (1984) which, in Australia, was shown as support to *Dune*. 'I was in despair at the conservatism of the Australian film industry,' says Keady. 'I described my ideas to [producer] James Vernon, who was looking for something new, different and rebellious.'

Keady's star is Rob Hartley, a heavy-metal singer from Perth. Hartley, a formidable presence on screen, plays Black Alice in the film; he is a working-class hero thrown into a time-warp when the world is destroyed. Keady employs staple sci-fi elements, like the need to reverse time to stop the accident that has caused the destruction, as a background to the songs and comic-strip action in this brash, lively picture. 'The video clip as a cinema experience is here,' says Keady. 'And it's an art form itself. I wanted to make *Sons of Steel* as colourful as possible and as bizarre as possible; but we couldn't afford a studio, so production designer Grace Walker used a variety of weird locations—we even filmed in tunnels under the city of Sydney.'

Sons of Steel is, indeed, a spectacular visual experience. The plot is all over the place, and it is almost impossible to decide what is going on, but it is all done with a brash self-confidence and fierce sense of humour that overcomes most misgivings. It never became the cult film it deserved to be, probably because of the innate caution and conservatism of the distribution and exhibition industry.

Moving away from heavy metal, we find a forgotten and rather sad attempt at a rock musical in *AT LAST . . . BULLAMAKANKA THE MOTION PICTURE* (1983). This was the brainchild of writer-director Simon Heath, and boasts a strong line-up of musicians: Australian Crawl, Jo Jo Zep, John Farnham, Donnie Sutherland, Skyhooks and Rose Tattoo among them. Their music is grafted on to a weak comedy plot about the visit of a government official to a small town, but the jokes are pitifully thin and the acting is uniformly abysmal. The film had a very troubled and lengthy production history, which presumably accounts for the first two words tacked on to the title.

Almost equally chaotic is Haydn Keenan's *PANDEMONIUM* (1987). The influence here seems to be *The Rocky Horror Show*, since the comedy is composed of deliberately freaky characters and near-blasphemous situations. David Argue is the innocent who stumbles

Pandemonium. *David Argue, Amanda Dole, Esben Storm.* (Photo: *Carolyn Johns.*)

into an old Bondi film studio once run by E. B. De Woolf (Esben Storm), who has a sadistic, crippled wife (Arna-Maria Winchester). There is also Amanda Dole as a big-bosomed, waif-like 'Dingo girl' clad only in a loin-cloth. She appears to be searching for her father, who turns out to be an Aboriginal Holy Ghost (Gary Foley) who impregnates her before she is crucified. Other characters include a diminutive Hitler clone and a pair of lesbian twins.

With all its nudity and blood and four-letter obscenities, the film tries hard to offend; but it simply is not funny enough, or pacy enough, to work on anything but the most primitive level, and it was never able to secure a cinema release.

L eaving behind the sound and fury of *Pandemonium*, we come to one of the most mysterious films of the 80s: a film involving tangled relationships, drug addiction and politics. *NIEL LYNNE* (1985) was planned as a comeback for David Baker (b. 1925 in Tasmania), a director whose one major feature of the 70s, *The Great MacArthy* (or *The Great McCarthy* if you prefer—there seems to be some dispute about the title), was made in 1975. Despite its promising subject matter and cast, that film had been a lamentable failure, and eclipsed Baker's earlier success with one sequence of *Libido*, *The Family Man* (scripted by David Williamson and starring Jack Thompson and Max Gillies), and the curious short film, *Squeaker's Mate*.

Baker's idea with *Niel Lynne* seems to have been to explore the era of radical change in the 60s from the viewpoint of one, rather ordinary, young man from Ballarat. It is a fair enough starting point, and the screenplay was sufficiently encouraging to secure a pre-sale ('for a staggering sum', says one insider) to the Seven Network and to attract the support of the AFC's Special Production Fund, which was being administered at the time by Gilda Baracchi. (AFC Chairman,

Phillip Adams, had referred favourably to *The Great MacArthy* in his newspaper column, describing it as 'Felliniesque' and Baker as a talent deserving attention.) Some time later, Baracchi resigned from the AFC to work under Baker as co-executive producer on *Niel Lynne.*

The film was produced on a budget of $1.9 million, with a cast that included Paul Williams as the eponymous Lynne, Judy Morris as his cousin, Patricia, who defects to North Vietnam during the war; and Sigrid Thornton as Fenimore, the lover Lynne shares with his drug-addicted friend Eric (Brandon Burke). During production, it became clear that not much money was being spent on extras. One observer who attended rushes recalls: 'There was a scene of a riot outside a jail with about six people taking part. Some scenes looked as if they were from *On the Beach*, they were so underpopulated.'

When the film was completed, it had come in under budget. Under the terms of the contract, the management company of the film (Baker and Baracchi) was entitled to be reimbursed up to 10 per cent of the budget if production ran under: *Niel Lynne* ran under budget to almost exactly that amount, and the money was paid out as bonuses so that, by the time the Seven Network requested some changes to the film, including new music, there was no money left.

It is difficult to know just what went wrong with the film, but it was undoubtedly a very costly failure. With its apparent allusions to Joseph Conrad's *Heart of Darkness*, the film attempts an overview of fifteen years of Australian life but flounders because it is so very hard to believe in the characters. This is especially true of Patricia who works for a government department in Canberra, steals secrets to send to Hanoi, happens to be around when Lynne, wounded in the war, finds himself in a North Vietnamese hospital, and who winds up back home in prison. Try as she might, Judy Morris cannot make Patricia anything more than a rather peculiar cypher.

Baker also seems to be trying to inject passion into the film, but, apart from a few scenes in which Sigrid Thornton gets slapped around by one or other of her lovers, there is little conviction here either; Thornton seems uncomfortable, and rather strident, in her role. The film almost works in scenes in which Lynne, putting his radical past behind him, settles into the good life of a country lawyer; but, here again, Baker blows it by some last-minute cutting which removed eleven minutes from his original version, including a whole sub-plot involving Nicki Paull as Lynne's teenage bride who is killed in a car accident.

It is really no surprise that Baker was never able to find a theatrical distributor for his film. More surprising is the fact that, despite the pre-sale to the Seven Network, the film has (at the time of writing) never surfaced on television or, indeed, on video. It is another of those forgotten, unseen Australian films: and, sadly, it hardly deserves a better fate.

Another film in which the central characters are addicted to hard drugs is *WRONG WORLD* (1984), the second feature from Ian Pringle. Pringle gave Jo Kennedy her second screen role (after *Starstruck*), and she rewarded him with a performance so strong that she won the Best Actress prize at the Berlin Film Festival (but was not even nominated in the AFI awards that year). She plays Mary, a young addict who teams up with David (Richard Moir), an addicted doctor, on a trek across Victoria.

Pringle's fascination for odd couples and chilly, bleak landscapes is much to the fore in this, the best of his three features (though the flashbacks to Bolivia seem quite unnecessary). The Wim Wenders influence hangs heavy in the long scenes of cross-country driving, and the actors are strong enough, and interesting enough, to keep the viewer involved. Despite the Berlin prize, the film never managed an Australian cinema release.

O bsessive behaviour bordering on madness is the subject of another unreleased film, *THE DARK ROOM* (1982). It is the first, and so far only, effort of director Paul Harmon (b. 1951). He is the son of American-born Bill Harmon who came to Australia in 1961 and whose Cash-Harmon company produced the successful television series *Number 96* (and the feature film spin-off). Paul Harmon was at the Australian Film and Television School at the same time as Michael Brindley, and the two decided to collaborate on a film inspired by Harmon sen. (who died in 1981). Says Brindley: 'Paul had a storyline, but it was hard to pin the character down. The closer we got to the bone, the more difficult it became.' Brindley wrote a draft screenplay, which pleased Harmon; they spent 1980 trying to raise money for the film, a prospect which grew more likely with the introduction of 10BA. At one stage Basil Appleby came in as producer, the first of three who spent time on *The Dark Room*.

'At one stage Paul decided the script wasn't commercial enough,' remembers Brindley. 'He came up with a new ending in which the son burnt down the country house where his father had taken his mistress. I thought it was total bullshit, but I wrote it as best I could.'

Harmon took the revised screenplay to various people, and ended up with Filmco where John Fitzpatrick agreed to include it in a package the company was putting together. But he did not want Basil Appleby involved: apparently, during his tenure at the Australian Film and Television School, Appleby had failed a young woman doing a production management course; she subsequently became Fitzpatrick's assistant.

Malcolm Smith (formerly of the Tasmanian Film Corporation) became the new producer, and the budget for the film was set at $1.2 million; but then Filmco started dithering about contracts, and Smith gave Fitzpatrick an ultimatum: 'Sign by Friday, or I resign.' They did not sign, and he resigned. In the end, the film was produced by documentary filmmaker Tom Haydon—the only fiction film he worked on in this capacity.

Paul found Svet Kovich in the Sydney Acting School, and signed him to play Michael, the obsessed son, in the film. 'Svet was incredibly shy, awkward and sensitive,' Brindley recalls. Several actresses were tested for the role of Nicky, the father's mistress. One who was considered was Joy Smithers who, at the time, had never acted before. Harmon's first choice, Anne Tenney, was lost to *A Country Practice* during the inevitable funding delays; in the end, Anna Jemison, who had recently made an impact in Roger Donaldson's New Zealand-made *Smash Palace* opposite Bruno Lawrence, was given the role.

There was a two-week rehearsal period, and from the start things did not go well. The actors rewrote their dialogue, and treated Harmon without much respect. Finding a crew proved incredibly difficult because of the large number of films in production at the time. It was impossible to find an assistant director, so one was imported from England ('He was very experienced, but hard to get on with,' says Brindley. 'He'd simply cross shots out, saying, "Forget these for a start".')

Three weeks into the seven-week shoot, things were going badly wrong. 'It was going down the tubes,' says Brindley. 'Paul was losing control.' Brian Rosen and Sue Milliken, who were completion guarantors for the picture, saw the footage and suggested Harmon be fired. 'I can't do that,' said Haydon. 'It's Paul's film.' Haydon himself wanted to resign, but in the end agreed to become the completion guarantors' representative on the production.

The next blow that fell was the sudden death of film editor Rod Adamson. He was replaced by Don Saunders, whose initial reaction, on seeing the footage, was: 'I hope you've got a lot of money for the music.' When the film was completed, no distributor would touch it: a Hoyts representative claimed: 'This film has no potential at all.' In the end, it became part of a package of films Filmco sold to Roadshow, but Roadshow never released it; it has never been on television, though it has appeared on video. Svet Kovich has never made another film, but Anna Jemison went on to win Best Supporting Actress for *Silver City*.

The production problems can be seen clearly in the finished film. Though Alan Cassell (as the father) gives his usual professional performance, Svet Kovich is mannered and irritating as Michael: he plays the character on a single, rather crazy, note, and alienates the audience from scene one as a result. Nor is Anna Jemison at her best as Nicky; though she looks lovely, she overplays the big dramatic scenes. Though Harmon builds up a certain amount of tension in everyday surroundings, he makes some crucial mistakes, too. Despite all the problems, though, the film does manage to present an unsettling study of an obsession.

Obsession is also the central emotion of THE UMBRELLA WOMAN (1986), which was written by Peter Kenna and is set in a small town in 1939. Producer Jan Sharp originally intended her husband, Phillip Noyce, to direct: but Sharp was developing two projects at the time, and, in the end, Noyce directed the one she had scripted herself (*Echoes of Paradise*; see previous chapter). Instead, Sharp offered *The Umbrella Woman* to Ken Cameron. 'I thought I could do something with it,' Cameron says. 'I'd never done an historical film.' But the script had problems that were never fully resolved.

The basic message of Kenna's story was: Even if you find out what you want most in life, you cannot always get it. Marge, the central character in the film, is wracked by unfulfilled yearnings, but in the end wastes herself on the wrong man. Sharp cast the three leads herself: Rachel Ward as Marge; Bryan Brown as her loving, rather simple, husband, Sonny; and Sam Neill as Neville Gifford, the womaniser with whom Marge falls hopelessly in love. Cameron feels the casting of Brown thwarted the script's intentions: 'Bryan has such staunch qualities. He made a perfect bushman, tough as nails but tender. If he'd been a repellent man, or brutal towards her, the psychology might have worked. Audiences were left wondering what Marge's problem was.' Cameron cast the fourth leading role himself: Steve Vidler as Sonny's brother, Sugar.

Sam Neill recalls that the project had been around a long time. 'There were drafts and drafts and drafts,' he says. 'And the first draft

I read was better than the draft we ended up making. So it didn't come out the way I'd hoped, but I loved working with Ken. Peter Kenna wrote a great background history for my character, Neville. Like many womanisers, there was something deeply misogynistic about him.'

Despite misgivings about the casting, it was a happy shoot, marred only by the fact that cinematographer David Gribble was taken ill with hepatitis at just the wrong time. 'It was a blow for me,' says Cameron. 'I'd wanted David to shoot the film.' Instead, a New Zealand cameraman, James Bartle, was hired, and he worked with Gribble's regular crew; Gribble had actually recovered before the shoot began, but by that time it was too late to reinstate him. 'Jim shot the way I wanted,' says Cameron. 'Though, in hindsight, we might have gone for a leaner, starker look.'

Cameron hoped he would overcome the script's problems during shooting, but learnt that 'you can't escape fundamental problems'. Although he enjoyed making the film, he looks back on it with sadness. It was poorly received by many critics, and he has not made another feature since (though he has had good notices for his television work, including the Kennedy–Miller mini-series, *Bangkok Hilton*). The film did poor business at the Australian box-office and had limited overseas sales ('The Yanks couldn't figure it at all,' says Cameron).

Despite Cameron's reservations, which are understandable, his four excellent actors do make their characters work. Rachel Ward gives her best performance to date as poor, silly Marge; Sam Neill oozes sexual menace as Gifford; Bryan Brown and Steve Vidler are totally convincing as the strong, naive, brothers. If there is a criticism, it is in the look of the film: it is just too beautiful, too conscious of the perfection of every image.

There are extraordinarily beautiful images, too, in *THE RIGHT HAND MAN* (1986): but, in this case, they play a more vital role in the drama. This was the first feature directed by Di Drew (b. 1950), a director of prize-winning short films, who had worked at the ABC and co-directed *1915*. The film is based on a novel by Katherine Peyton, which was optioned by actors Steven Grives and Tom Oliver (who formed a company, Yarraman, to make the film). The $5.5 million budget was raised through UAA (see Chapter 1). Basil Appleby was line producer for the film, which was mainly shot on locations around Bathurst, NSW, where Abercrombie House stood in for the Ironminster family home.

Di Drew (left) *directing* The Right Hand Man, *with Jennifer Claire and Rupert Everett.*

British actor Rupert Everett was imported to play the young aristocrat, Harry Ironminster, who loses an arm in a coaching accident and is forced to rely on his groom, Ned (Hugo Weaving). The film has all the elements of a Gainsborough piece from 40s Britain: the anguished lives of the aristocracy seem a long way from the trends of Australian cinema in the mid-80s; you can almost see James Mason and Stewart Granger in the leading roles.

Apart from an unnecessarily gory amputation scene early on, the film works well until near the end, when Drew botches a couple of crucial scenes, one being the seduction by Ned of Harry's fiancée, Sarah (Catherine McClements) at Harry's request. The staging of this scene, with Harry sitting nearby while the woman he loves gives herself to another man, simply does not work. Nor does the scene of Harry's eventual death, which was filmed several times but never, apparently, with complete success.

But the film is memorable because of the splendour of Peter James' images (which won an AFI award, deservedly). James' lighting captures perfectly the limpid colours of another era, and the film is a constant delight for his work alone. Notable, too, are the scenes involving the giant coach, the Leviathan, which travels, laden with passengers and cargo, to Sydney and back. Weaving actually drove the Leviathan himself, a considerable feat given the horsepower involved. But despite all these positive elements, the film is burdened with too many implausibilities, and it never found a significant audience.

T here was more overheated, old-fashioned melodrama to be found in *AN INDECENT OBSESSION* (1985), the first of two cinema features produced by Kerry Packer's PBL Productions (the ill-fated *Bullseye* being the second). This was the first feature directed by Lex Marinos, and Denise Morgan's screenplay is based on a book by Colleen

An Indecent Obsession. Foreground:
*Jonathan Hyde, Bruno Lawrence, Mark
Little, Wendy Hughes.* Background: *Tony
Sheldon, Gary Sweet, Richard Moir.*

McCullough set in an army hospital on a Pacific island during World
War II. Wendy Hughes was cast as a nurse who brings tea and sympathy
to an assortment of psychiatric cases.

The film is unsubtle; it poses the question: is Gary Sweet really
homosexual (he killed a sergeant-major who made advances to him)
or will he succumb to Nurse Honour's charms? There are no prizes
for guessing the answer. Sweet's sadistic tormentor is played by Richard
Moir (whose colourfully named character, Luce Daggett, is an actor
in civilian life); it is quite obvious that he will meet a sticky end,
and in fact he is castrated.

There is more than a touch of Tennessee Williams in this sweaty
story of passion and torment. It all looks very stagebound, perhaps
because it was filmed as a telemovie, but subsequently blown up from
16mm to 35mm for cinema release. It was probably at about this time
that Wendy Hughes' admirers started wondering if she was making
the best career decisions, because the character she plays is pretty
unconvincing.

She is, however, a model of clarity compared to the characters and events in *THE EVERLASTING SECRET FAMILY* (1987), the only film Michael Thornhill directed in the 80s. Thornhill (b. 1941 in Sydney) had been film critic for *The Australian* (1969–73) before making his first feature, *Between Wars* (1974), which was written by Frank Moorhouse; the success of this was followed by the even more successful *The F.J. Holden* (1977), about teenagers in Sydney's western suburbs. But then Thornhill went into an alarming decline: his telemovie, *Harvest of Hate* (1978) and feature *The Journalist* (1979) were lamentably banal.

During the 80s, Thornhill served as a director of the NSWFC, and produced a number of television programmes. As a producer, he is highly regarded: his decision to return to directing seems to have been an unwise one.

The source material for his comeback film, like that of his first feature, was from the writings of Frank Moorhouse. Moorhouse's screenplay, based on his own stories, was a rich, dark, tragi-comic story of an organised society of homosexuals, with members in very high places, who recruit newcomers from exclusive boys' private schools. One could imagine that, with really imaginative direction (and, perhaps, in black-and-white rather than colour) and with first-rate casting, the film might have been a sensational, possibly scandalous, success on the art-house circuit: it might have given censors around the world cause for alarm, however.

Unfortunately, Thornhill (financed by Tony Ginnane's IFM as part of the Hemdale package) made all the wrong decisions. He chose to shoot in colour and Panavision, his casting was crucially wrong, and the direction, far from being deft and comic, is heavy-handed and stolid. Arthur Dignam is the Senator around whom the drama unfolds; it would have been interesting to see a very different type of actor (Jack Thompson, say, or Bruno Lawrence) cast in such a role. Dignam can be a fine actor, but here he plays the role in the most obvious, campy style.

Scenes of the members of the secret society, clad in Roman-style togas, are extremely silly; the sex scenes are awkward and coy and, in the case of Beth Child as an Earth Mother type, embarrassing. Mark Lee gives a stilted performance (his nomination for an AFI award remains a mystery) and John Meillon is a hoot as a judge into leather and bondage. A weird rejuvenation sub-plot allows Bogdan Koca (as a doctor) to give the film's most assured performance, but nothing can save such a misconceived affair.

As a former film reviewer himself, Thornhill must have known how reviewers might react to his film, because he (or his distributor) refused to have the usual advance press screenings for it. At the time, I was standing in for the *Sydney Morning Herald*'s Paul Byrnes (who wisely took a holiday the week the film opened), and I was obliged to review the film. The response was an advertisement in the next week's *Herald* headed: 'Shock Disclosure; Stratton Gets it Wrong'. The ad read: 'Avid readers of the *Sydney Morning Herald* learnt last week that stand-in film reviewer David Stratton detests this film. Sadly, convinced by his vehement condemnation, many will now choose not to see this remarkable work. Our advice is very simple: take a chance and see how wrong a reviewer can be! This film is a hugely enjoyable, melodramatic confection for adults. Played out at one remove from reality, it is a sly blend of preposterous nonsense and darkly intelligent speculation about the secret life of the senses. HURRY. LAST DAYS!'

Most of my fellow reviewers were hardly more generous than I was, and the film fared poorly in Australia, though in Britain it attracted a cult following. Hemdale reneged on its pre-sale deal, but Ginnane was able to find an alternative US distributor. *The Everlasting Secret Family* was a great idea which deserved better treatment.

The Everlasting Secret Family. *Mark Lee, Arthur Dignam.*

AUTHOR!

AUTHOR!

■

■

T he majority of Australian films are based on original screenplays, but, naturally, a number of novels and plays are brought to the screen each year. Some film versions of novels, such as *Robbery Under Arms*, *Monkey Grip* and *Puberty Blues*, and some adapted plays, like *Rebel*, have already been discussed in other chapters; this chapter is devoted to some of the more significant novels and plays which were filmed during the 80s, and also a few films in which the theatre formed an important backdrop to the drama.

At the end of the 70s, there was a great deal of interest in Christopher Koch's 1978 novel *The Year of Living Dangerously*; Phillip Noyce was but one filmmaker keen to tackle the story of an Australian radio journalist working in Indonesia during the crucial year in which the government almost fell to the Communists. In the end, film rights to the novel were optioned by Peter Weir for Jim McElroy to produce: *THE YEAR OF LIVING DANGEROUSLY* (1982) would become Weir's last Australian film of the 80s.

During the long period in which Weir and David Williamson worked on the script of *Gallipoli* (see Chapter 2), *Dangerously* was also very much in the director's plans. Koch had been asked to write a screen adaptation himself, but this had proved unsuccessful. The apparent reason was that Koch expected a film *of* the book whereas, quite naturally, Weir planned to make a film *from* the book—making the screenplay as cinematic as possible, which, of necessity, meant changes and modifications. Says Weir: 'I'd been so impressed with his writing, but somehow the experience of writing that first draft seemed to make him feel almost that he had a *right* to be involved. After all, he had sold us the rights, but he was unwilling to let the project go: to allow me to make *my* interpretation, or reinterpretation, of his vision. He certainly knew how to write a novel, but I knew how to make a film, and he didn't seem to understand that. Film is closer to opera than it is to the novel, but he couldn't see it that way. So I had to ask him to stand aside and go and see the movie.'

The Hollywood-based Scots writer, Alan Sharp (*Ulzana's Raid*, *Night Moves*) then wrote three drafts, which got further and further away from Weir's ideas, so he asked David Williamson if he would write the next draft. 'Peter and I worked together on a further four or five drafts,' says Williamson. 'I never worked with Koch, but I got input from him. I knew him, and he'd ring me and ask: "What's he [Weir] doing now?" I felt a bit like the meat in the sandwich in that situation, because I sympathised with both points of view. You can't literally make a film of a book: in the transition, certain things happen to the narrative line.'

Much later, at about the time of the film's release, Christopher Koch expressed his feelings about all this in a letter to *Cinema Papers*, which reads, in part: 'Peter Weir, when I originally approached him to direct the film, asked me to write a screenplay from my novel, collaborating with him in restructuring the material . . . I was always prepared for another writer to take over, provided he respected the material . . . Weir pronounced himself satisfied with my screenplay and in 1980 took it to CBS in America. They wanted Peter Weir; they wanted the novel; but not the script. As Americans so often do, they plainly had plans to debauch the property along commercial lines. Weir informed me that Alan Sharp . . . was to do a "polishing job", at the request of CBS. This polishing job turned out to be a total rewrite. It left nothing of my original novel but the names of the characters, and in my opinion it resembled a comic strip . . . I am not your sensitive novelist who thinks his book ought to be preserved *in toto*, as a film, . . . the Sharp script was a total, talentless betrayal of the book, and of the film I had envisaged . . . My protest was dismissed in a telegram, and Weir has ever since refused all contact with me, a situation not of my choosing . . . CBS then dropped the project. Weir then hired David Williamson to rework the material. Only a few lines of Sharp now remain; and by my estimate the final proportions are about 55 per cent Williamson–Weir and 45 per cent Koch . . . I believe he [Williamson] did a fine job under trying circumstances . . . The finished product, despite what I see as dialogue deficiencies, has all the imaginative and visual power I always knew Peter Weir would bring to it . . .'

As with *Gallipoli*, the SAFC was originally involved in backing the project, along with the AFC; and the McElroys had signed a deal with the American major MGM–UA for international distribution. However, again as with *Gallipoli*, the SAFC suddenly dropped out of the project and everything came apart; it was Weir's agent who suggested that MGM–UA step in and put up the entire $6 million budget, which is what eventually happened.

Weir was so pleased with his working relationship with Mel Gibson during *Gallipoli*, that he asked the actor to play the role of the journalist, Guy Hamilton. Gibson was hesitant at first: he wanted to work with Weir again, but felt the character was too old for him. Also it is, in some ways, a thankless part, because for much of the film the character is reacting to situations out of his control. However, Gibson was persuaded, and Sigourney Weaver was cast as Jill Bryant.

The big problem remained the casting of Billy Kwan, the tiny Chinese-Australian who befriends Guy and who is also in love with Jill. Says Weir, 'Apart from the fact that it's a fine story, Koch's greatest achievement in the novel was the creation of the Kwan character. Kwan was unique, and unless the character worked in the film, the film wouldn't work.' Weir considered every possible Australian actor who was short of stature, and in the end, after satisfactory make-up tests, cast David Atkins in the role. Atkins (see the discussion on *Squizzy Taylor* in Chapter 2) started rehearsals with Gibson, but Weir quickly saw that it was not going to work. He brought David Williamson in to look at tapes of the rehearsals, and they agreed the relationship between Guy and Billy was unconvincing. 'It wasn't Atkins' performance—he was giving his all. I began to think it was in the writing. You felt that there was real competition between those two,' says Weir. 'There was no way Guy would have tolerated Billy: he'd have kicked him out and got another cameraman. Billy had become an irritating character.'

The painful decision was made to recast. Sets were being built in Manila, where production was due to start shortly. Weir cleared his decision with Freddie Fields of MGM–UA and altered his flight to Manila so that he could make stopovers in New York and Los Angeles. At a casting session in New York, Weir and a casting agent pored over possible American actors. Several were brought in to audition, with Weir standing in for the Mel Gibson role: among them were Joel Grey, Bob Balaban and Wallace Shawn (the latter said: 'I'm not a dwarf and I'm not Chinese, but I had to come to audition because it's such a crazy idea'). 'I found the same problem as Mel had found in Sydney,' says Weir. 'These endless tests showed me that the relationship wasn't working. Audiences would never believe that these two men would become a team, would become friends. I very nearly gave it all up and started seriously thinking about the implications, in terms of money already spent, if we abandoned the project. And then I was shown this photo: it looked perfect. Height, right. No film experience, but plenty of theatrical experience. Available. Name, L. Phipps Hunt. I said, "What are we waiting for?" And the casting agent told me, "L. Phipps Hunt is a woman."

'A week later, when we were absolutely desperate, I was told that Hunt had been invited to audition. I thought it was a bad joke, and asked the casting agent to send her away, but he insisted I see her. So, in came Linda, into the film and into my life—and she subsequently won the Academy Award for playing Billy.' She impressed Weir at the outset by telling him how much sympathy she had for the character of Billy—no other actor had expressed such sentiments. She asked if it would be possible to rewrite the role for a woman, but Weir suggested she consider playing a man. Next day, she was given special make-up, which, says Weir, was dreadful: 'She didn't look like a man and she didn't look Chinese. But, as we went over those same lines, it started working. I was fascinated and intrigued by her Billy: as Guy, I would have listened to her and I'd have worked with her. So I flew her (without authorisation) to California, showed the tests to Fields and his executives, and it all worked.'

Absorbing the identity of Billy Kwan, who was basically a sad, painful character, proved agonisingly difficult for Hunt, but she brought it off brilliantly. There was great relief in Manila when Weir phoned the news of his unusual casting through to Mel Gibson, David Williamson and other key crew members.

Shooting commenced on schedule, but after only three weeks, disaster struck. A note was handed to a crew member on the street: it read: 'In the Name of Allah, The One, The Almighty. Cease your Imperialistic Filmmaking Activities. You make a Mockery of the Muslim People. Stop, Or We will Stop You.' The note was followed by telephone threats along similar lines. The threats were unsigned, and authorities suspected radicals among the 400 Iranian students studying at university in Manila.

The Year of Living Dangerously. *Linda Hunt.*

The Philippines authorities urged Jim McElroy and the crew to stay on, and Imelda Marcos offered the protection of her personal bodyguards, but Weir was concerned for the safety of his cast and crew: it was decided to leave immediately, and to finish the film in Sydney.

It was a costly move. The art department, with very little time at their disposal, had to create sets in the Sydney area. 'They did an amazing job,' says Weir. 'We didn't lose a day.' The canal in Glebe was used as a setting for an Indonesian village, and the exterior of Cranbrook School in Bellevue Hill became the British Embassy. 'Perhaps, in the end, we gained by the move,' says Weir. 'The shoot was more comfortable, we had more time, we got better performances. You're always under a certain amount of stress on location.'

A few lingering problems with the screenplay remained. Weir is happy with the ending (in which, in contrast to the book, Guy leaves his job to follow Jill out of Indonesia) but others were not. David Williamson blames himself for one unfortunate incident that strained the relationship between writer and director. 'It was the day *The Perfectionist* opened at the Theatre Royal. There was a press conference and afterwards I thought all the press had gone. I was in a back room talking to someone I thought was from the theatre, and he said: "How did you like working on *The Year of Living Dangerously*?", and I said "Oh, I was sandwiched between a writer with a big ego and a director with a big ego." It turned out I'd been talking to Dorian Wild [a Sydney gossip columnist], so there it was in print a few days later. Peter, quite rightly, wasn't very happy about that.'

As for the film itself, Williamson feels that the Guy–Jill relationship lacked electricity and that as a result Weir focused more on Billy Kwan. 'Most of the rewriting during the shoot involved increasing the number of scenes between Guy and Billy,' he says. 'So, in the end, it was a bit unbalanced.' He concedes, however, that 'maybe it was never quite balanced in the novel, either. You had Guy, an obsessive and Jill, a neurotic: their individual deficiencies were offset by the other's strengths. And that's very difficult to pull off on film.' Williamson also regrets the fact that Billy, in the film, is less complex than he was in the novel: 'Billy is quite malignant in the book,' he says. 'But Peter made him saint-like—the moral core of the film.'

Some of the problems experienced in production show in the finished film. The first two-thirds is brilliantly handled, but towards the end something goes awry; things seem to be missing, so that Billy's about-turn attitude towards President Sukarno, which leads to his death, seems too abrupt, and Guy's escape from Billy's house (surrounded by security guards) looks all too easy. The final image, of Guy and Jill reunited on the plane, is a bit banal, smacking of Hollywood endings of another era. But it remains a generally intelligent and exciting adaptation of a very difficult, challenging novel, and Linda Hunt's extraordinary performance deserved all the praise heaped upon it. There is a magical moment (typical of Weir) in which the wizened, diminutive Billy says to handsome Guy: 'We look alike.' Guy does an understandable double-take, and Billy continues: 'We've the same colour eyes.' The film did moderately well all over the world, was invited to compete at the Cannes Film Festival, and remains the only Australian feature film to date for which an Academy Award was won.

If Christopher Koch was unhappy about Weir's treatment of his novel, he was presumably even less happy about the other film of the 80s based on one of his books, *BOYS IN THE ISLAND* (1989). This semi-autobiographical work was first published in 1958, when the author was twenty-three (a revised, tightened edition was published in the mid-80s). Gillian Armstrong had wanted to film the book in 1984, but made *Mrs Soffel* in the US instead. At that point, Koch decided to develop a screenplay himself, working in collaboration with Tony Morphett, who was a friend. They interested director Carl Schultz and producer Jane Scott (who had worked together on *Goodbye Paradise*) in the subject.

Tony Ginnane became involved in the project, which was to have been another film financed through his IFM company with a pre-sale to Hemdale. But Schultz got tied up in lengthy post-production chores on his first Hollywood feature, *The Seventh Sign*, and, in the meantime, Hemdale started reneging on its pre-sale arrangements with other Ginnane films. At a meeting of investors held early in 1988, it was decided to press ahead with the production, without Hemdale and without Ginnane. In the event, they were without Schultz, too, although he was in the final stages of post-production on *The Seventh Sign* and could have rushed into *Boys in the Island* had he not needed a rest. He was replaced by newcomer Geoffrey Bennett, whose short film, *The Way She Moves*, was a finalist in the GU awards in 1979, and who had subsequently directed *On Loan*, one of the *Winners* series of children's telemovies.

Despite Koch's close ties with the project, somehow, along the way, the delicacy and originality of the original is lost in the transition.

For too much of its length the film smacks of a routine nostalgia coming-of-age-in-the-50s story, and the Tasmanian setting adds nothing very new. The characters remain on the surface, and newcomer Yves Stening, as Frank, lacks charisma. The second half of the film, set in a very strange Melbourne, is much better, thanks to James Fox as the gang-leader and, especially, Jane Stephens as the devious femme fatale, Keeva; but the difficulty the film has had in finding distribution is probably understandable given the tentative treatment. One of the people closely connected to the film believes it was spoilt in the editing: 'The rushes were great,' he says, 'but the inexperience of the director showed in the way it was cut together.'

A more formidable literary adaptation is the Ray Lawrence film of Peter Carey's *BLISS* (1985). Lawrence (b. 1947 in London's Bethnal Green), became one of Australia's top directors of commercials. His father was a painter who looked after the official carriages for Buckingham Palace, and he frequently took his son to the cinema (mostly Randolph Scott westerns). In 1958, when Lawrence was eleven, the family moved to Australia in search of a better climate and conditions; they settled in South Australia. When he was fifteen, Lawrence left school and home and came to Sydney eager to work in the arts (there seemed no chance of work in film or television). Young as he was, he found work in advertising and at the same time started writing. In 1966, he sent a story to Paramount and received in response a letter suggesting he come to New York. Somehow he scraped up the money for the trip, but by the time he got there his contact had moved on and nobody had even heard of him or his story. He travelled on to London, where he got a job in advertising and started producing commercials. Officially, he was unable to direct because he could not get a union card; unofficially, he would hire 'really bad' directors, and get them to read the paper while he made vacuum-cleaner commercials. He still wanted to work in feature films, and wrote letters to a number of film directors, including Orson Welles and Federico Fellini, seeking help; Fellini replied, in Italian, saying that, if Lawrence came to Rome, he would find him an unpaid job.

Meanwhile, he was writing screenplays, including one nearly produced with the assistance of the British Film Institute (about French girls coming to London to get abortions). 'I got worn down,' he says. 'And decided to come back to Australia.' This was the turning point: he started a company, Window Productions, with Glen Thomas, and, over

Bliss. *Sara de Teliga as 'The Vision Splendid'.*

a long period of time, became established as one of the country's top directors of television commercials, favouring the style of the mini-drama, using top actors (Angela Punch McGregor appears in his Setamol 500 commercial) with clients that included Australia Post, Telecom, IBM, State Bank of Victoria and the *Australian Financial Review*.

Lawrence met Peter Carey (who at the time was also working at an advertising agency) at a party; they became friends, and started writing scripts for commercials together. Both men wanted to make films, and they jointly wrote two screenplays, *Dancing on the Water* (based on Carey's short story *Life and Death in the South Side Pavilion*) and *Spanish Pink*, while Carey also worked on a novel, *Bliss*. Lawrence approached Phillip Adams to see if Adams–Packer would be interested in producing one of these scripts; Adams did express interest at first, but nothing came of it.

Meanwhile Anthony Buckley, whose last production, *Kitty and the Bagman*, was made with Adams–Packer, had been, as he says, 'in the wilderness' since the failure of that film. Buckley recalls: 'Ray Lawrence arrived on my doorstep one day to see if I could help get these films made. I thought they were terrific, and went to Melbourne to see Ken Watts [former Chief Executive of the AFC who was then managing Adams–Packer]. But Adams–Packer was out of money, and Watts

Ray Lawrence directing Bliss.

couldn't help.' Meanwhile, Carey's novel, *Bliss*, had won the Miles Franklin Award, and Lawrence gave Buckley a copy of the book: he read the entire book on an eight-hour flight to Kuala Lumpur to attend the Asian Film Festival, and immediately saw its film potential. He told Lawrence and Carey: 'Why are we trying to raise money on two scripts nobody's heard of, when we've got this?' The film rights for *Bliss* had been sold to a British producer, but they expired in January 1983: this was October 1982. Within an hour of the rights becoming available, Buckley had placed a deposit on them (provided by the NSWFC). Money was raised through 10BA, and one of the 360 investors was a 14-year-old girl!

Within the industry, there were quite a few who thought that the *Bliss* project was a foolhardy one, that the book was unfilmable. But Carey and Lawrence agreed on what material to use and what to omit; they started work on a screenplay, which came together quickly, given the complexities involved. Lawrence is disdainful of much of today's cinema: 'Films don't take themselves seriously enough, they don't fulfil their potential or, even, audience expectations, often enough.' He enjoyed tackling the grand ideas of the novel and devising visual equivalents for them. He and Carey met every day for two months at 6 a.m. and worked for three hours before Lawrence went off to work: they broke the story down onto cards, decided what to use and what new material needed to be added. 'Much of the dialogue was straight from the novel,' says Lawrence.

In hindsight, Peter Carey believes it was a mistake for him to work on the adaptation of his novel. 'I found writing the adaptation ridiculously easy at the time,' Carey says. 'But I think we went about it the wrong way. Probably the best way to adapt a novel is to treat it like a piece of pottery: to smash it, and then put the pieces together again as a screenplay. But we stuck closely to the book on one level— yet, really, the film has only a superficial resemblance to the novel.'

Lawrence decided he wanted Barry Otto to play Harry Joy almost from the beginning. Otto was an established theatre actor (he played Cooley in *Don's Party* and D. H. Lawrence in *Upside Down at the Bottom of the World* among many other stage roles), but had appeared only in supporting roles in a couple of films (*Norman Loves Rose* and *Undercover*). However, investors, and the NSWFC, needed convincing that the leading role in such a complex and important film should be given to a comparative unknown. Buckley managed to get money to shoot a 35mm screen test. In October 1983 (one year before production on the film commenced), Otto and Lynette Curran, cast as Harry's wife, went before the cameras in a Double Bay hotel; the scene shot was set in the asylum. A screening of that sequence, together with some of Lawrence's commercials, convinced investors that *Bliss* would be a feasible project.

Having cast Otto, Lawrence used him, wherever possible, to test with other potential actors. He recalls being in Melbourne, at the Windsor Hotel, when casting the role of Alex Duval: Tim Robertson was reading for the role, and the scene involved Harry and Duval in bed in the mental hospital. Lawrence was recording the test on video, when the maid walked in: the sight of two men in bed and another filming them was presumably an alarming one for the staff of the Windsor—she walked out very quickly.

Production of *Bliss* was elaborate and complicated. Lawrence spent two weeks rehearsing every scene in an empty flat in Lane Cove, filming on video. Later, he would replay the tapes for the actors when they came to shoot the scenes for the 35mm camera. Production commenced in October 1984, and lasted eleven weeks; the budget was $3.4 million and, although the film was delayed for a couple of days because of rain, it came in $16,000 under the budget.

There were 167 scenes in the film, a logistical nightmare: although the book is set in Queensland, the film was shot in New South Wales to save money. The house used as Harry's home was in Hunter's Hill, but the street where the house is apparently located was in the beach suburb of Bilgola. Much of the interior of the house was built at the Mort Bay studio in Balmain. The famous dream sequence at the beginning of the film, in which Harry sees his mother as The Vision Splendid, was filmed at Richmond; sets had to be built in the lake and shooting took place on a Friday afternoon, but no-one was very satisfied with the results, and it was reshot the following Wednesday. Some key crew members, including cinematographer Paul Murphy, were working on their first feature after a career in commercials.

Given the complex logistics of this, his first feature, Lawrence was understandably a little nervous, and he asked Peter Carey not to visit the set during shooting, but to join him in the editing room afterwards. 'This was a mistake,' Lawrence says in hindsight. 'I should have allowed Peter on set, because I could have shared my insecurities with him: but I was working with a crew of sixty people, and I was a bit freaked. I could have saved myself a lot of aggravation if I hadn't made that decision, and I'd never do it again.'

One of the many striking scenes in the film comes near the beginning when Harry suffers his heart attack. Lawrence planned the scene six months before it was filmed: 'I had a bucket on the end of a building crane: camera operator David Williamson [no relation to the writer] was in the bucket during the shot which started on a close-up of Harry's cigarette burning and then lifted high up into the sky.'

Lawrence was deeply depressed after viewing the first rough cut, or assembly: it ran well over three hours. Getting to fine-cut stage was a difficult process, but Buckley (himself a former editor) was supportive and gave valuable advice. At about this time, Buckley approached Gilles Jacob, director of the Cannes Film Festival, and sent him a video of the cutting copy (which was subtitled into French at SBS TV). Jacob expressed interest, so a video of the fine cut was sent to him a few weeks later. At this stage it ran just over two hours: 'Will it be shorter?' Jacob wanted to know. Buckley said it would be, but the version sent to Cannes was finally 135 minutes. Jacob was not very pleased to discover that the film was still so long, and until the last minute Lawrence was not sure he wanted to be in competition at all—after they arrived in the south of France he considered withdrawing it.

Bliss was screened towards the end of the festival, and the audience reaction was terrible. According to Gilles Jacob, walkouts were exceeded only by those for Michelangelo Antonioni's *L'Avventura* in 1960. Ray Lawrence faced the press conference with trepidation, but discovered that some people had appreciated the film; it was invited to the New York and London Film Festivals, and the NSWFC was able to arrange a good international distribution deal with New World. Lawrence was quite glad of the opportunity to recut the picture, which was shortened by 25 minutes to 110 minutes after Cannes. Peter Carey feels that these cuts helped the picture: 'It was strange,' he says, 'that in post-production Ray felt he couldn't cut another second. But, suddenly after Cannes, chunks could be cut.' The negative publicity from Cannes was turned to the film's advantage by the anti-French attitude in Australia at the time (the result of nuclear testing in the Pacific and the *Rainbow Warrior* affair).

Yet getting a release in Australia proved difficult: *Bliss* was rejected by every distributor. The film was saved by its success at the 1985 AFI awards: it won best film, director and adapted screenplay. The NSWFC had decided to distribute the film itself, and had arranged a booking at the tiny State 2 cinema in Sydney: after the awards,

GU offered a screen at the much larger Pitt Centre. The first week, the film took $42,000, and takings increased in subsequent weeks. *Bliss* took off, and ran several months at the Pitt: it remains the only film successfully released without an established distributor.

The film is extremely audacious, and Lawrence's depiction of the strange world of Harry Bliss (brilliantly portrayed by Barry Otto) mixes astonishing beauty, black humour, and the genuinely bizarre in almost equal proportions. The shorter, post-Cannes, version is a marked improvement: the hospital scenes especially are shortened so that they become funnier and less laboured, and several other scenes are sharpened. The uncompromising material (involving incest between brother and sister, sudden switches from comedy to tragedy, nightmares and visions) is shaped into a moving story of a man's break with his well-ordered, affluent past, at first into a world of dreams and nightmares, and then into a world of ecological peace and harmony. Some of the effects (cockroaches crawling out of the hole in Harry's chest) are extraordinarily powerful, and one cannot imagine even Fellini handling the material better.

Peter Carey looks back on the film version of *Bliss* with, as he puts it, 'a weird sense of loss'. 'I really can't see the film any more,' he says. 'But, then, I really can't see the book any more. Such a lot of work went into that film, but I just have no overview of it. I'd never adapt my own work again.' At the end of the decade, Carey was working with Wim Wenders on his massively ambitious project, *Until the End of the World* (a substantial amount of which would be filmed in Australia) and with Bill Bennett on *War Crimes*.

Sadly, Ray Lawrence has been unable to set up another feature, despite the success of *Bliss*. Says Buckley: 'It's a tragedy that Ray hasn't been able to make another film, and it's a reflection on our industry that talents like him can't get support.' Lengthy attempts to make a film of Robyn Davidson's *Tracks* (about a single woman trekking across the desert) came to nothing, but, in 1990, Lawrence and Buckley were hoping to team up to make *Sweetlip*, adapted from one of the short stories in Robert Drewe's collection, *The Bodysurfers*.

M rs Aeneas Gunn's novel *We of the Never Never* was, for generations, staple reading for every Australian child. As such, it was a natural choice to make *WE OF THE NEVER NEVER* (1982) the first production of the newly-formed Adams–Packer company. John B. Murray, head of production for Adams–Packer, assumed the role of producer of the film, which was budgeted at $2.5 million, with Igor Auzins directing. The screenplay was originally to have been written by John Dingwall, who started it and went to the Northern Territory to work on research. But he and Auzins did not get on, and Dingwall was replaced by Peter Schreck; it was Schreck who phoned Dingwall to tell him he was off the picture.

Angela Punch McGregor was ideal casting as Jeannie Gunn, who in 1900 joined her husband Aeneas at a cattle station in the remote outback. Arthur Dignam was less fortunately cast as Gunn, partly because he lacks the strength the role required, and partly because he never adequately conveys the devotion towards his wife that was essential to the relationship.

Auzins wanted to film entirely on location in the Northern Territory, interiors as well as exteriors; it was a thirteen-week schedule, lasting from April to June 1981. The homestead chosen was Mataranka, 172 kilometres from the nearest town, Katherine. Two blocks of motel units had been built at the homestead to house cast and crew, but the isolation was severe, catering appalling, morale low, and the film was running badly behind schedule. Four weeks into the shoot, Murray was replaced by Greg Tepper, who had been production manager for Fred Schepisi. Murray resigned from Adams–Packer, and Brian Rosen was brought in as associate producer.

The homestead was supposed to be in charge of catering, but supplies were erratic. The first task of Antonia Barnard, the new production manager brought in by Rosen, was to hire a Sydney caterer. There were other problems: every morning cast and crew had to drive forty-five minutes to location *into* the rising sun and drive back every evening *into* the setting sun—there were several accidents as a result.

Luckily, cinematographer Gary Hansen had an even temperament, and was very helpful in keeping things moving along. He was also coming up with stunningly beautiful wide-screen images, which remain the film's principal asset. Tragically, this was Hansen's final feature: before it could be released, he was killed in a helicopter accident while filming a commercial, a great loss to the film industry.

It took a long time for the film to see the light of day: a year after principal photography was completed, it screened in the market section of the Cannes Film Festival. The official world premiere took place, in the presence of Prime Minister Malcolm Fraser, at the Center Cinema in Canberra on 28 October 1982. The version unveiled for the Prime Minister ran 132 minutes; subsequently it was cut to 121 minutes, but in any version it is a ponderous effort, lethargically paced and lacking a genuinely interesting narrative to accompany the gorgeous images. Even in the longer version, there are indications that plenty of footage ended up on the cutting-room floor: for example, the first time we see Jack (Lewis Fitz-Gerald), the camera dollies in towards him very significantly as if he will play a major role in what follows— but, as the film progreses, his character is no more important than any of the other supporting roles.

Crucially, the climax, in which Jeannie is left alone after Aeneas has died of fever, is unmoving. She remains a remote character, probably because the film glosses over the hardships she must have faced (her biggest problems seem to be cleaning up the dirty homestead and waiting for the luggage to arrive). But there is always the photography: sunsets and daybreaks and more crane shots than even Delmer Daves in his heyday aspired to. There is also a sweeping music score from Peter Best.

When it finally opened, *We of the Never Never* did reasonably good business, and played well in Britain, too (after a good launch at the London Film Festival), where it must have all seemed terribly exotic.

There was, of course, a feminist message to *We of the Never Never*, as there had been to *My Brilliant Career*, another turn-of-the-century book successfully filmed. And so there is in *FOR LOVE ALONE* (1985), adapted from the novel by Christina Stead, which was for years the pet project of Margaret Fink, producer of *My Brilliant Career*. The two novels, and films, have something in common: both are period pieces dealing with young women, not conventionally attractive, who possess great talent but who are torn between relationships with men and a career.

Raising the $3.8 million budget took a number of years. Fink is bitter about the problems she faced: 'While people with little or no track record were getting countless millions to make films I, who had proved myself, couldn't get the money. And I really felt the injustice of that. It was heartbreaking, and I really don't know why it took so long. People said they didn't like the book, but frankly I think they hadn't read it. It's not an easy novel. But, then, they didn't like the idea of *My Brilliant Career* either. Could be because I'm a woman.' In the end, there was a generous pre-sale from GU, and UAA arranged the balance of the finance.

As with *My Brilliant Career*, there was a problem in casting the central character. At the outset, Fink thought about Judy Davis, who had been brought to international attention with the earlier film, but she felt in the end that such casting would be unadventurous, and decided to look for a newcomer. Nor did she want to use director Gillian Armstrong a second time: she saw *Stir* (see chapter 7), liked it a lot, and contacted its director, Stephen Wallace. 'He immediately responded to the book,' says Fink. 'And I thought he had the depth to cope with such unconventional material.' Hugo Weaving played Jonathan Crow and, at the last moment, Sam Neill replaced Peter Strauss, the American actor originally cast as James Quick.

Fay Weldon was originally brought in to adapt the book, but none of her drafts worked ('I don't think she liked the book,' says Wallace. 'She seemed to think the central character was an idiot.') There was no money to find another writer, so Fink urged Wallace to write it himself. 'I never wanted to write it,' says Wallace. 'And if I'd known then what I know now, I'd have insisted someone else do it.'

Genevieve Picot (before she was cast in *Undercover*) was tested ('One of the best tests I've done with anybody,' says Wallace), and tentatively cast; but it took two years to raise the money for the film, by which time she was considered to be too old for the part (moreover, *Undercover* had not launched Picot in the way that might have been expected.) Eventually, Helen Buday, a young actress fresh out of NIDA, was cast in the role.

New Zealand cinematographer Alun Bollinger was chosen to shoot the film because Russell Boyd dropped out (as he had with *My Brilliant Career*) and several cameramen contacted by Fink (Don McAlpine, John Seale, Dan Burstall, Andrew De Groot) were busy filming elsewhere. The shoot itself went smoothly enough, except for some differences of opinion over the approach to the subject. Wallace favoured a stylised approach: he wanted something vaguely expressionist, 'like *The Blue Angel*'. 'I wanted it to be rather bold,' he said. 'And at first Margaret agreed, but then, as we were under more and more pressure, she changed her mind. "Let's keep it simple," she told me. "When we've done a lot more films we can experiment." ' Some of the pressure came from UAA, the investment company, and some from GU, who had $1 million invested in the film (Wallace feels that GU's David Williams basically expected another *Brilliant Career*). Wallace still regrets that he capitulated: 'I *should* have been bolder,' he says. 'The problems with the film partly stem from the book, but if I'd kept to my original ideas, it could have been better.'

Half the film is set in Britain, but most of the English scenes were (convincingly) shot in Sydney. Wallace did go to Oxford for a four-day shoot; doubles stood in for the actors. Footage from trains was also shot in Britain for later front projection use. 'There are lots of model shots in the film,' says Wallace. 'And I defy anyone to pick them.' Fink praises the work of production designer John Stoddart, who built a wholly convincing street set in Balmain.

Despite all the care lavished on *For Love Alone* (the work of Bollinger and Stoddart is flawless), it remains a distant experience, far less spirited than *My Brilliant Career*. It has some memorable sequences, especially one in which Tess and Jonathan shelter from the rain in an old abandoned saw-mill which eerily starts working; and the principal actors are all good. But the uncertainty of style shows in, for example, the robust way Hugh Keays-Byrne plays Tess's father (doing an Emil Jannings?) and, in the end, it is fatally passionless. We never really care about Tess. The high expectations held for the film were largely unfulfilled, and its performance at the box-office was disappointing.

The relative failure of *For Love Alone* put paid to Margaret Fink's long-term plans to bring Sumner Locke Elliott's novel *Eden's Lost* to the screen; eventually, she made it as an acclaimed (and award-winning) mini-series. By the end of the 80s, the difficult novel was firmly the province of television (when, that is, the commercial networks could afford such things). Meanwhile, another Sumner Locke Elliott book had been successfully brought to the screen: *CAREFUL HE MIGHT HEAR YOU* (1983), which was produced by Jill Robb.

This autobiographical work had been around as a film project for years: in the mid-60s, American director Joshua Logan (*South Pacific*) wanted to film it with Elizabeth Taylor, and came to Sydney on a much-publicised search for a child actor to play P.S.; mercifully, perhaps, he could not find one. Robb (b. 1935 in London) had been involved in the film industry for several years, having been continuity girl (as they were then called) at Southern International, the Chips Rafferty–Lee Robinson production company. She had been production co-ordinator on the *Skippy* television series and marketing and distribution manager at the SAFC in the early 70s; in 1975 she became the first woman commissioner of the VFC and, later, its first Chief Executive. She had left to form her own production company, Syme International, and *Careful* was to be her first feature. Robb had long admired the book; she acquired the rights and hired Michael Jenkins to write the screenplay before approaching director Carl Schultz.

Schultz and Jenkins had worked together at the ABC. Schultz says:

Careful He Might Hear You. *Wendy Hughes, Nicholas Gledhill.*

'I liked the book very much, and I liked Michael's script too. I worked with him on the final draft.' Robb, like Margaret Fink, had a lot of trouble raising money for the film, but she was very determined; the NSWFC backed her, and its support was crucial in raising the $2.2 million budget.

As Logan had found nearly twenty years earlier, casting P.S. was crucial. Says Schultz: 'I saw hundreds of boys, but funnily enough Nicholas was the first one I actually tested.' Nicholas Gledhill was the son of actor Arthur Dignam, and one of Schultz's concerns was that, as time went by and the budget still had not been fully raised, the boy was growing and changing. 'At the time of the screen test he was absolutely perfect, but as each month passed I thought, "Oh God, he's getting older—we'll have to recast." There's a delicacy in a 7 or 8 year old that's no longer there in a 9 or 10 year old.' But eventually the money came through, and no recasting was necessary.

The film was shot on locations around Sydney. Vanessa's sumptuous house was located in Elizabeth Bay, while the much more modest home of Lila and George was in Undercliff St, Neutral Bay.

Schultz's challenge in the film was, as he puts it, 'to get inside the child. Looking back on my own childhood, I remember key incidents in a heightened way. A Sunday afternoon in a child's life is infinity. I wanted to create a sense of that kind of wonderment and mystery. So John Seale [the cinematographer] and I wanted to get visuals which had that kind of exploration.' To his great credit, Schultz also decided not to make the rather melodramatic story realistic: 'I wanted it to be bigger than life,' he says.

The films of Douglas Sirk come to mind while watching *Careful He Might Hear You*; the tortured family relationships, the contrast between the wealthy branch of the family (Vanessa, Ettie) and the working class (Lila, George), the family quarrels, the *deus ex machina* that seals Vanessa's fate (when the ferry on which she is travelling across the harbour sinks after a collision with another boat). All of it is shot with lots of smoke and lavish use of wide screen. It is splendid stuff. Wendy Hughes is ideally cast as Vanessa; in another era, Bette Davis or Joan Crawford would have made a formidable Vanessa, but Hughes' portrayal of the frigid, neurotic 'virgin queen' is perfect. So, too, is Robyn Nevin as the troubled, caring Lila, and Peter Whitford whose very face conveys the cares and problems of the dogged George. John Hargreaves has only two brief scenes but, as the father of P.S., makes an enormous impact, and the scene on a smoke-filled station platform at night, as he is about to leave his son's life for ever and the frustrated George suddenly lets fly and punches him, is one of the great moments in Australian cinema. Nicholas Gledhill, solemn and sensitive, is a perfect P.S.

The film is flawed only (slightly) by Ray Cook's operatic music score, which is 40s Hollywood style—fitting enough, but overdone at times. (Schultz now regrets he never had time to modify the score which, on a couple of occasions, underlines what is already on screen far too insistently.)

Hoyts distributed the film, which was quite a big success at a time when many Australian films were failing. 20th Century–Fox acquired US rights, and the film did surprisingly well in North America, especially Canada; as a result, Schultz received many offers to direct Hollywood films. The film made its European bow in competition at the Venice Film Festival which Schultz attended; Sumner Locke Elliott was also there. To Schultz's relief, the author was extremely happy with the film, which, though it won no prizes, was enthusiastically received.

T he filmed novels discussed above were all Australian. *DEVIL IN THE FLESH* (1985) was adapted by Scott Murray from the French novel *Le Diable au Corps*, by Raymond Radiguet (a disciple of Jean Cocteau); Claude Autant-Lara had made a version of the novel in 1947. Murray (b. 1951) was editor of the film magazine *Cinema Papers* for a number of years, but also made a number of short films and documentaries; like Schultz, he rejected a realistic approach to his subject. Murray (son of producer John B. Murray) had grown up attending the Melbourne Film Festival each year, and tended to prefer European cinema to American cinema.

As a critic who had often been forthright in his comments about Australian films, he acknowledged he was putting himself on the line: 'Perhaps it would be fair to ask Tim Burstall [whose work Murray had criticised] to review the film and have a chance to get even with me. I put my opinions forcefully in print, so expectations must be quite high.'

He was attracted to the novel when he first read it at school. 'It's the best book I've read about that time of one's life when one moves from childhood to adulthood,' he says. 'It can be a cruel time. A lot of books and films have romanticised a relationship between a youth and an older woman; Radiguet's book is crystalline hardness, and that's why I wanted to film it.' The book is set in France during World War I; Murray shifted the setting to rural Victoria during World War II. 'In the novel, the woman's husband was a soldier at the front, which was about 30 miles from where the story is set; we're 12,000 miles from the front, so I decided to make her married to an Italian who was interned at the beginning of the war. This solved the problem dramatically, and also allowed me to refer to specific Australian concerns.'

The film was budgeted at $1.6 million, and was filmed over a seven-week period in Central Victoria: locations in Bendigo, Castlemaine and the small town of Dunolly were used.

Devil in the Flesh is almost unique in that it combines a strong French influence with a very Australian flavour. As cinematographer, Murray chose Andrew De Groot, whose only previous feature had been Richard Lowenstein's *Strikebound*: 'I think Andrew is one of the great

Devil in the Flesh. *Keith Smith, Katia Caballero.*

talents of the Australian film industry,' says Murray. 'He has an ability to achieve even better results than the director might have expected.'

Casting was very difficult. Murray had anticipated he would have to cast the role of the Frenchwoman overseas, but after a search discovered Katia Caballero, who was French-born but lived in Sydney. 'We screen-tested her, and were just stunned by her,' he says. The role of the youth, Paul, was even more tricky: Murray found Keith Smith only two weeks before he started shooting. The South Australian actor had been seen in a small role in *Robbery Under Arms.*

Devil in the Flesh is one of the few genuinely erotic films made in Australia in the 80s. 'I like eroticism in films,' says Murray. 'But I found it wasn't easy to make those scenes work. The actors had to be totally at ease, because you can't act without clothes if you're nervous, plus, if the actors aren't relaxed, they impart a tension which spoils the scene.'

The French atmosphere is further enhanced by Murray's decision to use Philippe Sarde to score the music: 'I thought he would be best for the subject. French film composers use music quite differently from the way we do—they don't use it at obvious moments, they underscore differently.' Murray contacted Sarde in Paris via a mutual friend, Pierre Rissient, and Sarde agreed to write the music as long as he liked the film, which, fortunately, he did.

In *Devil in the Flesh*, the setting plays a vitally important role: in this small-town backwater, with its quiet streets, sleepy railway station, willows and gum-trees, the passionate affair between a schoolboy and a married woman seems even more disturbing. Katia Caballero is certainly a find as Marthe, but the love scenes, despite all the nudity, remain rather tentative. The same year that Murray made his film, Italian director Marco Bellocchio produced a much steamier, updated version of the novel, which received limited international release, probably because of the lack of inhibition of the sex scenes. Murray's film suffered lengthy delays in finding a cinema to show it: it was three years before it opened for, sadly brief, commercial runs.

I t is interesting to record how often producers faced daunting difficulties in bringing established novels to the screen. For much of the 80s, Patricia Lovell, despite *her* impressive track record, was unable to make a cherished adaptation of George Johnston's book *Clean Straw for Nothing*, although she had, at one time, both Gillian Armstrong and Mel Gibson attached to the project. Nor did Maurice Murphy's intention to make a new version of C. J. Dennis' *The Sentimental Bloke* (with a Bob Ellis screenplay and Phillip Quast as The Bloke) come to anything after it was first announced in 1982. In *The Last New Wave*, I detailed the problems connected with bringing Colleen McCullough's *The Thorn Birds* to the screen: that was originally to have been Peter Weir's first American feature, and, in 1979, he spent some months in Hollywood working on the script with Australian expatriate Ivan Moffatt: Robert Redford and Bette Davis were mentioned as possible starters. But Weir turned the project down, unhappy with the script, and in the end the book was made as a mini-series on locations in Arizona, Hawaii and the Simi Valley, 50 kilometres from Beverly Hills, with Bryan Brown about the only authentic bit of Australia involved (Canadian Daryl Duke directed). There were also plans, on the part of the South Australian Film Corporation, to produce a feature-film remake of the Peter Finch film *The Shiralee*, based on the novel by Darcy Niland; in 1985, Donald Crombie was announced as director. But this, too, became a mini-series, directed by George Ogilvie, with Bryan Brown and Rebecca Smart, both perfectly cast.

In terms of bringing a novel to the screen, one of the longest stop-start sagas was that of *KANGAROO* (1986), the 1922 D. H. Lawrence novel, which was being mooted as far back as 1972 (with Dirk Bogarde in mind for the central role). In 1981, the project resurfaced to be produced by David Roe, with Tim Burstall directing and Brian Probyn as cinematographer. It was several more years before Burstall managed to make the film, by which time Probyn was dead (Dan Burstall, son of Tim, photographed it). The adaptation was by Britisher Evan Jones, who had worked with Joseph Losey and who had previously adapted Kenneth Cook's novel *Wake in Fright* for Ted Kotcheff's successful 1971 film.

Lawrence wrote *Kangaroo* during the six weeks he spent in Australia, and in it he explored the possibility of the establishment of a right-wing secret army, composed of World War I veterans. 'Kangaroo' is the nom de plume used by the leader of that army, and Burstall cast Hugh Keays-Byrne, an actor with an imposing presence, in the role. For Judy Davis, it was her first Australian film since *Heatwave*; she had, meanwhile, played the lead in David Lean's *A Passage to India*. She stars as Harriet, and Colin Friels is Somers, the Lawrence surrogate.

Kangaroo, budgeted at $3.3 million, is an extremely handsome picture, and an intelligent adaptation of a difficult book. The sexual tension between Somers and Harriet and their neighbours, Vicki (Julie Nihill)

Kangaroo. *Hugh Keays-Byrne, Judy Davis.*

and Jack (John Walton) might have been more forcefully handlea, but the scenes involving Somers and Kangaroo (who 'wants to be loved') depict a strange courtship which is very faithful to the original. Judy Davis (not surprisingly) was named Best Actress at the AFI awards, but the film's only other acknowledgement was for Terry Ryan's costume design; Burstall might have expected more appreciation, because it is one of his best films.

Kangaroo actually went into release overseas before it opened in Australia, a trick used to try to get some kind of international prestige and thus persuade local audiences that a film has the approval of the Brits and Yanks. The cultural cringe lives on.

After *Kangaroo*, Burstall moved from D. H. Lawrence to Charles Dickens, with an ambitious attempt to tell what happened to the convict Magwitch during his years in Australia. This was *GREAT EXPECTATIONS: THE UNTOLD STORY* (1987), which was made simultaneously as a mini-series (co-produced by the ABC) and a feature

film; it was the first film Tony Ginnane made as part of his deal with
Hemdale. In the event, the feature film was never released in cinemas,
but appeared on video early in 1990.

Based on the feature-film version alone, *Great Expectations* is another
dire example of the incompatibility of simultaneous cinema and
television. The narrative has more holes than a cheap screen door,
and the picture is patched together so haphazardly that, at times, it
looks more like a trailer for a film than the film itself. As Estella,
Anne-Louise Lambert (with sixth billing) has not one word of dialogue,
but is briefly seen in one sequence dancing with Pip. Sigrid Thornton,
who has a credit as associate producer, fares little better with only
three scenes.

Perhaps Burstall would have done better to tell the story entirely
from the point of view of Magwitch; certainly, he was unwise to include
scenes taken directly from Dickens (by way of David Lean's great film
of the novel), because when the genuine article, with its wonderful
dialogue, occasionally peeps through, it only underlines the tawdriness
of the new material. Noel Ferrier is a Jaggers worthy of Dickens (and
of Francis L. Sullivan, who played him in the other two films of the
book), but, of the supporting cast, only Rod Haddrick as a kindly
colonialist, and Bruce Spence, as Joe Gargery, are the least bit authentic.
This was Tim Burstall's last feature film of the decade.

A dapting a novel to the screen is one thing; adapting a play is
quite another. By far the most filmed of Australian playwrights
is David Williamson, and he has worked on all the adaptations of
his work until now. In the 70s, film versions of *Stork* and *Don's Party*
were extremely successful, while *The Removalists* was a failure. Bruce
Beresford had directed *Don's Party*, and so he was a natural choice
for the film version of *THE CLUB* (1980), which was jointly produced
by the SAFC and the NSWFC immediately after production of *Breaker
Morant* was completed. *Morant*, though technically a 1979 film, was
released in Australia in 1980, and, by the end of the year, Beresford
had two films playing side by side in capital city theatres, which was
something of a record.

Says Williamson: 'Bruce does a very thorough job planning the film
with the cinematographer: he and Don McAlpine storyboard
exhaustively, and they like to layer their visual effects, so that there
are things going on in the foreground as well as the background.'
Beresford cast the film particularly well, giving a strong central role

*David Williamson: playright and
screenwriter.*

to Jack Thompson and allowing Graham Kennedy to steal the show
as the pork-pie manufacturer who is ruthlessly robbed of the presidency
of the football club by his devious colleagues. 'Kennedy's a very fine
comic actor,' says Williamson.

But, despite these qualities, *The Club* translates less easily to film
than *Don's Party* did. It is basically a committee-room story, and despite
valiant work from Beresford, McAlpine and the actors, it fails to work
on screen. Somewhat desperate efforts were made to make it more
cinematic: countless locations are used, to little effect; there are
unnecessary tracking shots, and some dizzying camerawork which
merely induces vertigo. On the whole, the play was funnier, but, then,
it is not Williamson's best play.

The film of *TRAVELLING NORTH* (1986), which was brilliantly
brought to the screen by Carl Schultz, is a play that lends itself better
to adaptation. Ben Gannon obtained an option on the film rights and
immediately contacted Leo McKern to play the role of Frank: this
would be the first Australian film for the celebrated expatriate. McKern
says: 'Ben sent me a copy of the play, and when I read it, I thought:
"That's me!" My wife read it and said: "Williamson must know you
backwards." '

It was originally intended that another Australian expatriate, Michael
Blakemore, would direct: Blakemore had a distinguished career as a
theatre director: he had directed *Don's Party* on stage in London, and
The Club in Washington and New York. He had made only one feature

film, the disappointing *Privates on Parade*, but Gannon felt he would be ideal for *Travelling North*. However, after casting was completed, Blakemore dropped out and was replaced by Schultz, who responded wholeheartedly to the sensitivity of the material. 'However,' says Schultz, 'I felt that, if it was to make a successful film, a lot of that snappy dialogue of David's, which worked so well on stage, would have to go. The film is much less funny than the play, deliberately so.' Williamson agreed to Schultz's suggestions, and the two had a harmonious working relationship.

'Schultz was a great choice to direct,' says Williamson. 'Carl is fond of atmosphere and mood. Bruce Beresford has a strong sense of pace and momentum: he often gets his actors, when they're walking, to move 50 per cent faster than normal; Bruce likes to get on with things, he hates longeurs. He was perfect for robust, satirical material like *Don's Party* and *The Club*; Carl is gentler, more whimsical, in his approach, and he was ideal to direct a poignant subject like *Travelling North*.' As for Leo McKern, Schultz reminded him of Fred Zinnemann, with whom he had worked on *A Man for All Seasons*: 'They have that same Central European sensitivity,' he says.

The film was shot with a budget of $2.5 million on location in Port Douglas, in northern Queensland, in July–August 1986. Everyone involved in the shoot agrees that it was a happy period. McKern, who sailed to Australia from Britain on a cargo-boat (he has a fear of flying), talks of the relaxed and happy atmosphere. Graham Kennedy, appearing in his third Williamson film (the first without Beresford), was equally contented: 'I was overawed by Leo at first: after all, he's one of the great character actors of our time. But he was charming, and he has a wonderful fund of stories about all the people he's worked with over the years.'

Schultz loved working with the actors. 'There's one moment when Graham Kennedy, who is quite superb in the film, says: "You'll find I'm a good neighbour"; that brings tears to my eyes. Graham's a nervous actor, terrified of forgetting his lines, but he had a great understanding of that character.'

Schultz's skill as a director is evident in every frame of the film. There is a scene in which, just before Frank and Frances leave Melbourne, they visit an art gallery for a last look at paintings they loved: and this sets the poignant mood for what follows. But, thanks to the crusty performance of Leo McKern, and the wonderfully sympathetic Julia Blake, the film never descends into sentimentality:

Travelling North. *Julia Blake, Leo McKern.*

it has pathos, and a certain amount of rather sad humour, but above all it is a film about real people. Graham Kennedy, who was mysteriously overlooked at the AFI awards in 1987, makes Freddie, the painfully lonely, chatty neighbour, a genuinely tragi-comic figure. Henri Szeps (who replaced Warren Mitchell, originally cast as the local doctor) is also fine. Schultz uses metaphors—the ferns which, like the prickly protagonist, close up when they are touched—with great skill.

The film was distributed by one of the smaller companies, CEL, and was consequently denied the best cinema outlets. Had it screened in, for example, GU cinemas, it might have become a major hit; as it was, it was a modest one. It won awards (Leo McKern was deemed Best Actor at the World Film Festival in Montreal, and also at the AFI awards, where David Williamson was awarded for his screenplay adaptation) but it deserved more, since it is undoubtedly another of the best Australian films of the decade.

In 1983, Patricia Lovell hoped to produce a feature film based on David Williamson's successful play, *The Perfectionist*; and Williamson was to have directed the film. He had directed his own work on stage, and, at the time, was keen to direct a film. But Lovell was unable to raise the money for the project: which, again, is mysterious, since so many substandard projects managed to attract funding in the early 80s. In the end, *The Perfectionist* was made as a telemovie in 1985, which Lovell produced in association with Roadshow, Coote & Carroll, and which Chris Thomson directed. Jacki Weaver, John Waters, Noel Ferrier, Steve Vidler and Kate Fitzpatrick appeared.

The final David Williamson play to be adapted for the screen during the 80s was *EMERALD CITY* (1988), which had been a huge success on stage. This jaundiced look at the differences between Sydney and Melbourne, and at the Americanisation of the Australian film industry, might have made a funny and important film. It was the last production backed by the NSW Film Corporation, and it was produced by Joan Long, whose long-standing interest in the film industry made her ideal to handle the subject.

Her first choice for director was Bruce Beresford, with whom she had worked very harmoniously on *Puberty Blues*; but he had just filmed a play (*Crimes of the Heart*) and was unwilling to do another immediately. In the end, Michael Jenkins was assigned to direct his second feature (after *Rebel*). David Williamson had written a screenplay which, as with *Travelling North* and his other play conversions, pared the dialogue down considerably: 'I think I know something about the difference between writing for the stage and writing for the screen after all these years,' he says. Most of the speeches cut in the adaptation had been in long scenes involving the characters of Colin and Kate Rogers; Joan Long says: 'Those cuts to the text were made by David with my full approval; they didn't represent the main thrust of the story.' But the actors who had been cast in the principal roles—John Hargreaves and Robyn Nevin—thought they knew better, and at rehearsals, Jenkins discovered that they wanted to restore many of the speeches which Williamson had cut for the screenplay.

Chris Haywood recalls: 'Johnny [Hargreaves] felt that some of the dialogue that had been dropped from the play was, in fact, funnier and had greater impact than dialogue in the screenplay. So he and Robyn kept suggesting things be put back, and maybe Michael didn't take a firm enough stand in support of his concept for the complete picture.'

Williamson had planned to attend these rehearsals, but unexpected pressure of work meant that he was out of the country for most of that period and could attend for only one day. He tried to reason with the actors, but they remained adamant. Faced with open revolt, Michael Jenkins was in a bind. Says Williamson: 'Michael sought my advice. I was dubious, but the actors were insisting the words went back in, and none of them were exactly shrinking violets. Michael didn't know whether to beat them over the head, or accept it as a challenge and go with it.'

Instead of pulling the rebellious actors into line, Jenkins decided to overcome the problem of so much verbal density by directing the dialogue in the style of Hollywood screwball comedies of a bygone era. He viewed classics like George Cukor's *The Philadelphia Story* and the Hecht–Macarthur films, and had the actors deliver their lines at a rapid-fire pace; just as *Rebel* is characterised by its decor (suffocating reds and pinks), so *Emerald City* shudders under the weight of its verbosity. During production, rumours abounded that the actors had taken over: visitors to the set, who asked members of the crew for the director's whereabouts, were greeted with remarks like 'Four of them are over there.'

We will never know how good a film based on Williamson's screenplay for *Emerald City* might have been, but Jenkins' film is a severe disappointment. The rapid-fire delivery does not work (Australians do not talk like characters from Hollywood films of the 40s) and some of the performances are embarrassingly theatrical; Hargreaves and Nevin did themselves no service by their insistence that so much of the play's dialogue be retained. Nicole Kidman is charming in a comparatively minor role, but Chris Haywood overcomes all the film's problems with a brilliantly funny characterisation as the dreadful Mike McCord who represents the crassest elements in the Australian film industry. The film's sentiments are in the right place, but (because it is so dialogue-oriented) it is preachy and pompous instead of being persuasive and witty.

Williamson was quite pleased with the result: 'I saw the film with a large audience, and I thought there was an energy on screen that I hadn't seen in an Australian film for a long while.' Joan Long notes that the actors worked very hard and put a lot into the film, but it seems evident that their wilfulness seriously unbalanced it.

D espite these reservations, the Williamson film adaptations tower over the other filmed plays of the 80s. Indeed, apart from them, there were not many others. *COMPO* (1989) is an adaptation of the play *Claim No. Z84*, by Abe Pogos but, as directed by Nigel Buesst, seems little more than a micro-budget exercise which mostly avoids opportunities for humour (such as the work carried out by investigators on dubious insurance claims—shades of Billy Wilder's *The Fortune Cookie*).

DEPARTURE (1986), based on Michael Gurr's *A Pair of Claws*, is even less appealing. Director Brian Kavanagh filmed this laborious piece (quite unnecessarily) in Tasmania, but scenes in which the play is opened out (lunch at an open-air restaurant, a visit to a football match) are superfluous. Nothing can disguise the appallingly theatrical dialogue and acting style, and only Sean Scully emerges from the film with any credit. It must be added that *Departure* was most cruelly treated by the audience at the AFI judging screenings, where it was almost hooted off the screen.

Apart from the Australian plays that were filmed, a few attempts were made during the 80s to adapt classics to the Australian environment. Ibsen was tackled in *THE WILD DUCK* (1983), and Liv Ullmann and Jeremy Irons were imported by first-time producer Philip Emanuel to play the leading roles. Henri Safran (b. 1932, in France) directs the material respectfully, but it remains an *unnecessary* film, adequately made, decent, respectable, but lacking fire. The Australian actors more than hold their own alongside the imported talents, and Arthur Dignam gives one of his best screen performances as Gregory Wardle. The story is relocated from Norway to turn-of-the-century Australia, making the casting of Liv Ullmann rather curious.

More ambitious, and much more worthwhile, is Neil Armfield's lively adaptation of Shakespeare's *TWELFTH NIGHT* (1986), which is essentially a film record of the director's successful modern-dress stage production. The sets are simple and patently artificial, the costumes are everyday Australian (one character wears bathing trunks), and the dialogue is adapted to Aussie slang.

Casting is superb. Gillian Jones is most effective as Viola and her twin, Sebastian; Ivar Kants is an imposing Orsino; Peter Cummins is a splendid Malvolio (especially when he goes courting in yellow shorts and socks); Kerry Walker is exceptional as The Fool. Best of all are John Wood, as a marvellously gross Sir Toby Belch, and Geoffrey Rush as the accident-prone Sir Andrew Aguecheek. It is, to be sure, just filmed theatre: but the sense of fun is infectious and it deserved to be better marketed than it was. Still, it should remain timeless.

This is more than can be said for the irredeemably ghastly *THE PIRATE MOVIE* (1982), the brainchild of actor and former Hollywood restaurateur Ted Hamilton, who was executive producer and who gives an embarrassingly narcissistic performance as The Pirate King. This is Gilbert and Sullivan updated, and Hamilton seems to have been responsible for employing a hand-me-down British director (Ken Annakin) and two less than memorable American leads (Kristy

McNichol and Christopher Atkins). Incidentally, when the project was first announced, Richard Franklin was attached as director.

The film is such a mess that it is almost bad enough to be funny—but not quite. Some of the original songs are tarted up and they are augmented by some dreadful new ones. The three principals are bad beyond belief; Garry McDonald should be ashamed for allowing himself to be talked into impersonating Peter Sellers as Clouseau; and only Bill Kerr brings any kind of dignity to the proceedings. Dialogue (by Trevor Farrant) is banal and sometimes juvenile (Mabel to Pirate King: 'You'll be hung.' Pirate King: 'I am. Well.')

The film opens with a sequence from an old Fox pirate picture, which is, needless to say, better than anything Annakin or Hamilton concocted. 'Lor', New York reviewer for *Variety*, called the film: 'A fiasco, an embarrassment to the Australian film industry and to distributor 20th Century–Fox.' There seems no reason to disagree with him. It was six years before Annakin made another film.

T his discussion of filmed theatre should also include films which use the theatre as a background. Pamela Gibbons' autobiographical *BELINDA* (1987) is not about legitimate theatre exactly: the setting is a Kings Cross nightclub in the late 60s where the teenage heroine, a ballet student, gets a job. Gibbons' film is a modestly appealing one, in which Belinda's safe suburban home is contrasted with the excitement (and danger) of the Cross. There are several good performances, not least 16-year-old Deanne Jeffs as the eponymous heroine. But it is the backstage scenes that are the best: the communal dressing room, where Doreen (Hazel Phillips), the ageing leader of the girls, is never seen without her poodle in her arms; the casual nudity, the seediness. Caz Lederman gives a powerful performance as a bullying waitress, and Mary Regan is also very good as the tragic Crystal. The film charts the end of an era, with the club closing to make way for a disco. Though small-scale, it is attractive and enterprising.

BACKSTAGE (1987) is more pretentious, and many times more expensive, but far less successful. The story behind the film is, however, of more than usual interest, and revolves around co-writer Frank Howson, whose passion for the theatre is evident in much of his work. Howson (b. 1952 in Melbourne), was a child actor (he was inspired by seeing *Yankee Doodle Dandy* when he was very young). As he grew older, he worked in numerous shows, including *Jesus Christ Superstar* in which he was lead dancer and Reg Livermore's understudy. At about this time (the early 70s) he also started to write songs, and one of his compositions, *Suicide Boulevard*, was recorded by Little River Band. He wrote four musical shows for children, including *Sinbad* (excerpts from which are featured in Howson's subsequent production, *What the Moon Saw*).

In 1981, Howson set up a company, Boulevard Films (named after his song) with his partner Peter Boyle; they wanted to make a film about the life of the Australian boxer, Les Darcy. Since he had never written a screenplay before, Howson felt he needed help. He approached Jonathan Hardy, a co-writer of *Breaker Morant*, which at the time was a big success. Hardy (b. 1941 in New Zealand) was an actor-singer who had played small roles in *The Devil's Playground*, *Mad Max* and *Lonely Hearts*; his contribution to *Breaker Morant* appears to have been marginal. He agreed to help Howson with the Les Darcy screenplay, which was titled *Something Great*, but, while Howson was away in Germany producing a record album, Hardy wrote a draft without his input which was submitted to Hoyts–Edgley. Simon Wincer of Hoyts–Edgley had been interested in the Darcy project, believing it had the makings of another *Phar Lap*, but he rejected Hardy's version.

Howson returned from Germany, wanting to have another attempt at the screenplay, a genuine collaboration. During this process, Hardy showed him several other scripts he had written, including *Backstage*. (Much later, Howson wrote a completely new script of *Something Great* which he hoped Richard Franklin would direct; when the project was announced, Hardy claimed the script as his own. A legal battle ensued, which was settled out of court.)

Meanwhile, Howson had been working with Hardy on the *Backstage* screenplay, and had suggested that the central character come from the music world. On a trip to Los Angeles, Howson met Laura Branigan and showed her the screenplay; she expressed interest in playing Kate, the American rock star who wants to become a serious actress. Boulevard Films was about to start raising money when they were approached by the Burrowes Film Group: Burrowes needed to make another film before the end of the financial year, and offered fund-raising facilities.

It was agreed that the Burrowes Group would be executive producers of the film but that Boulevard Films would have the creative input. 'I knew very well what audience we were aiming at,' says Howson. But as production neared, Howson says, Burrowes spent a lot more time on the project than his role as executive producer warranted; and further dissension was created when Howson, who was officially producing and co-writing the film, discovered a previously unseen script which was apparently written by Jonathan Hardy alone.

In the end, tensions on the production reached breaking point. Howson and Burrowes disagreed over who should compose the music: Howson wanted a Los Angeles-based musician, John Capek, while Burrowes insisted on Bruce Rowland. Capek, who had been brought to Melbourne, was fired by Burrowes. Conditions became intolerable: eventually, Burrowes bought Boulevard out of the picture. 'They made the film they wanted to make,' says Howson. 'And it was terrible. They left my name on it as co-producer and co-writer, yet, according to the contract, they had to screen me the final cut of the film so I could decide if I wanted to take credit. They never screened it for me: I first saw it at the American Film Market where it was shown to potential buyers. It was a packed screening at the start, but at the end only Peter and me and one other person were left.' Howson says that only two scenes he wrote remain in the film.

Backstage is, indeed, a terrible film. 'It's all the clichés you've ever heard,' someone says at one point: he is talking about the music business, but he might as well have been discussing this screenplay. In it Ms Branigan decides to try-out as a 'serious' actress in Melbourne (presumably because, to all intents and purposes, it is the end of the earth) and falls for a waspish theatre critic (Michael Aitkens). The film's love-hate attitude towards critics is its only interesting element: early in the film, Noel Ferrier (who overplays the producer character embarrassingly) tries to influence a newspaper owner to curb his critic, and later the film ridicules the Aitkens character for asking perfectly legitimate questions about why an American singer was imported to star in an Australian stage production. Yet this same critic is able to teach Branigan how to act, a talent few critics would possess. It is hard to decide what is worst in the film: Branigan's performance (especially at the end when we are expected to believe she plays a serious role in *The Seagull* on Broadway) or all the childish jokes about the name of the Ferrier character (Wynde).

Backstage was a ludicrously costly film, which, with other Burrowes Group productions, was the focus of an inconclusive investigation into alleged financial shenanigans by the ABC programme *Four Corners*. *Backstage* had been completed for a considerable period of time before it limped into cinemas for a mercifully brief release.

Howson was still keen to make *Something Great*, but he found it impossible to raise money for such an expensive project, especially for a production team without a track record. Ray Beattie, of the Seven Network, suggested it might make a successful mini-series, and so Howson rewrote the script with that format in mind. At that stage, he needed a director with television experience, and met Pino Amenta (who had directed or co-directed some top-rating television series, *The Sullivans*, *All the Rivers Run*, *Anzacs* and *Nancy Wake* among them). Nothing came of the Les Darcy project.

But Howson had another screenplay, which became *BOULEVARD OF BROKEN DREAMS* (1988). Stockbroker Malcolm Olivestone thought this script had potential and agreed to back it; Howson sent the screenplay to Amenta, who said it moved him to tears. The film was budgeted at $2 million, which included shooting in Los Angeles and New York, plus the acquisition of some expensive music rights for Tom Waits and Buddy Holly songs—music rights alone cost $15,000.

John Waters was cast as an expatriate writer, living in Los Angeles, who discovers he is dying of cancer and returns to Melbourne to see his wife and child (not telling them of his condition). Naturally, given the plot, Waters was expected to look gloomy for much of the film (his wife is living with another man and does not want him around), and the performance was chosen by the actor's peers as the best of the year: Waters won the AFI Best Actor award. Critics were not so kind, however, and attacked the film for its mawkishness and sentimentality. Howson was taken aback by the almost universal scorn levelled at the film: 'The film had screened for test audiences, and at the American Film Market, and those screenings had all gone over very well. People had been very positive about the film. So the reaction of the critics came as a shock, because we had a false sense of security, and we'd lived with it so long we'd lost any objectivity. Perhaps Hoyts could have handled the press screenings better: it was an audience reaction movie. [Actor] Kim Gyngell says you have to leave your cynicism at the door when you see this film.' Howson concedes that a darker ending might have made for a better film, but feels he has learnt a lot from the experience.

Soon after the release of *Boulevard of Broken Dreams*, there was some speculation that Boyle and Howson were considering taking legal action against some of the people who had reviewed the film negatively; nothing came of this, however.

Boulevard has a valid central idea, but is mishandled. John Waters is allowed to indulge himself, and his constant weeping on camera becomes self-defeating. Nor is it easy to identify with a character who

Boulevard of Broken Dreams. *John Waters.* (Photo: *Greg Noakes.*)

just cannot come out and tell his ex-wife the truth about his condition. The film has some powerful scenes, the best being a confrontation in which the couple's small daughter pleads with her mother (Penelope Stewart) to let her father come back and live at home, while the mother's new lover sits, in embarrassment, at the dinner table: it is a wrenching moment, but the immediate superimposition on the soundtrack of a Tom Waits song undercuts, rather than reinforces, it. The ending—

family renuion at the airport—is a dreadful piece of contrivance, and Kevin Miles is encouraged to give a fatuous performance as a theatre producer (compare Noel Ferrier in *Backstage*). Indeed, the theatre scenes, with the doleful hero visiting the local production of his latest hit play and briefly, chastely, dallying with leading lady Nicki Paull, seem like padding.

Boulevard returned money to its investors, and Boulevard Films was able to raise money to produce a package to make a further five films, the first of which was *WHAT THE MOON SAW* (1989), an autobiographical piece which reflects Howson's childhood affection for the theatre and for pantomime. Howson was aiming for an audience similar to that of *My Life as a Dog*; he wanted to make a film which parents would take their children to see, and which both would enjoy.

Apart from yet another theatrical caricature (this time from Max Phipps as the owner of the theatre), the film has a lot more charm than its predecessor. More could have been made of the relationship between the boy (Andrew Shepherd) and his grandmother: Pat Evison is a delight in the latter role, an elderly woman in charge of the theatre box-office but once, as she puts it, 'the best legs on the Tivoli circuit'. The theatre seen through the eyes of the boy is, indeed, a magical place, though Pino Amenta might have made a bit more of it. There are a few sharp lines of dialogue: when he receives a complaint that a particular play contains Communist propaganda, the theatre owner concedes, 'it was written by a member of the Writers' Guild.'

AND

JUSTICE

FOR

ALL

■
■

I t is generally accepted that films made for the cinema should stay away from social issues and politics; such subjects, it is said, are better suited to television, or should be made as documentaries. As a result, a relatively few films about social and political issues were produced during the 80s, and even fewer recovered their costs.

Perhaps the commercial failure and mixed critical reaction to Fred Schepisi's bold, full-frontal *The Chant of Jimmie Blacksmith* (1978) is the reason that so few films touched on Aboriginal themes during the decade; such films are seen to be commercially and politically risky.

In the light of this, Bruce Beresford's return to Australia to make *THE FRINGE DWELLERS* (1986) can be seen as both courageous and foolhardy. Beresford (b. 1940) had established himself during the 70s as a key figure of the Australian New Wave, starting with his Barry Humphries comedies, *The Adventures of Barry McKenzie* (1972) and *Barry McKenzie Holds His Own* (1974). He continued with successful adaptations, making *Don's Party* (1976) and *The Getting of Wisdom* (1977), and at the very end of the decade, he made one of the most famous and popular of all Australian films, *Breaker Morant* (1979), which won for Jack Thompson a special Best Supporting Actor award at the 1980 Cannes Film Festival. In 1982, Beresford made *Tender Mercies* in Texas with Robert Duvall, and then a biblical epic, filmed on locations in the south of Italy, *King David* (1985), starring Richard Gere, which proved to be an expensive failure for Dino de Laurentiis. During the late 80s, he would continue to work in Hollywood where he made *Crimes of the Heart* (1986), *Her Alibi* (1989) and *Driving Miss Daisy* (1989) and in Europe filming an episode for the multi-part *Aria* (1987). His return home, then, was welcomed in many quarters, even if his choice of project was questioned.

Beresford wanted to make a film of Nene Gare's 1961 novel because, as he said, 'I spent a lot of my childhood in western New South Wales and was always very interested in Aborigines; they really were outcasts, fringe dwellers. I read the book in 1974–5 and it gave me a tremendous understanding and appreciation of them and their way of life. I admired their sense of humour; that they could laugh when their lives were so sad. Their culture had broken up, they had problems with alcoholism, but they could always see the humour in things—they were able to laugh at the whites. I think that's really why they survived so well. I'd seen a lot of documentaries that emphasised the frightening aspects: the drunkenness and the brutality. They scared me, and I knew this wasn't the whole story, only part of the story. I knew the way the families were united was tremendously strong and I wanted to make a film that showed these people as likeable and admirable human beings.'

Getting finance for the film proved predictably difficult. Beresford discovered a considerable lack of enthusiasm when he presented the project to people in the film industry. 'It was an entertaining story,' he says. 'In many ways sad, but also very funny with a believable, likeable group of characters. I thought everyone would leap at it. I was wrong. A lot of people would rather the whole thing was swept under the carpet and just not mentioned.' Eventually, though, with considerable help from producer Sue Milliken and backing from the AFC and the QFC, the budget—a little over $1 million—was raised. Beresford had written a screenplay (in collaboration with his ex-wife, Rhoisin Beresford) and had made a decision which he probably later regretted: he updated the period from 1961, when the book was written, to the present day. 'I updated the things that had changed,' he says. 'Details of the Housing Commission house are different from the novel—but a lot of things really hadn't changed, like the fringe dwelling, humpy town existence.'

Casting director Alison Barrett spent almost three years (while Beresford was in Italy making *King David*) looking out for Aboriginal actors. She found Ernie Dingo and Kylie Belling in stage productions, but Kristina Nehm, for the key role of Trilby, was discovered at the very last minute. Casting Trilby's mother, Mollie, proved more difficult until Justine Saunders persuaded Barrett and Beresford she could play the role: 'Justine is young and very beautiful,' says Beresford. 'But we needed a middle-aged woman who wasn't very attractive.' Saunders felt she understood the character of Mollie, who reminded her of her mother; she did a test with grey hair and got the part. Aboriginal poet Kath Walker, cast as Eva in the film, notes that the Aboriginal actors 'tidied up' the screenplay.

Despite that, the film still has a curiously dated feel about it; the updating seems to have been a crucial mistake, because nowhere in the film is to be found reference to the political issues, such as land rights, which have been so much a factor in the 70s and 80s. Beresford, always good with actors, gets fine performances from his cast; Don McAlpine's camerawork beautifully captures the details of the small community; Tim Wellburn's editing crisply cuts from character to character. It is a beautifully *made* film, in which some sequences are flawless—driving to the new home in an overloaded, rickety truck

Bruce Beresford directing The Fringe Dwellers.

with dicy brakes; the discovery of a snake at the waterhole; old Eva frightening the children with Aboriginal legends; Mollie trying to remember the few Aboriginal words her mother taught her, or packing up her personal belongings prior to the move, inescapably evoking Jane Darwell in John Ford's *The Grapes of Wrath*. But the overall impression is of a tentative film, sincere but dated and even patronising.

Beresford defends himself on this point: 'Directing a film by definition means exploring someone's life that's not your own. I've made a film about soldiers in the Boer War, and another about Victorian schoolgirls; I made a film [*Crimes of the Heart*] about three sisters in the Deep South, and I'm not a woman and had never been before to the Deep South—you're always interpreting someone else's experience. I'm doing the same thing with Aborigines. One thing I have in common with all of them: I'm a human being.'

The Fringe Dwellers was invited to compete in the 1986 Cannes Film Festival; it had a generally positive reaction there (though three Aboriginal activists walked out of the official screening) but won no prizes. It was nominated for seven Australian Film Institute Awards,

The Fringe Dwellers. *Kristina Nehm, Kylie Belling, Denis Walker, Bob Maza, Justine Saunders.*

including Best Film, Director and Actress, but won only for best adapted screenplay: a curious decision in the circumstances, since the screenplay is the weakest element. Despite valiant efforts on the part of Roadshow, the distributors, it did only modest business. The controversy continued, with Aboriginal activists like playwright Bob Merritt (author of that remarkable drama *The Cake Man*) condemning the film as 'a figment of a non-Aboriginal's imagination' and 'an advertisement for the world to see exactly how Aboriginal people *aren't*.'

Before *The Fringe Dwellers* was made, Merritt himself had been involved in the scripting of two feature films. The first, *THE CITY'S EDGE* (1983), was written by Merritt in collaboration with Ken Quinnell, a critic-turned-screenwriter (*Hoodwink*) who made his debut as director with this project. Originally titled *Running Man*, the film focuses its attention mainly on the white characters, all of whom live in a sleazy Bondi flat; but there is a major Aboriginal character, Jack Collins (played by Tommy Lewis of *Jimmie Blacksmith* fame), who is the lover of Laura (Katrina Foster), a young woman once sexually involved with her brother, Jim (Mark Lee).

The film suffers from some embarrassingly hackneyed dialogue ('You're just another of the running men.' 'What are you doing in the company of the damned?') and is unremittingly sombre and one-key until it explodes into violence in the final reel. It was rumoured at the time that Quinnell had difficulty persuading his crew to try out some of his theoretical ideas. In any event, the film quickly faded into oblivion; it was never released in Australia though, oddly enough, Cannon picked it up for the UK. Merritt writes it off as necessary to create a track record.

The other feature on which Merritt worked (and on which Quinnell was also briefly involved) was *SHORT CHANGED* (1985). It was directed by George Ogilvie, who had met Merritt when he was teaching at Eora, an Aboriginal visual arts and performance centre in Redfern which Merritt had founded. Ogilvie had won Merritt's confidence, and that of the actors at the centre, and so was a natural choice to direct the screenplay, which, like *The City's Edge*, was supported by the NSWFC.

'I worked a great deal with Bob on the script,' says Ogilvie. 'It kept changing; I think Bob wanted to say 100,000 things, and we had to hone it down to 1,000. He had so much to say, and we had to discover a way to encapsulate what he wanted and still make a film that was possible to see, as opposed to something people can't bear looking at. I had to take on a great deal of responsibility, but as the director of the film my opinions were important too.'

Casting the part of Tommy, the child of a black father and a middle-class white mother, proved to be a problem until Justine Saunders suggested Jamie Agius, the son of a friend; Ogilvie met him and though the boy had no acting experience was immediately convinced he was right for the part.

The film went into production in April 1985, on a seven-week shoot using Super-16mm. Ogilvie, directing a film solo for the first time (after co-directing *Mad Max Beyond Thunderdome*) was not entirely at ease; this feeling was exacerbated by the fact that he met director of photography Peter Levy, on whom he would have to rely so much, only a little over a week before production began. 'As a white director,' Ogilvie says, 'trying to edge myself into a black world was very difficult. I had their confidence, and I loved working with the actors, but many times I said to Bob: "You have to find a way to direct your own work." Fortunately, *Short Changed* depicts a white world as well.'

An additional problem during production was technical. At rushes, the Super-16mm image seemed slightly out of focus, which naturally caused considerable alarm. It was decided to have the cameras overhauled and continue shooting on 35mm, which obviously added to the budget. After several days, Super-16mm shooting resumed, but the problems continued, and many scenes had to be reshot. Later it was discovered that the problem was not in the camera, but in the projector gate.

Perhaps because of his theatre training, Ogilvie tends to edit the film in his head, which results in a smaller-than-usual use of stock: his ratio is about eight to one. 'I can't shoot something without knowing how it will cut together. I've *got* to know how it will cut. If there's one thing I loathe, it's the reverse close-up: it's just to give you a way out in case the actor doesn't perform well enough. Well, that's no good; *get* the actor to perform well enough—work on it until he does.' Editing time is saved as a result. Ogilvie worked harmoniously with editor Richard Francis-Bruce and composer Chris Neal, and things proceeded well until the final mix. And then, again, there was a technical problem.

During the process of blowing up the Super-16mm footage to 35mm, which was carried out at Atlab, it was discovered that there was a disconcerting jerking of the image. It transpired that the problem was a faulty negative splicer used in the neg-cutting process; when enlarged to 35mm, each splice became obvious because of the jolt that occurred, and some damage was done to the negative. Eventually, producer Ross Matthews made the major decision to move from Atlab to another laboratory, Colorfilm, where a different printer coped better with the problem. These were relatively early days for Super-16mm, and such lessons were being learnt all the time.

These problems delayed the completion of the film, the release of which was further frustrated by the usual curious reluctance of the NSWFC to screen its productions for anyone who might be able to give support and advice. As a result, rumours spread around the industry that the film was a dud, which could not have been further from the truth. If *The Fringe Dwellers* presents a rose-coloured view of contemporary Aboriginal life, *Short Changed* confronts the problems head-on. The film depicts the everyday racism of white Australians unflinchingly: Stuart, given temporary access to his son by the court, is at first unable to rent an apartment solely because of his colour. White children are seen to have ingrained racial attitudes ('My dad says blacks are useless'), and the only barrister who will help Stuart in his struggle is Sri Lankan. Interestingly, the character of Alison comes across as less defined than that of Stuart, and we are never quite sure why she would have married him in the first place. Overall, though, *Short Changed* is a chilling reminder of the problems faced by urban Aborigines.

GU eventually bought *Short Changed* (in a package with other NSWFC productions), but the release, late in 1986, was half-hearted; the film was nominated in a couple of categories in the 1986 Australian Film Institute Awards, but won nothing. Its fate reinforced the commonly held opinion that films about blacks do not work, but with better handling and fewer delays it might have had the impact it deserved.

Perhaps the most authentic Aboriginal film of the 80s, however, is *WRONG SIDE OF THE ROAD* (1981), a dramatised documentary in which director Ned Lander (not to be confused with the actor of the same name who appears in *Puberty Blues* and *Starstruck*) takes us into the world of two Aboriginal rock groups, Us Mob and No Fixed Address. The idea was to recreate on film events the musicians had themselves experienced, mostly in small country towns. There is constant conflict with the law (Chris Haywood providing a sharp cameo as a racist cop) and a telling scene in which a small-town hotelkeeper breaks his contract with the band on discovering they are black. The music is good, and the film (shot on 16mm and made on the tightest of budgets) is filled with barely restrained anger but, at the same time, with an energy and optimism that is infectious. The screenplay was written in collaboration with the cast, who essentially play themselves, and the film unit was based in Adelaide, with shooting taking place all over South Australia.

Chris Haywood recalls: 'It was an important film at the time, and it was made on a very low budget. My accommodation was a couch in the editing room, which was in an Aboriginal hostel. The hostel seemed to catch fire every night, so I didn't get any sleep the first week.' Shortly after filming was completed, one of the musicians, John John, a drummer, had his hands smashed by police, indicating that the disturbing scenes shown in the film were all too close to reality.

Wrong Side of the Road won the Jury Prize at the 1981 AFI awards, enjoyed a limited theatrical release, and was screened (four-letter words and all) on SBS.

Given that the Aboriginal voice was heard so fleetingly in the Australian films of the 80s, it is to be regretted that at least one intriguing project never got off the ground. In 1980, it was announced that actor David Gulpilil had written a screenplay called *Billy West*, in which he hoped to act, together with Canadian singer Buffy St Marie, and co-direct (with Bill Leimbach). Nothing ever came of this.

The only other film of the 80s to present an Aboriginal character in any serious way was Bill Bennett's *BACKLASH* (1986). Production came about in an unusual way. Says Bennett, 'I'd raised $175,000 to make a documentary about a black tracker called Jimmy James. I had the money sitting in the trust account in Canberra for two years; I'd done a lot of research, but something prevented me making the film. Meanwhile, I'd had the idea for *Backlash*, and I suddenly wondered if it would be possible to make a feature film for $175,000.' In the event, it proved impossible; the final budget was $225,000, and Bennett had to add $50,000 of his own money.

It was a complicated procedure to obtain approval from the tax department, Home Affairs and investors for the switch, but Bennett achieved this, and also received money from J. C. Williamson (to replace funding originally promised by the BBC and the ABC for the black tracker film). Bennett wrote a 26-page treatment, hired his actors, and went off to Broken Hill with a crew of six.

'One thing I learnt from *A Street to Die*,' he says, 'was that if you want to tackle a heavy subject, it makes good sense to get some levity into it. For *Backlash*, I needed an actor with a real edge, and I'd always admired David Argue's work. I'd been warned that he was hard to

Backlash. *David Argue, Gia Carides, Lydia Miller.*

control, but I figured that if I treated him right, I'd be able to control him.' He saw Argue on stage in *Bouncers*, and was extremely impressed with his improvisational work (he had already planned to use improvisation on *Backlash*). At around the same time he saw Gia Carides in *Theatre Sports* at Belvoir Street. Casting the role of Kath, the Aboriginal prisoner, proved more difficult: in the end, Bennett found Lydia Miller, who was not an actress at all, but a nurse. 'She was a friend of a friend,' he says. 'Highly intelligent, with a very strong political and social outlook: I took a gamble.'

The first problem in the relationship between Bennett and David Argue occurred just a few days before they were due to leave for location: although this was to be a road movie entailing a lot of driving, Argue did not have a driver's licence, something he had omitted to tell Bennett. He passed his driver's test only with difficulty. Then, when the cast and crew arrived in Broken Hill, at a motel where special rates had been arranged, the manager was less than happy about Argue's presence: it appears that the same motel had been used as a base for *Razorback*, and Argue, who had also been in that film, had left a deep impression on the management. Moreover, he had brought with him a mangy-looking dog which Bennett barred from the set, and which then spent the days frightening the motel staff and destroying the room.

The first week of shooting passed without problems. To save money, rushes were sent back to Sydney where editor Denise Hunter synched them; they were then photographed by a video camera (on the editing machine) and the VHS tapes were sent back to the motel. Because the motel was small, and the crew had it virtually to themselves, these rushes were piped through the motel's central system to every room.

During the second week, the heat and the isolation started to affect people. Bennett's relationship with Argue started to break down; the actor refused simple instructions and they had some bitter and heated arguments, which sometimes became violent. 'It was a really tough time,' says Bennett. 'I was putting everybody under a lot of pressure. And some of what happened was my fault, because I could see the tensions building and I thought I could use those tensions in the film. So I didn't do anything to de-fuse them; in retrospect, that was an unwise thing.'

The inevitable explosion occurred on the day they shot the scene where Trevor (Argue) goes to interrogate the publican's wife. Antagonism between director and actor had become acute; the atmosphere was electric. The spark came over a simple matter of colour. 'The curtains in the room were green, and the bed-covers were green too,' says Bennett. 'I didn't want the room to look so green. In the next room there were orange bed-covers, and I wanted the green ones replaced with them.' Argue became angry, and the argument that followed could be heard all over the pub; the scene was completed only with the greatest of difficulty. Unfortunately, in the finished film the off-screen drama results in an extraordinarily unconvincing moment in an otherwise powerful movie.

The remainder of filming was strained. Bennett spent a lot of time locked in his motel room. 'At the end of *Backlash* I wanted to get out of film,' he says. 'It upset me terribly. One Sunday, locked in my room watching cricket on television, I checked my pulse—it didn't drop below 120 all day. For about six weeks, the palms of my hands peeled; I put it down to the tension. But I learnt a lot from the film. I realise I should have done the confession scene again, but I'd had a gutful by then.'

With a week of shooting left, Argue announced he was leaving. It was a crisis for Bennett: he had paid everyone working on the film (the actors were getting double the Equity minimum) but not only had he taken no money himself—he had invested $50,000. 'I phoned the production manager in Sydney,' says Bennett, 'and explained the situation. I said: "Look, David's signed a contract—he can't do this." There was an awful pause on the other end of the phone. I said: "He *has* signed his contract, hasn't he?" He hadn't signed it, and I hadn't been told. So I called everyone together and said: "That's it! Pack up! We're all going." Ten minutes later, David came to me and said: "I want to complete the film." We completed the film.'

The production problems are evident only towards the end; for almost all its length, *Backlash* is indeed a powerful variation on the road movie genre. The improvisation of Argue and Gia Carides works extremely well, and Bennett manages to fill the film with a barely defined menace that is extremely unsettling. Less successful are the scenes involving actors other than the principals. Tony Wilson's cinematography is handsome, and the editing of Denise Hunter is extremely precise. Above all it is a film filled with energy and vigour which, given its production history and the financial restrictions involved, is little short of miraculous.

The film was selected as the closing-night attraction in the prestigious 'Un Certain Regard' sidebar to the official Cannes Film Festival programme, and there was considerable international interest. Distributed by the Dendy group in Australia, the film received generally positive reviews, and attracted enough customers to cover its modest costs. But it left Bennett disenchanted with improvisation as a method of working with actors.

T here is, however, a considerable degree of improvisation in *MALPRACTICE* and *MORTGAGE* (both 1989), films Bennett directed for television and which would normally fall outside the scope of this book, were it not for the fact that, like *Backlash*, *Malpractice* was chosen to close the 'Un Certain Regard' section of Cannes. The films are part of a series of drama-documentaries produced at Film Australia for the Nine Network (others had been *Prejudice* and *Custody*), all of them dealing with social issues. 'Tristram Miall [the executive producer of the series] called me up out of the blue,' says Bennett, 'and asked me if I'd like to do one of the series. I was taken with the idea because it gave me a chance to work with improvisation again; I wanted to see if I could make it work this time. It requires a long

Malpractice. *Bob Baines, Caz Lederman.*
(Photo: *Jim Townley.*)

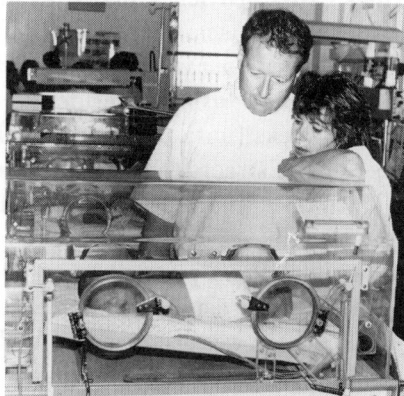

rehearsal period, precise casting and the right subject. And you have to have total commitment from the actors; they have to trust that you'll do the right thing by them.'

In *Malpractice*, the professional actors give extraordinary performances: Caz Lederman as Coral Davis, the woman who undergoes a traumatic confinement; Bob Baines as her stolid husband; Ian Gilmour as the inexperienced, harassed young intern; Pat Thomson as the troubled nursing sister; and Janet Stanley as a senior nurse (Stanley, sadly, died soon after shooting was completed). The scenes in which Coral Davis gives birth are so shattering, they tend to unbalance the film so that the climactic trial sequence (which employs a number of real-life members of the legal profession) comes as an anti-climax.

Mortgage, made later the same year, is even more effective, thanks to harrowingly good performances by Brian Vriends and (especially) Doris Younane as a married couple who, like Mr and Mrs Blandings in the famous American comedy, want to build their dream house. This is far from comedy, however, and the film is as much about the pressures on the marriage as it is about the pitfalls in building a home. One sequence, after the husband has stayed out all night, involves a painful, near-violent 'domestic' which ranks alongside scenes in *My First Wife* and *Phobia* in terms of sheer power. By this time, Bennett has perfected his improvisational techniques.

D uring the early 70s, there was a much-publicised series of confrontations between the Builders Labourers' Federation (led by Jack Mundey) and developers over 'green bans' placed on buildings by the union. The main focus of attention was Victoria Street in Sydney's Kings Cross district, a magnificent tree-lined street composed of large residential houses, many of which had been bought by a developer who planned to raze them and build modern apartments. The BLF, in an alliance with the residents, occupied the threatened houses for several weeks (until they were finally ousted by the police); eventually, most of the street (though not all of it) was saved. During this period, a journalist, Juanita Nielsen, who edited a small local newspaper disappeared: her body has never been found. In 1981, two films were made about these events.

The first to get under way was *THE KILLING OF ANGEL STREET* (1981), which was produced by Anthony Buckley and directed by Donald Crombie; it was their third film together, after *Caddie* and *The Irishman*.

Buckley recalls: 'We read about the case while we were on location for *The Irishman*, and Michael Craig [the lead actor in that film] tackled the first screenplay, which had the working title, *The Juanita Factor*. Later, Cecil Holmes was brought in and added a further political dimension. But we discovered it was a minefield of legal problems: each draft of the script was read by a QC, and every time something had to be deleted or changed.' During this period, word got out that a film on the subject was being planned. A representative of Frank Theeman, the developer involved in the Victoria Street events, requested a copy of the script: he was refused.

Eventually, the script was completely fictionalised and the names changed. The film was budgeted at $1.3 million, and the AFC advised Buckley that, for a budget of this size, it was advisable to bring in an international star. Crombie approached Julie Christie; despite a small battle with Actors Equity, triggered after a complaint to the union from someone connected with the other film then being planned on the same subject, a complaint Equity rejected, Christie seemed set for the part. But Buckley had been negotiating with David Thomas of UAA to finance the film, and when it came to the crunch, and Christie had to be paid, UAA did not come up with the money. 'So we lost Julie Christie,' says Buckley. 'We approached Helen Morse, but she didn't think the script was strong enough. We brought out Evan Jones [the British writer who had worked with Joseph Losey and had scripted Ted Kotcheff's *Wake in Fright*], and he spent a month working on added layers to the script; Helen was in regular contact with him. But then, for reasons I've never understood, she left a letter under my door saying she didn't want to do the film.' It was, coincidentally, at the launching of my book, *The Last New Wave*, that Buckley fell into conversation with actress Elizabeth Alexander and decided she would be right for the part.

With some difficulty, Buckley extracted himself from the UAA deal and raised the money for the film through a stockbroker (helped by the backing of GU).

The production company constructed, with bricks and mortar, an entire dummy row of houses at the bottom of a street in East Balmain. The New South Wales police authorities gave the filmmakers no co-operation in making the film, though the local Balmain police were extremely helpful and allowed filming of their vehicles. Buckley was also aware that the filming was being observed: 'A paddy wagon which didn't come from the Balmain police station would be parked at the

The Killing of Angel Street. *Elizabeth Alexander, John Hargreaves.*

end of the street on many nights watching us film. We never discovered where it came from.' But the most unusual warning came, in an oblique way, from a prominent State Liberal Party politician. Buckley was Deputy Chair of the Australian Film and Television School, and was asked if he could attend a meeting with the politician at the school. 'Storry Walton [Director of the school] was intrigued to know why this politician wanted to come to the school. We gave him a conducted tour, at the end of which he turned to me and said: "What's this film you're making on Juanita Nielsen?" I told him it wasn't about Juanita Nielsen. He said: "You'd better be very careful. You might come home and find that your dog's dead." It was very strange, because he obviously didn't want to see the Film School at all—he just wanted to find out about the film.'

The Killing of Angel Street pulls few punches, though it is a little soft at the edges. It depicts an apolitical woman gradually swept along by a tide of events involving the death of her father in a fire set in the terrace house which he refuses to sell to a developer. Jessica (a fine performance from Elizabeth Alexander) discovers more about the political background from Elliot (John Hargreaves), a communist. The script suggests that the developer is being used by criminals involved in sex-club operations: the police who harass Jessica (and, presumably, murder Elliot) are not real police but thugs in police uniform. But having made these points, the picture then ends on a startling scene in which a senior police officer (Norman Kaye) is talking on the phone to the Police Minister, who assures him a 'safe' judge will be selected to head the inevitable enquiry.

The film remains controversial to the last. 'It didn't open to very good figures,' says Buckley. 'But it was starting to build when it was suddenly taken off. I believe pressure was put on GU. David Williams always supported the film, but there were a lot of people around who didn't want it made; the subject matter was too close to the bone. And yet you look at it now, and it's probably just a good telemovie.' The film represented Australia at the 1982 Berlin Film Festival, where it received a special award and was particularly appreciated by audiences who identified with militant efforts to save old residential buildings from the developers' clutches.

The other film made at about the same time on the same subject was *HEATWAVE* (1981), which was the second feature directed by Phillip Noyce. This project was originally titled *King's Cross*, and was written by Tim Gooding and Mark Stiles, both of whom eventually dropped out; the final script was by Noyce and Mark Rosenberg.

The ground covered is very similar to that of *The Killing of Angel Street*, though the film is more melodramatic. The central character is a young activist (Judy Davis) who has an unlikely relationship with a yuppie architect (Richard Moir); the Juanita Nielsen character is called Mary Ford (Carole Skinner) and, like Nielsen, she publishes her own small newspaper: the last shot of the film reveals that Mary's body has been thrown into a drain on the site of the development.

The most interesting character in *Heatwave* is that of the developer, Peter Houseman, played to the hilt by Chris Haywood as a brash, ambitious Pom (a kind of Alan Bond in embryo). Interestingly, the script shares with *Angel Street* the idea that the developer is being used by a Mr Big of crime, in this case a very ethnic-looking man called Molnar (Frank Gallacher) who runs a sex club.

Noyce is a better director than Crombie, and most of *Heatwave* is brilliantly done, with the sweltering summer weather used to add to the increasing tension. The dialogue crackles, the performances are good (they include Bill Hunter as Moir's partner and Anna Jemison as his trendy wife) and the pace is vibrant. Unfortunately, it all spins out of control in the end, as if Noyce just did not know how to bring the story to a conclusion; the scene in which two avenging women, each carrying a gun, arrive simultaneously at Mr Big's club at the stroke of midnight on New Year's Eve is really a bit much to take, and the make-up used to depict the victims of the bloody shoot-out that follows is extremely unconvincing.

In the end, neither *The Killing of Angel Street* nor *Heatwave* are completely satisfactory, but they do represent exciting and provocative attempts to take important social issues and bring them to a wide audience.

Other films of the 80s that deal with social issues have been uneven.

Don McLennan's *HARD KNOCKS* (1980) is certainly one of the better ones. McLennan (b. 1950 in Leeton, NSW) spent most of his childhood on his parents' property on King Island in Bass Strait; he decided he preferred films to football, and eventually persuaded his parents that television (at the time the only real option) would make a viable career. At the age of seventeen he was taken to Sydney where he obtained a humble job at the ABC. A year later, he landed a job as unit runner on Fauna Productions' television series *Skippy* and, soon afterwards, was elevated to third assistant director on Fauna's feature, *The Intruders*. In 1970, he moved to Melbourne to work for Crawfords: he was assistant on *Division 4* for a time (which is where he met his future partner, Zbigniew Friedrich, who was also assistant director on the series). After hours, he managed the East End (Village) cinema in Bourke St, where he became fascinated with Andy Warhol–Paul Morrissey films. In 1974, he applied to the AFC for money from the Creative Development Branch; he remembers that Fred Schepisi was on the assessment panel. With the grant he made *Point of Departure*, a half-hour improvised drama, using film stock 'nicked from work and processed at Channel 10 after hours'. Friedrich photographed and edited the film. At about this time, the friends formed a company, Ukiyo Films; the name was derived from a Jade Warrior album—later they discovered 'ukiyo' is Japanese for 'floating world'.

Hard Knocks originally started out as *Sam*, and again used CDB funding. McLennan says: 'I came across a story in the paper about a girl who'd been in prison and later became a model; and I thought "That's a great idea for a film." So I concocted a storyline inspired by that idea and submitted it to the CDB for script development money, which they granted; and later they gave me $33,500 to make it as a 50-minute film. Then, I had an opportunity to go on my first overseas trip. I saw a lot of films in London and Paris that I'd never had a chance to see here; very stimulating. When I returned, I decided there wasn't any point making a 50-minute film nobody would want to see—so I revised the script, and we started shooting.' (In an interview in *Cinema Papers*, no. 30, McLennan states that he never intended to make a 50-minute film: 'I blatantly lied my way through the assessment.')

McLennan met Tracy Mann at an audition: she had appeared in the television series *The Box*, but had done little else at the time. 'She looked right,' he says, 'and her attitude was right. There was a vulnerability about her, but also a certain "Don't mess with me" toughness.' During a casting trip to Sydney, McLennan met several local actors, including Bill Hunter, Max Cullen and Tony Barry, in a bar; he told them about the film, and they expressed interest. 'I haven't got the money for you guys,' McLennan told them—but the three were so keen that they did it 'for beer money, plus air fares and accommodation.'

McLennan used all the CDB money, and paid for the final footage from the lab with his Bankcard. He and Friedrich bought an upright Movieola for $400 and spent six months editing the film in his bedroom; the first cut ran 100 minutes. 'We had a double-head screening for the CDB assessors and they said "Sorry. We contracted to make a 50-minute film, and this isn't what we wanted." ' The matter received publicity through the *Cinema Papers* interview in which McLennan was critical of the CDB assessors, who included director Donald Crombie. CDB manager Lachie Shaw, and Crombie, were given right of reply; Shaw in his comments criticised *Cinema Papers* for publishing McLennan's criticisms; Crombie accused McLennan of 'lacking professional morality' for 'his evident pleasure in (unsuccessfully) attempting to screw the system.'

The assessors' comments had, indeed, been harsh: *Hard Knocks* was described as being 'flawed', 'too long', 'unsaleable', and 'two-dimensional'. The assessors were 'very disappointed' and 'disheartened'. One felt: 'The applicant seems unaware of the moral delinquency he has perpetrated in spending his funds on shooting.' Another, that 'The filmmaker was more concerned to beat the system than attune himself to his material.'

McLennan's request for funds to proceed to a 16mm answer print, or, better still, a 35mm print, was denied. McLennan says: 'At that

Hard Knocks. *Tracy Mann.*

point, we had a fine-cut double-head feature for only $33,500. We'd done very well with the money we had—we just needed the money to finish it off. So, it sat on the shelf for six months; I was on the dole and it was tough.' By chance, McLennan met Trevor Lucas, an executive in a film company called Andromeda; Lucas liked the film, and eventually bought out the AFC and also paid for the completion.

Once the film was available for public screenings, it became evident that the AFC and its assessors had been more concerned with McLennan's attempts to 'screw the system' than with the quality of the product. *Hard Knocks* proved to be one of the outstanding films of 1980, it won for Tracy Mann the Best Actress prize at the AFI awards, as well as the Jury Award for the film itself. Mann is, indeed, heartbreakingly good as Sam, an independent young woman harassed by the police (Bill Hunter and Max Cullen in good form as the repulsive lawmen) yet succeeding in living her own life, being her own woman. Given appreciative reviews, the film had a modestly successful release.

A very different kind of independent woman, seen in a very different social context, was to be found in *SHAME* (1987), made in Western Australia by director Steve Jodrell, who had previously explored the world of macho men in his GU Award-winner, *The Bucks' Party* (1978). Jodrell (b. 1949 in Perth) was a stage actor and director, who, for ten years (1974–84), lectured on film and drama at Curtin University.

The screenplay for *Shame* was written by Sydney writers Beverly Blankenship and Michael Brindley; Blankenship had seen *Mad Max*, and became excited about the possibility of writing a film about a *woman* on a motorcycle. She and Brindley discussed ideas for such a character, which gradually took the form of a modern western with classic western themes: the stranger, the town secret (compare *Bad Day at Black Rock*). Blankenship wrote an 11-page outline, and money was received from the Women's Film Fund for the first draft screenplay; this decision was not without controversy, because some of the WFF assessors felt that a subject which dealt with violence should not be supported.

At the beginning, Blankenship and Brindley offered the screenplay to producer Joan Long, but she became involved in preparations for *Silver City* and did not renew her option. She had, meanwhile, left a copy of the screenplay with Perth-based producer Paul Barron who became enthusiastic about it. Not everyone was, however. Much later, when Brindley was head of the Script Development Branch at the

AFC, he discovered just how damning some of the assessments of *Shame* had been.

Barron showed the screenplay to Steve Jodrell. 'It was the best I'd read in a long time,' Jodrell says. 'I liked the western elements, the social commitment and the fact that this important message was contained within the formula of a drive-in style movie.'

'It was a very difficult film to get financed,' says Barron. 'I wanted Steve, a first-time feature director, to do it; we were still a relatively young company; there was no place for an American lead.' Eventually, UAA, the Perth-based finance company, agreed to back the film and provided the distribution guarantee; without them, says Barron, it would not have been made. Barron was determined to make the film: 'I was right behind it from Day One,' he says. 'And when I saw the finished film, I was very moved.'

Jodrell had wanted the same kind of small-town, dusty, isolated outback feeling Ted Kotcheff had captured in *Wake in Fright* (1971); but the film's budget ($1.7 million) would not allow such a distant location, so it was shot, on a six-week schedule, in the small country town of Toojay, about one hour out of Perth. One problem: Toojay was on a main highway, which sometimes had to be closed for filming.

Jodrell tested several actresses for the key leading role, and finally selected Deborra-Lee Furness, who is magnificent as the courageous, strong-willed outsider who discovers the town's nasty secret. The film was shot not without difficulty: the Super-16mm camera kept breaking down, causing loss of vital shooting time. The usual pressures of time and budget also weighed on the first-time director.

Shame exposes, like no feature film since *Wake in Fright*, the dark side of Australian mateship. The louts who terrorise the women in the town are of all ages: they are protected by the weak, vacillating cop, Cuddy (who performs much the same function as the sheriff, played by Robert Keith, in *The Wild One*) and even, for a while, by the menfolk of the frightened women (like Tim Curtis, played with all his customary strength and integrity by Tony Barry). When Furness, the out-of-town catalyst for all the violence, convincingly fights back, the stage is set for a *Straw Dogs*-style climax which is genuinely chilling. The combination of serious social comment and convincing drama is, indeed, rare in the Australian cinema.

Blankenship and Brindley were not entirely happy with the way their script had been filmed, however. 'The first eleven minutes of the film don't really work,' says Brindley, 'because only the central character's point of view is presented. Some of the casting could have been better, and, stylistically, we had envisaged more of a genre piece than a social realist piece.' Nevertheless, he says, 'women still come up to us and thank us for writing a film that means so much to them; it really did touch a lot of people.'

Shame should have scooped the pool at the 1988 AFI awards: instead, it was deemed to be ineligible by Institute officials. The film had been entered in the 1987 awards, but in an incomplete version; as soon as Paul Barron discovered this, he withdrew it with the approval of the AFI's Awards Manager, who assured him the film could be entered in its completed version the following year. Says Barron: 'We found out that the material supplied was inadequate. When you're based in Perth, it isn't always to easy to keep on top of that sort of thing. What we sent was a work print, with spaces still in it, which was in no way acceptable. But when it was rejected the following year, and I read in *Variety* an admission that we *had* been told we could resubmit it, but that the person who told us that was wrong . . . Well, I'm no longer a member of the AFI.' The AFI won no points at all in the industry for its ham-fisted decision over *Shame*, and the film's box-office career undoubtedly suffered as a result of the bureaucratic bungling.

Despite this, *Shame* had a reasonably good run at the box-office in Australia, was selected for several overseas festivals, and was released in a number of countries. Says Jodrell: 'Reactions to it were always very strong. It seems to have been a catharsis for a lot of women. I was taken to be some kind of expert in sexual abuse, which of course I'm not, and I was told some terrifying stories by women.'

N ot many feature films dealing with political subjects are made in Australia, but during the 80s, John Duigan directed two. *FAR EAST* (1982) started out as a much more austere project than it eventually became. 'I often think I should have stuck with my early intentions,' says Duigan, 'which were to make a film something like Volker Schlondorff's *Circle of Deceit* [which was set in war-torn Beirut]. It would have been much more gruelling, and dealt with a situation where members of the Philippines New People's Army surrounded the hall where an international business conference was going on.' But once Duigan and producer Richard Mason decided they wanted to work with Bryan Brown again (they had made *Winter of Our Dreams* together the previous year), they set the original idea aside and Duigan worked on a script whose starting point was inspired by the basic set-up of *Casablanca*. 'The moral realities in the Philippines are completely different from those during the Second World War, where the moral issues were much more clear-cut.'

The film is notable not least because it features the only cinema performance in the 80s of Helen Morse, who had made such an impression in *Caddie* (1976). Morse had just co-starred with Bryan Brown in David Stevens' mini-series *A Town Like Alice*, and Duigan decided to pair them again in his new film. 'The teaming of them was shouted about in the press at the time,' says Duigan. 'But my reason for using them was simply that they were perfect for the roles.'

To shoot the film, Duigan chose Brian Probyn, the British cinematographer whose work included *Poor Cow* and *Badlands*. Probyn, who was suffering from heart disease, had been living in Australia for a number of years, and had shot such films as *The Mango Tree* and Tom Cowan's *Sweet Dreamers*. *Far East* was his final film; he died later the same year.

Mason had financed the film through Filmco, on a budget of $1.3 million. It was a comparatively high budget for the time because of the necessity of Asian shooting. After Peter Weir's experiences of filming *The Year of Living Dangerously* in Manila, there was no question of filming in the Philippines; instead, Macao was used for eight days as a location. 'It was a difficult decision,' says Duigan, 'because Manila is such a unique city. But *Far East* was critical of the Marcos regime, and it would have been far too dangerous. It was a weakness of the film that we couldn't shoot there.'

In the end, though, politics in *Far East* take a back seat to good old-fashioned romance. The three leads are excellent; the third being John Bell, in an all-too-rare screen appearance as Morse's rather dry, intellectual husband. The dialogue is snappy, and the moral questions are unflinchingly raised. No other fictional film comments so forcefully on Australia's role in Asia, and this fact mitigates the disappointingly melodramatic ending, with its almost Rambo-like heroics. Says Duigan: 'I wanted to bring a serious theme to a mainstream audience. I wanted to remain within the logic of the genre, which seemed to call for that kind of resolution.'

Given the popularity of its lead actors, and the exoticism of the setting and plot, it is no wonder that *Far East* was a success. It is quite unlike Duigan's other films, which are usually far more cerebral, though he did tackle the morality of Third World politics again in his American film, *Romero* (1989). Meanwhile, his next Australian film, also produced by Richard Mason, dealt with a political theme in an altogether different way.

This was *ONE NIGHT STAND* (1984), which is also significant because it was the first production of Hoyts–Edgley, a production company formed in the wake of the success of *The Man from Snowy River* and *Phar Lap*; it is odd that such an uncharacteristic project should have been the first Hoyts–Edgley picture, because *One Night Stand* has no less a theme than the destruction of Sydney (and, presumably, the world) as a result of nuclear war.

'The film was a study of the naivete of our perceptions of the threat of nuclear war,' says Duigan. 'It was quite a subtle and elusive subject for a mainstream film.' The film was made not long after American films on the same subject (*The Day After*, *Testament*) had raised the question of nuclear war all over again, but Duigan emphasises the *banality* of the end of the world, and takes the point of view of four young people, three Australians and one American sailor, setting almost the entire film within the Sydney Opera House on a fateful New Year's Eve.

'We wanted to film all of it in the Opera House, but it was too expensive, so we shot about ten days there and the rest in the Seymour Centre.' But the film is not all interiors: there is some marvellous photography (by Tom Cowan) early in the film of a Sydney street that looks more like a set than a real street. 'I wanted to match the flimsiness and artificiality of the theatrical world inside the Opera House with the flimsiness of the real world,' explains Duigan. 'We found a location where we could film a corner building in such a way as to make it look like a theatre set.'

During the long night, the quartet spend some time watching Fritz Lang's *Metropolis*: 'Images of Armageddon of a different kind,' says Duigan. 'And another level of artificiality. Images of buildings tumbling down and water welling up from below. All part of the sense of dislocation and surreality. I also had them play Strip Jack Naked wearing costumes they'd found from a production of *Alice in Wonderland*.'

The four young actors, all of them newcomers, were cast after a series of auditions, and the acting is uneven. But the film's strange sense of humour, and the devastating impact of the final reel, more than compensate for uncertainties in the middle section of the film. An extraordinarily complex sound mix adds a further dimension.

One Night Stand was not a success. 'It was completely misunderstood,' says Duigan. 'I was told it was grossly immoral to ridicule an issue as important as nuclear war. The film never found an audience, so obviously I failed in that respect. I think the expressionistic devices I used, plus the heightened, slightly theatrical, acting style I wanted, puzzled and even annoyed people. I wanted the characters to become disjointed and even ludicrous, such as the scene in which they walk out carrying umbrellas to keep the fall-out off their heads. Audiences today are so conditioned by certain narrative forms that they don't want a mix of social realism and satire. I made a conscious attempt to try to give a different kind of challenge to audiences, and I know the film became a cult in some places, but generally people didn't respond. I saw it again recently, and parts of it are quite sluggish, especially near the start. But there are images I like, such as the lone wind-surfer on the Harbour.'

Many political films end up preaching only to the converted, of course. Martha Ansara, with *THE PURSUIT OF HAPPINESS* (1987) tried to reach a wider audience by embellishing her basic story—the radicalisation of an 'ordinary' Fremantle woman (Laura Black) whose teenage daughter (Anna Gare) becomes a member of an anti-nuclear rock group—with a domestic drama involving the woman's right-wing husband (Peter Hardy).

American-born Ansara had long been a radical member of Sydney's film community, active in politics and feminism. In 1987, she won the Byron Kennedy Award for her work in cinema.

Ansara has explained that the film, funded partly from the sale of a Victoria Cross which had been donated to the People for Nuclear Disarmament, originally started out as a more traditional documentary, but that a number of influences during production altered its course.

The film tries to cover quite a lot of ground: a family in crisis, the anti-nuclear movement, and a conspiracy theory suggesting a link between syndicates formed to defend the America's Cup and arms dealers. The most successful element of all these is the political awakening of the central character, convincingly played by Laura Black (who, with other cast members, contributed to the screenplay). It is an emotional subject, and that is what lifts it above the usual worthy, but didactic, low-budget political film.

A strong female character is also the focal point of *TRAPS* (1985), which, like *The Pursuit of Happiness*, mixes reality with fiction.   Carolyn Howard plays a dogged journalist investigating a conspiracy theory linking highly placed members of the Labor Party with the CIA, and she talks to a number of journalists who tell her things they are unable to use themselves for fear of libel laws. The film, co-written, produced and directed by John Hughes, accurately captures the disenchantment of traditional Labor voters with the policies of the Hawke government, and a scene in which a suave conservative castigates modern journalism as a whole is a scary look at the face of the Right.

The Pursuit of Happiness was distributed by the AFI and enjoyed a modest success; *Traps*, perhaps even more deserving of attention, seems to have had all too few public screenings. *AGAINST THE GRAIN* (1980), another low-budget political film, directed by Tim Burns, suffers from its self-conscious attempts to be 'experimental', and its anti-nuclear message gets lost in the shuffle. Burns' intentions, as expressed in interviews given at the time of the film's release, were ambitious, but the film is too incoherent to make much of an impact and too muddled in its approach: it appears to support acts of urban terrorism.

A ll these films take a left-wing view of the Australian political and social scene. Few films take a right-wing viewpoint, but *COOL CHANGE* (1985) is one that does. This is a production of Geoff Burrowes, and the director is George Miller (2), both of *Man from Snowy River* fame; the film was advertised as 'A modern love story . . .', but it seems more like an attempt to discredit the greenies.

Set in the same High Country of Victoria as *Snowy River*, the film centres on a clash between conservationists (all of them grubby, destructive and hippie-like) and the noble cattlemen of the region. The latter are heroes as colourful as the knights of old: they gallop spectacularly on magnificent horses as they round up their herds. The conservationists want the cattlemen out of the region; the cattlemen naturally object; and hero Jon Blake, a forest ranger whose family are cattlemen, is smack in the middle.

The greenies are seen to be in league with the villainous Labor government, and the Minister for Environment is sneaky enough to despatch a voluptuous aide (Deborra-Lee Furness) to seduce our hero, who prefers local girl Lisa Armytage. This is soap opera at its silliest, with a screenplay (by Patrick Edgeworth) burdened with almost unimaginable clichés, and acting as wooden as the forest in which most of it takes place. Miller's direction totally lacks the impact of the outdoor scenes in *Snowy River*, and the film quickly sank into deserved oblivion.

Patrick Edgeworth also scripted *A STING IN THE TALE* (1989), an odd little comedy about federal politics which, mysteriously, is set in Adelaide rather than Canberra. This Rosa Colosimo production was directed by Eugene Schlusser, whose background includes participation in Peter Watkins' epic documentary, *The Journey*; but this is closer to *Yes, Minister*, without the wit.

The film centres on the relationships between an ambitious woman politician (Diane Craig) with scruples; her married lover (Gary Day), a government minister who is scheming to become Prime Minister; and a ruthless newspaper baron who likes manipulating politicians. He is called Roger Monroe, and, as played by Edwin Hodgeman, there is no doubt what internationally-famous Australian-born media magnate with the same initials he is supposed to be. The fact that this character ends up ruined, earning a living selling newspapers on a Melbourne street, is a naive bit of wish-fulfilment.

But the film is pretty naive throughout, and not written or acted sufficiently sharply to make its ideas work. It is also curiously bitchy about the film industry; when the heroine becomes Arts Minister, with responsibility for film, there are a couple of heavily emphasised comments about what an ordeal it must be to have to watch Australian films or attend the AFI awards (though there might be more than a grain of truth in the latter observation).

More interesting, though hardly more satisfying, is *TO MARKET TO MARKET* (1987), an ambitious drama made by Virginia Rouse, a former stills photographer and assistant to Paul Cox. Rouse's father is a Tasmanian media baron, which possibly explains her jaundiced look at the moulding of a young capitalist, from his days in boarding school until his destruction at the hands of members of his own family.

The film seems needlessly elliptical; Rouse never allows us to get close to the characters, despite Phillip Quast's effective central performance. But there is a sharpness to some of the dialogue: the protagonist's father advises him, 'only create what you can sell' and his girlfriend adds: 'Life is to be got through, not enjoyed.' The film is a bit like that: not enjoyable, but capable of abstract admiration. It does not allow anything more.

Esben Storm's *WITH PREJUDICE* (1982) was made to change public opinion, though, again, its release was so limited that it was probably seen only by those who already supported its aim, which was to shed new light on the Ananda Marga trials. Three members of the sect—Dunn, Anderson and Alister—were accused of the 1978 bombing of the Sydney Hilton Hotel (aspects of the case continue even into the 90s).

Storm (b. 1950 in Fyn, Denmark) had made his reputation with prize-winning short films. His first feature, *27A* (1973), was a fine piece of social realism, and *In Search of Anna* (1978) was an attractive combination of road movie and love story. During the 80s, he worked mostly in television, and, apart from *With Prejudice*, made only one other feature, an uncharacteristic comedy called *Stanley* (see Chapter 10). He can regularly be seen as an actor, often in tiny roles.

With Prejudice takes the view that the three, who were found guilty, were the victims of massive injustice, and uses transcripts from the trials in an attempt to prove it. Despite the presence of several fine actors (including Chris Haywood as a controversial Sydney detective), the film reached only a most limited audience. Filled with speeches and dialogue, it would have fared better as a telemovie.

T he three accused in *With Prejudice* received lengthy prison sentences, so they might have identified with the two films of the decade which dealt with life behind bars. The first of these is *STIR* (1980), the very auspicious feature debut for Stephen Wallace. It was Martha Ansara who introduced Wallace to the original script, which was then titled simply *Bathurst*. She had seen *Love Letters from Teralba Road*, the tough short film Wallace had made with Bryan Brown in 1977 and, representing the Prisoners' Action Group, interested him in this story about the Bathurst Prison riot. At first unattracted to the project, Wallace attended a meeting of PAG and met the writer, Bob Jewson: 'I thought his writing was really good,' says Wallace. 'It was unformed and rough, but, I thought: "If he writes it, I'll do it." '

Jewson had been in Bathurst at the time of the riot (he was a convicted safebreaker) and his work was an accurate reflection of prison life. Wallace had been asked by the NSWFC to put in an application for a film (the Corporation was, at the time, encouraging low-budget features by new directors) and suggested the prison subject. They agreed, and Richard Brennan was brought in as producer. 'It took two years to get it off the ground,' says Brennan. 'There was no possibility that script could be filmed on the kind of money the NSWFC envisaged. Plus, I feared the prison authorities in NSW wouldn't co-operate with us and we'd have real trouble finding a prison.' In the end, private

Stephen Wallace (left) *directing* Stir.

investment, including money from the Atlab laboratory, topped up the budget, which was $425,000.

Bryan Brown was involved from the beginning, and several ex-convicts were cast in supporting roles; by the end of the decade, many of them, including Bob Jewson himself, were back behind bars.

One of the biggest problems was, as Brennan had predicted, to locate a suitable setting, a building that would pass for a prison in which the riot and fire could be staged. This took a long time, but eventually an abandoned prison at Gladstone in South Australia was located. 'We never told the SA government people the film was an attack on the prison system, or that we'd be using explosives,' says Wallace.

Since the film was to be shot in South Australia, and the production still needed some extra investment, Brennan and Wallace approached John Morris, Chief Executive of the SAFC, for help. Morris rejected the script on the grounds that it contained 'too many fucks'; ironically, at the same time, the SAFC was involved in the production of John Lamond's lame and leering sex comedy, *Pacific Banana*.

The shooting of *Stir* took five weeks, preceded by an intense four-week rehearsal period. 'It was the most gruelling shoot I've ever

Stir. *Bryan Brown.*

experienced,' says Wallace. 'Every shot, except one, was inside the jail and the tone of the film was so violent.' Cinematographer Geoff Burton, working within these limitations, did a remarkable job. During production the film was titled *The Promotion of Mr Smith* (a reference to a prison guard promoted at the end of the film), and it was Bob Jewson who suggested the simpler, and evocative, *Stir.*

The film is, as it should be, harsh and unrelenting. Its depiction of prison life is nightmarish, with the guards, if anything, more brutal than the prisoners. Max Phipps, in one of his best roles, is Norton, who seems, at first, to be the most sympathetic of the guards; but when the violent riot breaks out and the prison burns, it is Norton who goes berserk and, in the aftermath, beats China (the Bryan Brown character) almost to death.

As an exposé of prison life, *Stir* had impact, and was a courageous project for the NSWFC to support (after all, the Bathurst riot had taken place in New South Wales while Neville Wran was Premier; and he was still Premier when his Film Corporation backed the film). It was a tough film to sell to the public, and was never a great commercial success, but anyone who doubts Bryan Brown's acting abilities should take a look at *Stir.*

The other prison film of the 80s is equally challenging. *GHOSTS . . . OF THE CIVIL DEAD* (1988) is the work of two young filmmakers, writer-director John Hillcoat (b. 1961 in Queensland) and writer-producer Evan English (b. 1959, Melbourne). They met at

Swinburne Institute of Technology, after Hillcoat spent much of his life in North America. He subsequently made a couple of notorious student films, while English made rock videos for Men At Work, Elvis Costello and Nick Cave.

Their inspiration was a book, *In the Belly of the Beast*, which was written by an American convict, Jack Henry Abbott. Inspired by this dark vision, Hillcoat and Evans planned a film about the manipulation of officially sanctioned violence and the way prisoners are criminalised in prison. 'The point we wanted to make,' says English, 'is that prisons aren't isolated from the outside world.'

While researching the film, the pair met David Hale, a former prison guard at Marion, Illinois, a federal penitentiary known in the US as 'the new Alcatraz'; Hale's shocking revelations about life inside such a high-level security prison became the basis for the screenplay.

To make the film, the two men selected a cast composed of professional actors (including Dave Field, Vincent Gil, Bogdan Koca and Mike Bishop), musicians (Nick Cave, Dave Mason) and ex-convicts: fifty members of the cast had actually served time in prison.

Interiors for the film were shot in a disused government aircraft factory in Melbourne. Three large sets were constructed by production

Ghosts . . . of the Civil Dead. *Gary Francis.*

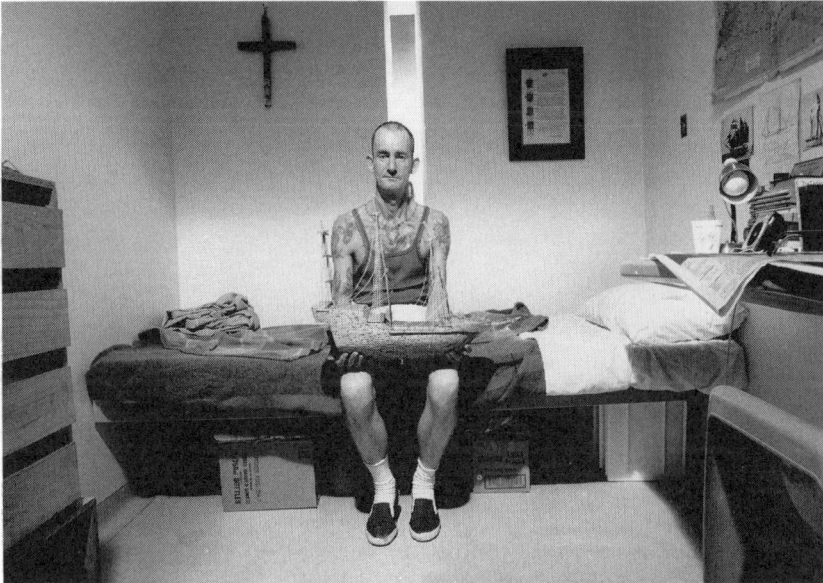

designer Chris Kennedy (whose extraordinary work was recognised at the 1989 AFI awards), each one representing a security level within the prison.

Like *Stir*, *Ghosts . . . of the Civil Dead* has an intensity and a harshness that is extremely unsettling. It is a film designed to confront audiences, and it is remarkably effective in achieving its aim. The filmmakers never flinch from depicting the ugliest aspects of prison life: there are bashings, stabbings, rape and drug abuse. The language is a constant stream of four-letter words, and the mixed cast meshes into an amazingly convincing ensemble. Above all, the film works: it has the power to challenge and disturb, and the final sequence, in which a freed convict strolls through a subway station in the outside world, is quite chilling.

Hillcoat and English promoted their film, which they distributed themselves, with the same passion as they made it. At the Venice Film Festival, where it was very well received, they were arrested for pasting posters on every available tree and wall. They followed the same procedure when the film opened commercially in Australia, and they succeeded in selling it to several countries.

Ghosts is one of the most powerful and disturbing of the socio-political feature films made in Australia during the 80s, its images and sounds reverberating long after the film itself is over. It is a credit to the courageous and uncompromising vision of its creators.

GUN

CRAZY

■
■

T he thriller is the staple of American cinema, but it is not so easy to make a successful thriller in Australia: Australian audiences will accept gun battles in the streets in Hollywood films, but jeer when similar situations are presented in movies set in Sydney or Melbourne. Nonetheless, a number of successful film thrillers have been produced in Australia, and the work of author Peter Corris shows that it is also possible to have a series of private-eye novels set in this country that are just as intriguing, well constructed and well written as anything by Ross McDonald.

Corris' hero is Cliff Hardy, a laconic bloke with a stubborn streak, a limited income, a host of personal problems, and good contacts among the honest cops in the police force. Bryan Brown seemed to be ideal for the role of Hardy, and the actor had enjoyed the books so much that he took an option on them. Originally, it was planned to film *White Meat* first, but in the end a different Corris–Hardy book was brought to the screen with Brown in the lead: this was *THE EMPTY BEACH* (1985), with Bob Weis as executive producer and Tim Read and John Edwards as producers.

Corris himself was hired to write the adaptation. He says: 'I worked happily with [script editor] Sandra Levy over several drafts of the screenplay. We did a soft one, then a tough one, then a mixture. I found out, however, that what the producers were telling me ("Great, Peter") was different from what they were telling themselves and others. I even got documentary proof of this in the form of a note left by accident in a draft. In fact, they didn't like the writing and they hired [former *Z Cars* scriptwriter Keith] Dewhurst. I wasn't too upset by this. I knew I was inexperienced, and that the script wasn't right. I thought putting a pro on the job was a good idea, and I'd have been happy with a joint credit.' Says Weis: 'Corris wrote the first couple of drafts, then begged to be excused. Chris Thomson [the director] and I worked on Keith Dewhurst's final draft.'

The Empty Beach was Thomson's first feature film. Says Weis: 'The film was a stepping stone towards trying to make a genre picture work in Australia without being dominated by the history of that kind of movie, a history that's so strongly American.'

When Corris saw the Dewhurst screenplay he was dismayed. 'I thought it silly and not in the spirit of the book at all,' he says. 'I hated the water death [of Henneberry, the investigative journalist], the car chase, and Bondi Pavilion shoot-out scenes.' Corris also disliked the emphasis on missing tapes that had been brought into the story,

The Empty Beach. *Anna Maria Monticelli, Bryan Brown.*

and what he saw as the rejection of the basic premise of the book: the spelling out of what happened to the missing Singer. 'The story was about deceit,' he says. 'Marion Singer's deceiving of Hardy, her deception of the crims, their deception of each other and, maybe, John Singer's deceiving of Marion. Deception is more interesting than tapes.'

It was not a trouble-free shoot. Anna-Maria Monticelli (formerly Anna Jemison), playing the femme fatale, Anne Winter, was pregnant by the time production actually began, and was fitted with flowing gowns to disguise the fact. Bryan Brown and Chris Thomson did not always see eye to eye, and nor did Thomson and cinematographer John Seale.

Corris was overseas when *The Empty Beach* was filmed, but was back in time to sit in on a rough cut; there was no music, but a tape of the score from *Blade Runner* played in the background. 'I was quite impressed,' says Corris. 'I still disliked a lot of it, but I thought Bryan was good, and I liked John Wood [as the cop]. I was flattered by the experience of hearing words I'd written [in the book] spoken. They [the filmmakers] said there would be more cuts and great music.'

But, when Corris saw the final film, 'dismay was back. I liked the opening song, but the wink at the nuns now looked clichéd and dumb. All the effects striven for were old-hat, done-often-before stuff. I still hated those "stand-out" scenes (water ski murder, car chase, shoot out) and the tapes. I still liked Bryan, especially when he warmed up a bit. I thought it was a mess.'

It is not a mess, by any means, but it could have been better. Like Corris, I saw an early (94-minute) version without music, which was, in fact, more successful than the final, 89-minute, version. The editor (Lindsay Frazer) seems to have cut the film to the bone, so that it speeds by at a pace which is occasionally too fast to take in. Bryan Brown is the perfect Cliff Hardy: cynical, witty, tough and resourceful. Anna-Maria Monticelli and John Wood are effective, too, though some of the supporting actors register less well. The mystery remains intriguing, though the final gun-battle at Bondi is pretty absurd. The title song is totally extraneous, and the jazzy music (Martin Armiger) sometimes intrusive.

The Empty Beach, released by Hoyts, did not perform as well at the box-office as had been hoped ('An absolute disaster,' says Jonathan Chissick), and plans to film other Cliff Hardy novels, with Brown, seem to have been permanently shelved. Still, as Weis points out, 'the film was seen all over the world. It had a known film star in the lead, so it travelled very easily.'

Ray Barrett plays a Mr Big of the Sydney crimeworld in *The Empty Beach*; in *GOODBYE PARADISE* (1982), the other significant private eye movie of the 80s, he plays the dogged hero. The screenplay was the work of Denny Lawrence and Bob Ellis. Says Ellis: 'Denny came to me, and said: "Raymond Chandler, Ray Barrett, Surfers Paradise, Carl Schultz." I said: "Never read any Raymond Chandler, Ray Barrett's too old, like Surfers Paradise, who's Carl Schultz?" Which shows how much you don't know. We went to Surfers, with Barrett (who was a local boy, and famous) and hung around low bars. We wrote it, and the NSWFC liked it. Paul Riomfalvy said: "We're going to make this film, but the director is going to be Mike Thornhill." I saw Thornhill, who said: "You've got to throw away all the voice-over narration and make the girl the main character." I said, "Why don't you make some other film?" '

Determined that Schultz, who had met Lawrence at the ABC, should direct their script, Ellis and Lawrence even offered to buy the project back from the NSWFC; in the end, it took six months before Riomfalvy would agree to Schultz. Schultz, meanwhile, was still recovering from the traumatic experience of his first feature, *Blue Fin*, which he had directed for the SAFC and from which, as outlined in *The Last New Wave*, he had been fired (with some scenes directed by an uncredited Bruce Beresford). He was delighted at the opportunity to direct a second feature. 'It was a very good script,' says Schultz, 'though ultimately rather ambitious for the amount of money we had to make it with. But it was a very happy experience after *Blue Fin*. And I enjoyed working with Bob. He isn't always easy to get along with, but we forged quite a strong friendship.'

The film was shot in the winter of 1981, on a budget of $1.1 million, on locations in and around Surfers. A number of Schultz' ABC colleagues left the Corporation to work on the film, including production designer

George Liddle, editor Richard Francis-Bruce and sound recordist Syd Butterworth.

Made when the Bjelke-Petersen National Party government was firmly in control in Queensland, *Goodbye Paradise* is a scathing satire of politics in the Sunshine State. With a very funny narration, in the best Raymond Chandler tradition, the film deals with an escort agency, religious cult, and an attempted coup (with the aim of seceding from the rest of the State) by a dissident army officer. Through it all staggers Stacey, the alcoholic ex-cop whose memoirs appear to contain some startling revelations about his fellow officers. Ray Barrett is magnificent in the role, and this is undoubtedly his finest screen performance; he won a well-deserved Best Actor award in 1982, and the screenplay also won an award. Robyn Nevin brings world-weary charm to her role as a barroom entertainer who takes Stacey home to bed and expires in his exploding car next day, and there are superb cameos from John Clayton, Robert (Tex) Morton, Lex Marinos, Kris McQuade, Paul Chubb and Carole Skinner.

The film goes right off the rails at the end, however, in an elaborate sequence depicting a pitched battle between army units. Says Ellis: 'The battle sequence was meant to be just a few random explosions while Stacey tottered through them drunkenly. But Schultz thought he had an opportunity to make *Apocalypse Now*, so he set aside a week of the schedule to shoot that sequence. It was wrong because the whole film until that point is seen from Stacey's point of view, and his point of view doesn't include helicopters. The way it was handled distanced the audience suddenly from the film.'

Goodbye Paradise. *Ray Barrett.*

Says Schultz: 'It was never intended to be a realistic film. It's to the credit of the actors, especially Ray Barrett and Robyn Nevin, that they created such realistic characters. So, although I intended it to be overstated right through, it didn't come out that way until the end, so the end came as a huge surprise to the audience.'

Unfortunately, *Goodbye Paradise* was distributed in a very half-hearted way by Filmways; it is a thoroughly entertaining and even crazy film, which could and should have found a wider audience than it did, especially given the AFI awards it won. 'I don't think the NSWFC got behind their films very well,' says Schultz. *Goodbye Paradise* was one of the NSWFC productions whose rights were sold to the mysterious Pepper Distribution Corporation described in Chapter 1. Tentative plans to make a sequel, *Goodbye Adelaide*, set during the Festival of Arts, never materialised.

In *BOOTLEG* (1985), John Flaus gets a starring role as Joe Hart, a Sydney private eye who wears the traditional trenchcoat and trilby but endures the nagging of a possessive mother. In John Prescott's rather self-conscious, ultra-low-budget movie, Hart gets involved with mistaken identity, thuggish cops and bootlegging rackets, but though Prescott obviously knows and loves his film noir, he is also maddeningly anxious to explore the latest trendy screen theories; the result, despite the usual strength Flaus brings to his role, is a confusing, slow, overlong mish-mash.

Though not exactly a private-eye movie, *THE SURFER* (1986) has a similar structure and opens in the same Surfers Paradise location as *Goodbye Paradise*; Gary Day plays a beach bum whose best friend is murdered and who becomes involved in a hectic cross-country chase accompanied by a beautiful, Hitchcockian blonde. This was the second feature of Frank Shields (b. 1947), whose first, *Hostage*, will be discussed later in this chapter. Shields is an energetic director not given to wasting time on unnecessary exposition. His work has been compared to that of the American Samuel Fuller, which explains why, to the amazement of many industry observers, *The Surfer* was invited to participate in the Directors Fortnight segment of the 1987 Cannes Film Festival— after it had been received with derision at the previous year's AFI judging screenings.

David Marsh wrote the female character with Gosia Dobrowolska in mind, and we can see in this film how much like a Hitchcock heroine this actress is: beautiful, with a cool exterior which belies a hot (and, in this case, sometimes treacherous) temperament. 'It was a difficult shoot on a very tight budget,' Dobrowolska says. 'We filmed on a great many different locations during a Queensland summer, so it was pretty tough.'

Her co-star, Gary Day, agrees: 'It was an incredible experience, like a circus. Here we were, making this road movie, changing location every day, in all that heat. I arrived at my motel and read the call sheet for the first day's schedule: I couldn't believe they were planning so many scenes in one day, and then I got to the bottom of the page and it said: "Lunch Break"!' The production was so short of money that, on one occasion, the caterer only had the money to cook spaghetti and chilli sauce!' Dobrowolska remembers asking a runner to buy some food from a local shop because she could not eat what was provided. She also recalls that the production could not afford $40 per day for a portable toilet: 'One day it rained, and they expected me to go, in costume and make-up, into the bush while an assistant held an umbrella over me!' She made such a fuss that a Portaloo was supplied next day. On one occasion, the production even ran out of cold water. 'I nearly fainted,' says Dobrowolska.

Gary Day had been filming the mini-series *The Great Bookie Robbery* for PBL before *The Surfer*; the *Bookie Robbery* wrap party was held on a launch at Surfers. 'I got a plastic bag and filled it with bottles of champagne and lobster and took it all back to *The Surfer* people,' he says. 'Kerry Packer didn't know that he'd put money in *The Surfer*.'

On more than one occasion, cast and crew shot a twelve-hour day in heatwave conditions, then drove to the next location: when they arrived at a motel, they leapt into the swimming pool, clothes and all. 'Some of the motel owners didn't exactly welcome us,' says Day.

The film was scheduled to allow a vital scene to be shot during the arrival of a cargo ship from Fiji at the wharves in Brisbane. The crew had just finished a typically frantic day's shooting about 200

The Surfer. *Gosia Dobrowolska, Gary Day.*

kilometres from Brisbane, when the first assistant arrived with the news that the ship was coming in early. 'How much time do we have to sleep?' asked Shields. 'We should have left three hours ago,' came the reply.

Given all this, it is surprising the cast and crew did not rebel. Day says: 'You'd go to the wall for Frank. He's so enthusiastic, and he works harder than anyone else. When we couldn't afford motel rooms, he had seven people in his room. He hustled money along the way. He was incredible.'

Despite the difficulties experienced in making the film, Shields' no-nonsense approach, allied to Michael Edols' excellent camerawork, makes *The Surfer* enthralling for most of its length. It is a pity that Tony Barry, as the best of the villains, gets killed off so early, and that Kris McQuade has such a small part. But the central chase section, softened only by the love scenes, is well handled, despite the lack of a substantial budget, and the denouement—that the 'McGuffin' is not drugs being imported, as we had supposed, but uranium being exported—comes as a genuine surprise.

In *GRIEVOUS BODILY HARM* (1988), one of the most satisfying thrillers made in Australia, Colin Friels plays an investigative journalist who is not above pocketing the illegal proceeds of a robbery when he stumbles across them. Richard Brennan produced the film for his company, Smiley Films, after his friend, Errol Sullivan, showed him the screenplay by Warwick Hind (a former executive of GU). 'I thought 80 per cent of it was really terrific,' says Brennan. 'It was very cleverly structured, people were haunted by memories, everybody trying to deceive everyone else—it had very clever twists and turns. The ending,

Grievous Bodily Harm. *Terry Markwell, John Waters,* (Photo: *Robert McFarlane.*)

I thought, was a disappointment, with bodies turning up everywhere.'

The film has a strong cast of male leads: Friels as the newspaperman, Bruno Lawrence as a corrupt cop, and John Waters as a deranged murderer. Brennan chose Mark Joffe to direct his first feature film (Joffe had previously scored a success with *The Great Bookie Robbery*) and Ellery Ryan to shoot his first large-scale 35mm feature as director of photography. Brennan went to Tony Ginnane for help with funding. 'I'd been working at the AFC until May 1987,' he says. 'And I had to have the film funded by the end of June. I had no time to try to raise money through other channels.' Ginnane was keen on the project, and had Brennan and Joffe meet John Daly of Hemdale (who was in Australia for a short visit); the two Australians were able to sell Daly on their ideas for all-Australian casting. This was also a film on which Ginnane did not raise the full amount of the $3.4 million budget (which included money paid to Hemdale—Brennan notes that the actual cost of the film was closer to $3 million): Brennan, with Errol Sullivan's assistance, had been able to raise some investment ('up to $1 million', says Ginnane) himself.

In making the film, Joffe set out consciously to refer to film noir classics of the past. 'We had another look at *Farewell My Lovely* and *Chinatown*, among others,' says Brennan. The film was shot over a six week period as, simply, *Bodily Harm*, with no-one aware that Margaret Atwood had written a book of that title. The additional word was a last-minute adjustment to prevent any legal wrangles. There was, however, always a problem with the ending: several were written, two were shot, and Richard Brennan, for one, was not entirely happy with the result.

Set in rain-swept Sydney, *Grievous Bodily Harm* is a most distinguished thriller. It is crisply directed and perfectly framed; Ellery Ryan's camerawork is outstanding. The film grabs you right from the start, with the very classy opening credits. True, the ending does not quite maintain the same level of surprise and invention, but it works nonetheless. Performances are strong, especially John Waters (starting to look a lot like Peter Finch) as the bereaved husband who goes on a murder rampage when he suspects his 'dead' wife may still be alive; and there are fine supporting cameos, like Kim Gyngell as Friels' photographer, and John Flaus as his editor. Above all, Joffe and writer Warwick Hind respect the conventions of the genre, and they certainly deliver the goods.

If ever there was a film that should have performed at the box-office, this was it. But it was ignored at the AFI awards, where it might have expected to win several acting and technical prizes, and it went into a surprisingly listless release. Meanwhile, Hemdale had rejected it (along with several others in the Ginnane package), though it was well received in market screenings at Cannes in 1988. In compensation, Ginnane received feelers from several distributors, including Universal and the art-house company Circle Releasing. In the end, though, the film was sold for America to Fries Entertainment for just over $US1 million, though the subsequent release was disappointing. Says Ginnane: 'If that picture had starred Jeff Bridges and Kathleen Turner it could well have taken $50 to $60 million; it really had the capacity to be another *Jagged Edge*. But it just didn't open because, in America, no-one goes to see pictures like that, mainstream pictures, when there's no name to get them in. Maybe we should have sold it to Circle Releasing and gone art-house, but we didn't see it as an art-house picture. Without the cast it was a mistake to try to sell it as a mainstream picture.'

On a much smaller scale, but also dealing with an investigative reporter, is *THE BIG HURT* (1986), which was made by the team of Barry Peak and Chris Kiely (for more details about this enterprising duo, see Chapters 9 and 10). As a change of pace from their two low-budget comedies, *Future Schlock* and *Channel Chaos*, Peak and Kiely wanted to make a thriller dealing with sado-masochism, but decided, in the end, that the subject was altogether too nasty. So they shifted the emphasis until it looked more like a traditional detective film, with the journalist (David Bradshaw) investigating a sex club apparently operated by ASIO.

Peak wrote the screenplay in collaboration with his wife, Sylvia Bradshaw, and Kiely produced (on a $690,000 budget) with Peak directing on a six-week shoot (the money was raised through 10BA in the normal way). Malcolm Richards photographed on Super-16mm, and the finished film was later blown up to 35mm.

The Big Hurt is a modestly satisfying thriller, well paced and passably intriguing, though short on action until the body-strewn climax. Bradshaw is adequate as the intrepid hero, but the supporting players steal the film: Simon Chilvers as a sinister ASIO man, John Ewart as the newspaper editor, and Alan Cassell as a scientist. The inexperience of the lead actress is a problem, but on the whole this is an enjoyable, if very modest, movie. It was shown in the Valhalla cinemas in Australia, and overseas video rights were sold in a number of countries.

In *The Big Hurt*, the investigative journalist is a hero; in *Grievous Bodily Harm* he is an anti-hero; in *THE HUMPTY DUMPTY MAN* (1986) he is a dead hero. This little-known feature, inspired by the David Combe affair, is the work of Paul Hogan (b. 1962 in Tweed Heads), a filmmaker who was accepted into the Australian Film, Television and Radio School at the age of seventeen (he had applied for entry to the school in Year 12, and went straight from high school in Tweed Heads to the AFTRS). In 1984, his short film, *Getting Wet*, won two AFI awards—best short fiction film, and best editing (he edited it himself). Buoyed by this success, and aware of the severe lack of employment for young filmmakers in Sydney, he decided to try his luck in Melbourne.

Producer Miranda Bain originally wanted to make a mini-series about the David Combe affair: Combe was a Labor Party stalwart with a consultancy business in Canberra and had a number of senior government people among his clients. He was accused of links with a KGB spy who was expelled from the Soviet Embassy, and suddenly found himself unable to work, shunned by his former friends. It proved impossible to raise finance for this project, but Hogan (who had been approached by Bain to make the mini-series) suggested the basis of the story be used for a fictional spy thriller. 'Combe's own story doesn't really come to a dramatic climax,' Hogan says. 'So I decided to push it further into the direction of spy fiction.' To help him write the screenplay, Hogan employed a friend from the AFRTS, Karl Zwicky.

Hogan and Zwicky wrote the screenplay very quickly, in only five weeks. And, suddenly, the project was up and running. 'We didn't even have time to do another draft,' says Hogan. 'We went straight into pre-production, and started shooting six weeks later. There wasn't time to catch my breath.' The film was budgeted at just under $1 million, and was shot on Super-16mm with the intention of blowing it up to 35mm for theatrical release; during shooting, the screenplay was constantly being rewritten. Originally, Hogan hoped to shoot in Canberra for ten days; in the end, it was possible to shoot in the capital for only two days.

Hogan never attempted to talk to David Combe, and never met him. 'I wasn't telling his story,' he says. 'Mine was an exaggerated story, pushed to the limit.' But he cast Frank Gallacher as his hero, called Gerry Shadlow in the film, 'because he bears a passing resemblance to Combe.' Curly black hair is really about all the two have in common.

Though *The Humpty Dumpty Man* starts out as what appears to be a dramatisation of the Combe scandal, it quickly takes a turn into John Le Carre territory. There is a KGB mole within the country's security agency (called AIS in the film). Calderwood (Frankie J. Holden), a journalist chasing the story, disappears and is later revealed to have been murdered. The bodies start falling thick and fast, most of them despatched by an assassin who works for the telephone company (which is named Intertel in the film, presumably because Telecom might have been perturbed about it all). Given its modest budget, and the rushed way it was made, the film emerges extremely well; suspense is maintained until the end, and there are some excellent performances (especially Gallacher himself as the rumpled, rather mournful hero and Frederick Parslow as the head of AIS who is ultimately revealed to be the KGB mole). The settings do not always look much like Canberra, but that is to be expected. Above all, the film works as a thriller.

Hogan is not sure what happened to the film after he completed it. At some stage, it was shortened by five minutes (removing a homosexual sub-plot) and remixed ('Cars sound like jet planes in the new mix,' says Hogan crossly.) It never saw the inside of a cinema, and, at the time of writing at least, has not been sold to television, though you would think such a subject would have been eminently exploitable in the media. At the end of 1989, it belatedly emerged on video, but until then few people seem even to have heard of it.

C raig Lahiff (b. 1947) is an 'Adelaide-based director who has brought an extra edge to the genre films he has made to date: his first was *Coda* (1986) (see the following chapter) and his second, a big advance, was *FEVER* (1987), for which he was nominated best director in the 1988 AFI awards.

Lahiff studied science at Adelaide University, and trained as a systems consultant before deciding on a change in career: he wanted to make films. He did a master of arts in film at Flinders University, and then tried to get work in the local industry. But it was difficult to get employment with the SAFC. 'They mostly imported their crews from interstate,' he says. The best he could do was work as dubbing assistant on *The Fourth Wish*, and as production assistant on SAFC documentaries.

Meanwhile, he applied for and received money from the Creative Development Branch of the AFI to make some short films: *Labyrinth* was a finalist in the GU awards at the 1979 Sydney Film Festival, and *The Coming* (1981) also won praise.

Fever. *Mary Regan, Gary Sweet, Bill Hunter.*

Fever was made under the influence of films like *Blood Simple* and film-noir classics like *The Postman Always Rings Twice*. Budgeted at $875,000 and shot on Super-16mm, the film was originally to have been set in a big industrial city like Port Pirie, but the budget did not allow shooting on such a distant location. Instead, Port Adelaide locations were used, but made to look as industrial as possible. 'I wanted a seedy, tacky atmosphere,' says Lahiff.

He always had Bill Hunter in mind as the leading character, the corrupt cop whose wife (Mary Regan) is having a steamy affair with another man. Shooting, which took five weeks, was in summer and the weather was very hot.

Fever is, for much of its length, an extremely taut thriller about passion, greed and violence, all taking place in a sweltering little town: *Blood Simple* territory indeed. With its scenes of sweaty passion, murder and mayhem, all taking place in the most mundane of urban settings, the film is first class as far as it goes: but then inspiration seems to run out, and the second half of the film—with Welles miraculously recovering from the wounds dealt him—loses conviction. It picks up again for a suspenseful sequence on a train, but the ending is a disappointment after the very powerful opening reels. Still, *Fever* is the work of a talented director and there seems little doubt that, given a really good script, Lahiff might one day surprise us all. He is obviously good with actors, because Bill Hunter is in top form as the wily, ruthless cop and Mary Regan is a most effective femme fatale.

Like so many interesting genre films, *Fever* failed to get a cinema release in Australia. 'J. C. Williamsons handled the sales,' said Lahiff, 'and though there were plenty of international sales, they were all video. We were told it just wasn't a big enough film.'

There is a crooked cop on the rampage, too, in *DANGEROUS GAME* (1988), another thriller which is well executed for most of its length, but which disappoints in the end. This is the work of Stephen Hopkins, a British-born rock-clip expert, and it boasts outstanding production design by Igor Nay whose department-store set is one of the most elaborate—and largest—sets ever seen in an Australian film. Steven Grives plays the cop, who traps five personable teenagers in the department store at night intending to terrorise them; he ends up accidentally killing one, leading to an escalation in the violence.

Until it goes over the top in the final reel, this is an unusually intelligent picture, with excellent stunt-work (a sequence on a ledge high above the city is a real heart-stopper). Given that Australian distributors release so many cheap, nasty and presumably barely commercial American thrillers, it is a wonder they passed over this unusually satisfying home-grown product, which became just one of many worthy local films denied commercial release. Hopkins and his cameraman, Peter Levy, went to Hollywood to make their next film, which was the fifth in the *Nightmare on Elm Street* series.

Directors like Lahiff and Hopkins clearly enjoy thrillers and know how to make them (it is the screenplays that do not quite deliver in both *Fever* and *Dangerous Game*). James Clayden's *WITH TIME TO KILL* (1987), which also features lawless cops, tries to intellectualise the genre, with dismal results. Though hailed in some quarters, and filled with Melbourne in-jokes, Clayden's effort is fresh from film school, shot on Super-8mm with a mini-budget. It sinks under the weight of its pretensions, despite flashes of grim humour ('Melbourne in winter— not far from Antarctica'). That quote is part of the narration used to bridge the holes in the narrative as the two cops go around the city meting out summary justice to a variety of villains. The body count is enormous, and such interesting actors as Barry Dickins and Tim Robertson barely register before they disappear.

Light-years away from the low-budget pretensions of this film is *HARBOUR BEAT* (1990), which is a superb example of how an Australian film can be 'international' without selling its soul. This was the first feature directed by David Elfick who, as we have seen in Chapter 2, is one of Australia's top producers. Elfick wanted to establish himself as a director, and took the opportunity of his twice reprised television

Harbour Beat. *Gary Day, John Hannah.*

mini-series, *Fields of Fire*, to do so: he directed half of the second series and all of the third. The vehicle he chose to launch himself as a feature-film director is a staple of genre cinema: the buddy-cop movie. During the 80s, American filmmakers churned out such films: white cop and black cop (*Lethal Weapon*), straight cop and gay cop (*Partners*), Chicago cop and Moscow cop (*Red Heat*) and, inevitably, human cop and dog cop (*K9* and *Turner and Hooch*). *Harbour Beat* belongs to the same formula: a streetwise Glasgow cop (John Hannah) is sent to Sydney and partnered with a surf-loving local cop (Steve Vidler).

There is nothing new here, but what is pleasing is the confident and entertaining way Elfick handles the material. Morris Gleitzman's script (his best so far) is filled with wisecracks, interesting characters,

David Elfick (left) *directing* Harbour Beat.

and intriguing situations. The cast is excellent: John Hannah dominates the film with a tough, funny performance; Vidler is also good, and so is Gary Day as the latter's former partner, now involved in drug rackets. Emily Simpson is fun to have around, too. She plays Mason, a policewoman naturally affronted when asked to make coffee for the male cops, but given to pithy dialogue; on learning that for three years Vidler never suspected his former partner was on the take she remarks: 'You didn't suspect him? You'd make a great wife.'

Ellery Ryan's sumptuous photography in spectacular Sydney locations (Bondi never looked better) adds to the enjoyment, and the stunts and action scenes are well staged. Elfick shows a relaxed style of handling this staple material, and demonstrates just how it should be done; his transition to direction is seamless.

As with the *Fields of Fire* programmes, *Harbour Beat* was made in association with the British company, Zenith; but any compromises required by this collaboration do not in any way detract from the film (in contrast to American collaborations during the 80s). As a genre piece, *Harbour Beat* is snappy, lively entertainment.

On the other hand, *KOKODA CRESCENT* (1988) is a mess. This film also deals with a corrupt cop (well played by Steve Jacobs) who is into drugs. It was the third film directed by Ted Robinson for producer Philip Emanuel, the others being *Those Dear Departed* and *Two Brothers Running* (see Chapter 10). Robinson's background was in television comedy: he had directed the second *Aunty Jack* series as well as *Flash Jack from Jindivik*, *Wollongong The Brave* and *The Gillies Report*. He also directed *Shout*, the 1985 mini-series about Johnny O'Keefe.

Kokoda Crescent, marketed overseas as *Mission Impractical*, is one of those totally misjudged projects that should never have got off the drawing board. The early scenes play as sentimental family comedy (Christmas by the sea, Easter at the RSL) marred only by some ugly racist jokes about blacks and Asians. But the mood changes with the death by drug overdose of Brett (Patrick Thompson, son of Jack), beloved grandson of World War II veteran Warren Mitchell, and the discovery that the detective in charge of the case is up to his ears in guilt. Mitchell and his two old buddies (Bill Kerr, Martin Vaughan), aided by the former's wife (Ruth Cracknell) decide to take the law into their own hands, and the film teeters off into *Death Wish* territory, though without an ounce of conviction.

It is no wonder that this had trouble getting a cinema release. Mitchell, Kerr and Vaughan are hardly the kind of geriatric heroes young cinemagoers identify with, and more mature fans of the actors would probably be repelled by the film's lack of morality and the violence of its climactic sequences. Patrick Cook, a talented satirist, wrote the unfortunate screenplay which, as directed by Robinson, is full of loose ends. The only bright moments are those in which the voice of Mike Carlton is heard impersonating a radio talk-back host who sounds a lot like John Laws.

A t the beginning of the decade, David Elfick had produced his second fictional feature (after *Newsfront*), *THE CHAIN REACTION* (1980). During production the film was known by the far more original title *The Man at the Edge of the Freeway*. Elfick, who thought the title a bit long and pretentious, wanted to call the film simply *Contaminated*; the compromise title was the suggestion of Spectrum Films' Hans Pomeranz. *The Chain Reaction* was the first feature directed by Ian Barry (see Chapter 3) and he had written it after reading newspaper stories speculating that Australia might take back nuclear waste from the uranium it had sold overseas. From this basic idea, Barry fashioned a suspenseful screenplay about a leak at a nuclear plant and a contaminated scientist (Ross Thompson) who tries to warn the outside world.

The screenplay had been written before *The China Syndrome* appeared, and also before the near-disaster at Harrisburg early in 1979 (later in the decade, the name Chernobyl became synonymous with this kind of man-made disaster). Elfick had earlier hoped to film another Barry screenplay, *Sparks*, about a blind film director, but decided it was too much of a risk. He budgeted the film at $600,000; the AFC insisted that this was too high, so an eventual budget was set at $450,000, which was raised from the AFC, Hoyts and the VFC. Elfick regrets the last-minute tightening of the budget, which, he feels, put undue stress on Ian Barry. Elfick invited George Miller(1), who had just scored an unexpected success with *Mad Max*, to join the project as associate producer. 'I wanted his expertise in the action car-chase sequences,' says Elfick. 'These were areas in which Ian and I had no experience. His career had really taken off by then, so his time was limited.'

Steve Bisley and Arna-Maria Winchester were cast as the husband and wife who help the fugitive scientist. In hindsight, Elfick, while acknowledging the fine work of both actors, wonders if different casting might have boosted the film's box-office chances. 'Casting's always very difficult,' he acknowledges.

The film was shot at Glen Davis, 60 kilometres from Lithgow, NSW. The place, once a thriving shale-mining centre, was a ghost town located at the end of a long, dead-end valley, accessible only by dirt road, and it was rumoured to be the site of an Aboriginal massacre. 'The place was supposed to be cursed,' says Elfick. 'And I can believe it, because we had a lot of accidents on location, including a couple of nasty car crashes. It was an uncomfortable, eerie place. Communications were poor (the telephone exchange closed at night) and because we were short of money, it was doubly difficult.'

Barry proved to be a meticulous, rather slow director, anxious to make the film visually striking (Russell Boyd was cinematographer) and full of impact. He devised some brilliant shots, which proved extremely time consuming. As a result, the picture fell behind schedule, and Miller agreed to direct a second unit (the car-chase scenes and stunts) on which, to save money, Elfick worked as first assistant director. When Miller ran out of time, Elfick directed some of this footage himself 'following closely the George Miller technique'. But money was saved in other ways: 'We conned the Air Force into landing a Hercules in a paddock for us: they did it for nothing.'

In the end, the film went 40 per cent over budget and cost the $600,000 originally predicted. Matters were complicated by disagreements between Barry and Elfick about where the emphasis should be placed: Barry did not want to lose sight of what he saw as a serious anti-nuclear theme, and feared that the thriller and chase aspects would swamp his message. Matters were not helped, in the post-production stage, by the input of the VFC's Ross Dimsey, who also wanted a say in the matter.

Hoyts took the film for Australia and, at the 1980 Cannes Film Festival market, the picture was sold to Warner Bros for the rest of the world; it performed well in several territories. In Australia, it was chosen as the closing-night film of the 1980 Sydney Film Festival.

The Chain Reaction works better as a thriller than it does as an anti-nuclear statement, because the message is all too often submerged under the dazzlingly staged car chases and stunts. Some subsidiary characters, like Richard Moir's very strange policeman, seem to have strayed in from another kind of film. Steve Bisley is so good in the lead that one wonders why he never became a popular actor like Mel Gibson and Bryan Brown; certainly he has all the attributes. Russell Boyd's camerawork is extremely stylish, but the film as a whole carries with it the whiff of compromise.

The other anti-nuclear thriller of the 80s was *GROUND ZERO* (1987). Michael Pattinson, who co-directed with actor Bruce Myles, says: 'Jan Sardi [the writer] and I wanted to make a thriller with something to say. Mac Gudgeon joined us early on, when we were storyboarding. It was a very easy script to write, because we had a very strong idea about the story: a contemporary story about the Maralinga nuclear tests, and we knew what our position would be on the subject. We worked out the storyline very quickly, because it all fell together. The characters in the film were based on a great deal of research.'

After a first-draft screenplay was completed, Pattinson made the decision to co-direct with Bruce Myles. 'I'd directed Bruce in a telemovie, *Just Friends*, for *The Winners* series,' he says, 'and we'd kicked ideas for the film around with him. I'd admired his work as director in the theatre, and I decided I wanted to work with him.' Myles had not directed a film before, but the two collaborated across the board: casting, design, later drafts of the script, and on-set direction. 'I did the hands-on direction,' says Pattinson. 'But we both worked on it. Bruce stood back and observed what I was doing, then suggested how to take it a step further. I learnt an enormous amount from working with him.' The collaboration seems to have worked in much the same way as the George Miller–George Ogilvie collaboration on *Mad Max Beyond Thunderdome*; Ogilvie was, of course, also a theatre director.

One of the most interesting pieces of casting was Jack Thompson as a sinister ASIO man. Co-writer Mac Gudgeon, who had worked with the actor on the mini-series *Waterfront*, suggested him for the part. 'It took some persuading to get him to play the role,' says Pattinson. 'But he brought a dangerous element to the character.' From the beginning, Pattinson hoped Donald Pleasence would agree to play the role of Prosper Gaffney, the British officer who stayed behind in the Australian desert after the tests were completed (a character based on a mixture of a number of different people the filmmakers had researched). 'We were fans of his work, and he took no convincing— he agreed to do it immediately.'

When production was due to commence, the Royal Commission into the Maralinga tests was still underway under Chairman Jim McClelland; there was some question that the material was sub judice, but McClelland readily signed a release form and, later, when he saw the film, was enthusiastic about it. Simon Chilvers, who played the Chairman of the enquiry, studied tapes of McClelland and the testimony before the Commission in the film consisted, to a large degree, of paraphrases

Ground Zero. *Colin Friels.*

of actual testimony brought before the real Commission; *Ground Zero* was certainly topical.

In the end, the film just misses out on being a really fine thriller. For most of the time, the audience is happy to go along with the twists and turns of the plot as Colin Friels, in an energetic performance, tries to unravel the mystery of his photographer father's death years earlier and the mysterious renewed interest in missing 16mm film he had taken at the Maralinga test site. Pattinson and Myles build up the tension with skill, until there is some botched business out in the desert: one moment Friels and the crippled Pleasence are being menaced by well-armed soldiers in a helicopter, the next they are— inexplicably—back in their car and on the road again. This is unfortunate, because it is a moment of such phoniness that whatever disbelief audiences have been willing to suspend, goes out the window.

Says Pattinson: 'I never thought that scene would be a credibility problem for the audience, but it has been frequently raised. I didn't think we needed to waste time showing how they actually got into the car, and I didn't want to trivialise the story with a chase at that point.'

The film won prizes for photography (Steve Dobson), editing, production design and sound at the 1987 AFI awards, but its theatrical release (through Hoyts) was disappointing. Subsequently, the film competed at the Berlin Film Festival, and was released in the US by Avenue Pictures (who insisted on replacing Chris Neal's subtle score with more obvious music by Tom Bähler). At the same time, Pattinson was able to do some fine-tuning on the picture ('I made it a better film'), and the version that screens on Australian television is the American release version, with the new music.

G *round Zero* was one of the more interesting films backed by the Burrowes Film Group which, also in 1987, released a film prosaically titled *RUNNING FROM THE GUNS*; during production (many, many months earlier) it had been known as *Free Enterprise*. This was the directorial debut of John Dixon, who also scripted (and had written the screenplay for Burrowes' hit *The Man from Snowy River*). Belonging to the genre of semi-comic buddy thrillers, the film boasts lively performances from Jon Blake and Mark Hembrow as the buddies and Nikki Coghill as the former's girlfriend. The pacing is also quite good; there is an exciting opening chase sequence and some excellent stunts.

But Dixon (or possibly Burrowes, who personally produced) spoil what is good in the film with a relentless soundtrack of deafening and inappropriate rock songs, and there are some badly directed supporting performances. Also, like so many Australian films, it runs out of conviction towards the end, in this case when dockworkers (hitherto lampooned by the film for marching with banners dating back to the Vietnam and Korean wars) suddenly come to the rescue of the heroes with an amazing supply of automatic weapons.

With rare exceptions, Australian audiences do not care for locally

Running from the Guns. *Mark Hembrow.*

made films in the thriller genre, and they did not care for *Running from the Guns* either, despite its very American style (though, mercifully, the characters and casting are authentically and distinctively Australian).

The Nikki Coghill character in the film works for a Crime Commission which is being undermined by a mole feeding information back to the crime lords. And large-scale criminal activity, understandably, features in a number of films of the decade. *DEAD EASY* (1982), which was never released in cinemas or on video, and which seems to have screened only on middle-of-the-night television, deals with rival Sydney gangs feuding, almost Chicago-style, over their Kings Cross territory. There is a well-established Jewish gang run by Sol (Joe Martin) which is opposed by a gang of brash all-Australian crims led by Lou (Tony Barry). Caught between the two are the young lovers who, as played by Scott Burgess and Rosemary Paul, make a pretty wan pair; but much of the film is excellent and director Bert Deling presents what seems to be (for the time) quite an outspoken picture of crime at the Cross, while depicting Sol in his luxurious waterfront mansion, living comfortably at a remove from the carnage for which he is responsible.

Crooked cops feature in the film too, with Max Phipps playing a particularly odious specimen of the breed, while Sandy Gore makes an impression as a lesbian brothel-owner. Well shot by Mike Molloy and Tom Cowan on authentic locations, the film deserved more attention than it ever received. Once again, the ending is unconvincing. Rather than allow Sol to have the young hero killed, his lifelong lieutenant (Jack O'Leary) tells his boss, 'We're worse now than the people we left Europe to escape', before he drives both himself and Sol in their silver Rolls-Royce, over a cliff. If the intention was to refer to a somewhat similar situation at the end of Orson Welles' *Touch of Evil*, the realisation is simply miles off the mark, but otherwise Deling, who had made two interesting experimental features in the 70s, *Dalmas* and *Pure Shit*, proves himself a strong director whose film deserved a better fate.

Melbourne director Chris Fitchett takes a more personal look at the underworld in *BLOOD MONEY* (1980), a short (62-minute) drama in which John Flaus and Bryan Brown play brothers, the former a hardened crim dying of cancer, the latter retired and trying to go straight. The opening jewel robbery sequence is tautly directed, and the film certainly does not overstay its welcome as it creates a touching portrait of a dying man trying to relive past happiness with his brother's wife (the handling of this theme compares very favourably to *Boulevard of Broken Dreams*). Flaus plays his world-weary character like Randolph Scott or Joel McCrea in their later films and proves, once again, that this film academic, at least, is a very fine actor.

John Hargreaves plays Martin, a hardened crim, in *HOODWINK* (1981), which was scripted by Ken Quinnell and which is based on a remarkable true story. Some years earlier, Rosemary Cresswell, the literary agent, had been doing some work for the Department of Corrective Services and met a convict, Carl Synnerdahl, who was serving a long prison sentence. Synnerdahl told Cresswell his story (how he had posed as a blind man to gain a lighter sentence and then been forced to keep up the deception) and she brought it to Errol Sullivan who made several visits to the prison over a long period to talk to Synnerdahl about his scam.

The NSWFC was keen on the screenplay which Quinnell fashioned from this material, and Sullivan and his partner, Pom Oliver, went ahead with plans for the film, which was budgeted at $950,000. But they were faced with a problem: they could not find a director. Several, including Bruce Beresford and Michael Thornhill, were approached, only to turn it down; Phil Noyce and Esben Storm both worked on the script, but both gave up, feeling it had insuperable structural problems. 'At that point we should have given up,' says Sullivan. 'We should have realised that Phil, Esben and the others were right. But I was committed to the story, and we'd put our own money into the development, so we decided to muscle it through and hire a foreign director. In hindsight, that was a mistake.'

The director they chose was Britisher Claude Whatham, mainly

Hoodwink. *John Hargreaves.*

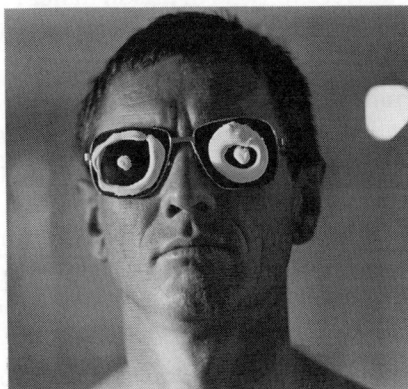

because Sullivan had loved his first feature, *That'll Be the Day* (he had subsequently directed three less successful films, *Swallows and Amazons*, *All Creatures Great and Small* and *Sweet William*). Whatham proved to be only a journeyman director. 'He took the money and ran,' says Sullivan. 'The final script was better than the film he made; he didn't enhance it.'

At the time, the hiring of Whatham caused a tremendous row, especially since it followed hard on the heels of Tony Ginnane's decision to employ another Britisher, David Hemmings, as director of *The Survivor*. Phil Noyce, particularly, was up in arms over the importation. Until this moment, film directors had been members of the Australian Theatrical and Amusement Employees' Association, and ATAEA had approved the Whatham importation. Now, Australian film directors (with a couple of exceptions) banded together to form the Australian Feature Film Directors Association, and elected Gillian Armstrong as Chair. AFFDA immediately decreed that Australian features with majority government funding must be directed by Australians, but members voted against taking action on *Hoodwink*. Armstrong wrote to the *National Times* to emphasise that: 'We hope in future no further permission will be granted [by ATAEA] to foreign directors without consultation with its director membership.'

Meanwhile, production of *Hoodwink* went ahead. This was Dean Semler's first major film as cinematographer, though he had shot the in-house Film Australia picture *Let the Balloon Go* in 1976. The particularly strong supporting cast, chosen by Sullivan and Oliver, included Judy Davis as Sarah, the dowdy wife of a country preacher. Colin Friels also appears in a tiny role in this, his first film. One problem with the screenplay is that Sarah's affair with Martin, the convict she visits in prison in her role as social worker, is barely credible. In the film's early, and much more energetic, sequences, Wendy Hughes and Kim Deacon as a couple of Martin's molls play their requisite nude scenes with elan.

The film's basic idea is a bit hard to swallow despite the fact that the story is true, but thanks to Hargreaves' stalwart performance it just about works.

Hoodwink falls uneasily into two halves: the first, amusing and quite suspenseful, has Martin bedding beautiful women and dodging corrupt cops and, later, equally corrupt prison guards. The prison scenes, in which he successfully hoodwinks the authorities into thinking he is blind, are also effective, if less so. But with the introduction of the

Judy Davis character, the film starts to take itself too seriously, the humour is lost, and it grinds to an unconvincing climax.

The film did modest business, and seems to have seriously disrupted Whatham's cinema career; after *Hoodwink*, he returned to Britain but his work for the remainder of the decade has been confined to television (in 1990, he directed a British musical, *Buddy's Song*, with Roger Daltrey).

In hindsight, Sullivan is sympathetic to the reaction of the AFFDA members. 'I think they were right,' he says. He recalls that both Stephen Wallace and John Duigan, though not as publicly angry as Noyce and Armstrong, expressed to him their private concerns. On the other hand, Richard Franklin, in *Cinema Papers*, characteristically stood in opposition to his fellow directors and in support of the Whatham importation.

There is a happy postscript to the story. After twenty-one years in prison, and facing another ten, Carl Synnerdahl was released on Errol Sullivan's bond. He moved north, married a doctor and had three children.

A few months later, Errol Sullivan was embroiled in another controversy, this time over *CROSSTALK* (1982): the controversy involved the dismissal of director Keith Salvat during the film's production and, almost ten years later, continues to stir passions and conflicting accounts of what actually happened.

Salvat (b. 1947) had made an acclaimed short film, *Sacrifice*, and a pioneering feature, *Private Collection*, in 1971 (this was a dramatic comedy, with Pamela Stephenson and Graham Bond, and was screened at the 1972 Sydney Film Festival); but he had had no success in getting another feature off the ground. In 1976, he nearly got to make *Palmer Street*, a thriller about a crooked cop and a prostitute: but investors backed away when rumours spread that the film was based on real-life characters. In 1979, Salvat wrote a screenplay he called *High Rise*, about a man trapped in a high rise building because of an injury; the inspiration was Hitchcock's *Rear Window*, but with variations, since Salvat was interested in the way technology was manipulating people into isolation. 'I really wanted to write a low budget thriller,' he says.

Salvat approached the NSWFC and received $10,000 for script development, plus the promise of $200,000 towards production. Feeling confident that the project would go ahead, he approached the producer of *Mad Max*, Byron Kennedy, who liked his ideas. At the time, *Mad*

Crosstalk. *Gary Day with the giant computer.*

Max was still in post-production, and Kennedy had just produced another film, *The Last of the Knucklemen*, directed by Tim Burstall. But before long, *Mad Max* was finished, picked up by Warners, and Kennedy left for America. 'We kept in touch,' says Salvat. 'Byron injected a lot of ideas into the script and had quite a bit of influence at that early stage. He helped turn it into something much better. He was creative, strong—an ideal producer.

By this time, the screenplay had been retitled *Wall to Wall*. Jenny Woods of the NSWFC suggested that Salvat bring Bob Jewson in to work on the script (Jewson had scripted *Stir*, which was currently in production).

This was twelve months before 10BA was introduced, and investors were reluctant to move on projects. Salvat approached Ross Matthews, who, until that time, had been working as a production manager but who had been associate producer on *The Chain Reaction* and had produced an hour-long Creative Development Branch film, *Just Out of Reach*: Matthews agreed to produce *Wall to Wall*. Salvat and Matthews spent much of 1980 in the US (funded by the NSWFC), working on further drafts of the script and exploring the possibility of casting an American actor in the lead role. At this stage, Hemdale almost came in as co-producer, and John Daly suggested John Savage for the leading role; but in the end nothing came of this.

On his return from America, Salvat concentrated on raising the rest of the budget. With the establishment of 10BA, the NSWFC agreed to undertake the full financing of the $1.2 million budget themselves.

Just as it seemed all the funds had been raised and the picture would finally be made, Ross Matthews announced that he was going to co-produce *Heatwave*. 'I didn't know Ross was working on *Heatwave* at the same time. I was really disappointed he had so little commitment to my project,' says Salvat. 'It's common practice for producers to develop two projects at the same time,' says Matthews. 'I'd been working on *Heatwave* with Hilary Linstead: unfortunately, the two pictures got up at about the same time. There was certainly no lack of commitment to Keith's film on my part. I'd spent a lot of time helping Keith, pushing Hemdale—all for very little income.' Matthews remained executive producer on *Wall To Wall*, and his friend Errol Sullivan stepped in as producer. 'I'd never have approached Errol myself,' says Salvat. 'Not because I didn't like him, but because I didn't think we were on the same wavelength. But I wasn't really worried.'

Just as the film was ready to go, the rush of 10BA-funded pictures went into production. As a result, prices escalated. 'The cost of the crew went up,' says Salvat. 'Everything went up—except our budget, which had not been redrafted since the original funding proposal— ten months before.' Vincent Monton joined the film as cinematographer, Larry Eastwood was production designer (and responsible for the huge, complex apartment set) and Mark Egerton was first assistant director. Casting was difficult: some actors Salvat had wanted had become unavailable. But he was pleased to have Gary Day, cast in his first starring role in a feature, as well as Penny Downie, John Ewart and Kim Deacon. Salvat rehearsed for three weeks with the actors. 'It was working well,' he says.

During pre-production, the problems really began, and the recollections of the different people involved come into conflict. Salvat feels that Errol Sullivan wasn't as available as he might have been. 'I rarely saw Errol to discuss the picture with him,' he says. Sullivan, however, says he was always on hand; 'I saw Keith every day.' There was also some dispute about the cost of the large apartment set Larry Eastwood was building: it eventually cost $100,000, and there is disagreement between Eastwood and Sullivan as to who authorised that amount.

There is also considerable dispute about the lack, or otherwise, of a completion guarantor and a contingency allowance. Salvat asserts that Sullivan told him, a week before production started, that no completion guarantor was in place and that the contingency allowance had been spent. Sullivan has no recollection of any such conversation.

The film centres on a computer designer (Day), confined to a wheelchair in his apartment after a car accident; he has a giant computer, which films its master's neighbours and visitors, and it is the computer that spots a murder that has taken place. At the beginning of the shoot, Salvat concentrated on filming material which would later be played back on the computer screens: these were mostly exterior shots of cars going past, or tenants of the other apartments in the building. He also shot a hospital sequence. While this was going on, Larry Eastwood was completing the main set.

Salvat shot for nineteen days, but faced a number of problems. His notes for Day 5 of the shoot, for example, state that: 'Time [was] lost when plans made in advance to film in the apartment opposite the location had to be aborted due to the fact that the owner of the apartment changed his mind at the last minute and wouldn't permit filming.'

Gary Day remembers that there was tension on the set: 'Keith was tense, but then so was I,' he says. 'Things were going slowly, but I didn't think that was unusual.' Vincent Monton remembers: 'We were behind schedule, but it was an incredibly complex film to make. We were shooting in Panavision, and there was a bank of seven TV monitors, all of them containing information which had to be taped or filmed first. They all had to cue up perfectly.' Sullivan, on the other hand, feels that the film wasn't all that complex: 'We hadn't started the really complicated scenes,' he says. Another crew member recalls: 'I don't think there'd been enough preparation. Keith was pushing the actors to give good performances, but he seemed to be disappointed with the rushes.' Salvat says: 'My preparation was complete—I can't speak for the producer.' Sullivan notes: 'But we had a real problem, because there was a stop date on Penny Downie: at the end of the scheduled shoot, she had to be elsewhere.'

On Sunday 31 May 1981, the day before shooting was due to start on the main set, Ross Matthews and Errol Sullivan had a meeting at the office of the NSWFC. They wrote Salvat a formal letter, and went to his home to deliver it personally. The letter stated: 'To meet the various difficulties which we have discussed in recent weeks we have decided that we must convene a meeting of directors [of Wall To Wall Pty Ltd] as a matter of urgency so that the company may make the correct decisions concerning the future direction of *Wall To Wall*. It is important that you attend this meeting and accordingly this letter serves as a notice convening the meeting.' The directors of Wall To Wall Pty Ltd were Salvat, Sullivan and Matthews. The letter went on to appoint that same afternoon as the date of the meeting, which would be held at Salvat's home in McMahon's Point.

'Errol came in with Ross,' says Salvat. 'They were looking pretty sombre. I offered them a drink: I'd been working out the scenes scheduled for the next day. They gave me this letter.' The meeting was in session, but, as Salvat says, 'I was completely floored: it was totally unexpected. I couldn't take in what was happening: it was like being hit over the head.' At the conclusion of the meeting, Salvat was handed a hand-written note, on official Wall To Wall Pty Ltd letterhead, stating that: 'In accordance with the meeting of the directors of Wall To Wall Pty Ltd held . . . on May 31/1981 we must inform you that a decision has been made pursuant to the agreement between Wall To Wall Pty Ltd, and Salvatfilm Pty Ltd and yourself dated April 12/1981 and in particular clause 7(a)(i) and 7(a)(vii) of Schedule A of that agreement terminating your engagement as Director of the film *Wall To Wall*.' The clauses referred to going over budget. The letter was signed by Sullivan and Matthews. Says Salvat: 'That was it. They left, and next day they rang up to tell me Mark Egerton was taking over as director.'

Sullivan says: 'Legally and contractually we had to do what we did. Maybe if the NSWFC had come up with more money, we could have let Keith continue: but we'd have gone way over budget. Morally, what happened still troubles me.' Says Matthews: 'The decision was forced on us, and it was one of the worst experiences of my life. Keith had a first class crew on that film.'

Production was shut down for a week while Egerton and Denis Whitburn rewrote the script. They included a new opening sequence, but eliminated most of the other exteriors, so that the film could be shot, as quickly as possible, mostly on the one set. They also cut back on Penny Downie's role (to enable her to leave on time) and gave some of her scenes to the character of the nurse, played by Kim Deacon. The actors were called together and told the news: there was a mixed reaction. When Gary Day saw the new screenplay, he hated it: 'It wasn't a film I wanted to do,' he says. 'But Errol said that unless I did, the production would be closed down. I talked to the other actors—John, Penny and Kim. They all agreed to go along with the situation, so I did too.'

Vincent Monton says: 'If I'd been directing that film, I'd have been nervous. I'd worked on other films by inexperienced directors: I did the first features of John Duigan, Richard Franklin and Phil Noyce. On Noyce's *Newsfront*, we had huge problems. There was a time when I remember we said: "What'll we do now?" But we stuck together, and finished it. I was very surprised when Keith was sacked, because I'd never experienced anything like that before. I thought we'd somehow get through the film, which was so extremely complex it would have fazed the most experienced director.' Errol Sullivan also worked on *Newsfront*, and says that, at no stage, was the situation on that film anywhere near as alarming as the situation on *Wall to Wall*. Another crew member says: 'I felt very sorry for Keith. It was his film, and they took it away from him. I was very surprised at what happened: we'd had a few problems, but I've worked with directors who were far worse, and they didn't get canned.'

The general feeling among crew members was the the film had gone into production too early, and that it was under-prepared. Sullivan says: 'It wasn't under-prepared. The people who organised that production—myself, Julie Monton and Mark Egerton—demonstrated their management skills on projects both before and after this one. It was an awful time. Cast and crew were divided about what happened; some weren't happy, others were relieved. In the end, Mark had only three weeks to shoot the entire film. We only used two or three scenes Keith had shot. Yet we came in on budget.'

Salvat took legal advice on his position, but was told that, unless he had a lot of money, his only recourse—an injunction—would be impossible. He had little money, and could only stand by while his film was taken over. He insisted that the title be changed (it became *Crosstalk*) and that his name be removed from the credits: he also took back his original screenplay, which he says has never been filmed. He never saw the finished film.

During post-production, great efforts were made by Matthews, Sullivan and Egerton to stitch *Crosstalk* together: Chris Neal's music played a vital role in this. Matthews notes that the picture was completed, and was released by GU: it also made overseas sales, and rated well on BBC television.

For the rest of the decade, Keith Salvat has made TV commercials while trying to get several other features off the ground. But he has never managed to touch first base with funding bodies and feels, probably correctly, that he's been blacklisted.

Crosstalk was finally released in the middle of 1982. The film is a mess, with an opening sequence which bears little or no relation to what follows, and a silly and complicated sub-plot which suggests that the wife-murderer (John Ewart) is in some way involved with the sinister forces trying to gain control of the central character's master computer. The film is confusing and derivative, with an irritating soundtrack filled with distorted computer voices and maddening beeps. It doesn't work on any level, and was a deserved commercial flop. The story behind the film is infinitely more interesting—and disturbing—than the film itself.

*R*ear *Window* was the inspiration for another thriller of the early 80s, *ROAD GAMES* (1981); director Richard Franklin had actually met Alfred Hitchcock, having studied film at the University of Southern California, where the director sometimes lectured. Franklin (b. 1948) had made three features during the 70s, one of them, the soft-core porno *Fantasm* (1976) under an alias: the others were *The True Story of Eskimo Nell* (1975) and a thriller produced by Ginnane, *Patrick* (1978). The first draft of *Road Games* was written in eight days by Everett De Roche in Fiji, where he was visiting the location of Randal Kleiser's *The Blue Lagoon*, which Franklin was co-producing. Franklin recalls: 'When we were working on *Patrick*, I'd given Everett a script of *Rear Window* as an example of how I wanted the script typed. And some time later he said: "Gee, it'd be great to do this story in a truck!" I don't know what prompted him to say that, but a year or so later I reminded him about it, and so he came to Fiji and we started writing.'

Road Games was budgeted at $1.75 million which, at that time, was the highest budget ever for an Australian film. The American company Avco Embassy paid a $500,000 pre-sale for all theatrical territories outside Australia, with the balance of the budget made up by GU, the AFC, the Victorian Film Corporation (later Film Victoria), and the Western Australian Film Council. Avco Embassy had script approval (but made no alterations to De Roche's final draft) and also had approval over the casting of the lead actor.

Perhaps because of his American training, Franklin was always an internationalist: *Patrick* had starred a little-known British actress, when an Australian actress could have played the role just as well if not better; for this story of a murder-hunt across the Nullarbor Plain, the director was determined to import two American stars—Stacy Keach and Jamie Lee Curtis. The Melbourne branch of Actors Equity approved both actors, and Franklin went ahead to sign contracts: but subsequently the Sydney branch of Equity overruled the Melbourne decision, and for a while the entire project was in jeopardy.

Franklin is a good thriller director, but his blinkered approach to his American actors is the weak link in *Road Games*. The problem is not that Keach and Curtis are not good—both of them are. Individually, either of them would have worked. There are probably American truck-drivers in Australia, and there are probably quite a few American hitch-hikers. The coincidence of an American truckie picking up an American hitch-hiker in such a remote place is bad enough, but it is confounded when writer and director are too lazy to include a simple line in the script which acknowledges that coincidence: something like 'Where are you from in America?' would have bridged the audience's credibility gap. Once audience credibility is undermined, the film falls apart.

Franklin must have been delighted to be directing a film starring the daughter of Hitchcock's *Psycho* star (and calling her character 'Hitch' into the bargain) but he was, and apparently remains, unable to see how his Americans made his film unbelievable. *Road Games* is, in many ways, an ingenious thriller; Franklin and cinematographer Vincent Monton use the wide screen to good effect, and there is another good score from Brian May. But the climax fails to work because, although it might have seemed a good idea on paper to have the highway chase slow down to a crawl in the narrow streets of Perth (actually filmed in Melbourne), it does not make for an enthralling ending. Grant Page is a rather colourless murderer, and Franklin and De Roche never explain why he lets Quid (Keach) catch up with him at the end. Again, it is a thriller that does not know how to resolve itself.

For all these reasons, *Road Games* was not the success it might have been. Franklin announced several other Australian projects during the 80s, including *Race for the 'Yankee Zephyr'* and *The Pirate Movie*, but they were directed by others. He left for Hollywood where he directed *Psycho II* and the excellent *Cloak and Dagger* (probably the best Hitchcock-style film made since Hitchcock's death) and then, in Britain, the sinister, much-troubled *Link*.

One of the most intriguing, and successful, thrillers made in Australia in the 80s is the Kennedy–Miller production, *DEAD CALM* (1988), an adaptation by Terry Hayes of the novel by Charles Williams first published in the late 50s. Orson Welles had started filming the book as *The Deep* (with himself, Jeanne Moreau and Laurence Harvey) but, as was the case with so many of Welles' later projects, it was never completed. The book had been brought to the attention of Phil Noyce by American producer-director Tony Bill, who had always hoped to buy the rights from Welles himself, but had never been successful. After Welles' death, Noyce told George Miller about the book, and he approached Welles' long-time companion, Oja Kodar who controlled the rights to the novel. She sold the rights to Kennedy–Miller, explaining at the time that she had refused to sell the book to Bill, or any other Hollywood producer, because she felt the Hollywood Establishment had persecuted Welles both personally and professionally.

Noyce's Kennedy–Miller connection had come about when he co-directed the mini-series *The Cowra Breakout*; this project, and the American series on which he worked during the 80s, *The Hitchhiker*, had broken him out of the mould of the kind of film he had made in the past (both *Newsfront* and *Heatwave* had strong political and social themes), and he was anxious to make more mainstream, commercial films. 'I decided I wanted to make different sorts of movies,' he says. 'And *Dead Calm* was different from any feature I'd made before.' Kennedy–Miller being the collaborative company it is, Noyce found himself working closely with Terry Hayes (who co-produced and scripted) and Miller himself who, though in America shooting *The Witches of Eastwick* in the period during which *Dead Calm* was being storyboarded, returned in time to direct some second unit material.

In making a film set on the ocean involving three people, a dog and two boats, Noyce was harking back to the simple but forceful elements of the first episode of *The Cowra Breakout*, which had a young Australian soldier pitted against a young Japanese soldier in a one-on-one struggle in the jungles of New Guinea. 'That drama,' says Noyce, 'contains a lot of similar elements to the drama of *Dead Calm*: two people, few props—an exercise in minimalism—less is more. This simplicity required me to draw on cinematic techniques that I didn't even know I could muster.'

Nicole Kidman was chosen for the female lead, though at first consideration she is too young to play the role of Rae, the wife threatened by the insane Hughie: Rae is thirty-six in the book. Noyce was persuaded

Dead Calm. *Nicole Kidman, Sam Neill.*

to cast Kidman by Terry Hayes who had been delighted with her performance in the Kennedy–Miller mini-series, *Vietnam*, directed by John Duigan (the actress would also play the lead in a later Kennedy–Miller series, *Bangkok Hilton*, directed by Ken Cameron). In fact, the casting makes the relationship between Rae and her husband, John (Sam Neill) unusually interesting. As for Neill, he had been an admirer of both Phil Noyce and Kennedy–Miller and had very much liked the *Dead Calm* script. An American newcomer, Billy Zane, was cast as the deranged Hughie.

The location used for the film was Hamilton Island, though a soundstage was used for the sets of both boats. 'It was a tough shoot,' says Neill. 'The sets were built in a big tank, and the water was cold and unfiltered. A lot of my scenes involved being in the water, often up to my bollocks, and it was uncomfortable and chilly. But, despite that, I really enjoyed it.' Shooting took place during the winter of 1987 and included a substantial amount of footage never used in the finished film. It had an unusually long post-production period, and was not released until the middle of 1989.

George Miller actually directed a number of scenes involving the sinking boat and the Sam Neill character. 'George didn't think John, who was isolated for much of the film, was in sufficient jeopardy,' says Sam Neill. 'Rae is in constant jeopardy from the Hughie character, while John was in this boat that was sinking. I'd always thought we should at least be aware of the shark menace, and George extended this idea by having a shark invade the boat itself through the rotting timbers. So that's what it did: it roared up through the floor boards into the saloon and started chasing me around—it was a fight to the death, me against the shark.' Three mechanical sharks were constructed and a great deal of time was spent on the sequence which, in the end, was dropped from the film. But, says Neill, 'It's the best unseen sequence from any Australian film, even if it was a bit extreme.'

The film's ending is in the now-tired tradition of *Carrie* and *Halloween* where the apparently dead villain returns for one last assault on the heroine. It is also a bit extreme and, for some people, ended this unusually well-sustained thriller on a disappointingly mundane note. The film originally ended with Rae successfully rescuing John; a 'sting' in which Hughie attacks Rae in the shower had been cut. But Warners felt the ending was too soft, and Miller and Noyce agreed. Seven months later, cast and crew reassembled to shoot the new ending (in the interim, Sam Neill had filmed *Evil Angels* and, in France, *The French Revolution*, in which he played Lafayette).

Until this conventional fadeout, *Dead Calm* is masterly. It grips from the opening sequence (in which the Ingram baby is killed when the car Rae is driving on a freeway crashes—a brilliantly directed sequence). Subsequently, Noyce creates and sustains astonishing tension from the most basic elements, thanks to a trio of splendid performances, and the scene in which the terrified Rae submits sexually to Hughie combines horror and pain to create a sequence that is difficult to forget. Dean Semler's superlative (and justly prized) Panavision photography is complemented by a first-class sound mix, and an unusual and impressive music score by Graeme Revill (also an AFI award recipient for his exemplary work on the film). 'We paid a great deal of attention to orchestrating the sound,' says Noyce. 'Roger Savage, who mixed the *Mad Max* films, did a fantastic job. As for the music, we spent a lot of time arguing about the kind of music we needed: but when we heard Graeme Revill's music we agreed that our months of searching were at an end.'

With its guaranteed worldwide release, *Dead Calm* is one of the most successful Australian films of the 80s; it shows technical mastery at its finest, but Noyce never allows the technical flourishes to overwhelm the trio of fine performances. The film made Nicole Kidman an international star: soon after its American release, she was cast opposite Tom Cruise in *Days of Thunder*. With his performance in this film, and in *Evil Angels* which was in release at about the same time, Sam Neill became firmly established as the best antipodean actor of the late 80s.

T he theme of the frightened woman and her unstable kidnapper turns up again in *HOSTAGE* (1983) but this time, as the opening titles remind us not once but twice, it is a true story. This was Frank Shields' first feature, and he was inspired by the case of Christine Maresch, a Wollongong teenager who made an unfortunate marriage with a visiting German with right-wing terrorist connections, who involved her in bank robberies both in Germany and in Australia.

Shields' front-on approach suits this subject, though he rushes so quickly through the early scenes that the audience barely has time to appreciate Christine's increasingly parlous situation. Once the action shifts to Munich, however, the film gets into its stride, and a sequence in which the couple try to escape by car through Turkey (filmed near Broken Hill) is genuinely exciting. The closing sequences, with the increasingly unstable Maresch back in Sydney, are also good. Kerry Mack seems just right as the beleaguered Christine, while Ralph Schicha makes Maresch himself a convincingly dangerous personality. The film closes with photos of the real-life characters.

Another real-life hostage story was told in *FORTRESS* (1985), which was based on the 1972 incident in which a teacher at a one-teacher country school was kidnapped, together with all her pupils, and held for ransom, but managed to escape. Gabrielle Lord wrote a book based on the story, and the television company Crawfords purchased the rights, intending to make it into a feature film for Australian release and a telemovie for America (on Home Box Office).

Everett De Roche had written the adaptation of Lord's novel, and Bruce Beresford was originally announced as director. When he passed on the project, producer Ray Menmuir brought the script to Arch Nicholson who, at the time, was working on *Special Squad* at Crawfords. The project immediately ran into trouble, because HBO insisted on a 'name' actress in the central role, and Actors Equity argued that an authentically Australian character should be played by an Australian actress. (The same argument might have been made some years later over the casting of Meryl Streep in *Evil Angels*, but Equity apparently felt then that Streep was an actress of such importance that no objection should be made.)

Crawfords and HBO wanted Bess Armstrong to play the character of Sally Jones: Equity rejected the actress, whose best-known role at the time was opposite Tom Selleck in the lacklustre adventure *High Road to China*. A compromise was finally achieved when HBO accepted Sigrid Thornton on the strength of her American success in *The Man*

Fortress. *Peter Hehir, Rachel Ward.*
(Photo: *Bill Bachman.*)

from Snowy River; but, two months before shooting, Thornton discovered she was pregnant.

At this point, Crawfords threatened to cancel the project unless Equity relented and allowed Bess Armstrong: the union stood firm in the face of mixed, sometimes hostile, press reaction, and pre-production on *Fortress* shut down. Three or four months later it was quietly reactivated when Rachel Ward proved to be acceptable to Equity. This British actress had appeared in two American features, *Dead Men Don't Wear Plaid* and *Sharky's Machine*, was married to Bryan Brown, whom she met when they played opposite each other in the mini-series *The Thorn Birds*, and had settled in Australia.

The shoot was not an easy one because every scene involved nine children, and there are restrictions on how many hours a day children can work. The film was made on location at Bairnsdale near the Gippsland coast, and in the Grampians, over twelve 5-day weeks in the winter of 1985: 'It was supposed to take place in summer, so Rachel and the kids were wearing summer gear,' says Nicholson. 'They got very cold.'

The film premiered on HBO in November 1985, and it was seven months (June 1986) before it was released in Australian cinemas. After all the trouble taken, the film is disappointing; Nicholson establishes the situation well enough, but goes for overkill at the end, and there is a particularly nasty climax in which children and teacher hack the surviving kidnapper to pieces and later threaten the police who come to rescue them. Such Hollywood-style exaggeration trivialises a true story in which a good deal of courage was displayed, and reduces the drama almost to the level of a horror film. The music is also misjudged, sounding at times appallingly crude.

SLATE, WYN AND ME (1987) also has a kidnap theme. Don McLennan read Georgia Savage's book *Slate and Me and Blanche McBride*, and liked it; he interested Tom Burstall, who agreed to produce. McLennan got script development money from Film Victoria, and set about trying to raise money. This proved extremely difficult: 'We couldn't get a nibble,' says McLennan. 'Not one person was interested in the film.' Burstall suggested they go to Tony Ginnane. 'Tony immediately said he'd try to put a deal together,' says McLennan. 'He went overseas and came back with three different pre-sale offers.' Eventually, the project became part of Ginnane's Hemdale package.

Some filmmakers had unhappy experiences on Ginnane-backed projects, but not McLennan. 'Tony was fantastic,' he says. 'He left me to my own devices. I think he liked what we were doing, though we had a bit of a squabble over the ending—but I brought that on myself. I knew the ending wasn't right, and I should have addressed it sooner than I did.'

Slate, Wyn and Me. *Martin Sacks, Simon Burke, Sigrid Thornton.*

The film was budgeted at $2.3 million, and the shoot lasted eight weeks; locations were mostly around Swan Hill. McLennan had a free hand in casting, except for the character of Blanche. Though in the book the character is only fifteen or sixteen years old, Hemdale insisted that Sigrid Thornton play the role: 'Part of the problem with the film was trying to change the age of the girl,' says McLennan.

The influence of the Terrence Malick film *Badlands* hangs heavily over *Slate, Wyn and Me*; Sigrid Thornton is the small-town schoolteacher who witnesses the murder of a policeman by the unstable Wyn (Simon Burke) and is kidnapped by him and his brother, Slate (Martin Sacks), a Vietnam vet. Thanks to David Connell's Panavision camerawork of hot, dusty, dry countryside, the ensuing, rather aimless, escape remains watchable, and a sequence in which the trio tries to cross a rickety bridge is a high point. But Blanche's motives in switching her affections from one brother to the other are not made very clear.

Nor is the ending satisfactory. Says McLennan: 'At the end we had a guy who'd murdered someone, but he's the lead character in the film. What do we do with him? Do you let him get away with it? Make him pay the price? In the book, he dies, but we'd digressed so much from the book at that point that we couldn't really refer back to it for any sort of guidance. The real question was, *How* should he die? John Daly wanted one solution; I wanted another. The problem was raised during shooting when I was under a lot of pressure, and we ended up shooting two endings; in the final film we cut together a combination of both those endings, which I think, looking back, says something about the film itself.'

Looking back on the film, McLennan feels a sense of frustration: 'It was my first 35mm feature, with a big budget and a large crew. I was working with people who had far more experience than I did. One problem was that my company, Ukiyo Films, was producing the film, and Tom Burstall, who was the producer, spent a lot of time in Sydney working on *Great Expectations: The Untold Story*. I got into some difficult political situations with Ginnane, Brian Burgess [the line producer] and Tom. If Tom had been around during the shoot, it would have been much easier for me. There were some clashes, and Tom wasn't there to adjudicate, and I think these political problems affected my direction. The actors helped get me through: Sigrid, Simon, Martin and I all got on very well.'

John Daly was sent a video tape of the director's cut, and professed to be very taken with it. It is, however, a flawed film, which McLennan readily acknowledges. 'I wasn't as adventurous or courageous as I should have been.' Although the film was released in several key territories, including Britain and America, it performed only modestly.

At the end of the decade, McLennan produced a feature with a similar theme, *Breakaway* (1990).

T he whodunit was not the most popular form of thriller in the 80s, and there are few examples of the genre. One is *GLASS* (1989), a low-budget, direct-to-video feature which was the debut of a former Sydney dentist, Chris Kennedy. Kennedy (b. 1949) followed his father into the dental profession, but soon discovered he preferred to write scripts. He was unable to get any of his work filmed, despite winning the Australian Writers' Guild award for the best unproduced script of 1983 and, decided to do it himself. He established a company, Oilrag Productions, in partnership with his businessman friend Patrick Fitzgerald, and used his savings to make *Glass* on a tiny budget.

The film strives to be an erotic thriller along the lines of the French classic *Les Diaboliques*: but the actors seem too young for their roles, and the suspense is only intermittently maintained, with the denouement rather easy to spot (until a second twist at the end, which is a real puzzler). Peter de Vries provides some sleek images of Sydney's high-rise glass office towers, where some of the mayhem takes place, and the best performances are those of the women: Lisa Peers as the scheming villain and Natalie McCurry as the hero's girlfriend, a make-up artist whose profession provides an all-too-obvious clue.

JIGSAW (1989) is a Rosa Colosimo production, directed by Marc Gracie. The first half of the film is quite intriguing, with the discovery of the corpse of heroine Rebecca Gibney's husband on a beach: since they have been married for only one day, after a whirlwind courtship, she is naturally distressed. The film then evolves into a drama about illegal land deals, with crooked politicians involved. As long as it sticks to uncovering clues about the dead man's past, it is entertaining enough, with good performances from Gibney and from Dominic Sweeney as the investigating policeman. But the action scenes are poorly handled, and the final chase (with Sweeney and villain Nico Lathouris, guns in hand, battling it out on top of Gibney's speeding car), is not so much exciting as exasperating.

GEORGIA (1988) is a cut above these, but still badly flawed. The genesis of the film is a painting: Albert Tucker's 1984 portrait of Joy Hester; she had died in 1961 and he had not seen her since 1947.

Producer Bob Weis acquired the painting and, together with Mac Gudgeon, decided to research Hester's life as a possible starting point for a film. Intriguingly, each of Hester's close contemporaries—ex-husband, children, lovers—all had very different visions of her. 'I realised they were all inventing her, out of their own needs,' says Weis.

Inspired by this research, and by an affection for *Rashomon*, and deciding that the Hester film was not getting anywhere, Weis decided instead to make a purely fictional film which would be about posing a question for the central character to answer—a question about her long-dead mother. 'In the script, we decided to explode the myth that the more you find out about something, the closer you get to the truth,' says Weis.

Weis offered the script to director Ben Lewin, with whom he had worked on the mini-series, *The Dunera Boys*. Lewin (b. 1946 in Poland) had come to Australia with his parents in 1949 and trained as a lawyer. But he was always interested in cinema, and a chance meeting with Colin Young, of Britain's National Film School, persuaded him to go to London. He studied at the NFS from 1971 to 1974, and then found work at the BBC. In 1975, he made a controversial independent documentary, *Welcome to Britain*, about the country's new immigration laws which were being enforced, in the most humiliating way, on Asians arriving at Heathrow.

Lewin returned to Melbourne in the early 80s, and kept busy working on television projects until he read the *Georgia* screenplay (originally titled *A Difficult Woman*). 'I felt it was very different, very intriguing,' he says. 'And the thought of making something very different appealed to me. I wanted to step out of my own, idiosyncratic style and work in a collaborative way on someone else's material. I had done a lot of comedy, and I knew how to make people laugh: but it was a challenge to make them gasp, to sit on the edge of their seats. I've always been a fan of thrillers and mysteries. There's a fine line between laughter and fear.'

Says Weis, 'From the beginning, we set out very deliberately to make a stylised, non-naturalistic picture. That's not easy to do in this country. We used a cryptic story-telling technique: we were interested in the four different characters and their versions of what happened in the past.' Says Lewin: 'I knew from the outset there'd be criticism about what was left unexplained, and I was prepared to face that. The general expectation of a whodunit is that someone did it. I know as an ex-lawyer, and as a human being, that's not the way life works.

The notion of the elusiveness of real truth is a very real notion, whereas the cinema notion, of the whodunit having a tight and unequivocal explanation, is an invention. I wanted to use the technique of the cinema, of the thriller, to make a comment on real life, namely that the truth *is* confusing. It's the search, the wandering through the maze, that's interesting.'

Judy Davis became involved in the project almost from the outset, even before Lewin. The actress has a reputation for being difficult; according to Lewin, she was, but not excessively so. 'I'm used to being the difficult one on set,' he says wryly. 'For someone else to be difficult is a taste of my own medicine.' Davis, incidentally, rejected the use of the film's working title, *A Difficult Woman*.

Yuri Sokol was cinematographer. 'We'd fight tooth and nail over technical things, artistic decisions,' says Lewin. 'Then we'd go and have lunch and talk about Chekhov. He has extraordinary genius, but like most gifted people there's a temperament associated with that— but he's a man of extraordinary vision.'

The film, which was made on a budget of $3 million, is visually very stylish indeed. Its stylishness offsets, in part, at least, the fact that, for all its good intentions, it does not deliver. It is all very well to raise questions about the meaning of Truth, but there are so many gaps and inexplicable occurrences in *Georgia* that, at the end, we are left with more questions that we started with. Judy Davis is, as usual, excellent in her dual roles as mother and daughter, but the structure of the film—with the same 'truth' told four times from different perspectives—gets repetitive, which *Rashomon* certainly never does.

Weis found the film difficult to sell to distributors for this very reason: 'I found people have difficulty seeing the film for what it is, not for what they'd like it to be,' he says. 'It's disheartening to a degree. It's a film that really polarised people: you either like it or hate it.' In subverting the whodunit genre, the film became merely confusing, and it lacks the brilliance in script or direction that might have made it work.

EARLY FROST (1981) was a more traditional whodunit, but the mystery was not so much Who was the murderer? as Who directed the film? This is the only Australian feature on which there is no director credit, not even a mythical name like 'Alan Smithee' (used on American films where, for whatever reason, the director does not want to be named). The director was, in fact, Brian McDuffie, who had worked in New Zealand television and made a few short films at Film Australia in the early 80s (with eye-catching titles like *The Federal Parliamentary System* and *A Cyclone Warning*). Producer David Hannay believes this was the first 10BA film, and it was part of a package of films financed by Filmco.

The project dates back to 1974, when Hannay was running the short-lived production arm of Greater Union. A GU publicist, Geoff Brown, brought Terry O'Connor's script to Hannay's attention, but it took seven years to get it off the ground. O'Connor lived in Blacktown, to the west of Sydney, and his story was very specifically set in this working-class western suburb. Once money had been raised through Filmco, Hannay tried to secure Brian Trenchard Smith as director (they had worked together on *The Man from Hong Kong*), but Trenchard Smith was unavailable and so were other possible starters.

Brian McDuffie, according to Hannay, assured the writer and producers that he could and would make the film they had in mind. 'But then he went off and shot his own film. We fought him every day. We'd look at a scene and tell him: "Look, you didn't get the emphasis right, will you please shoot it again." And he'd go off for a conference with the cast and crew and decide I was a philistine trying to take his picture away from him. I decided not to sack him— the sacking of Keith Salvat from *Wall to Wall* had just occurred, and had given such things a bad odour. I decided to try to make it right afterwards, but, of course, it was never going to be right.'

It was always intended that Blacktown would be almost a character in this film about a woman who, as a result of some disastrous relationships, had neglected her children who had then turned evil. The decision was made to shoot in Blacktown, with cast and crew commuting there every day. 'But McDuffie hated being in Blacktown,' says Hannay. 'And he decided to transform it into Paddington. He took a perfect Blacktown house, and made it trendy.' Nor did the film make much sense: 'McDuffie liked to extemporise,' says Hannay, 'so a lot of the logic got lost along the way.'

The original screenplay was titled *Something Wicked This Way Comes* (a quote from *Macbeth*), and during production it became, simply, *Something Wicked*. The film was shot during a State election campaign and one unwary politician, visiting the set, was photographed wearing a *Something Wicked* T-shirt; the photo appeared in the newspapers next day, and was a source of much mirth. However, Walt Disney owned the rights to the Ray Bradbury book of the same name and, to avoid a lawsuit, Hannay decided to change the title to *Early Frost*.

Early Frost. *David Franklin, Jan Kingsbury.*

Hannay received a letter from Disney's legal department, filled with ominous warnings about courtroom battles; the letterhead incongruously featured Mickey Mouse in one of his most endearing poses.

McDuffie was handed a letter at the wrap party informing him he was fired, and Hannay, Brown and O'Connor handled the post-production themselves. 'We assembled a director's cut to see if we could understand it; but we couldn't. So we started again and completely recut it. I personally worked on the sound design to try to bring back the sounds of Blacktown. But visually it wasn't what we intended at all. [Cinematographer] David Eggby gave it no feeling of place.'

Early Frost represents the worst kind of tax-shelter film produced in the early 80s. One crew member recalls: 'It was a film made for all the wrong reasons; a classic 10BA film. A rort from beginning to end. The crew was really pissed off having to drive all the way to Blacktown to shoot every night inside a house. No-one had any passion for the film, they only cared about the money. The original first assistant director was very inexperienced and only lasted a few days, but he learnt he was being fired only when he saw the call sheet for the next day with Stuart Freeman's [the replacement first] name on it. It was an example of everything that could go wrong; it was tainted from the word go. To top it all, it is supposed to be summer and boiling hot and the actors are so cold you can see the breath coming out of their mouths.'

Part of the film's problems were connected with the 'bunching' of films brought about by the way the tax scheme worked. So many films were produced at the same time that top people—directors, crews, actors—were in short supply and the result was often compromised productions like this one. It never had a cinema release and is justifiably forgotten, though Jon Blake, in one of his early roles, appears as one of the suspects. But the characters and situations, as presented here, are so laboriously one-dimensional that to call it comparable to a telemovie is to demean that modest art form.

T wo other films financed by Filmco were thrillers. Both of them were directed by Quentin Masters, the London-based brother of investigative journalist Chris Masters. *A DANGEROUS SUMMER* (1982) was a McElroy production that had its genesis in a particularly bad series of bushfires that plagued the outer suburbs of Sydney in the summer of 1979–80. John Seale was despatched to shoot footage of the blaze, which Brian Trenchard Smith subsequently constructed into a 25-minute short film, *The Dangerous Summer*, scripted by Anne Brooks-bank. Trenchard Smith was announced as director of the feature—originally titled *Bushfire* and, later, *A Burning Man*—which would incorporate the same material, and, for a while, Bruce Beresford was connected with the project; but Masters (b. 1949) eventually took over. He had been working overseas, and already had two features to his credit, *Thumb Tripping* (1972) and the Joan Collins vehicle *The Stud* (1978).

Two foreign leads were imported: Tom Skerritt as the rugged architect hero and James Mason as an insurance investigator. The latter at least gives the picture some class, but Skerritt is totally out of place and it seems unlikely that he would ever father the lovely Kim Deacon. Wendy Hughes makes a brief appearance before being drowned in the surf, and the arsonist is eventually revealed to be personable Ian Gilmour. Part of the film's many production problems involved Gilmour, who broke his leg during shooting. The plot cobbled together to fit in with the bushfire sequences is pretty thin, the thrills are sparse and the ending weak. The Panavision photography of the Blue Mountains, and the fire sequences—including a blazing train—look great on the big cinema screen, but since the film was never theatrically released, only a tiny number of people ever experienced them.

MIDNITE SPARES (also 1982) was also troubled, but even more disastrously; it is the only Australian film on which a crew member has been killed. This is an utterly routine thriller about a gang of car thieves, although there is a strong supporting cast. It includes gang leader John Clayton and bent cop Tony Barry, plus Bruce Spence and David Argue playing for light relief. The film would have been instantly forgettable had it not been for the fatal accident that killed camera operator David Brostoff.

Geoff Burton, director of photography on the picture, recalls: 'We'd had a large number of night shoots, and this was the final night; everyone was tired. It wasn't a complicated stunt scene; we had four cameras, and David was pulling focus on my camera, which was in the most exposed position. The scene involved sprint cars going round a racetrack: one car was supposed to lose control and roll over. The stunt was set up in the conventional way, where a ramp is erected and the offside wheels of the car run up the ramp which causes it to spin over. I've filmed a fair few of these, and we had an experienced stunt driver doing it. We placed the cameras accordingly in what I considered to be relatively safe positions.

'What was not taken into account was what the other cars were going to do when this particular car rolled over in front of them. It was, in my view, an oversight on the part of the people planning the stunt. We took into account the car that would spin out, but not how the other cars—all being driven by racing drivers—would react. As it happened, three or four of them went out of control, and one of them—not the stunt car—came straight towards our camera. I dived one way, David the other—and it went right over him.

'It was totally shattering. And it was made worse because it was the last night, and the picture had been problematic from the start—a project that wasn't really in anyone's heart, something routine. We were eager to finish it. After that, I stopped work for a while and taught at the Film School. But the accident brought about the introduction of an industry safety code, which still applies today.'

Midnite Spares is a dull and soporific film, typical of the early 80s. No wonder voices were being raised against the tax packages being patched together by Filmco and the others. By the time the film was released, the founder of Filmco, Peter Fox, was himself dead, and *Midnite Spares* is dedicated 'to Foxie'.

Midnite Spares. *Bruce Spence.*

THEM!

A s Hamlet said, 'There are more things in heaven and earth, Horatio, than are dreamt of in your philosophy.' The cinema has, from its beginnings, taken us into that dark fantasy world of dreams and nightmares, where the incredible becomes real and goblins and long-legged beasties prowl. Science fiction and horror films have been immensely popular in recent years, with *Star Wars* (1977) putting sci-fi well and truly on the map, and pictures like John Carpenter's *Halloween* (1978) and the endless *Friday the 13th* series doing their bit for deranged (and seemingly unstoppable) human monsters. Australian films of the 80s occasionally attempted to enter this territory (the *Mad Max* films, discussed in Chapter 3, at times combine sci-fi, horror and outdoor adventure).

By far the most ambitious, and expensive, science fiction film made in Australia is *THE TIME GUARDIAN* (1987), which was also one of the most troubled and, ultimately, bitter films ever made in this country. It was conceived originally by two friends, Brian Hannant (b. 1940 in Brisbane) and John Baxter, who had met when both were working at the Commonwealth Film Unit in the mid-60s. Baxter had written a number of sci-fi novels and short stories, as well as books about the cinema (including a 1970 publication, *Science Fiction in the Cinema*), and had been away from Australia during most of the 70s, working in Britain and America. Hannant had directed the central segment, *Judy*, of *Three to Go* (1971), and later made documentaries at the CFU and Film Australia as well as in South Australia. In 1981, he co-scripted and worked as second unit director on *Mad Max 2* (see Chapter 3).

The following year, Baxter returned to Australia to record a series of interviews for BBC radio; he met Hannant, who encouraged him to try to set up a film in this country. In two days, they wrote what was then called *Time Rider*, a sci-fi love story. While working on *Mad Max 2*, Hannant had been impressed with the unusual rock formations at Wilpena Pound, South Australia, and this location became a major element of the story. The plot involved a female geologist, a man from the future (trying to escape from a polluted world), and a tribe of evil brigands, the Jen-Diki. A crucial character in the story was Prenzler, an old man living in an outback town, who 'held the key to certain elements in her [the geologist's] future.'

'John and I worked on about five or six drafts,' says Hannant. There was interest in the subject from the beginning. The script was acquired by Chateau Productions—Norman Wilkinson and Robert Lagettie; Hannant, who had previously made a documentary for the duo in

The Time Guardian. *Tom Burlinson.*

Kakadu, describes them as 'a couple of song pluggers who'd made commercials and documentaries and decided they wanted to make features. They had a rough, no-frills quality about them, but they had absolutely nothing to do with the Australian film industry as we knew it. They had no contacts with the AFC, they were anti-intellectual—yet they got out and did it, and they were honest. But they never went to the movies—and they weren't John's type. I quite liked them.'

At one point, in 1985, New World became involved in the project and Hannant went to the US to work with a script editor ('John should have come too,' he says). But the New World deal fell through, and Tony Ginnane stepped into the breach. 'He told Wilkinson and Lagettie he'd get the picture up, and he did,' says Hannant. 'He made one of those deals with Hemdale; and that's where it all started to fall apart. Wilkinson and Lagettie were under-capitalised and had never worked on a budget of this size before.' A budget of $8 million was settled on. ('Worked out on the backs of envelopes over a weekend,' says Hannant.) An approach to the AFC for money for project development had been rejected, so the AFC was not approached again for help in budgeting. 'The basic problem,' says Hannant, 'was lack of money. We became saddled with that $8 million budget: the money was raised in two days, but $12 million could have been raised just as easily. People fought over themselves to put money in.'

The sum of $8 million sounds like a lot of money, but Hollywood spends much more than that on sci-fi films with elaborate special effects. Hannant admits 'We could have skated by on the original draft. But, from July 1, the money started to go. Nine per cent went immediately to the brokers, and that was just the start: $1 million went the first day.'

The project, now titled *The Time Guardian*, went into pre-production. Geoff Burton was assigned as cinematographer. 'We'd never done an effects picture on this scale before,' says Burton. 'We didn't have the facilities they have in LA. We didn't have 65mm cameras, for instance. We shot on Super-35mm and worked in conjunction with a local company, Mirage Effects, to make optical effects which were pretty good. But we knew from the outset that, with the facilities at our disposal, we couldn't make anything really stylish; we knew the limitations. We closely analysed every American effects picture which was around at that time, and worked out how their rotoscoping worked, how their matte shots and split screens worked, and we tried to do it as they did. Mirage acquired (at huge expense) a blue screen rear-projection set-up designed by Douglas Trumbull: we set it up in an old disused cinema in Port Adelaide. The blue screen effects worked very well, and it's a pity that the facility, which is still here, hasn't been used since.'

All this work—and expense—was well under way and the film was crewed (but not yet cast) when, eight weeks before shooting was due to start, a call came from Hemdale boss John Daly: 'I don't understand this script.' Says Hannant, 'Wilkinson and I went immediately to Los Angeles and on arrival met with Ginnane, who was already there, and who handed me a new script. This had been written by an American (whose bill for around $15,000 was enclosed).' 'I can't tell you how appalled I was,' says Hannant. 'It wasn't only bad, it was laughable, and the attempts at Australianisms were dreadful. We'd written a modest film which contained only one monster, and we'd set aside about $150,000 in the budget to make it well; arms that worked, a head that worked. The end of the film was a one-on-one between Ballard and the monster. And the Prenzler character was vitally important to the time-travel aspects of the love story. But Daly, the man whose company made *The Terminator* [another time-travel film, which had been a hit] claimed he didn't understand it! Leaving all the drivel aside, I could see what he wanted: lots of monsters, a big battle at the beginning, and a bigger one at the end. Interestingly, after we left the meeting with Daly, Wilkinson and I went to see *Aliens* [currently a big hit], and we realised Daly had seen that and wanted something like it.'

It was an impossible situation. The now depleted $8 million budget was not big enough to make the film Daly demanded; $150,000 might have made one decent monster, but not dozens. Hannant phoned Baxter in Australia, and he was shattered, and was all in favour of washing his hands of the whole thing. 'I would've loved to have done that,' says Hannant. But how? The money was being spent, the crew was at work, the blue screen had cost hundreds of thousands of dollars— if the film was cancelled, who would pay for all of that? And, of course, the investors did not want the money back.

Hannant decided, grimly, to proceed. But he needed more money, money that was never forthcoming. He wrote a new script incorporating Daly's demands, which proved acceptable. Then came the problem of casting. Hannant and Baxter had envisaged a tough character actor in the leading role of Ballard: Scott Glenn had been mentioned. But in the end, Daly decided he wanted two Americans in supporting roles instead of one lead, and the only available Australian whom Daly was willing to approve in the Ballard role was Tom Burlinson, a solid young actor but hardly the right casting for a grizzled, middle-aged warrior. Dean Stockwell was quickly cast as the boss of the city of the future: after long delays, Carrie Fisher's casting was announced after shooting had commenced. Hannant regrets that there was no time, or money, to cast the minor roles in Sydney: 'They were all cast in Adelaide,' he says.

It was at this stage that Hannant and Baxter fell out; Baxter came to Adelaide for two days to work on the new script, but the friends quarrelled, and Baxter (whose name is still on the screen as co-screenwriter) has since written bitterly about the film. Each one felt the other had let him down.

Making *The Time Guardian* was a nightmare for Hannant. He had to write a first draft of the new material which was tacked on to seventh draft material. The shoot, originally planned for thirteen weeks, was cut to nine. Whole pages of the script had to be arbitrarily dropped on orders from the producers and line producer Harley Manners. There had to be fifteen set-ups a day, there were numerous night shoots, and the final sequence was never shot. 'It was like watching the *Titanic* going down,' says Hannant.

Post-production was equally fraught: Hannant was frustrated at every turn. Daly arrived in Australia demanding to see the film before it was ready, and Hannant refused to show it to him. Hannant's contract gave him the right of first cut, but Ginnane insisted Daly see the film, and the screening was a disaster. Hannant left the project: 'They certainly didn't want me around,' he says. 'If I hadn't quit, I'd have been fired.' Film editor Andrew Prowse and camera assistant

282 THE AVOCADO PLANTATION

Steve Arnold subsequently shot some additional scenes in which neither Hannant nor Geoff Burton were involved (though Burton was consulted).

An entire book could probably be written about *The Time Guardian*, but the bottom line is that the ideas Hannant and Baxter originally conceived were lost in an unexciting and disappointing film. Tom Burlinson is, to say the least, inadequate as Ballard, and he is not helped by dialogue such as 'These creatures aren't plumbers you can bribe to get your bathroom fixed overnight'. Nikki Coghill is a charming heroine, Dean Stockwell has little to do as the city boss, and Carrie Fisher gets crushed by a monster. The monsters are an unthreatening lot, being obviously people inside rubber armour with horns and red eyes, and the time-travel love story involving Prenzler is gone with the wind (though Prenzler does make a fleeting appearance). The Wilpena Pound location that inspired it all is seen only in a brief aerial shot. Crucially, the final battle is a feeble affair, and a dismal end to the proceedings.

How could $8 million be wasted on such a fiasco? The story of *The Time Guardian* is an object lesson in how the deal-driven 10BA films could be white-anted by the non-creative people. Hannant and Baxter might have made a memorable sci-fi drama to stand alongside classics of the genre: but they had the wrong producers, the wrong deals, the wrong budget, the wrong cast and, in the end, the wrong script.

Ironically, in the same year, 1987, a much more modest and infinitely more successful time travel movie was produced: this was *AS TIME GOES BY*, the fourth production from the Peak–Kiely team which made *The Big Hurt*. Interestingly, this project, too, changed a lot from its initial concept. The original story was titled *The Cricketer*, and it was about a mythical cricketer in outback Australia; the Robert Redford film *The Natural* seems to have been the inspiration. Barry Peak and Chris Kiely gradually shifted towards a classic sci-fi story about a Sydney surfie (Nique Needles) who keeps a mysterious rendezvous in the outback with a time-travelling alien.

The film unit shot for three weeks on locations around Broken Hill and Silverton, with the modest but excellent special effects designed by Peter Stubbs. Max Gillies was cast as the quickwitted alien, Joe Bogart, and gives his best screen performance to date, including clever impersonations of famous voices of the 30s and 40s: Bogart, Cagney, Lorre, Greenstreet—even Garbo. Bruno Lawrence is a tough outback cop, who turns out to be the long-lost father of the hero; Ray Barrett is a landowner obsessed by the Greenhouse Effect, and there are a number of amusing supporting characters. The film is briskly paced, filled with classic time-travel ideas, and hugely entertaining. 'We just wanted to make a fun picture,' says Peak—and he certainly succeeded. *As Time Goes By* was a considerable success, not only in Australia but in world sales, though, at the time of writing, it had not been acquired for the US.

One problem was with the title, and once that was cleared, the use of the title song. Peak was originally quoted $5000 to use that, but then discovered that, for world rights, $100,000 was closer to the mark. The song is heard in the Australian version of the film, but not in overseas prints.

As Time Goes By is comic-clever sci-fi; the best example of suspense sci-fi made in Australia to date is *INCIDENT AT RAVEN'S GATE* (1988), produced by Marc Rosenberg and Rolf De Heer and directed by the latter. De Heer (b. 1951) had been given the basic script some years earlier by James Vernon: 'It had a central image I liked,' he says. De Heer and Vernon tried to get the project going for several years without success; Rosenberg subsequently acquired the project, and renewed efforts were made to get it off the ground. Says Rosenberg: 'We'd both seen a lot of sci-fi films, and we thought this could be a lot of fun. The limitations of the budget made it more interesting, because we realised we couldn't compete with American films. The challenge was to tell the story without having aliens in rubber suits.'

The film has one thing in common with *The Time Guardian*: finance was raised by Tony Ginnane's company. Says Rosenberg: 'People didn't bang on our doors to finance the film, and we tried unsuccessfully for three years. We got close several times, and then the tax laws changed and we had to start again. In 1985, I went to Britain, Japan

Incident at Raven's Gate. *Steve Vidler.*

and the American Film Market, and I thought I had a deal, but it fell through. Ginnane was really our last hope: we sold our soul to get the film made. Our experience closely parallels the Faust legend.'

The budget was $2.5 million, of which $1.1 million was actually used in production: the remaining $1.4 million was spent on fees for executive producers, writers and producers. With such a budget, De Heer and Rosenberg never seriously considered showing the aliens. De Heer says: 'I'd been out bush and talked to people who'd seen UFOs. And you often read of people missing from some remote farm and never find out what happened to them. That was the kind of thing I was after: we know something's happening, but what's causing it? What was important to me wasn't what people saw, but what they *thought* they saw. There are good films, like *Alien* and *E.T.*, in which the alien is seen—the audience has to accept them. I wanted audiences to make up their own mind about what was there.'

The film was shot on locations in farm country in South Australia, and depicts a place where waterholes mysteriously dry up, car engines die, and an elderly couple are discovered welded together. The story revolves around parallel love affairs: Eddie (Steven Vidler), fresh out of prison, falls in lust with the frustrated wife (Celine Griffin) of his dull brother (Richard Singer). Vincent Gil plays Skinner, the local cop who is passionately addicted to opera and who is jealous of Eddie's relationship with Annie (played by the producer's wife, Saturday Rosenberg). Somehow, the never-seen aliens are affecting the behaviour of these people: Skinner kills Annie in a fit of violent jealousy, and sings a forlorn aria as he dumps her body over a bridge.

The film is technically brilliant, with astonishing camerawork from Richard Michalak, who uses swooping crane shots and dazzling contrast between the very bright and the very dark (the film was shot in a wide screen system, and looks pitifully inadequate on video or television). There is also a magnificent and carefully constructed soundtrack, one of the most creative ever for an Australian film. Says Rosenberg: 'Money controlled our decisions. We couldn't compete with special effects, so we used sound to greater effect. A lot of filmmakers underestimate the power of sound, but the audience finds it very affecting.' The Adelaide sound team, led by mixer Jim Currie, was inspired by the radical use of sound De Heer and Rosenberg employed.

Says De Heer: 'For me, the question is: "What is cinema? Why go to the cinema as opposed to watching something on television?" The cinema has the potential to provide wonderful visuals and great sound that you can't experience on television or on video. Then it's a matter of using those elements to their fullest, going radical, because, if you don't it's all been seen before. We thought: "How dark can we afford to make this? How bright can we afford to make this?" The wide screen is cinema, not television, so let's use it; let's find the shapes and the angles. And it's a Dolby soundtrack, so, again, we used it: big sound, no sound at all. More than anything, the film's an attempt to be cinematic.'

The fact that the aliens are not seen makes for some genuinely spooky moments, but De Heer and Rosenberg also inject a black sense of humour: Rachel, seeing her husband drunk, remarks: 'I haven't seen him like this since our wedding night,' and as Felix, dressed for a visit to the Sydney Opera House, drives through town with Annie's body in his police car, a bystander remarks: 'He's dressed to kill!' Says Rosenberg: 'We often talked about films with similar budgets, like John Carpenter's *Dark Star* in which a beach ball was an alien, and, of course, *Blood Simple*; we could see that the tension would come out much stronger if it was juxtaposed with humour.'

There is no doubt that, on the big screen, *Incident at Raven's Gate* is cinema: *Blood Simple* certainly comes to mind, but so does George Miller's original *Mad Max*. These are all films made on modest budgets which transcend their limitations with the quality of the scripting and direction, performances, cinematography, sound and design. *Raven's Gate* should have followed the route taken by *Mad Max*; it should have been screened at science-fiction festivals, like Avoriaz in France, where it could have made an international reputation for itself. But it did not.

Says Rosenberg: 'Tony Ginnane never had much faith in the film, and we never knew why.' It was not a lack of distributor or exhibitor interest: Hoyts offered a wide release for the film, but were refused. 'Ginnane actively fought against a broad release,' says De Heer. Eventually, the film was booked into the Valhalla cinemas simultaneously with the video release. Ginnane has pointed out that the cost of launching a film in Australia (prints, advertising) is enormous, and presumably felt that *Raven's Gate* would not attract a large enough audience to justify such expenditure; but since it is one of the best films he was ever involved with, the lack of faith is, indeed, saddening.

The most elaborate and ambitious sci-fi movie ever planned for Australia was, in the event, never made. This was *Total Recall*, which was announced in 1987 as the first production for DEL (the Australian subsidiary of Dino De Laurentiis). The story, set on Mars in the twenty-first century, was to be filmed at the new De Laurentiis film studios on the Gold Coast; Bruce Beresford was to direct a screenplay by Dan O'Bannon and Ronald Shusett, with Sue Milliken producing, Peter James behind the camera and John Stoddart as editor. After numerous delays, the project was abandoned because of the financial problems of DEG (De Laurentiis' American company) and the film was eventually made, in America, by Paul Verhoeven.

In discussing futuristic films, we should exclude Roger Christian's British *Lorca and the Outlaws* (1985), a.k.a. *Starship*, which was shot in Australia and has a few local actors—Hugh Keays-Byrne, Joy Smithers—but is not Australian. For similar reasons, we will not consider here the dismal *Salute of the Jugger* (1989), by David Webb Peoples, which, again, uses Australian locations and supporting actors—Hugh Keays-Byrne yet again—as well as some key crew, but which is American. Only a couple of other futuristic films were made in Australia in the 80s and both were directed by Brian Trenchard Smith (b. 1947 in Britain), the most prolific director of Australian films in the 80s. And—a further coincidence—both deal with prison camps of the future.

The better of the two—by far—is *DEAD END DRIVE-IN* (1986), which

Brian Trenchard Smith (second from left), *the most prolific director of the 80s, on the set of* Dead End Drive-in.

Dead End Drive-in. *Ned Manning.*

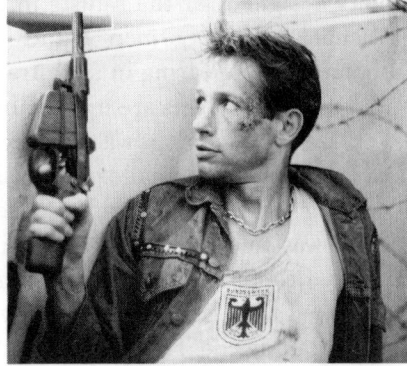

is set in the 1990s when unruly elements are incarcerated in a disused
drive-in cinema; the film was shot in a real drive-in in Sydney's south-
western suburbs. Based on *Crabs*, a short story by Peter Carey, the
film's plotting is a bit confusing, but the drive-in atmosphere is
convincingly presented, and there are better than average performances
from Ned Manning, as the rebellious hero, and Peter Whitford, as
the drive-in/prison's avuncular manager/warden. This was Manning's
only major film role of the decade, although on the strength of it
this former schoolteacher and playwright (*Us and Them*) deserved more
opportunities.

The film is famous chiefly for its climactic stunt, in which Crabs
apparently drives his car through a neon sign and right over the drive-
in wall. This was said at the time to be a world record (49.4 metres)
for stunt driver Guy Norris, and it is a pity that it has been edited
in such a way as to diminish its impact. Superbly shot by Paul Murphy,
and designed by Larry Eastwood, *Dead End Drive-in* maintains a mood
of subdued tension throughout. It might have fared better at the box-
office if it had been less moody and more action-packed; still, it is
several cuts above the average.

It is a veritable masterpiece when compared to *TURKEY SHOOT* (1981)
which is merely a catalogue of sickening horrors. This variation on
The Hounds of Zaroff, involving an island prison camp of the future,
includes scenes in which: a mutant is sliced in half by a bulldozer;
a man is shot full of arrows, then run over by a car; another man
is shot in the groin; Olivia Hussey chops the hands off a man; a woman's
body is found covered with lacerations, an arrow plunged into her
mouth; a man is literally decapitated by bullets; a woman is stabbed
in the face with an exploding arrow; and a woman is punched and
kicked to death. All of this is lovingly shot, and seems to be an exercise

solely designed for the sadists in the community. The actors involved (Michael Craig, Carmen Duncan, Noel Ferrier) should have been ashamed for appearing in such trash: some apparently were.

The special effects are undeniably well done, and the film is certainly slick. David Hemmings was co-executive producer (with Hemdale's John Daly), and Tony Ginnane produced (with William Fayman). Just before shooting started, the film's budget was suddenly cut and Trenchard Smith was told to eliminate the first seven minutes of the screenplay (neatly dropping all that irritating exposition as a result). It was also rumoured that Hemmings took over direction of a second unit which worked alongside Trenchard Smith and which helped cut the overall shooting schedule by two weeks; if this was the case, Hemmings worked without credit.

The film was shot on location in Cairns, and Ginnane saw it as 'a broadly-drawn black comedy'. He had wanted to work with Trenchard Smith after seeing *The Man from Hong Kong*: 'Brian is one of those "can do" sort of people I like associating with.' Ginnane asserts that my review in the New York-based international show-business journal, *Variety* (20 April 1983), in which I described the film as 'a sadistic bloodbath', lost him a sale to Malaysia when the censor there banned it, enclosing a cutting of the *Variety* review with his letter of rejection.

F rom the gruesome horrors of the future as depicted in *Turkey Shoot*, it is not a long step to the genre of films about terrorised people (invariably women) inspired by *Halloween* and its ilk. Most of these are low-budget efforts, and very occasionally a director of talent will cut his or her teeth on such material. Often the human monster who threatens the lovely heroine is a psychopath, but in the case of *FAIR GAME* (1985) he, or rather they, are just your average macho Aussie outdoorsmen. In fact, they are kangaroo hunters (compare *Wake in Fright* and *Razorback*) who just like a little simple fun, and Jessica (Cassandra Delaney) fills the bill: she is beautiful and she lives alone in an isolated homestead. Sunny, Ringo and Sparks first see her during a *Duel*-like encounter on the highway, and then increase their harassment of her and end up stripping her half-naked and destroying her home (though not, apparently, raping her). She retaliates by killing all of them.

First-time director Mario Andreacchio does his best with this material, but is hampered by a script (by Rob George) lacking motivation and characterisation; the film, shot in South Australia, is notable only for some clever stuntwork and a general atmosphere of nastiness.

RUN, CHRISSIE, RUN! (1984) is also set in South Australia—a State that seems to attract such damsel-in-distress subjects. But, unlike *Fair Game*, this dismal picture was produced by the SAFC, which should have known better: why executive producer Jock Blair thought this inept screenplay (by Graham Hartley) was worth filming is anyone's guess. Michael Aitkens is an ex-IRA hit-man who arrives in Adelaide looking for his ex-girlfriend, a former German terrorist (Carmen Duncan with the most uncertain of accents) and his daughter, a nubile teenager. The trio heads for the Barossa Valley, pursued by IRA terrorists plus Toe (Nicholas Eadie), a malodorous and malevolent oaf who seems to have strayed in from the *Mad Max* films.

The film brings back unwanted memories of Michael Thornhill's dire telemovie *Harvest of Hate* (1978) about Arab terrorists in the Barossa; it was equally silly, though not as tawdry, and was also produced by the SAFC. In this case the low point probably occurs when Duncan explains that she became a terrorist as a result of Vietnam and in protest against the Shah of Iran! Mercifully, the film seems not to have been distributed.

The title *LADY, STAY DEAD* (1981) just about sums up the whole genre. This has a sex-obsessed gardener-handyman (Chard Hayward) rape and then murder his employer, a precocious actress (Deborah Coulls), and later terrorise her sister (Louise Howitt). Filmed at a Palm Beach mansion, the film, as written, produced and directed by Terry Bourke, is a routine exercise in suspense which is never very gripping. Though the violence is downplayed, there is a fair amount of gratuitous nudity, which did not help the film find a cinema release— like so many in this category, it went straight to video.

DESOLATION ANGELS (1982) has three young women in trouble— Melbourne high-school students who 'borrow' a weekender at Portsea and head off there to have some fun, but who are terrorised by three dangerous youths. Chris Fitchett's film is a disappointment after his *Blood Money* (see Chapter 8); he seems uncertain whether he is making a horror film or a more serious drama, and includes not enough thrills for the former genre, and too many sadistic elements for the latter. The wintry seaside setting is nicely shot by Ellery Ryan (who co-scripted) and early scenes, especially those on the road, are effective. But later the film loses all plausibility, and a voice-over (spoken by one of the schoolgirls), at first merely irritating, becomes positively risible.

HOUSEBOAT HORROR (1989), co-directed by Ollie Martin and Kendal

Flanagan, is a thoroughly routine slasher film closely modelled on the *Friday the 13th* series. A film crew is shooting a rock video at a remote lake; one by one they are slaughtered by a horribly scarred maniac with a grudge against film people. There is the usual tired *Psycho* reference, a redundant, fleeting appearance from film 'personality' John Michael Howson (who turns out to be neither victim nor slasher) and attempts at grim humour in the various gimmicky ways the victims are despatched. The final image paves the way for a sequel one hopes will never be made.

MARAUDERS (1987) is another Victorian-produced low-budget film with a rural setting. This was produced by the aptly-named Savages: Mark Savage wrote, produced, photographed and directed, while Colin Savage plays the lead (and assisted Mark at the editor's bench). At least Savage displays a certain energy and visual slickness, but the nasty little story is a put-off, especially as the mindless violence is directed invariably at women: the rape and murder of an innocent girl is just one of the film's low points, while the fact that a group of small-town vigilantes who hunt down the rapists are led by women hardly redresses the balance.

The most that can be said for these films is that they are all trying to find Australian variations on a familiar genre. In contrast, *INNOCENT PREY* (1983), produced and directed by Colin Eggleston, is a mid-Pacific picture starring Americans P. J. Soles and Martin Balsam. The film opens in Dallas, Texas, where Joe (Kit Taylor), the husband of Cathy (Ms Soles) goes off the rails, apparently as the result of a bad business deal. He commits a series of murders, whereupon the terrified Cathy high-tails it for Sydney and the luxury harbourside apartment of a girlfriend, unaware that the landlord (John Warnock) is as crazy, and dangerous, as her old man.

The script (Ron McLean) is full of holes: how does Joe find Cathy in Sydney? Come to that, how does he get out of America in the first place, since all the police in the country are after him? The direction is merely functional: Eggleston even has the cheek to show blood draining down the plug-hole after a prostitute is murdered in a shower. The film is, at 100 minutes, also far too long, and very laboriously handled.

Eggleston also directed *CASSANDRA* (1987), a feeble combination of slasher movie and whodunit about a young woman whose mad brother has been in an asylum since he was a child but now is out and killing people. Again, the unanswered questions: how come the brother was sent to a mental home at what seems to be the ripe old age of three? But, does anyone care? Certainly not the filmmakers.

John Lamond's *NIGHTMARES* (1980) is also a slasher-whodunit, but it holds even fewer surprises. Set in a theatre, it combines a leering fondness of full frontal nudity with a series of particularly nasty knife killings, all centred on the deranged heroine, a would-be actress with an American accent. One of the victims is Max Phipps, as a theatre director; another is John Michael Howson, who provides an embarrassing caricature of a theatre critic. Nina Landis, who plays another victim, was subsequently seen to better advantage in *Rikky and Pete*. Roadshow released this one, but only in Melbourne.

The same year, Ross Dimsey directed *FINAL CUT* (1980), the first feature funded by the Queensland Film Corporation. Queensland bureaucrats being what they are (or were) it is perhaps no surprise that, in this most 'moral' of States, the QFC's first picture should be a sadistic thriller. It concerns a young filmmaker and his journalist girlfriend making a documentary about a businessman suspected of involvement in snuff movies. Lacking suspense and a credible narrative, the film is further burdened with lacklustre performances, though Jennifer Cluff does demonstrate a hint of the talent she would display in future films with her husband, Bill Bennett. *Final Cut* was Dimsey's last feature film as a director: a subsequent project, *The Unforgiven*, announced in 1980, seems never to have been made. He subsequently worked as an administrator (Victorian Film Corporation) and producer, and, more recently, was Head of the ABC's Melbourne Drama Unit.

Journeymen directors like Dimsey, Lamond, Eggleston and Bourke are unlikely ever to surprise us: Craig Lahiff might one day. As we saw in Chapter 8, the director of *Fever* has ideas, but they are muted in his first film, *CODA* (1987). It was produced by Tom Broadbridge who, by this time, had become an astute packager of video projects which occasionally have cinema potential. *Coda* was shot on Super-16mm on a budget of $600,000, mostly on locations at Flinders University. Its chief claim to fame is that all the central roles, including that of the police inspector, are women, though this was not the original intention. Says Lahiff: 'I was originally going to cast a Bill Hunter type as the policeman. But it's hard to get all the people you want when it's your first film, plus an exploitation thriller. So then I thought I'd cast a woman [Olivia Hamnett] in the role, and make it a little different.'

Otherwise, Lahiff borrows freely from Hitchcock (*Psycho*, inevitably,

Dial M for Murder) and shows a marked interest in defenestration (two such deaths in one picture). The climax, an endless chase down university corridors, is unduly protracted. Lahiff himself admits that the theme of obsessive (gay) love does not really work. But the actresses are all worth watching: Penny Cook as the threatened heroine; Arna-Maria Winchester as a butch music professor, obsessed with her brother, missing for years; Olivia Hamnett as the policewoman; Liddy Clark as Cook's best friend. The film sold very well on video.

In 1987, Broadbridge got together with another Sydney producer, David Hannay, and they agreed to make a package of four exploitation films, each with a budget of about $600,000, and all shot on 35mm with the aim of tapping the theatrical market if possible, the video market if not. The two had been discussing for some years the possibility of collaborating on low-budget films, and, during pre-production of the four, a video company, Medusa Communications, also became involved.

The four films were shot, more or less simultaneously, late in 1987. Of them, the best is *VICIOUS* (1988), later recut and retitled *To Make a Killing*; though it must be said that this is a terrifyingly nasty film. It was directed by Karl Zwicky (b. 1958 in Zurich): Zwicky had come to Perth with his family while still a baby. He became interested in film at an early age, and spent the years 1979–82 at the Film and TV School, where he met Paul Hogan (of *The Humpty Dumpty Man*, not *Crocodile Dundee*!) He co-scripted *The Humpty Dumpty Man* and made a successful short film, *The Bus Trip*, a slapstick comedy in Panavision. As a result, he was given the chance to direct his first feature, *Contagion* (read on).

Vicious was produced for $640,000, and was shot in four 6-day weeks on 35mm with the aim of possible theatrical release: but the principal market was video. Broadbridge handed Zwicky a formula script for

Vicious. *Kelly Dingwall, Craig Pearce.* (Photo: *Corrie Ancone.*)

a thriller: Zwicky suggested that, instead, he and Hogan write an original screenplay. 'The original brief was to get an R rating in America,' says Zwicky. 'But, after the film was finished, the market collapsed for that sort of stuff. You can never predict these things.'

Hogan and Zwicky wrote the screenplay in five weeks. Like Craig Lahiff, they found it very hard to cast actors in this kind of project: 'They read the script and it's confronting. A formula horror film isn't so bad, but this was so real. And Australians don't want to admit that their society has just as many shadowy nooks and crannies as the Americans. It's all right for the Americans to behave that way, but not for us. Plus, there was an element of perverseness in the way Paul and I wrote it.'

The film was shot in the northern suburbs of Sydney. 'It was a fascinating shoot,' says Zwicky. 'But I probably wouldn't do a film of that nature again. The massacre scene in the Price home took four days to shoot, and it was confronting even to film it. The actors respected the script, but they didn't like it. In the production office, some of our people who had read the script were convinced the film included a rape scene. There is no rape scene, but they were convinced there was.' Even Paul Hogan was somewhat shattered by the film he had co-written: 'Karl pushed it a bit too far,' he says. 'It was pretty nasty.'

After *Vicious* was completed, Broadbridge found sales resistance to it. 'It was just too strong,' says Zwicky. 'Though, actually, there's nothing to *see*, really, in the film: it's the horror that's implied.' Part of the film's extraordinary intensity stems from the dynamic, genuinely scary performance of Craig Pearce as Terry, the leader of the gang. 'He has an incredible screen presence,' says Zwicky. 'I'm surprised other producers haven't taken him up.'

Vicious is a quite terrifying film, the more terrifying because it is so believable. The casual violence of Terry, Felix and Benny, the three young hoodlums who raid the homes of the rich; rich boy Damon's initial attraction towards that violence, and his terrible realisation that his girlfriend, Sondra, and her family are in mortal danger; and the awful scenes in the Price house—all these elements are handled with a ruthless skill. The ultimate moralistic message is laid on a bit thick, but there is little doubt, after this film, that Karl Zwicky could become, if not Australia's John Carpenter, then at least Australia's Wes Craven. In Britain, *Vicious* was deemed 'a video nasty', and recutting was demanded before it could be released on video at all; in the US, it had a brief cinema release.

K arl Zwicky's first feature, also produced by Tom Broadbridge, belongs to a different category of horror film: the ghost story. Quite a few films involving ghosts have been made in Australia, none of them coming close to classics of the genre like the British *Dead of Night* or *The Innocents*, the American *The Uninvited* or the Japanese *Kwaidan*.

CONTAGION (1987) is a good try, though. Zwicky was approached to direct by Queensland writer Ken Methold, who had seen *The Bus Trip*. 'As that was all-out slapstick, I can't quite understand what connection he saw,' says Zwicky, 'unless it was the way I used the Panavision screen.' *Contagion* was budgeted at $750,000, and was shot, entirely around Brisbane, in thirty-five days. 'It wasn't 10BA,' says Zwicky. 'It was all direct investment. If it had been 10BA, it would have cost $1.5 million once all legal and broking fees had been added to it.'

Zwicky leapt at the opportunity to make his first feature, but was not crazy about the script. 'Ken spent his youth in England; he's now in his 50s, and his dialogue didn't ring very true, but he had fixed ideas about it. I tried to make it a bit tongue in cheek. Since it was written in 60s style, a bit like *The Avengers*, I thought I'd direct in that style. But the fundamental problem was that I had a very limited range of actors to draw on.'

Contagion starts out like a routine slasher film, until real-estate salesman John Doyle winds up in a mysterious, beautiful house in the woods where he is quickly seduced by two attractive young women (Pamela Hawksford, Nathalie Gaffney) and charmed by the lascivious head of the house, amusingly played by Ray Barrett. Only when it is too late does our hero realise that these three are ghosts, and that their beautiful home is a ruined and abandoned homestead. Bookended by ominous overhead shots of a car driving through the woods, the film already displays Zwicky's cinematic skills, though he is ill-served by the occasionally creaky plot development. Chilling scenes in the woods at night (with unexplained light sources illuminating the terrors) might not be everyone's cup of tea, but with these two films (unseen in Australian cinemas), Zwicky is clearly a talent for the future.

For proof of this contention, you have only to compare *Contagion* with the laboriously unthrilling *FRENCHMAN'S FARM* (1986), which also features Ray Barrett, and which has a vaguely similar idea. This time the ghost-affected protagonist is a young woman, Jackie (Tracey Tainsh) and the screenplay unwisely suggests she is top of her university law class, which requires a gigantic act of faith on the part of the audience. She is driving through the Queensland countryside in broad daylight when she witnesses a murder that apparently took place some forty years earlier; and the plot (such as it is) develops into a hunt for buried treasure and the revenge of a ghost from the French Revolution, with just about everyone meeting a sticky end. Barrett plays the owner of the haunted farm, John Meillon is a policeman and Norman Kaye is the local vicar, a rather mysterious gent; but this distinguished cast does not help, and nor does the presence of David Reyne as Ms Tainsh's boyfriend. The problem is the flat, television-style direction of Ron Way, and the unconvincing screenplay.

Returning to the package of four films produced by Broadbridge and David Hannay, of which *Vicious* is the most interesting, we find three more variations on the ghost story. *THE 13TH FLOOR* (1988), written and directed by newcomer Chris Roache, is the least of the bunch, an unconvincing thriller about a couple of women drop-outs (Lisa Hensley, Miranda Otto) squatting on the deserted (and apparently haunted) thirteenth floor of an office building. As a child, Hensley, whose corrupt businessman father owns the building, had seen a young boy electrocuted while his father was tortured; it is the ghost of the boy, a quite benign ghost, in fact, who comes to Hensley's aid when she is attacked by her father's hit-men. Roache makes heavy weather of all this nonsense, and the producers had to employ another director to shoot for five more days after principal photography was completed.

With his wealth of experience, Brian Trenchard Smith could be expected to do a better job with *OUT OF THE BODY* (1988), and indeed he does. He also has a stronger cast than Roache. Mark Hembrow stars as a music composer haunted by visions of death in which various young women are killed and their eyes plucked out. The killer, we discover eventually, is within Hembrow himself; but along the way, Trenchard Smith and writer Kenneth G. Ross provide some amusing red herrings and a neat final twist. There are also some engaging performances, especially John Clayton and John Ley as policemen and Mary Regan as one of the victims. Nor does the director wallow in gore, since the violence takes place mostly off-screen.

The fourth of the Broadbridge–Hannay productions belongs to a sub-genre of the ghost film: the Aboriginal legend film. *KADAICHA* (1988) is a *Poltergeist*-inspired yarn about a bunch of teenagers being killed by a variety of unseen monsters because, we eventually discover, they live on a housing estate built on an Aboriginal sacred site.

Queensland writer Ian Coughlan (who had written and directed another thriller, *Alison's Birthday*, for Hannay in 1979) provided the screenplay, and former rock drummer James Bogle directed. Bogle provides a few good moments of suspense, and the film is lifted out of the routine by some of the actors, especially Sean Scully as the local headmaster.

These four films, plus *Contagion*, are not great works of art, but they are useful examples of completely home-grown genre films that do not need has-been American actors in leading roles to succeed. Apart from Trenchard Smith, the film directors employed are new at the game, and were given a chance to cut their cinematic teeth with relatively inexpensive projects with results that are, on the whole, encouraging. It is in the area of the exploitation film that such experiments are most likely to succeed.

Another film in the Aboriginal ghost sub-genre is *THE DREAMING* (1988), which was Mario Andreacchio's second feature (after *Fair Game*). *Kadaicha* features a mystic stone, filled with power: *The Dreaming* has a bracelet which insensitive archaeologist Arthur Dignam discovers in an Aboriginal cave on an island, and it is his doctor daughter (Penny Cook) who starts to be plagued by ghost-like visions of a massacre of Aborigines by whalers which apparently took place 200 years earlier—the chief whaler looks horribly like her father.

The Dreaming was produced by the South Australian company Genesis Films (Craig Lahiff, Wayne Groom). They had originally written the story, and Lahiff had planned to direct; but Lahiff was exhausted after directing *Coda* and *Fever* one after the other, and was never very involved in the project. The money was raised through Tony Ginnane's FGH company, which then had approval of script and casting, and Lahiff was not happy with the way the script was being turned (by other writers) into, as he puts it, 'a B-grade horror film.' Lahiff decided not to direct it, and Mario Andreacchio was brought in at the last moment.

The Dreaming is depressingly poor. It is not very suspenseful, or well enough acted to make the final confrontation between frightened daughter and maddened father very gripping. Nor is it visually very interesting, with Michael Ralph's production design noticeably below standard (the Aboriginal cave is very plastic, and Cook and husband Gary Sweet live in an apartment of surpassing ugliness). Any hopes, based on his first film, that Mario Andreacchio had some talent for thrillers are quickly dashed with this one. Not surprisingly, it was released on video without benefit of cinema screenings. Says Lahiff, 'It didn't wind up at all the way I'd planned it.'

Much earlier in the decade, Ginnane was involved in a couple of films which also had ghostly elements; but these were both made in the period when he was producing films himself, rather than acting primarily as a raiser of finance for other producers and assuming executive-producer credit. *HARLEQUIN*, though released in 1980, was discussed in my earlier book, *The Last New Wave:* 'Inept and utterly absurd' were the words I used then, and there is no reason to change them. Writer Everett De Roche came up with the interesting idea of updating the Rasputin story to make a political thriller, but the thought of a priest with supernatural powers (which was the original concept) might have frightened off audiences in the Bible Belt of Middle America: and this film was, above all, tailored for middle-American audiences. It is the only Australian film which was thoroughly

Harlequin. *David Hemmings, Robert Powell.*

Americanised: the story is set, presumably, in America, American flags fly, cars drive on the right (but with Western Australian licence plates), telephones ring in the American style, Alan Cassell is crudely dubbed into American, and the screenplay is filled with references to the American political system.

Finance for *Harlequin* was raised from a number of sources: the AFC, GU, Ace Theatres of Western Australia, and the new company Pact Productions (Peter Fox and Bob Sanders): but the budget was $50,000 short. Ginnane was able to obtain that money from Larry Fredericks of Hemdale in return for foreign agency rights; this was the company which actor David Hemmings had originally formed in Britain with John Daly (though Hemmings was no longer involved at this stage, and Hemdale was in the process of shifting its activities from London to Los Angeles). *Harlequin* represented Ginnane's first link with Hemdale—a link which, as we have already seen, would assume greater importance as the decade wore on.

Three actors were imported for the film: David Hemmings had already acted in Ginnane's production *Thirst* (1979), a modern vampire story; Robert Powell plays the Rasputin figure, now reduced to the status of a magician and known as Wolfe; and Broderick Crawford, looking mummified, was brought in to play one of his final screen roles as a political hatchet-man. As a result of the casting, and the aforementioned attempts to Americanise the story, the film exists in a kind of no man's land. All the skills which director Simon Wincer— making his second feature, following on from *Snapshot*—and cinematographer Gary Hansen bring to the picture cannot deny the basic contempt shown for the audience. Nevertheless, the strategy seems to have worked, for *Harlequin* took $1.2 million overseas, a substantial figure. The fact that the film could have been so much better is a matter for regret.

Later the same year, 1980, Ginnane produced another film with supernatural elements, *THE SURVIVOR*, which David Hemmings directed; Hemmings had previously directed three films in Britain, *Running Scared*, *The 14* and *Just a Gigolo*. It seemed at the time incredible that the SAFC would invest in such a project, but, as we have seen, this was just one of many strange decisions made at the SAFC in the period after *Breaker Morant*. Given the success of *Harlequin*, it did not take much persuasion to get Hemdale to invest in the new film. Ginnane recalls: 'It seemed to me an opportunity to take advantage of what Hemdale was doing through an associate company: raise money in the UK under the Capital Allowances scheme, and match it to non-recourse lending and use the tax-exempt status of the SAFC, as a government body, to effectively shelter the money that was coming in. So on that basis we managed to put *The Survivor* together for about $1.2 million—the most expensive film we'd done up to that time. The SAFC was in for $350,000, the English tax group for about the same, Pact Productions for about the same, GU gave us an advance and we got a TV sale. The English investors got a complete write-off on the whole movie, and so did the Australian investors: a nice example of double-dipping.'

If the deal made on *The Survivor* was satisfactory, other elements were not. The film marked the real beginning of Ginnane's struggle with Actors Equity, which invoked Section 31A(b) of the Actors Feature Film Award to prevent Ginnane from importing four actors for the film: he had wanted Robert Powell, Joseph Cotten, Samantha Eggar and Susan George. An appeal by Ginnane to the Arbitration Commission met with no success, and in the end neither Eggar nor George was imported: Jenny Agutter was brought in for one of the roles, and local actress Angela Punch McGregor played the other (though most of her part seems to have landed on the cutting-room floor).

Ginnane's remarks about raising money for the film indicate how important was 'making the deal' in projects like this. In *The Survivor* a complicated financial structure results in another 'international' production: three imported actors and an imported director. The film is an even greater mish-mash than *Harlequin*, which at least told a coherent story. *The Survivor* is incomprehensible: there are numerous killings, but we never find out who is doing them. Is it Slater (overplayed by Ralph Cotterill), the villain who planted the bomb on the 747? (Why *did* he sabotage the plane, by the way?) Or is it the ghosts of the plane's passengers? What is fourth-billed Angela Punch McGregor doing in the film? The synopsis tells us she is the wife of the owner of the airline, and that she has had an affair with the pilot, but in her one tiny scene no such information is forthcoming. What is an ill-at-ease Joseph Cotten doing in the picture, since his role—a Catholic priest—seems totally extraneous? Is the pilot himself (woodenly played by Powell) also a ghost? It all remains a murky mystery.

Says Ginnane: 'During pre-pre-production, David and I had a long debate about whether we should go Gore or Cerebral. We thought, wrongly as it turned out, that the market was turning and that a picture in the style of Jack Clayton's *The Innocents* would be more appropriate than an exploitation horror film. So we went Cerebral, and the film got mucked about. It's quite hard to follow, and a bit of a disappointment. But it's amazing how you can sell one film off another film and, on the basis of *Harlequin*'s success, Hemdale did pretty well with *The Survivor*. It wasn't sold theatrically in the US, but the foreign income wound up between $600,000 and $700,000, so it was no disgrace.' Financially, maybe not: cinematically, disgrace is too mild a word.

There are some nice touches which fail to redeem this totally botched film: the sequence which follows the air-crash is imaginatively staged, thanks to the very inventive production design (Bernard Hides). John Seale, making another of his earliest films as director of photography, displays the skill of a veteran in the filming of this scene; it is shot in Panavision, with police, foremen and an opportunistic photographer (soon to fall victim to the unknown killer) stumbling through the wreckage.

The only other attempt at a ghost story in the 80s was *NEXT OF KIN* (1982), which is far closer to the mood of *The Innocents* than *The Survivor*. Director Tony Williams (b. 1942), a New Zealander, had previously made *Solo* (1978), an Australian–New Zealand co-production (produced by David Hannay): that was a love story, but *Next of Kin* involves an apparently haunted nursing home and a series of strange (and, frankly, rather confusing) occurrences. It is an odd film, lacking a clear vision of how to tell its slight little story; one imagines *Survivor*-style debates about Gore versus Cerebral. There is, however, a well-staged, and rather unexpected, climax at a roadside cafe, and Gary Hansen's cool, subtle photography is an important factor in creating the necessary mood.

Next of Kin. *Kristina Marshall.*

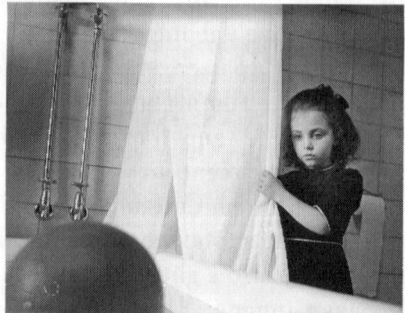

S ci-fi, mad killers, ghosts: the only other kind of exploitation film left to discuss is that involving the man-hunting animal, preferably

Razorback. *Bill Kerr.*

one that has grown to larger than usual size—the *Jaws* cycle. *RAZORBACK* (1984) is the first feature of Russell Mulcahy who trained at the ABC, made some award-winning short experimental films (*Delicious Dreams Despite Depression* won the General category of the Greater Union Awards at the Sydney Film Festival in 1976), and then forged a career making rock clips for Air Supply, Elton John, Rod Stewart, Duran Duran and others.

Mulcahy is a visual stylist, and his collaboration with cinematographer Dean Semler on the film ensures the quality of its Panavision images: much of this quality is deliberately stylised, such as the inevitable light sources in the outback which are manifestly impossible—there are even two moons in one shot. But Mulcahy is also, like George Miller, a physical director with a sense of humour. The film starts with a reference to the then-notorious Dingo Baby case, though in this case the baby is taken by a giant feral pig, a razorback, and the infant's grandfather (Bill Kerr) is forced to stand trial on a charge of killing the child. When he is released, he is determined to avenge himself on the porker.

Also out for revenge is an American, Carl, played by Gregory Harrison, a US television star employed by producer Hal McElroy with the American market in mind. Carl's wife (Judy Morris with very shaky accent), a television newswoman, has become another victim of the giant pig. What follows is a commendably inventive addition to the genre, though it must be admitted that the mechanical pig is not always 100 per cent convincing. Most of the time, though, Mulcahy forces us to forget such things, since he delights in a bravura display of technical skill, and Everett De Roche's screenplay (based on Peter Brennan's novel) is a good basis for the thrills. (It should be added that Arch Nicholson directed a second unit which filmed the pig.)

The film also boasts a couple of larger-than-life supporting performances from Chris Haywood and David Argue, playing brothers who carry on a thriving business turning kangaroos into petfood. Haywood and Argue, apparently emulating Strother Martin and L. Q. Jones in Sam Peckinpah movies like *The Wild Bunch*, make their manic characters wonderfully sleazy. In contrast, Harrison is a rather dull hero. At the 1984 AFI awards, *Razorback* was justifiably recognised for the quality of its photography and editing (William Anderson).

DARK AGE (1987), adapted by Sonia Borg from a novel by Grahame Webb, is also in the *Jaws* tradition, except this time the marauding monster is a giant crocodile. Arch Nicholson, who as we saw above had worked on *Razorback*, was approached by Tony Ginnane to direct the film. However, the picture had to be shot quickly and economically, and Nicholson agreed, though he felt there were problems with the screenplay and preferred aspects of the book (Webb was a Darwin-based crocodile expert).

RKO had cast approval but, in this instance, the American company approved an all-Australian cast. It was headed by John Jarratt, as a Northern Territory wildlife ranger, with Nikki Coghill as his girlfriend, Max Phipps as an evil crocodile hunter, and Aboriginal actors Burnam Burnam and David Gulpilil. Shooting (with Andrew Lesnie in charge of the Panavision camera) took place entirely in the north, five weeks in Cairns, one week in Alice Springs. The problem, as with *Razorback*, was always the mechanical creature, but, Nicholson says: 'We got away with it, though there are two or three shots where it stretches the imagination. We were always intercutting with footage of real crocs. In the end, I hoped the characters would be interesting enough to outweigh the croc.'

Dark Age does not have quite the impact of *Razorback*, but it comes close. The emphasis on Aboriginal legend and tradition is interesting, and the ending is strongly conservationist. Jarratt and Burnam Burnam (in the Robert Shaw role if we follow the *Jaws* analogy) transport the giant reptile to the safety of its breeding grounds despite the intervention of the deranged hunter, who kills Burnam before, inevitably, falling victim to the monster that, like Moby Dick with Ahab, already has one of his limbs. This is one of Phipps' better screen performances: the actor often overplays, but he makes John a thoroughly evil character without overstating anything.

Nicholson directs the action scenes adroitly. An early sequence, in which an Aboriginal boy is taken by the croc while swimming at a water-hole, is genuinely chilling. So is the sequence in which Phipps and two mates, in a boat on the croc-infested river, are attacked at night. There is also a pleasantly strong relationship between Jarratt and Coghill, an actress who deserved better roles in the 80s.

Unfortunately, *Dark Age* remains totally unseen in Australia as a result of one of those financial 'deals'. Ginnane notes: 'Rothschilds wanted a 60 per cent guarantee on that picture. I had done a two-picture deal with RKO [the second film was *The Lighthorsemen*], but they said they'd only put up 60 per cent in exchange for world rights, *including* Australia. Later, they licensed all foreign rights to Embassy. Embassy was dealing with CEL in Australia, but then Embassy got merged into Nelson and during that merge Nelson wanted to renegotiate their deal with CEL and get more money.' CEL was not prepared to pay more, so *Dark Age* remains unseen in the country of its origin, either in cinemas, or on television, or on video. Says Ginnane: 'Back when all those people were getting eaten by crocodiles in the Northern Territory I tried to buy it back. I thought it would be a terrific picture to bring out in the summer. I showed my personal print to the exhibitors here, but they didn't share my enthusiasm, so I dropped the idea.'

Finally, the spoof horror film, and Philippe Mora's *THE MARSUPIALS: THE HOWLING III* (1987). Joe Dante's original *The Howling* (1980) took advantage of the latest special effects make-up techniques to breathe new life into the werewolf genre, and the result was a genuinely thrilling horror film. Mora had directed the sequel, *The Howling II* (1984), rather lamely and with a straight face, in Europe. He returned to Australia to make fun of the genre with an engagingly preposterous plot about a tribe of marsupial werewolves who meet up with a traditional European werewolf. The latter is played by Dasha Blahova as a Russian ballerina who transforms into a hairy beast during a pas de deux on stage at the Sydney Opera House.

Barry Otto plays a scientist who falls for Blahova and tries to escape the marsupial werewolves with her. Imogen Annesley is a marsupial werewolf who gets pregnant by an assistant director of a film on which she worked as an extra: when the baby is born, and crawls up her stomach and into her pouch, her boyfriend seems unfazed by this intriguing piece of biology! The film is full of wonderfully wacky characters and situations: Frank Thring as the director of the film (*Shape Shifters Part 8*); film enthusiast and television movie presenter Bill Collins as a doctor who becomes a werewolf victim; even Dame Edna Everage as an Oscar presenter in the film's hilarious final scene. There is a priceless sequence in which werewolves disguised as nuns attend the movie's wrap party, where they undergo transformations and become wolfish, and a charming scene in which Annesley and her date go to the movies (the marvellously titled *It Came From Uranus*) and she keeps muttering: 'It doesn't happen like that' during all the horror bits.

This good-natured spoof, very much tongue-in-cheek, is a good antidote to more serious, and less successful, horror films. It is curious that it never found distribution in Australia (except on video) since it could have been a huge success on the Valhalla circuit if nowhere else. Mora knows his horror movies, and parodies them with elan, and the final title—'Adios Amigos'—brings the film to an end on a note of cheerful good humour.

COME

UP

SMILING

T he Australian New Wave began with comedies. At the beginning of the 70s, films like *Stork, The Adventures of Barry McKenzie* and *Alvin Purple* overcame the anti-Australian bias of the mass cinema audience. Within a few years, such films were considered distinctly infra dig; they were supplanted by prestige pictures like *Picnic at Hanging Rock, My Brilliant Career* and *Breaker Morant*.

The screen comedies of the 80s are a mixed bunch, which range from the most successful (the *Crocodile Dundee* films) to the least successful, of which *LES PATTERSON SAVES THE WORLD* (1987) must rank near the top (or bottom). The savage, confrontational humour of Barry Humphries has been delighting and appalling his stage audiences, especially in Australia and Britain, for nearly three decades now, and his two Barry McKenzie films, both directed by Bruce Beresford, were exceedingly popular.

Critics were not so kind to them, but *The Adventures of Barry McKenzie*, at least, had a raffish way of presenting its bad taste: Bazza could chunder live on BBC television and it was still funny. Humphries had wanted to make another film for a long time: 'I kept putting it off,' he says, 'and not only because I was busy with the stage shows. I was a bit daunted by the long period of high seriousness in the Australian film industry. Comedies were really out of fashion; by the time we made the second Barry McKenzie film, the backlash against the Ocker movement, which I'd inadvertently set in motion, had begun. Films had started representing Australians as highly refined, sophisticated people.'

The original intention was to produce the film in Britain, for Thorn-EMI; but, as a result of one of those upheavals in the British film industry, the company ceased producing movies, and Humphries bought it back, after which it was set up as a wholly Australian production with 10BA financing.

The screenplay, which was concocted by Humphries in collaboration with his wife, Diane Millstead, was the antithesis of refined and sophisticated, which in itself would not have mattered. But they made the crucial error of focusing attention on Humphries' least likeable creation, Sir Les Patterson, rather than on the identifiable Barry McKenzie or the ghastly, but genuinely comic, Dame Edna Everage. Sir Les is funny only in the smallest of small doses: Humphries sees him as a kind of latter-day Toby Belch, a larger-than-life caricature of a nouveau-riche bon vivant—belching, farting, womanising and

Les Patterson Saves the World. *Barry Humphries, Thaao Penghlis.*

chundering his way through life with scant regard for the sensibilities of others.

'His origins are in the trade union movement,' says Humphries. 'He was in the Plasterers' Union, he was born in the western suburbs of Sydney, he's Roman Catholic (his wife still practising). He was entertainments officer at St George Leagues Club and thus a bit of an authority on show business. Everyone liked him. He drifted into the Whitlam Cabinet, but his habits of gross intemperance suggested the ideal job for him might be the High Commissioner in London; instead he was made Cultural Attaché to the Court of St James.' Sir Les on stage was never a pretty picture, though Humphries claims that young audiences responded to the character: 'On one occasion, there was a rather attractive young woman spreadeagled across the seat in the front row saying: "Spit on *me*, Les!" '

Hoyts, the company that launched *Crocodile Dundee* so successfully the previous year, made a distribution deal, though not without some misgivings. Executive director Jonathan Chissick recalls that he tried to persuade Humphries and Millstead to angle the plot more towards Edna Everage and away from Sir Les. Chissick says: 'I always felt the Les Patterson character was all right on stage for five minutes but would be over the top in a two-hour movie.'

The strategy in preparing the screenplay seems to have been to introduce huge chunks of plot, much of it looking like rejects from the sub-James Bond cycle of the 60s. 'It has a complicated plot,' Humphries said before the film opened—he was putting it mildly, for once. 'Indeed, from time to time I have to get my wife to explain it to me.' The vulgarity of the material was such that at least one prominent actress turned down the role of Veronique Crudite, the glamorous assistant to Dr Herpes, and Sir Les' principal love interest. On the other hand, an actor who did accept a major role in the film (and wishes to remain anonymous) claims that the original screenplay *was* funny, and that the direction was to blame for the disastrous results.

There is no doubt that George Miller (2) was a surprising choice as director. With *The Man from Snowy River* as his chief claim to fame, it is hard to see why he was chosen to handle a large-scale comedy of this sort, though he was an admirer of Sir Les. 'He told me that asking him to make a film about Les Patterson was like asking a priest to make a film about God,' says Humphries. Humphries describes Miller as 'wily and astute, but not too artistic, not too cultural.' Certainly, he shows no skill in comedy timing. Though there are a few amusing moments in the first reel (including Paul Jennings' impersonation of Prime Minister Bob Hawke) the film quickly degenerates into a series of laboured and repetitive jokes about sexually transmitted diseases. It was also a bad mistake to create spectacular make-up effects for the victims of HELP (Humphries is trying to be funny about AIDS), who emit a yellow pus which would have better suited a horror film, while the attitude towards Russians (definitely Cold War) was hopelessly dated at the beginning of the *glasnost* era. Dame Edna's belated arrival gives the film a lift, but nothing can overcome the basic hideousness of the conception, or the awkwardness with which its handled. Only Graham (Grace) Walker's magnificent production design—the New York revolving restaurant, an Arab city— emerges from the fiasco with any honour.

'I was horrified when I saw the picture,' says Jonathan Chissick. Humphries hoped for a young audience, and felt the picture would appeal especially to gays and women. In the event, it appealed to very few people. 'It was a disaster of major proportions,' says Chissick. The gala opening was an embarrassing occasion, and it is still rumoured in the industry today that Federal Treasurer Paul Keating, who attended, was so angry that he decided to end rorts in the film industry. For George Miller (1), the film was embarrassing too. Until then, he had hardly worried about the career of his namesake: now, he was anxious about the confusion.

Humphries had hoped for an major American release to rival that of *Crocodile Dundee*; but test screenings were dire. The picture eventually opened in Britain late in 1988, in a slightly shortened version. Again, the reaction was disappointing, given Humphries' devoted British following. At the time of writing, the film has not even been released on video in Australia, an indication of the low esteem in which it is generally held.

Less shattering, because less expensive and with a lower profile, was an attempt to return to the other ocker cycle of the early 70s, the Alvin Purple films. *MELVIN, SON OF ALVIN* (1984), produced by McElroy and McElroy and directed by John Eastway of *The Norman Gunston Show*, was a case of too little, too late. Ten years after *Alvin Rides Again* we meet Melvin (Gerry Sont, looking bemused throughout) whose sexual problems differ radically from those of his father (Graeme Blundell, returning for an unwise reprise).

The new film lacks whatever qualities the earlier ones had; Morris Gleitzman's screenplay is devoid of humour and, presumably in order to qualify for an M rating (*Alvin Purple* was R-rated) exceedingly coy in the sex department: actors remain clad throughout. David Argue steals the picture in a typically wild performance as an accident-prone television cameraman, and Tina Bursill brings some style to her performance as a television journalist. There is also a splendid moment in which Ariathe Galani, as the black-clad mother of Melvin's Greek girlfriend, leaps on him from a first-floor balcony like some avenging harpy (the film does, at least, acknowledge the changing face of Australia by introducing this multicultural sub-plot). Roadshow released *Melvin* in time for Christmas 1984, and presumably regretted it.

The film *was* released, though. *PACIFIC BANANA* (1980), a film which represents perhaps the nadir of the once-illustrious SAFC, managed to play only a few days in a cinema in Melbourne and then a few nights in Sydney drive-ins before being hastily transferred to video. In the wake of *Breaker Morant*, the SAFC, apparently in the forlorn hope of making a lot of money, joined forces with sex film director John Lamond to make this specious comedy. The screenplay was by Alan Hopgood (who had written both the original *Alvin Purple* films), and Alvin himself, Graeme Blundell, appeared as an airline pilot who is attractive to women but who always has fits of uncontrolled sneezing at the wrong moment. The title song ('It wants to go up, up, up; Instead it goes down, down, down') says it all. Mercifully, few people saw this turkey.

B ookending the decade were two strikingly similar, and equally poor, films about groups of women: *TOUCH AND GO* (1980) and *LUIGI'S LADIES* (1989). Both starred Wendy Hughes, one of the country's finest actresses, and they represent her weakest screen performances.

In *Touch and Go*, feebly scripted by Peter Yeldham and even more feebly directed by Peter Maxwell, she plays Eva, an actress who, together with her women friends, becomes involved in a series of robberies. The film aims to be an exciting, serio-comic thriller along the lines of Hollywood heist films; but the plot development is predictable, the jokes witless and the pacing slack. The actresses are left to flounder hopelessly; Chantal Contouri, who had appeared in a few minor thrillers in the late 70s, quit Australia not long afterwards to appear in Hollywood soaps. The casting of singer Jon English, as a gardener with almost nothing to do, is a blatant (and, as it turned out, unsuccessful) attempt to reach a youth audience.

With the experience of *Touch and Go* behind her, you would think Wendy Hughes would have had misgivings about a project like *Luigi's Ladies*, which also involves a trio of women friends and their problems. Again, the idea was to make a smart, sophisticated comedy from a woman's perspective; Hughes executive-produced for Tra La La Films, the company owned by herself and her husband, Patric Juillet. She also co-scripted with Judy Morris, who made her directorial debut, and played the leading role.

The result was another complete disaster: a strident, only fitfully amusing affair in which Morris' inexperience as a director leads to embarrassingly theatrical performances all round, with Hughes herself the worst offender. Even the normally reliable Sandy Gore is unable to do anything with her character, and Max Cullen overplays the eccentric French chef in Luigi's restaurant as if he was doing a turn on *The Muppet Show*. Given that the film deals with quite painful subjects (the stockmarket crash, male infidelity and impotence) its attempts at humour seem doubly feeble ('My Dunlop Rubber shares are the only ones holding up'). Flat camerawork and uninspired editing are the final straw. Hoyts did an excellent job of promotion on the film which was, however, greeted with critical disdain and public indifference. ('It came and went,' says Chissick.)

It was disappointing to see a talented actress like Judy Morris floundering at her first attempt at direction, but there were several other disappointments in store during the 80s. In 1983, many hailed Brisbane-based Jackie McKimmie for her GU prizewinning short *Stations*, which featured Noni Hazlehurst and Tim Burns; the film screened in cinemas in the same programme as *Careful, He Might Hear You*, and so was widely seen. McKimmie, a playwright and media teacher, decided to write another vehicle for Hazlehurst, and the result was *AUSTRALIAN DREAM* (1986). The film started out as a 50-minute project, and in hindsight it was probably a mistake to expand it to feature length because the material simply is not there. McKimmie became one of several directors of the 80s who made exciting short or medium-length films, and then failed to make the quantum leap to feature production.

There were other problems with *Australian Dream*; the budget ($600,000) was so small that only a four-week shoot was possible: two weeks out of the four were night shoots. Cast and crew were forced to work at a feverish pace, there was no time for rehearsal with the supporting actors, and the pressure was constant. Such a gruelling schedule could be expected to affect the quality of the final product, and, unfortunately, it did.

Set in the suburbs of Brisbane, the film has moments of comic brilliance (the weekend car-washing ritual) and insight (scenes between bored housewife Noni Hazlehurst and her daughter). But McKimmie, in attempting to depict the ugly banalities of suburban life, falls into the trap of making an ugly, banal film.

And it is a predictable film, too. It is not hard to foresee that Hazlehurst, as the frustrated wife of a butcher with political ambitions (a good role for Graeme Blundell) should be disappointed when she finally has a fling with John Jarratt, the object of her lustful fantasies: 'Is that *it*?' Less foreseeable was the director's inability to control her material, so that the endless fancy-dress party (Come as your Fantasy) which forms the second half of the film, is numbingly dull.

A more successful satire of suburban life is *EMOH RUO* (1985), one of producer David Elfick's consistently interesting forays into comedy. The screenplay was written by Paul Leadon and David Poltorack; in 1981 these two had written and directed an amusing short film, *Making Weekend of Summer Last*, which cheerfully lampooned some of the more prestigious Australian films of the 70s. Leadon and Poltorack wanted to direct the new film, and received AFC funding to shoot a couple of scenes on video. This was not a success, since too much time was spent on set with the co-directors discussing who would do what, while actors and crew cooled their heels. 'They just weren't experienced enough,' says Elfick. Instead, he hired Denny Lawrence to direct his first feature.

Emoh Ruo was financed by UAA when another Elfick project, *Cane* (scripted by Miranda Downes) fell through; Elfick had been on a location hunt in northern Queensland and flew to Perth to meet with UAA executives, only to be told that *Cane* was too expensive and too risky (it later became the hugely successful television mini-series *Fields of Fire*). But UAA was willing to back *Emoh Ruo* which was cheaper ($1.5 million).

Elfick was interested in discovering new talent. Phillip Quast was given the role of hero Des' awful brother, Les; he was little known at the time but has since become a star of stage musicals (*Les Misérables*, Paris). Elfick met Martin Sacks when he (briefly) went to acting classes—Sacks was also little-known, though he had acted in theatre and television soaps. Joy Smithers was another discovery, and proved to be a real find who gave an exuberant, funny performance. She had been a model since the age of twelve, a singer, and star of numerous television commercials; ironically given the theme of *Emoh Ruo*, these included a commercial for a building society! She had also played a supporting role in *Stanley*, a comedy made two years earlier.

Filming took place mostly at Baulkham Hills in Sydney's western suburbs, and production designer Robert Dein did a particularly good job with the house itself which, though supposedly newly built, is filled with electrical and plumbing malfunctions and eventually collapses altogether. The inspiration goes back to *Mr Blandings Builds his Dream House*, and a year later a similar plot formed the basis for the Spielberg production *The Money Pit*. *Emoh Ruo* provides plenty of laughs. Its trick opening sequence discovers Smithers in a luxurious home which, we later find out, she has been hired to clean—there is an uncredited guest spot here from Anna-Maria Monticelli. The humour is sustained through the jokes about weekend barbecues, building societies, banks, television advertisements and nosy neighbours. Jack Ellis, son of Bob Ellis and Anne Brooksbank, is amusing as the Tunkley child.

Elfick was not happy with the way the film was released by GU— it opened at a bad time of the year (October) at the climax of the football season. It was also saddled with a silly title (UAA is said to have offered it overseas as *House Broken*). But despite a disappointing cinema career, *Emoh Ruo* has been a big success on video.

Elfick's subsequent *AROUND THE WORLD IN 80 WAYS* (1986), is genuinely eccentric and one of the best comedy films of the 80s. This opinion is not shared by everyone; Hoyts released the film eventually, but Jonathan Chissick admits: 'I never understood the picture.' There was no government support at all for the $2.5 million film, which

Around the World in 80 Ways. *Gosia Dobrowolska, Kelly Dingwall, Allan Penney.*

was financed by a merchant bank; this proved to be a problem later since the bank retained all distribution rights and proved slow in assigning them.

Stephen Maclean, screenwriter of *Starstruck*, had written an offbeat, original tale about a fake trip around the world; the inspiration came from an old man Maclean had known when he was young. 'He was a little bit senile,' he says, 'and my mother used to visit him. He always wanted to bet on horses, so she'd pretend to ring up the TAB. Sometimes he'd think he'd won a lot of money, but later he'd forget about it. Then he decided he wanted to go away on a trip, and I thought "You could really do it here, at home." And the idea for the film just grew from that.' Maclean's work has been entirely in the comedy genre: 'I heard Barry Humphries on the radio one day when I was about ten years old—and he was the first one to give me a sense of Australian identity. From that springs just about everything I've done.'

Elfick, ever willing to try new talent, was happy for Maclean to make his directorial debut on the film. Maclean the director quickly learnt how to deal with Maclean the writer: 'Before, when I'd written a script and it was directed by someone else, a lot of changes were made,' he says. 'But I discovered, when I directed myself, that *I* made a lot of changes; it gets outside your hands as a writer and takes on a life of its own. So, you work out a scene, you storyboard it, you've got fifteen shots but you've only got two hours before you have to move on and the sun goes, so you've really only got two shots. It was exciting for me to be able to change things like that on the spot. Circumstances are very seldom ideal.'

It was a complicated film to make, not so much in the staging of the fake trip, but in the shooting of the 'real' trip. 'We used Kings

Cross for Italy, for instance. The irony is that the "real" trip had to be just as fake as the "fake" trip. I enjoyed doing the "fake" trip more.'

Philip Quast appears in his second Elfick production, this time centre stage as the gay, entrepreneurial Wally; John Dingwall's actor son, Kelly, plays the younger brother, Eddie; veteran Allan Penney gets the role of a lifetime as Roly, the senile old man rejuvenated as a result of his wholly imaginary world trip; and Diana Davidson makes Mavis, his long-suffering wife, a very likeable character. The most interesting casting, though, was Gosia Dobrowolska as the nurse who becomes part of the plot. This was Dobrowolska's second film (after *Silver City*) and at the time her Polish accent was still quite strong. She was not the most obvious choice for the role, which was her first comedy part, but she is a delight and enters into the madcap spirit of the film with a cheerful elan that adds a lift to all her scenes.

Maclean and Elfick originally had in mind a more conventional kind of actress. But, after a great many auditions and tests, they failed to come up with anyone. 'I was their last choice,' says Dobrowolska. 'Co-producer Steve Knapman had liked me very much in *Silver City* and suggested me; and funnily enough the accent helped. They just wrote a line in the script to explain it.' 'She was an inspired piece of casting,' says Elfick. 'She relished the chance to play comedy.'

Undoubtedly the other star of the film was Lissa Coote, the production designer. The details of the Davis home and, more importantly, that of lecherous next-door neighbour Alec Moffatt, which forms the Honolulu, Rome and Tokyo settings for the imaginary trip, and which eventually is destroyed by flood, are cleverly handled, and it is a wonder Coote's work was not recognised at the AFI awards. Perhaps the delays in the film's release were partly responsible; the bank that financed the picture spent nearly two years negotiating distribution deals, finally settling for Hoyts in Australia. As it happened, the film was released in the US first. A deal had been struck with the Alive distribution company, but, unfortunately, by the time the film went into release, the executive who had made the deal, and who liked the picture, had left and his replacement was unsympathetic. Nevertheless, *Around the World* . . . was warmly received at the World Film Festival in Montreal, and got mostly favourable reviews from American critics. Some months later, when it opened in Australia, it failed to attract a large audience, despite generally positive reviews.

Looking back, David Elfick feels the biggest flaw in the film is the title. 'Titles are extraordinarly important, and this one doesn't work,' he says. 'People got it confused with the real *Around the World in 80 Days*, and there was apparently a notorious porno film in America with the same title as ours. We had a bad title, and it made it difficult for the film's identity.'

E moh Ruo and *Around the World in 80 Ways* deserved to succeed better than they did. One thing they both lacked was a determined and supportive distributor with complete faith in the films. Another eccentric first feature, *YOUNG EINSTEIN* (1986–8) had just that. During its three-year post-production period, Graham Burke of Village–Roadshow never wavered in his support for the film and its energetic young writer-producer-director-star.

Yahoo Serious (who changed his real name, Greg Pead, by deed-poll at the conclusion of a three-day binge while at art college) was a Newcastle tyre-fitter and painter who wanted to break into films. He got the idea for *Young Einstein* during a trip down the Amazon: an Indian delivering beer on board the river boat wore a T-shirt with the famous picture of Albert Einstein, aged seventy-two, poking out his tongue at the camera. The image set off various trains of thought, which resulted in young Albert Einstein growing up on a Tasmanian apple farm and, eventually, inventing rock 'n' roll.

'In scripting, we based a lot of our Albert's adventures around those of the real Albert Einstein,' says Serious. 'In 1905, he was a long-haired 26-year-old rebel—and the greatest genius in the history of scientific thought. Also, he was a violin player—but not a very good one.'

Serious had never written a screenplay before, but, together with collaborator David Roach, he came up with a joke-filled outline on which he was able to raise money. 'I always knew my taste was pretty weird,' he says. 'But then I discovered that the taste of Australians in general is pretty weird.' Incredibly, Serious was able to persuade an American company Film Accord, to come up with a $2 million pre-sale. This was quite a feat, given that he had no previous filmmaking experience except for one short film, *Knightmare*, that played the Hoyts circuit in the days when short films were still being screened. The film's original budget of $2.2 million was easily raised, given this unprecedented pre-sale.

Serious wanted to direct, edit and act in the film himself ('It's the only way to go in comedy,' he says, citing Chaplin, Tati and Woody

Allen as examples), and to his credit he sold himself and his project and retained creative control. During pre-production, the screenplay changed a lot: originally, there was even a role for Hitler, but this character was dropped.

The film went into production late in 1985. Jeff Darling, twenty-three years old at the time, became the youngest cameraman to have worked on an Australian feature film. The Tasmanian sequences that top and tail the film were not, in fact, filmed in Tasmania, but in Wollombi, near Cessnock in the Hunter Valley in New South Wales. In order to film the comic sequence of Einstein's trip to Sydney via Ayers Rock and the Snowy Mountains, production manager Antonia Barnard managed to persuade a travel agent to fly Serious, assistant Lulu Pinkus and Darling to Alice Springs and Cooma free of charge. Many of the old Sydney streets seen in the film were actually shot on Newcastle locations.

Alterations to the script during production, especially those involving costume changes, taxed the budget. For Serious, the strain of fulfilling four roles—producer, director, writer and lead actor—was enormously demanding. The seven-week shoot was a muddle, but in many ways an exhilarating one.

Serious entered a 91-minute version of the film in the 1986 Australian Film Institute Awards, and it won Best Music for William Motzing. 'That was very unexpected,' says Serious. 'We never thought we were an award-type film.' At this stage, the basics were all in place, though sumptuous camerawork and production design tended to overwhelm a gentle, amusing, eccentric comedy about an inventor, naive in the ways of the world, who travels to the Australian mainland, falls foul of a scoundrelly patents-pincher (John Howard) and falls for Marie Curie (Odile Le Clezio). The first half of the film was definitely better than the second half, and the ending was anti-climactic.

When Graham Burke saw the film, he was sufficiently impressed to persuade Serious and co-producer Warwick Ross to delay the planned February 1987 release and spend additional money on reshooting, re-editing and rescoring. Village–Roadshow bought out Film Accord and persuaded Warner Bros to take the film for international distribution outside Australia. More than the entire original budget was spent on reshooting and post-production, so that the final budget was close to $5 million.

Serious has claimed that about an hour of material was reshot; certainly he came up with a better, more up-beat ending (Einstein

Young Einstein. *Yahoo Serious and friends.*

playing his rock 'n' roll for the folks back home in Tasmania), and he restaged the climax of the Science Academy Awards (shot in Sydney's State Theatre) to provide a more spectacular explosion. The additional (and expensive) music is a considerable asset; a Mental As Anything number was one of the notable additions (the additions to the music are ironic, given that the film had already won a Best Music prize).

The film was finally released in time for Christmas 1988, with a generous publicity budget. Critics were generally appreciative, and the film was a hugely popular success; after the *Crocodile Dundee* films, it is the most successful Australian comedy of all time. Overseas, the story was not quite so happy. Neither the Americans nor the British critics proved eager to embrace Serious or the film. Typical was Kim Newman in *Monthly Film Bulletin*, who wrote: 'The film . . . misfires on every cod-scientific cylinder . . . [a] mix of sloppy farce, period name-dropping . . . and eyeball-rolling obviousness . . . Most of the gags fall flat . . . [the film] manages to be innocuous and appalling at the same time.' Nevertheless, *Young Einstein* did excellent business in Britain; it became the fourth most successful release for Warners in the UK in 1989, a magnificent achievement. Even in the US, where it was a relative failure, it grossed $13 million.

Other comedies of the 80s were less ambitious. Bill Bennett, after the rigours of *Backlash*, decided on a change of pace with *DEAR CARDHOLDER* (1987). This is a promising yarn starring Robin Ramsay as Hec Harris, a forlorn Everyman who loses control of his life when he overspends on his credit cards. The film was made quickly and economically on a $500,000 budget. It suffers partly from the fact that Bennett seems ill-attuned to comedy; he sets up an interesting situation, and attempts to find humour in the serious theme of burgeoning personal (and national) debt. But then the seriousness of it swamps the comedy, leaving a sour taste in the viewer's mouth. Robin Ramsay's overly solemn performance does not help much.

'When it was finished, I thought it was wonderful,' says Bennett. 'So I was pretty upset when I started to get reaction to the contrary. Now, I guess it's a failure.' It was at the American Film Market that the bitter truth came to him: 'Most people who saw it at screenings didn't like it. They didn't think it was funny. And it unnerved me. My other two films had been well received, but now I started to doubt my judgement.' He was unable to find a distributor for the film in Australia.

'I guess I would have liked Hec to be a little more compassionate. I sometimes wonder how Chris Haywood would have played that role. I cast Robin because he had an irrationality which the character needed.' As far as his experiment in comedy is concerned, Bennett says: 'It gets back to the Avocado Plantation. I guess with 10BA we felt we had a right to fail sometimes, but in retrospect that's a pretty irresponsible attitude to take.' Nevertheless, *Dear Cardholder* was popular on video and also on network television.

S everal of the comedies of the 80s, though apparently made with cinema release in mind, were made on such small budgets they seemed destined from the start for the small screen. Yet *WARMING UP* (1983), produced by JNP (the team that makes the television soap, *A Country Practice*), did get the briefest of cinema releases. Producer James Davern provides a screenplay which goes for mildly amusing sentiment, and there are few sparks between Henri Szeps, as a small-town policeman, and Barbara Stephens, as a sophisticated, strong-willed divorcee from the city. Bruce Best directs without flair.

Equally modest is *FANTASY MAN* (1984), written and directed by John Meagher, and produced by Basil Appleby and Darrell Lass. This is one of those mid-life crisis films in which Harold Hopkins plays an office worker bored with his job, his wife (Jeanie Drynan) and his apartment. His fantasies feature Kerry Mack, playing a fast-food salesperson, and they involve prancing around the fields with her most indecorously. The final solution, to leave Sydney and go to live in Brisbane, brought guffaws from the few audiences that saw the film. Perhaps it should have been screened in double bills with *Australian Dream*.

Jeanie Drynan also appears in both of Anthony Bowman's comedies, *RELATIVES* (1985) and *CAPPUCCINO* (1989), which are equally modest in scope, but have altogether more content. *Relatives*, first announced as a project in 1980, was a long time in the works, and made less impact than it deserved when it was finally screened. As the title suggests, it is a family reunion film. Bowman has an excellent cast: Bill Kerr as the family patriarch; Norman Kaye, who also composed the music, as a gay priest; Ray Barrett as a bitter landowner; Alyson Best as his fun-loving daughter; Drynan as the adulterous wife of stupid, cricket-loving Ray Meagher; Rowena Wallace as another bored wife; and others. A sex scene between Best and her Czech boyfriend was, perhaps, a bit too explicit to sit comfortably alongside the generally blander events in the film, but otherwise *Relatives* proves to be an enjoyable, unpretentious entertainment.

Cappuccino, unlike its predecessor, managed a theatrical release. It has some of the same cast members (Drynan, Wallace) but the comedy this time revolves around a group of (mostly out-of-work) actors who meet regularly at the same coffee-shop. The characters of Ann (Rowena Wallace) and Maggie (Jeanie Drynan) are particularly sympathetic: close friends, the women are frequently rivals for the same role and sometimes for the same man. The film's jokes about auditions and theatre people hit the target, though a sub-plot, involving a crooked cop and some incriminating tapes, is a bit laboured. The film also boasts a delightful performance from John Clayton as a taxi-driver turned stand-up comic who ends up in prison. Once again, Bowman's ear for dialogue and skill with actors result in a pleasant, low-key movie.

Brendan Maher's *THE BIT PART* (1987) is equally low-scale but even more successful (and funny) in its depiction of the acting profession. Chris Haywood (whose name is unaccountably misspelled 'Heywood' in the opening credits) gives a tremendously likeable performance as Michael Thornton, a careers counsellor, who decides to become an actor. He takes speech and deportment classes (there is a marvellous moment in which he is seen learning to tap dance, surrounded by little girls) and gets himself a formidable agent, but still only manages to be cast as the hand in a chocolate commercial. His co-star is Nicole Kidman who plays an ambitious actress (to whom Thornton is understandably attracted) who is whisked off to Hollywood to appear in something called *Wormwood*.

The film, very well written by Steve Vizard, Peter Herbert and Ian McFadyen, is filled with smart industry in-jokes, and the slightly sleazy director of the television commercial ('You see where I'm coming from?') is neatly satirised. One hilarious sequence has Thornton cast as an extra in a war film being directed by an extremely butch woman with an equally butch first assistant: he sneezes when he is supposed to be a corpse, and, when playing a waiter, is afflicted with a growling stomach which reduces the scene's principal actors to hysterics. Haywood's climactic, impassioned speech, in which he heaps praise on the acting profession, looks heartfelt. It is a pity that this little gem could not have been more widely seen.

Haywood recalls the film with great affection and feels 'it does give people a real sense of what it's like to try to break into the industry as an actor. Brendan Maher is a gem of a director, and I'm surprised we don't hear more of him.'

Chris Haywood is well suited to comedy, and also appears to advantage in *THE CLINIC* (1982). This was director David Stevens' first feature film; his direction of the television mini-series *A Town Like Alice* had made him 'hot'. He brought the screenplay, a comedy set in a VD clinic, to producer Bob Weis, who liked the fact that it contained a great many interesting characters from all walks of life 'just brought together by this accident in their sexual lives'.

Raising the money was not unduly hard, despite the unusual theme; not only was Stevens' reputation riding high, but Weis had just produced the television series *Women of the Sun*, which was also a prestige success. But there was still criticism in the industry of the project: 'A lot of people thought we should still be making prestigious costume dramas,' says Weis. 'Australians aren't very tolerant of non-naturalistic films in a local setting—they're prepared to accept them from abroad, but very suspicious about films that depart from that realist norm. *Sweetie* is a good example of this.'

Luckily, the film was well distributed by Roadshow, with a lively advertising campaign and a funny tagline ('A Highly Infectious Comedy') so that it was quite widely seen. It was also appreciated in many overseas countries. It is almost unique among Australian films in that Greg Millin's excellent screenplay takes a deadly serious subject and fools around with it: in one scene, we laugh, initially, when a rather plump and seemingly silly woman explains to the doctor that she is afraid she might have caught something from a man who did not wash afterwards. The doctor laughs, too, but then she goes on to explain, painfully, how uncomfortable and unhappy she is, and the laughter is stilled.

Sexually transmitted diseases are discussed throughout with disarming frankness; indeed, the film is almost educational. And the revelation that the chief doctor (a marvellous performance from Chris Haywood) is gay comes as a jolt to us and also to Simon Burke, who plays the young intern spending a day at the clinic.

An elaborate set of the interior of the clinic was built at a Melbourne studio, and shooting was very fast and efficient. In *The Clinic*, David Stevens not only succeeds in the difficult task of juggling comedy and drama, but he also puts across a serious message about prejudice in all its forms; as a result, *The Clinic* remains one of the most satisfying films of the 80s.

Another 80s film to deal substantially with sex is Dusan Makavejev's *THE COCA-COLA KID* (1985). I suppose I must claim a godfatherly kinship to the film in that I originally brought Frank Moorhouse's marvellous book, *The Americans Baby*, to Makavejev's attention. In the late 60s and early 70s, Makavejev (b. 1932 in Belgrade) was one of the world's most exciting directors. His collage-style of editing and ebullient love for mixing sex and politics (very much in that order) in films like *Love Dossier, or The Tragedy of a Switchboard Operator* (1967) and *W.R.: Mysteries of the Organism* (1971) created an international stir and led to his (temporary) banishment from Yugoslavia. In 1975, I invited him to attend the Sydney Film Festival with *Sweet Movie*, which he had made in Canada; and when he left, I gave him a copy of Moorhouse's book to read on the plane—I felt that he would respond to the humour and the blend of sex and politics in the linked short stories.

He did, and immediately became interested in filming some of them; but it was ten years before his idea was fulfilled. David Roe, himself a former film festival director (Perth) produced the film. One of his immediate problems was to clear the title with the Coca-Cola company; hence the long disclaimer seen in the film.

It was not a happy shoot because, although Roe was naturally familiar

The Coca-Cola Kid. *Bill Kerr, Eric Roberts, Greta Scacchi.*

with Makavejev's work, he was reluctant to let him have his head. Makavejev was first puzzled, then frustrated: after all, Roe knew what kind of filmmaker he was. Why hire him and then stop him doing what he did best? Part of the problem seems to have been that the carefully budgeted and scheduled Australian production methods were at odds with Makavejev's cheerfully disorganised way of working. He says: 'At the beginning, I thought it would be my film, my fantasy. But once the finance was raised, the doors started to close. The film became less and less mine. A schedule was arranged, timetables had to be followed. I became a navigator, a conductor—I became less and less important to the making of the film.' On-set arguments between director and producer became increasingly bitter as filming continued. Denny Lawrence was hired to work alongside Makavejev, in accordance with the requirements of the Australian Screen Directors Association.

Some of the Australian actors and technicians who worked with Makavejev were excited by his methods. Chris Haywood recalls that he admired the director's earlier films so much that 'when I heard he was here I went to see him and said "I'd do anything to work with you." ' Makavejev cast Haywood as Greta Scacchi's violent ex-husband, and the actor was interested to discover on set that the director's wife, Bojana Marijan (who is credited as first assistant director on the film) tended to direct the actors' performances, while Makavejev himself worked with the crew. 'I enjoyed working with him immensely,' says Haywood, and the relationship was so good that Makavejev cast him in his subsequent film, *Manifesto* (1988), which was shot in Yugoslavia.

On the other hand, there was friction between the director and his leading lady, Greta Scacchi; but that was nothing new for Makavejev. Actresses had regularly criticised him for the way he presented them on screen, especially in the nude scenes he loves so much. It must be said that, although the shower scene involving Scacchi and her daughter, Rebecca Smart, is quite gratuitous, it is very sweet and very beautiful.

Unfortunately, the finished film lacks Makavejev's outrageousness. He packs the film with interesting characters, including the indispensable Chris Haywood. Max Gillies as the head of Coca-Cola in Australia, Ian Gilmour as a spy called Marjorie, and Tony Barry as an unlikely-looking bushman who is first seen riding a camel through the Blue Mountains. But the results are fairly chaotic, and not in the positive sense of the director's earlier films. Nor is the imported American actor Eric Roberts a great success in the leading role; an actor with a better sense of comedy timing would have helped enormously.

Makavejev's political barbs are muted, too, as if he was unsure of himself in this alien territory. He says: 'When I was here in 1975, everyone was talking politics. It was an exciting time, a hot time. When I came back to make the film, that excitement was dead. People had become conservative, tame.' Still, he was not completely unhappy with the film: 'I was very happy with the minor characters, that gallery of Australian eccentrics: they're like Australia itself—independent, interesting, antagonistic, funny and whimsical.'

The film was selected for competition at the Cannes Film Festival in 1985, but was generally felt to be one of the director's lesser works. Still, it had a respectable commercial career around the world, especially in the American South (where Coca-Cola still obviously stands for something).

T he success of *MALCOLM* (1986) was one of the happiest surprises of the decade. The film seemed to come from nowhere; there was little hype during production; and suddenly there it was, a fresh, clever, touching comedy which scooped the pool at the 1986 AFI awards.

It was the creation of Nadia Tass and David Parker, a husband-and-wife team based in Melbourne. Parker was born in 1947 in Brisbane. Tass was born in Macedonia, northern Greece, in 1956 (her father's side of the family was Russian; she came to Australia with her family in 1963. By 1980, Parker was a prominent stills photographer specialising in show business and movies. Tass, meanwhile, had been acting and directing in the theatre, and was about to appear in a production of *Antigone* at the Playbox; she needed some photos of herself, called Parker and hassled him until he made an appointment to photograph her. 'The photographs were lousy,' he says. 'But we fell in love.'

Through the early 80s, Parker worked as stills photographer on several important films, among them *The Man from Snowy River*, *Phar Lap*, *The Coolangatta Gold*, *Burke and Wills* and *High Tide*. 'A lot of the films being made in the early 80s were pretty awful,' he says. 'They were just tax driven. I thought it was crazy that millions of dollars were being spent on junk like that. It came to a head on *The Coolangatta Gold*—I thought, "I can do better than this." The stumbling block was always: "Who could write the script I wanted?" It was Colin Friels, who was working on the film, who said: "Why don't you write it yourself?" That had never occurred to me.'

The character of Malcolm was inspired by Tass's brother, John. 'We picked him,' says Parker, 'because we found so many of the characters in Australian films so very bland. Yet this country is full of wonderful eccentrics from a variety of backgrounds. Here was a man, very close to home, with so much warmth and humour—that's what we wanted to capture. We didn't want to make an art film about a retarded boy— we wanted to make a film that was very funny, but without belittling that character. People can be unwittingly condescending to the retarded; we wanted to face the character head on.' Tass says: 'There's a lot of John in *Malcolm*: his behaviour, the way he relates to people, his love of trains and trams. All we imposed on the character was his ability to create those mechanical toys.'

Despite Colin Friels' initial encouragement, the role of Malcolm was not written with him in mind. 'I never write for a particular actor,' says Parker. 'I have an image, but it's not based on a person I know.' Once Friels saw the script, however, he was very keen to play the role. And, in keeping with his aim of not making a serious film of limited appeal, Parker tried to keep the humorous aspects of the script in the foreground. The screenplay was written in the desert where Parker was working on *Burke and Wills*, and then the task of raising money began.

The couple formed a company called Cascade Films (says Tass, 'It's a beautiful image of running water suggesting continuity and also freshness—hopefully our productions are fresh') and started making contact with investors. One was Ray Beattie of the Seven Network in Sydney. Says Parker: 'I spoke to him on the phone and he said: "I may be able to do something for you—can you be in my office on Monday morning?" We were completely broke, but we got on a bus for Sydney. Nadia was sick at the time, and it was an awful trip.

Malcolm. *The famous split-car sequence.*

We arrived in Sydney and went straight from the bus depot to Beattie's office at Epping—and his secretary said: "He hasn't got your appointment down in his diary, but he's here somewhere." She found him, he apologised, we went into his office and he said: "I don't think there's anything I can do for you people." And that was it! So we came back down to Melbourne on the bus.'

More successful was an approach to Gary Fenton, programme manager of HSV7 in Melbourne; Parker had shot stills for Channel 7 for many years, so was known to Fenton, who enjoyed the script and offered a $175,000 pre-sale. Film Victoria came up with 10 per cent of the $1 million budget, but there was still a hefty sum of money to raise by the 10BA route. Parker and Tass believed so much in the project that they sold everything they had, including Parker's precious Leica cameras, and mortgaged their house. Then they discovered Ian Johnson of D. & D. Tolhurst who was that rare thing—a stockbroker with a sense of humour. Parker had already made up one of the remote-control ashcans which feature in the film, and they steered this into Johnson's office by remote control, the lid flipped up and a gun came out while a taped message said: 'Give us $1 million, or we'll blow your balls off!' 'He took the first option,' says Parker.

Even with Johnson's help, it was not plain sailing. Three days before the end of the financial year, the underwriters pulled out. But the money was eventually raised at five o'clock on 30 June 1985. 'It was very hairy,' says Parker. 'We were already in pre-production. I rushed back and forth between meetings with high-flying stockbrokers and cutting Hondas in half.'

When shooting began, Nadia Tass initially had to overcome the crew's suspicions of her; she was, after all, from the theatre. But after the first screening of rushes, she had full support ('They weren't questioning me because I was a woman,' she says. 'Only because I hadn't made a film before.') Tass believes in rehearsing the actors and thoroughly understanding the psychology of the characters; she feels the actors responded to this approach.

Actor Chris Haywood fulfilled an unusual function on *Malcolm*; he was unit manager. 'He wanted to do it, to support us,' says Parker. 'He had a very small role in the film, but he wanted to work on the production. And he brought that energy he has as a performer to his role as unit manager—we were looked after beautifully. He did the same on *Burke and Wills*—he didn't have a big role there either, and we'd get back to base after shooting and discover he'd set up a whole beer garden in the middle of the desert with umbrellas and bunting.' 'He offers so much to our industry,' says Tass. 'He comes up with the goods over and over again.'

During post-production, Tass and Parker showed the film to Jonathan Chissick whom Parker knew as a result of his work on the Hoyts–Edgley productions. Chissick had reservations about the project, and when he and his staff saw the completed film, told Parker: 'We're all pretty cool on it.' Chissick passed up the film. Next day, Tass and Parker had a cast and crew screening in Melbourne and invited several other friends including Simon Wincer who at that time was working with Hoyts–Edgley. The response at the screening was extremely positive, and Wincer promised to talk to Chissick about it. Immediately afterwards, it was screened at the American Film Market, again with positive results. Chissick called Tass: 'What *is* it with your film?' he asked—and they did a deal. Chissick says: 'I didn't think the picture was particularly funny until I saw it with an audience. Then, I thought it was hilarious.'

Hoyts did an excellent job of marketing the film which was considerably boosted by its success in the 1986 AFI awards—it won eight prizes, including Best Film, Director, Original Screenplay and Actor, and Tass and Parker won the Byron Kennedy Award. Audiences loved the film, and no wonder. Colin Friels is quite wonderful as Malcolm, one of the most endearing characters in any Australian film. He is perfectly complemented by John Hargreaves as the tough crim who comes to stay in Malcolm's house and, against the odds, befriends the painfully shy inventor. As Hargreaves' girlfriend, Linda Davies rounds out a trio of quite perfect performances. The sequence in which Malcolm demonstrates to Frank his getaway car, which divides into two self-contained mini cars, confounding the pursuing police, is a gem of invention, and the climactic robbery by remote control also combines ingenuity with great good humour. Above all, though, *Malcolm* succeeds because of the fine performances and the warmth of characters—it was a film with entertainment value that surpassed many a more elaborate, expensive production.

'It was a phenomenal success,' says Chissick. 'It did almost $1 million in rentals.' It also sold around the world, and went into profit in just over a year. It was the first theatrical release of Vestron in the US: company executives were very keen on the film and strongly supported it, but the film never took off in America the way it did in other countries. Parker feels that the Vestron people did not have the expertise to 'platform' the film successfully—to break out of limited big-city art-house release and find a wider audience. With this one reservation, the *Malcolm* story is as cheerful and successful as the film itself.

Given the enormous goodwill in the film industry towards *Malcolm*, the second Tass–Parker film was awaited with unusually high expectations: and when it became known that Cascade Films had come to an agreement with United Artists for a worldwide release, apparently with few strings attached, there was widespread admiration. It would have been difficult to fulfil those expectations but, in the event, *RIKKY AND PETE* (1988) fell far short of the mark.

The aim was to make a film about a family, a film in which the central characters were not lovers, but brother and sister. Tass's family had once again proved an inspiration to Parker; the close-knit group provided a strength he had not previously experienced, but he also saw the negative side. The basis, then, was a story about a brother and sister who move away from their parents; but this concept proved a stumbling block, since most backers wanted a love story.

Early overseas deals, with Spectrafilm and later with Virgin, fell through, but finally Parker and Tass found one American company willing to back the project. Tony Thermopoulos and Beth Brand, respectively President and Vice-President of United Artists, liked the screenplay, saw *Malcolm*, and offered a whacking 75 per cent presale ($3 million of the film's $4 million budget). The dealmaking was extremely difficult: 'UA wasn't used to dealing with a director and cinematographer-writer who were also the film's producers. We'd go from creative meetings to confabs with the business affairs manager. But once we'd done the deal, they really didn't interfere. They were willing to let us make the film our way.' The rest of the budget was raised in Australia by 10BA: 'People belted down the door,' says Parker.

UA wanted approval of the lead actors, and for a while there was pressure to cast an American actress as Rikky (justified by having the character return to Australia after studying in New York with, of course, a perfect American accent). 'But we insisted on total creative control,' says Tass. 'What's the point of spending three years of your life and then not being happy at the end of it?' In the end, UA accepted the choices of Tass and Parker: two virtual unknowns. Rikky was played by Polish-born Nina Landis (she had attended the famous Lodz Film School when she was eighteen and played the role of a victim in John Lamond's nasty horror film, *Nightmares*, in 1980). Comedian Steve Kearney, one of the Melbourne comedy team Los Trios Ringbarkus, was cast as Pete.

Shooting took place in Melbourne and Broken Hill, and rushes were videotaped and sent off every day to UA in Los Angeles (first having been transferred from PAL to NTSC, the American video system). The fax machine ran red-hot, because UA had no other film in production at the time, and *Rikky and Pete* was treated as an in-house production, not as a pick-up. 'They had seven floors of people,' says Parker, 'and they had nothing to do but check on what was happening here.' 'On an individual level, they were very supportive,' says Tass, 'but we were a small film being produced by a large studio.'

The result is a grave disappointment after *Malcolm. Rikky and Pete* is a surprisingly incoherent film, which has the feeling of an abridged version of a much longer movie: the charm of the earlier film is conspicuously absent. This is partly due to the performances which, while perfectly competent, are uninspired. There are far too many characters vying for attention, including Bruno Lawrence as Sonny, a miner who forms a tentative friendship with Rikky, and Bruce Spence, with a Swedish accent, as Ben, another miner. Crucially, the brother–sister relationship never sparks, so that the most basic concept of the film remains stillborn.

The reviews were generally lukewarm (television critic Peter

Thompson, generally supportive of the Australian film industry, refused even to mention the film on his Nine Network *Sunday* programme). Tass and Parker still vigorously defend the film, feeling the poor reaction was, in part, due to overly high expectations. Tass points out that, with *Malcolm*, she was working on an emotional level, but 'with *Rikky and Pete*, I wasn't working on that level at all. My intention was to stimulate the mind. People came to the cinema with the wrong expectations.' Says Parker, 'Enough people have told me they prefer *Rikky and Pete* to *Malcolm* to show me we at least partially succeeded. But I'm not going to write another character with such a subtle psychological condition as that of Pete's—I think you've got to be more overt. Pete's anti-authoritarian attitude was the result of his anger against his parents; to have a character like that in a comedy is something I like very much. But I wouldn't do it again.' '*Malcolm* holds a very dear place in my heart,' says Tass. 'But I think *Rikky and Pete* is a cleverer film.'

Parker notes that the decision to cast a name actor such as Bruno Lawrence in a relatively minor role was the result of the small number of good character actors in Australia. 'People complain about the quality of scripts,' he says. 'I'd like to see better screen actors here.' Tass agrees: 'Many actors in Australia arrive for audition expecting the director to discover their qualities, rather than preparing the role for which they're auditioning, and then they often arrive on set without any preparation. We desperately need to improve that attitude.'

Despite the mixed reviews, *Rikky and Pete* did respectable business, though nowhere near the level *Malcolm* had achieved. At the end of 1989, the team was busy shooting a new comedy, *Mark Clark Van Ark*, with Steve Bisley, Claudia Karvan and Ben Mendelsohn in the leading roles. Again, there were problems raising the money; as with *Malcolm*, Tass and Parker were so convinced of the quality of their material that they mortgaged their house to get funds. Their faith and tenacity is formidable.

J ewish humour has never occupied centre stage in Australian comedy, though Roy Rene brought his 'Mo' character to the screen in Ken Hall's *Strike Me Lucky* (1934) and Alan Finney (later Village-Roadshow's Marketing Manager) played a Jewish tailor in Tim Burstall's *Stork* (1971). Three comedies of the 80s, however, had specifically Jewish themes.

NORMAN LOVES ROSE (1982) was written and directed by Henri

Safran whose biggest success of the 70s had been *Storm Boy*. It has
a storyline similar to that of the 1972 Israeli film, *I Love You Rosa*,
an early Menahem Golan–Yoram Globus production, written and
directed by Mozhe Mizrahi. The basic theme of both films is the
relationship between a frustrated wife and the young brother of her
husband. For the Australian film, Carol Kane was imported to play
Rose, married to boring David Downer; British Warren Mitchell plays
Downer's sympathetic father.

Mitchell, who won Best Supporting Actor at the AFI awards, steals
the film: he has precious little material to work with, but is often
quite funny and ultimately moving in the sequence in which he recalls
how little he remembers of his own father back in Poland. Ms Kane,
though she received an AFI nomination for Best Actress, seems all
at sea in the film, with an extraordinary accent and an almost complete
lack of conviction. Young Tony Owen is stilted and stiff as Norman,
and David Downer's performance seems inspired by television soaps.
On the other hand, Sandy Gore is astringent as the betrayed wife
of randy dentist Barry Otto, though she is cruelly photographed by
Vince Monton (whose camerawork is oddly unattractive throughout).
Safran's screenplay is padded out with overlong scenes of marginal
interest (the Bar Mitzvah), and the funniest moment comes when
Warren Mitchell advises his impotent son to think of another woman
when he makes love to his wife. 'Who?' asks Downer. 'Jane Fonda,'
says Mitchell. 'Will she mind?' Downer asks. A dismal title song adds
nothing to the picture.

Jewish brothers and their problems are also at the centre of *TWO
BROTHERS RUNNING* (1988), the second Phillip Emanuel-Ted Robinson
production. Tom Conti was imported to play Moses Bornstein, opposite
Ritchie Singer as brother Ben, and Elizabeth Alexander as Moses' wife
in this Morris Lurie screenplay. Despite the promising elements, the
film disappeared for two years after being screened to negative reactions
in the 1988 Cannes Festival market. And no wonder, because Lurie's
screenplay is an endless series of speeches, delivered by Conti with
enthusiasm but no conviction.

Moses, as played and written, is a crashing bore: there is a running
gag that people to whom he tells his awful jokes on the phone have
already heard them, and the film as a whole is a bit like that. We
know what to expect (a dismal time at his brother's wedding, adultery
with Deborra-Lee Furness) but we might have expected it all to be
lighter and brighter. Conti wears funny hats, adopts an oddly

unconvincing New York Jewish accent, gazes soulfully at the camera and gabbles on for what seems like hours on end; but it all adds up to precisely nothing. How this script ever got filmed is another of the film industry's mysteries. Poor Liz Alexander: she deserves a lot better than this.

The best of the Jewish comedies remains the low-budget *BACHELOR GIRL* (1987), co-written and directed by Rivka Hartman who had previously made an excellent medium-length film ironically titled *A Most Attractive Man* (1982). Originally titled *Once Upon a Weekend*, *Bachelor Girl* stars Lyn Pierse as Dot Bloom, thirty-two years old, single, and with eighty-two pot plants to support. She is unable to decide between her work as a writer, a computer nut (Bruce Spence) she fancies, and Karl (Kim Gyngell), a friend from university days, now divorced and a successful lawyer, so she spends a weekend devoting time to all three. Well-acted, sharply written and directed, and genuinely enjoyable, the film's best scene is a moment of embarrassment in a smart restaurant where Dot's knickers somehow get mixed up with her table napkin. Fortunately, the waiter is a man of the world.

S ix years before *Two Brothers Running* an attempt had been made to import Tom Conti for an Australian comedy: the film was *STANLEY* (1983) and producer Andrew Gaty still recalls the letter he received from Actors Equity refusing permission for this 'American' actor to be imported. The film marked a change of pace for writer-director Esben Storm, who had been previously associated with low-budget serious films like *With Prejudice*. The casting of an actor such as Conti had been seen as insurance against a relatively high ($3 million) budget, but after the Equity rejection Peter Bensley, star of *The Young Doctors* (a local television soap), was given the title role—and was mobbed wherever he went on location.

A yacht was needed for the film, since Stanley's father (Michael Craig) was a multi-millionaire businessman; the yacht rented by the production company had a helipad, so Storm thought it would add to production values to have a 'copter land on the boat. A black 'copter would look especially effective, and so the production approached Byron Kennedy for the chopper used on *Mad Max 2*; that one image, of the 'copter landing on the boat in the middle of Sydney Harbour, was the most complicated shot in the film.

Stanley is an uneven comedy and, at 107 minutes, far too long. The viewer quickly tires of the joke of Stanley going everywhere on roller skates and calling his titled father 'Sir Dad'; and Peter Bensley simply is not a sufficiently stylish actor to bring it off. On the other hand, there is a splendid supporting cast, including Graham Kennedy, whose impeccable sense of comedy timing insures he gets most of the laughs, and the volatile David Argue. Jon Ewing does a clever cameo as a shoe salesman: 'There are twice as many feet in the world as there are people—in this job, you have to love feet.' Joy Smithers is seen to advantage in an early role as Kennedy's pregnant daughter. Also amusing is Stanley's suggestion to his father's Board of Directors that their petfood be marketed for humans under the label, 'His Master's Choice'. Russell Boyd's cinematography ensures the film has a lush look, but the sluggish pacing, and central performance, are crippling liabilities.

The Phillip Emanuel-Ted Robinson team that made *Two Brothers Running* produced another comedy during the 80s: *THOSE DEAR DEPARTED* (1987). This was Emanuel's third production (after *The Wild Duck* and *Rebel*) and the first of three films he made with Robinson.

Garry McDonald, whose Norman Gunston creation will probably live with him forever, undoubtedly deserved a starring role in a comedy. Pamela Stephenson, after an initial appearance in the lead role of Keith Salvat's pioneering comedy *Private Collection* (1972), had become a celebrity in Britain; she returned to make this film and also *Les Patterson Saves the World*.

The screenplay, by Steve J. Spears (author of the successful play, *The Elocution of Benjamin Franklin*) is a good one about death and hauntings, possibly inspired by the Ealing school of comedy. The efforts of actress Stephenson and her secret lover and chauffeur (Marian Dworakowski) to eliminate her unwanted and egotistical actor-spouse (McDonald)—by means of glass in the pasta, poison in the nightcap— could have been turned into an amusing black comedy; but the handling is too strident and undisciplined and, as in many recent American films, the unnecessary special effects take centre stage instead of genuinely interesting people and funny situations. Attempts to jazz up the early scenes with rapid editing devices as if this were a movie from the swinging 60s are merely intrusive. Robinson describes the humour in the film as 'subtle and whimsical', but there is nothing subtle or whimsical about his handling of it.

D uring the 80s, Melbourne became firmly established as the home of comedy via a series of successful television programmes (*The*

Comedy Company, *Fast Forward*, et al.). A few modest, and enterprising, movie comedies were made in Melbourne, too, like *FUTURE SCHLOCK* and *CHANNEL CHAOS* (both 1984), which were produced by Barry Peak and Chris Kiely, operators of the Valhalla repertory cinemas in Melbourne and Sydney. Peak and Kiely were both born in Sydney in 1951; they met at school and ran a film club at Sydney University in the late 60s. Later, they rented the Union Theatres in both Sydney and Melbourne to screen films they liked to the public: they were very successful with repeat screenings of favourites featuring the Marx Brothers, W. C. Fields, Buster Keaton and Charles Chaplin. They also screened more recent films which had been and gone quickly in the regular cinemas.

The two found they could earn a modest living from these screenings, and decided to expand their activities. Peak had moved to Melbourne in 1975, and eventually signed a lease on a cinema in Richmond which became the Valhalla (or movie heaven). Repertory programming there was also successful, but it seemed to be easier to find such locations in Melbourne than in Sydney, and it was 1981 before the partners were able to take over the New Art Cinema in Glebe and transform it into Sydney's Valhalla. (Kiely now owns the Glebe cinema.) Among the biggest successes screened by the Valhallas were *Steppenwolf*, David Lynch's first film, *Eraserhead*, and the Italian animated feature *Allegro Non Troppo*. Attempts to start Valhallas in other cities—Brisbane, Perth, Adelaide—resulted in losses.

From the beginning, Peak and Kiely wanted to produce films themselves. Eventually they decided to go ahead on minuscule budgets with movies made for the cinema audiences they knew. *Future Schlock*, which was originally titled *The Ultimate Show*, cost $40,000, which the partners raised themselves. They wrote and directed the film together, on 16mm with a crew of four (plus lots of friends) over three weeks in the Melbourne suburbs. The largest costs in the budget were the fees paid to the actors, who all received union rates. 'It was a pretty slapdash effort,' says Peak. 'But we made the sort of film we'd like to see, given what was possible on such a small budget.'

Future Schlock is, indeed, on the amateurish side, but its cheerful anarchy makes it fun viewing. This was an early role for Maryanne Fahey (later seen on television as Kylie Mole), and she gives an exuberant performance as, with her partner, Michael Bishop, she brings havoc to the suburbanites of the future. The pair put lobsters into police lavatories, pose as government officials to announce that all

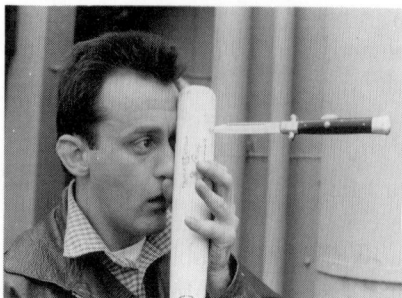

Channel Chaos. *Tim Scally*

brick veneer houses are about to collapse, and announce new guidelines for the populace that will involve painting children green, undressing at parties, and burying the family car. Groucho himself might have approved, despite the dodgy lip synch and chaotic structure.

Peak and Kiely were able to afford only one 16mm answer print of the film, and that is what they showed, with great success, in their cinemas. Unfortunately, TAA eventually lost the print somewhere in transit, and though the negative exists in Peak's garage, it is now no longer possible to see the film (except on video). In the end, Peak and Kiely got half their money back; they were determined to try again.

Channel Chaos, formerly *A Hatful of Arseholes*, was actually written before *Future Schlock*. Again, Peak and Kiely collaborated on the screenplay, but Peak takes a sole credit as director. This time, the budget was considerably larger—$400,000—and the money was raised through 10BA. Set in a television station, the film involves a series of murders investigated by the actors who play the station's cops in a long-running series. The goings-on at GRRS-TV are as anarchic as the events in the earlier film: the newsreader has a chronic stutter, the evening talk-show host is a deaf-mute; there is a game in which footballers face a team of bewildered chickens, a quiz show for girls with large breasts, and a mini-series about nudists with leukemia. The station's Chairman, Sir Ninian, likes to dress up in a sailor's uniform and ogle the girls, and there are some choice dialogue exchanges between this character and the station director, for example:

Director: 'Bugger the ratings!'

Sir Ninian: 'That was all very fine at sea . . .'

Some of the actors are better than others, and the concluding chase, involving the entire cast, is tiresome, but *Channel Chaos* has plenty of ideas and cheerfully rude comedy. However, when it was finished, Peak and Kiely hated it. 'We misjudged it during production,' says

Peak. 'It just wasn't funny. We were ashamed of it, and decided we didn't want to screen it at the Valhallas.' So the partners voluntarily shelved the film, and went on to make *The Big Hurt* (see Chapter 8) and *As Time Goes By* (Chapter 9).

A handful of comedy films of the 80s spoofed particular genres and even non-comedy films: films like *Wills and Burke, Bullseye* and *The Marsupials: The Howling III* are dealt with in other chapters. None of these was successful and, indeed, few comedies of the 80s worked at the box-office. The massive, almost unbelievable, exceptions are *CROCODILE DUNDEE* (1986) and its sequel. These two blockbusters were principally the creation of Paul Hogan (b. 1940), a cheerful, outgoing, blue-collar entertainer whose father had been a professional soldier, and who laboured at various jobs (on the railways, for the Water Board, in an abattoir, on the docks, in a flour mill and, most famously, on the Sydney Harbour Bridge) until he was over thirty.

Hogan was a family man with five children and he had no particular love for movies, and no great interest in them. He became famous sending up the judges on *New Faces*, was a frequent guest on Mike Willesee's *A Current Affair*, and did a series of humorous television commercials, notably for Winfield cigarettes: 'Any how, 'ave a Winfield.' His own television show, produced by his mate John Cornell, directed by another mate, Peter Faiman, was a big success, and he graduated to acting, playing a soldier in the mini-series *The Anzacs*. He had a reputation in the US, because of his amusingly laconic advertisements for the Australian Tourist Board, and in the UK (ads for Foster's). And when he decided to make a film, he knew exactly what kind of film he wanted to make. 'A *real* movie,' or 'a *proper* movie' were phrases he used in interview after interview. He was not interested in the 'wankers' who comprise the Australian film industry (though Peter Weir was originally approached to direct *Crocodile Dundee*): not for Hogan such arty fare as *Picnic at Hanging Rock* or *My Brilliant Career*. He did not see why the government should subsidise the industry at all, though he took advantage of 10BA to raise the $8.8 million needed for his first feature (which, incidentally, had been rejected at script stage by an assessor for Hoyts–Edgley as 'not funny'). He was aiming to produce a film that would be as popular as *Arthur* or *Back to the Future*. And he succeeded.

Hogan was clever about choosing his collaborators. Cornell, his television producer, produced. Faiman, his television director, directed.

He wrote the film himself, together with Ken Shadie, a regular co-writer. But on the technical side, he hired the very best people: Russell Boyd as director of photography, Jane Scott as line producer, David Stiven as editor, Graham (Grace) Walker as production designer, Peter Best as composer, and so on. The character he dreamed up, that of the laid-back Northern Territory larrikin guide, teller of tall tales and all-round good guy, was tailored for his personality, and the story—the old fish-out-of-water theme—that has Mick Dundee journey to New York City, was shrewdly tailored for the American audience (anyone less ambitious might have made the city Sydney or Melbourne, and the effect would not have been the same). The crew shot for seven weeks in the Territory, mostly in Kakadu, partly near Cloncurry, and for a further six weeks in New York.

The film is divided evenly between the two locations, the outback and the Big Apple. The humour comes entirely from Dundee's naivete and innocence, and Hogan plays with a relaxed charm that is disarming and endearing. He fought Actors Equity to import Linda Kozlowski, the little-known actress who plays the New York journalist who travels to the outback (compare *Razorback*), and in real life wound up leaving his wife for her.

Hogan's antipathy towards the Australian film industry's 'wankers' can only have been confirmed by the reaction of Phillip Adams, Chairman of the Australian Film Commission, who was shown the film at a small, private preview. Adams was unimpressed, and went into print in the *Australian* to say so (as he had done, some years earlier, with *Mad Max*, which he similarly underrated). Adams' was about the only (public) attack on the film, though. The opening night (22 April 1986) in Sydney was a great event in the history of the industry: everyone seemed to know they had seen a major hit. Just how major, nobody could have foreseen. Hoyts, despite their pre-

Crocodile Dundee. *Paul Hogan, Linda Kozlowski.*

production rejection, distributed the film in Australia, but Jonathan Chissick admits that 'nobody could have predicted the film would do $20 million in rentals in Australia and hundreds of millions overseas. I originally predicted $5 million in rentals in Australia, which would have been a huge figure: I never guessed it would do four times as much. The film was one in a million, a mega-hit. People loved the picture. The very first public session was practically full, and it went on to run a year.'

It was a mega-hit all around Australia, but would it play (as they say in the trade) in Peoria? Hogan was confident about that, too. 'I've made a very good movie,' he said in Montreal on the eve of the film's North American premiere as the World Film Festival's closing night attraction. 'It's feelgood stuff, pure entertainment. It's going to be a big hit in America like it was in Australia.' And it was, but not quite in the same version as it had been in Australia. Paramount had bought the North American rights, and during the (northern) summer of 1986 worked together with Hogan on minor modifications to the film which would make it more acceptable to mainstream American audiences. These modifications included the rather odd addition of inverted commas to the 'Crocodile' of the title, but also some re-editing (losing approximately five minutes) and redubbing of some typical Australian slang (so that 'stickybeak' becomes 'busybody' and 'billabong' becomes 'lake'). For full details of this fascinating transformation, see Stephen Crofts' invaluable report in the January 1990 issue of *Cinema Papers*.

Even with all this doctoring, the executives at Paramount were undoubtedly amazed to find the film became the top grossing foreign (i.e. non-American) film ever released in the US—bigger even than the British James Bond movies. Americans, many of whom undoubtedly thought the film was American, flocked to see it in such numbers that it ended up with a gross rental, in the US and Canada alone, of $US70 million. Subsequent video cassette sales were also astronomical. When 20th Century–Fox released the film in the rest of the world the success was repeated: in Scandinavia and Italy, Britain and Germany, even France and Japan, people laughed at the film and cheered as its hero won the girl at the end.

Hogan refused to enter *Crocodile Dundee* in the 1986 AFI awards, probably because of his aforementioned distrust of anything 'arty'; this decision prevented the film winning any technical awards, and there was speculation that John Meillon—wonderful as Dundee's offsider—could have won a Supporting Actor award, had Hogan not been so stubborn. Hogan won an honorary award from the AFI, whether he liked it or not.

Once the roller-coaster success of the film was in motion, it was obvious there would be a sequel, but Hogan always said he would not do a second film unless it was better than the first. *'CROCODILE' DUNDEE II* (1988)—the inverted commas cropped up in Australia this time—was far from being as good as the first, since the thriller plot (Dundee and Sue pursued back to Australia by sinister drug runners) was banal. Hogan scripted with one of his sons, Brett, and made a couple of significant changes in personnel: Peter Faiman was replaced by John Cornell as director, and Graham Walker by Larry Eastwood on production design. Ernie Dingo played the Aboriginal role taken by David Gulpilil in the first film.

'Croc' II was a hit, but not quite such a big one. It became the No. 2. film ever released in Australia with $12.2 million rentals (nearly $8 million less than its predecessor) and it garnered a further $US57.3 million in North America. Perhaps significantly, video sales were way below those for the first film. Still, it made more millions worldwide, and Hogan, on the strength of the two films, became a multi-millionaire. Early in 1990, he commenced work on his third feature, *Almost an Angel*, entirely American-based, with Cornell directing, Kozlowski co-starring, and most of the same key Australian crew members; it will be interesting to see if lightning strikes a third time, especially as the new film is not about the character of Michael J. 'Crocodile' Dundee.

A success like the *Crocodile Dundee* films is something every filmmaker strives for: that is the big pay-off, the crock of gold. But it has happened once only, in the history of the Australian cinema. That is not to say it could not happen again: Yahoo Serious tried with *Young Einstein*, but did not make it. It takes talent, up to a point, but Paul Hogan's success went beyond talent: it was his supreme, almost brazen, self-confidence that brought him such phenomenal success. Making people laugh can be an astronomically profitable business: more often, as all too many Australian filmmakers can testify, it is not a funny business at all.

THE

KID

STAKES

■
■

F ilms made specifically for children are very much in the minority in Australia, as they are elsewhere, though the admirable work of Yoram Gross and his animation team (which falls outside the scope of this book) should not be underestimated. Also of note are the children's films made for television—the *Winners* series (which has attracted many top film directors, including Paul Cox) is the best example.

In the cinema, though, the pickings have been relatively slim. One of the most ambitious is *PLAYING BEATIE BOW* (1985), the last feature (to date) from the South Australian Film Corporation (which made *Storm Boy*, one of the best children's films of the 70s). Based on a popular novel by Ruth Park, this lavish time-travel yarn is notable for the award-winning production design of George Liddle: Sydney streets and homes—and Circular Quay itself—in the 1870s, are marvellous creations, all constructed in studios in Adelaide.

Imogen Annesley is appealing as the present-day teenager who travels back over 100 years in time, but director Donald Crombie seems uncertain as to what age-group he is aiming at: scenes in a brothel are a bit strong for the younger ones. Also, some of the supporting actors and the extras are noticeably poorly directed. But the relatively poor performance of the film can probably be put down to the fact that it was made in the same year as *Back to the Future* which is, in some ways, the archetypal time-travel film.

FLUTEMAN (1982) takes a familiar children's story—that of the Pied Piper of Hamelin—and relocates it in a drought-stricken outback town. Peter Maxwell's film was made on a very modest budget, but the film does boast a lovely performance from John Ewart as one of the town's senior citizens: mysteriously, and frustratingly, Ewart drops out of the picture without explanation before the climax. John Jarratt is the hippie-influenced piper, with beard, ear-ring and a line in archaic dialogue. Several missed opportunities here.

The same year, 1982, the same team—director Peter Maxwell and producer Brendon Lunney—made another family film, *RUN, REBECCA, RUN!* It is a modest adventure in which a plucky child (Simone Buchanan) is 'kidnapped' by a refugee (Henri Szeps) from a South American dictatorship. John Ewart plays Australia's Minister for Immigration in this one, and is easily persuaded by young Rebecca that Manuel is a good candidate for Australian citizenship, despite the way he treats her at the outset.

FROG DREAMING (1985) is much more ambitious than either of these, and was made on a much bigger budget. Financed by UAA, the film started shooting under the direction of Russell Hagg, who was replaced by Brian Trenchard Smith during production. The intriguing story, redolent of Australian bush yarns, is about an apparently haunted lake and an Aboriginal legend. Trenchard Smith's craftsmanship ensures that the sunlit, peaceful lake has a sinister aura to it, and the combination of humour and tension is well maintained. There is also a strong supporting cast, including John Ewart (again) as the local policeman and Tony Barry as the guardian of the 14-year-old hero. Some of the dialogue is designed to amuse adults (a professor, asked if he knows anything about monsters, replies that he has been married to one for twenty years), and the frequent close-ups of animals in the wild (including a shot of a huge lizard consuming a mouse) add to the sense of primeval mystery.

Sadly, *Frog Dreaming* is crippled by the opportunistic casting of American child actor Henry Thomas (fresh from his success in *E.T.*) in the lead. The boy is totally out of place in this Australian bush story, and no attempt is made to disguise his accent, even though he seems to have been living in the township for some time (since the death of his American parents). As is usually the case with this kind of casting, made with a view to future marketing and with no serious thought, apparently, given to how this will affect the film as a whole, a promising film is critically undermined.

Trenchard Smith's energetic skills are also on display in *BMX BANDITS* (1983), an exuberant teenage adventure in the tradition of the Ealing classic, *Hue and Cry*. Russell Hagg was marginally involved in this one, too (Patrick Edgeworth's screenplay was based on Hagg's original), but the film is notable mainly for providing an important early role for Nicole Kidman, who was fifteen years old at the time. She plays one of the trio of BMX bike fanatics who become involved in some exciting comic chases with villains David Argue and John Ley on spectacular locations in Sydney's northern beach suburbs: Trenchard Smith revels in the expertly staged chase sequences. John Seale's outstanding cinematography undoubtedly helped establish him at this early stage of his career.

Kidman's first film, made when she was fourteen, was actually *BUSH CHRISTMAS* (1983), a remake of the 1947 Children's Film Foundation production. Ralph Smart, who wrote, produced and directed the original, is not mentioned in the credits of the new film, which Henri Safran directed for producers Paul Barron and Gilda Baracchi. (At one time,

Howard Rubie was announced as director.)

Handsomely shot on location in Lamington Plateau, Queensland, this was Barron's first feature production, and is another superior family film. Kidman is impressive in her first role as the oldest of the children who, with an Aboriginal farmhand (Manalpuy) track down the thieves who have stolen her father's horses. John Ewart is a villain this time, and a most engaging one; John Howard is effective, too, as his offsider. In comparison, the 'honest' adult characters are a dull lot. There is suspense (the children trapped in a cave that fills with water) and humour (having to eat lizards or witchetty grubs, the way Manalpuy does, to survive), but the film did not fare as well as it deserved to at the box-office. Barron suggests this was the result of a hardening of audience attitude at around the time the film was released.

BUSHFIRE MOON (1987) is also set at Christmas, but is a vastly inferior production. From a screenplay by Jeff Peck, George Miller (2) fumbles this tall tale, set in 1891 in the drought-stricken outback, in which a little boy mistakes an old derelict (Charles Tingwell) for Father Christmas. The family here is an uninteresting one, and the film is marred by another piece of miscasting with Dee Wallace Stone (also ex-E.T.) as Mum (the excuse for this was a sale to the Disney television channel, and it is explained away by having the character hail originally from San Francisco). Nadine Garner is the inevitable young teen, and John Waters (who has been in more bad films than most other actors around) struggles as the head of the family. A few bright moments are provided by Bill Kerr as an Anglophile landowner determined to enjoy Christmas with all the trimmings—including yule log and roast suckling pig—despite the stifling heat.

J udging from his remarkable sci-fi feature, Incident at Raven's Gate, Rolf De Heer is a director of considerable talent. His first feature, TAIL OF A TIGER (1984), is a modest, amiable family film about a little boy (Grant Navin), mad about aeroplanes, who befriends an old-timer (Gordon Poole) who owns an ancient Tiger Moth. The climax, in which the pair soar over Sydney in the refurbished plane, is sure to bring joy to the heart of many a likely lad, but the film is almost stolen by Dylan Lyle, as the young hero's cheeky little brother.

In much the same mood is I OWN THE RACECOURSE (1985), another Paul Barron production, in which Gully Coote plays a youngster who thinks he has purchased the racecourse in the inner-Sydney suburb of Glebe from an old derelict (a surprising performance from Norman

Kaye). Tony Barry is, once again, a tower of strength, this time as a sympathetic groundsman; and there are a couple of shambling villains (Bob Ellis, Les Murray) who provide the comedy. Stephen Ramsey directed this pleasant wish-fulfilment fantasy.

After Tiger Moths and racecourses, an old ferryboat might seem like small (ginger) beer, and, indeed, *SAVE THE LADY* (1981), the second (and final) feature production of the Tasmanian Film Corporation (after *Manganinnie*) is slight indeed. There is the usual clutch of eager youngsters, and an unusually strong batch of old-timers in the character roles: coincidentally, John Ewart, Bill Kerr, Desmond Tester and Wallas Eaton had all been child actors themselves. Hobart locations are the chief attraction here. Leon Thau directed a screenplay based on a book by animator Yoram Gross, who distributed through his Young Australia Films company.

In the early 80s, two films based on popular cartoon characters emerged: *FATTY FINN* (1980) and *GINGER MEGGS* (1982). *Fatty Finn* was produced by John Sexton for the Children's Film Foundation, with a screenplay by Bob Ellis and Chris McGill. It is significant as the first feature on which John Seale worked as director of photography; he returned to operate for Russell Boyd the following year on *Gallipoli*. *Fatty Finn* is larger than life: colours are bright, costumes are fanciful, and the acting of the adults is deliberately broad—Bert Newton, as Fatty's father, is made up to look like Oliver Hardy, and Gerard Kennedy's Tiger Murphy wears emerald green throughout. Ben Oxenbould is a robust Fatty, and Noni Hazlehurst brings class to the role of his mother.

The original locations of Woolloomooloo were no longer available, so the film was shot, to good effect, around Glebe; as befits the fact that the story is set in 1930, the opening (black-and-white) image is of the uncompleted Harbour Bridge. The director, Maurice Murphy (b. 1939), had previously worked on such television comedy staples as *The Aunty Jack Show* and *The Norman Gunston Show*.

Ginger Meggs was also produced by John Sexton, this time for his own company. Jonathan Dawson, who directed, was a lecturer in film at Queensland University, and his prior claim to feature-film fame was the dubious one of providing the screenplay for Ross Dimsey's atrocious thriller, *Final Cut* (1979).

Unfortunately, the later film completely misses the charm of *Fatty Finn*; colourful sets and costumes are used again, but look merely garish on this occasion; the children are dull and amateurish; and the adults overplay their roles without elan or conviction. John Seale photographed on locations around Bowral. The film is set in the 40s, and nostalgia is laid on with a trowel, including a scene in which a travelling cinema visits town for a projection of *Forty Thousand Horsemen*. However, it is all undercut by a painfully inappropriate soundtrack of 80s rock. The plot is thin, and is made to seem thinner by the film's inordinate length (100 minutes).

In the interim, Maurice Murphy joined forces with producer Brian Rosen to form Universal Entertainment Corporation, for which he directed *DOCTORS AND NURSES* (1981), a major comedown after *Fatty Finn*. A lame attempt to cash in on the success of Alan Parker's *Bugsy Malone*, the film casts children as doctors and nurses in a hospital where the patients are adults. Attempts to Americanise the film reek of desperation (one VIP patient is discovered to be the US President) and the actors, adults and children alike, are uniformly weak. They include Pamela Stephenson, making an unfortunate return to Australian cinema, Bert Newton (as a derelict), Graeme Blundell (a man who has lost his memory), Andrew McFarlane, June Salter and others. Make-up is noticeably poor and even John Seale cannot make the film look interesting. A running gag (borrowed from *M*A*S*H*—the film is very short on originality) has a series of hospital announcements over the PA involving famous medicos from Dr Who to Dr Strangelove—Dr Livingstone is informed Mr Stanley is looking for him! No less than five writers, including Morris Gleitzman and Murphy himself, laboured on this turkey.

After this fiasco, Murphy and Rosen embarked on what sounded like an interesting project. Two films, *Horror Movie* and *Goose Flesh*, were designed to be made back-to-back, with the same crew (John Seale again behind the camera) and cast (Drew Forsythe, Paul Chubb, John Derum, David Argue, Sara de Teliga). Murphy and Geoffrey Atherden had written two screenplays with identical plotlines, one (*Horror Movie*) handled straight, the other (*Goose Flesh*) comic. Budgeted at $1 million for the two films ($500,000 each), production commenced in April 1981, in Sydney: a scene would be shot for the first film, then reshot as comedy for the second.

It sounds like a rather odd concept, but we will never know how it might have turned out. This was a period when 10BA was getting under way, and the financing of films was changing dramatically. After a week's shooting, lack of funds brought production to a halt. Since the film had to be completed by June 1981, the delays resulted in a complete shutdown. The actors were fully paid, and Brian Rosen was left with a $700,000 debt, which took years to pay off. The footage that was shot remains in Maurice Murphy's possession. He has not made another feature since (attempts to film *The Sentimental Bloke* in 1982 came to nothing, as already noted in Chapter 6), but is kept busy making television commercials.

T he formula for a children's film, at least as defined in many of the Australian films discussed above, is simple enough: take a child, or group of children, aged anywhere from eight to fifteen, pit them against some very mild villains, and cast some good character actors as those villains. Quite the strangest film to employ this formula is *MOLLY* (1983); and in this case the title refers not to the diminutive heroine but to (wait for it!) a singing dog.

Molly had built up something of a reputation for herself by howling in such a way that the generously disposed could at times discern the hint of a tune. She was the property of Phillip Roope, who had encouraged her in her warbling and created an 'act' with her (which had featured on the Mike Walsh television show). Roope and his friend, Mark Thomas (who had been assistant director on Ian Pringle's *The Plains of Heaven*), had, meanwhile, written the script of a short film, *The Applicant*. At the AFC office in North Sydney, Roope showed *The Applicant* to Hilary Linstead (who was working as an assessor) and she seems to have been more taken with Molly, who was brought along by her master to attend the screening. Linstead encouraged Roope and Thomas to write a screenplay structured around Molly, and managed to raise the money after three drafts. She wanted Gillian Armstrong to direct, but Thomas suggested Ned Lander, because he had admired

Molly. *Claudia Karvan, Garry McDonald and Molly.* (Photo: *Carol Ruff.*)

Lander's *Wrong Side of the Road*; Roope and Thomas wanted to make the film in a co-operative fashion.

Richard Brennan was brought in as executive producer, and Lander worked on further rewrites with Roope and Thomas. It was originally conceived as a modestly-budgeted ($500,000) picture, but Lander was keen to introduce new elements into the story, notably some elaborate circus scenes; the Flying Fruit Fly Circus, based at Coogee, became involved. As Lander's ideas became more elaborate, intense pressure was put on both schedule and budget; but the ideas kept coming and the budget kept ballooning (eventually up to $1 million). The scheduling—the responsibility of Mark Thomas—became extremely difficult; and, all the time, the rewriting continued. Claudia Karvan (daughter of restaurateur Arthur Karvan) was cast in her first screen role as Maxie, the little girl who befriends the singing dog.

Mark Thomas looks back on the whole affair with some dismay. 'We were on a rollercoaster,' he says. 'Nobody told Ned to stop.' A few days before the shoot was due to begin, with the schedule still not properly resolved, Thomas was removed as first assistant director by Richard Brennan, and left the project feeling bitter. 'Ned hijacked the film,' he says. 'He completely changed the concept.' Says Brennan: 'Gradually, the script got more and more dismembered. I thought the finished film was a hideous mess.' Brennan recalls having a dispute with Lander about a scene in which the villain, played by Garry McDonald, is chasing Maxie. 'Ned told me: "A child would never be able to outrun an adult." I reminded him of the tortoise and the hare, but that didn't satisfy him. He came up with an "accident", in which Garry slashed his bare foot open with a razor-blade which he stepped on: the film was filled with hideous scenes like that.'

Indeed, the razor scene *is* hideous, and totally out of place in a 'family' film. Garry McDonald plays the villain in a variety of disguises (including circus clown and nun) and gives such an intense performance that at times it seems as if he is in a horror film, not a children's picture. Lander's direction is deficient in terms of pace, too: the film moves with desperate slowness—the characters even seem to *move* slowly, and this lassitude even affects the delivery of the lines. Lander has not directed another feature since *Molly*.

About the only positive thing that can be said about this most peculiar film is that the production design (by Robert Dein) deserved a better vehicle. Added to that is the fact that Molly does not assault our eardrums on too many occasions.

THE

CHILDREN

ARE

WATCHING

US

■
■

T he films discussed in the previous chapter were made for children: in this final chapter, we consider a number of films made *about* children, or teenagers, and the way they relate to their parents.

John Duigan's *THE YEAR MY VOICE BROKE* (1987) is generally considered one of the finest Australian films of the decade. It won five AFI awards in 1987 (including Best Film, Director and Original Screenplay) and its insight into the world of teenagers growing up in a small country town in the early 60s is acute and tender. The film represents an interesting and important marriage of a large production house, Kennedy–Miller, with a serious, even radical, director like Duigan.

After the commercial failure of *One Night Stand* (see Chapter 7), Duigan found himself unable to realise his ambition to make a film called *Flirting*, about life at a boarding school in the mid-60s. Subsequently, he wrote the screenplay for *The Year My Voice Broke* (which eventually became a prequel to *Flirting*). He then accepted an offer from Kennedy–Miller to co-direct (with Chris Noonan) the mini-series *Vietnam* (1987). 'I knew George [Miller] slightly,' says Duigan, 'because he'd been editing *Mad Max* at the same time I'd been editing *Mouth to Mouth* in Melbourne.'

After the success of *Vietnam*, Duigan mentioned to Terry Hayes that he had a feature script he would like to do. Hayes, Miller and Doug Mitchell liked the screenplay, and agreed to produce it. Kennedy–Miller had planned to make four telemovies for the Ten Network and it was decided to include *The Year My Voice Broke* in this package, while agreeing that Duigan could make it on the budget of a modest feature film, and shoot in 35mm (the other three telemovies were shot on 16mm).

Though not exactly autobiographical, the character of Danny does express some of Duigan's own sensibilities and views of the world. 'But Danny's background is completely different from mine,' he says. 'And he has very different relationships.' Duigan spent his school holidays in a country town, and worked on his uncle's farm, so scenes like the hay-baling were taken from personal observation.

As he had done in *Mouth to Mouth* and *One Night Stand*, Duigan chose young unknown actors to play the leading roles: Noah Taylor as Danny; Loene Carmen as Freya, the girl he adores; and Ben Mendelsohn as Trevor, the high-spirited boy with whom Freya becomes involved. In supporting roles, he cast a whole gallery of well-known Australian actors, many of whom he had worked with before: 'Graeme

Blundell had directed me as an actor at The Pram Factory and La Mama; I'd acted in plays with Bruce Spence and Tim Robertson, and they'd both been in *Dimboola*; I hadn't worked with Nick Tate before, but it was great to get someone of his stature to play the policeman.'

Duigan worked with cinematographer Geoff Burton for the first time on *Vietnam*, and chose him to shoot *The Year My Voice Broke*. 'I really enjoyed working with him,' he says. The film was shot in Braidwood, on the New South Wales tablelands.

When it was completed, *Year* was entered in the AFI awards. This sparked a protest from the Screen Producers Association of Australia, a group of which Kennedy–Miller is not a member, on the grounds that the film was a telemovie, not a feature, and therefore ineligible. Duigan was easily able to prove that the film was shot on 35mm and designed as a feature, so the film remained in contest and, as mentioned earlier, won many of the major awards that year. As a direct result of this success, it was picked up by Hoyts and enjoyed an excellent cinema release, buoyed by enthusiastic reviews.

The touching central situation of *The Year My Voice Broke* is Danny's difficulty in coping with the fact that Freya, whom he has adored since childhood, prefers the company of an older boy, and is becoming sexually active. Duigan elicits painfully real performances from Noah Taylor and Loene Carmen, and also provides a richly observed background for the small town with its dark little secret: Freya's mother had been a prostitute who had slept with most of the local men; she had lived in what is now known as the 'haunted house' where, ironically, Freya and Trevor go to make love. The ending, as Freya leaves by train for Sydney after Trevor's death, and Danny says goodbye to her, is one of the most affecting and satisfying conclusions to any

The Year My Voice Broke. *Loene Carmen, Ben Mendelsohn, Noah Taylor.*

Australian film. We feel for these characters because Duigan and the actors have made them so painfully real.

In the wake of this success, Duigan made a telemovie for Kennedy–Miller (*Fragments of War*, 1988, which was about photographer Damien Parer) and then, in Mexico, made the political drama *Romero* (1989) for an American company founded by radical Catholics who wanted to tell the story of the assassinated Archbishop of El Salvador. Meanwhile, Duigan reworked his *Flirting* screenplay so that it became a sequel to *The Year My Voice Broke*, with Noah Taylor returning as Danny. This film was shot for Kennedy–Miller at the end of 1989, with a third film in the trilogy planned for 1991.

Reality is not the great strength of *THE DELINQUENTS* (1989), another film about small-town teenage love from another era (the 50s); but comparisons between this film and Duigan's are particularly odious. However, *The Delinquents* represents a couple of significant firsts. It was the first of a programme of features to be produced by Village–Roadshow; and it was the first film to go into release with the logo of the Film Finance Corporation.

First-time producers Alex Cutler and Michael Wilcox acquired rights to Criena Rohan's 1962 book. They discovered David Bowie was also interested in it and persuaded him to write the music, but he later dropped out, pleading pressure of other work. Cutler is an American lawyer who worked as business affairs manager at Grundy's and then with Hoyts; Wilcox, also a lawyer, was business affairs manager for McElroy and McElroy.

The Delinquents. *Charlie Schlatter, Kylie Minogue.*

With initial support from both the NSWFC and the AFC, Lex Marinos wrote the first draft and was joined by playwright Dorothy Hewett on subsequent drafts. Cutler and Wilcox managed to interest Greg Coote and John Tarnoff, of Village–Roadshow Pictures, in the project Tarnoff, another American (ex-De Laurentiis) has described how he wanted to make not a small Australian film, but an international film. Coote suggested Kylie Minogue, popular star of *Neighbours* and the song charts, for the role of Lola. With Village–Roadshow involved, it was an easy decision to base the film at the Gold Coast studios which the company (in partnership with Warners) had acquired from the ailing Dino De Laurentiis company, even though basing a film at those studios has been estimated by one producer to add at least $1 million to the budget of any film. *The Delinquents* had an announced budget of a very substantial $9 million.

To achieve the 'internationalism' which the producers wanted, major compromises were made. A young American actor called Charlie Schlatter was cast as Brownie, the youth with whom Minogue's Lola has a passionate relationship in Bundaberg, Queensland, in 1957. Schlatter's previous films (including the lumbering George Burns comedy *18 Again*) gave no indication that he was an actor of note; and he was obviously miscast as a teenager from the small Australian sugar town. Actors Equity, quite understandably, attempted to block Schlatter's casting, and the matter went to arbitration with the arbitrator, unfortunately, finding in the producers' favour. Schlatter makes no attempt to modify his accent: there is a laboured little scene in which he explains his Dad was American and that he lived a while in Seattle, but it does not convince and he appears to have lived in Bundaberg long enough for some kind of Australian accent to filter through. Nor does he have the look or style of a teenager from a provincial town in the 50s.

It is ironic, because production designer Larry Eastwood and cinematographer Andrew Lesnie take great pains to get the film looking right, only to have credibility dashed by this piece of grossly opportunistic casting. Many in the industry at the end of the 80s feared that the incongruous presence of actors like Schlatter would become the norm in high-budget Australian films in a vain attempt to make them appealing to middle America. If so, it is an incredibly stupid policy.

The screenplay is credited to Mac Gudgeon and Clayton Frohman, the latter an American writer; during pre-production, Dorothy Hewett and Lex Marinos were still listed as Gudgeon's co-writers, and the fact that they have been replaced by Frohman is a further indication of the direction *The Delinquents* took during production. In any event, the script, as filmed, is repetitive and trite.

Director Chris Thomson brings less conviction to the film than he has to anything he has tackled before. There is so little chemistry between these 'delinquents' that their co-stars easily overwhelm them in terms of interest, despite having less screen time. Authority figures in the film are brutal to the point of caricature. The spirit of Charles Dickens constantly hovers over scenes at the welfare hostel, the hospital and at the home of the mean-spirited do-gooder (Melissa Jaffer) with whom poor Lola is forced to live—a character that might have been played, in another era, by that distinguished interpreter of Dickensian characters, Edna May Oliver. Dickensian, too, is the amazing coincidence that allows Brownie to be reunited with a sadder but wiser Lola in a Melbourne bar.

The Delinquents was launched with a big advertising campaign in Australia and Britain simultaneously in time for 1989 Christmas audiences. Though understandably savaged by the critics (who were not permitted to see it before its opening), the film opened to strong business, which was in no way dampened by Kylie Minogue's new hairstyle, or her much-publicised relationship with rock star Michael Hutchence. However, its takings were well below those of *Young Einstein*, which had been launched with similar fanfare twelve months earlier.

R *AW NERVE* (1988), also known as *Things and Other Stuff*, is an infinitely more modest and appealing film about more traditional delinquents: three teenagers who break into the home of a wealthy man. Tony Wellington's film is confined almost entirely to one location—the interior of the house—and is interesting chiefly for the performances of the actors. Kelly Dingwall plays the ringleader, who has his own secret motives for robbing this particular house; Rebecca Rigg is his girl, still suffering the trauma of having secretly had a baby, which was adopted; and John Polson is the slightly paranoid Billy, jealous of the other two and ashamed of his working-class parents.

Produced by Michael Lynch, who is better known as a casting director, *Raw Nerve* is a good example of low-budget filmmaking, but it also demonstrates the difficulty of finding an audience for such very modest material. Cinemas were not interested in the film, which was also (surprisingly) bypassed for AFI nominations, and so, at the time of writing, languishes unseen.

One drawback in *Raw Nerve* is that the actors, good as they are, seem too old to be playing high-school kids. No such reservations can be held about *FAST TALKING* (1983), Ken Cameron's very fine second feature. Cameron (see Chapter 5) was a schoolteacher before he became a film director, and he wrote the *Fast Talking* screenplay before that of *Monkey Grip*, which was made first. 'Fast Talking developed out of my short films,' he says. 'It's my favourite of my films, the most free and the most joyful.' Had it been a commercial success, which, sadly, it was not, Cameron had hoped to continue to explore the life of his young hero, Steve, much in the same way Francois Truffaut returned time and again to the life of Antoine Doinel, whom we first met as a child in *Les Quatre Cents Coups* (*The 400 Blows*). Cameron envies John Duigan's success in being able to continue the story of Danny in *The Year My Voice Broke*, *Flirting* and the planned third feature.

Cameron spent months looking for a boy who could play Steve; he went to a great many schools to talk to youngsters interested in drama. He finally found Rod Zuanic, fourteen years old at the time, living in Blacktown (west of Sydney), half Yugoslav, half French. 'He was a very cheeky, funny, unselfconscious kid,' says Cameron. 'And he was happy to do the film because he wanted to get out of doing maths.'

Fast Talking. *Rod Zuanic.*

Ross Matthews produced the film, which was budgeted at $1 million. It was a risky project, because there were no name actors, and the story was generally considered not very commercial. Filming was scheduled to last six weeks: though location work was done at Botany, the film in the school is actually Balmain High: 'I knew the headmaster from my teaching days,' says Cameron. 'These days we'd need permission from the Education Department to film at a school, but then it was easier. He was happy for us to shoot there, but we had to hide the film crew when school inspectors arrived.' He adds, 'The kids were a joy to work with. The filming became a game for them.' Adult roles were taken by Steve Bisley and Tracy Mann; David Gribble, who had photographed *Monkey Grip*, was cinematographer.

Fast Talking is an extraordinarily impressive film: funny, honest, sad, and superbly acted by its mostly young cast. Rod Zuanic in particular is a find as the lively, likeable Steve (the young actor was subsequently cast in *The Tale of Ruby Rose* and *Warm Nights on a Slow Moving Train*). Above all, Cameron does not patronise: he knows these youngsters well, and allows us to see the world from their point of view. The open ending, with Steve, alone, facing an uncertain future, is an acknowledged tribute to the final image of *The 400 Blows*.

Sadly, despite its life and energy and great good humour, the film fared poorly at the box-office. The major distributors didn't want it, and so it was handled by Filmways—and it never really got off the ground. 'It polarised people,' says Cameron. 'It wasn't oozing with charm—it was tough. But there was no rock 'n' roll, and people seemingly couldn't accept its mood. I can't see how it could ever have been a hit, but it could have been marketed more imaginatively than it was.'

FIGHTING BACK (1982) covers similar territory and also centres on a boy, Tom (Paul Smith) in his early teens. The fourth of the Adams–Packer films (and the last to be released), this was produced by Tom Jeffrey and directed by Michael Caulfield (b. 1949), a versatile character whose one feature film this is. Caulfield's work in the industry includes composing music for *Stockade* and the television series *The Godfathers*; writing for television (*The Restless Years*) and working as actors' coach (on *The Chant of Jimmie Blacksmith* among other films).

The source material here was a book, *Tom*, written by a young technical school teacher, John Embling; the book was adapted for the screen by Jeffrey and Michael Cove. Lewis Fitz-Gerald plays Embling (the names are not changed in the film), with Kris McQuade giving an award-winning performance as Tom's mother.

The film presents a rather chilling portrait of young Sydney teens (like *Fast Talking*, the location is the Botany area). Tom is anti-social, destructive and violent: he cannot read or write, but drinks and smokes, steals cars, and terrorises his mother and sister (his father has left the family long ago). The film, in the tradition of *Blackboard Jungle* and *To Sir With Love*, has a naive young teacher, fresh from university, gain the confidence and respect of the boy. Tough as nails when dealing with the boy and his friends, the film is a bit too gentle in its depiction of the guileless, saintly Embling. It lacks the resonances of Ken Cameron's film, perhaps because his background in the teaching profession almost guaranteed maximum authenticity.

In *SEBASTIAN AND THE SPARROW* (1988), a half-Vietnamese boy, living by his wits on the Adelaide streets, is taken in hand by Sebastian, a 15-year-old from an affluent background. The director is Scott Hicks (b. 1953 in Uganda), whose first feature, *Freedom*, is discussed later in this chapter. Hicks came to Australia with his family at the age of fourteen, graduated in drama, and entered the film industry as a production assistant on several SAFC features, including *Storm Boy* and *The Last Wave*. After *Freedom*, made in 1981, he co-wrote and directed the telemovie *Call Me Mr Brown* (mentioned in Chapter 2) and then worked on children's films before he wrote, produced and directed *Sebastian*.

Two 15-year-olds were cast in the film, and Jeremy Angerson (as Sparrow) far overshadows his co-star Alexander Bainbridge in what is, admittedly, a flashier role. It is a well-meaning film, but fatally

Sebastian and the Sparrow. *Alexander Bainbridge, Jeremy Angerson.*

soft, and the cosy climax smacks of a sentimental Hollywood confection. Elizabeth Alexander (far too seldom on the screen these days) and Robert Coleby, as Sebastian's worried parents, are immensely professional, but deserve stronger material.

If young Sebastian's parents are comfortably off, they seem like paupers compared to the mother of John Kirkland in THE BOY WHO HAD EVERYTHING (1984) who lives in a splendid beachfront house in what looks like the Palm Beach area of Sydney. This was the second feature film directed by Stephen Wallace and, by any yardstick, was a considerable disappointment after Stir. 'It was a mini-disaster for me,' says Wallace.

Wallace, like Duigan in The Year My Voice Broke, used elements of his own experience in his screenplay for the film. 'But the original script started when the character was twenty-eight years old,' he says. 'I was persuaded to start earlier, when John was at university. It would have been a much dirtier film if I'd stuck to my original idea.' Like Duigan's One Night Stand, made the same year, the film was produced by Richard Mason for Hoyts–Edgley, with Julia Overton as co-producer. 'The story was, to be honest, always flawed,' says Wallace, 'but there was a lot of pressure on me, even though it was a low-budget film, to change the script to make it more appealing to the public. People thought it was too bald, too raw, too cutting: they said it needed a cloak, and persuaded me to include the college scenes. That was a

The Boy Who Had Everything. *Diane Cilento, Jason Connery.*

mistake, and I think everyone involved would agree with me now. What was lost was a sense of reality; the college scenes gave it an air of unreality. The original had a grittiness and sordidness that I rather liked. John's whole attitude to life was more despairing.'

Julia Overton thinks, 'the film fails for the same reason *Boys in the Island* fails: to have a film about someone going through a catharsis is extremely difficult. I've seen English films, American films and Polish films on the subject that work: but I've never seen an Australian film about catharsis that worked. It was based on Stephen's own experiences, and that made it difficult for him; we even shot in his old college.'

Also involved in the production was Multi Films, a company established by Russell Bennett (father of Bill Bennett): the idea was to establish a producers' company, and Dick Mason had been invited to participate along with David Elfick and the McElroys. In the end, Multi Films raised only enough money to make *The Boy Who Had Everything*, which was produced on a budget of $1.1 million.

One of the interesting things about the film is the casting of real-life mother and son, Diane Cilento and Jason Connery. Connery was cast first, and it was only then someone suggested his real mother play his mother in the film. 'I got carried away with what I thought was a great idea,' says Wallace. 'But, on reflection, the casting of Diane Cilento was wrong. I should have had someone more ordinary-looking, less glamorous, [because] then I had to alter the character to fit the actress.' Ironically, after all these rather strained attempts to make the film 'more commercial', *The Boy Who Had Everything* never had a cinema release in Australia, though it did in Britain.

It is, indeed, a rather sad film, which manages to be neither very original nor very interesting. The 60s backgrounds (the beginning of the Vietnam involvement and Prime Minister Menzies' bland, arrogant speeches) promise more than they deliver. The endless college scenes at the beginning are precious and dull, despite good performances (the film launched the career of Nique Needles, who won Best Supporting Actor at the AFI awards), and the more interesting mother–son scenes are marred by Diane Cilento's one-dimensional portrayal. There is also at least one alarming continuity gaffe.

Another commercial disappointment, but of much more serious proportions in terms of the money involved, was another Hoyts–Edgley picture, *THE COOLANGATTA GOLD* (1984) which also deals with conflict between sons and parents. For a while, Peter Schreck's screenplay was being touted around as The Great Australian Script:

The Coolangatta Gold. *Josephine Smulders, Joss McWilliam.* (Photo: *David Parker.*)

this is hard to credit in the light of the finished film, which is little short of abysmal.

During their collaboration on *We of the Never Never*, Schreck and director Igor Auzins decided on their next project: a film about love and sport. This modest idea soon ballooned into a $5.6 million epic, shot on the Gold Coast, in which Joss McWilliams and Colin Friels vie for the love and attention of their father, Nick Tate, while mother, Robyn Nevin, wrings her hands on the sidelines.

Igor Auzins and his team (including cinematographer Keith Wagstaff) pour slick gloss over a basically novelettish story which contains elements of *Gallipoli* (in scenes with the gruff father badgering his favourite son to perform better) as well as *Flashdance* (the absurd appearance of a winsome ballet dancer, wanly played by Josephine Smulders). The script is never certain whether to make the father a Great Australian or a Crashing Bore (he is more suited to the latter role), and it incorporates every cliché known. *This* is a great screenplay?

The Coolangatta Gold is not a film made with conviction or passion; it is obviously a package, and is sadly typical of some of the worst excesses of the 10BA period. Colin Friels, though oddly cast, gives the only acceptable performance; Joss McWilliam seems bewildered as the supposedly 'sensitive' younger son; Robyn Nevin is completely wasted; and the Bill Conti score is redundant. Not surprisingly, the film did very poorly at the box-office, and overseas distributors proved, in the main, unresponsive. Igor Auzins has not made a feature film since this fiasco.

There are more familial tensions to be found in MOVING OUT (1982), the very fresh and appealing first feature of Michael Pattinson. The screenplay was by Jan Sardi, whom Pattinson had met via his brother, Peter Sardi, an actor; like Ken Cameron, Jan Sardi was a schoolteacher and was teaching in a school similar to the one featured in *Moving Out*. 'At the time,' says Pattinson, 'young directors were supposed to go through stages, and my next stage would have been a 50-minute film funded by the Creative Development Branch of the AFC. I was looking for a subject for a 50-minute film, and Jan was talking about his experiences teaching Italian kids. I could see the potential there, and encouraged him to develop a script, which we worked on over a long period of time.'

Pattinson had been working at Grundy's since 1979, first as a trainee. 'It was the unhappiest eighteen months of my life,' he says. 'I learnt a great deal, but I left under unfortunate circumstances. And then I worked full time on getting Jan's script off the ground. We weren't experienced filmmakers, so we had a lot of trouble raising money. I went to all the usual funding bodies, but didn't have much success. Also, it was a film of moments, small details and observations, so it was hard for people to see the emotional line.'

By now, it was clear that *Moving Out* would be a feature. Pattinson

Moving Out. *Vince Colosimo, Emilica Vera.*

had been earning money directing television commercials, and met Jane Ballantyne through his work; she agreed to co-produce with him. 'Jane had a yen to work in drama; she hadn't done a feature before.' Money was raised through private investment under 10BA: 'We roamed the streets, knocking on the offices of solicitors and accountants,' says Pattinson. 'I didn't want to go through Filmco, or one of those companies; and, anyway, they wouldn't have seen it as a very commercial picture.' At the eleventh hour, when the $540,000 budget was still lacking a relatively small amount of money, the AFC put in $50,000, which enabled the film to go ahead.

Hundreds of Italian Australian teenagers were auditioned before Pattinson found Vince Colosimo, who plays the role of Gino. Coincidentally, Colosimo is related by marriage to producer Rosa Colosimo who, on *Moving Out*, worked as dialogue coach.

The film was shot over six weeks in various schools in inner Melbourne: Brunswick Tech, St Joseph's, Marist Brothers in North Fitzroy (where Jan Sardi was teaching). Vincent Monton shot on Super 16mm, and it was later blown up to 35mm.

After completion, the film was shown to the big three distributors: Hoyts and Roadshow passed on it, but GU agreed to handle it. The film was well reviewed and did good business, eventually returning most of its costs. 'It sold to about thirty or forty countries,' says Pattinson, 'and it's frequently shown on the BBC.'

Moving Out captures with what appears to be total accuracy the world of a teenager of Italian background trying to assimilate into the Australian mainstream. Gino wants to be 'an Aussie'; he refuses to 'speak wog' at home. He is furious that his father has decided the family shall move from Fitzroy, in the inner city, to the outer suburbs; he does not want to leave his mates behind. The style of the film is gentle and anecdotal. Pattinson does not impose a storyline on the film (as he would do in his next picture, *Street Hero*); instead, he is content to explore Gino's world in a casual, genuinely affectionate, style. Vince Colosimo gives a natural and unaffected performance, and Vince Monton's camerawork complements the naturalistic mood.

The troubled teenager at the centre of *BREAKING LOOSE* (1988) is a far less interesting character than Gino in *Moving Out*. The film is a sequel to *Summer City* (Christopher Fraser, 1977) which, though totally undistinguished, introduced a young Mel Gibson to the screen. It was set in the 60s, and the new film, in consequence, deals with the next generation. The project was originally announced in 1985 as *The End of Innocence*, when it was to be written and directed by Alan Dickes and to star Christopher Pate, with Tony Barry in the role eventually played by John Clayton.

Ross (Peter Phelps) is intrigued by Robbie, one of his mother's old friends, and heads north to visit him at his surf-beach home. Robbie was played in the first film by producer Phil Avalon, but in the sequel Vince Martin takes the role.

Breaking Loose fails on almost every count. Peter Phelps is far too old to play the tormented teen hero. His adventures are totally uninvolving: they include a rapacious female (Abigail), her jealous husband (John Clayton) and an evil bikie gang who look as if they have strayed in from Roger Corman's *The Wild Angels*. Significance is introduced by means of an Aboriginal character talking about the Dreamtime but, apart from a few moments of carefree surfing, it is a long plod to the anti-climactic fadeout. The script is full of loose ends; the camerawork (by the usually reliable Richard Michalak) and the sound are uneven, and the actors are noticeably uninspired. The writer-director, Rod Hay (b. 1947), was formerly partnered with Terry Bourke and works chiefly as a film editor, spending much of his time in South Africa.

Mike (Terry Serio), the hero of *RUNNING ON EMPTY* (1982), which is also known as *Fast Lane Fever* and *Wild Wheels*, lives with his dad (Robin Ramsay), a leftover from the Flower Power generation: but Mike seems to yearn for the 50s, and references to Jack Kerouac and *Rebel Without a Cause* are littered through this dumb little picture about drag-racers. The trouble here is that writer Barry Tomblin and director John Clark want to appeal to everyone, and end up appealing to no-one.

To begin with, the characters beggar belief. Why is an apparently well-off model with a mind of her own (Debbie Conway) hanging around with these unlovely dragsters? What does she see in Terry? Come to that, what does she see in Terry's rival for her affections, Fox (Richard Moir, trying to be sinister and hip, and failing lamentably)? What is Max Cullen doing giving such an embarrassing performance as a blind hepcat uttering jive-talk? And what about the comic cops played by Graeme Bond and Penne Hackforth-Jones? Only the stunts provide any relief from the tedium of this one.

The lure of the fast car as an escape from everyday reality is also the theme of *FREEDOM* (1981), the first feature directed by Scott Hicks. Jon Blake, in his first starring role, is the basically good-natured young hero who is laid off from his job and starts to get angry with the Establishment. The first half of John Emery's screenplay accurately depicts the frustrations of unemployed youth, but later it goes off the rails borrowing from other movies. Like the Jean-Pierre Leaud character in Jerzy Skolimowski's *Le Depart*, our young hero is determined to get himself a Porsche, even if it means stealing one and, like Goldie Hawn in Spielberg's *The Sugarland Express*, the lithe hitchhiker—Jad Capelja—he picks up along the way wants to be reunited with her baby.

Given that the lamentable *Pacific Banana* was released only briefly in Melbourne, *Freedom* was the first SAFC production widely seen after *Breaker Morant*. It is a pity that it tails away so badly towards the end, because the early scenes are really effective and there is an extremely strong supporting cast, including Max Cullen, Chris Haywood (as the hero's best friend), Charles Tingwell, Candy Raymond and John Clayton.

T he films mentioned above all centre on teenage boys: there are also a significant number of films about young girls—many of them, not surprisingly, directed by women. Jane Oehr's ON THE LOOSE (1984) actually deals with both, because it is a three-parter, funded by Media Health Productions. The first and third stories, *Exit Eddie Leech* and *Beginners' Luck*, are linked by the character of Eddie (Steve Bergan), a crippled boy who longs to leave school; the first story was scripted by Ken Cameron. The middle story, *Ring of Confidence*, revolves around a school leaver (Tamsin Hardman) who suffers sexual harassment in her first job, which is working as assistant to a smug dentist (John Hamblin).

All three stories are sympathetically handled, with wonderfully naturalistic performances from the young actors. Though very modest in scale, Oehr brings to her material such sensitivity that one regrets she has not been able to make a more ambitious feature. *On the Loose* was hardly seen by the public, except by those who attended a screening at the 1985 Sydney Film Festival, where the film was warmly received.

Almost equally modest in scale is THE STILL POINT (1985), the first feature produced by Rosa Colosimo. At the time she had been trying to finance a much more ambitious film (*Blowing Hot and Cold*, see Chapter 3), and had found an investor who was willing to give her $100,000, provided the money was spent by the end of the financial year. This was April: Colosimo had until 30 June.

She brought an old friend on to the project, Barbara Boyd-Anderson with whom she had studied philosophy at university. Boyd-Anderson had been making films for the Education Department: the two women wrote the script together, and Boyd-Anderson directed. The final budget was $262,000.

Nadine Garner, who had appeared in *The Henderson Kids* on television, was cast as 14-year-old Sarah, who suffers from deafness and is also troubled by her mother's new lover. Garner is excellent, but the character of Sarah is a rather irritating one, and the film, although well-meaning, is tentative and unformed. It might have been more effective as a 50-minute featurette rather than as an 80-minute feature. Colosimo distributed it herself, and had some success in Canberra (where it did better than *Moving Out*); but in Sydney and Melbourne the film attracted tiny audiences.

Nadine Garner also stars in *MULL* (1988), which was directed by Don McLennan. McLennan discovered Bron Nicholls' book, *Mullaway*, in the same Lygon Street bookshop where he had found the book that he had earlier filmed as *Slate, Wyn and Me*: 'I read it at a sitting,' he says. 'And thought it would make a wonderful film. The challenge was to externalise what in the book was internal—without relying on voice-over.'

Mull. *Kymara Stowers, Nadine Garner, Bill Hunter.*

Tony Ginnane and Hemdale had been satisfied with *Slate, Wyn and Me*, and were ready to work with McLennan again. 'Tony liked the book,' says McLennan, 'and his head of production, Howard Grigsby, came on board to produce it. Film Victoria was strongly supportive, too. It all happened quickly: sixteen months after I found the book, we were making the film.'

Somewhat surprisingly, Hemdale did not quibble about the casting of *Mull*: 'It was almost as if they just gave me the money to make another film,' says McLennan. 'They didn't seem terribly concerned about the subject matter, or who was in it. They backed me as a director, which was fantastic. I didn't want to make it an "international" film; I wanted it to be intrinsically Australian.'

Nadine Garner was McLennan's first choice to play Phoebe Mullens. 'I'd seen her in *The Still Point*,' he says, 'which my partner Peter [Zbigniew] Friedrich edited. He said: "You've gotta watch this girl— she's great." I thought from the start, "She's Mull." But I still went through the casting process in case there was someone else.'

The budget for *Mull* was $3 million. 'But,' says McLennan, 'I actually had only about $1.7 million to make the film. That's what happened in the days of 10BA!' Stylistically, McLennan decided to give the film a documentary feel instead of moving closer to the emotions of the characters. 'I wanted to stand back from it, I didn't want it to be poetic; I wanted it to be hard.'

This may not have been the right decision, because although *Mull* is a film of considerable merit, it desperately needs a touch of poetry in the cinematography (also by Friedrich). Comparisons with such different films as *The Year My Voice Broke* and *Monkey Grip* are instructive: they both affected audiences deeply because the depth of emotion provided by the director and the actors was reinforced by the beauty (not the prettiness) of the images. This is what *Mull* lacks, though Nadine Garner (who won Best Actress at the AFI awards for this role) is excellent as the teenage girl trying to look after her fractious family while her mother is dying, but also trying to cope with her own emotional problems.

Surefire scenes like the mother's death go for surprisingly little (McLennan has said he did not want to linger over the scenes, but he does not linger long enough) and Mull's eventual romance with a deaf-mute also lacks impact. The director seems constantly to be pushing the viewer away, and as a result *Mull*, despite its qualities, does not touch the heart. Maybe this is why it never found much

The Place at the Coast. *John Hargreaves, Heather Mitchell, Tushka Bergen.*

of an audience, but the half-hearted release by Filmpac is also to blame.

The Bee Eater, by Jane Hyde, another novel about the problems of a pubescent girl, was brought to the screen by director George Ogilvie as *THE PLACE AT THE COAST* (1986), and proved to be another disappointment. The theme here is similar to that of *The Member of the Wedding*, or Claude Miller's French film *L'Effrontée*: Ellie (Tushka Bergen) is a teenager holidaying with her widowed father (John Hargreaves). She becomes jealous when the woman (Heather Mitchell) she has befriended falls in love with him.

Producer Hilary Furlong adapted Hyde's material for the screen, and despite the care Ogilvie lavishes on the material, it remains stillborn. The sub-plot, about the destruction of the coastal environment, seems grafted on. The actors are unsure of themselves: Bergen shrieks unintelligibly in moments of crisis. The whole thing is smothered with self-consciously clever camerawork by Jeff Darling, with the camera seemingly forever on the move to the extent that the viewer craves a moment when the eye is not assaulted by some new cinematic trick. And why cast a well-known comic like Garry McDonald (as the husband of a troubled shopkeeper) and then do absolutely nothing with him?

It is the sort of film that, with less self-conscious treatment and a firmer grip on the actors, might have worked extremely well; but audiences failed to respond to the film, and it performed badly at the box-office. Ogilvie more than redeemed himself with his beautiful handling of the SAFC mini-series, *The Shiralee*, the following year.

The heroine of *EMMA'S WAR* (1985) is aged fourteen, and there is a strong element of autobiography in this story set in Sydney in 1942. First-time director Clytie Jessop is a former actress: she played Miss Jessel, one of the ghosts in Jack Clayton's *The Innocents* and had made a number of short films, including the well-regarded *Flamingo Park* (about fashion at the end of the 70s). She wrote *Emma's War* in collaboration with her husband, Peter Smalley, and, to begin with, they received little encouragement: she was told the story was too gentle, needed more sex, and so on. Originally, she wanted Michelle Fawdon to play the role of Anne, the mother: but the usual funding delays forced her to change her plans.

By the time the film was finally made, Andrena Finlay was co-producer. Finlay's friend Robin Dalton, an Australian expatriate living in London (who would subsequently produce John Schlesinger's *Madame Sousatzka*), arranged a pre-sale with the British distribution and exhibition company Curzon; the pre-sale was conditional on Lee Remick playing the role (apparently, films starring Ms Remick were always popular at the Curzon in Mayfair). Even though, as an American, Ms Remick was entirely wrong for the role, Jessop accepted.

Any director will tell you how crucial casting is, and *Emma's War* does not survive the weight of this particular piece of miscasting, even though Miranda Otto, as Emma, positively blooms in the film, and Pat Evison is wonderful in the kind of role Margaret Rutherford used to play. Originally, Jessop wanted Brian Probyn as cinematographer, but he was dead by the time the film went into production and Tom Cowan shot the film, giving it a warm, nostalgic glow. The final scenes, with Emma's crippled father (Terence Donovan) returning from the war and the crowds celebrating victory in Martin Place, are by far the best in this slow-moving, tentative film.

Despite the international success of *My Brilliant Career*, Gillian Armstrong directed only three feature films during the 80s: *Starstruck*, *Mrs Soffel* (in the US) and *HIGH TIDE* (1987), which reunited her with Judy Davis. The film was scripted by Laura Jones, with the close collaboration of Armstrong and producer Sandra Levy; and it was written with a male leading character. Says Armstrong: 'Lilli was originally to have been a man who came back to find his daughter, Ally. We raised the money on that script, and a couple of months before we started shooting, when I'd just started casting, I had the feeling something was wrong. I thought: "I'm sick to death of seeing alienated, selfish modern men, how about we do it as a woman?" I thought, too, it would add a lot more to the story, because there'd been a number of films, like *Paris, Texas* and *Paper Moon*, in which a man had been touched by a small child: I thought that making the central character the mother would make it tougher. Society doesn't condone a woman who behaves that way, who's abandoned her baby.'

Having made this change, Armstrong approached Judy Davis to play the role. 'Her first reaction was that Lilli was such a despicable character that no-one would like her,' says Armstrong. 'But there was a challenge to make the character sympathetic. It was good to work with her again: there was a bond between us because of so much water under the bridge. I'm a great admirer of Judy's work.' Davis won another AFI Award for this role. Claudia Karvan, the young actress who had survived working on *Molly*, was cast as Ally, and Jan Adele memorably plays her grandmother. The character of Lilli's lover, Mick (played by Colin Friels), was originally to have been the hero's girlfriend: 'Just about everyone did a sex change,' says Armstrong.

The production was based at Eden, a southern coastal town in New South Wales. 'I remembered it from long ago when I'd stayed in a caravan park there,' says Armstrong. 'It was a terrible place, but I thought it would make a marvellous setting for the story.'

High Tide. *Judy Davis, Claudia Karvan.*

High Tide is a film in which emotions run very deep, and it contains some of Armstrong's most satisfying work. The opening scenes (with Davis as one of a trio of blonde-wigged back-up singers for Elvis imitator Frankie J. Holden) look like something out of *Starstruck*; but the bleak setting of the seaside resort in winter (beautifully shot by Russell Boyd) casts a spell over the drama. The three women are splendid, and the climactic scenes are as emotionally draining as any in Australian cinema. Worth commending, too, are the film's beautifully designed opening credits.

Returning to Australia after making *Mrs Soffel* for MGM, Armstrong was glad to be given so much creative independence again. 'The producer and I had final control over everything to do with the film,' she says. 'It's very different from the politics and the battles I had to go through with MGM. Every extra dollar a film costs, you lose some of your power. I ended up in a reasonably happy position with Metro, and made a film I wanted to make: but it was great not to have to worry about playing those games on *High Tide*. I could concentrate on making the film.' Nevertheless, Armstrong's next feature after *High Tide*, and her first film of the 90s, is another Hollywood studio picture, *Distant Shores*, produced by Cannon–Pathe for Warner Bros release and starring Jimmy Smits, Greta Scacchi and Vincent D'Onofrio.

Brief mention should be made here of *Bingo, Bridesmaids and Braces* (1988), a feature documentary Armstrong completed after *High Tide*. It was composed partly of footage shot eleven years earlier for an SAFC documentary, *Smokes and Lollies*, about three Adelaide schoolgirls, which was updated in 1981 as *14's Good, 18's Better*. It is a revealing panorama of the development of three ordinary women, something like British director Michael Apted's equally daring *28 Up*. Armstrong's obvious affection for her three subjects allows her to capture some revealing and memorable moments in this fine documentary.

The title character in Ann Turner's *CELIA* (1988) is younger than Ally and her parents live together, but she has troubles of her own. The film is set in Melbourne in the 50s, and Celia (Rebecca Smart) loses not only her friends next door (whose parents are communists) but her beloved pet rabbit as a result of the overly-protective Bolte government.

Turner (b. 1960 in Adelaide) studied law before enrolling in the film course at Swinburne. The screenplay for *Celia* was actually written in 1984, when it won an AWGIE Award for Best Unproduced Screenplay. At the time, Turner was working at Film Victoria: later she was senior

Celia. *Rebecca Smart.*

script consultant at the AFC. The idea for the film was triggered by a newspaper article about the rabbit plague of the 50s and the round-up of pet rabbits. 'It was about 1981, and rabbits were finally being legalised: I hadn't realised they'd been banned till then. It was such a bizarre story. Later, I discovered that a friend of mine had to leave Melbourne in the 50s because her father was a communist and was blackbanned—the two stories fitted nicely together. Scapegoating and intolerance were the links. The government had a problem with rabbits in the country, but pet rabbits weren't a part of that. It was the same with the Communist Party: the government scapegoated a group of people who were really no threat at all.'

Telling the story through the eyes of a child was part of the challenge. 'I didn't want to make judgements: I wanted the film to be open to interpretation. It was fun to write from a child's perspective.' The film was produced by the Melbourne company, Seon Films.

'As soon as I met Rebecca Smart,' says Turner, 'I knew I wanted her to play Celia. I'd seen her other work, and she was perfect; she's intuitive and intelligent.' The other children were cast after an extensive search lasting several months. 'They were a delight to work with,' says Turner. Victoria Longley, cast as the next-door neighbour whose warm-heartedness contrasts with that of Celia's own, rather severe, mother, won Best Supporting Actress for her role. The mother herself was played by Maryanne Fahey who, by the time the film was released, had gained a certain fame as the Kylie Mole character on *The Comedy Company*, a popular series on the Ten Network.

Celia is, until near the end, a very fine film about childhood, and Rebecca Smart is amazingly good as the precocious child at its centre. Turner captures the mood of the 50s effectively, and the games the children play neatly counterpoint the adult games enacted by parents and governments alike. Where the film falters is in the closing scenes, when Celia suddenly turns a gun on her hated uncle, the local policeman, and shoots him dead. To succeed in this dramatic shift away from family cinema, the film needed a treatment that would have been consistently far blacker than it is: it is perhaps asking too much to expect a first-time director to be another Luis Bunuel, but perhaps only a Bunuel would have successfully carried off this screenplay, with its hatred of officialdom and its swipes at the conservatism of the church.

Some critics saw the ending as an endorsement of the child's crime. Says Turner: 'I didn't see it that way at all. The undercurrent of violence, oppression and intolerance generated by that society is appalling, and the way the adults respond to the murder is also a tragedy—they sweep it under the rug. In doing that, they create a dangerous person out of Celia. To me the fact that society hasn't faced the problems it's created gives the ending its power.'

The film was invited to the Panorama section of the Berlin Film Festival early in 1989. 'It was interesting to see how universal childhood problems are,' says Turner. 'People from a lot of other cultures saw resonances in it.' The film was sold theatrically to several countries, including Britain.

We have been discussing films in which the central characters have been teenagers or children, all of whom came into conflict with their parents. In *JENNY KISSED ME* (1985), the emphasis is on the adults, though the child, the eponymous Jenny, plays a crucial role. This was written by Warwick Hind, but it is greatly inferior to his subsequent screenplay, *Grievous Bodily Harm*. Tamsin West plays 10-year-old Jenny, daughter of Carol (Deborra-Lee Furness) who lives with, but is not married to, Lindsay (Ivar Kants). The relationship is on the rocks and Carol, who tends to wear a wet T-shirt and little else, gets sexually involved with her randy next-door neighbour.

Brian Trenchard Smith apparently wanted a change from his usual action subjects, and so, unwisely, took on this soppy effort (which ends with Lindsay expiring from a terminal disease). He seizes every chance to inject a bit of action (even a car chase) and sex into the desultory material, but to no avail. The actors seem to be having difficulty delivering their lines with straight faces.

Thank goodness, then, for *FRAN* (1985), which has a similar theme but which, for all its tiny budget, is light-years better. This Western Australian film, executive-produced by Paul Barron and written and directed by Glenda Hambly, centres on a woman, Fran (Noni Hazlehurst) who never seems to choose the right man and whose children suffer for her mistakes.

Hambly was commissioned by the WA Department for Community Welfare to make a film about the problems of a single mother; she convinced them to let her make it as a drama, and started research. She approached Barron with a treatment, and he agreed to support her, but it was not easy, because the AFC refused her script development money. Says Barron: 'We didn't have the financial resources at the time to commission Glenda, but she went ahead and wrote the script anyway. The script sang off the page.'

Hambly and her producer, David Rapsey, persuaded Noni Hazlehurst to play the title role: Barron made a pre-sale arrangement with the Seven Network's Ray Beattie. The budget for the film was $700,000, and the film was shot on 16mm.

When *Fran* was finished, Barron decided it was strong enough to deserve theatrical exposure before it went to television. 'Glenda and David didn't agree,' he says. 'They thought it should go straight to television. But I persuaded them. I knew they'd conceived it as a telemovie, but what they made was a feature good enough for the cinema. It was an emotional thing. I didn't want to see it broken up by Omo ads.'

Fran got its cinema release: it also won three AFI awards: Best Actress for Hazlehurst, Best Supporting Actress for Annie Byron (wonderful as Fran's supportive friend and neighbour) and Best Screenplay (Hambly). The frequently corrosive Neil Jillet, in the Melbourne *Age*, called it the best Australian film of the year.

The year 1985 was a good one for low-budget features: *A Street to Die* and *Unfinished Business* were also produced that year. Hambly's film is right up alongside the others. She tackles a number of difficult themes and makes no attempt to gloss over the shortcomings of her protagonist. Fran has, in fact, made a complete mess of her life: as a result of her complicated love affairs, she allows the same fate that befell her to befall her children—childhood in a welfare home. Hazlehurst makes Fran a sexy, sensual woman, unstable and annoying, but believable and understandable. Her children (all of them beautifully acted) suffer for her sins, as Marge, her sympathetic friend, knows they will. It is a sad little film but, again, the level of emotion is high. Limited in scope as it is, it is preferable to, say, *Mull*, in depicting everyday problems with insight and heart.

It is appropriate to conclude this survey of Australian films of the 80s with the work of a maverick: Jane Campion. As noted in Chapter 1, she came to Sydney from New Zealand and enrolled in the AFRTS. Apart from, as she puts it, falling in love with fellow student Gerard Lee, she found the school frustrating: 'They thought I was arrogant,' she says. 'When they saw the first cut of *Peel*, they told me not to bother finishing it.' *Peel* (1984) went on to win the Palme d'Or for Best Short Film at the 1986 Cannes Film Festival. Campion's other short films, *Passionless Moments* and *A Girl's Own Story* were also shown at Cannes—and just about everywhere else in the world, as was *TWO FRIENDS* (1986), though it is undeniably an ABC telemovie. The film wins a place in this book because of its film festival exposure, not to mention its importance in terms of the future of the industry as a whole, and because Campion is an important new figure on the scene, a genuine original who, with luck, will be impressing us with her films right through the 90s.

Campion has a very odd sense of humour, an oblique vision of the world. She deals with ordinary people and situations: inner-cities, families, friends, lovers. But she brings to her films a perspective that is all her own. *Two Friends* was written by Helen Garner and, like the Harold Pinter film *Betrayal*, is told backwards: it begins in July and ends the previous October. The friends are Louise (Emma Coles) and Kelly (Kris Bidenko): Louise is the steady, studious one, better able to cope with life than her neurotic friend, while Kelly leaves home (after a mate of her father makes a pass at her) and lives, punk-style, in a communal flat in Bondi.

The film is composed of a whole series of telling moments, and Campion is just as successful in presenting the adult characters as in presenting the teenagers. The adults make plenty of mistakes in dealing with their children, but they are well meaning and have problems of their own. The two young women simply drift apart; their interests divide, their destinies are very different. The final freeze-frame (for once the device works to perfection) of the two, in their school uniforms, toasting their future, is wrenchingly sad. *Two Friends* was the best Australian telemovie of the decade.

SWEETIE (1989) was one of the best feature films of the decade, though you would never know it from the way it was (ill)treated at the AFI awards. Its genesis came from Campion's first trip to Cannes, in 1986: 'My short films received a lot of attention,' she says. 'When I made them, I never thought in the future I'd have the opportunity to make such personal, off-the-wall, films. But then I saw how people enjoyed them, and I thought I'd like to make a feature which went even further than they did. I decided I didn't want to ape the kind of films made by other people: I wanted to invent my own. I decided to make a film about love and romance, sex and family. I wanted to provoke, but at the same time to touch people.'

Sweetie was produced by another New Zealander, John Maynard, who had also produced Vincent Ward's films *Vigil* and *The Navigator*. 'I have always had a strong belief in the value of a small, indigenous film industry,' he says. The film was made on a modest budget, and pre-sold to Filmpac.

The film involves two sisters and their parents, but the structure is far from conventional: the younger sister, Kay (Karen Colston) is introduced and established well before her hated sibling, Dawn, better known as Sweetie (Genevieve Lemon) appears on the scene. The mother and father who raised these strange daughters appear last of all.

Says Campion: 'One of the sad things in my life has been the search for love. Love is a right: after the 60s, everyone should have a successful love life. In writing *Sweetie*, the characters of Kay and her boyfriend, Louis [Tom Lycos] came first: then Sweetie emerged and started taking

Sweetie. *Karen Colston.*

over. She just grew.' The film isn't really *about* Sweetie, though: if anything, Kay is the central character. But it is the impact Sweetie has on her family that earns her the title of the film. 'For Kay, Sweetie is what she might become if she lost control,' says Campion. 'Kay is very afraid that things will get out of control.'

Campion saw Genevieve Lemon in a stage production of *When I Was a Girl I Used to Scream And Shout* (the actress had also appeared on stage in *Steaming* and *Steel Magnolias*). Karen Colston was working at an actors' co-op. 'Jane's initial vision of Sweetie was much darker than she turned out to be,' says Lemon. 'She wanted Sweetie to be angry: I'm not an angry person, and Jane constantly encouraged me to make her as angry as possible.'

Kay is frightened of trees, a fear stemming back to childhood and her sister's tree-house. When Louis uproots her Hills hoist (a marvellously funny scene) to plant a woebegone tree in the middle of a concrete backyard, Kay is very distressed and removes the offending shrub, vainly trying to hide it under the spare bed. Her fears prove well founded: Sweetie dies after a fall from a tree-house and at her funeral the grave-diggers have trouble with tree roots which encroach, menacingly, on the grave.

One of the enjoyably odd characters in the film is Bob (Michael Lake) whom Sweetie introduces to Kay as her 'producer', though he is clearly her lover, and a very spaced-out one at that. 'I like Bob,'

Jane Campion, director of Sweetie.

says Campion. 'Sweetie loves him. She believes in him, and he believes in her. In a way.' Another example of Campion's off-beat humour is the outback sequence involving dancing jackaroos, one of them a dwarf. 'I wanted to make a film with likeable men,' says Campion. 'And this was a bit like Snow White and the Seven Dwarfs. Mother goes out there and these men heal her: it's a celebration of the gentle side of men. They all love their Mummies. It's adorable. The girls on the crew loved that scene: they all wanted to help select the men to play the jackaroos.'

Filled as it is with off-centre characters, *Sweetie* is shot by Sally Bongers (who worked on Campion's film school shorts, but not on *Two Friends*) in an equally off-centre way. 'We came on this way of filming intuitively,' says Campion. 'It didn't seem right to shoot in the straightforward way, especially in a film like this. When I saw the first cut of the film, I thought it looked as if it had been made by Martians!'

The music for the film is unusual, too, much of it being choral. 'I love singing,' says Campion. 'I originally wanted a whole soundtrack made up of the noises people can make. But time ran out, and the best I could do was choral music. I just love that music.'

Sweetie is an extraordinarily audacious and witty film, but it polarised audiences in a remarkable way. At Cannes, where it was invited to compete, it was almost as badly received, by some sections of the audience, as *Bliss* had been. And yet it was widely distributed all over the world, admired by many serious critics, and invited to many other festivals, including New York and London. It opened in New York in January 1990 to rave reviews, including a glowing one in the crucially important *New York Times*.

Sweetie is refreshingly original, but it is confronting and disturbing; and it is also very funny, though some people do not seem to see the joke. Says Campion: 'I think humour's a great way to connect with people. I use humour to create intimacy with the audience: once you have the audience on side, once you have their trust, you can whip them off somewhere they never expected to go, and might never have gone. I like to be entertained in the cinema, and I feel I have a responsibility to entertain audiences: and, at the same time, challenge them.'

We can all do with the kind of challenges Jane Campion poses in her films: she is a breath of fresh air. Who knows why *Sweetie* was not even nominated for best film or best director in the 1989 AFI awards? In future years, eyebrows will continue to be raised about that. The film did win the Best Original Screenplay award, and Campion won the Byron Kennedy Award, a prize most richly deserved. She made her next film, *An Angel at My Table* (1990), based on the autobiography of Janet Frame, in New Zealand. But this Kiwi will surely be back to enrich the Australian film industry, along with all the other talented men and women who told their tales and spun their dreams in the Australian films of the 80s.

• AFTERWORD •

S o there they are, the Australian films of the 80s, the films of
10BA, the tax-incentive, packaged, deal-driven, pre-sold films of
The Avocado Plantation.

A significant number of them are films to be proud of. Others have
raised healthy debate and controversy. Some were enormously
successful; some were not; others were simply never seen where they
were supposed to be seen—on cinema screens. A few of them deserved
this fate; several others did not.

There are heroes and villains in the Australian film industry, but
mostly there are a great many people just trying to survive and pay
their bills. Governments have tried to help the industry, but constant
shifting of official policy has caused only confusion and alarm.

There is no doubt that the Film Finance Corporation and its policies
will have a crucial effect on the film industry in the 90s. The FFC's
Chair, Kim Williams, predicts: 'The 90s will see a slightly smaller
film industry, which will be much more focused on quality.' Williams
foresees an average of sixteen to eighteen features with medium to
large budgets produced each year. 'The FFC has no creative involvement
in the films,' he notes. 'Filmmakers must accept responsibility for the
films that are made.'

Graham Burke of Village–Roadshow takes a commercial perspective.
'We will tap into world markets and make profits with successful
Australian films,' he predicts. 'We have to make films which will
compete with films from other countries. We've got to be good enough
to get into the cinema complexes being built around the world, and
we have to have the best films in those complexes.'

Another important new player in the field at the beginning of the
new decade is the Beyond International Group, producers of George

*In production for the 90s: Beyond
International's* The Crossing, *with George
Ogilvie directing Danielle Spencer.*

Ogilvie's *The Crossing* (1990), a film about young people living in a country town. Beyond's chairman and managing director, Phil Gerlach, was formerly in the music business, and the company's head of production and development, Al Clark, was head of production for the British company, Virgin. In addition to *The Crossing*, Beyond put up guarantees for two other FFC-backed films, Jerzy Domaradzki's *Struck by Lightning* and Craig Lahiff's *Strangers*, and as a result will market these films internationally. At the end of 1989, Gary Hamilton resigned from the AFC's London office to run Beyond's marketing department. The talents involved in Beyond International are such that there is every reason to expect sensible and effective production and marketing decisions will be made in the future.

There is also hope to be found in the policy of the AFC's Peter Sainsbury, noted in Chapter 1: the full funding of a number of relatively low-budget ($1 million) high-quality films each year. This programme could be of vital importance during the 90s if it is allowed to develop.

In the meantime, there is no doubt that, at the beginning of a new decade, Australian films have largely lost the international reputation they had ten years ago; we are no longer the flavour of the month. But our filmmakers can regain the prestige of the past: we need only the recklessness described by Peter Weir, the tenacity and dedication of Paul Cox, the vision of Jane Campion: these attributes must be embraced and encouraged by the bureaucrats of the FFC and the AFC. In the 90s, we need, more than ever, exciting and innovative movies— not deals and packages in which the end result, the film, takes a back seat to a host of quarrelling production executives. The 90s must be a decade for filmmakers, not avocado farmers.

• APPENDIX •

T he following is an alphabetical listing of feature films produced in Australia during the 1980s. Films completed in 1990 are listed in a separate alphabetical sequence, commencing on page 442.

The page numbers after the film title refer to the discussion of the film in the main text.

Films made specifically as telemovies, documentaries and animated films are not included: nor are films running less than one hour. This listing contains: Principal crew credits. Principal cast. Brief synopsis.

The date listed at the end of the crew credits is the copyright date as printed on the film: it is not necessarily either the date of production or the date of release.

The following abbreviations are used in these listings:

a.d.:	first assistant director	**mins:**	minutes (running time)
a.p.:	associate producer	**p:**	producer
choreog.:	choreographer	**p.c.:**	production company
cost:	costume designer	**p.d.:**	production designer
d:	director	**ph:**	director of photography (cinematographer)
dist:	distributor		
ed:	editor	**p.m.:**	production manager
ex.p	executive producer	**sc:**	screenwriter
line p.:	line producer	**sd:**	sound recorder
m:	music composer	**sp.ef.:**	special effects

AFRAID TO DANCE (page 107)
p.c.: Andrena Finlay Production. **ex.p.**: Grahame Jennings, Juliet Grimm. **p**: Andrena Finlay. **d**: Denny Lawrence. **sc**: Paul Cockburn. **ph**: Steve Arnold. **ed**: Richard Hindley. **m**: Chris Neal. **p.d.**: Jane Norris. **sd**: Bob Clayton. **p.m.**: Sue Seeary. **a.d.**: Jake Atkinson. Eastmancolour. 89 mins. Direct to video release. 1988.

Nique Needles (The Male), Rosey Jones (The Female), Grigor Taylor (Jim Pratt), Tina Bursill (Driving Woman), Annie Byron (Betty), Mervyn Drake (Terry), Tom Richards (Don Chapman), Steve Spears (Garage Man), Allan Penney (Newsagent).

A devil-may-care young man decides to leave the city and his roach-infested flat. He is given a lift by a woman whom he plans to rob, but she turns the tables on him. Stranded, he tries to steal a car belonging to a young woman who has been pilfering from a grocery store. They become friends, and she tells him her story (abandoned by her father, raped by office colleagues, a boyfriend who abandoned her). Back in the city, the couple rob a mail van to steal security cheques, but find only letters, which they read while hiding in an empty house. They are inspired by a video sent by Jim Pratt to his unborn daughter, and finally make love. Next day, attempting to return the stolen letters, the young man is killed.

AGAINST THE GRAIN (page 224)
p.c.: Nightshift Films. **d**: Tim Burns. **sc**: Tim Burns, Michael Callaghan. **ph**: Louise Irving. **ed**: Peter Gailey, Melissa Woods, Chris Cordeaux. **sd**: Dasha Ross, Laurie Fitzgerald. Colour. 76 mins. Aust. dist: AFI. 1980.

Michael Callaghan (Ray), Sandy Edwards (Paula), Mary Burns (Mary), Joy Burns (Elsie), Letham Burns (Letham), George Sutton (Devac).

An urban terrorist leaves Sydney to visit his family in rural Western Australia.

ANNIE'S COMING OUT (page 57)
p.c.: Film Australia. **ex.p.**: Don Harley. **p**: Don Murray. **d.**: Gil Brealey. **sc**: John Patterson, Chris Borthwick (based on the book by Rosemary Crossley, Anne McDonald). **ph**: Mick Van Borneman. **ed**: Lindsay Frazer. **m**: Simon Walker. **p.d.**: Mike Hudson. **sd**: Rodney Simmons. **p.m.**: Colleen Clarke. Eastmancolour. 93 mins. Aust dist: Hoyts. US dist: Universal (US title: *A Test Of Love*). UK dist: Enterprise. 1984.

1984 Australian Film Awards: best film; best actress (Angela Punch McGregor); best adapted screenplay.

Angela Punch McGregor (Jessica Hathaway), Tina Arhondis (Annie O'Farrell), Drew Forsythe (David Lewis), Liddy Clark (Sally Clements), Monica Maughan (Vera Peters), Philippa Baker (Sister Watermann), Mark Butler (Dr John Monroe), John Frawley (Harding), Wallas Eaton (Dr Rowell), Lyn Collingwood (Mrs O'Farrell), Laurie Dobson (Mr O'Farrell), Simon Chilvers (Warren Metcalf), Charles Tingwell (Judge), Bill Bennett (Court Clerk), Nikki Coghill (University Girl).

Jessica Hathaway, newly appointed teacher at a Melbourne institution for the handicapped, discovers that Annie O'Farrell, a 14-year-old unable to move or talk, actually has a lively intelligence. Jessica befriends Annie and teaches her to read and communicate, devoting her entire time to the child (and alienating her boyfriend, David). At the age of eighteen, Annie communicates her desire to leave the institution, and Jessica takes the matter to court when the hospital authorities refuse. She wins.

AROUND THE WORLD IN 80 WAYS (page 312)
p.c.: Palm Beach Entertainment, in ass. with Australian European Finance and Commonwealth Bank of Australia. **p**: David Elfick, Steve Knapman. **d**: Stephen Maclean. **sc**: Stephen Maclean, Paul Leadon. **ph**: Louis Irving. **ed**: Marc van Buuren. **m**: Chris Neal. **p.d.**: Lissa Coote. **cost**: Clarissa Patterson. **sd**: Paul Brincat. **p.m.**: Catherine Phillips Knapman. **a.d.**: Ian Page. Colour. 91 mins. Aust dist: Hoyts. US dist: Alive. 1986.

Phillip Quast (Wally Davis), Allan Penney (Roly Davis), Gosia Dobrowolska (Nurse Ophelia Cox), Diana Davidson (Mavis Davis), Kelly Dingwall (Eddie Davis), Rob Steele (Alec Moffatt), Judith Fisher (Lotte Boyle), Jane Markey (Miserable Midge), John Howard (Dr Proctor), Nell Schofield (Scottish Scrooge), Kaarin Fairfax (Checkout Chick).

Mavis Davis is fed up with living with her senile old husband Roly, and embarks on a world tour with her lustful neighbour, Alec, in tow. Roly, abandoned to an old people's home, decides to take a tour himself, and his two sons, anxious to save what money the family still has, decide to fake it for him. With the help of his pretty nurse, Ophelia Cox, Wally, a gay entrepreneur who is good at impersonations, and Eddie, a sound technician, convince Roly he is in Hawaii, Las Vegas, Rome and Tokyo—though he actually never leaves his own Sydney suburb. Alec and Mavis return to discover Alec's house completely wrecked; Eddie and Ophelia, meanwhile, have fallen in love.

AS TIME GOES BY (page 282)

p.c.: Monroe Stahr Production. **ex.p.**: Phillip J. Dwyer. **p**: Chris Kiely. **d, sc**: Barry Peak. **ph**: John Ogden. **ed**: Ralph Strasser. **m**: Peter Sullivan. **p.d.**: Paddy Reardon. **sd**: Steve Haggerty, Tim Chau. **p.m.**: Ray Pond. Colour. 97 mins. Aust dist: Valhalla. 1987.

Bruno Lawrence (Ryder), Nique Needles (Mike), Max Gillies (Joe Bogart), Ray Barrett (J. L. Weston), Marcelle Schmitz (Connie Stanton), Mitchell Faircloth (James McCauley), Deborah Force (Cheryl), Christine Keogh (Margie), Don Bridges (Ern), Ian Shrives (Greaser).

Mike, complete with surfboard, travels from the city to the outback to keep a rendezvous made twenty-five years earlier by his mother; he has to meet a certain Joe Bogart at a spot miles from anywhere, and he does not know why. He becomes involved with an outback cop, Ryder; Connie, a young woman running a property single-handed; and J. L. Weston, a landowner who hopes cracks in the ozone layer will turn his desert property into an oasis. Joe Bogart turns out to be an alien trapped in a time-warp, whose spaceship is in the form of a 1940s diner, and it turns out that Ryder's son, accidentally killed years before by a cricket ball, is, in fact, Mike. Bogart is able to return to his own planet.

AT LAST . . . BULLAMAKANKA THE MOTION PICTURE (page 154)

p.c.: Bullamakanka Film Prod. **p**: David Joseph. **d, sc**: Simon Heath. **ph**: David Eggby. **ed**: John Scott. **m**: Australian Crawl, Tony Catz, The Expression, Jo Jo Zep, Moving Pictures, The Radiators, Rose Tattoo, Skyhooks, Sunnyboys, Wendy and the Rocketts, Uncanny X Men. **p.d.**: Terry Stanton. **sd**: Ross Linton. **a.p.**: Murray Francis. Eastmancolour. 89 mins. Direct to video release. 1983.

Steve Rackman (Rhino Jackson), Gary Kliger (Waldo Jackson), Alyson Best (Clare Hampton), Robert Baxter (The Senator), Angry Anderson (Senator's aide), Bassia Carole (Sister Mary), Debbie Matts (Maureen), John Stone (Wally), Mark Hembrow (L.D.), Iain Gardiner (T.M.), Frank Thring (TV Producer).

Rhino Jackson, corrupt mayor of the small town of Bullamakanka, up for re-election, invites a federal politician to attend a beauty parade and a horse race, but the visit is dogged by noisy demonstrations and disturbances. Various musical groups also participate.

ATTACK FORCE Z (page 42)

p.c.: John McCallum Productions, Central Motion Pictures Corp. (Taipei). **p**: Lee Robinson. **d**: Tim Burstall. **sc**: Roger Marshall. **ph**: Lin Hung-Chung. **ed**: David Stiven. **sd**: Don Connolly, Tim Lloyd. **p.m.**: Me Chang Kwen. Colour. 84 mins. Aust dist: Roadshow. 1980.

John Phillip Law (Lt Jan Veitch), Mel Gibson (Capt. Paul Kelly), Sam Neill (Sgt Danny Costello), Chris Haywood (Able Seaman Bird), John Waters (Sub-Lt King), Sylvia Chang.

During World War II, five members of Z Force arrive on an island occupied by the Japanese with a mission to help a friendly Japanese diplomat. In an initial skirmish, King is wounded and Sgt Costello kills him rather than leave him behind. Despite help from friendly islanders, the assault team is decimated by the enemy, and even the diplomat they came to help is killed. Only Capt. Kelly survives.

AUSTRALIAN DREAM (page 311)

p.c.: Filmside. **ex.p.**: Ross Matthews. **p**: Susan Wild, Jacki McKimmie. **d, sc**: Jacki McKimmie. **ph**: Andrew Lesnie. **ed**: Sara Bennett. **m**: Colin Timms. **p.d.**: Chris McKimmie. **sd**: Ian Grant. **p.m.**: Susan Wild. **a.d.**: David Munro. Colour. 86 mins. Aust dist: Ronin. 1986.

Noni Hazlehurst (Dorothy Stubbs), Graeme Blundell (Geoffrey Stubbs), John Jarratt (Todd), Barry Rugless (Sir Bruce), Jenny Mansfield (Tracy), Caine O'Connel (Jason), Margaret Lord (Sex-aids Demonstrator), Lil Kelman (Sandra), James Ricketson ('Baby').

Dorothy and Geoffrey Stubbs live in the suburbs of Brisbane; Geoffrey, a butcher, is an aspiring National Party politician, while Dorothy opts out of her boring life in erotic daydreams involving the spunky Todd (whom she met at a sex-aids demonstration). However, when she finally makes love to her dream-lover (during a raucous fancy dress party at the Stubbs home), it proves to be a disappointing experience.

BACHELOR GIRL (page 331)

p.c.: Yarra Bank. **p**: Ned Lander. **d**: Rivka Hartman. **sc**: Rivka Hartman, Maggie Power, Keith Thompson. **ph**: John Witteron. **ed**: Tony Stevens. **m**: Burkhart Von Dallwitz. **p.d.**: Ro Cooke. **sd**: John Phillips. **p.m.**: Lynda House. **a.d.**: Phil Jones. Colour. 83 mins. Direct to video release. 1987.

Lyn Pierse (Dot Bloom), Kim Gyngell (Karl Stanton), Jan Friedl (Helen Carter), Bruce Spence (Alistair Dredge Jr), Doug Tremlett (Charles), Ruth Yaffe (Aunt Esther), Jack Perry (Uncle Isaac), Monica Maughan (Sybil), Tim Roberston (Grant).

Dot is a nice, single, Jewish girl, aged thirty-two, whose Aunt Esther thinks she should get herself a man. When a friend from uni days, Karl, turns up, Dot drags herself away from her word-processor (she is a writer) long enough for a dinner date and a seduction, but decides in the end that Karl is not for her, and nor is Alistair, a preoccupied computer buff whom she quite fancies.

BACKLASH (page 208)

p.c.: Mermaid Beach Productions, Multifilms. **p, d, sc**: Bill Bennett (with dialogue improvised by the actors). **ph**: Tony Wilson. **ed**: Denise Hunter. **m**: Michael Atkinson, Michael Spicer **sd**: Leo Sullivan. **p.m.**: Sue Seeary. Colour. 89 mins. Aust dist: Dendy. US dist: Samuel Goldwyn. UK dist: Blue Dolphin. 1986.

David Argue (Trevor Darling), Gia Carides (Nikki Iceton), Lydia Miller (Kath), Brian Syron (Lyle), Anne Smith (Publican's wife), Don Smith (Publican), Jennifer Cluff (Waitress).

In Sydney, Kath, an Aboriginal, is arrested for the murder of Don Smith, publican from the outback town of Quondong, who had tried to rape her. Two police officers, Trevor Darling and Nikki Iceton, are assigned to take Kath back to Quondong (and are unaware they are being followed by the mysterious Lyle). When Trevor tries to take a short cut, their car breaks down, and the trio reveal more about each other. Trevor and Kath make love, Kath escapes, but is recaptured. Trevor and Nikki force Anne Smith, the murdered man's wife, to confess that she killed her husband. Stopping off at a sheep station on the homeward trip, Trevor is killed by Lyle.

BACKSTAGE (page 195)

p.c.: Burrowes Film Group. **ex.p.**: Dennis Wright, Kent C. Lovell. **p**: Geoff Burrowes. **co-p**: Frank Howson. **d**: Jonathan Hardy. **sc**: Jonathan Hardy, Frank Howson (based on a story by John Lamond). **ph**: Keith Wagstaff. **ed**: Ray Daley. **m**: Bruce Rowland. **p.d.**: Leslie Binns. **sd**: Terry Rodman, John Schiefelbein. **p.m.**: Bill Regan. **a.d.**: Bob Donaldson. Colour. 91 mins. Aust dist: Hoyts. 1987.

Laura Branigan (Kate Lawrence), Michael Aitkens (Robert Landau), Noel Ferrier (Mortimer Wynde), Rowena Wallace (Evelyn Hough), Phillip Holder (Bill French), Len Kaserman (Milton), Kim Gyngell (Paarvo), David Letch (Steven Williams), Mary Ward (Geraldine Woollencraft), Henry Cuthbertson (Miles Frewe), Ian Mune (Mangin), John Frawley (Metheny), James Condon (Frank Turner).

Kate Lawrence is a popular American singer who wants to be taken seriously as an actress. Against her agent's advice, she goes to Melbourne to appear in a hopelessly dated play, and falls in love with critic Robert Landau, who teaches her how to act and writes a review in *Variety* which helps her get the starring role in a Broadway production of *The Seagull*.

BELINDA (page 195)

p.c.: Fontana. **p**: Bedrich Kabriel. **d, sc**: Pamela Gibbons. **ph**: Malcolm McCullogh. **ed**: David Huggett. **p.d.**: Herbert Pinter. **sd**: Tim Lloyd. **ch**: Robyn Moase. **p.m.**: Sue Wild. **a.d.**: Adrian Pickersgill. Colour. 97 mins. Aust dist: Greater Union. 1987.

Deanne Jeffs (Belinda), Mary Regan (Crystal), Kaarin Fairfax (Sandra), Nicos Lathouris (Benny), Hazel Phillips (Doreen), John Jarratt (Graeme), Elizabeth Lord (Mandy), Gerda Nicholson (Belinda's mother), Alan Cassell (Belinda's father), Tim Burns (Jamie), Caz Lederman (Rhonda), John Haddon (Jeremy Shaw), Joy Smithers (Liz), Jeff Rhoe (Tim).

1968. Belinda, a 16-year-old ballet student, gets a job at a seedy nightclub in Sydney's King's Cross where she befriends Crystal who works there to keep her son at a Swiss boarding school. She also falls foul of the bullying Rhonda. When the club is abruptly closed (to make way for a disco), Crystal commits suicide.

THE BEST OF FRIENDS (page 109)

p.c.: Friendly Film, with NSW Film Corp. **p**: Tom Jeffrey. **d**: Michael Roberston. **sc**: Donald Macdonald. **ph**: David Gribble. **ed**: Ron Williams. **m**: Brian King. **p.d.**: John Carroll. **sd**: Tim Lloyd. **p.m.**: Su Armstrong. **a.d.**: Eddie Prylinski. Colour. 95 mins. Aust dist: Hoyts. 1981.

Angela Punch McGregor (Melanie), Graeme Blundell (Tom), Ruth Cracknell (Iris), Henri Szeps (Lilo), Sonja Tallis (Pammie), Serge Lazareff (Colin), Alan Becher (Jim), Graham Rouse (Father James), Les Foxcroft (Mr Malone), Moya O'Sullivan (Mrs Malone), Deborah Gray (Grace), Mark Lee (Bruce), Maggie Dence (Shop Assistant).

Melanie and Tom have been friends since childhood; she is a television personality, he is an accountant (and practising Catholic)—both are single. On the occasion of the twentieth anniversary of their friendship they get drunk and sleep together for the first time. He wants to continue the sexual relationship; she does not, but discovers she is pregnant, and they move in together. But they have little in common, and who knows if they will actually get married?

THE BIG HURT (page 240)

p.c.: Ultimate Show, Big Hurt Ltd. **ex.p.**: Phillip Dwyer. **p**: Chris Kiely. **d**: Barry Peak. **sc**: Barry Peak, Sylvia Bradshaw. **ph**: Malcolm Richards. **ed**: Ralph Strasser. **m**: Allan Zavod. **p.d.**: Paddy

Reardon. **sd**: Ralph Strasser. **p.m.**: Ray Pond. **a.d.**: Ross Hamilton. Eastmancolour. 93 mins. Aust dist: Valhalla. 1986.

David Bradshaw (Price), Lian Lunson (Lisa), Simon Chilvers (Algerson), John Ewart (Harry), Alan Cassell (Brake), Nick Waters (McBride), Abbe Holmes (Jenny).

Price is an investigative journalist who has just spent twelve weeks in prison for refusing to divulge his sources. Harry, his editor, welcomes him back, and before long he is up to his neck in a new investigation when Lisa asks him to check out a sex club run by ASIO. Price discovers that Lisa's 'father, a scientist experimenting in hormonal changes, who was believed to have suicided, may be alive after all; and meets Algerson, a sinister ASIO man. At the climax it is revealed Lisa wanted to locate her father (still experimenting) in order to kill him; she also kills Algerson before herself being gunned down.

THE BIT PART (page 319)

p.c.: Comedia Ltd. **p**: Stephen Vizard, John Gauci, Peter Herbert. **d**: Brendan Maher. **sc**: Stephen Vizard, Peter Herbert, Ian MacFadyen. **ph**: Ellery Ryan. **ed**: Scott McLennan. **m**: Paul Grabowsky, Red Symons. **p.d.**: Carole Harvey. **sd**: John Phillips. **p.m.**: Frank Brown. **a.d.**: Katherine Hayden. Colour. 87 mins. Direct to video release. 1987.

Chris Haywood (Michael Thornton), Nicole Kidman (Mary McAllister), Katrina Foster (Helen Thornton), John Wood (John Bainbridge), Maurie Fields (Peter), Maureen Edwards (Bev Howard), Deborra Lee-Furness (Acting Teacher).

Michael Thornton works as a careers counsellor, but has always yearned to be an actor. With the approval of Helen, his understanding wife (who has a good job), Michael switches careers, and undergoes acting courses. He acquires an agent, but finds those great roles— preferably Shakespeare—elusive. He is attracted to Mary McAllister, a beautiful young actress, and they plan to perform in some intellectual play readings—until she is lured to Holywood and a horror film. Michael winds up as the 'star' of a television commercial in which only his hand is actually seen.

BLISS (page 172)

p.c.: Window III Productions, with NSW Film Corp. **p**: Anthony Buckley. **d**: Ray Lawrence. **sc**: Peter Carey, Ray Lawrence (from Carey's novel). **ph**: Paul Murphy. **ed**: Wayne Le Clos. **m**: Peter Best. **p.d.**: Owen Paterson. **sd**: Gary Wilkins. **p.m.**: Carol Hughes. **a.d.**: Keith Heygate. Colour. 110 mins (At Cannes Film Festival: 135 mins). Aust dist: Self-dist. UK dist: Entertainment. US dist: New World. 1985.

1985 Australian Film Awards: Best film; best director; best adapted screenplay.

Barry Otto (Harry Joy), Lynette Curran (Bettina Joy), Helen Jones (Honey Barbara), Gia Carides (Lucy Joy), Miles Buchanan (David Joy), Jeff Truman (Joel), Tim Robertson (Alex Duval), Bryan Marshall (Adrian Clunes), John Ewing (Aldo), Kerry Walker (Alice Dalton), Paul Chubb (Reverend Des), Sara De Teliga (Harry's mother), Saskia Post (Harry's daughter), George Whaley (Vance Joy), Robert Menzies (Damian), Nique Needles (Ken McLaren), Les Foxcroft (Paul Bees), Allan Penney (Bettina's father), Rob Steele (Hastings), Manning Clark (Preacher), Peter Carmody (Dr Hennessey).

Adman Harry Joy suffers a heart attack at a family celebration and 'dies' for several minutes. When he recovers, he is a changed man. He realises that his wife, Bettina, is having an affair with Joel, his business partner; that his children David and Lucy are involved in drugs and incestuous sex; and that his biggest client's product causes cancer. Aldo, the maître d'hôtel at his favourite restaurant has cancer; an elephant sits on Harry's car; and Harry's family decides to place him in an asylum. Fortunately, he meets Honey Barbara, an earthy young prostitute, and after Bettina's suicide (she, too, has cancer) Harry ends up in the bush where an eight-year courtship of Honey Barbara brings him final happiness.

BLOOD MONEY (page 252)

p.c.: Lunar Prods. **p**: Tom Broadbridge, Chris Oliver. **d**: Chris Fitchett. **sc**: Chris Fitchett, John Ruane, Ellery Ryan. **ph**: Ellery Ryan. **ed**: Chris Oliver. **m**: Mark McSherry. **sd**: Lloyd Carrick. **a.d.**: Andrew Friedman. Colour. 62 mins. Aust dist: Greg Lynch Film Dists. 1980.

John Flaus (Pete Shields), Chrissie James (Jeannie Shields), Bryan Brown (Brian Shields), Peter Stratford (Curtis), Caroline Cassidy (Lisa Curtis), Peter Curtain (Dan), Jay Mannering (Jim), John Proper (Jack), Sue Jones (Doctor), Sophie Murphy (Kathy), Tom Broadbridge (Parking officer).

Veteran criminal Pete Shields carries out a bungled jewel robbery in Sydney, resulting in the deaths of his two partners. Discovering that he has terminal cancer, he returns home to Melbourne to see his younger brother, Brian, Jeannie, his ex-girlfriend (now Brian's wife), and their daughter, Kathy (who may be his). He kidnaps the daughter of gangster Curtis and robs Curtis to secure Kathy's future before stoically facing death at the hands of the gangster's gunmen.

BLOWING HOT AND COLD (page 89)

p.c.: Chancom Ltd—A Rosa Colosimo Production. **ex.p.**: Kevin Moore, Reg McLean, Rosa Colosimo. **p**: Rosa Colosimo. **d**: Marc Gracie. **sc**: Rosa Colosimo, Reg McLean, Luciano Vincenzoni, Sergio Donati. **ph**: Jaems Grant. **ed**: Nicolas Lee. **m**: Joe Dolce. **sd**: Joe Wilkinson. Colour. 85 mins. Self-dist in Australia. 1988.

Peter Adams (Jack Phillips), Joe Dolce (Nino), Kate Gorman (Sally Phillips), Elspeth Ballantyne (Shelagh McBean), Bruce Kane (Jeff Lynch).

Nino, who sells porno magazines and sex aids, tries to cheat country garage-owner Jack Phillips, but they become friends and get together to find Sally, Jack's teenage daughter, who has run off with a drug-runner.

BMX BANDITS (page 341)

p.c.: Nilsen Premiere. **p**: Tom Broadbridge, Paul F. Davies. **d**: Brian Trenchard Smith. **sc**: Patrick Edgeworth, based on a screenplay by Russell Hagg. **ph**: John Seale. **ed**: Alan Lake. **m**: Colin Stead, Frank Strangio. **p.d.**: Ross Major. **sd**: Ken Hammond. **p.m.**: Carolynne Cunningham. **a.d.**: Bob Howard. Panavision. Colour. 90 mins. Aust dist: Filmpac. UK dist: Rank. US dist: Comworld Intl. 1983.

David Argue (Whitey), John Ley (Moustache), Nicole Kidman (Judy), Angelo D'Angelo (P.J.), James Lugton (Goose), Bryan Marshall (Boss), Brian Sloman (Creep).

Teenagers P.J. and Goose, avid BMX riders, befriend supermarket employee Judy, also a biker, when they accidentally cause chaos in the store where she works. Later, the trio accidentally become involved with a gang of bank robbers and, after a hectic chase, is instrumental in capturing them. As a reward, the police agree to support the establishment of a biking track in the district.

BOOTLEG (page 236)

p.c.: Bootleg Films. **p**: Trevor Hawkins, John Prescott, Jeanne Taylor. **d, sc**: John Prescott. **ph**: Stephen Frost. **ed, a.d.**: Trevor Hawkins. **sd**: Kieran Knox. **p.m.**: Jeanne Taylor. Colour. 105 mins. 1985.

John Flaus (Joe Hart), Ian Nimmo (Lucan), Ray Meagher (Lawker), Carmen Duncan (Rita), Max Meldrum (Walter Stone), Shelley Friend (Netha), John Gregg (T. C. Brown) Iain Gardiner (Miko), Penny Jones (Deslene), Tracey Tainsh (Linda).

Joe Hart, a Sydney private eye with a possessive mother, goes to Brisbane to search for a missing woman. At the airport, he is mistaken for someone else, pursued by criminals involved in record piracy, and also by some violent cops. The case becomes a nightmare.

BOULEVARD OF BROKEN DREAMS (page 198)

p.c.: Boulevard Films. **ex.p.**: Peter Boyle. **p, sc**: Frank Howson. **d**: Pino Amenta. **sc**: Frank Howson. **ph**: David Connell. **ed**: Phil Reid. **m**: John Capek. **p.d.**: Tel Stolfo. **sd**: Andrew Ramage. **p.m.**: John Suhr. **a.d.**: John Powditch. **a.p.**: Barbi Taylor. Eastmancolour. 95 mins. Aust dist: Hoyts. 1988.

1988 Australian Film Awards: Best actor (John Waters); best supporting actor (Kim Gyngell).

John Waters (Tom Garfield), Penelope Stewart (Helen Garfield), Nicki Paull (Suzy Daniels), Kim Gyngell (Ian McKenzie), Kevin Miles (Geoff Borman), Andrew McFarlane (Jonathan Lovell), Ross Thompson (Cameron Wright).

Tom Garfield, an Australian writer, has carved a successful career for himself in Los Angeles but has, in the process, lost his wife, Helen, and daughter. Discovering that he is dying of cancer, Garfield returns to Melbourne to find his wife is now living with Jonathan Lovell. Without telling Helen about his illness, Garfield checks out the local production of his hit play, and seems attracted to actress Suzy Daniels. He decides to return to LA, but Helen rushes to the airport to see him . . .

BOUNDARIES OF THE HEART (page 117)

p.c.: International Film Management, Tra La La Films, FGH Films. **ex.p.**: Antony I. Ginnane. **p**: Patric Juillet. **d**: Lex Marinos. **sc**: Peter Yeldham. **ph**: David Sanderson, Geoff Simpson. **ed**: Philip Howe. **m**: Sharon Calcraft. **p.d.**: Melody Cooper. **sd**: Ken Hammond. **a.p.**: Wendy Hughes, Norman Kaye. **p.m.**: Michael Fuller. **a.d.**: Robert Kewley. Eastmancolour. 99 mins. Aust dist: Filmpac (direct to video). 1988.

Seattle Film Festival (1989): Best actress (Wendy Hughes).

Wendy Hughes (Stella Marsden), John Hargreaves (Andy Ford), Norman Kaye (W. H. [Billy] Morgan), Julie Nihill (June Thompson), Max Cullen (Blanco White), Michael Siberry (Arthur Pearson), John Clayton (Riley), Robert Faggater (Ted Mason).

Olwyn's Boundary (pop. 49) is a tiny township in Western Australia. Stella Marsden, single and nearly forty, works at the hotel owned by her father, Billy, a once-famous cricketer, disgraced after a sex scandal. Cowboy Andy Ford comes to the hotel every year at Christmas to ask Stella to marry him, but till now she has always refused. When Arthur, a salesman from the city whose car has broken down, is forced to stay at the hotel, Stella seduces him, but he flees next day, and Andy is alienated forever. Meanwhile, Billy decides to marry June, recently sacked from her job as nanny at a nearby property after being found in bed with the boss.

THE BOY WHO HAD EVERYTHING (page 356)

p.c.: Alfred Road Films, Multi Films. **p**: Richard Mason, Julia Overton. **d, sc**: Stephen Wallace. **ph**: Geoff Burton. **ed**: Henry Dangar. **m**: Ralph Schneider. **p.d.**: Ross Major. **sd**: Tim Lloyd. **p.m.**: Rod Allan. **a.d.**: Mark Turnbull. Colour. 92 mins. Aust dist: Hoyts (direct to video). UK dist: Enterprise. 1984.

1985 Australian Film Awards: Best supporting actor (Nique Needles)

Jason Connery (John Kirkland), Diane Cilento (Mother), Laura Williams (Robin), Lewis Fitz-Gerald (Peter Vandervelt), Ian Gilmour (Pollock), Nique Needles (Graham Cummerford), Michael Gow (Roger Kaplin), Tim Burns (Bookmaker), Caz Lederman (Prostitute), David Slingsby (Father in play), Jo Kennedy (Zenobia in play).

1965. John Kirkland, star pupil at grammar school, enters Sydney University and undergoes various initiation rites. He lives with his alcoholic, divorced, mother and has a tentative relationship with Robin, who comes from a similar, privileged, background. But John rebels against the university rules and traditions, and starts going to prostitutes. After a confrontation with his mother, John quits university.

BOYS IN THE ISLAND (page 171)

p.c.: Great Scott. **ex.p.**: Brian Rosen. **p**: Jane Scott. **d**: Geoffrey Bennett. **sc**: C. J. Koch, Tony Morphett (from the novel by Koch). **ph**: Andrew Lesnie. **ed**: Suresh Ayyar. **m**: Sharon Calcraft. **p.d.**: Igor Nay. **sd**: Gary Wilkins. **p.m.**: Fiona McConaghy. **a.d.**: Steve Andrews. Eastmancolour. 107 mins. 1989.

Yves Stening (Frank), Jane Stephens (Keeva), James Fox (George Farrell), Lexa Murphy (Heather), Joseph Clements (Louis), Steve Jacobs (Heather's father), Daniel Pollock, Daniel Heath.

The 1950s. Frank, a teenager with little family life, lives in Tasmania but, together with his friends, longs to leave the island and live in Melbourne. After an ineffectual romance with Heather, whom he meets at a dance, Frank follows Louis, leader of his group, to the mainland, to discover Louis is a member of a gang of petty criminals led by George Farrell. Farrell's mistress, Keeva, makes a play for Frank and steals Farrell's money; Farrell accuses her of the theft, there is a struggle, and Farrell is killed. Frank returns to Tasmania.

BREAKFAST IN PARIS (page 111)

p.c.: Cinema Enterprises, John Lamond Motion Pictures. **p, d**: John D. Lamond. **sc**: Morris Dalton. **ph**: Ross Berryman. **ed**: Jill Rice. **m**: Brian May. **p.d.**: Stephen Walsh. **sd**: John Rowley. **p.m.**: John Chase. **a.d.**: Ross Hamilton. Eastmancolour. 94 mins. Aust dist: Roadshow. 1981.

Barbara Parkins, Rod Mullinar, Jack Lenoir. Elspeth Ballantyne, Jeremy Higgins, Graham Stanley.

A Melbourne dress-designer, on the rebound, flies to Paris, meeting an accident-prone man on the plane. In Paris, they have an affair; he wants to marry her, she declines and returns to Melbourne. She has second thoughts and goes back to Paris for a romantic reconciliation.

BREAKING LOOSE (page 360)

p.c.: Avalon Films. **ex.p.**: Eric Jury, James M. Vernon. **p**: Phillip Avalon. **d, sc**: Rod Hay. **ph**: Richard Michalak. **ed**: Ted Otton. **m**: Jan Preston. **p.d.**: Andrew Paul. **sd**: Bob Clayton. **p.m.**: Andrew W. Morse. **a.d.**: Carolynne Cunningham. Colour. 87 mins. Aust dist: Hoyts. 1988.

Peter Phelps (Ross Cameron), Vince Martin (Robbie Woods), Abigail (Helen), David Ngoobumjarra (Davie), John Clayton (Williams), Gary Waddell (Bill), Shane Connor (Samson), Sandra Lee Patterson (Caroline Dixon), Tom Richards (Rick Dixon), Angela Kennedy (Girlfriend).

Ross, a troubled teenager, leaves the city (where he has had a run-in with a bikie gang) and heads north to meet Robbie Woods, an old friend of his mother, who lives by a surf beach. He is seduced by Helen, a middle-aged woman, and beaten up by her husband, Williams. Then the bikies, who have kidnapped Ross's girlfriend, arrive and destroy Robbie's beach-house before they are overcome.

BROTHERS (page 136)

p.c.: Areflex Pictures. **ex.p.**: Frank Wilkie, Brock Halliday. **p, d, sc**: Terry Bourke (from the book *Reflex* by Roger Ward). **ph**: Ray Henman. **ed**: Ron Williams. **m**: Bob Young. **p.d.**: Paul Tolley. **sd**: Bob Clayton. Eastmancolour. 103 mins. Direct to video release. 1982.

Chard Hayward (Adam Wild), Ivar Kants (Kevin Wild), Margaret Lawrence (Lani Aveson), Jennifer Cluff (Allison Levis), Alyson Best (Jenine

Williams), Ricky May (Bill Mason), Joan Bruce (Mrs Williams), Les Foxcroft (Jim Williams), Ken Wayne (Bureau Chief), Desmond Tester (Journalist), Roger Ward (Cameraman).

Timor, 1975. Adam and Kevin Wild, newsmen, narrowly escape the massacre of five of their colleagues by Indonesian soldiers. Five years later, the brothers become involved with a prostitute, Lani (who commits suicide) and Allison, a 'nice girl' who is killed in a coach crash.

BUDDIES (page 88)

p.c.: J.D. Productions, in ass. with Queensland Film Corp. **p, sc**: John Dingwall. **d**: Arch Nicholson. **ph**: David Eggby. **ed**: Martyn Down. **m**: Chris Neal. **p.d.**: Philip Warner. Panavision. Colour. 99 mins. Aust dist: Self-dist. 1983.

1983 Australian Film Awards: Best original screenplay.

Colin Friels (Mike), Harold Hopkins (Johnny), Kris McQuade (Stella), Bruce Spence (Ted), Dennis Miller (Andy), Simon Chilvers (Alfred), Norman Kaye (George Spencer), Lisa Peers (Jennifer Spencer), Andrew Sharp (Peter), Dinah Shearing (Merle).

Mike and Johnny, friends and rivals, are prospectors in Queensland diamond fields. Mike occasionally sleeps with Stella, another prospector. Matters are complicated when the villainous Andy covets the friends' sapphire claim, and is only defeated, in the end, during a battle between two front-end loaders. Meanwhile a family of tourists, the Spencers, arrive, and daughter Jennifer falls for Mike; and Alfred, a light-aircraft salesman, decides to stay on in this remote spot and live the simple life with the willing Stella.

BULLSEYE (page 69)

p.c.: PBL Productions, Dumbarton Films. **p**: Brian Rosen. **d**: Carl Schultz. **sc**: Robert Wales (additional dialogue by Bob Ellis). **ph**: Dean Semler. **ed**: Richard Francis-Bruce. **m**: Chris Neal. **p.d.**: George Liddle. **p.m.**: Carol Hughes. **a.d.**: Charles Rotherham. System 35 Widescreen. Eastmancolour. 95 mins. Aust dist: Hoyts. US dist: Cinema Group. 1986.

Paul Goddard (Harry Walford), Kathryn Walker (Lily Bond), John Wood (Billy McGurk), Paul Chubb (Don McKenzie), Lynette Curran (Dora McKenzie), Bruce Spence (Purdy), David Slingsby (Spence), John Meillon (Merritt), Kerry Walker (Mrs Gootch), Rhys McConnochie (Judge).

The 1860s. Harry Walford, accompanied by his mate, Billy, steals 1000 head of cattle, including a priceless white bull, from the property of Don McKenzie in Roma, Queensland. Dogged by the treacherous Purdy and Spence, the rustlers head for Adelaide across the centre of Australia and, miraculously, survive to sell the cattle. Meanwhile, Lily, the McKenzies' housemaid, whom Harry loves, has got into the clutches of Mrs Gootch, who runs an Adelaide brothel. Harry saves Lily from a fate worse than death, but is arrested and brought to Roma for trial. He is acquitted.

BURKE AND WILLS (page 29)

p.c.: Hoyts–Edgley. **ex.p.**: Terry Jackman. Michael Edgley. **p**: Graeme Clifford, John Sexton. **d**: Graeme Clifford. **sc**: Michael Thomas. **ph**: Russell Boyd. **ed**: Tim Wellburn. **m**: Peter Sculthorpe. **p.d.**: Ross Major. **cost**: George Liddle. **sd**: Syd Butterworth. **a.p.**: Greg Ricketson. **p.m.**: Carolyne Cunningham. **a.d.**: Mark Turnbull. Panavision. Eastmancolour. 140 mins. Aust dist: Hoyts. US dist: Hemdale. 1985.

Jack Thompson (Robert O'Hara Burke), Nigel Havers (William John Wills), Greta Scacchi (Julia Matthews), Matthew Fargher (John King), Ralph Cotterill (Charley Gray), Drew Forsythe (William Brahe), Chris Haywood (Tom McDonagh), Monroe Reimers (Dost Mahomet), Barry Hill (George Landellis), Roderick Williams (Bill Wright), Hugh Keays-Byrne (Ambrose Kyte), Arthur Dignam (Sir William Stawell), Ken Goodlet (Dr John Masadam).

1860. Robert O'Hara Burke, a fiery-tempered Irishman in love with Julia Matthews, a beautiful opera singer, leads an expedition to cross central Australia from Melbourne to the Gulf of Carpentaria, supported by important businessmen and politicians. Eager to beat a rival expedition, Burke is joined by the British scientist, William Wills, and sets off with a party of nineteen men, plus horses, specially imported camels and tons of equipment. The expedition reaches the northern sea, but frustrating delays on the way back mean they miss a crucial rendezvous by a few hours. One by one the members of the expedition perish, with young John King, who is helped by Aborigines, the only survivor. King returns to Melbourne and makes a moving public speech about the fate of the Burke and Wills expedition.

BUSH CHRISTMAS (page 341)

p.c.: Bush Christmas production, in ass. with Queensland Film Corp. **p**: Gilda Baracchi, Paul Barron. **d**: Henri Safran. **sc**: Ted Roberts. **ph**: Malcolm Richards, Ross Berryman. **ed**: Ron Williams. **m**: Mike Perjanik. **p.d.**: Darrell Lass.

sd: Don Connolly. Colour. 91 mins. Aust dist: Hoyts. 1983.

John Ewart (Bill), John Howard (Sly), Nicole Kidman (Helen), Mark Spain (Michael), Manalpuy (Manalpuy), James Wingrove (Johnny), Peter Sumner (Father).

A hot Christmas in the lush Korrabyn Valley in Queensland. Helen's father is looking forward to the coming New Year's Day horserace, since he hopes to win, on Prince, and save his farm with the prize money. But his hopes are dashed when Bill and Sly, a couple of thieves, steal Prince. Helen, together with the English visitor Michael, young Johnny and Aboriginal Manalpuy, sets out to track down the thieves. After difficulties and dangers, the youngsters get Prince back, and father wins the vital race.

BUSHFIRE MOON (page 342)
p.c.: Entertainment Media, in ass. with The Disney Channel, Children's Film and TV Foundation, Film Victoria. p: Peter Beilby, Robert Le Tet. d: George Miller (2). sc: Jeff Peck. ph: David Connell. ed: Tim Wellburn. m: Bruce Rowland. p.d.: Otello Stolfo. cost: Rose Chong. sd: Andrew Ramage. p.m.: Helen Watts. a.d.: Brian Giddens. Colour. 98 mins. Aust dist: Roadshow. 1987.

Dee Wallace Stone (Elizabeth O'Day), John Waters (Patrick O'Day), Bill Kerr (Trevor Watson), Charles Tingwell (Max Bell), Nadine Garner (Sarah O'Day), Andrew Ferguson (Ned O'Day), Grant Piro (Angus Watson), Rosie Sturgess (Miss Daly), Kim Gyngell (Hungry Bill).

On a drought-stricken property around the turn of the century, the O'Days face a bleak Christmas of dust storms and dying stock. Patrick appeals to his miserly neighbour Watson, a British traditionalist, for help with water, but is rebuffed. But young Ned O'Day sees a white-bearded drifter, Max Bell, whom he assumes is Father Christmas, and appeals to him for help. Despite a threatening bushfire, everything turns out well: Watson has a change of heart, the rains come, and Ned's sister Sarah sees a happy future with Watson's son, Angus.

CACTUS (page 95)
p.c.: Dofine. ex.p.: Jeannine Seawell. p: Jane Ballantyne, Paul Cox. d: Paul Cox. sc: Paul Cox, Bob Ellis. ph: Yuri Sokol. ed: Tim Lewis. p.d.: Asher Bilu. sd: Ken Hammond. p.m.: Milanka Comfort. a.d.: Virginia Rouse. a.p.: Tony Llewellyn-Jones. Colour. 93 mins. Aust dist: Roadshow. UK dist: Blue Dolphin. US dist: Spectrafilm. 1986.

Isabelle Huppert (Colo), Robert Menzies (Robert), Norman Kaye (Tom), Monica Maughan (Bea), Banduk Marika (Banduk), Sheila Florance (Martha), Peter Aanensen (George), Julia Blake (Club Speaker), Jean-Pierre Mignon (Jean-François), Ray Marshall (Kevin), Maurie Fields (Maurie), Sean Scully (Doctor).

Colo, a Frenchwoman taking an Australian holiday away from her husband, Jean-François, and staying with her friends Tom and Bea near Melbourne, is badly injured in a car accident. As a result, she loses the sight of one eye, and is warned that the sight of her other eye will eventually be affected. Colo meets Robert, blind from birth, and a collector of cacti. The two become friends, then lovers, though Robert is troubled when Jean-François pays an unexpected visit. Colo sends her husband away.

CANDY REGENTAG (page 135)
(Alternative title: *Kiss The Night*)
p.c.: Rainy Day. ex.p., sc: Don Catchlove. p: Graeme Isaac. d: James Ricketson. ph: Michael Edols. ed: Tony Stephens. m: Graeme Isaac. p.d.: Rob Ricketson. sd: Ross Linton. p.m.: Brenda Pam. a.d.: John Warran. Fujicolor. 99 mins. Self-dist in Aust. 1987.

Patsy Stephens (Candy Regentag/Jenny), Warwick Moss (Reg), Garry Aron Cook (Ian), Rainee Skinner (Fleur), Maxine Klibingaitis (Bibi), Toni Scanlon (Gail), Jacqui Phillips (Wendy), Beth Child (Lola), Imogen Annesley (Sacha).

Jenny, who calls herself Candy Regentag, works at a King's Cross brothel, Bambi's, and lives with Ian, her surly boyfriend. One night, out on the street, she meets Reg, who later becomes a client at Bambi's. Candy finds herself falling in love with Reg, and breaks off with Ian, but discovers, too late, that Reg only wants her if he is in a customer–client situation. In a moment of agonised fury, she stabs him to death.

CAPPUCCINO (page 319)
p.c.: Archer Films. p: Anthony Bowman, Sue Wild. d, sc: Anthony Bowman. ph: Danny Batterham. ed: Richard Hindley. m: William Motzing. p.d.: Darrell Lass. sd: Ross Linton. p.m.: Sue Wild. a.d.: Corrie Soeterboek. Colour. 84 mins. Aust dist: Ronin.

John Clayton (Max), Rowena Wallace (Anna French), Jeanie Drynan (Maggie Spencer), Barry Quin (Larry), Cristina Parker (Celia), Ritchie Singer (Bollinger), Simon Matthew (Nigel), Ernie Dingo (Himself).

Max, a former taxi-driver turned stand-up comedian, tells his story from a prison cell. He met regularly in a coffee shop with actress friends

Anna and Maggie, who were often rivals for the same roles (and men). Max's latest girl, Celia, falls for Anna's actor boyfriend, Larry. A crooked cop, Bollinger, leaves an incriminating tape in Max's cab, leading to various complications. In the end, the story we have been seeing turns out to be the script for a movie.

CAREFUL HE MIGHT HEAR YOU
(page 181)
p.c.: Syme Entertainment, in ass. with NSW Film Corp. **p**: Jill Robb. **d**: Carl Schultz. **sc**: Michael Jenkins, from the novel by Sumner Locke Elliott. **ph**: John Seale. **ed**: Richard Francis-Bruce. **m**: Ray Cook. **p.d.**: John Stoddart. **sd**: Syd Butterworth. **cost**: Bruce Finlayson. **p.m.**: Greg Ricketson. **a.d.**: Colin Fletcher. Panavision. Eastmancolour. 116 mins. Aust dist: Hoyts. US dist: 20th Century-Fox. UK dist: Cannon-Gala. 1983.

1983 Australian Film Awards: Best film; director; actress (Wendy Hughes); supporting actor (John Hargreaves); photography; adapted screenplay; production design; costume design.

Wendy Hughes (Vanessa), Robyn Nevin (Lila), Nicholas Gledhill (P.S.), John Hargreaves (Logan Marriott), Geraldine Turner (Vere), Isabelle Anderson (Agnes), Peter Whitford (George), Colleen Clifford (Ettie), Edward Howell (Judge), Jacqueline Kott (Miss Pile), Julie Nihill (Diana), Michael Long (Mr Hood), Beth Child (Mrs Grindel), Colin Croft (Magician).

The 1930s. P.S. (so-called because he was a 'postscript' to his late mother's life), lives with his working-class Aunt Lila and Uncle George and has never met his larrikin father, Logan Marriott. The boy's wealthy aunt Vanessa returns to Sydney from Europe and wants to take control of the boy's education and future; her lifestyle is totally different from that of the impoverished Lila and George. Logan reappears, briefly meets his son, then rejects Vanessa's advances before disappearing again. Vanessa wants full guardianship of P.S., and a legal battle results which she wins, but she dies when a harbour ferry sinks. P.S., back with Lila and George, demands that from now on he be known by his real name, Bill.

CASSANDRA (page 290)
p.c.: Parrallel [sic] Films. **ex.p.**: Philip Gerlach, Mikael Borglund. **p**: Trevor Lucas. **d**: Colin Eggleston. **sc**: Colin Eggleston, John Ruane, Chris Fitchett. **ph**: Gary Wapshott. **ed**: Josephine Cooke. **m**: Trevor Lucas, Ian Mason. **p.d.**: Stewart Burnside. **sd**: Robert Clayton. **a.p., p.m.**: Steve Amezdroz. **a.d.**: Michael Faranda. Agfacolor. 93 mins. 1987.

Tessa Humphries (Cassandra), Shane Briant (Steven Roberts), Briony Behets (Helen Roberts), Susan Barling (Libby), Tim Burns (Graham).

Cassandra is plagued with horrifying nightmares in which she sees a small boy drive a woman to suicide. Her father's mistress is found stabbed to death, and Cassandra discovers that her parents are actually brother and sister and that her twin brother had been responsible for their mother's death when the children were only three years old. The boy has been in a mental home ever since, but now he is out and ready to kill ... But who is he? Her father's new assistant? Or Cass's new boyfriend? (The latter, as it turns out.)

CELIA (page 368)
p.c.: Seon Films. **ex.p.**: Bryce Menzies. **p**: Timothy White, Gordon Glenn. **d**, **sc**: Ann Turner. **ph**: Geoffrey Simpson. **ed**: Ken Sallows. **m**: Chris Neal. **p.d.**: Peta Lawson. **sd**: Lloyd Carrick. **p.m.**: Lynda House. **a.d.**: Phil Jones. Colour. 102 mins. Aust dist: Hoyts. US dist: Seven Gables. UK dist: Electric Pictures. 1988.

1989 Australian Film Awards: Best supporting actress (Victoria Longley).

Rebecca Smart (Celia), Nicholas Eadie (Ray), Maryanne Fahey (Pat), Victoria Longley (Alice), William Zappa (Uncle John), Deborra-Lee Furness (Teacher).

The 1950s. Celia, aged nine, is distressed by the death of her beloved grandmother, a life-long radical, and is haunted by nightmares resulting from a book she reads at school. An only child, she befriends the children of new neighbours (while her father, Ray, makes a pass at the attractive young mother, Alice); but when it is discovered that the neighbours are active Communists, they are hounded out of the district. Celia is given a pet rabbit but has to surrender it (to her policeman uncle, John), when the Victorian government, in an effort to combat a rabbit plague, orders domestic rabbits be impounded. The ban ends, but Celia's rabbit is dead. Her uncle tries to make amends, but Celia shoots him with her father's gun. The policeman's killer is not discovered, though Celia's mother suspects; the child continues playing with her friends, though her games have become more macabre ...

CENTRESPREAD (page 137)
p.c.: Australian Film Productions. **p**: Wayne Groom. **d**, **ed**: Tony Paterson. **sc**: Michael Ralph, Robert Fogden. **ph**: Geoffrey Simpson. **p.d.**:

Michael Ralph, Robert Fogden. **sd**: James Currie **p.m.**: Jenny Day. **a.d.**: Chris Williams. colour. 82 mins. Aust dist: Greg Lynch Film Distribs. 1981.

Paul Trahair, Kylie Foster, Ivor Louis, Jack Neate, Mark Watson, Edson Annan, Paula Carter, Sarah Collins, Deanne Carsas, John Nobbs. Carmen McCall.

In the near future, a magazine photographer (who specialises in graphic shots for a sex magazine), meets the love of his life (and a conscience) in an antique shop.

THE CHAIN REACTION (page 247)

p.c.: Palm Beach Pictures. **p**: David Elfick. **d, sc**: Ian Barry. **ph**: Russell Boyd. **ed**: Tim Wellburn. **m**: Andrew Thomas Wilson. **p.d.**: Graham Walker. **sd**: Lloyd Carrick. **a.p.**: George Miller (1), Ross Matthews. **p.m.**: Lynn Gailey. **a.d.**: Chris Maudsen. Eastmancolour. 87 mins. Aust dist: Hoyts. US (and rest of world) dist: Warner Bros. 1980.

Steve Bisley (Larry), Arna-Maria Winchester (Carmel), Ross Thompson (Heinrich), Ralph Cotterill (Gray), Hugh Keays-Byrne (Eagle), Richard Moir (Piggott), Lorna Lesley (Gloria), Patrick Ward (Oates), Kim Gyngell (Crabs).

In central Australia, an accident occurs at a nuclear waste facility. Heinrich, a scientist who works at the plant is exposed to radiation, but escapes and tries to warn the outside world. He is taken in by Larry and Carmel, who run a repair shop; but security agents Gray and Oates are determined to kill Heinrich and anyone with whom he has come in contact. They close in on Heinrich, Larry and Carmel, and a furious chase ensues, with a television newsteam arriving on the scene in the nick of time. But the three have been fatally exposed to radiation.

CHANNEL CHAOS (page 333)

p.c.: Hatful Prods. **ex.p.**: Phil Dwyer. **p**: Chris Kiely. **d**: Barry Peak. **sc**: Barry Peak, Chris Kiely. **ph**: Malcolm Richards. **ed**: David Hipkins. **m**: John Rees, Bernadette Holloway, Greg Macainsh. **p.d.**: Ian McWha. **sd**: John Rowley. **p.m.**: Ray Pond. **a.d.**: Ross Hamilton. Eastmancolour. 85 mins. Direct to video release. 1984.

Jay Hackett (Mike), Tim Scally (Kookie), Lyn Semmler (Helen), Clive Hearne (George), Peter Thompson (Sir Ninian Richards), Peter Hosking (Sullivan), Brenda Clarke (Valerie), David Beresh (Johnny), Lydia Knight (Kathy Kowalski).

GRRS TV is losing ratings. When a scriptwriter for the station's cop show is found stabbed to death, the actors who play the TV cops are assigned to investigate, while a television crew covers their adventures.

THE CITY'S EDGE (page 205)

p.c.: CB Films, in ass. with NSW Film Corp. **p**: Pom Oliver, Errol Sullivan. **d**: Ken Quinnell. **sc**: Robert Merritt, Ken Quinnell (based on a novel by W. A. Harbinson). **ph**: Louis Irving. **ed**: Greg Ropert. **p.d.**: Robert Dein. **sd**: Noel Quinn. **a.p.**: Barbara Gibbs. Colour. 86 mins. UK dist: Cannon. 1983

Hugo Weaving (Andy White), Mark Lee (Jim Wentworth), Tommy Lewis (Jack Collins), Katrina Foster (Laura Wentworth), Ralph Cotterill (Cripple).

Andy White arrives in Sydney by train from his country home and moves into a cockroach-infested flat at Bondi Beach. There he meets Jim Wentworth, a drug addict, who blames himself for his father's death; his sister, Laura, still troubled over the abortion she had at the age of sixteen; and her Aboriginal lover, Jack Collins. Andy falls in love with Laura, but is horrified to learn that her weak-willed brother was the father of her baby. Jim throws himself under a train and is killed, and Jack, after killing a white bigot during a fight on the beach, is gunned down by police.

THE CLINIC (page 320)

p.c.: The Film House, Generation Films. **p**: Robert Le Tet, Bob Weis. **d**: David Stevens. **sc**: Greg Millin. **ph**: Ian Baker. **ed**: Edward McQueen-Mason. **m**: Redmond Symonds. **p.d.**: Tracy Watt. **sd**: John Rowley. **p.m.**: Michael Lake. **a.d.**: David Clarke. Colour. 91 mins. Aust dist: Roadshow. UK dist: Eagle. 1982.

Chris Haywood (Dr Eric Linden), Simon Burke (Paul Armstrong), Gerda Nicolson (Linda), Rona McLeod (Dr Carol Young), Suzanne Roylance (Pattie), Veronica Lang (Nancy), Pat Evison (Alda), Max Bruch (Hassad), Gabrielle Hartley (Gillian), Jane Clifton (Sharon), Ned Lander (Warwick), Mark Little (Basil).

A Melbourne VD clinic. Paul Armstrong, a medical student doing work study, observes the work of Drs Eric Linden, cheerfully permissive, and Carol Young (who is pregnant, but has separated from her ardent lover). Patients include a middle-aged widow, a Chinese with limited English, and a distraught young man, Warwick, fired because he has syphilis (he later suicides). Paul discovers that Dr Linden is gay, and is shocked, but later, concerned that he may have a disease himself, submits to an examination in the toilet of a nearby bar.

CLOSER AND CLOSER APART (page 119)

p.c.: Rosa Colosimo Prods. **p**: Rosa Colosimo.

d: Steve Middleton. **sc**: Angelo Salamanca (inspired by *La Cavalleria Rusticana*). **ph**: Vladimir Osherov. **ed**: Catherine Birmingham. **m**: Joe Dolce. **p.d.**: Maria Ferro. **sd**: Peter Clancy. **p.m.** Alison Sadler. **a.d.**: Rick Lappas. Eastmancolour. 88 mins. 1989.

Steve Bastoni (Sam), George Harlem (Alfio), Marie-Louise Walker (Lola), Linda Hartley (Angie), Kate Jason-Omodei (Mrs Macca), Yvette Bentana (Connie), George Kapiniaris (Enza Vozza), Bettina Spivakovsky (Vittoria Serini), Dino Nicolosi (Carmelo Serini), Vince D'Amico (Mr Giblisco).

Sam and Alfio are best friends in their early twenties. Alfio is having an affair with easy-going Lola, who works in the same electrical shop as Sam; Sam is dating virginal Angie. Lola is bored with Alfio and makes a pass at Sam, who succumbs. Angie finds out and tells Alfio, who challenges his friend to a knife fight, but finds himself unable to kill Sam.

THE CLUB (page 188)

p.c.: SA Film Corp., NSW Film Corp. **p**: Matt Carroll. **d**: Bruce Beresford. **sc**: David Williamson (based on his play). **ph**: Don McAlpine. **ed**: William Anderson. **m**: Mike Brady. **p.d.**: David Copping. **sd**: Gary Wilkins. **a.p.**: Moya Iceton. **a.d.**: Scott Hicks. Colour. 96 mins. Aust dist: Roadshow. 1980.

Jack Thompson (Laurie), Graham Kennedy (Ted), Frank Wilson (Jock), Harold Hopkins (Danny), John Howard (Geoff), Alan Cassell (Gerry), Maggie Doyle (Susy).

Behind the scenes at an Australian Rules football club in Melbourne. Laurie—a former star player, now team coach—is witness to the struggles between two factions of the club's board. Ted, club president (and pork-pie manufacturer) falls foul of business manager Gerry, who conspires with former president (and latently violent) Jock to strip him of his position.

THE COCA-COLA KID (page 321)

p.c.: Grand Bay Films, Cinema Enterprises, Smart Egg Prods. **p**: David Roe. **d**: Dusan Makevejev. **sc**: Frank Moorhouse (based on his short stories); additional ideas, dialogue: Denny Lawrence. **ph**: Dean Semler. **ed**: John Scott. **m**: Bill Motzing. **p.d.**: Anni Browning. **sd**: Mark Lewis. **p.m.** Susan Wild. **a.d.**: Bojana Marijan. Eastmancolour. 94 mins. Aust dist: Roadshow. US dist: Cinecom. UK dist: Palace Pictures. 1985.

Eric Roberts (Becker), Greta Scacchi (Terri), Bill Kerr (T. George McDowell), Max Gillies (Frank), Kris McQuade (Juliana), Tony Barry (Bushman), Chris Haywood (Kim), Paul Chubb (Fred), David Slingsby (Waiter), Tim Finn (Phillip), Colleen Clifford (Mrs Haversham), Rebecca Smart (DMZ), Esben Storm (Hotel Manager), Gia Carides (Chambermaid), Ian Gilmour (Marjorie), Jon Ewing (McCorvey), Annie Semler (Cindy Lou), Linda Nagle, Julie Nihill, Fiona Hallett (Marching Girls).

Becker is sent from the head office of the Coca-Cola company in the US to Sydney to discover from the firm's Australian manager, Frank, why sales are slow. He discovers that in Anderson Valley, T. George McDowell manufactures an immensely popular soft drink. Frank's secretary Terri, a divorced mother attracted to Becker, is revealed to be McDowell's daughter. Becker is determined to take over McDowell's bottling plant, but is waylaid by Terri, who eagerly seduces him. McDowell destroys his plant, Becker resigns from Coca-Cola and stays on in Sydney with Terri and her daughter.

CODA (page 291)

p.c.: Premiere Film Marketing, Genesis Film. **ex.p.**: Tom Broadbridge. **p**: Terry Jennings. **d**: Craig Lahiff. **sc**: Craig Lahiff, Terry Jennings. **ph**: David Foreman. **ed**: Catherine Murphy. **m**: Frank Strangio. **p.d.**: Anni Browning. **p.m.**: Elspeth Baird. **a.d.**: Gus Howard. Colour. 102 mins. Direct to video release. 1987.

Penny Cook (Kate Martin), Arna-Maria Winchester (Dr Steiner), Liddy Clark (Sally Reid), Olivia Hamnett (Det.-Sgt Turner), Patrick Frost (Mike Martin), Vivienne Graves (Anna).

A female music student is attacked in her room at a university and falls from a high window, but miraculously survives. However, she is murdered by an unseen intruder while recovering in hospital. Police suspect the dead woman's ex-husband, but her best friend Kate swears he is innocent. Kate and her friend, the ebullient Sally, are threatened by a mystery man; the dead woman's tutor (and lesbian lover), Dr Steiner, acts suspiciously, and the investigating police-woman, Det.-Sgt Turner, is murdered. The killer turns out to be Dr Steiner, a psychotic who dresses up (as the brother she had killed years before) to commit the murders.

COMPO (page 193)

p.c.: Sunrise Pictures. **p**: Nigel Buesst, Joanne Bell, Matthew Lovering. **d**: Nigel Buesst. **sc**: Abe Pogos (based on his play *Claim No. Z84*). **ph**: Vladimir Osherov. **ed**: Nubar Ghazarian. **m**: Iain Mott. **sd**: Ray Boseley. **p.m.**: Joanne Bell. **a.d.**: Matthew Lovering. Colour. 83 mins. 1989.

Jeremy Stanford (Paul Harper), Bruce Kerr (David Bartlett), Christopher Barry (Carlo

Garbanzo), Elizabeth Crockett (Gina), Cliff Neate (Dale Bradley), Rowan Woods (Tom Little), Peter Hosking (Vince Caruana), Leo Regan (Eddie).

Paul Harper arrives for work at a workers' compensation office, to find the bureaucracy, under manager David Bartlett, is stultifying. Despite a romance with fellow-worker Gina, Paul decides eventually to leave.

CONTAGION (page 294)
p.c.: Premiere Film Marketing, Reef Films. **ex.p**: Tom Broadbridge. **p**: Leo Barretto, Ken Methold. **d**: Karl Zwicky. **sc**: Ken Methold. **ph**: John Stokes. **ed**: Roy Mason. **m**: Frank Strangio. **sd** Tony Vaccher. **a.d.**: David Munro. Colour. 90 mins. 1987.

John Doyle (Mark), Nicola Bartlett (Cheryl), Ray Barrett (Bael), Nathalie Gaffney (Cleo), Pamela Hawksford (Helen), Jacqueline Brennan (Trish).

Real-estate salesman Mark is lured to a rundown mansion by two blonde beauties where he meets Bael who urges Mark to bring him a woman. Eventually, Mark discovers Bael is a ghost.

COOL CHANGE (page 224)
p.c.: Delatite. **ex.p.**: Geoff Burrowes. **p**: Dennis Wright. **d**: George Miller (2). **sc**: Patrick Edgeworth. **ph**: John Haddy. **ed**: Philip Reid. **m**: Bruce Rowland. **p.d.**: Leslie Binns. **sd**: Terry Rodman. **p.m.**: Bill Regan. **a.d.**: John Powditch. Eastmancolour. 90 mins. Aust dist: Hoyts. 1985.

Jon Blake (Steve), Lisa Armytage (Joanna), Deborra-Lee Furness (Lee), David Bradshaw (Hardwicke), Alex Wilson (Raddick), James Wright (Senior Ranger), Mark Albiston (Mitchell), Robert Bruning (Minister).

Steve, a young forest ranger based in Victoria's High Country, is caught up in a feud between cattlemen and conservationists. He has to deal with Lee, sent by the government's conservation minister to cause trouble, and also with Joanna, with whose family Steve's family has long feuded. All ends well, with the cattlemen triumphing over the conservationists.

THE COOLANGATTA GOLD (page 357)
p.c.: Hoyts-Edgley. **ex.p.**: Terry Jackman, Michael Edgley. **p**: John Weiley. **d**: Igor Auzins. **sc**: Peter Schreck. **ph**: Keith Wagstaff. **ed**: Tim Wellburn. **m**: Bill Conti. **p.m.**: Bob Hill. **sd**: Phil Judd. **p.m.**: Rosslyn Abernathy. **a.d.**: Colin Fletcher. Panavision. Eastmancolour. 112 mins. Aust dist: Hoyts. 1984.

Joss McWilliam (Steve Lucas), Nick Tate (Joe Lucas), Josephine Smulders (Kerri Dean), Robyn

Nevin (Robyn Lucas), Colin Friels (Adam Lucas), Grant Kenny (Himself), Melanie Day (Gilda), Melissa Jaffer (Ballet teacher).

Back in 1960, Joe Lucas finished second in The Coolangatta Gold, a contest involving swimming, running and surfing on Queensland's Gold Coast; Joe is determined his sons will win the coveted prize, but favours his older son, Adam, in favour of his more sensitive younger son, Steve. Steve falls for Kerri, a ballet dancer, and determines to win the race himself to prove to his father he is a man. At the climax of the gruelling contest, however, he allows Adam to win.

CROCODILE DUNDEE (page 335)
(International title: 'Crocodile Dundee')
p.c.: Rimfire Films. **p**: John Cornell. **d**: Peter Faiman. **line p.**: Jane Scott. **sc**: Paul Hogan, Ken Shadie, John Cornell. **ph**: Russell Boyd. **ed**: David Stiven. **m**: Peter Best. **p.d.**: Graham (Grace) Walker. **sd**: Gary Wilkins, Bill Daley. **p.m.**: Peter Sjoquist, Kelly Van Horn. **a.d.**: Mark Turnbull, Craig Bolles. Panavision. Colour. 104 mins. Aust dist: Hoyts. US dist: Paramount. UK (and rest of the world) dist: 20th Century-Fox. 1986.

Paul Hogan (Michael J. Crocodile Dundee), Linda Kozlowski (Sue Charlton), John Meillon (Walter Reilly), David Gulpilil (Neville Bell), Ritchie Singer (Con), Maggie Blinco (Ida), Steve Rackman (Donk), Mark Blum (Richard Mason), Michael Lombard (Sam Charlton).

Sue Charlton, journalist for the New York magazine *Newsday*, arrives in northern Australia and meets Mick Dundee, nicknamed Crocodile because he claims to have killed one with his bare hands. Sue accompanies Mick on a safari, where they encounter snakes and a croc—Mick saves Sue's life. She persuades him to return with her to New York, where he manages to cope well with the alien environment. Due to a misunderstanding, Mick leaves, but Sue catches up with him on a crowded railway station platform and tells him she loves him.

'CROCODILE' DUNDEE II (page 338)
p.c.: Rimfire Films. **ex.p.**: Paul Hogan. **p**: John Cornell, Jane Scott. **d**: John Cornell. **sc**: Paul Hogan, Brett Hogan. **ph**: Russell Boyd. **ed**: David Stiven. **m**: Peter Best. **p.d.**: Lawrence Eastwood. **sd**: Gary Wilkins, Tom Brandau. **p.m.**: Fiona McConaghy, Kelly Van Horn. **a.d.**: Mark Turnbull, Chitra Mojtabai. Panavision. Colour. 110 mins. Aust dist: Hoyts. US dist: Paramount. UK (and rest of world) dist: UIP. 1988.

Paul Hogan (Mick 'Crocodile' Dundee), Linda Kozlowski (Sue Charlton), John Meillon (Walter

Reilly), Ernie Dingo (Charlie), Steve Rackman (Donk), Gus Mercurio (Frank), Maggie Blinco (Ida), Mark Blum (Richard Mason), Hechter Ubarry (Rico), Stephen Root (DEA Agent), Marilyn Sokol (Doris).

Mick Dundee is living with Sue Charlton in her New York apartment; meanwhile, in Colombia, Sue's ex-boyfriend, Richard Mason, is murdered by drug-dealers after mailing her vital evidence. Sue is kidnapped by Rico, but Mick rescues her from his fortified HQ, and takes off with her to Australia with Rico and some of his men in hot pursuit. In the remote north of the country, Rico and his gang catch up with Mick and Sue, but good triumphs.

CROSSTALK (page 255)

p.c.: Wall to Wall P/L, in ass. with NSW Film Corp. **ex.p.**: Ross Matthews. **p**: Errol Sullivan. **d**: Mark Egerton. **sc**: Linda Lane, Mark Egerton, Dennis Whitburn. **ph**: Vincent Monton. **ed**: Colin Waddy. **m**: Chris Neal. **p.d.**: Larry Eastwood. **sd**: John Phillips. **p.m.**: Julie Monton. **a.d.**: Steve Andrews. Panavision. Eastmancolour. 81 mins. Aust dist: Greater Union. 1982.

Gary Day (Ed Ballinger), Penny Downie (Cindy), Brian McDermott (Whitehead), Peter Collingwood (Hollister), Kim Deacon (Jane), Jill Forster (Mrs Stollier), John Ewart (Stollier), Judith Woodruffe (Clair).

At computer expert Ed Ballinger's country home, things are going wrong: eggs fail to boil, toast burns. Ed is involved in a car accident which results in his confinement to a wheelchair in his plush city apartment which houses the advanced computer he has invented. Ed is visited regularly by girlfriend Cindy and nurse Jane. But he suspects that his upstairs neighbour, Stollier, may have murdered his wife; when he sends Jane to investigate, she is beheaded. Eventually, Ed discovers that Stollier is in league with sinister forces trying to gain control of the computer. When two killers gain access to the apartment, the computer manages to vanquish them.

DAISY AND SIMON
(Alternative title: *Where The Outback Ends*) (page 91)

p.c.: Executive Producers Ltd, Falcon Films, Barron Films. **ex.p.**: Charles E. Wolnizer. **p**: Pamela Borain, Paul Barron. **d**: Stasch Radwanski Jr. **sc**: Anthony Wheeler. **ph**: John McLean. **ed**: Mark Norfolk. **m**: Andrew Hagan, Morton Wilson. **p.d.**: Kelvin Sexton. **sd**: Les McKenzie. **p.d.**: Bill Hughes. **a.d.**: Steve Jodrell. Colour. 106 mins. Aust dist: Hoyts. 1988.

Jan Adele (Daisy), Sean Scully (Simon), Colin McEwan (Vince), Loith Taylor (Susie), Shaunna O'Grady (Joan), Tony Wager (Cuthbert).

Simon, a Perth accountant, drives into the outback and, when his car breaks down, meets Daisy, an elderly woman who lives in filthy conditions in a shack. Suspicious at first, Daisy eventually softens towards the stranger, who stays on, does odd jobs, and helps her clean up the place and herself. Daisy's snobbish daughter correctly suspects Simon is an embezzler on the run, but when Daisy is taken ill, it is Simon who helps her fulfil her last wish—to see the Perth beach where, forty years before, she had spent her honeymoon.

DANGEROUS GAME (page 244)

p.c.: Quantum Films, Virgo Productions. **ex.p**: Robert Mercieca. **p**: Judith West, Basil Appleby. **d**: Stephen Hopkins. **sc**: Peter West. **ph**: Peter Levy. **ed**: Tim Wellburn. **m**: Les Gock, Steve Ball. **p.d.**: Igor Nay. **sd**: Philip Keros. **p.m.**: Cathy Flannery. **a.d.**: Keith Heygate. Colour. 102 mins. 1988.

Miles Buchanan (David Forrest), Marcus Graham (Jack Hayward), Steven Grives (Patrick Murphy), Sandie Lillingston (Ziggy), Kathryn Walker (Kathryn), John Polson (Tony).

Murphy, a psychotic cop, terrorises teenager Jack Hayward (because he believes Hayward's dead father, once his superior, was responsible for his demotion in the force). Murphy tracks Hayward and four friends to a large department store, which they have broken into to test a security computer system, and accidentally kills one of them. He then determines to finish off the other four . . .

A DANGEROUS SUMMER (page 275)

p.c.: Filmco Ltd, McElroy & McElroy. **p**: James McElroy. **d**: Quentin Masters. **sc**: David Ambrose, Quentin Masters (based on the novel by Kit Denton). **ph**: Peter Hannan. **ed**: Ted Otten. **m**: Groove Myers. **p.d.**: Bob Hilditch. **sd**: Don Connolly. **p.m.**: Peter Appleton, Greg Ricketson. **a.d.**: Michael McKeag. Panavision. Colour. 88 mins. Aust dist: Roadshow (unreleased). 1982.

Tom Skerritt (Howard Anderson), Ian Gilmour (Steve Adams), James Mason (George Engles), Wendy Hughes (Sophie McCann), Ray Barrett (Webster), Guy Doleman (Julian Fane), Kim Deacon (Maggie Anderson), Shane Porteous (Sgt Goodwin), Norman Kaye (Percy Farley), Martin Harris (Curly Chester).

In the Blue Mountains, architect Howard Anderson and his partner, Julian Fane, are planning a tourist resort, but Fane is out to double-cross Anderson with an insurance fraud.

Insurance investigator Sophie McCann catches on, but is murdered while surfing. George Engels arrives from Lloyds. Meanwhile, Anderson's daughter Maggie is having an affair with unstable Steve Adams who turns out to be hired by Fane to destroy the project. Adams causes a massive bushfire, and perishes in the ensuing conflagration.

DARK AGE (page 302)

p.c.: RKO Pictures, FGH. **ex.p.**: Antony I. Ginnane. **p**: Basil Appleby. **d**: Arch Nicholson. **sc**: Sonia Borg (based on *Numunwari* by Grahame Webb). **ph**: Andrew Lesnie. **ed, 2nd unit d**: Adrian Carr. **m**: Danny Beckerman. **p.d.**: David Copping. **sd**: Garry Wilkins. **p.m.**: Renate Wilson. **a.d.**: Barry Hall. Panavision. Eastmancolour. 91 mins. 1987.

John Jarratt (Steve), Nikki Coghill (Cathy), Max Phipps (John), Burnam Burnam (Oondabund), David Gulpilil (Adjaral), Ray Meagher (Rex), Jeff Ashby (Mac), Paul Bertram (Jackson).

Steve, a wildlife ranger based in the Northern Territory, is trying to save crocodiles from hunters. John, an unscrupulous hunter, has lost an arm (and two companions) to a giant croc, and vows to kill the reptile. Steve, encouraged by the return of his girl Cathy, who had earlier left him, and by the advice of a wise Aboriginal, Oondabund, who believes the giant croc has the soul of a man, decides to try to capture the animal and relocate it in safe breeding grounds. Helped by another Aboriginal, Adjaral, they manage to capture the beast, but are surprised by John, who kills Oondabund before being killed himself by the croc.

THE DARK ROOM (page 157)

p.c.: Filmco, Nadira, Artis Films. **p**: Tom Haydon. **d**: Paul Harmon. **sc**: Michael Brindley, Paul Harmon. **ph**: Paul Onorato. **ed**: Rod Adamson. **m**: Cameron Allan. **p.d.**: Richard Kent. **sd**: Ken Hammond. **p.m.**: Michael McKeag. **a.d.**: David Bracknell. Eastmancolour. 95 mins. 1982.

Alan Cassell (Dr Ray Sangster), Anna Jemison (Nicky), Svet Kovich (Michael Sangster), Diana Davidson (Martha Sangster), Rowena Wallace (Liz Llewellyn), Oriana Panozzo (Susan Bitel), Ric Hutton (Sam Bitel), Hayes Gordon (Himself).

Michael Sangster, a highly-strung arts student, discovers his doctor father is having a secret love affair with Nicky, a beautiful dress designer. He follows them obsessively, and photographs them making love through their bedroom window. He contrives to meet Nicky without telling her who he is, but when a chance to make love to her is offered, he proves to be impotent.

Now completely deranged, he kidnaps Nicky and takes her to his father's country house, setting fire to the place. Nicky escapes, but Michael dies in the blaze.

DAY OF THE PANTHER

p.c.: Virgo Productions, TVM Studios, in ass. with The Mandemar Group. **ex.p.**: Judith West, Grahame Jennings. **p**: Damien Parer. **d**: Brian Trenchard Smith. **sc**: Peter West; additional dialogue, Brian Trenchard Smith. **ph**: Simon Akkerman. **ed**: David Jaeger, Kerry Regan. **m**: Gary Hardman, Brian Beamish. **sd**: David Glasser. **p.m.**: Deb Copland. **a.d., 2nd unit d**: Stuart Wood. Colour. 84 mins. Direct to video release. 1988.

Edward John Stazak (Jason Blade), John Stanton (William Anderson), Jim Richards (Jim Baxter), Paris Jefferson (Gemma Anderson), Michael Carman (Damien Zukor), Zale Daniel (Colin), Linda Megier (Linda Anderson).

Hong Kong. Jason Blade is trained in martial arts by The Panthers, a Chinese society, and wings to Perth on a secret mission against drug-lord Damien Zukor. His assistant, Linda, is quickly killed by Zukor's men, and Blade teams up with her cousin, Gemma, finally meeting Zukor's henchman, Jim Baxter, in one-on-one conflict.

DEAD CALM (page 263)

p.c.: Kennedy–Miller. **p**: George Miller (1), Terry Hayes, Doug Mitchell. **d**: Phillip Noyce. **sc**: Terry Hayes (from the novel by Charles Williams). **ph**: Dean Semler. **ed**: Richard Francis-Bruce. **m**: Graeme Revill. **p.d.**: Graham (Grace) Walker. **sd**: Ben Osmo. **2nd unit d**: George Miller (1), Vincent Monton. **p.m.**: Narelle Barsby, Barbara Gibbs. **a.d.**: Colin Fletcher, Tony Wellington. Panavision. Eastmancolour. 96 mins. World-wide dist: Warner Bros. 1988.

1989 Australian Film Awards: Best photography, editing, music, sound.

Sam Neill (John Ingram), Nicole Kidman (Rae Ingram), Billy Zane (Hughie).

Recovering from the death, in a car accident, of their baby, naval officer John Ingram and his young wife Rae are sailing the Pacific north-east of Australia on their yacht when they see another yacht, apparently in distress. They take on board Hughie, a young American, who tells them that everyone else on the cruise yacht died of food poisoning. While Hughie sleeps, John goes to investigate and finds dead bodies and a video suggesting Hughie went berserk. Meanwhile, Hughie awakens, overpowers Rae, and sets sail in the opposite direction. Forced to submit to Hughie's sexual advances in order to seize the advantage, Rae finally manages to turn the yacht around, while John, trapped below decks on the other boat, has managed to force his way out. Hughie falls overboard, but returns to threaten Rae and is killed by John with a flare gun.

DEAD EASY (page 252)

p.d.: Firebird Films. **p**: John Weiley. **d**: Bert Deling. **sc**: Bert Deling, Danny Sankey. **ph**: Michael Molloy, Tom Cowan. **ed**: John Scott. **m**: William Motzing. **p.d.**: Jon Dowding. **sd**: Peter Barker. **p.m.**: Greg Ricketson. **a.d.**: Tony Wellington. Eastmancolour. 92 mins. 1982.

Scott Burgess (George), Rosemary Paul (Alex), Tim McKenzie (Armstrong), Max Phipps (Francis), Joe Martin (Sol), Jack O'Leary (Morry), Barney Combes (Jack), Tony Barry (Lou), Bobby Noble (Lou), David Bracks (Arnoe), Sandy Gore (Frieda), Rosemary Butcher (Jenny).

George is an ambitious young man hired to front a nightclub owned by Sol, the Mr Big of Sydney's Jewish mafia. George falls in love with Alex, a heroin-addicted prostitute, and gets caught in the crossfire between Sol's gang and that of rival gang-leader, Ozzie. George's only ally is Armstrong, an honest cop. After a violent car chase, the lives of George and Alex are only saved by the intervention of Sol's long-time friend and chauffeur, who drives his master over a cliff.

DEAD END DRIVE-IN (page 286)

p.c.: Springvale Productions, in ass. with NSW Film Corp. **p**: Andrew Williams. **d**: Brian Trenchard Smith. **sc**: Peter Smalley (from the short story *Crabs*, by Peter Carey). **ph**: Paul Murphy. **ed**: Lee Smith. **m**: Frank Strangio. **p.d.**: Larry Eastwood. **sd**: Leo Sullivan. **a.d.**: Adrian Pickersgill. **stunts**: Guy Norris. Eastmancolour. 90 mins. Aust dist: Greater Union. US dist: New World. 1986.

Ned Manning (Crabs), Natalie McCurry (Carmen), Peter Whitford (Thompson), Wilbur Wilde (Hazza), Brett Climo (Don), Ollie Hall, Sandy Lillingstone, Lyn Collingwood, Nikki McWaters, Melissa Davis.

The 1990s. The authorities have started herding unemployed youngsters into makeshift prison camps. Crabs borrows his brother's '56 Chevy to take his girl, Carmen, to the Star drive-in, unaware it is a prison camp. Once in, Crabs and Carmen cannot get out. Carmen accepts her fate, but Crabs refuses to conform and, despite the warnings of camp manager Thompson, makes a spectacular break-out.

DEAR CARDHOLDER (page 318)

p.c.: Mermaid Beach, in ass. with Multifilms. **p, d, sc**: Bill Bennett. **ph**: Tony Wilson. **ed**: Denise Hunter. **m**: Michael Atkinson. **sd**: Danny Cooper. **p.m.**: Debbie Samuels. **a.d.**: Philip Rich. **a.p.**: Jenny Day. Colour. 90 mins. Direct to video release. 1987.

Robin Ramsay (Hec Harris), Jennifer Cluff (Aggie Smith), Marion Chirgwin (Jo Harris), Russell Newman (Afred Block), John Ewart (Hart), Patrick Cook (Ardent), Bob Ellis (Terence), Arianthe Galani (Antoinette).

Hec Harris, a widower, lives with his 12-year-old daughter Jo, and works as a clerk in a tax office. He decides to buy a computer on credit, and runs up a series of credit card debts, acquiring new cards to pay off the debts accrued on the old ones. He also falls in love with Aggie, a struggling chicken farmer. Eventually, his debts catch up with him: he loses his job and his apartment, and Jo is placed in a foster home. In the end, however, he is offered a good job with a large computer company.

DEATH OF A SOLDIER (page 44)

p.c.: Suatu Film Management. **ex.p.**: Oscar Scherl, Richard Tanner. **p**: David Hannay, William Nagle. **d**: Philippe Mora. **sc**: William Nagle. **ph**: Louis Irving. **ed**: John Scott. **m**: Alan Zavod. **p.d.**: Geoff Richardson. **cost**: Alexandra Tynan. **co-p**: Lance Reynolds. **p.m.**: David Clarke. **a.d.**: Brian Giddens. Panavision. Eastmancolour. 96 mins. Aust dist: Open Eye. US dist: Scotti Bros. UK dist: Vestron. 1985.

James Coburn (Maj. Patrick Dannenberg), Reb Brown (Edward J. Leonski), Bill Hunter (Det.-Sgt Adams), Maurie Fields (Det.-Sgt Martin), Belinda Davey (Margot Saunders), Max Fairchild (Maj. William Fricks), Jon Sidney (Gen. Mac-Arthur), Michael Pate (Maj.-Gen. Sutherland), Randall Berger (Gallo), Nell Johnson (Maisie), John McTiernan (Col. Williams), Frank Thring (Preacher), Terence Donovan (John Curtin).

Melbourne, May 1942. 48,000 US soldiers, under the command of General MacArthur, arrive in the city, and there are occasional violent confrontations between the Americans and Australian soldiers. Several women are found murdered, and US liaison officer Major Dannenberg joins forces with local police officers Adams and Martin when a GI is the suspect. The killer is actually Edward Leonski, a gentle giant who confesses his crimes to his friend, Gallo, who reports him to the authorities. Dannenberg, believing Leonski to be insane, assists his defence, but Leonski is found guilty by an American military court, and executed.

THE DELINQUENTS (page 350)

p.c.: Delinquents P/L. **ex.p.**: Greg Coote, John Tarnoff, Graham Burke. **p**: Alex Cutler, Michael

Wilcox. **d**: Chris Thomson. **sc**: Mac Gudgeon, Clayton Frohman (from the novel by Criena Rohan). **ph**: Andrew Lesnie. **ed**: John Scott. **m**: Miles Goodman. **p.d.**: Laurence Eastwood. **sd**: Paul Brincat. **line p**: Irene Dobson. **p.m.**: Rosslyn Abernathy. **a.d.**: Colin Fletcher. Agfacolor. 101 mins. Aust dist: Greater Union. 1989.

Kylie Minogue (Lola), Charlie Schlatter (Brownie), Desiree Smith (Mavis), Todd Boyce (Lyle), Angela Punch McGregor (Mrs Lovell), Lynette Curran (Mrs Hansen), Melissa Jaffer (Aunt Westbury), Bruno Lawrence (Bosun).

The 1950s. Lola and Brownie, two teenagers from Bundaberg, fall in love. Lola gets pregnant and they plan to elope together, but are separated by her alcoholic mother and she is forced into an abortion. Brownie goes to sea, finds Lola in a Melbourne bar, and they live together until she is arrested and, eventually, placed in a home. When their friend Mavis dies in childbirth, Lola (now released) and Brownie take care of the child.

DEPARTURE (page 193)

p.c.: Cineast Prods, Rychemond Film. **ex.p.**: William Oswald. **p**: Christine Suli, Brian Kavanagh. **d**: Brian Kavanagh. **sc**: Michael Gurr (based on his play, *A Pair Of Claws*). **ph**: Bob Kohler. **ed**: Ken Sallows. **m**: Bruce Smeaton. **p.d.**: Paddy Reardon. **sd**: John Rowley. **p.m.**: Damian Brown. **a.d.**: Ross Hamilton. Eastmancolour. 93 mins. 1986.

Patricia Kennedy (Sylvia Swift), Michael Duffield (Presley Swift), June Jago (Frances), Serge Lazareff (Simon Swift), Sean Scully (Alex Rowan), Jon Sidney (Joseph).

Presley Swift, a retired diplomat living in Hobart with his domineering wife Sylvia, is about to leave on a trip to Rome. The couple spend their last weekend in Tasmania with their son Simon, an aspiring Labor Party politician. Then an old scandal surfaces, involving Presley and a young girl (who died). Scared of the effect that it will have on his own political future, Simon betrays his father.

DESOLATION ANGELS (page 289)

p.c.: Winternight Productions. **p**: Chris Oliver. **d**: Christopher Fitchett. **sc**: Ellery Ryan, Christopher Fitchett. **ph**: Ellery Ryan. **ed**: Tony Stephens. **m**: Mark McSherry. **p.d.**: Josephine Ford. **sd**: Laurie Robinson. **p.m.**: Miranda Bain. **a.d.**: Tony MacDonald. Colour. 88 mins. 1982.

Kim Trengove (Jilly), Kerry Mack (Joanna), Marie O'Loughlin (Liz), Karen West (Pamela Wilkinson), Monica Maughan (Liz's mother), Jay Mannering, Nick Forster, Nick Lathouris, Niel Schneider, Paul Alexander, Louise Howitt.

Three Melbourne schoolgirls, Jilly, Joanna and Liz, go off for a weekend together, staying in a 'borrowed' weekender in Portsea. Along the way, they are harassed by louts in two black panelvans. When they arrive at their destination, the louts are there too, and the 'game' gets nasty. Meanwhile Pamela, a con-artist who has stolen her partner's loot, arrives in the next-door house with her vengeful partner in pursuit . . .

DEVIL IN THE FLESH (page 183)

p.c.: J. C. Williamson Film Management, World Film Alliance. **ex.p.**: Peter Collins. **p**: John B. Murray. **d, sc**: Scott Murray (based on the novel *Le Diable au Corps*, by Raymond Radiguet). **ph**: Andrew De Groot. **ed**: Tim Lewis. **m**: Philippe Sarde. **p.d.**: Paddy Reardon. **sd**: Laurie Robinson. **p.m.**: John Hipwell. **a.d., line p.**: Tom Burstall. Eastmancolour. 103 mins. Aust dist: Hoyts/ Premium. 1985.

Katia Caballero (Marthe), Keith Smith (Paul Hansen), John Morris (John Hansen), Jill Forster (Jill Hansen), Colin Duckworth (Pierre Fournier), Reine Lavoie (Madeleine Fournier), Luciano Martucci (Ermanno), Louise Elvin (Blonde model), Jeremy Johnson (Simon Greene), Odile Le Clezio (Simone), Peter Cummins (Disciplinarian Brother).

1943. Paul Hansen, a shy schoolboy, lives with his parents in a small Victorian country town. He meets Marthe, a Frenchwoman whose Italian husband has been interned for the duration of the war. Marthe, an artist, befriends the boy and they become lovers; she eventually becomes pregnant. But the war ends, the husband is freed and Marthe returns to him. Some time later, Paul sees Marthe—and his child.

DOCTORS AND NURSES (page 344)

p.c.: Universal Entertainment Corp. **p**: Brian Rosen. **d**: Maurice Murphy. **sc**: Morris Gleitzman, Doug Edwards, Robyn Moase, Tony Sheldon, Maurice Murphy. **ph**: John Seale. **ed**: Greg Ropert. **m**: Mike Harvey. **p.d.**: Bob Hill. **sd**: Tim Lloyd. **a.d.**: Charles Rotherham. Eastmancolour. 89 mins. Aust dist: Classic Films. 1981.

Rebecca Rigg (Dr Mercia King), Miguel Lopez (Dr Juan Peron), Jeremy Larsson (Sir Rupert Young), Joshua Samuels (Dr Bud Abel), Brent Gowland (Dr Bernard Christian), Mary Anne Davidson (Dr Isabel Gold), Sarah Lambert (Sister Mary Gray), Bert Newton (Kenneth Cody), Pamela Stephenson (Permanent Wave), June Salter (Lady Clicquot), Andrew McFarlane (Milligan), Graeme Blundell (Mister X), Drew Forsythe (Rupert Katz), Richard Meikle (President of the U.S.).

The setting is a hospital in which the patients include derelict Ken Cody, rock star Permanent

Wave, amnesiac Mister X and the US President. The doctors and nurses (played by children) have their own personal problems.

DOGS IN SPACE (page 142)

p.c. Entertainment Media, Burrowes Film Group, Central Park Films. **ex.p.**: Robert Le Tet, Dennis Wright. **p**: Glenys Rowe. **d**, **sc**: Richard Lowenstein. **ph**: Andrew De Groot. **ed**: Jill Bilcock. **m**: Ollie Olsen. **p.d.**: Jody Borland. **sd**: Dean Gawen. **p.m.**: Lynda House. **a.d.**: Ross Hamilton. Scope. Colour. 105 mins. Aust dist: Hoyts, Ronin. UK dist: Recorded Releasing. US dist: Skouras. 1986.

Michael Hutchence (Sam), Saskia Post (Anna), Nique Needles (Tim), Deanna Bond (The Girl), Tony Helou (Luchio), Chris Haywood (Chainsaw man), Peter Walsh (Anthony), Laura Swanson (Clare), Adam Briscomb (Grant), Sharon Jessop (Leanne), Gary Foley (Barry), Fiona Latham (Barbara).

1978. Inner-suburban Melbourne. Sam, Anna, Tim, Luchio and others share a terrace house and an interest in music, though Luchio is a student trying (rather vainly) to study. People come and go at all times of the day and night, and drugs are freely available. A teenage girl from the country arrives and simply moves in. Anna, who has vague plans to become an air-hostess, is in love with the unpredictable Sam and it is to please him that she eventually takes the drug overdose that kills her.

DOUBLE DEAL (page 90)

p.c.: Filmco, Pact Productions, Rychemond Films. **p**: Brian Kavanagh, Lynn Barker. **d**, **sc**: Brian Kavanagh. **ph**: Ross Berryman. **ed**: Tim Lewis. **m**: Bruce Smeaton. **p.d.**: Jill Eden. **sd**: John Phillips. **p.m.**: John Chase. **a.p.**: Carlie Deans. Panavision. Colour. 89 mins. US dist: Samuel Goldwyn. 1981.

Louis Jourdan (Peter Stirling), Angela Punch McGregor (Christine Stirling), Diane Craig (June Stevens), Warwick Comber (Young man), Peter Cummins (Det. Mills), Bruce Spence (Doug Mitchell), June Jago (Mrs Coolidge), Kerry Walker (Sibyl Anderson).

Wealthy businessman Peter Stirling has been married for four years to a beautiful model, Christina. One day, a macho bikie breaks into the Stirling home, romances Christina, and rides off with her on a crime spree which turns into a kidnap drama when the (unnamed) bikie demands as ransom a valuable jewel. But it transpires that Peter was in league with June, his devoted secretary, to get rid of Christine, since he no longer loves her, and that June, in

turn, hates Peter for spurning her to marry Christine in the first place, and is planning a double-double-cross.

THE DREAMING (page 296)

p.c.: FGH, International Film Management, Genesis Film. **ex.p.**: Antony I. Ginnane. **p**: Craig Lahiff, Wayne Groom. **d**: Mario Andreacchio. **sc**: Rob George, Stephanie McCarthy, John Emery (from a story by Lahiff and Groom). **ph**: David Foreman. **ed**: Suresh Ayyar. **m**: Frank Strangio. **p.d.**: Michael Ralph. **sd**: Rob Cutcher. **p.m.**: Ron Stigwood. **a.d.**: Gus Howard. Colour. 88 mins. Aust dist: Filmpac (direct to video release). 1988.

Arthur Dignam (Prof. Bernard Thornton), Penny Cook (Dr Cathy Thornton), Gary Sweet (Geoff Douglas), Laurence Clifford (Najira), Kristina Nehm (Warindji).

Prof. Thornton discovers an ancient Aboriginal artefact in a cave and places it in an Adelaide museum. Warindji, a young Aboriginal woman, breaks into the museum to steal the treasure, and is mortally wounded. Thornton's daughter Cathy, a doctor, treats the dying woman and then starts seeing visions of a massacre of Aborigines by whalers 200 years earlier; in her dreams, the leader of the whalers looks like her father. She visits the site of the massacre, followed by her father who turns into the ancient whaler and attacks her . . .

DUET FOR FOUR (page 116)

p.c.: Burstall Associates, in ass. with Victorian Film Corp. **p**: Tom and Tim Burstall. **d**: Tim Burstall. **sc**: David Williamson. **ph**: Dan Burstall. **ed**: Edward McQueen-Mason. **m**: Peter Sullivan. **p.d.**: Herbert Pinter. **sd**: Phil Stirling. **p.m.**: Helen Liston. **a.d.**: James Parker. Panavision. Eastman-colour. 96 mins. Aust dist: Greater Union. 1981.

Mike Preston (Ray Martin), Wendy Hughes (Barbara Dunstan), Michael Pate (Al Giesman), Diane Cilento (Margot Martin), Gary Day (Terry Byrne), Vanessa Leigh (Dianne Byrne), Sigrid Thorton (Carolina Martin), Arthur Dignam (Doug Quincey), Rod Mullinar (Ken Overlord), Warwick Comber (Cliff Ingersoll), Claire Binney (Jacki Nesbitt).

Ray Martin, a 48-year-old toy manufacturer in partnership with Terry Byrne, is separated from his first wife, Margot, and lives with Barbara, who has three small children of her own; Margot, meanwhile, lives with Cliff, a much younger sculptor. Ray and Terry are trying to obtain exclusive Australian rights to a line of American toys whose representative, Giesman, on a quick visit to Melbourne, is Australian-born. The deal is jeopardised when Ray's secretary, Jacki, refuses

Giesman's sexual advances. Meanwhile Caroline, Ray's daughter by Margot, has an abortion and Ray makes a play for his partner's wife, Dianne, which adds to the tension all round.

DUSTY (page 73)
p.c.: Kestrel Films, in ass. with Film Victoria. **p**: Gil Brealey. **d**: John Richardson. **sc**: Sonia Borg (from the novel by Frank Dalby Davison). **ph**: Alex McPhell. **ed**: David Greig. **m**: Frank Strangio. **p.d.**: Ivana Perkins. **sd**: John Phillips. **p.m.**: Mark Ruse. **a.d.**: Colin Fletcher. Eastmancolour. 88 mins. Aust dist: Filmways. 1982.

Bill Kerr (Tom), Noel Trevarthen (Harry), Carol Burns (Clara), John Stanton (Railey Jordon), Nick Holland (Jack).

Tom, an old station hand, buys Dusty as a pup, believing him to be pure kelpie: actually, he is half-dingo. Tom trains Dusty successfully, until the dog starts killing sheep, and the old man quarrels with his boss, Harry, as a result. Man and dog head off, followed by dingo-hunter Railey Jordan, who spares Dusty once they reach cattle country. Old Tom is taken ill and Dusty goes for help—too late. The old man dies, and Dusty heads for the wild.

EARLY FROST (page 272)
p.c.: Filmco, David Hannay Productions. **ex.p**: John Fitzpatrick. **p**: David Hannay, Geoff Brown. **d**: Brian McDuffie. **sc**: Terry O'Connor. **ph**: David Eggby. **ed**: Tim Street. **m**: Mike Harvey. **p.d.**: Bob Hilditch. **sd**: Mark Lewis. **p.m.**: Julia Overton. **a.d.**: Stuart Freeman. Eastmancolour. 90 mins. 1981.

Diana McLean (Val Meadows), Jon Blake (Peter Meadows), Jan Kingsbury (Peg Prentice), David Franklin (David Prentice), Daniel Cumerford (Joey Meadows), Guy Doleman (Mike Hayes), Joanne Samuel (Chris), Kit Taylor (Paul Sloane).

Blacktown. Val's husband was drowned some years ago trying to save their youngest son; she lives with her other son, Peter. A series of murders is taking place in the area, and David, son of Val's friend Peg, is keeping a scrapbook on the crimes which include the decapitation of Val's lover. Hayes, a detective, dies when his car explodes. Eventually, the killer's identity is revealed.

ECHOES OF PARADISE
(Alternative title: *Shadows of the Peacock*) (page 112)
p.c.: Laughing Kookaburra Production, in ass. with Australian European Finance Corp. **ex.p**: Jan Sharp. **p**: Jane Scott. **d**: Phillip Noyce. **sc**: Jan Sharp (add. material: Anne Brooksbank). **ph**:

Peter James. **ed**: Frans Vandenburg. **m**: William Motzing. **p.d.**: Judith Russell. **sd**: Tim Lloyd. **cost**: Clarissa Patterson. **p.m.**: Antonia Barnard. **a.d.**: Chris Webb. Colour. 90 mins. Aust dist: Roadshow. US dist: Quartet Films. 1987.

Wendy Hughes (Maria McEvoy), John Lone (Raka), Steven Jacobs (George McEvoy), Peta Toppano (Judy), Rod Mullinar (Terry), Gillian Jones (Mitty), Claudia Karvan (Julia McEvoy), Rebecca Smart (Tessa), Matthew Taylor (Simon), Vithawat Bunnag (Sali), Prasert (Kasem), Lynda Stoner (Beth Mason), Ray Harding (Paul Mason).

Maria, married to philandering lawyer George McEvoy, is distressed at the death of her father. She impulsively decides to join her friend, Judy, on a holiday at a beach resort in Thailand, run by a fellow Australian, Terry. There she meets Raka, a dancer and refugee from his native Bali, and a passionate love affair ensues. The holiday over, Maria reluctantly returns to Sydney.

EMERALD CITY (page 192)
p.c.: Limelight Productions, in ass. with NSW Film Corp. **p**: Joan Long. **d**: Michael Jenkins. **sc**: David Williamson (based on his play). **ph**: Paul Murphy. **ed**: Neil Thumpston. **m**: Chris Neal. **p.d.**: Owen Williams. **sd**: Ben Osmo. **p.m.**: Brenda Pam. **a.d.**: Chris Webb. Eastmancolour. 93 mins. Aust dist: Greater Union. 1988.

John Hargreaves (Colin Rogers), Robyn Nevin (Kate Rogers), Chris Haywood (Mike McCord), Nicole Kidman (Helen Davey), Ruth Cracknell (Elaine Ross), Dennis Miller (Malcolm Bennett), Ella Scott (Penny Rogers), Hayden Samuels (Sam Rogers), Michelle Torres (Kath Mitchell).

Colin Rogers, a successful Melbourne writer, moves to Sydney with his wife, Kate, and children. When producer Elaine Ross shows a lack of interest in his latest screenplay, he teams up with hustler Mike McCord to make a TV film, which fails in the ratings. Meanwhile, Kate, who works for a publisher, is able to have a radical tome by an Aboriginal woman published only through McCord's intervention; later, McCord buys the film rights to the book, intending to sell it to an American producer. Colin is attracted to Helen, Mike's mistress, but fails to follow through and, on a London trip, Kate has an affair with her boss.

EMMA'S WAR (page 366)
p.c.: Belinon Productions. **ex.p**: Robin Dalton. **p**: Clytie Jessop, Andrena Finlay. **d**: Clytie Jessop. **sc**: Clytie Jessop, Peter Smalley. **ph**: Tom Cowan. **ed**: Sonia Hofmann. **m**: John Williams. **p.d.**: Jane Norris. **sd**: Ross McKay. **p.m., a.p.**: David Hannay. **a.d.**: Mick Coleman. Colour. 94 mins. Self-distrib.

in Australia. UK dist: Curzon. 1985.

Lee Remick (Anne Grange), Miranda Otto (Emma Grange), Mark Lee (John Davidson), Terence Donovan (Frank Grange), Donal Gibson (Hank), Bridey Lee (Laurel), Pat Evison (Miss Arnott), Grigor Taylor (Dr Friedlander), Noeline Brown (Mrs Mortimer), Rebel Russell (Miss Gunz), Ashley Grenville (Brian).

1942. Fourteen-year-old Emma Grange is at a Sydney boarding school; her father, Frank, is in New Guinea and her American mother, Anne, is a lonely alcoholic. When she nearly succumbs to the advances of an American sailor, Anne removes Emma, and her other daughter, Laurel, from school and takes them to the country. Emma stumbles upon John Davidson, a conscientious objector hiding out in the bush; later, he is taken away by police. Frank returns home, an amputee, and Emma joins the crowds in Martin Place celebrating the end of the war.

EMOH RUO (page 311)

p.c.: Palm Beach Pictures, in ass. with UAA Films. **ex.p.**: David Thomas, John Picton-Warlow. **p**: David Elfick. **d**: Denny Lawrence. **sc**: David Poltorak, Paul Leadon. **ph**: Andrew Lesnie. **ed**: Ted Otton. **m**: Cameron Allen. **p.d.**: Robert Dein. **sd**: Paul Brincat. **a.p.**: Steve Knapman. **p.m.**: Catherine Phillips Knapman. **a.d.**: Michael Falloon. Eastmancolour. 93 mins. Aust dist: Greater Union. 1985.

Joy Smithers (Terri Tunkley), Martin Sacks (Des Tunkley), Philip Quast (Les Tunkley), Genevieve Mooy (Margaret York), Louise Le Nay (Helen Tunkley), Max Phipps (Samson Tregardo), Jack Ellis (Jack Tunkley).

Terri and Des Tunkley live with their small son Jack in a caravan by the sea. Terri yearns for a proper home and, with help from a building society, the Tunkleys move far out into the western suburbs into a new house, which quickly proves to be jerry-built. When Des, a bus driver, loses his licence, things get even tougher; the family's only neighbours are nosy bigots, and the final straw comes when the house totally collapses.

THE EMPTY BEACH (page 232)

p.c.: Jethro Films. **ex.p.**: Bob Weis. **p**: Timothy Read, John Edwards. **d**: Chris Thomson. **sc**: Keith Dewhurst (from the book by Peter Corris). **ph**: John Seale. **ed**: Lindsay Frazer. **m**: Martin Armiger, Red Symonds. **p.d.**: Laurence Eastwood. **sd**: Max Hensser. **p.m.**: Adrienne Read. **a.d.**: Colin Fletcher. Eastmancolour. 89 mins. Aust dist: Hoyts. 1985.

Bryan Brown (Cliff Hardy), Anna-Maria Monticelli (Anne Winter), Ray Barrett (MacLeary),

John Wood (Parker), Nick Tate (Brian Henneberry), Belinda Giblin (Marion Singer), Peter Collingwood (Fred Ward), Kerry Mack (Hildegard), Sally Cooper (Sandy Modesta), Joss McWilliam (Tal), Steve J. Spears (Manny).

Marion Singer employs private detective Cliff Hardy to investigate the disappearance of her rich husband, supposedly drowned two years earlier. The trail leads to investigative journalist Brian Henneberry, who is murdered, but who has apparently left incriminating tapes behind. Henneberry's girlfriend, Anne Winter, becomes Hardy's ally, and suspects include the missing man's drug-addicted mistress, Sandy; MacLeary, a powerful criminal with a liking for young girls; and the urbane Ward. One trail leads Hardy to a racket to defraud the government of pension cheques, but rival criminals eventually confront each other in a shoot-out on Bondi Beach.

THE EVERLASTING SECRET FAMILY (page 163)

p.c.: Indian Pacific Films, FGH, International Film Management. **ex.p**: Antony I. Ginnane. **p**, **d**: Michael Thornhill. **sc**: Frank Moorhouse (based on his book of short stories, *The Everlasting Secret Family and Other Secrets*). **ph**: Julian Penney. **ed**: Pam Barnetta. **m**: Tony Bremner. **p.d.**: Peta Lawson. **co-p**: Sue Carleton. **p.m.**: Elizabeth Symes. **a.d.**: Keith Heygate. Panavision. Eastmancolour. 94 mins. Aust dist: Filmpac. UK dist: Cannon. 1987.

Arthur Dignam (Senator), Mark Lee (Youth), Heather Mitchell (Senator's wife), Dennis Miller (Eric), Paul Goddard (Son), Beth Child (Pottery woman), John Clayton (Mayor), Nick Holland (New chauffeur), Bogdan Koca (Medical Specialist), John Meillon (Judge), Anna Volska (Wife's friend), Allan Penney (Gardener), Louis Nowra (Shop assistant).

A handsome youth is selected by a Senator from a private boys' school, and initiated into homosexual activity. The youth becomes devoted to the Senator, while realising he has replaced Eric, now the Senator's chauffeur. Realising that marriage will further his career, the Senator marries; the youth visits a doctor specialising in rejuvenation. Years pass, and the youth becomes companion to the Senator's son, who is in turn initiated in the secret fraternity of homosexuals (which includes a prominent judge). The youth and the son become lovers.

EVIL ANGELS

(International title: *A Cry In the Dark*)
(page 59)

p.c.: Evil Angels Films, for Cannon Films Inc., Cannon International. **ex.p**: Menahem Golan,

Yoram Globus. **p**: Verity Lambert. **d**: Fred Schepisi. **sc**: Robert Caswell, Fred Schepisi (based on the book by John Bryson). **ph**: Ian Baker. **ed**: Jill Bilock. **m**: Bruce Smeaton. **p.d.**: Wendy Dickson, George Liddle. **sd**: Gary Wilkins. **p.m.**: Carol Hughes. **a.d.**: Steve Andrews. **line p**: Roy Stevens. Panavision. Colour. 118 mins. Worldwide dist: Warner Bros. 1988.

1989 Australian Film Awards: Best film, director, adapted screenplay, actor (Sam Neill), actress (Meryl Streep), AFI Members Prize.

Meryl Streep (Lindy Chamberlain), Sam Neill (Michael Chamberlain), Dorothy Alison (Avis Murchison), Brian Jones (Cliff Murchison), Maurice Fields (Barritt), Charles Tingwell (Justice Muirhead), Bruce Myles (Barker), Neil Fitzpatrick (Phillips), Dennis Miller (Sturgess), Lewis Fitz-Gerald (Tipple), Brendan Higgins (Kirkham), Sandy Gore (Joy Kuhl), Kevin Miles (Prof. Cameron), Jon Finlayson (Prof. Boettcher), John Howard (Lyle Morris), Frank Holden (Leslie Thompson), Tim Robertson (Wallace), Patsy Stephen (Anne Houghton), Ian Gilmour (John Buckland), Deborra-Lee Furness (Magazine reporter), Chuck Faulkner (Conrad Grey), Nick Tate (Charlwood), Mervyn Drake (Gilroy), Vincent Gil (Roff), Mark Little (Morris), Debra Lawrance (Sally Lowe).

1980. Lindy and Michael Chamberlain, Seventh Day Adventists, are holidaying at Ayers Rock in Central Australia, with their children Aidan and Reagan and baby Azaria, ten weeks old. Lindy discovers that Azaria is missing from their tent, and claims to see a dingo with the baby in its mouth. Since the body is not found, and there have been no previous reports of dingos taking children, the incident becomes a major news story, although an inquest puts the blame on the dingo. Forensic evidence, however, suggests that the rips in the baby's blood-stained clothing were not caused by a dingo (the matinee jacket the child was wearing has not been found) and the Chamberlains are arrested. In Darwin, the pregnant Lindy is tried for murder and found guilty (although Justice Muirhead directs for an acquittal). After three and a half years in prison, Lindy is released when the matinee jacket is found at the Rock.

FAIR GAME (page 288)

p.c.: Southern Films International. **p**: Ron Saunders, Harley Manners. **d**: Mario Andreacchio. **sc**: Rob George. **ph**: Andrew Lesnie. **ed**: A. J. Prowse. **m**: Ashley Irwin. **p.d.**: Kimble Hilder. **sd**: Toivo Lember. **p.m.**: Gay Dennis. **a.d.**: Chris Williams. Eastmancolour. 85 mins. Aust dist: CEL. 1985.

Cassandra Delaney (Jessica), Peter Ford (Sunny), David Sandford (Ringo), Garry Who (Sparks).

Jessica, who lives alone on an isolated property, is terrorised by three kangaroo shooters, who try to run her off the road. Later the three, smooth Sunny and scungy Ringo and Sparks, ogle her as she lies naked on her bed in the midday heat. The trio leave a dead kangaroo in her car, then tie her, almost naked, to the front of their truck and drive wildly through the scrub. When they set about destroying her home, she retaliates and manages to kill all three.

FANTASY MAN (page 318)

p.c.: Centaur Enterprises. **p**: Basil Appleby, Darrell Lass. **d, sc**: John Meagher. **ph**: Andrew Lesnie. **ed**: Ron Hibberd. **m**: Adrian Payne. **p.d.**: Darrell Lass. **sd**: Ross Linton. Colour. 79 mins. 1984.

Harold Hopkins (Nick Bailey), Jeanie Drynan (Liz Bailey), Kerry Mack (Donna), Kate Fitzpatrick (Neighbour), John Howitt (Howard), Colin Croft (Teacher).

Office worker Nick Bailey is bored with his job and his wife Liz. He has fantasies about Donna, a girl who sells hamburgers from a street stall. He enrols in art classes, also attended by Donna, while Liz dallies with Howard, an old flame. The final solution is a move to Brisbane.

FAR EAST (page 220)

p.c.: Filmco, Alfred Road Films. **p**: Richard Mason. **d, sc**: John Duigan. **ph**: Brian Probyn. **ed**: Henry Dangar. **m**: Sharon Calcraft. **p.d.**: Ross Major. **p.m.**: Julia Overton. **a.d.**: Michael Falloon. Eastmancolour. 106 mins. Aust dist: Roadshow. 1982.

Bryan Brown (Morgan Keefe), Helen Morse (Jo Reeves), John Bell (Peter Reeves), Raina McKeon (Rosita), Henry Duval (Rudolf De Cruz), Sinan Leong (Nene), Bill Hunter (Walker), John Clayton (Alsop).

In an unnamed Asian city, French-born Jo Reeves and her husband, Peter, a journalist, come to The Koala Klub, an Australian bar, and meet its owner Morgan Keefe, an Australian who stayed on in Asia after the Vietnam War. Jo and Morgan, who had been lovers years earlier in Saigon, resume their relationship, while Peter becomes involved in local politics and is arrested. Morgan agrees to help rescue him from the headquarters of the secret police, and succeeds: but he is subsequently gunned down and killed.

FAST TALKING (page 353)

p.c.: Oldata. **p**: Ross Matthews. **d, sc**: Ken Cameron. **ph**: David Gribble. **ed**: David Huggett. **m**: Sharon Calcraft. **p.d.**: Neil Angwin. **sd**: Tim Lloyd. **p.m.**: Dixie Betts. **a.d.**: John Rooke.

Eastmancolour. 93 mins. Aust dist: Filmways. UK dist: Merchant Ivory Productions, Filmtrax. 1983.

Rod Zuanic (Steve Carson), Toni Allaylis (Vicki), Chris Truswell (Moose), Gail Sweeny (Narelle), Steve Bisley (Redback), Peter Hehir (Ralph Carson), Tracy Mann (Sharon Hart), Dennis Moore (Yates), Julie McGregor (Steve's mother), Garry Cook (Al Carson), Peter Collingwood (Principal), Genevieve Mooy (Secretary).

Fifteen-year-old Steve Carson lives with his bitter, drunken father (his mother left with another man) in the western suburbs of Sydney. A born larrikin, Steve and his pals Vicki and Moose are often in trouble at school, despite a sympathetic new teacher, Miss Hart. Steve is befriended by Redback, an ex-con who runs a motor-bike repair yard. Expelled after being suspected of selling drugs on behalf of his older brother, and distraught because his father has poisoned his beloved dog, Steve, together with his friends, destroys the headmaster's study during an end-of-term party. Vicki and Moose are arrested, but Steve rides away on a bike 'borrowed' from Redback.

FATTY FINN (page 343)
p.c.: Children's Film Corp. **ex.p**: John Sexton. **p**: Brian Rosen. **d**: Maurice Murphy. **sc**: Bob Ellis, Chris McGill. **ph**: John Seale. **ed**: Bob Gibson. **m**: Graham Bond, Rory O'Donohue. **p.d.**: Lissa Coote. **sd**: Tim Lloyd. **cost**: Norma Moriceau. **p.m.**: Su Armstrong. **a.d.**: Mark Egerton. Eastmancolour. 89 mins. Aust dist: Hoyts. 1980.

Ben Oxenbould (Fatty Finn), Bert Newton (Mr Finn), Noni Hazlehurst (Mrs Finn), Gerard Kennedy (Tiger Murphy), Greg Kelly (Bruiser Murphy), Lorraine Bayly (Maggie McGrath), Henri Szeps (Mr Zilch), Frank Wilson (Lord Mayor), Peter Carroll (Teacher), Ross Higgins (Radio Announcer), Tony Llewellyn-Jones (Dunny Man).

1930. Fatty Finn, an ebullient youngster, longs for his own crystal set (so he can listen to the Test Match from England). Meanwhile, his adventures include a frog race, a goat race and encounters with various Woolloomooloo characters, like the local policeman, Mrs McGrath (who runs a sly-grog shop) and the dunny man.

FEVER (page 242)
p.c.: J. C. Williamson. **ex.p**: Ron Saunders, Craig Lahiff. **p**: Terry Jennings. **d**: Craig Lahiff. **sc**: John Emery. **ph**: David Foreman. **ed**: Denise Haratzis. **m**: Frank Strangio. **p.d.**: Derek Mills **sd**: Rob Cutcher. **p.m.**: Elspeth Baird. Eastmancolour. 92 mins. 1987.

Bill Hunter (Jack Welles), Gary Sweet (Jeff), Mary Regan (Leanne Welles), Jim Holt (Morris).

In a small town in summer, police officer Jack Welles observes a drug sale, kills the drug-runner and scores a suitcase filled with $100 bills. He returns home to find his wife, Leanne, with her lover, Jeff, who attacks Jack and apparently kills him. The couple dump the body down a deep shaft, but Jack recovers and escapes. The couple try to escape by train, having discovered the money, but are followed by Morris, Welles' deputy. Welles kills Morris and Jeff, but is himself killed by a sinister Asian hit-man.

FIGHTING BACK (page 354)
p.c.: Samson Productions, in ass. with Adams–Packer Films. **ex.p**: Phillip Adams. **p**: Tom Jeffrey, Sue Milliken. **d**: Michael Caulfield. **sc**: Tom Jeffrey, Michael Cove (from the book *Tom* by John Embling). **ph**: John Seale. **ed**: Ron Williams. **m**: Colin Stead. **p.d.**: Christopher Webster. **sd**: Tim Lloyd. **p.m.**: Su Armstrong. **a.d.**: Steve Andrews. Eastmancolour. 100 mins. Aust dist: Roadshow. 1982.

1982 Australian Film Awards: Best supporting actress (Kris McQuade).

Lewis Fitz-Gerald (John Embling), Paul Smith (Tom), Kris McQuade (Tom's mother), Robyn Nevin (Mary), Caroline Gillmer (Rosemary), Ben Gabriel (Moreland), Wyn Roberts (Payne), Rob Steele (Truscott).

Thirteen-year-old Tom lives with his deserted mother and sister in the suburb of Botany. Unable to read or write, and violently anti-social, Tom is involved with a gang of older boys who like to steal cars and share the favours of their girls. At a technical school, Tom is taken in hand by John Embling, fresh out of university. Gradually, the teacher wins the boy's confidence, and they become friends.

FINAL CUT (page 291)
p.c.: Wilgar Productions. **ex.p**: Frank Gardiner. **p**: Mike Williams. **d**: Ross Dimsey. **sc**: Ross Dimsey, Jonathan Dawson. **ph**: Ron Johansen. **ed**: Tony Patterson. **m**: Howard Davidson. **p.d.**: James Penny. **sd**: John Rowley. **p.m.**: Terrie Vincent. **a.d.**: Scott Hicks. Eastmancolour. 81 mins. Aust dist: Greater Union. 1980.

David Clendenning (Dominic), Louis Brown (Chris), Jennifer Cluff (Sarah), Narelle Johnson (Yvette), Carmen J. McCall (Julie/Lyn), Thaddeus Smith (Mick).

Chris, a journalist, and his girlfriend Sarah are given permission to make a video documentary about tycoon Dominic. Suspecting that their subject is involved in snuff movies, the couple aim to expose him but find themselves in danger.

FISTS OF BLOOD

p.c.: Virgo–TVM Studios, in ass. with The Mandemar Group. **ex.p**: Judith West, Grahame Jennings. **p**: Damien Parer. **d**: Brian Trenchard Smith. **sc**: Peter West, Ronald Allan. **ph**: Simon Akkerman. **ed**: Kerry Regan, David Jaeger. **m**: Garry Hardman, Brian Beamish. **sd**: David Glasser. **p.m.**: Deb Copland. Eastmancolour. 84 mins. 1988.

Edward John Stazak (Jason Blade), John Stanton (William Anderson), Rowena Wallace (Lucy Andrews), Jim Richards (Jim Baxter), Paris Jefferson (Gemma Anderson), Zale Daniel (Colin), Mathew Quartermaine (Lambert).

Jim Richards, nemesis of martial arts hero Jason Blade [see *Day Of The Panther*] escapes from prison and kidnaps Blade's girlfriend, Gemma. Blade, after many conflicts, manages to rescue her.

FLUTEMAN (page 340)

p.c.: Independent Productions. **p**: Brendon Lunney. **d**: Peter Maxwell. **sc**: Charles Stamp. **ph**: Phil Pike. **ed**: Tim Wellburn. **m**: John Sangster. **p.d.**: Ken James. **sd**: Rowland McManis. **p.m.**: Jan Tyrrell. **a.d.**: Tony Wellington. Eastmancolour. 84 mins. 1982.

John Jarratt (Fluteman), Debra Lawrence (Sally Cooper), Patrick Dickson (David Hanson), John Ewart (Clarence Quint), Michael Caton (Oswald Snaith), Peter Gwynne (Mayor Cooper), Sheila Kennelly (Myra Hanson), Emil Minty (Toby), Aileen Britton (Beatrice Peachley).

In a drought-stricken outback town, the council treasurer, Quint, and undertaker, Snaith, have embezzled public money. A mysterious stranger calling himself Fluteman arrives and offers to end the drought for a fee of $5000. He succeeds, but payment is withheld, whereupon Fluteman plays his music and all the town's children—except for Tony, who is deaf— follow him and disappear.

FOR LOVE ALONE (page 179)

p.c.: Waranta, in ass. with UAA. **ex.p**: David Thomas. **p**: Margaret Fink. **d, sc**: Stephen Wallace (from the novel by Christina Stead). **ph**: Alun Bollinger. **ed**: Henry Dangar. **m**: Nathan Wax. **p.d.**: John Stoddart. **sd**: Syd Butterworth. **cost**: Jennie Tate. **p.m.**: Susan Wild. **a.d.**: Mark Turnbull. Eastmancolour. 104 mins. Aust dist: Greater Union, 1985.

Helen Buday (Teresa Hawkins), Sam Neill (James Quick), Hugo Weaving (Jonathan Crow),

Huw Williams (Harry Girton), Hugh Keays-Byrne (Andrew Hawkins), Odile Le Clezio (Kitty Hawkins), Linden Wilkinson (Miss Havilland), Judi Farr (Aunt Bea), Anna Phillips (Ann), John Polson (Leo Hawkins), Fiona Stewart (Martha), Jennifer Hagan (Manette).

England, 1936. Just before he leaves to fight in the Spanish Civil War, Harry Girton spends a night with an Australian woman, Tess Hawkins. Some years later, in Sydney, Tess is living with her overbearing father, sister Kitty, and brothers. She falls in love with the aloof Jonathan Crow, a university lecturer, and after he leaves for England, she saves her money to follow him. On the ship, she meets James Quick, a banker, who employs her. The affair with Crow comes to an end, and Tess and Quick become engaged, with Quick condoning her relationship with Girton. As she leaves the church on her wedding day (in heavy rain), Tess sees Crow pass by in the street—he does not see her.

FORTRESS (page 266)

p.c.: Crawford Productions. **ex.p**: Hector Crawford, Ian Crawford, Terry Stapleton. **p**: Ray Menmuir. **d**: Arch Nicholson. **sc**: Everett De Roche (from the novel by Gabrielle Lord). **ph**: David Connell. **ed**: Ralph Strasser. **p.d.**: Phil Warner. **sd**: Andrew Ramage. **p.m.** Helen Watts. **a.p.**: Michael Lake. Eastmancolour. 88 mins. Aust dist: UIP. 1985.

Rachel Ward (Sally Jones), Dennis Miller ('Father Christmas'), David Bradshaw ('Pussy-cat'), Vernon Wells ('Daffy Duck'), Roger Stephen ('Mac The Mouse'), Sean Garlick (Sid O'Brien), Rebecca Rigg (Narelle), Anna Crawford (Sarah), Beth Buchanan (Leanne).

A quartet of criminals, wearing comic masks, invade a one-teacher school in a small community and kidnap the teacher, Sally Jones, and entire class. The hostage victims, after much difficulty, manage to outwit their kidnappers, who are killed one by one—but the effect of the killings on the children is horrific.

FRAN (page 371)

p.c.: Barron Films. **ex.p.**: Paul Barron. **p**: David Rapsey. **d, sc**: Glenda Hambly. **ph**: Jan Kenny. **ed**: Tai Tang Thien. **m**: Greg Schultz. **p.d.**: Theo Mathews. **sd**: Kim Lord. colour. 99 mins. Aust dist: Barron Films. 1985.

1985 Australian Film Awards: Best actress (Noni Hazlehurst); supporting actress (Annie Byron); original screenplay.

Noni Hazlehurst (Fran), Annie Byron (Marge), Alan Fletcher (Jeff), Narelle Simpson (Lisa), Travis Ward (Cynthia), Rosie Logie (Cynthia), Danny

Adcock (Ray), Rosemary Harrison (Carol), Colin McEwan (Graham).

Fran and her husband have split up after he discovered she was having an affair with one of his mates. She is left to care for three children, one, Lisa, in her early teens. She starts an affair with Jeff, a barman, and they go off together leaving Marge, Fran's friend and neighbour, to care for the children. But it transpires that Jeff made sexual advances towards Lisa; the welfare department takes the children from Fran, who quarrels with Marge, breaks with Jeff, and is left alone to face an uncertain future.

FREEDOM (page 361)

p.c.: SA Film Corp., Endeavour Films. **ex.p**: Jim George. **p**: Matt Carroll. **d**: Scott Hicks. **sc**: John Emery. **ph**: Ron Johansen. **ed**: Phil Reid. **m**: Don Walker. **p.d.**: Herbert Pinter. **sd**: Tim Lloyd. **p.m.**: Valerie Hardy. Colour. 99 mins. Aust dist: Roadshow. 1981.

Jon Blake (Ron), Candy Raymond (Annie), Jad Capelja (Sally), Charles 'Bud' Tingwell (Cassidy), Max Cullen (Factory Clerk), Chris Haywood (Phil), Reg Lye (Farmer), John Clayton (Employment Officer), Greg Rowe (Service Station Attendant).

Ron loses his job in a factory, becomes frustrated by unfeeling bureaucrats, and dreams of owning a Porsche. Eventually, he steals one belonging to Annie, mistress of businessman Cassidy. Along the way, Ron picks up 16-year-old Sally, who wants to reclaim her baby from a foster-home. The police are after the runaways, and, despite the fact that they become lovers, Ron is forced to leave Sally behind. He loses the car, too, but manages to escape . . .

FRENCHMAN'S FARM (page 294)

p.c.: Mavis Bramston Productions. **ex.p**: Colin Worner. **p**: James Fishburn, Ron Way. **d**: Ron Way. **sc**: James Fishburn, Ron Way, Matt White (based on a screenplay by William Russell). **ph**: Malcolm McCulloch. **ed**: Pippa Anderson. **m**: Tommy Tycho. **p.d.**: Richard Rooker. **sd**: Max Bowring. **p.m.**: Penny Wall. **a.d.**: Dorian Newstead. Eastmancolour. 95 mins. Aust dist: CEL. US dist: Goldfarb. 1986.

Tracey Tainsh (Jackie Grenville), David Reyne (Barry Norton), Ray Barrett (Benson), Norman Kaye (Rev. Aldershot), John Meillon (Bill Dolan), Andrew Blackman (Det. Mainsbridge), Phil Brock (John Hatcher), Tui Bow (Old Lady), Kyn Lynch (George Slater).

Driving from her parents' Queensland property to Brisbane, law student Jackie Grenville takes a detour and winds up at Frenchman's Farm where she witnesses the murder of a World War II soldier by a man in French Revolutionary garb. Discovering the soldier was killed in 1944, Jackie and boyfriend Barry Norton return to the farm to investigate. They uncover an ancient curse and a recurring series of murders and themselves fall victim to the horror.

THE FRINGE DWELLERS (page 202)

p.c.: Fringe Dwellers Productions. **ex.p**: Hilary Heath. **p**: Sue Milliken. **d**: Bruce Beresford. **sc**: Bruce Beresford, Rhoisin Beresford (from the novel by Nene Gare). **ph**: Don McAlpine. **ed**: Tim Wellburn. **m**: George Dreyfus. **p.d.**: Herbert Pinter. **sd**: Max Bowring. **p.m.**: Helen Watts. **a.d.**: Mark Egerton. Eastmancolour. 98 mins. Aust dist: Roadshow. UK dist: Virgin. US dist: Atlantic. 1986.

1986 Australian Film Awards: Best adapted screenplay.

Kristina Nehm (Trilby Comeaway), Justine Saunders (Mollie Comeaway), Bob Maza (Joe Comeaway), Kyle Belling (Noonah Comeaway), Denis Walker (Bartie Comeaway), Ernie Dingo (Phil), Malcolm Silva (Charlie), Marlene Bell (Hannah), Marlene Torres (Audrena), Kath Walker (Eva).

The Comeaways live on the edge of an outback town alongside other Aboriginal families. Joe, who never got round to marrying Mollie, hates work, preferring to spend money on drink. The Comeaway daughters, Trilby, a teenage schoolgirl, and Noonah, a trainee nurse, persuade their parents to move to a Housing Commission home in a white area, despite the obvious prejudices. But they cannot keep up with payments, family members arrive for an extended visit, and the Comeaways lose their home. Meanwhile, Trilby is pregnant as a result of an affair with a black drover; the baby is born, but dies. Noonah's nursing career looks promising, but Trilby heads for the city . . .

FROG DREAMING (page 340)

p.c.: Western Film Productions, for UAA Films, Middle Reef Production. **ex.p**: David Thomas, John Picton-Warlow. **p**: Barbi Taylor. **co-p**: Everett De Roche. **d**: Brian Trenchard Smith. **sc**: Everett De Roche. **ph**: John McLean. **ed**: Brian Kavanagh. **m**: Brian May. **p.d.**: Jon Dowding. **sd**: Mark Lewis. **p.m.**: Jan Tyrrell. **a.d.**: Terry Needham. Colour. 93 mins. Aust dist: Greater Union. UK dist: ICA Projects. 1985.

1985 Australian Film Awards: Best editor.

Henry Thomas (Cody Walpole), Tony Barry (Gaza), Rachel Friend (Wendy). Tamsin West (Jane), Dempsey Knight (Charlie Pride), John

Ewart (Sgt Ricketts), Chris Gregory (Wheatley), Dennis Miller (Cannon), Peter Cummins (Neville).

Fourteen-year-old Cody Walpole, an American orphan, lives with Gaza, his father's best friend, in a small Australian town. Cody becomes convinced that there is an underwater monster in a mysterious lake known to Aborigines as Donkegin Hole and, during his investigations, disappears. The 'monster' turns out to be some ancient mining machinery, and Cody, trapped in an air pocket, emerges safely.

FUTURE SCHLOCK (page 333)
p.c.: Ultimate Show P/L. **p, d, sc**: Barry Peak, Chris Kiely. **ph**: Malcolm Richards. **ed**: Robert Martin, Ray Pond. **m**: John McCubbery, Doug Sanders. **p.d.**: Ian McWha. **sd**: Murray Tregonning. **p.m.**: Ray Pond. Colour. 75 mins. Aust dist: Valhalla. 1984.

Maryanne Fahey (Sarah), Michael Bishop (Bear), Tracey Callander (Ronnie), Tiriel Mora (Alvin), Simon Thorpe (Sammy), Peter Cox (Cap'n Fruitcake), Keith Walker (Sgt Tatts), Mitchell Faircloth (Dr Allen).

Melbourne, the 21st century. In a post-civil-war society controlled by suburbanites, nonconformists are confined to an inner-city ghetto. At Alvin's Bar, Sarah and Bear are known as performers but secretly moonlight as Cisco and Pancho, who harass police and suburbanites each night. The couple are joined in their subversive campaign by Ronnie, a suburbanite who changes sides.

GALLIPOLI (page 22)
p.c.: Associated R & R Films. **ex.p**: Francis O'Brien. **p**: Robert Stigwood, Patricia Lovell. **a.p**: Martin Cooper, Ben Gannon. **d**: Peter Weir. **sc**: David Williamson. **ph**: Russell Boyd. **ed**: William Anderson. **m**: Brian May. **p.d.**: Wendy Weir. **sd**: Don Connolly. **p.m.**: Su Armstrong. **a.d.**: Mark Egerton. Panavision. Eastmancolour. 108 mins. Aust dist: Roadshow. US dist: Paramount. UK (and rest of world) dist: CIC. 1981.

1981 Australian Film Awards: Best film; actor (Mel Gibson); supporting actor (Bill Hunter); screenplay; photography; editor; production design; sound.

Mel Gibson (Frank Dunne), Mark Lee (Archy Hamilton), Bill Hunter (Maj. Barton), Robert Grubb (Billy Lewis), Tim McKenzie (Barney Wilson), David Argue (Snowy), Bill Kerr (Uncle Jack), Ron Graham (Hamilton), Harold Hopkins (McCann), Gerda Nicolson (Rose Hamilton).

1915, Western Australia. Youthful sprinter Archy Hamilton, trained by his uncle, Jack, wins the 100 yards at a local sports meeting and decides to enrol in the Light Horse. Rejected because of his age, he meets up with another runner, Frank Dunne, less idealistic about the war; but, eventually, both wind up at the front where they befriend Billy, Barney and Snowy. At Gallipoli, Frank is appointed Major Barton's personal runner. The British order the Australians to provide a diversion, and as a result many, including Billy, Barney and Snowy are killed. Barton sends Frank to the General for permission to withdraw, but, despite an heroic run, Frank returns too late to save Archy from a pointless death.

GEORGIA (page 270)
p.c.: Jethro Films. **p**: Bob Weis. **d**: Ben Lewin. **sc**: Joanna Murray-Smith, Ben Lewin, Bob Weis. **ph**: Yuri Sokol. **ed**: Edward McQueen-Mason. **m**: Paul Grabowsky. **p.d.**: Jon Dowding. **sd**: John Phillips. **p.m.**: Simon Rosenthal. **a.d.**: Tom Burstall. Fujicolor. 93 mins. Aust dist: Hoyts. 1988.

Judy Davis (Nina/Georgia), John Bach (William Karlin), Julia Blake (Elizabeth), Alex Menglet (Laszlo), Marshall Napier (Frank LeMat).

Nina, a tax investigator, is disturbed by a photo she sees of a young woman with a baby. Elizabeth, her mother, reveals that Georgia, the woman in the photo, was Nina's real mother, who died in a mysterious accident. Nina investigates her mother's death, shadowed by a masked man with a knife. Witnesses to the incident tell different stories: they include LeMat, the shady cop who investigated; Karlin, Elizabeth's husband at the time; and Laszlo, her current lover (who was also there). Eventually, Nina discovers her mother died accidentally, and that the masked man was LeMat, who is killed when he runs on to a busy road.

GHOSTS . . . OF THE CIVIL DEAD (page 228)
p.c.: Correctional Services Film Prods. **p**: Evan English. **d**: John Hillcoat. **sc**: Nick Cave, Gene Conkie, John Hillcoat, Evan English. **ph**: Paul Goldman. **ed**: Stewart Young. **m**: Nick Cave. **p.d.**: Chris Kennedy. **sd**: Bronwyn Murphy. **p.m.**: Denise Patience. **a.d.**: Phil Jones. Eastmancolour. 92 mins. Aust dist: Outlaw Values. UK dist: Electric Pictures. 1988.

1989 Australian Film Awards: Best production design.

Dave Field (Wenzil), Mike Bishop (Hale), Chris de Rose (Greschner), Nick Cave (Maynard), Vincent Gil (Ruben), Bogdan Koca (Waychek), Kevin Mackey (Glover), Ian Mortimer (Jack),

Freddo Dierck (Robbins), Dave Mason (Lilly), John Flaus (Armstrong).

In the ultra-modern Central Industrial Prison, inmates are housed in different sections according to their crimes and are closely watched by TV monitors. Glover is in solitary, Wenzil in a unit where drug-taking and sex are practised openly, and guard-killer Grezner in the Segregation Unit. The prisoners have formed gangs, and the authorities make a series of raids, confiscating drugs and private property. Maynard, a psycho killer, starts trouble and is suspected of being a provocateur. Grezner is hanged in his cell by guards, Wenzil attacks the prison 'queen', Lilly, and Waychek, a Polish addict, also dies. There's a riot, and the prison is locked-down. Later, a number of prisoners, including Wenzil, are freed and move out into society . . .

GINGER MEGGS (page 343)
p.c.: John Sexton Productions. **p**: John Sexton. **d**: Jonathan Dawson. **sc**: Michael Latimer, based on the cartoon strip by Jim Bancks. **ph**: John Seale. **ed**: Philip Howe. **m**: Front (John Stuart, Ken Thraves). **p.d.**: Larry Eastwood. **sd**: Tim Lloyd. **p.m.**: Jill Nicholas **a.d.**: James Parker. Eastmancolour. 100 mins. Aust dist: Hoyts. 1982.

Paul Daniel (Ginger Meggs), Garry McDonald (Mr Meggs), Coral Kelly (Mrs Meggs), Ross Higgins (Floggswell), Hugh Keays-Byrne (Capt. Hook), Gwen Plumb (Miss Leach), Drew Forsythe (Tiger Kelly), Terry Camilleri (Mr Crackett), Mark Spain (Benny), Miranda Latimer (Polly), Shelley Armsworth (Minnie).

In a country town in the 40s, Ginger Meggs is an unruly youngster who plays truant, gets involved in fights and tells tall tales. While searching for his stolen monkey, he manages to capture a jewel thief, and also to impress his girlfriend, Minnie.

GLASS (page 270)
p.c.: Oilrag Productions. **p**: Patrick Fitzgerald, Chris Kennedy. **d, sc**: Chris Kennedy. **ph**: Peter de Vries. **ed**: James Bradley. **m**: Mario Gregorie. **p.d.**: Kerry Ainsworth. **sd**: David Glasser. **p.m.**: Cathy Flannery. **a.d.**: Corrie Soeterboek. Eastmancolour. Direct to video release. 93 mins. 1989.

Alan Lovell (Richard Vickery), Lisa Peers (Julie Vickery), Adam Stone (Peter Breen), Natalie McCurry (Alison Baume), Julie Herbert (Brenda Fairfax), Bernard Clisby (Insp. Ambrosoll), Richard Gilbert (Reg), Marilyn Thomas (Alice), Felicity Copeland (Veronica), Rowan Jackson (Charlie).

Businessman Richard Vickery's secretary, Veronica, is murdered with a piece of glass. Julie, Richard's wife, returns from abroad and resumes her affair with her husband's scheming lawyer, Peter Breen. With the help of his girlfriend Alison, a make-up artist, Richard fakes his death; Julie and Peter fall victim to the mystery killer.

GOING DOWN (page 144)
p.c.: X Productions. **p, d**: Haydn Keenan. **sc**: Julie Barry, Moira Maclaine-Cross, Melissa Woods. **ph**: Malcolm Richards. **ed**: Paul Healey. **sd**: Lloyd Carrick. **p.m.**: Mitou Pajaczkowska. **a.d.**: Peta Lawson. Eastmancolour. 94 mins. Self dist. in Australia. 1982.

Tracy Mann (Karli), David Argue (Greg/Trixie), Vera Plevnik (Jane), Moira Maclaine-Cross (Ellen), Julie Barry (Jackie), Esben Storm (Michael), Ian Gilmour (Shadow), Henk Johannes (Ian), Mercia Dean-Johns (Ned), Ian Nimmo (John), Ralph Cotterill (Karli's father).

Four young women, Karlie, Jane, Ellen and Jackie, share a house at King's Cross. Karli's father has given her $2000 cash for a trip to the US, but it has been stolen. Was the thief one of her girlfriends, or one of several men who visit the place? Jane is a hedonist obsessed by death; Jackie has turned to prostitution because she cannot get a job; and Ellen is a scatty type who picks up the nerdy Greg in an employment office. There is also Michael, a would-be writer; Shadow, a mysterious hanger-on; and Trixi, a transvestite. Michael turns out to be the thief, and Karli 'borrows' a car from out-of-town newly-weds to get to the airport in time.

GOING SANE (page 110)
p.c.: Sea Change Films, in ass. with NSW Film Corp. **ex.p**: John Sanford, **p**: Tom Jeffrey. **d**: Michael Robertson. **sc**: John Sanford. **ph**: Dean Semler. **ed**: Brian Kavanagh. **m**: Cameron Allan. **p.d.**: Igor Nay. Eastmancolour. 93 mins. Aust dist; Greater Union. 1985.

John Waters (Martin Brown), Judy Morris (Ainslee Brown), Linda Cropper (Irene Carter), Kate Raison (Nosh), Frank Wilson (Sir Colin Grant), Jim Holt (Irwin Grant), Tim Robertson (Owen Owen), Anne Semler (Marta Owen).

Martin Brown, an executive in a mining company owned by Sir Colin Grant, is having a mid-life crisis: he is bored with Ainslee, his wife, and ambivalent towards his lustful secretary, Irene Carter. After bringing Irene home to meet Ainslee, and locking himself in Sir Colin's office, Martin sets out, with Irene, for the outback seeking a mystical experience. This he finds with Nosh, a greenie, who persuades Martin to take up the ecology cause against his old company.

GOODBYE PARADISE (page 234)

p.c.: Petersham Productions, in ass. with NSW Film Corp. **p**: Jane Scott. **d**: Carl Schultz. **sc**: Bob Ellis, Denny Lawrence. **ph**: John Seale. **ed**: Richard Francis-Bruce. **m**: Peter Best. **p.d.**: George Liddle. **sd**: Syd Butterworth. **p.m.**: Jill Nicholas. **a.d.**: Neill Vine-Miller. Eastmancolour. 119 mins. Aust dist: Filmways. 1982.

1982 Australian Film Awards: Best original screenplay; actor (Ray Barrett).

Ray Barrett (Michael Stacey), Robyn Nevin (Kate), Janet Scrivener (Cathy), Kate Fitzpatrick (Mrs McCredie), Robert 'Tex' Morton (Sir Ted Godfrey), Don Pascoe (Les McCredie), John Clayton (Todd), Guy Doleman (Quiney), Lex Marinos (Con), Paul Chubb (Curly).

Alcoholic ex-cop Michael Stacey, has written a book exposing the Queensland police force but it has been stopped by his publisher. He is hired by Les McCredie, a politician who wants the Gold Coast to be established as a separate state, to help find Cathy, his missing daughter. The trail leads to the headquarters of a religious cult and then to an escort agency before Stacey becomes involved in the murder of a woman, apparently killed when she is mistaken for Cathy. Kate, Stacey's barmaid mistress, is also killed and Stacey badly beaten before the case develops into a violent political struggle culminating in an attempted coup led by Quiney, a dissident army officer.

GREAT EXPECTATIONS: THE UNTOLD STORY (page 187)

p.c.: International Film Management, Australian Broadcasting Corporation, for Hemdale. **ex.p**: Antony I. Ginnane, Ray Alchin. **p**: Tom Burstall. **d, sc**: Tim Burstall. **ph**: Peter Hendry. **ed**: Tony Kavanagh, Lyn Solly. **m**: George Dreyfus. **p.d.**: Laurie Johnson, L. Pryce-Jones. **sd**: Peter Barber. **p.m.**: Debbis Kiely. **a.d.**: Wayne Barry. Colour. 107 mins. Direct to video release. 1987.

John Stanton (Abel Magwitch), Sigrid Thornton (Bridget Tankerton), Robert Coleby (Roger Compeyson), Noel Ferrier (Jaggers), Todd Boyce (Pip), Anne-Louise Lambert (Estella), Ron Haddrick (Tankerton), Bruce Spence (Joe Gargery), Jill Forster (Miss Havisham), Gerard Kennedy (Tooth), Danny Simmonds (Young Pip), Leah Richardson (Young Estella), Serge Lazareff (Courtney), Alexander Hay (Judge), Annie Byron (Mrs Joe Gargery), Les Foxcroft (Gaoler), Steven Grives (Sedley), Nell Schofield (Biddy).

Convict Abel Magwitch has a lifelong hatred for upper-class forger Roger Compeyson. Transported to Australia, Magwitch is unable to prevent Bridget, daughter of his kindly employer Tankerton, from entering into a bigamous marriage with Compeyson. She later dies, and Magwitch becomes rich when he strikes gold. Through his British lawyer Jaggers, he makes an anonymous allowance to Pip, who, as a child, had helped him when he escaped the hulks. Returning to England to see Pip, he runs foul of Compeyson again, but manages to kill him and, though taken for dead himself, survives.

GRIEVOUS BODILY HARM (page 238)

p.c.: International Film Management, Smiley Films, FGH. **ex.p**: Antony I. Ginnane, Errol Sullivan. **p**: Richard Brennan. **d**: Mark Joffe. **sc**: Warwick Hind. **ph**: Ellery Ryan. **ed**: Marc Van Buuren. **m**: Chris Neal. **p.d.**: Roger Ford. **sd**: Andrew Ramage. **p.m.**: Julie Forster. **a.d.**: Even Keddie. Eastmancolour. 96 mins. Aust dist: Filmpac. US dist: Fries Entertainment. 1988.

Colin Friels (Tom Stewart), John Waters (Morris Martin), Bruno Lawrence (Det.-Sgt Ray Birch), Joy Bell (Claudine), Chris Stalker (Allen), Kim Gyngell (Mick), Shane Briant (Stephen Enderby), Caz Lederman (Vivian Enderby), Sandy Gore (Barbara Helmsley), Kerry Armstrong (Annie Stewart), John Flaus (Bradshaw).

Tom Stewart, an unscrupulous crime reporter, steals a large sum of money from a dying criminal; Det.-Sgt Birch, an equally unscrupulous cop, suspects Stewart. Meanwhile, Morris Martin, a schoolteacher depressed about the death in Paris some time earlier of his beautiful wife, Claudine, sees a woman who looks like her at a nightclub. While quizzing Vivian Enderby, a woman involved in sexual threesomes with Claudine (captured on the videos Martin obsessively watches), he loses control and kills her. This leads to other murders, investigated by both Stewart and Birch, but it is the former who tracks Claudine down—to a high-class brothel in the Blue Mountains. Martin has followed him, however . . .

GROUND ZERO (page 249)

p.c.: BDB Productions, with Burrowes Film Group. **p**: Michael Pattinson. **d**: Michael Pattinson, Bruce Myles. **sc**: Jan Sardi, Mac Gudgeon. **ph**: Steve Dobson. **ed**: David Pulbrook. **m**: Chris Neal (US version: Tom Bähler). **p.d.**: Brian Thomson. **sd**: Gary Wilkins. **p.m.**: Narelle Barsby. **a.d.**: Stuart Freeman. Panavision. Eastmancolour. 109 mins. Aust dist: Hoyts. US dist: Avenue Pictures. 1987.

1987 Australian Film Awards: Best cinematography, editing, production design, sound.

Colin Friels (Harvey Denton), Jack Thompson (Trebilcock), Donald Pleasence (Prosper Gaffney), Natalie Bate (Pat Denton), Simon Chilvers (Commission President), Neil Fitzpatrick (Hooking), Bob Maza (Wallemate), Peter Cummins (Ballantyne), Kim Gyngell (Detective).

Harvey Denton, a film cameraman, is in the process of transferring to video his dead father's 16mm film material (his father, who had filmed the British nuclear tests at Maralinga in the early 50s, had died in 1953, apparently in an accident). When his apartment is ransacked, Denton is told by Trebilcock, an ASIO agent, that his father was murdered. Determined to solve the mystery, Denton travels to the test site where he meets a crippled Englishman, Gaffney, who shows him where his father hid film which showed that Aborigines had been killed during the tests; Gaffney is killed helping Denton escape British agents. During an inquiry into the testing, ASIO's demands for secrecy prevent the truth being told, but Denton finally gets to see the film his father died for.

HARD KNOCKS (page 216)

p.c.: Andromeda Films, Ukiyo Films. **sc**: Don McLennan, Hilton Bonner. **d**: Don McLennan. **ph, ed**: Zbigniew Friedrich. **sd**: Lloyd Carrick. **p.m., a.d.**: Rod McNicol. Colour. 79 mins. Aust dist: Greg Lynch Distributors. 1980.

Tracy Mann (Sam), John Arnold (Wally), Bill Hunter (Brady), Max Cullen (Newman), Tony Barry (Barry), Hilton Bonner (Frank), Kirsty Grant (Debbie), Jack Allen (Father), Penelope Stewart (Raelene), Liz Stevenson (Joan).

1980 Australian Film Awards: Best actress (Tracy Mann); Jury prize.

Sam, a Melbourne teenager just out of prison, is trying to survive independently in a world of unemployment and police harassment.

HARLEQUIN (page 297)

p.c.: FG Film Productions. **ex.p.**: William Fayman. **p**: Antony I. Ginnane. **d**: Simon Wincer. **sc**: Everett De Roche. **ph**: Gary Hansen. **ed**: Adrian Carr. **m**: Brian May. **p.d.**: Bernard Hides. **sd**: Gary Wilkins. **sp.ef.**: Conrad Rothmann. **a.p., p.m.**: Jane Scott. Panavision. Eastmancolour. 95 mins. Aust dist: Greater Union. US dist: New Image Releasing. 1980.

Robert Powell (Gregory Wolfe), Carmen Duncan (Sandra Rast), David Hemmings (Nick Rast), Broderick Crawford (Doc Wheelan), Gus Mercurio (Mr Bergier), Alan Cassell (Mr Porter), Mark Spain (Alex Rast), John Frawley (Dr Lovelock), Alyson Best (Alice).

Alex, son of Senator Nick Rast and his wife Sandra, suffers from leukemia. Doctors have given him no chance until a mysterious magician, Gregory Wolfe, appears from nowhere and cures the boy. Wolfe moves into the Rast home,

becoming close to mother and son. Meanwhile, Doc Wheelan, an unscrupulous political manipulator, is grooming Rast for the position of deputy governor (the former deputy has mysteriously drowned, and the governor himself is gravely ill). Wheeler and his men try to implicate Wolfe in the rape and burning by acid of Alice, the Rasts' maid, and he is imprisoned, but escapes and tries to convince Rast that Wheeler was responsible before being gunned down by Wheeler's men.

HEATWAVE (page 215)

p.c.: A Preston Cruthers–M & L production. **p**: Hilary Linstead. **co-p**: Ross Matthews. **d**: Phil Noyce. **sc**: Marc Rosenberg, Phil Noyce. **ph**: Vincent Monton. **ed**: John Scott. **m**: Cameron Allan. **p.d.**: Ross Major. **p.m.**: Lynn Gailey. **a.d.**: Steve Andrews. Eastmancolour. 91 mins. Aust dist: Roadshow. US dist: New Line Cinema. UK dist: Mainline. 1981.

Judy Davis (Kate Dean), Richard Moir (Stephen West), Chris Haywood (Peter Houseman), Bill Hunter (Robert Duncan), John Gregg (Phillip Lawson), Anna Jemison (Victoria West), John Meillon (Freddy Dwyer), Dennis Miller (Mick Davies), Peter Hehir (Bodyguard), Carole Skinner (Mary Ford), Gillian Jones (Barbie Lee Taylor), Frank Gallacher (Dick Molnar), Tui Bow (Annie), Don Crosby (Jim Taylor), Lynette Curran (Evonne Houseman), Graham Rouse (1st Detective), Paul Chubb (2nd Detective), Robert Menzies (Student).

Stephen West, an up-and-coming architect, is designing the Eden project for developer Peter Houseman, but the ambitious luxury apartment block is the target of protesters (since local housing is being destroyed to make way for it). An activist journalist, Mary Ford, disappears about the same time an old man, Jim Taylor, dies in a fire in his house (which he refused to sell to Houseman). Mary's friend Kate Dean enlists Stephen's help, and they become lovers (though he is married); when Houseman abruptly leaves the country, ownership of the project passes to a shady businessman and nightclub-owner Molnar, whose thugs beat up Stephen and threaten Kate. On a hot New Year's Eve, Kate (just out of prison after being accused of arson) goes to Molnar's club just in time to see him shot dead by his former mistress, Barbie, Taylor's daughter.

HEAVEN TONIGHT (page 153)

p.c.: Boulevard Films. **ex.p**: Peter Boyle. **p**: Frank Howson. **d**: Pino Amenta. **sc**: Frank Howson, Alister Webb. **ph**: David Connell. **ed**: Phil Reid.

m: John Capek. p.d.: Jeannie Cameron. sd: Andrew Ramage. co-p: James Michael Vernon. line p: Barbi Taylor. p.m.: Deborah Samuels. a.d.: John Powditch. Colour. 95 mins. 1989.

John Waters (Johnny Dysart), Rebecca Gilling (Annie Dysart), Kim Gyngell (Baz Schultz), Sean Scully (Tim Robbins), Guy Pearce (Paul Dysart), Sarah de Teliga (Secretary), Ted Hepple (Caretaker), Bruce Venables (Policeman), Syd Conabere (Priest).

Johnny Dysart, forty, is a former rock star who had one big hit (*Heaven Tonight*) in the 60s and is now struggling to make a comeback and more than a little jealous of his son Paul, eighteen, who is starting a music career himself. Matters are not helped by the return from overseas of Baz, a former member of the band, who is hooked on drugs. Police close in on Baz, and he is gunned down in a back alley. Johnny and his loyal wife, Annie, go to see Paul perform.

HIGH TIDE (page 366)

p.c.: FGH, SJL, for Hemdale. ex.p: Antony I. Ginnane, Joseph Skrzynski. p: Sandra Levy. d: Gillian Armstrong. sc: Laura Jones. ph: Russell Boyd. ed: Nick Beauman. m: Peter Best. p.d.: Sally Campbell. sd: Ben Osmo. a.p.: Greg Ricketson. p.m.: Julie Forster. a.d.: Mark Turnbull, Eastmancolour. 104 mins. Aust dist: Filmpac. US dist: Tri-Star. UK dist: Ritzy. 1987.

1987 Australian Film Awards: Best actress (Judy Davis).

Judy Davis (Lilli), Jan Adele (Bet), Claudia Karvan (Ally), Colin Friels (Mick), John Clayton (Col), Frankie J. Holden (Lester), Toni Scanlon (Mary), Mark Hembrow (Mechanic).

Eden, NSW. Lilli, back-up singer to Lester (a Presley imitator) is fired and left with a broken-down car and little cash. She rents a caravan at a local caravan park and goes on a drunken binge. Coincidentally, Lilli's young daughter, Ally, lives in a nearby caravan with her paternal grandmother, Bet (after her husband's death, Lilli left Ally in Bet's care). Bet fears Lilli wants the girl back, but at first Lilli is concerned mainly with a new love affair, with the divorced Mick, whom she tells about Ally. When she ends the affair, Mick tells Ally who her mother is (hitherto she had been kept in the dark). Ally confronts her mother, who offers to take the girl away with her. Ally goes to say an emotional farewell to her grandmother.

HOODWINK (page 253)

p.c.: CB Films, in ass. with NSW Film Corp. p: Pom Oliver, Errol Sullivan. d: Claude Whatham. sc: Ken Quinnell. ph: Dean Semler. ed: Nick

Beauman. m: Cameron Allan. p.d.: Ross Major. sd: Gary Wilkins. Colour. 93 mins. Aust dist: Hoyts. 1981.

John Hargreaves (Martin), Judy Davis (Sarah), Dennis Miller (Ralph), Max Cullen (Buster), Les Foxcroft (Baldy), Wendy Hughes (Lucy), Kim Deacon (Marian), Wendy Stehlow (Sister).

Martin, a hardened criminal, is arrested at the home of Lucy, his girlfriend, but manages to escape. He robs a bank and hides out with a dancer, Marian, who makes love with him but then betrays him to the police. To get a lighter sentence, he feigns blindness, hoodwinks the initially sceptical authorities, and ends up in a minimum security prison in the country. Sarah, wife of the local priest, visits him at the prison and they fall in love.

HOSTAGE (page 266)

p.c.: Frontier Films, Klejazz Productions. p: Basil Appleby. d: Frank Shields. sc: Frank Shields, John Lind. ph: Vincent Monton. ed: Don Saunders. m: Davood Tabrizi. p.d.: Phil McLaren. sd: Bob Allen. p.m.: Sue Wild. a.d.: Bob Howard. Colour. 90 mins. Aust dist: Roadshow. 1983.

Kerry Mack (Christine), Ralph Schicha (Walter Maresch), Judy Nunn (Mrs Lewis), Doris Goddard (Mrs Hoffman), Claire Binney (Freda Hoffman), Henk Johannes (Wolfgang).

Christine Lewis, seventeen, leaves an unhappy home to join a carnival where she meets Walter Maresch, an unstable German immigrant. They become lovers, and he forces her to marry him (threatening suicide if she refuses). They have a daughter, but soon she is desperately unhappy—even more so when, pregnant again, Walter suddenly takes her off to Munich, where she discovers he is a member of a neo-Nazi group involved in armed robberies. She secretly has an abortion in Holland, and then the couple, with child, flee Germany (narrowly escaping death from hostile villagers in a Turkish stopover). Back in Australia, Walter forces Christine to commit another bank robbery, but is eventually captured by the police.

HOUSEBOAT HORROR (page 289)

p.c.: P.M. Terror Productions. ex.p: Greg Petherick. p, sc: Ollie Martin. d: Ollie Martin, Kendal Flanagan. ph: Bill Parnell. ed: Clayton Jacobson. m: Brian Mannix, Steve Harrison, Ross McLean. p.d.: Brian Gunst. sd: Scott Findlay. p.m.: Warren Amster, Bosley Spry. a.d.: Collin Morris. a.p.: Rick Lappas. Colour. 85 mins. Direct to video release. 1989.

Alan Dale (Grant Evans), Christine Jeston (Tracy), Craig Alexander (Sam), Des 'Animal'

McKenna (Ziggie), Gavin Wood (Costello), John Michael Howson ('J'), Louise Siversen (Zelia), Peppie D'Or (Teresa), Steve Whittacker (Bernie), Julie Thompson (Jennie), Mark Muggeridge (Dagger).

A film crew, making a rock clip at remote Lake Infinity, is decimated by a mad, scarred killer seeking vengeance after being badly burnt during a previous film shoot. Most of the filmmakers, including director Grant Evans, are killed, but just as it seems the murderer has been vanquished (by fire) he returns . . .

THE HUMPTY DUMPTY MAN
(page 241)
p.c.: A Quantum Films presentation of a Capital Films production. **ex.p**: Robert Mercieca. **p**: Miranda Bain. **d**: Paul Hogan. **sc**: Karl Zwicky, Paul Hogan. **ph**: Martin McGrath. **ed**: Murray Ferguson. **m**: Peter Sullivan. **p.d.**: Neil Angwin. **p.m.**: Elizabeth Symes. **a.d.**: Phil Jones. Colour. 94 mins. Direct to video release. 1986.

Frank Gallacher (Gerry Shadlow), Frederick Parslow (Symes), Rod Mullinar (Stewart Brax), John Frawley (Gordon Morris), Deborra-Lee Furness (Carmel DeVries), Jim Holt (Russell Wilks), Robin Harrison (Alex Galkin), Frankie J. Holden (Noel Calderwood), Sue Jones (Adele Shadlow), Greg Moorhouse (The Technician), Agnieska Perepeska (Yelena), Clare Crowther (Ruth).

Gerry Shadlow, who runs a trade office in Canberra and has close ties with government ministers, is friendly with Alex Galkin, a Soviet diplomat. When the Australian government decides to end the role of the AIS (Security), the KGB, which has a highly-placed mole, uses Galkin and businessman Gordon Morris to discredit Shadlow, who is accused of espionage. Meanwhile Carmel, secret mistress of senior AIS officer Stewart Brax, has been stealing secrets: she is murdered, and an investigating journalist, Noel Calderwood, disappears (also murdered). AIS head Symes has Brax and Morris killed by an assassin, The Technician, but Shadlow, also a target, escapes. Symes is revealed as the KGB mole and is killed by his deputy, Russell Wilks. But Shadlow has taped evidence of the whole messy affair.

HUNGRY HEART (page 118)
p.c.: Lions Den Productions, for Chancom. **p**: Rosa Colosimo, Reg McLean. **d, sc**: Luigi Acquisto, based on a screenplay by Rosa Colosimo, Josie Arnold, Angelo Salamanca. **ph**: Jaems Grant. **ed**: Courtney Page. **m**: David Bridie. **p.d.**: Michael Kourri. **sd**: Mark Tarpey. **p.m.**: Rosa Colosimo.

a.d.: Kath Hayden. Eastmancolour. 95 mins.

Nick Carrafa (Sal Bono), Kimberley Davenport (Katie), Lisa Schouw (Jane), Dasha Blahova (Mrs Bono), Norman Kaye (Mr O'Ryan), John Flaus (Mr Maloney), Sheila Florance (Grandmother), Osvaldo Maione (Vito), Gaetano Scollo, Mark Rogers, Greg Caves.

Sal Bono has finished his medical training, but is reluctant to start work as a doctor. Drifting about Melbourne with his friend Charlie (a postman who steals money from letters) he meets Katie and falls in love with her. They move in together, but he quickly becomes jealous of her past life and her lack of inhibition. She leaves to visit her parents in the country (and perhaps an ex-boyfriend) so Sal spends the night with her friend, Jane. Next morning Katie returns to find Sal guilty and Jane gone.

I OWN THE RACECOURSE (page 342)
p.c.: Barron Films. **ex.p**: Paul Barron. **p**: John Edwards, Timothy Read. **d**: Stephen Ramsey. **sc**: Stephen Ramsey, John Edwards, from the book by Patricia Wrightson. **ph**: Geoff Burton. **ed**: Denise Haslem. **m**: Red Symonds, Martin Armiger. **p.d.**: Richard Roberts. **sd**: Kevin Kearney. **p.m.**: Adrienne Read. **a.d.**: Corrie Soeterboek. Eastmancolour. 77 mins. 1985.

Gully Coote (Andy Hoddel), Tony Barry (Bert Hammond), Norman Kaye (Drunken Old Man), Rodney Burke (Joe), Paul Bertram (Connelly), Brett Climo (Const. Eadie), Gillian Jones (Mrs Hoddel), Les Murray (Creevy), Bob Ellis (Renehan).

Gullible youngster Andy Hoddel is convinced that an old drunk has sold him the Glebe racecourse in inner Sydney. Racetrack employees, including sympathetic groundsman Bert Hammond, are tolerant when the new 'boss' makes regular appearances at the track. When a couple of crooks, Creevy and Renehan, involved in a doping scheme, enlist Andy's help, they discover he is not as simple as they supposed.

IN TOO DEEP (page 132)
p.c.: Media World. **p, d**: John Tatoulis, Colin South. **sc**: Deborah Parsons. **ph**: Mark Gilfedder, Peter Zakharov. **ed**: Michael Collins. **m**: Jex Saarelaht. **p.d.**: Phil Chambers. **sd**: John Wilkinson. **p.m.**: Yvonne Collins. **a.d.**: Stephen Saks. **a.p.**: Deborah Parsons, Peter Bain Hogg. Eastmancolour. 106 mins. 1989.

Hugo Race (Mack Dunolly), Santha Press (Wendy Lyle), Rebekah Elmalogou (Jo-Jo Lyle), John Flaus (Det. Miles Konitz), Dominic Sweeney (Det. Dinny Collins), Craig Alexander (Ivan Friedrich), Ian Rae (Pike), Richard Aspel

(Barman), Tassos Ioannides (Mella).

Wendy, a spoilt jazz singer, and Jo-Jo, her adoring 15-year-old sister, become involved with Mack, a rock musician and punk criminal who is wanted by both the police and the mob.

INCIDENT AT RAVEN'S GATE
(UK title: *Encounter at Raven's Gate*)
(page 283)

p.c.: FGH, International Film Marketing, Acquabay. **ex.p**: Antony I. Ginnane. **p**: Marc Rosenberg, Rolf De Heer. **d**: Rolf De Heer. **sc**: Marc Rosenberg, Rolf De Heer, from an original screenplay by James Michael Vernon. **ph**: Richard Michalak. **ed**: Suresh Ayyar. **m**: Graham Tardif, Roman Kronen. **p.d.**: Judith Russell. **sd**: Rob Cutcher. **sp. ef.**: Jon Armstrong. **p.m.**: Ron Stigwood. **a.d.**: Carolynne Cunningham. Super 35mm. Colour. 93 mins. Aust dist: Filmpac. UK dist: Castle Premier Releasing. 1988.

Steven Vidler (Eddie Cleary), Celine Griffin (Rachel Cleary), Ritchie Singer (Richard Cleary), Vincent Gil (Felix Skinner), Saturday Rosenberg (Annie), Terry Camilleri (Dr Hemmings), Max Cullen (Sgt Taylor).

In the area around the South Australian property Raven's Gate, strange things are happening. Electrical equipment is malfunctioning, motors cut out, wells run dry, a homestead is flooded. Humans are affected, too. Eddie Cleary, out on parole in custody of his older brother, Richard, starts a passionate affair with Richard's frustrated wife, Rachel. Simultaneously, Eddie is attracted to barmaid Annie, who is forlornly wooed by opera-loving cop, Felix Skinner. When she rejects him, Felix kills Annie and heads for Sydney and a performance at the Opera House. The Cleary farmhouse is destroyed and Richard killed, but Eddie and Rachel make a temporary escape. Some time later, a policeman, Taylor, and scientist, Dr Hemmings, speculate over the remains of Raven's Gate.

AN INDECENT OBSESSION (page 161)

p.c.: A PBL production, presented by Hoyts-Edgley International. **ex.p**: Michael Edgley, John Daniell. **p**: Ian Bradley. **d**: Lex Marinos. **sc**: Denise Morgan, from the book by Colleen McCullough. **ph**: Ernest Clark. **ed**: Philip Howe. **m**: Dave Skinner. **p.d.**: Michael Ralph. **a.p.**: Maura Fay. Colour. 104 mins. Aust dist: Hoyts. 1985.

Wendy Hughes (Honour Langtry), Gary Sweet (Michael Wilson), Richard Moir (Luce Daggett), Jonathan Hyde (Neil Parkinson), Bruno Lawrence (Matt Sawyer), Mark Little (Benedict Maynard), Bill Hunter (Col. Chinstrap), Julia Blake (Matron), Caroline Gillmer (Sally).

In an army hospital on a Pacific island towards the end of World War II, nurse Honour Langtry cares for the patients in the psychiatric ward. They include Luce Daggett, a sadistic former actor; Matt Sawyer, who tries to prevent his wife discovering the fact that he has been blinded; Benedict Maynard, a nervous schizophrenic; and Nuggett Jones, a chronic hypochondriac. New arrival Michael Wilson seems more normal than most, until it is revealed he killed a sergeant-major for making homosexual advances towards him. Daggett makes a play for Wilson but Honour discovers, during a night of sweaty passion, that he is capable of heterosexual love. Daggett, meanwhile, is castrated and murdered.

INITIATION (page 90)

p.c.: International Film Management, Filmbar. **ex.p**: Antony I. Ginnane. **p**: Jane Ballantyne. **d**: Michael Pearce. **sc**: James Barton. **ph**: Geoffrey Simpson. **ed**: Denise Haratzis. **p.d.**: Jon Dowding. **sd**: Toivo Lember. **p.m.**: Robert Kewley. **a.d.**: Euan Keddie. Eastmancolour. 92 mins. Direct to video release. 1987.

Bruno Lawrence (Nat Molloy), Rodney Harvey (Danny Molloy), Arna-Maria Winchester (Sal), Miranda Otto (Stevie), Barry Smith (Kulu).

Danny Molloy, a New York youngster, comes to Australia in search of his father after his mother's death. He locates Nat Molloy living in the bush with Sal and her daughter, Stevie; Nat is smuggling marijuana for the Italo-Vietnamese mafia to make ends meet. Danny is befriended by Kulu, a wise old Aboriginal, who teaches him about Aboriginal lore and initiation ceremonies. These come in useful when Nat's light aircraft crashes (after Nat is bitten by a snake placed on board by the Italians), and Danny has to help his father get back to civilisation.

INNOCENT PREY (page 290)

p.c.: Crystal Films Corp. **ex.p.**: David G. B. Williams. **p, d**: Colin Eggleston. **sc**: Ron McLean. **ph**: Vincent Monton. **ed**: Pippa Anderson. **m**: Brian May. **p.d.**: Larry Eastwood. colour. 100 mins. 1983.

P. J. Soles (Cathy Wills), Kit Taylor (Joe), Grigor Taylor (Rick), Martin Balsam (Sheriff Virgil Baker), John Warnock (Phillip), Susan Stenmark (Gwen), Richard Morgan (Ted), Debi Sue Voorhous (Hooker).

Dallas. Cathy Wills' businessman husband, deranged after a bad business deal, slashes a hooker to death in a motel bathroom. Cathy turns him in to the police, but he escapes, killing several policemen and decapitating a policewoman, and starts to terrorise his wife, who decides to leave for Sydney, Australia, to visit a friend. Phillip, landlord of the luxury harbourside apartment where the women stay, spies on his tenants and kills Cathy's husband when he arrives in search of her. For Cathy, the nightmare continues . . .

ISLAND (page 127)

p.c.: Illumination Films. **ex.p**: William Marshall, Jeannine Seawell. **p**: Paul Cox, Santhana K. Naidu. **d, sc**: Paul Cox. **ph**: Michael Edols. **ed**: John Scott. **m**: Anil Acharya. **p.d.**: Neil Angwin. **sd**: Jim Currie. **p.m.**: Paul Ammitzboll. **a.d.**: Alexandra Christou. **a.p.**: Takis Emmanuel. Colour. 93 mins. Aust dist: New Vision. US dist: Atlantis Releasing. 1989.

Eva Sitta (Eva), Irene Papas (Marquise), Anoja Weerasinghe (Sahana), Chris Haywood (Janis), Norman Kaye (Henry), Francois Bernard (Frenchman).

Eva, a Czech-born Australian drug addict, arrives on a Greek island in winter, and rents a small house. She is soon befriended by Marquise, a refugee from the mainland, with tragic memories of war and dictatorship, and by Sahana, a Sri Lankan woman who waits in vain for the return of her husband, a political refugee. Eva also meets Janis, one of the deaf-mute fishermen who work on the island. When her former lover, a French drug-dealer, turns up, Eva resists him and is beaten. Janis kills him, and the body is dumped into the sea. The three women increasingly find strength from one another.

JENNY KISSED ME (page 370)

p.c.: Nilsen Premiere. **p**: Tom Broadbridge. **d**: Brian Trenchard Smith. **sc**: Judith Colquhoun, Warwick Hind. **ph**: Bob Kohler. **ed**: Alan Lake. **m**: Trevor Lucas, Ian Mason. **p.d.**: Jon Dowding. **sd**: Paul Clark. **p.m.**: Andrew Morse. **a.d.**: Ross Hamilton. Colour. 98 mins. 1985.

Ivar Kants (Lindsay Fenton), Deborra-Lee Furness (Carol Grey), Tamsin West (Jenny West), Paula Duncan (Gaynor), Mary Ward (Grace), Steven Grives (Mal), Nicki Paull.

Lindsay lives in the Melbourne hills with his girlfriend, Carol, and her daughter, Jenny. Jenny adores her 'father', and is disturbed when her mother makes a play for next-door neighbour, Mal. Carol takes Jenny with her to Melbourne where they stay with her friend Gaynor, a prostitute. Lindsay comes searching for 'his' daughter, though he is suffering increasingly from dizzy spells, caused by cancer of the brain. Carol finally agrees to marry Lindsay on his deathbed.

JIGSAW (page 270)

p.c.: Rosa Colosimo Films. **p**: Rosa Colosimo. **d**: Marc Gracie. **sc**: Marc Gracie, Chris Thompson.

ph: Jaems Grant. **m**: Dalmazio Babare. **p.d.**: Chris Kennedy. **sd**: John McKerrow. **p.m.**: Simon Rosenthal. **a.d.**: Paul Healey. Eastmancolour. 89 mins. 1989.

Rebecca Gibney (Virginia York), Dominic Sweeney (Det.-Const. Broulle), Gary Day (Gordon Carroll), Terence Donovan (Jack McClusky), Nico Lathouris (Ed Minter), Michael Coard (Aaron York), James Wright (Ray Carpenter), Peppie D'Or (Laura Carpenter), Peter Black (Ted Lanski), David Bradshaw (Alex York), Brenda Addie (Jean).

Real-estate developer Alex York is found dead—apparently by accident—one day after his marriage to Virginia. Det.-Const. Broulle investigates, while Virginia is followed by sinister hitman Ed Minter. She discovers Alex had a son, Aaron, she knew nothing about. Also involved are an MP, Gordon Carroll, and an unscrupulous mayor, Jack McClusky. Virginia discovers her brother-in-law Ray was involved with Alex in a land deal and that he was killed by Minter. Minter kills Ray, but, after a chase, is shot dead by Broulle.

JILTED (page 104)

p.c.: Mermaid Beach. **p**: Bill Bennett, Jenny Day **d, sc**: Bill Bennett. **ph**: Geoff Simpson. **ed**: Denise Hunter. **m**: Michael Atkinson. **sd**: Tovio Lember. **p.m.**: David Joyce. **a.d.**: Phil Rich. Colour. 89 mins. Direct to video release. 1987.

1988 Australian Film Awards: Best supporting actress (Tina Bursill).

Richard Moir (Al), Jennifer Cluff (Harry), Steve Jacobs (Bob), Tina Bursill (Paula), Helen Mutkins (Cindy), Ken Radley (Doug).

At the holiday resort of Fraser Island, there is tension among the staff of a tourist hotel. The chef, Al, is having an affair with waitress Cindy; hotel manager Bob is attracted to Paula, the accountant, but she rejects him. Enter Harriet, a refugee from a broken marriage; tough and independent, Harry—as she prefers to be called—becomes passionately involved with Al until her husband, Doug, arrives on the scene. Paula finally succumbs to Bob, who accuses her of being the cause of his impotence; her suicide attempt brings matters to a head.

KADAICHA (page 295)

p.c.: Premiere Film Marketing, Meausa Communications. **ex.p**: Tom Broadbridge. **p**: David Hannay, Charles Hannah. **d**: James Bogle. **sc**: Ian Coughlan. **ph**: Stephen F. Windon. **ed**: Andrew Aristedes. **m**: Peter Westheimer. **sd**: Pam Dunne. **line p**: Lynn Barker. **p.m.**: Julia Ritchie. **a.d.**: Deuel Droogan. Eastmancolour. 88 mins. Direct to video release. 1988.

Zoe Carides (Gail Sorensen), Tom Jennings

(Matt), Eric Oldfield (Alex Sorensen), Natalie McCurry (Tracey), Fiona Gauntlett (Fizz), Sean Scully (Mr Fitzgerald).

In a Sydney suburb, high-school students are dying mysterious deaths: by spider, savage dog, eel-like creature etc. The deaths are linked to an Aboriginal legend and a magic stone, or *kadaicha*. Gail Sorenson discovers that her developer father Alex has built houses and a shopping mall atop an Aboriginal sacred site, and that this is the cause of the killings.

KANGAROO (page 186)

p.c.: Naked Country Productions. **ex.p**: Mark Josem, William Marshall, Peter Sherman, Robert Ward. **p**: Ross Dimsey. **d**: Tim Burstall. **sc**: Evan Jones, based on the novel by D. H. Lawrence. **ph**: Dan Burstall. **ed**: Edward McQueen-Mason. **m**: Nathan Waks. **p.d.**: Tracy Watt. **sd**: Paul Clark. **p.m.**: Darryl Sheen. **a.d.**: Stuart Freeman. Panavision. Eastmancolour. 108 mins. Aust dist: Filmways. UK dist: Enterprise. US dist: Cineplex Odeon. 1986.

1986 Australian Film Awards: Best actress (Judy Davis), best costume design (Terry Ryan).

Colin Friels (Richard Somers), Judy Davis (Harriet Somers), John Walton (Jack Calcott), Julie Nihill (Vicki Calcott), Hugh Keays-Byrne (Kangaroo), Peter Hehir (Jaz), Peter Cummins (Struthers), Tim Robertson (O'Neill), Malcolm Robertson (Publisher).

1922. Richard Somers, an English writer who was found unfit for medical service during the war, and is disillusioned with life in Britain, arrives in a small NSW town with his wife, Harriet. Their neighbour, Jack Calcott, a VC winner, is member of a paramilitary organisation (led by Kangaroo) which aims to infiltrate the Left and gain political power. Somers rejects Kangaroo's offer to be the movement's 'voice', and also rejects overtures from Struthers, the Socialist leader. Vicki is attracted to Somers, who rejects her; and Jack makes a play for Harriet, who is horrified. At a riot instigated by Kangaroo's men, Kangaroo is fatally injured; to the last, Somers rejects his overtures of love and friendship.

THE KILLING OF ANGEL STREET (page 212)

p.c.: Forest Home films. **p**: Anthony Buckley. **d**: Donald Crombie. **sc**: Michael Craig, Evan Jones, Cecil Holmes. **ph**: Peter James. **ed**: Tim Wellburn. **m**: Brian May. **p.d.**: Lindsay Hewson. **sd**: John Phillips. **p.m.**: Jacqueline Ireland. **a.d.**: Andrew Williams. Eastmancolour. 96 mins. Aust dist: Greater Union. 1981.

Liz Alexander (Jessica Simmonds), John Hargreaves (Elliot), Alexander Archdale (B. C.

Simmonds), Reg Lye (Riley), Gordon McDougall (Sir Arthur Wadham), David Downer (Alan Simmonds), Ric Herbert (Ben), Brendon Lunney (Scott).

Jessica Simmonds returns home to Angel Street, East Balmain, after a long stay overseas. She finds her father, B.C., actively involved in efforts to save the street from being redeveloped. Jessica is unimpressed, and moves to a trendy suburb to live with her brother and sister-in-law; but when her father dies in his blazing house (a fire apparently deliberately set), she regrets her inaction. Elliot, a local Communist Party member, tells her about the links between the developers, criminals, corrupt police and government officials; they become lovers before he, too, is murdered and Jessica terrorised by thugs. She goes on television to reveal everything she knows about the Angel Street killings.

KITTY AND THE BAGMAN (page 37)

p.c.: Forest Home Films, in ass. with Adams–Packer Film Productions. **ex.p**: Phillip Adams. **p**: Anthony Buckley. **d**: Donald Crombie. **sc**: John Burney, Philip Cornford. **ph**: Dean Semler. **ed**: Tim Wellburn. **p.d.**: Owen Williams. **cost**: Judith Dorsman. **sd**: John Phillips. **p.m.**: Lynn Gailey. **a.d.**: Stuart Freeman. Panavision. Colour. 99 mins. Aust dist: Greater Union. 1982.

Liddy Clark (Kitty O'Rourke), John Stanton (The Bagman), Val Lehman (Lil Delaney), Gerard Maguire (Cyril Vikkers), Colette Mann (Doris de Salle), Reg Evans (Chicka Delaney), Kylie Foster (Sarah Jones), Danny Adcock (Thomas), Ted Hepple (Sam), John Ewart (Engine driver).

1920. Kitty O'Rourke's husband has been arrested for cutting up a lady-friend. She becomes involved in the Sydney underworld, helped by her prostitute friend, Doris, and by The Bagman, a crooked cop on the take. The Bagman helps Kitty establish herself as a rival gang leader to Lil Delaney, but not before plenty of gun battles and punch-ups between the rival gangs.

KOKODA CRESCENT (page 246)

p.c.: Phillip Emanuel Productions. **p**: Phillip Emanuel. **d**: Ted Robinson. **sc**: Patrick Cook. **ph**: Dan Burstall. **ed**: Rob Gibson. **m**: Peter Best. **p.d.**: Leslie Binns. **sd**: Syd Butterworth. **p.m.**: Lesley Parker. **a.d.**: Phil Rich. Eastmancolour. 83 mins. Aust dist: Roadshow (direct to video release). 1989.

Warren Mitchell (Stan), Bill Kerr (Russ), Ruth Cracknell (Alice). Madge Ryan (Margaret), Martin Vaughan (Eric), Patrick Thompson (Brett), Steve Jacobs (Detective), Penne Hackforth-Jones (Carol), Lisa Rhodes (Jackie).

Stan, Russ and Eric, three World War II

veterans, are troubled by the modern world and especially by the drug scene. When young Brett dies of a heroin overdose, their attempts to enlist help from the media and their local politician yield no result. They take up arms to assault the heavily guarded home of the policeman they consider responsible for Brett's death.

LADY STAY DEAD (page 289)

p.c.: Ryntare. **ex.p**: Alex Hopkins. **p, d, sc**: Terry Bourke. **ph**: Ray Henman. **ed**: Ron Williams. **m**: Bob Young. **p.d.**: Bob Hill. **sd**: Bob Clayton. **a.p**: John Hipwell, Eric Cook. Colour. 95 mins. Direct to video release. 1981.

Chard Hayward (Gordon Mason), Louise Howitt (Jenny Nolan), Deborah Coulis (Marie Coleby), Roger Ward (Ollings), Les Foxcroft (Billy Shepherd), James Elliott (Dunbar).

Gordon Mason, who works as a gardener, is a dangerous psychotic. He is employed by Marie, a bitchy actress, and he rapes and murders her. He then turns his attention to her sister, Jenny, who barricades herself inside her beach-house. Collings and Dunbar, two policemen, arrive on the scene; Mason kills Dunbar but it seems he has been finished off by Collings when he makes an unexpected recovery and final attack on Jenny.

LEONORA (page 137)

p.c.: Revolve Party Productions. **p**: Geoffrey Brown. **d, sc, ph, m**: Derek Strahan. **ed**: Anthony Egan. **sd**: Peter Morton. **a.p.**: Paul Watson, Ruth Redmond. Eastmancolour. 85 mins. Direct to video release. 1985.

Mandi Miller (Leonora), Leon Marvell (Mark), David Evans (Simon), Angela Menzies-Wills (Helena), Ron Beck (Dogon).

When Leonora's car salesman husband, Simon, suggests an open marriage, Leonora responds by starting an affair with Mark, a film director who makes her husband's television commercials. From this, she graduates to lesbian relationships and becomes a disciple of Helena, who practises witchcraft.

LES PATTERSON SAVES THE WORLD (page 306)

p.c.: Humpstead Productions. **ex.p**: Diane Millstead. **p**: Sue Milliken. **d**: George Miller [2]. **sc**: Barry Humphries, Diane Millstead. **ph**: David Connell. **ed**: Tim Wellburn. **m**: Tim Finn. **p.d.**: Graham (Grace) Walker. **cost**: Anna Senior. **sd**: Syd Butterworth. **p.m.**: Tony Winley. **a.d.**: Brian Giddens. Panavision. Eastmancolour. 95 mins. Aust dist: Hoyts. UK dist: Recorded Releasing. 1987.

Barry Humphries (Sir Les Patterson, Dame Edna Everage), Pamela Stephenson (Veronique Crudite), Thaao Penghlis (Col. Richard Godowni), Andrew Clarke (Neville Thonge), Henri Szeps (Dr Herpes, Desiree), Hugh Keays-Byrne (Insp. Farouk), Elizabeth Lemvor (Nancy Borovansky), Garth Meade (Mustafa Toni), Josef Drewniak (Mossolov), Joan Rivers (US President), Esben Storm (Russian Scientist), Joy Westmore (Lady Gwen Patterson), Connie Hobbs (Madge Allsop), Paul Jennings (Australian PM), Graham Kennedy (Brian Lannigan), John Clarke (Mike Rooke).

When Australia's ambassador to the UN, Sir Les Patterson, suffers an attack of flatulence during a debate and thereby sets fire to an Arabian delegate, he is posted to Abu Niveah to make amends. His arrival coincides with a coup which ends with rebel leader Richard Godowni assuming control; Sir Les becomes Australian ambassador. He meets Dr Herpes who has discovered a drug which can cure the severe skin ailment HELP (spread by infected toilet seats, exported by Godowni to the West). KGB agents are after the antidote, as is CIA representative Dame Edna Everage (who arrives in the country escorting a group of housewives— the Possums For Peace tour). Helped by Herpes' glamorous assistant, Veronique, Sir Les foils the villains and saves the free world from the scourge of HELP.

THE LIGHTHORSEMEN (page 27)

p.c.: An RKO Pictures presentation of a Picture Show Production. **ex.p**: Antony I. Ginnane. **p**: Ian Jones, Simon Wincer. **d**: Simon Wincer. **sc**: Ian Jones. **ph**: Dean Semler. **ed**: Adrian Carr. **m**: Mario Millo. **p.d.**: Bernard Hides. **sd**: Lloyd Carrick. **cost**: David Rowe. **stunts**: Grant Page. **p.m.**: Phillip Corr. **a.d.**: Bob Donaldson. Panavision. Eastmancolour. 128 mins. Aust dist: Hoyts. US dist: Cinecom. UK dist; Medusa. 1987.

1988 Australian Film Awards: Best music, sound.

Jon Blake (Scotty), Peter Phelps (Dave Mitchell), Tony Bonner (Lt Col. [Swagman Bill] Bourchier), Bill Kerr (Lt Gen. Sir Harry Chauvel), John Walton (Tas), Gary Sweet (Frank), Tim McKenzie (Chiller), Sigrid Thornton (Anne), Anthony Andrews (Major Meinertzhagen), Anthony Hawkins (Gen. Sir Edmund Allenby), Gerard Kennedy (Ismet Bey), Shane Briant (Reichert), Serge Lazareff (Rankin), Ralph Cotterill (Von Kressenstein), John Heywood (Mr Mitchell).

Dave Mitchell enlists in the Australian Light Horse in 1917 and is posted to Palestine to replace the popular Frank, who has been fatally wounded. At first, Dave is not popular with Scotty, Tas and Chiller, Frank's mates, especially as he finds himself unable to fire on the enemy. A romance with Anne, a nurse, lightens his load, and Dave becomes an unarmed stretcher bearer. At the legendary charge of the Light Horse against the German positions at Beersheba, Tas is killed but Dave manages to save Chiller's life, almost at the cost of his own.

LONELY HEARTS (page 94)

p.c.: Adams–Packer Film Productions. **ex.p**: Phillip Adams. **p**: John B. Murray. **d**: Paul Cox. **sc**: Paul Cox, John Clarke. **ph**: Yuri Sokol. **ed**: Tim Lewis. **m**: Norman Kaye. **p.d.**: Neil Angwin. **sd**: Ken Hammond. **a.p.**: Erwin Rado, Fran Haarsma. **p.m.**: Jane Ballantyne. **a.d.**: Bernard Eddy. Eastmancolour. 94 mins. Aust dist: Greater Union. US dist: Samuel Goldwyn Co. UK dist: Gala. 1981.

1982 Australian Film Awards: Best film.

Wendy Hughes (Patricia Curnow), Norman Kaye (Peter Thompson), John Finlayson (George), Julia Blake (Pamela), Jonathan Hardy (Bruce), Chris Haywood (Detective), Kris McQuade (Rosemarie), Irene Inescourt (Patricia's mother), Vic Gordon (Patricia's father).

Fifty-year-old bachelor Peter Thompson, a piano tuner, feels lonely after his mother's death and meets shy, dowdy, thirtyish Patricia Curnow through a dating service. He persuades her to join him on stage in an amateur production of Strindberg's *The Father*, but his tentative sexual approaches are met with horror. Peter's friend, George, tries to reconcile the couple, and Patricia finally stands up to her overly protective parents and goes to see Peter again . . .

LUIGI'S LADIES (page 309)

p.c.: Tra-La-La Films. **ex.p**: Wendy Hughes. **p**: Patric Juillet. **d**: Judy Morris. **sc**: Jennifer Claire, Ronald Allan, Wendy Hughes, Judy Morris. **ph**: Steve Mason. **ed**: Pamela Barnetta. **m**: Sharon Calcraft. **p.d.**: Melody Cooper. **sd**: Ken Hammond. **a.p.**: Rachel Symes. **p.m.**: Brenda Pam. **a.d.**: Charles Rotherham. Colour. 94 mins. Aust dist: Hoyts. 1989.

Wendy Hughes (Sara), Sandy Gore (Cee), Anne Tenney (Jane), David Rappaport (Luigi), John Walton (Steve), Serge Lazareff (Trev), Ray Meagher (Lance), Joe Spano (Nick), Max Cullen (Chef), Maggie Dence (Shandra), Brian Adams (Tom Stoker), Genevieve Lemon (Debbie).

Three yuppie women, Sara, Cee and Jane, meet regularly for lunch at Luigi's, a fancy Italian harbourside restaurant. Sara, editor of a glossy women's magazine, is married to Steve, a stockbroker, and embarks on an affair with Nick, a wealthy Italian Australian. Cee is divorced and lonely: she spends all her money on expensive clothes. She starts an affair with Lance, a policeman she meets at a gym, but he has sexual hang-ups. Jane has three children with another on the way and (rightly) suspects her wine-dealer husband Trev of having affairs. All three, and Luigi, are wiped out in the 1987 stockmarket crash and have to change their lifestyles.

MAD MAX BEYOND THUNDERDOME (page 85)

p.c.: Kennedy-Miller Productions. **p**: George Miller (1). **co-p**: Terry Hayes, Doug Mitchell. **d**: George Miller, George Ogilvie. **sc**: George Miller, Terry Hayes. **ph**: Dean Semler. **ed**: Richard Francis-Bruce. **m**: Maurice Jarre. **p.d.**: Graham (Grace) Walker. **sd**: Lloyd Carrick. **sp. ef.**: Mike Wood. **stunts**: Grant Page. **p.m.**: Antonia Barnard. **a.d.**: Steve Andrews. Panavision. Colour. 106 mins. Aust dist: Roadshow (Warner Bros). US dist: Warner Bros. UK dist: Columbia–EMI-Warner. 1985.

Mel Gibson (Mad Max), Tina Turner (Aunty Entity), Bruce Spence (Jedediah), Frank Thring (The Collector), Angry Anderson (Ironbar), Robert Grubb (Pigkiller), George Spartels (Blackfinger), Edwin Hodgeman (Dr Dealgood), Bob Hornery (Waterseller), Angelo Rossitto (The Master), Paul Larsson (The Blaster), Helen Buday (Savannah Nix), Mark Spain (Mr Skyfish), Rod Zuanic (Scrooloose), Justine Clarke (Anna Goanna), Tom Jennings (Slake), Ollie Hall, Tushka Hose (Guards).

In post-holocaust Australia, ex-cop Mad Max is robbed of his car by Jedediah, and pursues him to Bartertown, a community where everything is for sale and where gladiatorial combats are staged. Dictator Aunty Entity enlists Max's help in destroying Master-Blaster, the dwarf-giant who rules the underground. Max challenges Blaster to mortal combat in the Thunderdome, and wins—but refuses to kill. Abandoned in the desert, Max is found by Savannah Nix, member of a lost tribe awaiting the return of the pilot who flew them there before the holocaust. Max leads them to Bartertown, rescues Master from Aunty's clutches, and sets off with Aunty and her guards in pursuit. The survivors fly over the ruins of Sydney, while Max returns to the desert.

MAD MAX 2 (US title: *The Road Warrior*) (page 80)

p.c.: Kennedy-Miller Entertainment. **p**: Byron Kennedy. **d**: George Miller (1). **sc**: Terry Hayes,

George Miller, Brian Hannant. **ph**: Dean Semler. **ed**: David Stiven, Tim Wellburn. **m**: Brian May. **p.d.**: Graham Walker. **sd**: Lloyd Carrick. **stunts**: Max Aspin. **2nd unit d, a.d.**: Brian Hannant. **p.m.**: Patrick Clayton. Panavision. Colour. 93 mins (in Australia). 96 mins (elsewhere). Aust dist: Roadshow (Warner Bros). US dist: Warner Bros. UK dist: Columbia–EMI–Warner. 1981.

1982 Australian Film Awards: Best director, editing, production design, costume design (Norma Moriceau), sound.

Mel Gibson (Max Rockatansky), Bruce Spence (Gyro Captain), Vernon Wells (Wez), Emil Minty (Feral Kid), Mike Preston (Pappagallo), Kjell Nilsson (Humungus), Virginia Hey (Warrior Woman), Syd Heylen (Curmudgeon), Moira Claux (Big Rebecca), David Slingsby (Quiet Man), Arkie Whiteley (Lusty Girl), Steve J. Spears (Mechanic), Max Phipps (Toadie), David Downer (Wounded Man), Max Fairchild (Broken Victim).

Left alone in the Australian desert after avenging the murder of his wife and child, Max Rockatansky, an ex-policeman, overpowers the Gyro Captain who tells him where he can find petrol, which has become a precious commodity. He finds the refinery, which is under the control of Pappagallo, besieged by Humungus and his vicious bike warriors. Max agrees to help Pappagallo's peaceful followers break the blockade, and risks his life to bring back a huge truck which can carry the petrol supplies. At first Max refuses to lead the escape, but after an attack from Humungus and his gang (after which he is aided by the Gyro Captain), he agrees. In the ensuing chase, Pappagallo and several of his followers are killed: eventually, Humungus is also killed. Max goes off alone into the desert.

MALCOLM (page 323)
p.c.: Cascade Films. **ex.p**: Bryce Menzies. **p**: David Parker, Nadia Tass. **d**: Nadia Tass. **sc, ph**: David Parker. **ed**: Ken Sallows. **m**: Simon Jeffes. **p.d.**: Rike Kullack. **sd**: Paul Clark. **a.p.**: Timothy White. **p.m.**: Chris Haywood. **a.d.**: Tony Mahood. Colour. 86 mins. Aust dist: Hoyts. US dist: Vestron. UK dist: Enterprise. 1986.

1986 Australian Film Awards: Best film, director, original screenplay, actor (Colin Friels), supporting actor (John Hargreaves), supporting actress (Lindy Davies), editing, sound, Byron Kennedy Award (David Parker, Nadia Tass).

Colin Friels (Malcolm Hughes), John Hargreaves (Frank Baker), Lindy Davies (Judith), Chris Haywood (Willy), Charles 'Bud' Tingwell (Tramways Supervisor), Beverley Phillips (Mrs T.), Heather Mitchell (Barmaid), Katerina Tassopoulos (Jenny's mother), Judith Stratford (Jenny).

Malcolm Hughes is a painfully shy, slightly retarded man with an amazing gift for practical mechanics: the house in which he lives (alone since the death of his mother) is filled with clever gadgets. When he loses his job on the tramways, Mrs T., a friendly local shopkeeper, persuades him to advertise for a lodger. Enter Frank Baker, a petty criminal who arrives with his girlfriend Judith in tow. After initial reservations on both sides, Frank is won over by Malcolm's 'getaway car', which splits in two when the police give chase. Malcolm subsequently devises an ingenious way to rob a bank, and the trio wind up in Lisbon with the loot.

MALPRACTICE (page 211)
p.c.: Film Australia. **ex.p**: Bruce Moir, Aviva Ziegler. **p**: Tristram Miall. **d**: Bill Bennett. **sc**: Jenny Ainge (and the cast). **ph**: Steve Arnold. **ed**: Denise Hunter. **m**: Michael Atkinson. **sd**: Max Hensser. **p.m.**: John Russell. **a.d.**: Carrie Soeterboek. Colour. 91 mins. 1989.

Caz Lederman (Coral Davis), Bob Baines (Doug Davis), Ian Gilmour (Dr Frank Harrison), Pat Thomson (Sr Margaret Beattie), Charles Little (Dr Tom Cotterslow), Janet Stanley (Sr Diane Shaw), Dorothy Alison (Maureen Davis).

Coral and Doug Davis, a working-class couple, have two small girls and hope that Coral's latest pregnancy will result in a son. Coral goes into labour on a Saturday when her regular gynaecologist, Dr Cotterslow, is out on his boat. At the overcrowded hospital, an overworked and over-confident young doctor, Harrison, makes a series of wrong decisions which result in the baby (a boy) being born brain-damaged. Following complaints from Coral and some of the nursing staff, Harrison is brought before a medical tribunal.

THE MAN FROM SNOWY RIVER (page 64)
p.c.: Michael Edgley International–Cambridge Films. **ex.p**: Michael Edgley, Simon Wincer. **p**: Geoff Burrowes. **d**: George Miller (2). **sc**: John Dixon (from an original script by Fred (Cul) Cullen, based on the poem by A. B. 'Banjo' Paterson). **ph**: Keith Wagstaff. **ed**: Adrian Carr. **m**: Bruce Rowland. **p.d.**: Leslie Binns. **sd**: Gary Wilkins. **p.m.**: Michael Lake. **a.d.**: Murray Newey. **2nd unit d**: John Dixon. Panavision. Eastmancolour. 102 mins. Aust dist: Hoyts. US, UK dist: 20th Century-Fox. 1982.

1982 Australian Film Awards: Best music.

Kirk Douglas (Spur, Harrison), Jack Thompson (Clancy), Tom Burlinson (Jim Craig), Sigrid Thornton (Jessica Harrison), Lorraine Bayly

(Rosemary), Terence Donovan (Henry Craig), June Jago (Mrs Bailey), Gus Mercurio (Frew), David Bradshaw ('Banjo' Paterson), Tony Bonner (Kane), Chris Haywood (Curly).

1888. Jim Craig's father is killed during a hunt for wild horses, and the youth is helped by old Spur, a mysterious mountain man. Jim is hired by Harrison, a property owner, and befriends his employer's daughter, Jessica, but is despised by the cattlemen because he hails from the mountains. Jim rescues Jessica when she is caught in a storm in the mountains; and he discovers that Spur and Harrison are brothers and that Jessica's mother had loved them both. Jim joins a hunt for a stolen prize horse, and recovers a valuable herd of wild horses into the bargain—he has made his mark.

THE MAN FROM SNOWY RIVER II
(US title: *Return to Snowy River Part II*)
(page 67)
p.c.: Burrowes Film Group–Hoyts Entertainment. **ex.p**: Dennis Wright, John Kearney. **p, d**: Geoff Burrowes. **sc**: Geoff Burrowes, John Dixon. **ph**: Keith Wagstaff. **ed**: Gary Woodyard. **m**: Bruce Rowland. **p.d.**: Leslie Binns. **sd**: Gary Wilkins. **2nd unit d, 2nd unit ph**: David Eggby. **cost**: Jenny Arnott. **p.m.**: Stuart Menzies. **a.d.**: John Powditch. Panavision. Eastmancolour. 97 mins. Aust dist: Hoyts. US dist: Buena Vista. 1988.

Tom Burlinson (Jim Craig), Sigrid Thornton (Jessica Harrison), Brian Dennehy (Harrison), Nicholas Eadie (Alistair Patton), Bryan Marshall (Harry Hawker), Rhys McConnochie (Patton Sr), Mark Hembrow (Seb), Peter Cummins (Jake), Cornelia Francis (Mrs Darcy), Tony Barry (Jacko).

Jim Craig returns to the High Country after spending time in the outback mustering wild horses. He finds that his sweetheart, Jessica, has been forced by her father, Harrison, to become engaged to Alistair Patton, the snobbish son of a local banker to whom Harrison is in debt. Reviled by the landed gentry as a 'hick' and a 'drifter', Jim has to prove himself all over again, and win over Jessica. He defeats Alistair in a race, survives a fall from his horse (shot from under him by the vengeful Alistair) and recovers in time to defeat his unscrupulous rival and win Jessica's hand.

MAN OF FLOWERS (page 124)
p.c.: Flowers International. **p**: Jane Ballantyne, Paul Cox. **d**: Paul Cox. **sc**: Paul Cox, Bob Ellis. **ph**: Yuri Sokol. **ed**: Tim Lewis. **p.d.**: Asher Bilu. **sd**: Lloyd Carrick. **a.p.**: Tony Llewellyn-Jones. Fujicolor. 92 mins. Aust dist: Roadshow. US dist: Spectrafilm. UK dist: Palace. 1983.

1983 Australian Film Awards: Best actor (Norman Kaye).

Norman Kaye (Charles Bremer), Alyson Best (Lisa), Chris Haywood (David), Sarah Walker (Jane), Julia Blake (Art Teacher), Bob Ellis (Psychiatrist), Barry Dickins (Postman), Patrick Cook (Coppershop man), Victoria Eagger (Angela), Werner Herzog (Father), Hilary Kelly (Mother), James Stratford (Young Charles), Tony Llewellyn-Jones (Church Warden).

Charles Bremer, wealthy and reclusive since the death of his beloved mother (to whom he still writes long letters) pays Lisa, a model he met at life classes, to undress for him while he listens to an aria from *Lucia di Lammermoor*. Lisa lives with her violent lover, David, an action painter, but leaves him for Jane, a lesbian. David tries to blackmail Charles into buying one of his paintings: Charles kills him, and has his body covered in bronze. The resulting statue is presented to the city.

MANGANINNIE (page 35)
p.c.: Tasmanian Film Corp. **ex.p**: Malcolm Smith. **p**: Gilda Baracchi, **d**: John Honey. **sc**: Ken Kelso, from the novel by Beth Roberts. **ph**: Gary Hansen. **ed**: Mike Woolveridge. **m**: Peter Sculthorpe. **sd**: John Schiefelbein. **p.m.**: Pamela Vanneck. **a.d.**: Robert Hynard. Eastmancolour. 88 mins. Aust dist: Greater Union. 1980.

1980 Australian Film Awards: Best music.

Mawuyul Yanthalawuy (Manganinnie), Anna Ralph (Joanna Waterman), Phillip Hinton (Edward Waterman), Elaine Mangan (Mrs Waterman), Yunupingu (Meenopeekameena), Reg Evans (Quinn), Jonathan Elliott (Simon Waterman), Timothy Latham (William Waterman).

Tasmania, the 1830s. During the infamous 'black drive', in which Aborigines were systematically slaughtered, Manganinnie is separated from her family. She stumbles across Joanna, a little white girl, and 'adopts' her, taking her with her on a long journey across the island, and teaching her Aboriginal language and lore. Eventually, Joanna is returned to her parents.

MARAUDERS (page 290)
p.c.: A Magic Men production. **p, d, sc, ph**: Mark Savage. **ed**: Paul Harrington, Colin Savage, Mark Savage. **m**: John Merakovsky, Mark Horpinitch. **sd**: Paul Harrington. **stunts**: Shaun Sullivan. Colour. 76 mins. 1987.

Colin Savage (Emilio East), Zero Montana (Jamie [JD] Kruger), Megan Napier (Becky Howard), Paul Harrington (David Fraser), Janie Fearon, Sam Davies, Michael Deflorid, Audrey Davies, Kerry Harrington, James Cain, Richard

Wolstencroft, Anthony Artman.

Emilio East murders his wife because she will not give him the keys to the car: they were in his pocket all along. Meanwhile, Jamie Kruger, who has been bringing bodies home to 'play with', stabs his mother to death when she calls the police. Emilio and Jamie team up and pursue schoolgirl Becky and her womanising lover David, who drive out of the city. The lovers hide out in a house in the woods, attacked by the killers and also by vigilantes seeking revenge for a rape-murder committed by Emilio and Jamie. They hang Jamie, and Emilio shoots himself to avoid capture.

THE MARSUPIALS: THE HOWLING III (page 303)

p.c.: Bacannia Entertainment. **ex.p**: Edward Simons, Steve Lane, Robert Pringle. **p**: Charles Waterstreet, Philippe Mora. **d, sc**: Philippe Mora (from the book *Howling III* by Gary Brander). **ph**: Louis Irving. **ed**: Lee Smith. **m**: Allan Zavod. **p.d.**: Ross Major. **sd**: Bob Clayton. **sp. ef.**: Bob McCarron. **co-p**: Gilda Baracchi. **p.m.**: Rosslyn Abernathy. **a.d.**: Stuart Wood. Colour. 94 mins. Direct to video release in Australia. US dist: Manson International. 1987.

Barry Otto (Prof. Harry Beckmeyer), Imogen Annesley (Jerboa), Dasha Blahova (Olga Gorki), Max Fairchild (Thylo), Ralph Cotterill (Prof. Sharp), Leigh Biolos (Donny Martin), Frank Thring (Jack Citron), Michael Pate (US President), Barry Humphries (Dame Edna Everage), Carole Skinner (Yara), Brian Adams (General Miller), Bill Collins (Doctor), Christopher Pate (Security agent).

Professor Harry Beckmeyer is a scientist obsessed with discovering more about a species of uniquely Australian marsupial werewolves, Jerboa, member of a werewolf tribe, wanders into Sydney and gets a job as extra in a horror film, *Shape Shifters Part 8*, being directed by Jack Citron; three female members of the tribe come looking for her disguised as nuns, but turn into werewolves at the film's wrap party. Meanwhile, Olga Gorki, a Russian ballerina and secret (European) werewolf, plans to marry Thylo, leader of the marsupial werewolves, but falls instead for Beckmeyer, and they try to escape the vengeance of the werewolves. Meanwhile, Jerboa has given birth to a baby by Donny Martin, an assistant director.

. . . MAYBE THIS TIME (page 111)

p.c.: Cherrywood Films, in ass. with NSW Film Corp. **p**: Brian Kavanagh. **d**: Chris McGill. **sc**: Anne Brooksbank, Bob Ellis. **ph**: Russell Boyd.

ed: Wayne Le Clos. **p.d.**: Chris Webster. **sd**: Lloyd Carrick. **p.m.**: Sue Milliken. **a.d.**: Elizabeth Knight. Eastmancolour. 96 mins. Self-distributed. 1980.

1980 Australian Film Awards: Best supporting actress (Jill Perryman).

Judy Morris (Fran), Bill Hunter (Stephen), Mike Preston (Paddy), Jill Perryman (Fran's mother), Ken Shorter (Alan), Michele Fawdon (Margo), Leonard Teale (Minister), Jude Kuring (Meredith), Rod Mullinar (Jack), Chris Haywood (Salesman), Lyndall Barbour (Miss Bates), Lorna Lesley (Susy Williams), Tessa Mallos (Sarah), Celia de Burgh (Paddy's girl).

The Whitlam Era. Fran, 29, who comes from a country town, has moved to Sydney leaving behind her Country Party boyfriend, Alan. She has an affair with Stephen, a married secretary of a government minister, then has a fling with Paddy, her boss at Sydney University (but he is unfaithful). Meanwhile, her sister, Margo, is unhappily married with three children, and her widowed mother is lonely. Fran decides to go to Europe to meet up with Jenny, her close friend: but at the airport she hears Jenny has been killed in a car accident.

MELVIN, SON OF ALVIN (page 309)

p.c.: McElroy and McElroy. **p**: James McElroy. **d**: John Eastway. **sc**: Morris Gleitzman. **ph**: Ross Berryman. **ed**: John Holland. **m**: Colin Stead. **p.d.**: Jon Dowding. **a.p.**: Tim Sanders, Wilma Schinella. **p.m.**: Tim Sanders. **a.d.**: David Clarke, Colour. 85 mins. Aust dist: Roadshow. 1984.

Gerry Sont (Melvin Simpson), Lemita Psillakis (Gloria Giannis), Graeme Blundell (Alvin Purple), Jon Finlayson (Burnbaum), Tina Bursill (Dee Tanner), Colin McEwan (Mr Simpson), Abigail (Mrs Simpson), David Argue (Cameraman), Arianthe Galani (Mrs Giannis), Greg Stroud (Ferret), Katy Manning (Estelle).

Melvin Simpson has inherited the sexual prowess of his father, Alvin Purple (of *Alvin Purple* and *Alvin Rides Again*), though he is terrified of women. A TV station assigns journalist Dee Tanner to do a story on Melvin's reunion with his father, while Melvin befriends Gloria, a cinema usherette, who wants to help him overcome his phobias.

MIDNITE SPARES (page 275)

p.c.: Filmco, Wednesday Investments. **ex.p**: John Fitzpatrick. **p**: Tom Burstall. **d**: Quentin Masters. **sc**: Terry Larsen. **ph**: Geoff Burton. **ed**: Andrew Prowse. **m**: Cameron Allan. **p.d.**: George Liddle. **sd**: Lloyd Carrick. **stunts**: Vic Wilson. **p.m.**: Jenny Day. **a.d.**: Derek Seabourne. Colour. 88 mins. Aust dist: Roadshow. 1982.

James Laurie (Steve), Gia Carides (Ruth), Max Cullen (Tomas), Bruce Spence (Wimpy), David Argue (Rabbit), Tony Barry (Howard), John Clayton (Vincent), Graeme Blundell (Sidebottom), Terry Camilleri (Uncle Harry), Jonathan Coleman (Wayne), Amanda Dole (Janelle), Ray Marshall (Panton), John Godden (Chris the Rat).

Steve returns to Sydney in search of his father, who has disappeared after refusing to join a gang of thieves who steal and strip cars. He teams up with his father's old partner, Tomas, and mechanics Wimpy and Rabbit, and also falls for free-spirited Ruth, a Greek girl whose mother is overly protective. Steve and his friends run foul of Howard and Vincent, who run the gang of car thieves, but manage to overcome them.

MINNAMURRA (Alternative title: Outback) (page 68)

p.c.: International Film Management, Burrowes Film Group, John Sexton Productions. **ex.p**: Antony I. Ginnane, Kent Lovell. **p, sc**: John Sexton. **d**: Ian Barry. **ph**: Ross Berryman. **ed**: Henry Dangar. **m**: Mario Millo. **p.d.**: Owen Paterson. **sd**: Ben Osmo. **cost**: Terry Ryan. **line p**: Su Armstrong. **p.m.**: Grant Hill. **a.d.**: John Wild. Eastmancolour. 91 mins. Aust dist: Hoyts. US dist: Samuel Goldwyn, 1988.

Jeff Fahey (Creed), Tushka Bergen (Alice Richards), Steve Vidler (Jack Donaghue), Richard Moir (Thompson), Shane Briant (Allenby), Drew Forsythe (Henry Iverson), Sandy Gore (Aunt Maude), Fred Parslow (Richards), Cornelia Francis (Caroline Richards).

At the turn of the century, Alice Richards, a wilful young woman, lives with her parents in the gracious old homestead of Minnamurra, but her father is going bankrupt. Alice is adored by Creed, a rich American businessman, who secretly buys up the property, but she initially prefers Jack Donaghue, a d' over who is into union politics (the union fails when its treasurer, Thompson, absconds with the funds). Creed's ships are sabotaged by Alice's jealous neighbour, Allenby, but the trio join forces to drive 100 horses across country to sell to Kitchener (for the Boer War), and Alice settles for Creed.

MOLLY (page 345)

p.c.: Troplisa Productions, in ass. with NSW Film Corp., M & L P/L. **ex.p**: Richard Brennan. **p**: Hilary Linstead. **d**: Ned Lander. **sc**: Phillip Roope, Mark Thomas, Ned Lander, Hilary Linstead. **ph**: Vincent Monton. **ed**: Stewart Young. **m**: Graeme Isaac. **p.d.**: Robert Dein. **sd**: Greg Bell. **p.m.**: Barbara Gibbs. Eastmancolour. 84 mins. Aust dist: Greater Union. 1983.

Claudia Karvan (Maxie Ireland), Garry McDonald (Jones), Reg Lye (Old Dan), Melissa Jaffer (Aunty Jenny), Ruth Cracknell (Mrs Reach), Leslie Dayman (Bill Ireland), Robin Laurie (Stella), Tanya Lester (Gina), Molly (Herself).

Maxie, freshly arrived in Sydney, meets old Dan at Central Railway Station when he collapses: the sick old man entrusts his singing dog Molly to the little girl. However, Molly is coveted by the evil Jones, a former short-order cook, who assumes various guises (circus clown, nun) to gain Maxie's confidence. Eventually, circus folk step in to help Maxie and Molly escape from Jones.

MONKEY GRIP (page 139)

p.c.: Pavilion Films. **ex.p**: Danny Collins. **p**: Patricia Lovell. **d**: Ken Cameron. **sc**: Ken Cameron, Helen Garner (based on the novel by Helen Garner). **ph**: David Gribble. **ed**: David Huggett. **m**: Bruce Smeaton. **p.d.**: Clark Munro. **sd**: Mark Lewis. **a.p.**: Treisha Ghent. **p.m.**: Will Davies, **a.d.**: Stuart Freeman. Eastmancolour. 100 mins. Aust dist: Roadshow. US dist: Cinecom. UK dist: Mainline. 1981.

1982 Australian Film Awards: Best actress (Noni Hazlehurst).

Noni Hazlehurst (Nora), Colin Friels (Javo), Alice Garner (Gracie), Harold Hopkins (Willie), Candy Raymond (Lillian), Michael Caton (Clive), Tim Burns (Martin), Christina Amphlett (Angela), Cathy Downes (Eve), Lisa Peers (Rita), Vera Plevnik (Jessie), Don Miller-Robinson (Gerald), Justin Ridley (Roaster), Pearl Christie (Juliet), Esben Storm (Record Producer).

Nora, thirty-three and single, lives with her 10-year-old daughter, Gracie, in the Melbourne suburb of Carlton. Her affair with Martin comes to an end when she meets Javo, an actor with a drug habit; when he is taken ill, Nora looks after him. Recovered, Javo leaves for Asia with Martin and ends up in prison in Bangkok. Nora becomes involved with members of a rock group and with other men until Javo returns and they get back together for a while, but it does not work out. Nora tries to resume her life and starts writing: she moves in with Gerald, a musician; Javo moves in with Nora's friend, Lillian. Some time later, Nora and Javo meet again, their relationship now apparently more stable.

THE MORE THINGS CHANGE . . . (page 105)

p.c.: Syme International, in ass. with NSW Film Corp. **p**: Jill Robb. **d**: Robyn Nevin. **sc**: Moya Wood. **ph**: Dan Burstall. **ed**: Jill Bilcock. **m**: Peter Best. **p.d.**: Josephine Ford. **sd**: John Phillips. **a.p.**:

Greg Ricketson. **p.m.**: Trish Hepworth. **a.d.**: Adrian Pickersgill. Panavision. Eastmancolour. 95 mins. Aust dist: Hoyts. 1985.

Judy Morris (Connie), Barry Otto (Lex), Victoria Longley (Geraldine), Lewis Fitz-Gerald (Barry), Peter Carroll (Roley), Louise Le Ney (Lydia), Owen Johnson (Nicholas), Brenda Addie (Angela), Joanne Barker (Bridesmaid), Bill Bennett (Eric).

Lex and Connie are trying a new lifestyle. Lex has given up his job, though Connie has kept hers (she is a publisher) and commutes daily to Melbourne from the farm they have bought in the country. Lex looks after their small son, Nicholas, and works on the farm, planning for them to be self-sufficient. Things get too much for him, so Connie hires Geraldine as a live-in babysitter: Geraldine is pregnant (but not, unfortunately, by her fiancé, Barry). Geraldine plans to have her baby without Barry's knowledge, and eventually gives birth to a girl who is taken away for adoption. At the wedding ceremony, young Nicholas spills the beans about the baby. Connie, who has been jealous of the easy-going relationship between Lex and Geraldine, decides she is fed-up with being the bread-winner and that the farm must be sold.

MORTGAGE (page 211)
p.c.: Film Australia. **p**: Bruce Moir. **d, sc**: Bill Bennett. **ph**: Steve Arnold. **ed**: Sara Bennett. **m**: Michael Atkinson. **sd**: Max Hensser. **p.m.**: Hilary May. **a.d.**: Nikki Long. Colour. 90 mins. 1989.

Brian Vriends (Dave Dodd), Doris Younnane (Tina Dodd), Bruce Venables (George Shooks), Andrew Gilbert (Kevin Grant), Paul Coolahan (Jack Napper), Bob Ellis (Philosophical Drunk).

Dave and Tina Dodd want a home of their own. They make a contract with the shifty Jack Napper who runs a company selling standard homes. Napper suggests builder George Shooks, who proves to have an unreliable assistant, Kevin, and to be in financial difficulties. Everything goes wrong with the home-building, placing a great strain on the Dodd marriage.

MOVING OUT (page 359)
p.c.: A Pattinson–Ballantyne Production. **p**: Jane Ballantyne, Michael Pattinson. **d**: Michael Pattinson. **sc**: Jan Sardi. **ph**: Vincent Monton. **ed**: Robert Martin. **m**: Danny Beckerman. **p.d.**: Neil Angwin. **sd**: Geoff White. **a.p., p.m.**: Julie Monton. **p.cons**: Rosa Colosimo. **a.d.**: Robert Kewley. Eastmancolour. 89 mins. Aust dist: Greater Union. 1982.

Vince Colosimo (Gino), Peter Sardi (Lino Condello), Kate Jason (Mrs Condello), Nicole Miranda (Maria), Luciano Catenacci (Maria's father), Sylvie Fonti (Maria's mother), Brian James (Mr Aitkens), Sandy Gore (Miss Stanislaus), Maurice Devincentis (Renato), Tibor Gyapjas (Allan), Sally Cooper (Sandy), Desiree Smith (Helen), Thomas Falla (Franca), Julio Dalleore (Pippo), Ivar Kants.

Fifteen-year-old Gino lives in the Melbourne suburb of Fitzroy with his sister and traditional Italian family; he wants to be an Aussie and not even talk 'wog', and is horrified when his father, Lino, announces the family is moving to the outer suburbs. Police become involved when Gino, two mates and two girls break into a house. Gino is also torn between Maria, his cousin, newly-arrived from Italy, and Sandy, the Aussie girl who seems to fancy him. Eventually, though, father's will prevails, and the Condellos move out of Fitzroy.

MULL (Alternative title: *Mullaway*) (page 363)
p.c.: International Film Management, Ukiyo Films. **ex.p**: Antony I. Ginnane. **p**: D. Howard Grigsby. **d**: Don McLennan. **sc**: Jon Stephens (from the novel by Bron Nicholls). **ph, ed**: Zbigniew Friedrich. **m**: Trevor Lucas, Michael Atkinson. **p.d.**: Patrick Reardon. **sd**: Lloyd Carrick. **p.m.**: Andrew Wiseman. **a.d.**: Bob Donaldson. Eastmancolour. 90 mins. Aust dist: Filmpac. 1988.

1988 Australian Film Awards: Best actress (Nadine Garner); AFI Members Prize.

Nadine Garner (Phoebe Mullens), Bill Hunter (Mr Mullens), Sue Jones (Mrs Mullens), Craig Morrison (Steve Mullens), Bradley Kilpatrick (Alan Mullens), Kymara Stowers (Jodie Mullens), Dominic Sweeney (Jim), Juno Roxas (Guido), Mary Coustas (Helen).

The Mullens family live in the Melbourne suburb of St Kilda. When Mrs Mullens is taken ill (terminally as it proves), it is up to 17-year-old Phoebe ('Mull') to drop out of school and care for her father, a security guard and fanatical born-again Christian, and three siblings. She loses touch with best friend Helen (whose wedding turns out to be a strangely sad affair) and is attracted to Guido, a friend of her older brother Steve—until she discovers Guido is gay and that Steve is on heroin. Her mother dies, and Mull faces an uncertain future.

MY FIRST WIFE (page 99)
p.c.: Dofine Productions. **p**: Jane Ballantyne, Paul Cox. **d, sc**: Paul Cox (with script collaboration from Bob Ellis). **ph**: Yuri Sokol. **ed**: Tim Lewis. **m**: (Various). **p.d.**: Asher Bilu. **sd**: Ken Hammond.

a.p.: Tony Llewellyn-Jones. **p.m.**: Santhana Naidu. **a.d.**: Erwin Rado. Colour. 95 mins. Aust dist: Roadshow. US dist: Spectrafilm. UK dist: Artificial Eye. 1984.

1984 Australian Film Awards: Best director, original screenplay; actor (John Hargreaves).

John Hargreaves (John), Wendy Hughes (Helen), Lucy Angwin (Lucy), David Cameron (Tom), Anna Jemison (Hilary), Charles Tingwell (Helen's father), Betty Lucas (Helen's mother), Robin Lovejoy (John's father), Lucy Uralov (John's mother), Jon Finlayson (Bernard), Julia Blake (Kirstin), Renee Geyer (Barmaid), Tony Llewellyn-Jones (Doctor), Neela Dey (Migrant Teacher).

John, a composer and host of a late-night classical music radio programme, is told by Helen, his wife of fourteen years, that she loves somebody else and wants to leave him. He is shocked and angry, especially when Helen no longer allows him to make love to her. He loses his grip, attempts suicide, kidnaps their daughter Lucy, returns her, and causes a disturbance at the home of his wife's lover, Tom. To no avail: the marriage is over. Helen and John meet again at the funeral of John's Russian-born father, and as they leave the cemetery, John takes Helen's hand . . .

THE NAKED COUNTRY (page 72)

p.c.: Naked Country Productions, in ass. with Queensland Film Corp. **ex.p**: Mark Josem, Robert Ward, Bill Marshall. **p**: Ross Dimsey. **d**: Tim Burstall. **sc**: Ross Dimsey, Tim Burstall (from the novel by Morris West). **ph**: David Eggby. **ed**: Tony Paterson. **m**: Bruce Smeaton. **p.d.**: Philip Warner. **sd**: Max Bowring. **p.m.**: Patricia Blunt, Helen Watts. **a.d.**: John Warren. Colour. 92 mins. Aust dist: Filmpac. 1985.

John Stanton (Lance Dillon), Rebecca Gilling (Mary Dillon), Ivar Kants (Sgt Neil Adams), Tommy Lewis (Mundara), John Harratt (Mick Conrad), Simon Chilvers (Insp. Poole), Neela Dey (Menyan).

North Queensland, 1955. Lance Dillon, a tough property owner, neglects his pretty wife, Mary. Conflict with local Aborigines, and especially renegade Mundara, come to a head with the killing of Dillon's prize Brahman bull. Inspector Poole sends Sgt Neil Adams, a weak, vacillating cop freshly returned from work as a mercenary in Africa, to help Dillon: but the alcoholic Adams soon makes a play for Mary. Conrad, Dillon's foreman, is killed by the blacks, and Dillon himself badly speared. However, he survives and manages to overcome Mundara. Adams, however, is killed by the blacks.

THE NAVIGATOR: A MEDIEVAL ODYSSEY (page 77)

p.c.: Arenafilm-Film Investment Corp (New Zealand), Australian Film Commission. **p**: John Maynard. **d**: Vincent Ward. **sc**: Vincent Ward, Kelly Lyons, Geoff Chapman. **ph**: Geoffrey Simpson. **ed**: John Scott. **m**: Davood Tabrizi. **p.d.**: Sally Campbell. **sd**: Dick Reade. Colour & b/w. 93 mins. 1988.

Bruce Lyons (Connor), Chris Haywood (Arno), Hamish McFarlane (Griffin), Marshall Napier (Searle), Noel Appleby (Ulf), Paul Livingston (Martin), Sarah Pierse (Linnet).

Cumbria, England, 1348. The inhabitants of a mining village are fearful of the Black Death. Nine-year-old Griffin is haunted by a vision of a cathedral in a celestial city, a cross, and a fall. When his brother Connor returns from the outside world and hears Griffin's story, he leads an expedition which travels through underground tunnels and arrives in Auckland, NZ, in the present day. The journey to place a home-made cross on top of the cathedral tower is a hazardous one, but finally achieved. Only when the time travellers return home do they discover the source of the plague.

NEXT OF KIN (page 300)

p.c.: Filmco-Film House, SIS Production. **p**: Robert le Tet. **d**: Tony Williams. **sc**: Tony Williams, Michael Heath. **ph**: Gary Hansen. **ed**: Max Lemon. **m**: Klaus Schultze. **p.d.**: Richard Francis. **sd**: Gary Wilkins. **co-p**: Timothy White. **p.m.**: Michael Lake. **a.d.**: Philip Hearnshaw. Eastmancolour. 88 mins. Aust dist: Roadshow. 1982.

Jackie Kerin (Linda Stevens), John Jarratt (Barney), Gerda Nicolson (Connie), Alex Scott (Dr Barton), Charles McCallum (Lance), Bernadette Gibson (Rita, Mrs Ryan), Robert Ratti (Kelvin), Debra Lawrance (Carol).

Linda Stevens returns to take charge of her family home (which has been turned into a nursing home) after the death of her mother. Her mother's diary reveals strange incidents which seem to be repeated: lights go out, bathtubs are mysteriously filled, patients start to die. Barney, Linda's boyfriend, is no help, and the mystery gets increasingly dense with the arrival of Aunt Rita, who was thought to have been dead . . .

NIEL LYNNE (page 155)

p.c.: Niel Lynne Production. **ex.p**: David Baker, Gilda Baracchi. **p, a.d.**: Tom Burstall. **d**: David Baker. **sc**: David Baker, Paul Davies. **ph**: Bruce McNaughton. **ed**: Don Saunders. **m**: Chris Neal.

p.d.: Robie Perkins. **sd**: Phil Sterling. **a.p.**: Brian Burgess. **p.m.**: Rosslyn Abernathy. Colour. 105 mins. 1985.

Sigrid Thornton (Fennimore), Paul Williams (Niel Lynne), Judy Morris (Patricia), Brandon Burke (Eric), David Argue (Reg), Alan Cinis (Mather), Tony Rickards (Tim Marsh), John Howard (Read), Marie Redshaw (Phillipa), [Nicki Paull (Melissa)].

1966. Niel Lynne, son of a Ballarat lawyer, is attracted to his older cousin Patricia; his best friend Eric is a radical would-be artist. Niel becomes a student at Monash University, while Eric is trying to survive as a painter and has a rich, hysterical mistress, Fennimore. Niel becomes editor of the student newspaper and Patricia, now working for a government department in Canberra, sends him top-secret documents about the Vietnam War. Niel loses his position at the paper, Eric and Fennimore retreat into drugs, and Patricia, fearing arrest, heads for Hanoi. Niel and Fennimore have a brief affair. [Niel marries Melissa, an 18-year-old schoolgirl, and they are blissfully happy until she is killed in a car accident.] Eric dies of a drug overdose. Niel enlists in the war, is wounded and captured. In a North Vietnam hospital, he is visited by Patricia.

1981. Back in Australia, Patricia is released from prison (after serving a sentence for her wartime activities); Niel is there to meet her.

NIGHTMARES (page 291)

p.c.: John Lamond Motion Picture Enterprises. **p**: John Lamond, Colin Eggleston. **d**: John Lamond. **sc, ed**: Colin Eggleston. **ph**: Gary Wapshott. **p.d.**: Paul Jones. **sd**: John Phillips. **p.m.**: Michael Hirsh. **a.d.**: Denise Paterson. Colour. Aust dist: Roadshow. 1980.

Jenny Neumann (Helen, Cathy), Gary Sweet (Terry), Nina Landis (Judy), Max Phipps (George Dalberg), John Michael Howson (Bennett Collingswood), Sue Jones (Fay), Briony Behets (Angela).

A thriller set in a theatre.

NORMAN LOVES ROSE (page 329)

p.c.: Norman Films. **p**: Henri Safran, Basil Appleby. **d, sc**: Henri Safran. **ph**: Vincent Monton. **ed**: Don Saunders. **m**: Mike Perjanik. **p.d.**: Darrell Lass. **sd**: Ross Linton. **p.m.**: Basil Appleby. **a.d.**: Steve Connard. Colour. 97 mins. Aust dist: Greater Union. UK dist: Direct Hit. 1982.

1982 Australian Film Awards: Best supporting actor (Warren Mitchell).

Carol Kane (Rose), Tony Owen (Norman), Warren Mitchell (Father), Myra De Groot (Mother), David Downer (Michael), Barry Otto (Charles), Sandy Gore (Maureen), Virginia Hey (Girlfriend), Louise Pajo (Shirley), Johnny Lockwood (Sam).

Thirteen-year-old Norman is preparing for his bar mitzvah. His older brother Michael, who lives next door, is married to Rose, but everyone in the family knows that Michael's sperm count is abnormally low. Norman spends more and more time with Rose and eventually sleeps with her; Rose becomes pregnant. Norman turns his attentions to Maureen, wife of Michael's womanising partner, Charles.

NOW AND FOREVER (page 115)

p.c.: Now and Forever Film Partnership. **p**: Treisha Ghent, Carnegie Fieldhouse, **d**, **ed**: Adrian Carr. [Original **d**], **sc**: Richard Cassidy (based on the novel by Danielle Steel). **ph**: Don McAlpine. **m**: Bruce Rowland. **p.d.**: Rene Rochford. **sd**: Kevin Kearney. **a.p.**: Rea Francis. **p.m.**: Carol Williams. **a.d.**: Stuart Freeman. Panavision. Colour. 89 mins. Aust dist: Roadshow. US dist: Interplanetary Pictures. 1982.

Cheryl Ladd (Jessie Clarke), Robert Coleby (Ian Clarke), Carmen Duncan (Astrid Bonner), Christine Amor (Margaret Burton), Aileen Britton (Bethanie), Alex Scott (Andrew Wyndham), Kris McQuade (Matilda Spencer), Rod Mullinar (Geoffrey Bates), Tim Burns (Kent Adams), Henri Szeps (Barry York), John Allen (Martin Harrington).

Boutique owner Jessie Clarke is happily married to novelist Ian. One day, Ian is picked up in a restaurant by Margaret Burton who seduces him, then accuses him of rape (it seems he reminded her of a former lover who cheated on her); despite his protests, he is sentenced to a year in prison. Jessie resorts to booze and pills, and almost has an affair with Geoffrey Bates, a handsome stranger: but all ends well.

ON THE LOOSE (page 362)

p.c.: Health Media Production. **p**: Lyn Norfor. **d**: Jane Oehr. **sc**: Ken Cameron (#1), Jane Oehr, Mark Stiles (#2), Tim Goodwin, Tom McPartland (#3). **ph**: Tom Cowan. **m**: Todd Hunter. **p.d.**: David Trethewey. **sd**: John Franks. Colour. 83 mins. 1984.

Steve Bergan (Eddie Leech), Ray Meagher (Russell Leech), John Smythe (Mr Stenning), Ron Hackett (Mr Cutler), Tamsin Hardman (Nicole Jones), John Hamblin (Noel Poulson), Maria da Costa (Stella), Carole Skinner (Mrs Jones), Jim Filipovski (Nick Malinowski), Garry Who (Cane Toad).

#1: *Exit Eddie Leech*. Eddie Leech, a crippled

boy who hates school, provokes his teacher into expelling him. #2: *Ring of Confidence*. 16-year-old Nicole gets a job as nursing assistant to a (married) dentist: when he makes sexual advances to her, she resists and is demoted. She quits, and joins the ranks of unemployed. #3: *Beginner's Luck*. Nick gets a job with a security firm, though he lies about being able to drive a car. His friend, Cane Toad, covers for him.

ONE NIGHT STAND (page 222)

p.c.: A Michael Edgley International presentation of an Astra Production. **ex.p**: Simon Wincer. **p**: Richard Mason. **d, sc**: John Duigan. **ph**: Tom Cowan. **ed**: John Scott. **m**: William Motzing. **p.d.**: Ross Major. **sd**: Peter Barker. **a.p., p.m.**: Julia Overton. **a.d.**: Deuel Droogan. Colour. 94 mins. Aust dist: Hoyts. 1984.

Tyler Coppin (Sam), Cassandra Delaney (Sharon), Jay Hackett (Brendan), Saskia Post (Eva), Midnight Oil (Themselves).

Sydney, New Year's Eve. American nuclear ships are anchored in the harbour and demonstrations against them are on-going. Sharon, who works at the Opera House (where Midnight Oil is playing in concert) meets up after the show with her flatmate Eva. But before they can leave they hear an announcement that nuclear war has broken out in Europe and North America, and that US facilities in Australia have been attacked. The young women are joined by Brendan, an Opera House cleaner, and Sam, an American sailor who jumped ship. They spend the night exploring the deserted building, play games (including strip poker) and indulge in small-talk. Next morning, Sydney is totally destroyed.

OUT OF THE BODY (page 295)

p.c.: A Premiere Film Marketing, Medusa Communications presentation of a David Hannay production. **ex.p**: Tom Broadbridge. **p**: David Hannay, Charles Hannah. **d**: Brian Trenchard Smith. **sc**: Kenneth G. Ross. **ph**: Kevan Lind. **ed**: Allen Woodruff. **m**: Peter Westheimer. **p.d.**: Darrell Lass. **sd**: Tim Lloyd. **line p**: Lynn Barker. **p.m.**: Barbi Taylor. **a.d.**: Jake Atkinson. Eastmancolour. 89 mins. 1988.

Mark Hembrow (David Gaze), Tessa Humphries (Neva St Clair), Carrie Zivetz (Dr Lydia Langton), Linda Newton (Carla Dupre), John Clayton (Det.-Sgt Whitaker), John Ley (Sgt Delano), Helen O'Connor (Barbara), Mary Regan (Mary Mason), Margi Gerard (Maggie).

Composer David Gaze finds to his horror that he can foresee the deaths of various beautiful women who are being murdered and their eyes removed. He eventually discovers that the killer is a monster from inside himself, and his girlfriend, Neva, only just manages to escape.

PACIFIC BANANA (page 309)

p.c.: Pacific Banana Production, in ass. with SA Film Corp. **ex.p**: John Chase. **p, d**: John Lamond. **sc**: Alan Hopgood. **ph**: Gary Wapshott. **ed**: Ray Daley. **p.d.**: Herbert Pinter. **sd**: John Phillips. **a.p.**: John Pruzanski. **a.d.**: Michael Hirsch. Colour. 84 mins. 1980.

Graeme Blundell (Martin), Robin Stewart (Paul), Deborah Gray (Sally), Alyson Best (Mandy), Helen Hemingway (Julia), Luan Peters (Candy).

Martin, an airline pilot flying the Pacific route, is attractive to women but has a problem sustaining his erections. His pal, Paul, is far more successful with the numerous beautiful women who cross their paths.

PANDEMONIUM (page 154)

p.c.: KFM Pandemonium Production, in ass. with Smart Street Films, Tra-La-La Films. **ex.p**: Patric Juillet. **p**: Alex Cutler, Haydn Keenan. **d**: Haydn Keenan. **sc**: Haydn Keenan, Peter Gailey. **ph**: David Sanderson. **ed**: Paul Healy. **m**: Cameron Allan. **p.d.**: Melody Cooper. **sd**: Phillip Keros. **sp. ef.**: Monte Fieguth. Eastmancolour. 88 mins. 1987.

David Argue (Kales Leadingham, Ding the Dingo), Amanda Dole (The Dingo Girl), Esben Storm (E. B. De Woolf), Arna-Maria Winchester (P. B. De Woolf), Rainee Skinner (1st twin), Kerry Mack (2nd twin), Ashley Grenville (Little Adolph), Mercia Deane-Jones (Morticia), Haydn Keenan (Dr Doctor), Lex Marinos (Det. Sgt Dick Dickerson), Gary Foley (The Holy Ghost), Henk Johannes (The Count), Greg Ham (Marvo the Magician), Pete Smith (Peter Kong), Ignatius Jones (Marriage Celebrant), Ian Nimmo (Mr David).

Clad only in a loin-cloth, a beautiful young woman arrives at Bondi Beach claiming to have been raised in the desert by dingos after being abandoned by her parents; she arrives at the disused, haunted film studio occupied by lecherous film director E. B. De Woolf and his crippled ex-beauty queen wife, P. B. Kales Leadingham ('a cross between Indiana Jones and Daffy Duck') tries to help her find her real parents in a bizarre world peopled with a diminutive descendant of Hitler, neo-Nazi twin girls, vampires, a corrupt cop and an Aboriginal Holy Ghost who seems to be the girl's father, but has sex with her anyway.

PHAR LAP (US title: *A Horse Called Phar Lap*) (page 39)
p.c.: John Sexton Productions, in ass. with Michael Edgley International. **ex.p**: Richard Davis. **p**: John Sexton. **d**: Simon Wincer. **sc**: David Williamson. **ph**: Russell Boyd. **ed**: Tony Paterson. **m**: Bruce Rowland. **p.d.**: Laurence Eastwood. **sd**: Gary Wilkins. **p.m.**: Paula Gibbs. **a.d.**: Murray Newey. **2nd unit ph**: Keith Wagstaff. Panavision. Colour. 118 mins (Internationally: 107 mins). Aust dist: Hoyts. US & UK dist: 20th Century-Fox. 1983.

1983 Australian Film Awards: Best editing; music; sound.

Tom Burlinson (Tommy Woodcock), Martin Vaughan (Harry Telford), Judy Morris (Bea Davis), Celia De Burgh (Vi Telford), Ron Liebman (Dave Davis), Vincent Ball (Lachlan McKinnon), John Stanton (Eric Connolly), Peter Whitford (Bert Wolfe), Robert Grubb (William Nielson), Georgia Carr (Emma), Warwick Moss (McCready).

1932. Champion racehorse Phar Lap dies in the US of a mysterious disease. 1928. Harry Telford, a horse trainer, buys Phar Lap (Siamese for 'Lightning') sight unseen for his employer, businessman Dave Davis. Groom Tommy Woodcock cares for the horse, but it proves a slow starter until an unprecedented series of wins. Telford opens his own stables, and Davis plans a crooked deal in which Phar Lap will be withdrawn from the Caulfield Cup but allowed to win the Melbourne Cup. Bookies try unsuccessfully to shoot the horse. McKinnon, who heads the Racing Commission, orders Phar Lap be burdened with increasingly heavy handicaps. An offer to race at Agua Caliente, on the Mexican-American border, is accepted.

PHOBIA (page 101)
p.c.: Jadee. **ex.p**: Will Davies. **p, ed**: John Mandelberg. **d, sc**: John Dingwall. **ph**: Steve Newman. **m**: Ross Edwards. **p.d.**: Robert Michael. Colour. 85 mins. 1988.

Gosia Dobrowolska (Renate Simmons), Sean Scully (David Simmons).

Polish-born Renate Simmons, who suffers from agoraphobia, lives in a waterside Sydney suburb with her psychiatrist husband, David, who drinks to excess. The marriage is breaking up, and Renate plans to leave to stay with a girlfriend; but David blackmails the friend (with whom he has had an affair) into refusing his wife accommodation. Increasingly desperate, but unable to leave, Renate shuts herself in her bedroom while David obsessively watches old videos taken earlier in the marriage. He becomes violent, beats his wife and attacks her with a knife. Renate manages to escape to the garden (to find David has slaughtered her chickens) with her husband in pursuit. She attacks him with a pitchfork, and summons up the will to escape. David returns to the house and commits suicide.

THE PIRATE MOVIE (page 195)
p.c.: Joseph Hamilton International productions. **ex.p**: Ted Hamilton. **p**: David Joseph. **d**: Ken Annakin. **sc**: Trevor Farrant (based on *The Pirates of Penzance*, by Gilbert and Sullivan). **ph**: Robin Copping. **ed**: Kenneth W. Zemke. **m**: Peter Sullivan. **songs**: Terry Britten, Kit Hain, Sue Shifrin, Brian Robertson. **p.d.**: Jon Dowding, Tony Wollard. **sd**: Paul Clark. **a.p.**: David Anderson. **a.d.**: Murray Newey. **stunts**: Grant Page. **choreog.**: David Atkins. Colour. 100 mins. International dist: 20th Century-Fox. 1982.

Kristy McNichol (Mabel), Christopher Atkins (Frederic), Ted Hamilton (Pirate King), Bill Kerr (Major-General), Maggie Kirkpatrick (Ruth), Garry McDonald (Policeman).

Mabel, an American tourist in Sydney, sees Frederic, a fellow American, on an old ship in the Harbour. Soon after narrowly surviving being drowned, she dreams of pirates invading her home and Frederic coming to the rescue.

THE PLACE AT THE COAST (page 365)
p.c.: Daedalus II Production, in ass. with NSW Film Corp. **p, sc**: Hilary Furlong (based on the novel *The Bee Eater* by Jane Hyde). **d**: George Ogilvie. **ph**: Jeff Darling. **ed**: Nicholas Beauman. **m**: Chris Neal. **p.d.**: Owen Paterson. **sd**: Phil Stirling. **p.m.**: Fiona McConaghy. **a.d.**: Lynn Gailey. Colour. 92 mins. Aust dist: Ronin. 1986.

John Hargreaves (Neil McAdam), Heather Mitchell (Margot Ryan), Tushka Bergen (Ellie McAdam), Margot Lee (May Ryan), Willie Fennell (Fred Ryan), Garry McDonald (Dan Burroughs), Julie Hamilton (Enid Burroughs), Ray Meagher (Uncle Doug), Michele Fawdon (Aunt Helen), Sue Ingleton (Nan Montgomery), Aileen Britton (Gran), Brendon Lunney (Seymour Steele), Rod Zuanic ('King').

Ellie McAdam, a young teenager who blames herself for her mother's death years earlier in a car accident, travels with her busy doctor father, Neil, to their 'place at the coast', an idyllic spot threatened by commercial development. Bored when her father spends his time fishing, Ellie befriends Margot Ryan, a sophisticated neighbour recently back from England. When Margot and her father fall in love, she feels doubly betrayed.

THE PLAINS OF HEAVEN (page 73)

p.c.: Seon Films. **p**: John Cruthers. **d**: Ian Pringle. **sc**: Ian Pringle, Doug Ling, Elizabeth Parsons. **ph, ed**: Ray Argall. **m**: Andrew Duffield. **sd**: Bruce Emery. **a.p.**: Brian McKenzie. **p.m.**: Mark Thomas. Fujicolor. 80 mins. Aust dist: AFI. 1982.

Richard Moir (Barker), Reg Evans (Cunningham), Gerard Kennedy (Lenko), John Flaus (Land Rover owner), Jenny Cartwright (Nurse).

In the Victorian High Country, Barker and Cunningham work at a satellite relay station. Barker, the younger, seldom goes outside, preferring to watch television quiz shows. Cunningham, who loves bird watching, sets his pet ferrets after rabbits. After a while, Cunningham loses control, smashes the equipment, and runs off into the rocky wilderness. Called to Melbourne to explain, Barker is freaked by the city. He returns to the mountains to find Cunningham cowering in a catatonic state in a mountain cave.

PLAYING BEATIE BOW (page 340)

p.c.: SA Film Corp. **ex.p**: John Morris. **p**: Jock Blair. **d**: Donald Crombie. **sc**: Peter Gawler (from the novel by Ruth Park). **ph**: Geoffrey Simpson. **ed**: A. J. Prowse. **m**: Garry McDonald, Laurie Stone. **p.d.**: George Liddle. **sd**: Robert Cutcher. **a.p.**: Bruce Moir. **p.m.**: Pamela Vanneck. **a.d.**: Philip Hearnshaw. Eastmancolour. 89 mins. Aust dist: CEL. 1985.

1986 Australian Film Awards: Best production design.

Imogen Annesley (Abigail), Peter Phelps (Judah, Robert), Mouche Philips (Beatie Bow), Nikki Coghill (Dovey), Moya O'Sullivan (Granny), Don Barker (Samuel), Lyndel Rowe (Kathy), Barbara Stephens (Justine), Su Cruickshank (Madam).

In present-day Sydney, 16-year-old Abigail is undergoing teen traumas (her parents are divorced, she has no boyfriend). She observes children playing a traditional game called Beatie Bow, then spies a little lost girl and follows her— into 1873 where Beatie Bow lives with her handsome older brother, Judah, and her mystical old Granny. Trying to return to the present, Abigail is kidnapped and delivered to a brothel, but rescued by Jonah. Eventually, she returns to the present day where she discovers that Judah's descendant, Robert, is just as charming as his ancestor.

THE PRISONER OF ST PETERSBURG (page 112)

p.c.: Seon Films, Panorama Film (West Berlin).

p: Daniel Scharf, Klaus Sungen. **d**: Ian Pringle. **sc**: Michael Wren. **ph**: Ray Argall. **ed**: Ursula West. **m**: Paul Schutze. **p.d.**: Peta Lawson. **sd**: Eckhardt Kuchenbecker. **p.m.**: Jolanda Darbyshire. Black and white. 80 mins. 1988.

Noah Taylor (Jack), Solveig Dommartin (Elena), Katja Teichmann (Johanna), Rene Schonenberger (Businessman), Dennis Staunton (Irishman), Johanna Karl-Lovy (Old woman), Olivier Picto (Stefan), Christian Zertz (Lorenzo), Hans-Martin Stier (Truckdriver), Manfred Salzgeber (Russian man with coat).

Jack arrives in West Berlin from Russia: he speaks only Russian, quoting from Gogol and Dostoyevsky. He attacks an old woman, and later is nearly picked up by a gay businessman. Two older women, Elena and Johanna, befriend him. To Jack, Elena is Sonya, his Russian dream woman: he falls in love with her. Speaking English, the three wander around the city, encountering an Irishman in a bar, a truckdriver and other characters. Jack retreats more and more into his dreamworld, a 'prisoner of St Petersburg'.

PUBERTY BLUES (page 145)

p.c.: Limelight Productions. **p**: Joan Long, Margaret Kelly. **d**: Bruce Beresford. **sc**: Margaret Kelly (based on the book by Kathy Lette and Gabrielle Carey). **ph**: Don McAlpine. **ed**: William Anderson. **m**: Les Gock. **p.d.**: David Copping. **sd**: Gary Wilkins. **p.m.**: Greg Ricketson. **a.d.**: Mark Egerton. Panavision. Eastmancolour. 85 mins. Aust dist: Roadshow. UK dist: 20th Century-Fox. US dist: Universal. 1981.

Nell Schofield (Debbie Vickers), Jad Capelja (Sue Knight), Geoff Rhoe (Garry Hennessy), Tony Hughes (Danny Dickson), Sandy Paul (Tracey), Leander Brett (Cheryl), Jay Hackett (Bruce), Ned Lander (Strach), Joanne Olsen (Vicky), Julie Medana (Kim), Kirrily Nolan (Mrs Vickers), Alan Cassell (Mr Vickers), Rowena Wallace (Mrs Knight), Charles Tingwell (Bishop), Kate Shiel (Mrs Yelland), Pamela Gibbons (Jazz Ballet Teacher).

Fifteen-year-olds Debbie Vickers and Sue Knight are eager to be accepted as members of a band of surfer groupies. Once accepted they have to obey the rules: girls do not surf, but they look after their boy's gear, and 'go with him' when he wants. Debbie's first boyfriend, Danny, cannot penetrate her; her second, Garry, a brickie, is a heroin addict, and for an alarming time she thinks she may be pregnant. Garry dies of his addiction. Debbie persuades Sue (whose love affairs have been more successful) to join her in defying the rules—by surfing.

THE PURSUIT OF HAPPINESS
(page 223)

p.c.: Jequerity Films. **ex.p**: Richard Mason. **p, d**: Martha Ansara. **sc**: Martha Ansara, Alex Glasgow, Laura Black and the cast. **ph**: Michael Edols. **ed**: Kit Guyatt. **p.m.**: Gail McKinnon. **a.d.**: Madelon Wilkens. Colour. 85 mins. Aust dist: AFI. 1987.

Laura Black (Anna), Peter Hardy (John), Anna Gare (Mandy), Jack Coleman (Stan).

Fremantle, WA. Anna, middle-aged and just starting a career as a journalist, is married to John, an ambitious businessman. Mandy, the couple's 15-year-old daughter, has taken up with a peace group which John bitterly opposes. Anna tries to find out more about her daughter's activities, and becomes a peace activist herself.

RACE FOR THE 'YANKEE ZEPHYR
(US title: *Treasure of the 'Yankee Zephyr*) (page 77)

p.c.: Endeavour Productions (Auckland), FGH Film Consortium (Melbourne), for Pact Productions, Fay, Richwite and Hemdale. **ex.p**: John Daly, Michael Fay, William Fayman. **p**: Antony I. Ginnane, John Barnett, David Hemmings. **d**: David Hemmings. **sc**: Everett De Roche. **ph**: Vincent Monton. **ed**: John Laing. **m**: Brian May. **p.d.**: Bernard Hides. **sd**: Graham Morris. **p.m.**: Tim Sanders. **a.d.**: Murray Newey. Panavision. Eastmancolour. 100 mins. Aust dist: Greater Union. US dist: Artists Releasing Corp. UK dist: Enterprise. 1981.

Ken Wahl (Barney Whittaker), Lesley Ann Warren (Sally Gibson), Donald Pleasence ('Gibbie' Gibson), George Peppard (Theo Brown), Bruno Lawrence (Barker), Grant Tilly (Collector).

In the South Island of New Zealand, deer hunter Gibbie Gibson discovers the wreck of the *Yankee Zephyr* in a lake (the aircraft, which crashed in 1944, was, unknown to Gibbie, carrying the payroll for the American South Pacific Fleet—$50 million in cash and gold). Gibbie, his daughter Sally, and his buddy Barney, team up to salvage the plane, but are confronted by Theo Brown and his henchmen (who know about the loot). They capture Gibbie and force him to guide them to the wreck, but he is rescued by Barney and Sally, and Brown and his men are killed accidentally by their own incompetent gunfire.

RAW NERVE (Alternative title: *Things and Other Stuff*) (page 352)

p.c.. Lynchpin & Tosh, in ass. with Australian Film Commission. **p**: Michael Lynch. **d, sc**: Tony Wellington. **ph**: Kim Batterham. **ed**: Marcus D'Arcy. **m**: Dale Barlow. **p.d.**: Judith Harvey. **p.m.**. Dixi Betts. **a.p.**: Richard Harper. Colour. 88 mins. 1988.

Kelly Dingwall (David), Rebecca Rigg (Michelle), John Polson (Billy).

David and his reluctant girlfriend, Michelle, break into a plush house looking for cash. They are followed by David's unstable friend, Billy, whose methods of burglary are very different.

RAZORBACK (page 301)

p.c.: Western Film Productions, UAA. **p**: Hal McElroy. **d**: Russell Mulcahy. **sc**: Everett De Roche (based on the novel by Peter Brennan). **ph**: Dean Semler. **ed**: William Anderson. **m**: Iva Davies. **p.d.**: Bryce Walmsley. **sd**: Tim Lloyd. **a.p.**: Tim Sanders. **2nd unit d**: Arch Nicholson. **p.m.**: Fiona McConaghy. **a.d.**: Stuart Freeman. **sp.ef.**: Mark Canny. Panavision. Colour. 94 mins. Aust dist: Greater Union. UK dist: Columbia-EMI-Warner. US dist: Warners. 1984.

1984 Australian Film Awards: Best photography, editing.

Gregory Harrison (Carl Winters), Arkie Whiteley (Sarah Cameron), Bill Kerr (Jake Cullen), Chris Haywood (Benny Baker), David Argue (Dicko Baker), Judy Morris (Beth Winters), John Howard (Danny), John Ewart (Turner), Don Smith (Wallace), Mervyn Drake (Andy), Redmond Phillips (Magistrate), Beth Child (Louise Cullen).

Near Gamulla, in the outback, Jack Cullen's grandson is carried off by a mysterious creature and never seen again: Jack is tried for murder, but acquitted for lack of evidence. Beth Winters, an American television journalist investigating the slaughter of kangaroos, falls foul of the unstable Baker brothers; later, she is attacked and killed by a giant feral pig, a razorback. Her husband Carl arrives to investigate her disappearance and also meets the Bakers, who abandon him in the desert, where he has an encounter with the razorback. He arrives at the property of Sarah Cameron, where he meets Jake, now obsessed with killing the monster. Suspecting (rightly) that the Bakers know more than they are saying (but not knowing they have crippled Jack and left him to the razorback), Carl extracts information from Benny and confronts Dicko in his meat-packing plant. Dicko is killed by the monster, which Carl then lures into the machinery.

REBEL (page 114)

p.c.: Phillip Emanuel Productions, in ass. with Village-Roadshow. **ex.p**: Robyn Campbell-Jones, Bonnie Harris. **p**: Phillip Emanuel. **d**: Michael

Jenkins. **sc**: Michael Jenkins, Bob Herbert (based on the play *No Names, No Pack Drill* by Bob Herbert). **ph**: Peter James. **ed**: Michael Honey. **m**: Chris Neal. **songs**: Peter Best. **p.d.**: Brian Thomson. **sd**: Mark Lewis. **choreog.**: Ross Coleman. **a.p.**, **p.m.**: Susan Wild. **a.d.**: David Evans. Panavision. Eastmancolour. 106 mins. (International running time: 93 mins). Aust dist: Roadshow. UK dist: Miracle. 1985.

1985 Australian Film Awards: Best photography, production design, costumes (Roger Kirk), music, sound.

Matt Dillon (Rebel), Debbie Byrne (Kathy McLeod), Bryan Brown (Tiger Kelly), Bill Hunter (Browning), Ray Barrett (Bubbles), Julie Nihill (Joycie), John O'May (Bernie), Kim Deacon (Hazel), Isabelle Anderson (Mrs Palmer), Sheree Da Costa (Barbara), Joy Smithers (Mary), Cassandra Delaney, Nikki Coghill (Band girls), Annie Semler (Madam), Beth Child (Bea Miles).

Sydney 1942. Rebel, a US Marine on R & R from the war, meets Kathy McLeod, lead singer in an all-female band. Kathy is married, and her husband is fighting: Rebel decides to desert, after experiencing the horrors of Guadalcanal. They become lovers and he hides from the police in her apartment. Tiger Kelly arranges for a passage out of the country, just as Kathy learns that her husband has been killed. Rebel is arrested, but escapes; Tiger ups the price of passage and attacks Rebel for his cowardice. Rebel returns to Kathy's club for one last glimpse of her as the military police lead him away.

RELATIVES (page 319)

p.c.: Archer Films. **p**: Basil Appleby, Henri Safran. **d**, **sc**: Anthony Bowman. **ph**: Tom Cowan. **ed**: Colin Greive. **m**: Norman Kaye. **p.d.**: Darrell Lass. **sd**: Bob Clayton. **p.m.**: Francis Durham. **a.d.**: Kim Anning. Colour. 89 mins. 1985.

Bill Kerr (Grandfather), Rowena Wallace (Nancy Peterson), Carol Raye (Joan Hedges), Ray Barrett (Geoffrey), Norman Kaye (Uncle Edward), Alyson Best (Clare), Jeannie Drynan (Catherine Taylor), Michael Aitkens (Peter Peterson), Robin Bowering (Alfred Hedges), Brett Climo (Ross), Ray Meagher (Herb Taylor), Marian Dworakowski (Alex).

Grandfather leaves a home for the aged to celebrate his eightieth birthday with members of his family. These include Geoffrey, who is being forced by hard financial times to sell the family property; Edward, a tipsy, effeminate priest; Alfred and Joan, an unhappily married couple, plus Alfred's mistress, Catherine, and her oafish spouse, Herb; bored Peter and Nancy Peterson and their snotty children; and Clare,

Geoffrey's independent daughter (who brings along her Czech boyfriend, Alex), and her punk brother, Ross. There are plenty of family upsets during the day, all endured stoically by the old patriarch, who finally expires while feeding chickens.

RETURN HOME (page 120)

p.c.: Musical Films. **p**: Cristina Pozzan. **d, sc**: Ray Argall. **ph**: Mandy Walker. **ed**: Ken Sallows. **p.d.**: Keith Holmes. **sd**: Bronwyn Murphy. **a.p.**: Daniel Scharf. **p.m.**: Eliza Argenzio. **a.d.**: Euan Keddie. Fujicolor. 86 mins. 1989.

Frankie J. Holden (Steve), Dennis Coard (Noel), Micki Camilleri (Jude), Ben Mendelsohn (Gary).

Steve and Noel, brothers, have drifted apart and live in separate cities. After ten years, they are reunited.

THE RETURN OF CAPTAIN INVINCIBLE (page 79)

p.c.: Willarra–Seven Keys Films. **p**: Andrew Gaty. **d**: Philippe Mora. **sc**: Steven E. De Souza, Andrew Gaty. **ph**: Mike Molloy. **ed**: John Scott. **m**: William Motzing. **p.d.**: David Copping. **sd**: Ken Hammond. **a.p.**: Brian D. Burgess. **a.d.**: Bosie Vine-Miller. Panavision. Eastmancolour. 91 mins. Aust dist: Seven Keys. UK dist: Media Releasing. 1982.

Alan Arkin (Captain Invincible), Christopher Lee (Mr Midnight), Kate Fitzpatrick (Patty Patria), Bill Hunter (Tupper/Coach), Michael Pate (President of the US), David Argue (Italian salesman), John Bluthal (Deli Owner), Chelsea Brown (Tour Guide), Max Cullen (Italian Man), Arthur Dignam (Lawyer), Noel Ferrier (Air Force General), Hayes Gordon (Kirby), Chris Haywood (Maitre d'hôtel), Graham Kennedy (Prime Minister), Gus Mercurio (Noisy Garbageman), Max Phipps (Admiral), Bruce Spence (Midnight's doctor), Henri Szeps (Security Officer).

During the anti-communist purge of the 50s, Captain Invincible (his red cape cited as evidence of his political leanings, despite his heroic work in the past) gives up his career and disappears. Thirty years later he is down-and-out in Sydney, but rallies to the cause when evil Mr Midnight steals a top-secret ray from an Australian research establishment. Though his magical flying skills have become rusty, Invincible, together with Sydney policewoman Patty Patria, heads for New York and a final encounter with his evil adversary.

THE RIGHT HAND MAN (page 160)

p.c.: A UAA presentation of a Yarraman production. **ex.p**: David Thomas. **p**: Steven

Grives, Basil Appleby, Tom Oliver. **d**: Di Drew. **sc**: Helen Hodgman (from the book by Kathleen Peyton). **ph**: Peter James. **ed**: Don Saunders. **m**: Allan Zavod. **p.d.**: Neil Angwin. **sd**: Syd Butterworth. **cost**: Graham Purcell. **p.m.**: Renate Wilson. **a.d.**: Phil Rich. Eastmancolour. 100 mins. Aust dist: Greater Union. US dist: New World. 1986.

1986 Australian Film Awards: Best photography.

Rupert Everett (Harry Ironminster), Hugo Weaving (Ned Rowlands), Catherine McClements (Sarah Redbridge), Arthur Dignam (Dr Redbridge), Jennifer Claire (Lady Ironminster).

Harry Ironminster, a sickly young aristocrat, is unwittingly responsible for the coaching accident that kills his father: as a result of the accident, Harry's right arm is amputated by Dr Redbridge. Unable to ride his beloved horses, Harry becomes more and more withdrawn and morose until he employs dashing Ned Rowlands, driver of the huge Leviathan stagecoach. Ned becomes Harry's 'right hand man', and even agrees to sleep with Sarah Redbridge, the doctor's scientifically-minded daughter, and Harry's fiancée. Sarah becomes pregnant, and Harry kills himself.

RIKKY AND PETE (page 327)

p.c.: United Artists, Cascade Films. **ex.p**: Bryce Menzies. **p**: Nadia Tass, David Parker. **d**: Nadia Tass. **sc, ph**: David Parker. **ed**: Ken Sallows. **m**: Phil Judd, Eddie Raynor. **p.d.**: Josephine Ford. **sd**: Lloyd Carrick. **p.m.**: Linda House. **a.d.**: Tony Mahood. Eastmancolour. 101 mins. Aust (and rest of the world outside US) dist: United International Pictures. US dist: MGM-UA Communications. 1988.

Stephen Kearney (Pete), Nina Landis (Rikky), Tetchie Agbayani (Flossie), Bill Hunter (Whitstead), Bruno Lawrence (Sonny), Bruce Spence (Ben), Dorothy Alison (Mrs Menzies), Don Reid (Mr Menzies), Lewis Fitz-Gerald (Adam), Peter Cummins (Delahunty), Peter Hehir (Police Officer), Ralph Cotterill (George).

Pete, a young inventor, is having a vendetta with Whitstead, a Melbourne cop; his sister Rikky is tired of singing in a bar, and of her boyfriend, Adam. When the siblings quarrel with their stuffy father, they leave the city in their mother's old Bentley and head for the outback. Pursued by Whitstead, they arrive in a mining town and buy a small lease. Pete has an affair with Flossie, a pretty Filipino girl, while Rikky befriends Sonny, a taciturn miner. Pete winds up in prison, but all ends well.

ROAD GAMES (page 261)

p.c.: Quest Films, Essaness Pictures. **ex.p**: Bernard Schwartz. **p, d**: Richard Franklin. **sc**: Everett De Roche. **ph**: Vincent Monton. **ed**: Edward McQueen-Mason. **m**: Brian May. **p.d.**: Jon Dowding. **sd**: Paul Clark, Raymond Phillips. **stunts**: Grant Page. **co-p**: Barbi Taylor. **p.m.**: Greg Ricketson, Barbara Gibbs. **a.d.**: Tom Burstall. Panavision. Eastmancolour. 98 mins. Aust dist: Greater Union. US dist: Avco Embassy. UK dist: Barber International. 1981.

Stacy Keach (Patrick Quid), Jamie Lee Curtis (Pamela Rushworth), Marion Edward (Madeleine Day), Grant Page (Smith or Jones), Thaddeus Smith (Abbott), Stephen Millichamp (Costello), Alan Hopgood (Lester).

Truckdriver Pat Quid makes up fanciful names for fellow travellers as he crosses the Nullarbor: the driver of a green van he calls 'Smith or Jones'. Gradually, he begins to suspect that 'Smith or Jones' may be the Jack-the-Ripper-style killer the police are after. He picks up a hitch-hiker, Pamela Rushworth (whom he dubs 'Hitch') and she goes along with his theories. Later, 'Hitch' is kidnapped by 'Smith or Jones', and Pat's suspicions are confirmed; he chases the green van to Perth, overpowers the killer, and is reunited with 'Hitch', who turns out to be a runaway heiress.

ROBBERY UNDER ARMS (page 71)

p.c.: SA Film Corp. **ex.p**: John Morris. **p**: Jock Blair. **d**: Donald Crombie, Ken Hannam. **sc**: Graeme Koestveld, Tony Morphett (from the novel by Rolf Boldrewood). **ph**: Ernest Clark. **ed**: Andrew Prowse. **m**: Garry McDonald, Laurie Stone. **p.d.**: George Liddle. **sd**: Lloyd Carrick. **cost**: Anna Senior. **sp. ef.**: Brian Cox, **stunts**: Bill Stacey. **a.p.**: Pamela Vanneck, Bruce Moir. **p.m.**: Barbara Ring. **a.d.**: Philip Hearnshaw, Brian Giddens. Colour. 141 mins. Aust dist: ITC Entertainment. 1985.

Sam Neill (Captain Starlight), Steven Vidler (Dick Marston), Christopher Cummins (Jim Marston), Liz Newman (Gracey), Deborah Coulls (Kate), Susie Lindeman (Jeannie), Tommy Lewis (Warrigal), Ed Devereux (Ben Marston), Jane Menelaus (Aileen Marston), Robert Grubb (Sir Frederick Morringer), Elaine Cusick (Mary Marston), Michael Duffield (Mr Falkland), Roger Ward (McIntyre), Paul Chubb (Mungo).

Dick and Jim Marston join their father, Ben, a member of the outlaw gang led by aristocratic Captain Starlight. After numerous adventures, during which Starlight invariably bests his nemesis, Sir Frederick Morringer, the bushranger is cornered by the constabulary and killed.

RUN, CHRISSIE, RUN! (page 289)
p.c.: SA Film Corp. **ex.p**: Jock Blair. **p**: Harley Manners. **d**: Chris Langman. **sc**: Graham Hartley (based on the novel *When We Ran* by Keith Leopold). **ph**: Ernest Clark. **ed**: Andrew Prowse. **p.d.**: Alistair Livingstone. **sd**: Lloyd Carrick. **a.p.**: Ron Saunders. **p.m.**: Jan Tyrrell. **a.d.**: Robert Kewley. Eastmancolour. 91 mins. 1984.

Carmen Duncan (Eve), Michael Aitkens (Riley), Shane Briant (Terrier), Redmond Symons (Pitt), Nicholas Eadie (Toe), Annie Jones (Chrissie).

Riley, an IRA militant, performs an execution in London, then heads for Australia to find Eve, his German girlfriend, and a former terrorist. Eve lives with her daughter, teenage Chrissie (who is Riley's daughter, too, though he does not know it) and still has the money Riley had stolen years before. Riley tracks Eve and Chrissie down in the Barossa Valley, pursued by IRA assassins and also a vicious youth, Toe. Events build up to a suspenseful climax.

RUN, REBECCA, RUN! (page 340)
p.c.: Independent Productions. **ex.p**: Gene Scott. **p**: Brendon Lunney. **d**: Peter Maxwell. **sc**: Charles Stamp (from a story by Gary Deacon). **ph**: Phil Pike. **ed**: Bob Cogger. **m**: Simon Walker. **p.d.**: Jakob Horvat. **sd**: Rowland McManis. **p.m.**: Peter Abbott. **a.d.**: Kevin Powell. Colour. 80 mins. 1982.

Simone Buchanan (Rebecca), Henri Szeps (Manuel Cortes), Adam Gernett (Rod), John Stanton (Bob Porter), Mary Ann Severne (Jean Porter), John Ewart (Minister for Immigration).

Rebecca is photographing a cockatoo on a lonely island when she is kidnapped by Manuel Cortes, an illegal political refugee from a South American dictatorship. Rod, Rebecca's Boy Scout friend, tries to find her, and helps her escape. Cortes is arrested, but Rebecca pleads his cause with the Minister for Immigration.

RUNNING FROM THE GUNS (page 251)
p.c.: Burrowes Film Group. **ex.p**: Dennis Wright. **p**: Geoff Burrowes. **d, sc**: John Dixon. **ph**: Keith Wagstaff. **ed**: Ray Daley. **m**: Bruce Rowland. **p.d.**: Leslie Binns. **sd**: John Schiefelbein. **stunts**: Chris Anderson. **sp. ef.**: Brian Pearce. **p.m.**: Bill Regan. **a.d.**: Bob Donaldson. colour. 87 mins. Aust dist; Hoyts. 1987.

Jon Blake (Dave Williams), Mark Hembrow (Peter), Nikki Coghill (Jill), Terence Donovan (Bangels), Bill Kerr (Gilman), Peter Whitford (Terence), Warwick Sims (Martin), Gerard Kennedy (Big Jim), Toni Lamond (Dave's mum), Greg Ross (Mallard), Gus Mercurio (Chazza), Ken

Snodgrass (Ocker), Barry Hill (Sir Julian), Delilah (Marathon Mandy).

Dave and Peter pick up a container of what they suppose to be Taiwanese-made toys at Melbourne docks: but Bangels, a middle-level crook, has switched containers and the partners find themselves with a stash of laundered cash. Dave befriends Jill, who works for a Commission into crime, and whose father, Sir Julian, is a politician. Martin, hatchet-man for Gilman, a shady businessman, murders Bangels. Dave, Jill and Peter are threatened, too, but dock workers come to their rescue.

RUNNING ON EMPTY (page 361)
p.c.: Film Corp. of WA. **ex.p**: David Roe. **p**: Pom Oliver. **d**: John Clark. **sc**: Barry Tomblin. **ph**: David Gribble. **ed**: Stuart Armstrong. **m**: Peter Crosbie. **p.d.**: Greg Brown. **sd**: Syd Butterworth. **p.m.**: Barbara Gibbs. **a.p., a.d.**: Mark Egerton. **stunts**: Frank Lennon. Eastmancolour. 85 mins. Aust dist: Roadshow. 1982.

Terry Serio (Mike), Vangelis Mourikis (Tony), Debbie Conway (Julie), Warren Blondell (Lee), Geoff Rhoe (Ram), Kris Greaves (Starter), Richard Moir (Fox), Gerry Sont (Victor), Keli Roberts (Sheryl), Grahame Bond (Jagger), Penne Hackforth-Jones (Dave), Max Cullen (Rebel), Anne Semler (Joan), Robin Ramsay (Dad).

Mike, an up-and-coming member of a drag-racing gang, falls for Julie, who is also admired by the sinister Fox. The rivals agree to a best of three competition. Mike loses the first race, goes bush with Julie, and meets Rebel, a former dragster (who speaks 60s vernacular) who was blinded in a crash. In Race 2, Mike's 1970 Dodge Challenger is destroyed, so he borrows Rebel's old Chevy and wins Race 3, whereupon Fox suicides.

SAVE THE LADY (page 343)
p.c.: Tasmanian Film Corp. **ex.p**: John Honey. **p**: Barry Pierce. **d**: Leon Thay. **sc**: John Palmer, Yoram Gross. **ph**: Gert Kirchner. **ed**: Mike Wolveridge. **m**: Peter McKinley. **p.d.**: Jon Bowling. **sd**: John Schiefelbein. **p.m.**: Damian Brown. **a.d.**: Jack Zalkains. Colour. 76 mins. Aust dist: Young Australia Films. 1981.

Robert Clarkson (Specs), Miranda Cartledge (Jo), Matthew Excell (Ben), Kim Clifford (Gina), Wallas Eaton (Trotter), John Ewart (Uncle Harry), Bill Kerr (MacDuff), Desmond Tester (Captain Playfair), John Cobley (Menial).

Lady is an 80-year-old Hobart ferryboat, doomed to destruction on orders of a heartless bureaucrat, Trotter. Four children—Specs, Jo, Ben and Gina—persuade a couple of elderly seamen—Captain Playfair and Engineer MacDuff—to help them save the ship, aided by Uncle Harry, whose job as a cleaner in the bureaucrat's office allows him to become a spy. After the motley group sets sail with *Lady*, and they are pursued by police boats, all ends well and the vessel will sail on.

SEBASTIAN AND THE SPARROW
(page 355)
p.c.: Kino Film, A Colour & Movement Film. **ex.p**: Terry Ohlsson. **p, d, sc**: Scott Hicks. **ph**: David Foreman. **ed**: Pip Karmel. **m**: Allan Zavod. **p.d.**: Anni Browning. **sd**: Toivo Lember. **a.p.**: Darryl Sheen. **a.d.**: Gus Howard. Colour. Aust dist: self-dist. 90 mins.

Alexander Bainbridge (Sebastian Thornbury), Jeremy Angerson (Sparrow), Robert Coleby (Peter Thornbury), Elizabeth Alexander (Jenny Thornbury), Vincent Gil (Mick), John Clayton (Country Cop), Alice Ramsay (Maude Thornbury), Jethro Heysen-Hicks (Jethro Thornbury), Chris Roberts (Turbo), Peter Crossley (Red), Patrick Frost (Schoolteacher).

Sebastian Thornbury, fifteen, goes to a private school in Adelaide and is rehearsing for an upcoming concert at which he plays the piano. He meets Sparrow, a half-Vietnamese street kid who lives by his wits and is searching for his mother. The boys team up and head for the country to find Sparrow's mother.

THE SETTLEMENT (page 110)
p.c.: Queensland Film Corp, Bruning Productions. **p**: Robert Bruning. **d**: Howard Rubie. **sc**: Ted Roberts. **ph**: Ernest Clark. **ed**: Henry Dangar. **m**: Sven Libaek. **p.d.**: John Watson. **sd**: Max Bowring. **a.p.**: Anne Bruning. **p.m.**: Sally Ayre-Smith. **a.d.**: Les Currie. Eastmancolour. 98 mins. Aust dist: Self dist. 1983.

Bill Kerr (Kearney), John Jarratt (Martin), Lorna Lesley (Joycie), Tony Barry (Crowe), Katy Wild (Mrs Crowe), Alan Cassell (Lohan), Elaine Cusack (Mrs Lohan), David Downer (Fr Kleran), Babette Stephens (Mrs Gansman).

The mid-50s. On the edge of a small country town, old friends Kearney and Martin live in a small shack. Joycie, a young former prostitute trying to go straight, is harassed by Lohan, owner of the pub where she works; when Kearney is taken ill, she helps him and soon moves in with the two, causing a town scandal. Angry women burn down the shack, but the three decide to continue to live together.

SHAME (page 218)
p.c.: Barron Films, in ass. with UAA Films. **p**: Paul Barron, Damien Parer. **d**: Steve Jodrell. **sc**:

Beverly Blankenship, Michael Brindley. **ph**: Joseph Pickering. **ed**: Kerry Regan. **m**: Mario Millo. **p.d.**: Phil Peters. **sd**: David Glasser. **a.p.**: Phil Peters. **p.m.**: Deb Copland. **a.d.**: Stuart Wood. Eastmancolour. 94 mins. Aust dist: Hoyts. UK dist: Metro. US dist: Skouras. 1987.

Deborra-Lee Furness (Asta Cadell), Tony Barry (Tim Curtis), Simone Buchanan (Lizzie Curtis), Gillian Jones (Tina Farrel), Peter Aanensen (Sgt Wal Cuddy), Margaret Ford (Norma Curtis), David Franklin (Danny Fiske), Bill McClusky (Ross), Allison Taylor (Penny), Phil Dean (Gary).

Motorbiking in the Western Australian countryside, Perth lawyer Asta Cadell has an accident and arrives in a small town where garage owner Tim Curtis allows her to stay at his place. Appalled by the sexist taunts of men in the town, Asta is shocked to discover Tim's young daughter Lizzie has been gang-raped. Threatened herself, Asta fights back and defeats her attackers. Asta persuades Lizzie to press charges against her assailants; but the youths in question are quickly released. Defending his daughter, Tim is badly beaten and his mother Norma kidnapped; Lizzie dies in another fracas and Lorna, another rape victim, agrees to testify.

SHORT CHANGED (page 205)
p.c.: Magpie Films, presented by NSW Film Corp. **p**: Ross Matthews. **d**: George Ogilvie. **sc**: Robert J. Merritt. **ph**: Peter Levy. **ed**: Richard Francis-Bruce. **m**: Chris Neal. **p.d.**: Kristian Fredrikson. **sd**: Peter Barker. **a.p., p.m.**: Barbara Gibbs. **a.d.**: Steve Andrews. Eastmancolour. 104 mins. Aust dist: Greater Union. 1985.

David Kennedy (Stuart Wilkins), Susan Leith (Alison Wilkins), Jamie Agius (Tommy Wilkins), Ray Meagher (Marshall), Mark Little (Curly), Ronald Merritt (Uncle), Rhys McConnochie (Headmaster), Ron Haddrick (Garrick), 'Lucky' Wikramanayake (Gopowalia), Alan McQueen (Cummings).

Stuart Wilkins, an Aboriginal, is married to Alison, a middle-class white woman, and they have a son, Tommy. After the death of his father in prison, Stuart leaves the city and returns some years later; meanwhile, Alison, urged on by Marshall, her father, has divorced him. A legal battle ensues for custody of the boy.

SILVER CITY (page 49)
p.c.: Limelight Productions. **p**: Joan Long. **d**: Sophia Turkiewicz. **sc**: Sophia Turkiewicz, Thomas Keneally. **ph**: John Seale. **ed**: Don Saunders. **m**: William Motzing. **p.d.**: Igor Nay. **sd**: Mark Lewis. **p.m.**: Susan Wild. **a.d.**: Michael Falloon. Panavision. Eastmancolour. 101 mins. Aust dist: Filmways. UK dist: Artificial Eye. US

dist: Samuel Goldwyn. 1984.

1984 Australian Film Awards: Best supporting actress (Anna Jemison), supporting actor (Steve Bisley), costume design (Jan Hurley).

Gosia Dobrowolska (Nina), Ivar Kants (Julian), Anna Jemison (Anna), Steve Bisley (Viktor), Debra Lawrance (Helena), Ewa Brok (Mrs Bronowska), Joel Cohen (Young Daniel), Tim McKenzie (Roy Jenkins), Dennis Miller (Max), Annie Byron (Dorothy), Steve Jacobs (Stefan), Halina Abramowicz (Ella), Josef Drewniak (Priest), Ron Blanchard (Arthur Calwell).

In 1962, Nina, a schoolteacher, meets Julian, whom she has not seen for many years, on a train. They had met in 1949 as immigrants from Poland; Julian, married to Anna, is attracted to Nina when they all live in Silver City, a migrant compound outside Sydney. Nina meets penfriend Roy Jenkins, a simple farmer, but is not attracted to him. She is sent to work as a maid in a country hospital, but is desperately unhappy and is transferred to Sydney where she meets Julian again and starts an affair with him. However, he elects to return to his wife. Back in the present, the train arrives in Sydney and Anna is there to meet her husband; Nina goes off alone.

SKY PIRATES (page 80)

p.c.: John Lamond Motion Pictures. **p, ed**: John Lamond, Michael Hirsh. **d**: Colin Eggleston. **sc**: John Lamond. **ph**: Garry Wapshott. **m**: Brian May. **p.d.**: Kristian Fredrikson. **sd**: Gary Wilkins. **2nd unit d**: Ross Hamilton. **stunts**: Max Aspin. **p.m.**: Kevin Powell. **a.d.**: John Powditch. Panavision. Colour. 86 mins. Aust dist: Roadshow. US dist: International Film Marketing. 1985.

John Hargreaves (Harris), Meredith Phillips (Melanie Mitchell), Max Phipps (Savage), Bill Hunter (O'Reilly), Simon Chilvers (Rev. Mitchell), Alex Scott (Gen. Hackett), David Parker (Hayes), Adrian Wright (Valentine), Peter Cummins (Col. Brien), Tommy Dysart (Barman).

1945. Harris, a top pilot, is flying from Sydney to Washington (his passengers include priest/scientist Rev. Mitchell) when the aircraft enters a time warp. Some time later, Harris tells the story at a court martial: the adventure involves Savage, a villain eager to obtain a powerful tablet left on Earth by prehistoric spacemen. Mitchell's feisty daughter, Melanie, falls in love with the intrepid Harris, who eventually defeats Savage and saves the world.

SLATE, WYN AND ME (page 268)

p.c.: Ukiyo Films, for Hemdale, International Film Management. **ex.p**: Antony I. Ginnane, William Fayman. **p**: Tom Burstall. **d, sc**: Don McLennan

(from the novel *Slate and Me and Blanche McBride* by Georgia Savage). **ph**: David Connell. **ed**: Peter [Zbigniew] Friedrich. **m**: Bluey & Curly Productions. **p.d.**: Paddy Reardon. **sd**: Andrew Ramage. **stunts**: Bill Stacey. Panavision. Eastmancolour. 90 mins. Aust dist: Filmpac. US dist: Hemdale. UK dist: Palace. 1987.

Sigrid Thornton (Blanche McBride), Simon Burke (Wyn Jackson), Martin Sacks (Slate Jackson), Tommy Lewis (Morgan), Lesley Baker (Molly), Harold Baigent (Sammy), Michelle Torres (Daphne), Murray Fahey (Martin), Taya Stratton (Pippa), Julia MacDougall (Del Downer), Peter Cummins (Old Man Downer).

Wyn and Slate Jackson rob a bank in a small country town, and Wyn shoots Wilkinson, the local policeman. Schoolteacher Blanche McBride witnesses the incident and is kidnapped by the brothers. There follows a lengthy cross-country chase during which Blanche turns first to Wyn, later to Slate (who had, at first, wanted to kill her). Finding Blanche and Slate in bed together, Wyn orders her away at gunpoint; Slate is gunned down, but Wyn escapes. Much later, Wyn finds Blanche, pregnant by Slate; she promises to wait for him . . .

SONS OF STEEL (page 154)

p.c.: Jet Films. **ex.p**: Charles Waterstreet, Klaus Sellinger. **p**: James Michael Vernon. **d, sc, m**: Gary L. Keady. **ph**: Joe Pickering. **ed**: Amanda Robson. **p.d.**: Graham (Grace) Walker. **sd**: Paul Radcliffe. **p.m.**: Brigitte Zeisig. **a.d.**: Peter Fitzgerald. Colour. 104 mins. Self-distributed. 1988.

Rob Hartley (Black Alice), Roz Wason (Hope), Jeff Duff (Secta), Dasha Blahova (Honor), Mark Hembrow (Mal), Elizabeth Richmond (Djard), Ralph Cotterill (Karzoff), Wayne Snell (Ex).

Oceana, the near future. Black Alice, a rock star, and Hope, his girlfriend, become involved in an attempt to reverse time and so prevent a nuclear accident in Sydney Harbour.

SOUTHERN CROSS (Japanese title: Minami Jujisei. UK title: The Highest Honour: A True Story) (page 44)

p.c.: Southern International Films (Sydney), Shinihon Eija (Tokyo). **ex.p**: John McCallum, [Kanji Mochimaru]. **p**: Lee Robinson, [Takeyo Otoh]. **d**: Peter Maxwell, [Seiji Moriyama]. **sc**: Lee Robinson, [Katsuya Suzaki, Takeo Ito]. **ph**: John McLean, [Kozo Okazaki]. **ed**: David Stiven, [Yoshitari Kuroiwa]. **m**: Eric Jupp, [Masaru Satoh]. **p.d.**: Bernard Hides, [Shigeichi Ikuno]. **sd**: Syd Butterworth, [Shin Tokai]. **p.m.**: Michael McKeag. **a.d.**: David Bracknell, [Koichi Nakajima]. Colour. 108 mins. [In Japan: 143

mins]. UK dist: Enterprise. Japanese dist: Toho. 1982.

John Howard (Capt. Robert Page), Atsuo Nakamura (Minoru Tamiya), Stuart Wilson (Lt-Col. Ivan Lyon), Steve Bisley (Falls), Michael Aitkens (Maj. Ingleton), George Mallaby (Lt-Comm. Don Davidson), Tony Bonner (Lt Carey), John Ley (Lt Sargent), Harold Hopkins (Corp. Stewart), Garry Waddell (Corp. Fletcher), Allan Cassell (Lt Ted Carse), Slim De Grey (McDowell), Mark Hembrow (Marsh), Vincent Ball (Marsham), Kinya Kitaoji (Tachibana), Jiro Sakagami (Kimura), Hosei Komatsu (Yabe), Takuya Fujioka (Matsumoto), [Diane Craig (Mrs Page), Veronica Lang (Mrs Lyon)].

In 1942, members of the Australian Z force, including Lyon and Page (whose father is a Japanese POW) destroy several Japanese ships before being captured. Lyon is killed, but Page is interrogated by the sensitive Minoru Tamiya, who befriends him and tries to save him from torture at the hands of the *Kempetai* (security police). Finally, Tamiya tricks Page into revealing secret information, and a month before the end of the War, Page and the others are ceremonially beheaded, with Tamiya personally executing his friend.

SPIRITS OF THE AIR, GREMLINS OF THE CLOUDS (page 74)

p.c.: Meaningful Eye Contact. **p**: Andrew McPhail, Alex Proyas. **d, sc**: Alex Proyas. **ph**: David Knaus. **ed**: Craig Wood. **m, sd**: Peter Miller. **p.d.**: Sean Callinan. **cost**: Angela Tonks. Colour. 93 mins. Self-distributed. 1988.

Michael Lake (Felix Crabtree), Melissa Davis (Betty Crabtree), Norman Boyd (Smith).

The desert, some time in the future. Felix and his sister, Betty, who have a religious fixation, are seemingly trapped in a wood house in the middle of nowhere; they are trying to build a primitive aircraft in which to escape. A stranger, Smith, arrives, and he helps them, but by the time a viable aircraft is built, Betty has gone mad and Felix elects to stay with her. Smith flies off alone.

SQUIZZY TAYLOR (page 36)

p.c.: Simpson Le Mesurier Films. **ex.p, sc**: Roger Simpson. **p**: Roger Le Mesurier. **d**: Kevin Dobson. **ph**: Dan Burstall. **ed**: David Pulbrook. **m**: Bruce Smeaton. **p.d.**: Logan Brewer. **sd**: Phil Sterling. **p.m.**: Christine Suli. **a.d.**: Philip Hearnshaw. Eastmancolour. 98 mins. Aust dist: Filmways. US dist: Satori. 1982.

David Atkins (Leslie 'Squizzy' Taylor), Jacki Weaver (Dolly), Alan Cassell (Brophy), Michael Long (Piggott), Kim Lewis (Ida), Steve Bisley (Snowy Cutmore), Robert Hughes (Reg Harvey), Cul Cullen (Henry Stokes), Tony Rickard (Dutch), Simon Thorpe (Paddy).

Melbourne, 1919. Squizzy Taylor, a diminutive small-time pimp, thief and gambler, cunningly starts a war between the rival Fitzroy and Richmond gangs, stepping into the breach himself. He gives self-glorifying interviews to newspaperman Reg Harvey, and is in the pay of Brophy, a cop. He decides to throw over his moll, Dolly, in favour of the upper-class Ida, but is drawn back into the gang struggles and killed by his chief rival, Snowy Cutmore, in 1921.

STANLEY (page 331)

p.c.: Seven Keys. **ex.p**: Brian Rosen. **p**: Andrew Gaty. **d, sc**: Esben Storm. **ph**: Russell Boyd. **ed**: William Anderson. **m**: William Motzing. **p.d.**: Owen Williams. **sd**: Mark Lewis. **a.p.**: Warwick Ross. **p.m.**: Antonia Barnard. **a.d.**: Steve Andrews. Colour. 107 mins. Aust dist: Seven Keys. 1983.

Peter Bensley (Stanley Dunstan), Graham Kennedy (Norm Norris), Nell Campbell (Amy Benton), Michael Craig (Sir Stanley Dunstan), Max Cullen (Berger), David Argue (Morris Norris), Susan Walker (Dorris Norris), Lorna Leslie (Sheryl Benton), Betty Lucas (Lady Dunstan), Joy Smithers (Patty Norris), Jon Ewing (Reg), Harold Hopkins (Harry), Johnny Lockwood (Flasher).

Stanley, whose father Sir Stanley Dunstan is a very wealthy businessman, is eccentric. Told by his father to be 'normal', he takes a room in the home of a totally average family who live in the suburbs. He discovers that Norm Norris is a closet homosexual, his wife Dorris is having an affair with the President of the Bowling Club (who has absconded with the funds), son Morris is a pusher, and daughter Patty is pregnant by an Aboriginal. After many adventures, and romance with Amy, who works in an employment exchange, Stanley comes to realise that 'there's no such thing as normal'.

STARSTRUCK (page 147)

p.c.: Palm Beach pictures. **p**: David Elfick, Richard Brennan. **d**: Gillian Armstrong. **sc, a.p.**: Stephen Maclean. **ph**: Russell Boyd. **ed**: Nicholas Beauman. **m**: Mark Moffatt. **p.d.**: Brian Thomson. **sd**: Phil Judd. **choreog.**: David Atkins. **cost**: Luciana Arrighi. **p.m.**: Barbara Gibbs. **a.d.**: Mark Turnbull. Eastmancolour. 103 mins (International version: 94 mins). Aust dist: Hoyts. US dist: Cinecom. UK dist. Entertainment. 1982.

Jo Kennedy (Jackie Mullens), Ross O'Donovan (Angus Mullens), Margo Lee (Pearl), Max Cullen (Reg), Pat Evison (Nana), John O'May (Terry

Lambert), Dennis Miller (Lou), Norman Erskine (Hazza), Melissa Jaffer (Mrs Booth), Ned Lander (Robbie), Carol Burns (Teacher).

Eighteen-year-old Jackie Mullens lives with her parents and cousin Angus, fourteen, in a pub by the Sydney Harbour Bridge. She wants to be a punk singer, and teams up with a group called The Wombats; Angus, a budding publicist, has her stage a dangerous stunt in which she walks a tightrope across a city street. Television star Terry Lambert has Jackie on his show, without The Wombats: to her disappointment, he turns out to be gay, and she is consoled by Robbie, her boyfriend. Angus' father steals the takings from the pub, but Jackie and The Wombats, disguised as stagehands, enter a talent contest staged at the Opera House on New Year's Eve— and win the $25,000 prize.

THE STILL POINT (page 362)

p.c.: Colosimo Films. **p**: Rosa Colosimo. **d**. Barbara Boyd-Anderson. **sc**: Barbara Boyd-Anderson, Rosa Colosimo. **ph**: Kevin Anderson. **ed**: Zbigniew Friedrich. **m**: Pierre Pierre. **p.d.**: Paddy Reardon. **sd**: Geoffrey White. **p.m.**: Robert Kewley. Colour. 82 mins. Self-distributed. 1985.

Nadine Garner (Sarah), Lyn Semmler (Barbara), Robert Cuming (Grandfather), Alex Menglet (Paul), Steve Bastoni (David), Kirsty Grant (Simone).

Sarah, fourteen, has suffered a hearing impairment from birth, but can lip-read perfectly. Upset because her parents have divorced and her mother Barbara has a new lover, she goes to stay with her grandfather, meets some older girls (involved in drugs) and attracts the boyfriend of one of them.

A STING IN THE TALE (page 225)

p.c.: Rosa Colosimo Films. **p**: Rosa Colosimo, Reg McLean. **d**: Eugene Schlusser. **sc**: Patrick Edgeworth. **ph**: Nicholas Sherman. **ed**: Zbigniew Friedrich. **m**: Allan Zavod. **p.d.**: Lisa (Blitz) Brennan. **sd**: Michael Piper. **p.m.**: Alison Sadler. **a.d.**: Arthur D'Aprano. Eastmancolour. 96 mins. Self-distributed in Australia. 1989.

Diane Craig (Diane Lane), Gary Day (Barry Robbins), Lynne Williams (Louise Parker), Edwin Hodgeman (Roger Monroe), Don Barker (Prime Minister), John Noble (PM's Minder), Tony Mack (Michael Meadows), Bob Newman (Permanent Secretary), Patrick Edgeworth (Editor).

Newly-elected government MP Diane Lane wants to become Australia's first woman Prime Minister. Her married lover, Barry Robbins, the Minister for Health, is plotting to unseat the incumbent PM. Meanwhile, Diane's best friend, Louise Parker, a journalist working on a paper owned by ambitious Roger Monroe, is assigned to write a story she'd rather not.

STIR (page 226)

p.c.: Smiley Films, in ass. with NSW Film Corp. **p**: Richard Brennan. **d**: Stephen Wallace. **sc**: Bob Jewson. **ph**: Geoff Burton. **ed**: Henry Dangar. **m**: Cameron Allan. **p.d.**: Lee Whitmore. **sd**: Gary Wilkins. **p.m.**: Barbara Gibbs. **a.d.**: Mark Turnbull. Eastmancolour. 100 mins. Aust dist: Hoyts. 1980.

Bryan Brown (China), Max Phipps (Norton), Dennis Miller (Redford), Michael Gow (Andrew), Phil Motherwell (Alby), Gary Waddell (Dave), Ray Marshall (Chalmers), Ted Robshaw (Partridge), James Marsh (Webster), Paul Sonkkila (McIntosh), Robert 'Tex' Morton (Governor).

China, an ex-prisoner, gives a television interview about recent prison riots and the brutalities that led up to them. Three years later, he is back in prison, trying to play it cool: but when a new riot occurs, it is Norton, seemingly the most sympathetic of the guards, who turns ugly and beats China almost to death.

STREET HERO (page 150)

p.c.: Paul Dainty Films. **ex.p**: Paul Dainty. **p**: Julie Monton. **d**: Michael Pattinson. **sc**: Jan Sardi. **ph**: Vincent Monton. **ed**: David Pulbrook. **m**: Bruce Smeaton. **p.d.**: Brian Thomson. **sd**: Gary Wilkins. **p.m.**: Helen Watts. **a.d.**: Stuart Freeman. Eastmancolour. 100 mins. Aust dist: Roadshow. 1984.

1984 Australian Film Awards: Best music, sound.

Vince Colosimo (Vinnie), Sigrid Thornton (Gloria), Sandy Gore (Bonnie Rogers), Bill Hunter (Det. Fitzpatrick), Ray Marshall (George), Amanda Muggleton (Miss Reagan), Peta Toppano (Vinnie's mother), Peter Sardi (Joey), Luciano Catenacci (Ciccio).

As a child, Vinnie witnessed the murder of his father. Now seventeen, he plans a career as a boxer, acts as courier for gangster Ciccio, and lives with his mother and brutal de facto father. At school, he falls for Gloria and comes under the influence of music teacher Bonnie Rogers, who encourages him in his musical ambitions.

A STREET TO DIE (page 54)

p.c.: Mermaid Beach Productions, in ass. with Multifilms. **p, d, sc**: Bill Bennett. **ph**: Geoff Burton. **ed**: Denise Hunter. **m**: Michael Atkinson, Michael Spicer. **p.d.**: Igor Nay. **sd**: Leo Sullivan. **a.p., p.m.**: Jenny Day. **a.d.**: Phil Rich. Colour. 91 mins. Aust dist: Octopus. UK dist: The Other Cinema. 1985.

1985 Australian Film Awards: Best actor (Chris Haywood).

Chris Haywood (Colin Turner), Jennifer Cluff (Lorraine Turner), Peter Hehir (Peter Townley), Andrew Chirgwin (Paul Turner), Peter Chirgwin (Jason Turner), Robin Ramsay (Tom), Susannah Fowle (Julie), Peter Kowitz (Craig), Arianthe Galani (Dr Walsea), Pat Evison (Sister Sweet), Don Crosby (Deputy President).

In 1966, Colin Turner served for ten months (as a conscript) in Vietnam, where he was exposed to the Agent Orange defoliant. In 1979, Colin, his wife Lorraine, and their two sons, move into a War Service home in the Sydney suburb of Whalan. They note that other Vietnam vets living in the street are sickly, and soon Colin's health deteriorates (lassitude, skin rashes, pain). Convinced his condition is related to Agent Orange, Colin seeks compensation with the help of Peter Townley from the Vietnam Veterans Association, but he dies before his case is heard. Lorraine continues the fight, and eventually receives a favourable finding from the Repatriation Tribunal.

STRIKEBOUND (page 40)
p.c.: TRM Productions. **ex.p**: Erik Lipins, **p**: Miranda Bain, Timothy White. **d**, **sc**: Richard Lowenstein (based on the book *Dead Men Don't Dig Coal* by Wendy Lowenstein). **ph**: Andrew De Groot. **ed**: Jill Bilcock. **m**: Declan Affley. **p.d.**: Tracy Watt. **sd**: Dean Gawen. **p.m.**: Julie Stone. **a.d.**: Robert Kewley. Colour. 101 mins. Aust dist: Ronin Films. UK dist: Mainline. 1983.

1984 Australian Film Awards: Best production design.

Chris Haywood (Wattie Doig), Carol Burns (Agnes Doig), Hugh Keays-Byrne (Idris Williams), Rob Steele (Charlie Nelson), Nik Forster (Harry Bell), David Kendall (Birch), Anthony Hawkins (Sergeant), Marion Edward (Meg), Reg Evans (Ernie), Rod Williams (Tom).

Korumburra, the 30s. Wattie Doig, a coal miner, works in the Sunbeam Colliery and is an active Communist; Agnes, his wife, is a teacher and member of the Salvation Army. Wattie organises the miners in a demand for a minimum wage; the management lock the miners out and hire scab labour. Hired killers try to kill Wattie. Agnes forms a Women's Auxiliary. The striking miners flood the shaft to flush out the scabs, and then barricade themselves inside the main tunnel. The miners win the day.

THE SURFER (page 236)
p.c.: Frontier Films, in ass. with The Producers Circle. **ex.p**: Grahame Jennings. **p**: James M.

Vernon, Frank Shields. **d**: Frank Shields. **sc**: David Marsh. **ph**: Michael Edols. **ed**: Greg Bell. **m**: Davood Tabrizi. **p.d.**: Martin O'Neill. **sd**: Max Bowring. **p.m.**: Penny Wall. **a.d.**: John Warren. Eastmancolour. 96 mins. Aust dist: Self-distributed. 1986.

Gary Day (Sam Barlow), Gosia Dobrowolska (Gina), Rod Mullinar (Hagan), Tony Barry (Calhoun), Gerard MacGuire (Jack), Kris McQuade (Trish), Stephen Leeder (Slaney), David Clendenning (Murph).

Sam Barlow, a Vietnam vet, operates a stall on the beach at Surfers Paradise. Visiting the home of his best friend, he meets Gina, a mysterious woman, and then discovers his friend has been murdered, apparently by Asian hit-men. He further discovers a blackmail plot against a government minister involving Hagan, a mercenary. Determined to avenge his friend, and pursued by crooked cop Calhoun, Sam heads north with Gina, as the arrival of a ship appears to be an important clue. Though Gina proves not entirely trustworthy, the couple fall in love. At their destination, they discover that illegal exportation of minerals is the reason behind the events that have occurred.

THE SURVIVOR (page 298)
p.c.: Tuesday Films, F.G. Film Productions. **ex.p**: William Fayman. **p.**: Antony I. Ginnane. **d**: David Hemmings. **sc**: David Ambrose (from the novel by James Herbert). **ph**: John Seale. **ed**: Tony Patterson. **m**: Brian May. **p.d.**: Bernard Hides. **sd**: Tim Lloyd. **a.p.**, **p.m.**: Jane Scott. **a.d.**: Mark Egerton. Panavision. Eastmancolour. 87 mins. Aust dist: Greater Union. 1980.

Robert Powell (Keller), Jenny Agutter (Hobbs), Joseph Cotten (The Priest), Angela Punch McGregor (Beth Rogan), Ralph Cotterill (Slater), Peter Sumner (Tewson), Adrian Wright (Goodwin), Lorna Lesley (Goodwin's assistant).

A 747 airliner crashes soon after taking off: Keller, the pilot, is the sole survivor. A mysterious woman, Hobbs, persuades Keller she can help him discover who planted the bomb (apparently it was the deranged Slater), but a series of mysterious murders occur, the victims including Keller's friend Tewson, and Goodwin, a photographer, and his assistant. Eventually it seems that Keller is a ghost on a mission of vengeance.

SWEET DREAMERS (page 120)
p.c.: T.C. Productions. **p**: Lesley Tucker. **d**, **sc**, **ed**: Tom Cowan. **ph**: Brian Probyn. **m**: Ralph Schneider. **p.d.**: Lesley Tucker. **sd**: Paul Schneller. 82 mins. Self-distributed in Australia. 1981.

Richard Moir (Will), Sue Smithers

(Joesephine), Adam Bowen (Stuart), Frankie Raymond (Landlady).

In London, Will, an Australian film cameraman who wants to write and direct a love story, meets Josephine, an Australian woman who works for a film producer; they have an affair. He returns home and soon she joins him in his scungy, under-furnished flat. His efforts to get the AFC to support his project fail; Josephine becomes involved in a café for students. Will is offered an assistant's job on an American film, but Josephine begs him to stay. They part. Much later, she discovers that, in his film he uses the same dialogue they had spoken to each other when they first met.

SWEETIE (page 373)

p.c.: Arenafilm. **p**: John Maynard. **d**: Jane Campion. **sc**: Jane Campion, Gerard Lee. **ph**: Sally Bongers. **ed**: Veronica Heussler. **m**: Martin Armiger. **p.d.**: Peter Harris. **sd**: Leo Sullivan. **p.m.**: Patricia L'Huede. **a.d.**: John Fretz. Colour. 97 mins. Aust dist: Filmpac. US dist: Avenue Pictures. 1989.

1989 Australian Film Awards: Best original screenplay.

Genevieve Lemon (Dawn [Sweetie]), Karen Colston (Kay), Tom Lycos (Louis), Jon Darling (Gordon), Dorothy Barry (Flo), Michael Lake (Bob), Andre Pataczek (Clayton).

Kay, who is frightened of trees and believes in fortune tellers, is told that the man of her life will have a question mark on his forehead. She meets Louis, who has just become engaged to marry a workmate: his kiss-curl and mole convince her he was the man the fortune teller described. Louis moves in with Kay and all is well until Kay's unstable sister Dawn, known as Sweetie, also moves in with her 'producer'/lover, Bob. The relationship between Kay and Louis deteriorates; Bob leaves and Gordon, the sisters' father, moves in (his wife Flo having left him to cook at an outback property). Concerned by Sweetie's increasingly irrational behaviour, Kay, Louis and Gordon leave her in Sydney when they go to collect Flo. Sweetie moves back with her parents, but one day strips naked and climbs a tree in the back yard; she suffers a fatal fall.

TAIL OF A TIGER (page 342)

p.c.: Producers Circle. **ex.p**: Grahame Jennings. **p**: James M. Vernon. **d**, **sc**: Rolf De Heer. **ph**: Richard Michalak. **ed**: Surresh Ayyar. **m**: Steve Arnold, Graham Tardif. **p.d.**: Judi Russell. **sd**: Penn Robinson. Colour. 82 mins. 1984.

Grant Navin (Orville Ryan), Gordon Poole (Harry), Caz Lederman (Lydia Ryan), Gayle Kennedy (Beryl), Peter Feeley (Spike), Dylan Lyle (Rabbit), Walter Sullivan (Stan), Basil Clarke (Jack).

Ten-year-old Orville Ryan is obsessed with vintage airplanes. He comes across old Harry, who has a wrecked Tiger Moth in a shed near the docks. Overcoming Harry's initial suspicions, Orville helps the old man restore the plane, and they eventually take off on a joyride over the city.

THE TALE OF RUBY ROSE (page 74)

p.c.: Seon Films, in ass. with FGH. **ex.p**: Basia Puszka, Antony I. Ginnane. **p**: Bryce Menzies, Andrew Wiseman. **d**, **sc**: Roger Scholes. **ph**: Steve Mason. **m**: Paul Schutze. **p.d.**: Bryce Perrin. **sd**: Bob Cutcher. **a.p.**: Ian Pringle. **p.m.**: Christine Gallagher. **a.d.**: James Legge. Eastmancolour. 101 mins. Aust dist: Filmpac. US dist: Hemdale. 1987.

1987 Australian Film Awards: Best music.

Melita Jurisic (Ruby Rose), Chris Haywood (Henry Rose), Rod Zuanic (Gem), Martyn Sanderson (Bennett), Sheila Florance (Grandma).

1933. In a remote, mountainous region of Tasmania, Ruby Rose lives with her fur trapper husband, Henry, and their adopted son, Gem. Terrified of the dark as the result of a childhood trauma, Ruby retreats into a world of illusion and fantasy. She treks down the mountain and, in the valley, meets her elderly grandmother, who dies soon after.

TENDER HOOKS (page 145)

p.c.: Tru Vu Picture. **p**: Chris Oliver. **d**, **sc**: Mary Callaghan. **ph**: Ray Argall. **ed**: Tony Stevens. **m**: Graham Bidstrup. **p.d.**: Kerri Brown. **sd**: Pat Fiske. **a.p.**, **p.m.**: Anna Grieve. **a.d.**: Ian Page, Colour. 95 mins. Aust dist: Ronin. 1988.

Jo Kennedy (Mitch), Nique Needles (Rex Reeson), Anna Phillips (Gaye), Robert Menzies (Yawn), John Polson (Tony), Ian Mortimer (Vic), Toni Scanlon (Lorraine), Kim Deacon (Connie), Shane Conner (Wayne).

Mitch, a hairdresser who lives alone in a King's Cross flat, becomes involved with Rex Reeson, a drifter involved in petty crime. Her friends include Gaye, a prostitute, Tony, her pimp, and Yawn, a drug addict in an almost permanent state of inertia. Rex is arrested and jailed after a robbery, but escapes with a friend and picks up Mitch for a final fling before the police close in.

THE 13TH FLOOR (page 295)

p.c.: Premiere Film Marketing, Medusa Communications. **ex.p**: Tom Broadbridge. **p**: David Hannay, Charles Hannah. **d**, **sc**: Chris

Roache. **ph**: Steve Prime. **ed**: Peter McBain. **m**: Mick Coleman. **p.d.**: Darrell Lass. **sd**: David Glasser. **p.m.**: Julie Ritchie. **a.d.**: Ian Astridge. Eastmancolour. 90 mins. Direct to video release. 1988.

Lisa Hensley (Heather Thompson), Miranda Otto (Rebecca), Tim McKenzie (John Burke), Jeff Truman (Bert), Vic Rooney (Brenner), Tony Blackett (Thompson), Michael Caton (Dr Fletcher), Paul Hunt (Nick).

Unscrupulous businessman Thompson causes the death of the son of a business rival on the 13th floor of a building he is constructing: his daughter Heather is a secret witness. Years later Heather, a dropout with evidence against her father, together with Rebecca, an addict, squats on the deserted 13th floor of the building; they are haunted by the friendly ghost of the dead boy, and hunted by Thompson's thugs.

THOSE DEAR DEPARTED (page 332)

p.c.: A Phillip Emanuel Production. **p**: Phillip Emanuel. **d**: Ted Robinson. **sc**: Steve J. Spears. **ph**: David Burr. **ed**: Robert Gibson. **m**: Phil Scott. **p.d.**: Roger Ford. **sd**: Phil Keros. **a.p.**: Barbara Gibbs. **p.m.**: Rosanne Andrews-Baxter. **a.d.**: Steve Andrews. Eastmancolour. 90 mins. Aust dist: Village–Roadshow. 1987.

Garry McDonald (Max Falcon), Pamela Stephenson (Marilyn Falcon), Su Cruickshank (Norda Thompson), Marian Dworakowski (Richard Kowalski), John Clarke (Insp. Jerry), Ignatius Jones (Phil Rene), Antonia Murphy (Phoebe Furlong), Graeme Blundell (Dr Howie), Arthur Dignam (The Producer), Jonathan Biggins (Sgt Steve), Patrick Cook (Tristan), Maureen O'Shaughnessy (Bronwyn).

Egotistical actor Max Falcon, currently starring in a musical about Freud, is unaware that his sexy wife, Marilyn, is having an affair with his chauffeur, Richard. The lovers plot to murder Max, but various attempts fail until his manager, Norda Thompson, drinks a poisoned nightcap intended for Max. Finally the lovers succeed, but Max finds himself in a strange theatre where dead people with business on earth wait to return as ghosts. Together with Norda and his father, Max returns to haunt Marilyn and Richard.

THE TIME GUARDIAN (page 278)

p.c.: FGH, Chateau, Jen-Diki Film. **ex.p**: Antony I. Ginnane. **p**: Norman Wilkinson, Robert Lagettie. **co-p**: Harley Manners. **d**: Brian Hannant. **sc**: John Baxter, Brian Hannant. **ph**: Geoff Burton. **ed, add. d**: Andrew Prowse. **m**: Allan Zavod. **p.d.**: George Liddle. **sd**: Toivo Lember. **vis. ef.**: Andrew Mason. **p.m.**: Stephanie Jones. **a.d.**: Philip

Hearnshaw. Panavision. Colour. 85 mins. Aust dist: Filmpac. US dist: Hemdale. 1987.

Tom Burlinson (Ballard), Nikki Coghill (Annie), Carrie Fisher (Petra), Dean Stockwell (Boss), Harry Salter (Prenzler), Jo Fleming (Tanel), Tim Robertson (Sgt McCarthy), Jim Holt (Rafferty).

In the 24th century, the ferocious Jen-Diki attack the citizens of a peaceful city. Ballard and Petra (the latter an expert on the twentieth century) are sent to Australia in 1987 to locate a new site for the city; the Jen-Diki follow, and Petra is wounded. Ballard meets up with Annie, a geologist, and meets the puzzled and hostile people of the mining town of Midas. Annie and Ballard fall in love and she decides to return with him to the future; in a final battle with the Jen-Diki, she kills the leader of the enemy.

TO MARKET TO MARKET (page 225)

p.c.: Goosey Ltd. **p, d, sc, p.d.**: Virginia Rouse. **ph**: Jaems Grant. **ed**: Tony Paterson. **m**: Ben Fitzgerald, Kate Reid, Fincina Hopgood. **sd**: Laurie Robinson. **a.p., p.m.**: Trish Carney. **a.d.**: Katherine Hayden. Fujicolor. 85 mins. 1987.

Phillip Quast (Edward Riat), Marcus Gollings (Edward Riat, aged thirteen), Noel Trevarthan (William Riat Sr), Kate Reid (Jackie), Maureen Edwards (Mother), Tony Llewellyn-Jones (Richard), Genevieve Picot (Susanna), Wayne Cull (William Riat Jr).

1965. Thirteen-year-old Edward Riat befriends an Asian boy at the traditional boarding school which both attend: traumatised by the racism of his classmates, the boy kills himself. 1987. Edward, though he tries to stay aloof from his wealthy family and their dubious business dealings, agrees to help his older brother in a scheme which, he later discovers, involves laundering drug money. Edward is exposed as a criminal, disgraced and humiliated, while his family escape without censure.

TOUCH AND GO (page 309)

p.c.: Mutiny Pictures. **ex.p**: Peter Maxwell, Peter Yeldham. **p**: John Pellatt. **d**: Peter Maxwell. **sc**: Peter Yeldham. **ph**: John McLean. **ed**: Sara Bennett. **m**: Jon English. **sd**: Brian Morris. **p.m.**: Michael McKeag. **a.d.**: Ken Ambrose. Eastmancolour. 92 mins. Aust dist: Greater Union. 1980.

Wendy Hughes (Eva Gilmour), Chantal Contouri (Fiona Latham), Carmen Duncan (Millicent Hoffman), Jeanie Drynan (Gina Tesoriero), Liddy Clark (Helen Preston), Christine Amor (Sue Fullerton), Jon English (Frank Butterfield), John Bluthal (Anatole

Sushinsky), Brian Blain (George Latham), Vince Martin (Steve Godfrey), Barbara Stephens (Julia Henderson).

Three women—an actress, a socialite and a locksmith—are anxious to keep a kindergarten open and to do so commit a series of robberies. Later, they recruit other women and plot to rob a holiday resort on a Queensland island.

TRAPS (page 223)

p.c.: Hughes Production. p, d: John Hughes. sc: Paul Davies, John Hughes. ph: Jaems Grant, Erika Addis. ed: Zbigniew Friedrich. p.d.: Clair Jager, Susan Weis. sd: Pat Fiske, Lou Hubbard. Colour. 98 mins. 1985.

Carolyn Howard (Judith Campbell), Gwenda Wiseman' (Gwenda), John Flaus (Father Coughlan), Paul Davies, Lesley Stern, Sylvie Le Clezio, Marian Wilkinson.

Judith Campbell, a journalist, is preparing a review of a documentary film about the CIA in Australia (Allies) when she becomes so intrigued with the subject that she begins an investigation of her own.

TRAVELLING NORTH (page 189)

p.c.: View Pictures. p: Ben Gannon. d: Carl Schultz. sc: David Williamson (based on his play). ph: Julian Penney. ed: Henry Dangar. m: Alan John. p.d.: Owen Paterson. sd: Syd Butterworth. p.m.: Julia Overton. a.d.: Colin Fletcher, Eastmancolour. 96 mins. Aust dist: CEL. US dist: Cineplex Odeon. UK dist: Recorded Releasing. 1986.

1987 Australian Film Awards: Best actor (Leo McKern), adapted screenplay.

Leo McKern (Frank), Julia Blake (Frances), Graham Kennedy (Freddie), Henri Szeps (Saul), Michele Fawdon (Helen), Diane Craig (Sophie), Andrea Moor (Joan), Drew Forsythe (Martin), John Gregg (Jim), Rob Steele (Syd).

Frank retires from his job as a local government engineer in Melbourne and travels to Northern Queensland with Frances, his mistress, a middle-aged divorcee. Despite the presence of a talkative neighbour, Freddie, Frank and Frances are happy in their isolated new home, until Frances decides to go to Melbourne to see her fractious daughters, accompanied by a reluctant Frank. They return to the north where the local doctor, Saul, becomes concerned about Frank's health. The couple decide to marry, and spend a blissful weekend in Sydney. Soon after, Frank dies listening to the classical music he loves so much.

TURKEY SHOOT (US title: Escape 2000) (page 287)

p.c.: Hemdale, FGH, Filmco. ex.p: John Daly, David Hemmings. p: Antony I. Ginnane, William Fayman. d: Brian Trenchard Smith. sc: Jon George, Neill Hicks. ph: John McLean. ed: Alan Lake. m: Brian May. p.d.: Bernard Hides. sd: Paul Clark. stunts: Kerry Rossall. p.m.: Mike Fuller. a.d.: Terry Needham. Panavision. Eastmancolour. 92 mins (87 mins in UK). Aust dist: Roadshow. US dist: New World. UK dist: Enterprise. 1981.

Steve Railsback (Paul Anders), Olivia Hussey (Chris Walters), Michael Craig (Charles Thatcher), Carmen Duncan (Jennifer), Noel Ferrier (Mallory), Lynda Stoner (Rita Daniels), Roger Ward (Ritter), Gus Mercurio (Red), John Ley (Dodge), Michael Petrovitch (Tito), Steve Rackman (Alph).

The year 2000. At Camp 97, a 're-education' centre run by the urbane Charles Thatcher, a 'turkey shoot' is arranged for Mallory, a visiting politician. The victims are Chris, a shopgirl, Paul, a freedom fighter, Rita, a suspected prostitute, Dodge, a deranged myopic, and Griffin, who has made numerous efforts to escape. Thatcher's sadistic guards, led by Ritter, pursue the victims, and Dodge, Griffin and Rita are killed, but in the process several guards, plus Mallory, also perish. The camp is bombed, Ritter and Thatcher are killed, and Paul and Chris escape.

TWELFTH NIGHT (page 194)

p.c.: A Twelfth Night production. p: Don Catchlove. d, sc: Neil Armfield (from the play by William Shakespeare). ph: Louis Irving. ed: Nicholas Beauman. m: Alan John. p.d.: Stephen Curtis. sd: Ron Staider. p.m.: Steven Salgo. a.d.: Corrie Soeterboek. Agfacolour. 120 mins. Aust dist: Greater Union. 1986.

Gillian Jones (Viola, Sebastian), Ivar Kants (Orsino), Jacqy Phillips (Olivia), Peter Cummins (Malvolio), Kerry Walker (The Fool), John Wood (Sir Toby Belch), Geoffrey Rush (Sir Andrew Aguecheek), Tracy Harvey (Sarah), Stuart McCreery (Antonio), Odile Le Clezio (Olivia's maid).

A modern-dress, Australianised version of Shakespeare's play.

TWO BROTHERS RUNNING (page 330)

p.c.: Phillip Emanuel Productions. p: Phillip Emanuel, Martin Cohen. d: Ted Robinson. sc: Morris Lurie. ph: Dan Burstall. ed: Robert Gibson. m: Phillip Scott. p.d.: Leslie Binns. sd: Laurie Robinson. line p: John Hipwell. p.m.: Jan Stott. a.d.: Brian Giddens. Colour. 87 mins. Aust dist: Hoyts. 1988.

Tom Conti (Moses Bornstein), Elizabeth Alexander (Barbara Bornstein), Ritchie Singer (Ben Bornstein), Asher Keddie (Ruthie

Bornstein), Martin Lewis (Silas Bornstein), Dorothy Alison (Mrs Widmore), John Gregg (Nelson), Deborra-Lee Furness (Silver's secretary), Rachel Levita (Aunt), Mark Zandie (Uncle).

A comedy about the relationship between Moses and his brother, Ben.

TWO FRIENDS (page 372)

p.c.: ABC. **p**: Jan Chapman. **d**: Jane Campion. **sc**: Helen Garner. **ph**: Julian Penney. **ed**: Bill Russo. **p.d.**: Janet Patterson. **sd**: Chris Alderton. **p.m.**: Carol Chirlian. **a.d.**: Kate Woods. Eastmancolour. 76 mins. 1986.

Emma Coles (Louise), Kris Bidenko (Kelly), Kris McQuade (Janet [Louise's mother]), Debra May (Chris [Kelly's mother]), Peter Hehir (Malcolm [Stepfather]), Tony Barry (Charlie), Steve Bisley (Kevin), Kerry Dwyer (Alison), Stephen Leeder (Jim), Sean Travers (Matthew).

Fifteen-year-old Louise, together with Janet, her divorced mother, attends the funeral of a friend who died of a drug overdose. Meanwhile, Louise's former friend, Kelly, lives in a communal beachfront house. Earlier, it transpires that Louise and Kelly were inseparable friends.

THE UMBRELLA WOMAN (UK title: The Good Wife) (page 159)

p.c.: Laughing Kookaburra Prods. **p**: Jan Sharp. **d**: Ken Cameron. **sc**: Peter Kenna. **ph**: James Bartle. **ed**: John Scott. **m**: Cameron Allan. **p.d.**: Sally Campbell. **sd**: Ben Osmo, **cost**: Jennie Tate. Eastmancolour. 97 mins. Aust dist: Roadshow. UK dist: Entertainment. US dist: Atlantic. 1986.

1987 Australian Film Awards: Best costume design.

Rachel Ward (Marge Hills), Bryan Brown (Sonny Hills), Sam Neill (Neville Gifford), Steven Vidler (Sugar Hills), Jennifer Claire (Daisy), Bruce Barry (Archie), Peter Cummins (Ned Hopper), Carole Skinner (Mrs Gibson), Clarissa Kaye-Mason (Mrs Jackson), Barry Hill (Mr Fielding), Oliver Hall (Mick Jones).

Corrimandel, 1939. Marge Hills, married to woodsman Sonny, and childless, helps other women in the area, sometimes acting as midwife. Sonny's younger brother, Sugar, moves in with them and is attracted to Marge: he asks her to make love to him, she suggests he get permission from his brother, which he does, causing gossip in the town. When a new barman, Neville Gifford, arrives in town, Marge is instantly attracted to him, but he is put off by her eagerness. She develops an obsession for Gifford, and is shocked when he is found in flagrante with Mrs Fielding, wife of the bank manager, and ordered to leave

town. Marge tries to follow him, but Gifford rejects her. She returns to Sonny.

UNDERCOVER (page 38)

p.c.: Palm Beach Pictures, Filmco. **ex.p**: Richard Toltz. **p**: David Elfick. **d**: David Stevens. **sc**: Miranda Downes. **ph**: Dean Semler. **ed**: Tim Wellburn. **m**: William Motzing, Bruce Smeaton. **p.d.**: Herbert Pinter. **sd**: Peter Barker. **cost**: Kristian Fredrikson. **p.m.**: Lynn Gailey. **a.d.**: Mark Turnbull, Panavision. Colour. 87 mins. Aust dist: Roadshow. 1983.

Genevieve Picot (Libby McKenzie), John Walton (Fred Burley), Michael Pare (Max Wylde), Sandy Gore (Nina), Peter Phelps (Theo), Andrew Sharp (Arthur Burley), Caz Lederman (May Burley), Susan Leith (Alice), Wallas Eaton (Lionel), Barry Otto (Professor).

Ambitious young Libby McKenzie leaves the small country town where she grew up to try to succeed in Sydney. She gets a job with Fred Burley, designer of women's underwear, and is inspired by Nina, the company's head designer. Burley embarks on a campaign to promote locally manufactured and designed goods; meanwhile, after various misunderstandings, Libby falls in love with Max Wylde, a brash American publicist.

UNFINISHED BUSINESS (page 107)

p.c.: Unfinished Business Prod. **ex.p**: Andrena Finlay. **p**: Rebel Penfold-Russell. **d, sc**: Bob Ellis. **ph**: Andrew Lesnie. **ed**: Amanda Robson. **p.d.**: Jane Johnston. **sd**: Gerry Nulifora. **p.m.**: June Henman. **a.d.**: Jake Atkinson. **a.p.**: Patric Juillet. Eastmancolour. 78 mins. Self dist. in Australia. 1985.

John Clayton (Geoff), Michele Fawdon (Maureen), Norman Kaye (George), Bob Ellis (Geoff's flatmate), Andrew Lesnie (Telegraph Boy).

Geoff, a fortyish journalist, returns to Australia after fifteen years overseas, leaving behind in the US a failed marriage and three children. He accidentally meets Maureen, an ex-girlfriend, now married to George, an older man. Maureen has been unable to become pregnant and proposes Geoff join her for a weekend of scientifically controlled lovemaking. At first, the relationship is purely clinical: later, love blossoms. But Maureen, happily pregnant, returns to her husband.

VICIOUS (page 292)

p.c.: Premiere Film Marketing, Medusa Communications. **ex.p**: Tom Broadbridge. **p**: David Hannay, Charles Hannah. **d**: Karl Zwicky. **sc**: Paul J. Hogan, Karl Zwicky. **ph**: John Stokes.

ed: Roy Mason. m: Robert Scott, John Sleith. p.d.: Marc Ryan. sd: David Glasser. line p: Lynn Barker. p.m.: Barbi Taylor. a.d.: Bob Howard. stunts: Bernie Ledger. Colour. 88 mins. US dist: SVS Films. 1988.

Tamblyn Lord (Damon Kennedy), Craig Pearce (Terry), Tiffany Dowe (Sondra Price), John Godden (Felix), Kelly Dingwall (Benny), Leather (Claire), Joanna Lockwood (Diane Kennedy), Ralph Cotterill (Professor), John Clayton (Price).

Damon Kennedy, a rich kid, falls in with three young thugs and joins them in breaking into the home of Price, a wealthy man. Matters get out of hand when the young criminals start killing the homeowner's family.

VINCENT: THE LIFE AND DEATH OF VINCENT VAN GOUGH (page 127)

p.c.: Illumination Films, Look Films, Ozfilms, Dasha Films (Netherlands). p: Tony Llewellyn-Jones. d, sc, ph, ed: Paul Cox. m: Vivaldi, Rossini, Norman Kaye. p.d.: Neil Angwin. cost: Jennie Tate, Beverly Boyd. sd: Jim Currie. co-p: Will Davies. Fujicolor. 103 mins. Aust dist: Roadshow. US dist: Roxy Releasing. UK dist: Artificial Eye. 1987.

John Hurt (Voice of Vincent).

The story of Vincent Van Gogh, seen through his paintings and heard via the letters written to his brother, Theo.

WARM NIGHTS ON A SLOW-MOVING TRAIN (page 134)

p.c.: Western Pacific Films. ex.p: William T. Marshall, Peter Sherman, Robert Ward. p: Ross Dimsey, Patric Juillet. d: Bob Ellis. sc: Bob Ellis, Denny Lawrence. ph: Yuri Sokol. ed: Tim Lewis. m: Peter Sullivan. p.d.: Tracy Watt. sd: Gary Wilkins. p.m.: Darryl Sheen. a.d.: Robert Kewley. Colour. 91 mins. Aust dist: Filmpac. US dist: Miramax. 1987.

Wendy Hughes (The Girl), Colin Friels (The Man), Norman Kaye (The Salesman), John Clayton (The Football Coach), Rod Zuanic (The Soldier), Lewis Fitz-Gerald (The Brother), Steve J. Spears (The Singer), Grant Tilly (The Politician), Peter Whitford (The Steward), Chris Haywood (Stationmaster), John Flaus (Taxi-driver), Peter Carmody (2nd-class Passenger).

A young woman, who works as a teacher in Melbourne and looks after her crippled brother (a former athlete), has made an arrangement with a steward on the Southern Aurora which allows her use of the Judy Garland suite. Each weekend, she solicits a customer on the train, adjusting her style and personality to suit her prospective client. She is approached by a mysterious man,

apparently from a government agency, and falls in love with him. He persuades her to assassinate a visiting politician, which she does. He then abandons her.

WARMING UP (page 318)

p.c.: JNP Films. p, sc: James Davern. d: Bruce Best. ph: Joseph Pickering. ed: Szolt Kollanyi. m: Mike Perjanik. p.d.: Michael Ralph. sd: Ross Linton. a.p.: Terri Vincent. Colour. 84 mins. 1983.

Barbara Stephens (Juliet Cavanagh-Forbes), Henri Szeps (Sgt Peter Sullivan), Queenie Ashton (Mrs Marsh), Adam Fernance (Randolph), Lloyd Morris (Ox), Tim Grogan (Snoopy), Ron Blanchard (Lennie).

Juliet, a divorcee, leaves Sydney with her 10-year-old son Randolph, and arrives in a small country town where she has purchased a ballet school which has, unfortunately, burned down. At first she falls foul of the local policeman, Peter Sullivan, but they eventually fall in love, and Juliet (who has trained the local football team to move like ballet dancers) allows Sullivan to train Randolph as a footballer.

WE OF THE NEVER NEVER (page 177)

p.c.: Adams–Packer Film Productions, Film Corp. of WA. ex.p: Phillip Adams. p: Greg Tepper. d: Igor Auzins. sc: Peter Schreck (from the novel by Mrs Aeneas Gunn). ph: Gary Hansen. ed: Clifford Hayes. m: Peter Best. p.d.: Josephine Ford. sd: Laurie Robinson. co-p: John B. Murray. a.p.: Brian Rosen. p.m.: Antonia Barnard. a.d.: Tim Higgins. Technovision. Eastmancolour. 132 mins. Aust dist: Hoyts. UK dist: Mainline. 1982.

1982 Australian Film Awards: Best photography.

Angela Punch McGregor (Jeannie Gunn), Arthur Dignam (Aeneas Gunn), Tony Barry (MacLennan), Tommy Lewis (Jackeroo), Lewis Fitz-Gerald (Jack), Martin Vaughan (Dan), John Jarratt (Dandy), Tex Morton (Landlord), Mawuyul Yanthalawuy (Rosie).

1900. Jeannie, aged thirty, marries Aeneas Gunn, a librarian who has taken on the job of overseer at the remote Elsey cattle station. At first, the station hands are suspicious (women do not usually accompany their husbands to such a remote spot). But eventually they come to respect Jeannie, though her friendly attitude towards Aborigines is seen as strange. Superstition is rife when an itinerant stockman dies; Aeneas becomes ill and also dies. Jeannie stays on.

WHAT THE MOON SAW (page 200)

p.c.: Boulevard Films. ex.p: Peter Boyle. p, sc:

Frank Howson. **d**: Pino Amenta. **ph**: David Connell. **ed**: Marc Van Buuren. **m**: John Capek. **p.d.**: Otello Stolfo. **sd**: Andrew Ramage. **cost**: Rose Chong. **line p**: Barbi Taylor. **co-p**: James Michael Vernon. **p.m.**: Deborah Samuels. **a.d.**: John Wild. Colour. 96 mins. 1989.

1989 Australian Film Awards: Best costume design.

Andrew Shepherd (Steven Wilson), Pat Evison (Pearl Wilson), Max Phipps (Mr Zachary), Danielle Spencer (Emma Pearce), Kim Gyngell (Jim Shilling), Mark Hennessy (Tony), Jan Friedl (Mrs Melrose), Kurt Ludescher (George), Ross Thompson (Hardy), Gary Sweet (Wilson), Nicki Paull (Night).

Young Steven is sent by his parents from the country to spend school holidays in Melbourne with Pearl, his grandmother, a former showgirl who now sells tickets at a city theatre. Steven becomes entranced with the world of the stage, particularly the current production of *Sinbad*, and befriends the young lead actors before reluctantly returning home.

THE WILD DUCK (page 194)

p.c.: Tinzu P/L. **p**: Phillip Emanuel. **d**: Henri Safran. **sc**: Henri Safran, Peter Smalley, John Lind (based on the play by Henrik Ibsen). **ph**: Peter James. **ed**: Don Saunders. **m**: Simon Walker. **p.d.**: Darrell Lass. **sd**: Syd Butterworth. **p.m.**: Susan Wild. **a.d.**: David Munro. **co-p**: Basil Appleby. Colour. 92 mins. Aust dist: Roadshow. US dist: Orion. 1983.

Liv Ullmann (Gina Ackland), Jeremy Irons (Harold Ackland), Lucinda Jones (Henrietta Ackland), John Meillon (Major Ackland), Arthur Dignam (Gregory Wardle), Michael Pate (George Wardle), Colin Croft (Mollison), Rhys McConnoche (Dr Roland), Marion Edward (Bertha Summers), Jeff Truman (Johnson).

Turn-of-the-century Australia. Harold Ackland, a failed scientist, works as a photographer and lives with his wife Gina, former housekeeper to the Wardle family, their daughter Henrietta, and his ex-soldier father. Harold's former friend, Gregory Wardle, returns after a long absence intent on proving that Gina once had an affair with his father, the wealthy merchant George Wardle, and that Henrietta is the result of that liaison.

WILLS AND BURKE (page 34)

p.c.: Stony Desert Prod. **p**: Bob Weis, Margot McDonald. **d**: Bob Weis. **sc**: Philip Dalkin. **ph**: Gaetano Nino Martinetti. **ed**: Edward McQueen-Mason. **m**: Red Symonds. **p.d.**: Tracy Watt. **sd**: Ian Ryan. **cost**: Rose Chong, Karen Markel. **a.d.**:

John Wild. Panavision. Eastmancolour. 101 mins. Aust dist: Greater Union. 1985.

Garry McDonald (Robert O'Hara Burke), Kim Gyngell (William John Wills), Jonathan Hardy (John Macadam), Peter Collingwood (Sir William Stawell), Mark Little (John King), Roy Baldwin (Charley Grey), Nicole Kidman (Julia Matthews), Roderick Williams (George Landellis), Alex Manglet (William Brahe), Chris Haywood (Constable).

The Burke and Wills story as comedy.

WINDRIDER (page 151)

p.c.: Barron Films. **p**: Paul Barron. **d**: Vincent Monton. **sc**: Everett De Roche, Bonnie Harris. **ph**: Joe Pickering. **ed**: John Scott. **m**: Kevin Peak. **p.d.**: Phil Monaghan. **sd**: Mark Lewis. **a.p.**: Bonnie Harris. **p.m.**: Terri Vincent. **a.d.**: Steve Jodrell. Eastmancolour. 92 mins. Aust dist: Hoyts. 1986.

Tom Burlinson (P. C. Simpson), Nicole Kidman (Jade), Charles Tingwell (Simpson Sr), Jill Perryman (Miss Dodge), Simon Chilvers, Penny Brown.

P.C., son of wealthy businessman Simpson, lives in a lavish beach house, drives a fast car, and loves to surf. He becomes passionately involved with Jade, a hard-driving rock star. P.C. arrives only just in time for an important surfing contest, and patches up a quarrel with Jade.

THE WINDS OF JARRAH (page 116)

p.c.: Film Corp. of WA. **p**: Mark Egerton, Marj Pearson. **d, sc**: Mark Egerton (based on a screenplay by Bob Ellis and Anne Brooksbank from the book *The House in the Timberwoods* by Joyce Dingwall). **ph**: Geoff Burton. **ed**: Sara Bennett. **m**: Bruce Smeaton. **p.d.**: Graham Walker. **sd**: Gary Wilkins. **p.m.**: Su Armstrong. **a.d.**: Michael Falloon. Eastmancolour 104 mins. 1983.

Terence Donovan (Marlow), Susan Lyons (Diana Venness), Harold Hopkins (Jock Farrell), Steve Bisley (Clem Matheson), Martin Vaughan (Ben), Dorothy Alison (Mrs Sullivan), Isabelle Anderson (Helen Marlow), Emil Minty (Andy).

1946. Diana Venness, a young Englishwoman recovering from a broken love affair, takes a job as tutor to children who live in rugged timber country with their embittered uncle, Marlow. Spurning the advances of Jock Farrell, Diana eventually winds up in the arms of her employer, but not before Andy, one of the children, has succumbed to a fatal disease.

WINTER OF OUR DREAMS (page 137)

p.c.: Vega Film Prods. **p**: Richard Mason. **d, sc**: John Duigan. **ph**: Tom Cowan. **ed**: Henry Dangar. **m**: Sharon Calcraft. **p.d.**: Lee Whitmore. **sd**: Lloyd

Carrick. **p.m.**: Julia Overton. **a.d.**: Andrew Williams. Eastmancolour. 89 mins. Aust dist: Greater Union. US dist: Satori. UK dist: Enterprise. 1981.

1981 Australian Film Awards: Best actress (Judy Davis).

Judy Davis (Lou), Bryan Brown (Rob McGregor), Cathy Downes (Gretel McGregor), Baz Luhrmann (Pete), Peter Mochrie (Tim), Mervyn Drake (Mick) Margie McCrae (Lisa Blaine), Mercia Deane-Johns (Angela), Joy Hubry (Marge), Kim Deacon (Michelle), Caz Lederman (Jenny), Virginia Duigan (Sylvia).

Rob McGregor is owner of a Balmain bookshop and involved in an open marriage with his wife Gretel, who is having an affair with Tim, one of her students. He is distressed to hear of the death of Lisa, whom he had known in the 60s when both were radical student activists. He befriends Lou, a prostitute and friend of Lisa, and tries to persuade her to give up drugs. Lou goes cold turkey at Rob's home, moves into Lisa's old room, and hopes for an affair with Rob; but he rejects her.

WITH LOVE TO THE PERSON NEXT TO ME (page 119)

p.c.: Standard Films. **p**: John Cruthers. **d, sc**: Brian McKenzie. **ph, ed**: Ray Argall. **p.d.**: Kerith Holmes. **sd**: Mark Tarpey. **p.m.**: Daniel Scharf. **a.d.**: Deborah Hoare. Fujicolor. 98 mins. Aust dist: AFI. 1987.

Kim Gyngell (Wallace), Paul Chubb (Sid), Barry Dickins (Bodger), Sally McKenzie (Gail), Beverley Gardiner (Irene), Phil Motherwell (Drunk).

Wallace, a Melbourne taxi-driver, lives alone in a small apartment near the sea. He secretly tapes the conversations he has with his passengers. Meanwhile, his neighbour Gail, a factory-worker, is fed up with her relationship with Sid who, with his friend Bodger, is forever stealing electrical goods. But nothing comes of her relationship with Wallace.

WITH PREJUDICE (page 225)

p.c.: Sirocco Visual Prod. **ex.p**: Jim George. **p**: Don Catchlove. **d**: Esben Storm. **sc**: Leon Saunders. **ph**: Peter Levy. Colour. 73 mins. Aust dist: AFI. 1982.

Scott Burgess (Ross Dunn), John Ley (Tim Anderson), Terry Serio (Paul Alister), David Slingsby (Richard Seary), Chris Haywood (Det. Rogerson), Max Cullen (Det. Krawczyk), Richard Moir (Det. Middleton), John Clayton (Det. Burke), Redmond Phillips (Judge Nagle), Tony Barry (Adams), David Downer (Einfeld), Tim McKenzie (Tueno), Peter Whitford (Bodor).

The trial of Ross Dunn, Tim Anderson and Paul Alister, accused of the 1978 Hilton Hotel bombing. Evidence is given by Richard Seary, a police informer who infiltrated the Ananda Marga sect of which the three were members.

WITH TIME TO KILL (page 244)

p.c.: Chair Films. **p, d, sc**: James Clayden. **ph, a.d.**: Laurie McInnes. **ed**: Gary Hillberg. **m**: Chris Knowles, Stephen Cummings, Ollie Olsen. **sd**: Steve Burgess. **a.p.**: Fred Harden. Colour. 71 mins. 1987.

Ian Scott (Lt Nick Yates), Elizabeth Huntley (Louise Yates), James Clayden (Sgt Max Clements), Lin Van Hek (Janet Golding), Peter Green (The Laundryman), John Howard (Adam Sayer), Barry Dickins (Terry Bendix), Tim Robertson (Jack Keane), Nigel Buesst (Wilson Man

Tw   policemen, Yates and Clen   courts are not doing their job and that it is time to 'get rid of the garbage'; their targets include crime kingpin The Laundryman.

WRONG SIDE OF THE ROAD (page 207)

p.c.: Imma Prods. **p, sc**: Ned Lander, Graeme Isaac. **d**: Ned Lander. **ph**: Louis Irving. **ed**: John Scott. **m**: Us Mob, No Fixed Address. **p.d.**: Jan Mackay. **sd**: Lloyd Carrick. Colour. 79 mins. Aust dist: AFI. 1981.

1981 Australian Film Awards: Jury Prize.

Les Graham, Peter Butler, Bart Willoughby, Ronnie Ansell, Veronica Rankine, Leila Rankine, Veronica Brodie, Gayle Rankine (Us Mob/No Fixed Address), Chris Haywood (Cop).

Two Aboriginal rock bands, Us Mob and No Fixed Address, tour Australia meeting hostility and harassment from white authorities along the way.

WRONG WORLD (page 157)

p.c.: Seon Films. **ex.p**: Basia Puska. **p**: Bryce Menzies. **d**: Ian Pringle. **sc**: Doug Ling. **ph, ed**: Ray Argall. **m**: Eric Gradman. **p.d.**: Christine Johnson. **sd**: Bruce Emery. **p.m.**: Andrew Wiseman. **a.d.**: Lucy McLaren. Colour. 97 mins. Aust dist: AFI. 1984.

1985 Berlin Film Festival: Best actress (Jo Kennedy).

Richard Moir (David Trueman), Jo Kennedy (Mary), Nicolas Lathouris (Rangott), Robbie McGregor (Robert), Esben Storm (Laurence), Tim Robinson (Psychiatrist).

David Trueman, a doctor recently returned from Bolivia, where he became hooked on drugs, meets up with Mary, a country girl who became addicted in Melbourne. The two team up to drive to Mary's sister's home, and find out more about each other along the way.

THE YEAR MY VOICE BROKE
(page 348)

p.c.: Kennedy Miller. **p**: Terry Hayes, Doug Mitchell, George Miller (1). **d, sc**: John Duigan. **ph**: Geoff Burton. **ed**: Neil Thumpston. **m**: Christine Woodruff. **p.d.**: Roger Ford. **sd**: Ross Linton. **a.p.**: Barbara Gibbs. **p.m.**: Dixie Betts. **a.d.**: Charles Rotherham. Colour. 103 mins. Aust dist: Hoyts. US dist: Avenue. UK dist: Palace Pictures. 1987.

1987 Australian Film Awards: Best film, director, original screenplay, supporting actor (Ben Mendelsohn), AFI Members Prize.

Noah Taylor (Danny Embling), Loene Carmen (Freya Olsen), Ben Mendelsohn (Trevor), Graeme Blundell (Nils Olsen), Lynette Curran (Anne Olsen), Malcolm Robertson (Bruce Embling), Judi Farr (Sheila Embling), Tim Robertson (Bob Leishman), Bruce Spence (Jonah), Harold Hopkins (Tom Alcock), Anja Coleby (Gail Olsen), Kylie Ostara (Alison), Kelly Dingwall (Barry), Colleen Clifford (Gran Olsen), Vincent Ball (Headmaster), Mary Regan (Miss McCall), Allan Penney (Martin), Queenie Ashton (Mrs O'Neil), Nick Tate (Sgt Pierce).

1962. Danny Embling, fifteen, lives with his parents, who run the only hotel in a small NSW town. Since childhood, he has been a close friend of Freya Olsen, but now she wants the company of older boys, especially the raucous Trevor. Increasingly unhappy about being left on the outside, Danny discovers that Freya was actually the daughter of a young prostitute who died giving birth to her. Trevor goes on a foolish rampage and is imprisoned. He escapes, and is killed in the ensuing police chase. Now pregnant, Freya decides to leave for the city, and says a sad goodbye to Danny.

THE YEAR OF LIVING DANGEROUSLY (page 166)

p.c.: McElroy & McElroy Prods, for MGM-UA. A Freddie Fields presentation. **p**: James McElroy. **d**: Peter Weir. **sc**: David Williamson, Peter Weir, C. J. Koch (from the novel by C. J. Koch). **ph**: Russell Boyd. **2nd unit ph**: John Seale. **ed**: William Anderson. **m**: Maurice Jarre. **p.d.**: Herbert Pinter. **sd**: Gary Wilkins. **p.m., a.d.**: Mark Egerton. Panavision. Metrocolor. 113 mins. Aust (and Intl) dist: UIP. US dist: MGM-UA. 1982.

1983 Australian Film Awards: Jury Prize to Peter Weir and Linda Hunt.

Mel Gibson (Guy Hamilton), Sigourney Weaver (Jill Bryant), Linda Hunt (Billy Kwan), Bembol Roco (Kumar), Domingo Landicho (Hortona), Michael Murphy (Pete Curtis), Noel Ferrier (Wally O'Sullivan), Bill Kerr (Col Henderson).

Indonesia, 1965. Guy Hamilton, a journalist employed by the Australian Broadcasting Service, arrives in Jakarta and is overwhelmed by the complexities of the political situation. Billy Kwan, a diminutive Chinese-Australian photographer, acts as his colleague and tutor, arranging an interview with the head of the Communist Party and a meeting with beautiful Jill Bryant from the British Embassy. Billy becomes increasingly disillusioned with President Sukarno when a child he has been supporting dies: during a protest, Billy is killed. Guy and Jill, by now in love, decide to leave, but with the declaration of martial law, Guy is arrested and badly beaten. Knowing he may lose an eye unless he has hospital treatment, Guy heads for the airport and makes the last plane out.

YOUNG EINSTEIN (page 315)

p.c.: Serious Productions. **ex.p**: Graham Burke, Ray Beattie. **p**: Yahoo Serious, Warwick Ross, David Roach. **d, ed**: Yahoo Serious. **sc**: Yahoo Serious, David Roach. **ph**: Jeff Darling. **m**: William Motzing, Martin Armiger, Tommy Tycho. **p.d.**: Steve Marr. **sd**: Geoff Grist. **p.m.**: Antonia Barnard. **a.d.**: Keith Heygate. **a.p.**: Lulu Pinkus. **choreog.**: Aku Kadogo. Colour. 89 mins. Aust dist: Roadshow. Intl dist: Warner Bros. 1986–8.

1986 Australian Film Awards: Best music.

Yahoo Serious (Albert Einstein), Odile Le Clezio (Marie Curie), John Howard (Preston Preston), Peewee Wilson (Mr Einstein), Su Cruickshank (Mrs Einstein), Lulu Pinkus (Blonde), Kaarin Fairfax (Brunette), Michael Lake (Hotel manager), Jonathan Coleman (Wolfgang Bavarian), Roger Ward (Cat Pie Cook), Max Meldrum (Mr Curie), Rose Jackson (Mrs Curie), Basil Clarke (Charles Darwin), Esben Storm (Wilbur Wright), Tim McKew (Sigmund Freud), Phillipa Baker (Freud's mother).

Tasmania, 1905. Young Albert Einstein, son of a simple apple farmer, is a prodigious inventor who formulates a theory of relativity and succeeds in splitting a (beer) atom. He heads for mainland Australia, meeting charming Marie Curie and devious businessman Preston Preston en route. At the Lonely Street hotel, he invents rock 'n' roll before being thrown into a lunatic asylum at the behest of Preston (out to steal his patents). Albert escapes and follows Marie to Paris where Preston is about to unveil a dangerous atomic beer barrel at the 1906 Science Academy Awards. Albert's electric guitar defuses the dangerous energy source.

ZOMBIE BRIGADE

p.c.: CM Films. **p**: Carmelo Musca. **d, sc**: Barrie Pattison. **ph**: Alex McPhee. **ed**: Tan Thien Tai. **m**: John Charles, Todd Hunter. **p.d.**: Julieanne Mills. **sd**: Hugo Cleverly. **p.m.**: Frances Walker. **a.d.**: Gerard Letts. Colour. 95 mins. 1988.

John Moore (Jimmy), Khym Lam (Yoshie), Geoff Gibbs (Mayor Ransom), Adam A. Wong (Kinoshita), Maggie Wilde West (Madam Rita), Bob Faggetter (Wild), Leslie Wright (Const. Bill Jackson), Michael Fuller (Uncle Charlie).

Lizard Gully, WA. Mayor Ransom has solved the rural depression by selling land to a Japanese company to build a theme park, not caring that the area includes a memorial to veterans of the Vietnam War. When the memorial is destroyed, vets emerge in the form of fanged zombies, after human blood. Jimmy, an Aboriginal, seeks the advice of Uncle Charlie and succeeds in defeating the zombies and winning the hand of Yoshie, assistant to the Japanese developers.

There follows a provisional list of feature films completed in 1990. Credits and other information may be incomplete.

AYA

p.c.: Goshu Films. **p**: Denise Patience, Solrun Hoaas. **d, sc**: Solrun Hoaas. **ph**: Geoff Burton. **ed**: Stewart Young. **p.d.**: Jennie Tate. **sd**: Ben Osmo. **p.m.**: Robert Kewley. **a.d.**: Euan Keddie. Fujicolor. Aust dist: Ronin Films. 1990.

Eri Ishida (Aya), Nicholas Eadie (Frank), Chris Haywood (Mac), Miki Oikawa (Junko), John O'Brien (Karo), Mayumi Hoskin (Nancy), Marion Heathfield (Lorna), Tim Robertson (Willy).

Frank marries Aya at the end of the war and brings her back to live in Melbourne.

BEYOND MY REACH

p.c.: Boulevard Films. **ex.p**: Peter Boyle. **p**: Frank Howson. **d**: Dan Burstall. **sc**: Frank Howson, Philip Dalkin. **ph**: Peter Bilcock. **ed**: Peter Carrodus. **p.d.**: Tel Stolfo. **sd**: John Phillips. **line p**: Barbi Taylor. **p.m.**: Lesley Parker. **a.d.**: Brian Giddens. Colour. 1990.

Terri Garber (Terri Neilson), David Roberts (Christopher Brookes), Alan Fletcher (Alex Gower), Nicholas Hammond (Steven Schaffer), Nancy Black (Jennifer Sellers), Belinda Davey (Emma), Christine Harris (Jade), Nicki Wendt (Pam), Jon Craig (Curt D'Angelo), Constance Landsberg (Sally), Chuck McKinney (Phil).

Christopher Brookes, a film director, is a close friend of Alex Gower, a writer. After success in Australia, they decide to try their luck in Hollywood, but the pressures there result in a breach of the friendship. Years later, they meet again.

THE BIG STEAL

p.c.: Cascade Films. **p**: Nadia Tass, David Parker. **d**: Nadia Tass. **sc, ph**: David Parker. **ed**: Peter Carrodius. **p.d.**: Patrick Reardon. **sd**: John Wilkinson. **co-p**: Timothy White. **a.p.**: Bryce Menzies. **p.m.**: Catherine Bishop. **a.d.**: Tony Mahood. Colour. 1990.

Ben Mendelsohn (Danny Clark), Claudia Karvan (Joanna Johnson), Steve Bisley (Gordon Farkas), Angelo D'Angelo (Vangeli Petrakis), Damon Herriman (Mark Jorgensen), Marshall Napier (Mr Clark), Maggie King (Mrs Clark), Tim Robertson (Mr Johnson).

Seventeen-year-old Danny buys an old Jag to impress his girlfriend, Joanna; but the car is nothing but trouble.

BLOODMOON

p.c.: Village Roadshow Pictures. **ex.p**: Graham Burke, Greg Coote. **p**: Stanley O'Toole. **d**: Alec Mills. **sc**: Robert Brennan. **ph**: John Stokes. **ed**: David Halliday. **m**: Brian May. **p.d.**: Philip Warner. **sd**: Ian Grant. **ass. p**: David Munro. **p.m.**: Judy Hamilton. **a.d.**: Bruce Redman. colour. 102 mins. Aust dist: Roadshow. 1990.

Leon Lissek (Myles Sheffield), Christine Amor (Virginia Sheffield), Ian Williams (Kevin), Helen Thomson (Mary Huston).

An unseen killer is garrotting teenage couples who attend neighboring schools.

BLOOD OATH (page 47)

p.c.: Blood Oath Productions. **p**: Charles Waterstreet, Denis Whitburn, Brian Williams. **line p**: Richard Brennan. **d**: Stephen Wallace. **sc**: Denis Whitburn, Brian Williams. **ph**: Russell Boyd. **ed**: Nicholas Beauman. **p.d.**: Bernard Hides. **sd**: Ben Osmo. **co-p**: Annie Bleakley. **p.m.**: Helen Watts. **a.d.**: Chris Webb. Eastmancolour. Aust dist: Roadshow. 1990.

Bryan Brown (Capt. Robert Cooper), George Takei (Vice-Admiral Baron Takahashi), Deborah Unger (Sister Littell), Nicholas Eadie (Sgt Keenan), John Clarke (Sheedy), Ray Barrett (Judge), Jason Donovan (Talbot), John Polson (Jimmy Fenton), Russell Crowe (Lt Corbet), Terry O'Quinn (Beckett).

Ambon Island, 1945. The war is over, and Capt. Cooper has been assigned the task of prosecuting Japanese in charge of the POW camp on the island. Cooper is convinced the island's commandant, Baron Takahashi, ordered the beating of prisoners and the execution of captured pilots; but Takahashi is protected by an American security man, Beckett, and exonerated. Tanaka, a Japanese Christian and signals officer, gives himself up and eventually confesses he executed Eddie Fenton, a captured pilot, on Takahashi's orders. Tanaka is executed.

BREAKAWAY

p.c.: Ukiyo Films, Breakaway Films, in ass. with Smart Egg–Cinema Enterprises. **ex.p**: Les Lithgow. **p, d**: Don McLennan. **sc**: Jan Sardi. **ph, ed**: Zbigniew Friedrich. **p.d.**: Paddy Reardon. **sd**: Lloyd Carrick. **co-p**: Jane Ballantyne. **p.m., a.d.**: Euan Keddie. Colour. 1990.

Bruce Boxleitner (Joey), Bruce Myles (Reginald), Deborah Unger (Marion), Toni Scanlan (Hilda), Terry Gill (Hank Stardust).

Joey, a convict on the run, kidnaps Reginald, a mild-mannered accountant.

CONFIDENCE

p.c.: Confidence Productions. **p**: Ben Gannon. **d**: Michael Jenkins. **sc**: Tony Morphett (from an idea by Morphett and Bryan Brown). **ph**: Russell Boyd. **ed**: Neil Thompson. **p.d.**: John Stoddart. **sd**: Gary Wilkins. **p.m.**: Adrienne Read. **a.d.**: Chris Webb. Colour. 1990.

Bryan Brown (Harry), Karen Allen (Julie), Justin Resnick (David), Bill Kerr (Cec), Chris Haywood (Bostock), Bruce Spence (Foster), Bruce Myles (Scraper), Ben Franklin (Larsen), Paul Chubb (Billy), Peter Hehir (Giles).

Harry Reynolds, a con-man, arrives in Beachport to ply his trade but becomes attached to the people of this small community.

THE CROSSING

p.c.: Beyond International Group. **ex.p**: Al Clark, Phil Gerlach. **p**: Sue Seeary. **d**: George Ogilvie. **sc**: Ranald Allan. **ph**: Jeff Darling. **ed**: Henry Dangar. **p.d.**: Igor Nay. **sd**: David Lee. **p.m.**: Debbie Samuels. **a.d.**: Chris Webb. Colour. Aust dist: Hoyts. 1990.

Russell Crowe (Johnny), Robert Mammone (Sam), Danielle Spencer (Meg), Rodney Bell (Shorty), Emily Lumbers (Jenny), John Blair (Billy), Megan Connelly (Kathleen), Warren Coleman (Clag), Patrick Ward (Nev), May Lloyd (Peg), Daphne Gray (Jean), George Whaley (Sid).

A small country town in the early sixties. During the Anzac Day dawn service, teenage Meg is making love in a barn with her boyfriend, Johnny, when they're discovered by her father. Meanwhile, Meg's previous boyfriend, Sam, who had left to find work as an artist in the city, makes a surprise return. During the course of the day, Meg has to decide between the two, but in the end tragedy intervenes.

DEAD SLEEP

p.c.: Village Roadshow Pictures. **p**: Stanley O'Toole. **d**: Alec Mills. **sc**: Michael Rymer. **ph**: John Stokes. **ed**: David Halliday. **p.d.**: Phil Warner. **ass.p**: David Munro. **p.m.**: Rose Spokes. Aust dist: Roadshow. 1990.

Tony Bonner, Sueyan Cox, Linda Blair, christine Amor.

A thriller set in a psychiatric hospital.

DEAD TO THE WORLD

p.c.: Huzzah Prods. **p**: John Cruthers. **d,sc**: Ross Gibson. **ph**: Jane Castle. **ed**: Andrew Plain. **p.d.**: Edie Kurzer. **sd**: Bronwyn Murphy. **co-p, p.m.**: Adrienne Parr. **a.d.**: Corrie Soeterboek. Fujicolor. 1990.

Richard Roxburgh (Johnny), Agnieszka Perepeczko (Alexandra), Tibor Gyapjas (Manny), Lynette Curran (Pearl), John Doyle (Mr Keats), Gandhi MacIntyre (Lester), Noah Taylor (Skip), Kris Greaves (Kogarah), Paul Chubb (Sgt. Jack Grant), Paul Goddard (Bobby).

A drama set around a gym in a Sydney inner suburb and the world of boxing.

DEATH IN BRUNSWICK

p.c.: Meridian Films. **ex. p**: Bryce Menzies. **p**: Timothy White. **d**: John Ruane. **sc**: John Ruane, Boyd Oxlade. **ph**: Ellery Ryan. **ed**: Neil Thumpston. **p.d.**: Chris Kennedy. **sd**: Lloyd Carrick. **ass. p, p.m.**: Lynda House. **a.d.**: John Wild. Eastmancolour. 1990.

Sam Neill (Carl Fitzgerald), Zoe Carides (Sophie Papafagos), John Clarke (Dave).

Carl, chef in a seedy rock club, becomes involved with Sophie, an attractive young Greek-Australian.

DINGO

p.c.: Gevest Australia-AO Prods/SARL (Paris). **ex. p**: Giorgio Draskovic, Marie Pascale Osterrieth. **p**: Marc Rosenberg, Rolf de Heer. **d**: Rolf de Heer. **sc**: Marc Rosenberg. **ph**: Denis Lenoir. **ed**: Surresh Ayyar. **m**: Michel Legrand, Miles Davis. **p.d.**: Judi Russell. **p.m.**: Dixie Betts. **a.d.**: Christian Faure. 1990.

Colin Friels, Miles Davis, Helen Buday, Bernadette Lafont, Joe Petruzzi.

A young outback Australian travels to Paris to play jazz.

FATHER

p.c.: Transcontinental Films. **ex.p**: Paul Barron. **p**: Damien Parer, Tony Cavanaugh, Graham Hartley. **d**: John Power. **sc**: Tony Cavanaugh, Graham Hartley. **ph**: Dan Burstall. **ed**: Kerry Regan. **m**: Peter Best. **p.d.**: Phil Peters. **sd**: Andrew Ramage. **p.m.**: John Wild. **a.d.**: Stuart Wood. Eastmancolour. Dist: Left Bank Productions. 1990.

Max Von Sydow (Joe Mueller), Carol Drinkwater (Anne Winton), Julia Blake (Iya Zetnick), Steve Jacobs (Bobby Winton), Tim Robertson (George Coleman).

The normal life of Anne and Bobby Winton is shattered when Anne's father Joe, who lives with them, is accused by Iya Zetnick of being involved in Nazi war crimes.

FLYNN

p.c.: Boulevard Films. **ex.p**: Peter Boyle. **p**: Frank Howson. **d**: Brian Kavanagh. **sc**: Frank Howson, Alister Webb. **ph**: John Wheeler. **ed**: Tim Lewis. **p.d.**: Brian Dusting. **sd**: John Rowley. **line p**: Barbi Taylor. **p.m.**: Tatts Bishop. **a.d.**: Carolynne Cunningham. Colour. 1990.

Guy Pearce (Errol Flynn), Paul Cantoni (Klaus Reicher), Rebecca Rigg (Penelope Watts), John

Frawley (Headmaster), Jan Friedl (Deirdre Watts), Sue Jones (Elsa Chauvel).

The young Errol Flynn enjoys wild times as a young man in Tasmania before becoming involved with Sydney's notorious razor gangs. He then travels to New Guinea to take part in the gold rush. He scores a small role in the Australian film, *In the Wake of the 'Bounty'*, and heads overseas in search of fame and fortune.

FLIRTING

p.c.: Kennedy-Miller. **p**: George Miller (1), Terry Hayes, Doug Mitchell. **d, sc**: John Duigan. **ph**: Geoff Burton. **ed**: Robert Gibson. **p.d.**: Roger Ford. **sd**: Ross Linton. **a.p., p.m.**: Barbara Gibbs. **a.d.**: Charles Rotherham. Eastmancolour. 1990.

Noah Taylor (Danny Embling), Tandy Newton (Thandiwe Adjewa), Nicole Kidman (Nicola), Kym Wilson (Melissa), Naomi Watts (Janet), Bartholomew Rose (Gilby), Marshall Napier (Mr Elliott), Jeff Truman (Mr Cutts), Jane Harders (Miss Anderson), Maggie Blinco (Miss McCready).

Danny Embling leaves his home in the NSW tablelands to go to boarding school, where he meets, and falls in love with, Thandiwe, daughter of an African academic (temporarily in Australia on a lecture assignment). At the end of his school years, in 1968, Danny finds himself in Paris during the student demonstrations.

GOLDEN BRAID (page 129)

p.c.: Illumination Films. **ex.p**: William Marshall. **p, d**: Paul Cox. **sc**: Paul Cox, Barry Dickins (from a story by Guy de Maupassant). **ph**: Nino Martinetti. **ed**: Russell Hurley. **p.d.**: Neil Angwin. **sd**: Jim Currie. **line p**: Paul Ammitzboll. **p.m.**: Santhana Naidu. Eastmancolour. 1990.

Chris Haywood (Bernard), Gosia Dobrowolska (Terese), Paul Chubb (Joseph), Norman Kaye (Psychiatrist), Monica Maughan (Antique Shop Owner), Marion Heathfield (Cleaning Woman), Barry Dickins (Barber), Mark Little (Nazi Punk), Robert Menzies (Ernst), Jo Kennedy (Paradise), Paul Cox (Priest).

Bernard, an eccentric collector of clocks, is having a secret affair with Terese, wife of a Salvation Army Major, Joseph. He also becomes besotted with a braid of golden hair, which he sleeps with.

HARBOUR BEAT (page 244)

p.c.: Palm Beach Pictures. **p**: David Elfick, Irene Dobson. **d**: David Elfick. **sc**: Morris Gleitzman. **ph**: Ellery Ryan. **ed**: Stuart Armstrong. **p.d.**: Michael Bridges. **sd**: Paul Brincat. **p.m.**: Catherine Knapman. **a.d.**: Colin Fletcher. Eastmancolour. 1990.

John Hannah (Neal McBride), Steven Vidler (Lancelot Cooper), Gary Day (Walker), Bill Young (Cimino), Emily Simpson (Mason), Peta Toppano.

Neal McBride, a Glasgow policeman, is transferred to Sydney where he teams up with local cop Lance Cooper.

HOLIDAYS ON THE RIVER YARRA

P.C.: Jungle Pictures. **p**: Fiona Cochrane. **d, sc, ed**: Leo Berkeley. **ph**: Brendan Lavelle. **m**: Sam Melet. **p.d.**: Margaret Eastgate, Adele Flere. **p.m.**: Peter Jordan. 1990.

Craig Adams, Luke Elliott, Tahir Cambis, Alex Menglet.

A pair of unemployed teenagers become involved with a gang of mercenaries planning to fight in Africa.

HUNTING

p.c.: Boulevard Films. **ex.p**: Peter Boyle. **p, d, sc**: Frank Howson. **ph**: David Connell, Dan Burstall. **ed**: Philip Reid. **p.d.**: Jon Dowding. **sd**: John Rowley. **line p**: Barbi Taylor. **p.m.**: Lesley Parker. **a.d.**: John Powditch. Colour. 1990.

John Savage (Michael Bergman), Kerry Armstrong (Michelle Harris), Jeffrey Thomas (Larry Harris), Rebecca Rigg (Debbie McCormick), Rhys McConnochie (Mr Stockton), Ian Scott (Holmes), Stephen Whittaker (Roberts), Guy Pearce (Sharp), Nicholas Bell (Piggott), Stacey Valkenburg (Young Michelle).

A young married secretary from a stockbroking firm falls in love with the company's most important client. She is dazzled by his wealth and glamorous lifestyle until she agrees to stay at his secluded country estate. It is there that events come to a surprising and explosive climax, leaving her longing for the safety of the world she has turned her back upon.

A KINK IN THE PICASSO

p.c.: Rosa Colosimo Productions. **ex.p**: Rosa Colosimo. **p**: Will Spencer. **d**: Mark Gracie. **sc**: Hugh Stuckey. **ph**: Jaems Grant. **ed**: Edward McQueen Mason. **p.m.**: Veronica Toole. **a.d.**: Ray Hennessy. Eastmancolour. 1990.

Jane Menz (Alex), Jane Clifton (Bella), Jon Finlayson (Lionel), Andrew Daddo (Nick), Tiriel Mora (Stan), Peter Farago (Harvey), Michael Bishop (Tony), Femi Taylòr (Nadia), Peter Hosking (Minister).

A comedy about a stolen Picasso.

THE PUNISHER

p.c.: New World Pictures (Aust.). **p, sc**: Robert Kamen. **d**: Mark Goldblatt. **ph**: Ian Baker. **ed**: Tim Wellburn. **p.d.**: Norma Moriceau. **sd**: David

Lee. **co-p**: Su Armstrong. **p.m.**: Tony Winley. **a.d.**: Philip Hearnshaw. **sp. ef.**: Steve Courtley. **stunts**: Chris Anderson. Eastmancolour. Aust dist: Roadshow. US dist: New World. 1990.

Dolph Lundgren (Frank Castle, The Punisher), Lou Gossett (Berkowitz), Jeroen Krabbe (Franco), Kim Miyori (Lady Tanaka), Nancy Everhard (Sam Leary), Barry Otto (Shake), Bryan Marshall (Moretti), Brian Rooney (Tommy), Todd Boyce (Tarrone), Stan Kouros (Deleo).

Frank Castle, a cop, goes underground when his family is killed by crime lords. When the Yakuza move in on the local criminals, Castle is able to step aside—until the Yakuza kidnap the children of their rivals.

QUIGLEY DOWN UNDER
p.c.: Quigley Down Under Prods. **ex.p**: Stanley O'Toole. **p**: Alex Rose. **d**: Simon Wincer. **sc**: John Hill. **ph**: David Eggby. **ed**: Adrian Carr. **p.d.**: Ross Major. **sd**: Lloyd Carrick. **p.m.**: Stephen Jones. **a.d.**: Bob Donaldson. Colour. Aust dist: Roadshow. 1990.

Tom Selleck (Matthew Quigley), Laura San Giacomo (Crazy Cora), Alan Rickman (Elliot Marston), Tonny Bonner (Dobkin), Chris Haywood (Major Ashley Pitt).

Quigley, an American cowboy, comes to Australia and becomes involved with Crazy Cora and a landowner out to exterminate Aborigines.

THE RETURNING
p.c.: Matte Box–David Hannay Prods. **ex. p**: David Hannay. **p**: Trishia Downie. **d**: John Day. **sc**: Arthur Baysting, John Day. **ph**: Kevin Haywood. **ed**: Simon Clothier. **m**: Clive Cockburn. **p.d.**: Mike Beacroft. **sd**: Mike Westhgate. **p.m.**: Kate Curtis. **a.d.**: Stewart Main. Eastmancolour. 1990.

Phillip Gordon (Allan Steadman), Alison Routledge (Jessica), Max Cullen (Donahue), Jim Moriarty (George), Terrance Cooper (Allan's father), Judie Douglas (Miriam), Grant Tilly (Dr Pitts).

SHER MOUNTAIN KILLINGS MYSTERY
p.c.: Intertropic Films. **ex. p**: Peter Taylor. **p**: Phillip Avalon. **d**: Vince Martin. **sc**: Dennis Whitburn. **ph**: Ray Henman. **ed**: Ted Otten. **m**: Art Phillips. **p.d.**: Keith Holloway. **sd**: Bob Clayton. **p.m.**: Veronica Sive. **a.d.**: Robin Newell. Colour. 86 mins. 1990.

Tom Richards (Alex Cordeaux), Phil Avalon (Caine Cordeaux), Abigail (Muriel), Elizabeth McIvor (Dianne), Ron Beck (Sole), Joe Bugner (The Ranger), Jeffrey Rhoe (Davy Joe).

Caine who possesses mystic powers though he is retarded, is taken on a hunting trip by his brother; meanwhile, a trio of villains seeking a valuable stone, arrive in the area.

STRANGERS
p.c.: Genesis Films. **p**: Craig Lahiff, Wayne Groom. **d**: Craig Lahiff. **sc**: John Emery. **ph**: Steve Arnold. **ed**: Denise Haratzis. **p.d.**: Derek Mills. **sd**: Mike Piper. **p.m.**: Ron Stigwood. **a.d.**: Soren Jensen. Colour. 1990.

James Healey (Gary), Anne Looby (Anna), Melissa Docker (Rebecca), Tim Robertson (King), Jim Holt (Graham), Geoff Morrell (Frank), Mary Regan (Joanne), John Clayton (Agent).

Gary, a young stockbroker, meets Anna on a plane: he becomes involved in a passionate liaison which leads to ruin and death.

STRUCK BY LIGHTNING
p.c.: Dark Horse Pictures. **ex. p**: Terry Charatsis. **p, sc**: Trevor Farrant. **d**: Jerzy Domaradzki. **ph**: Yuri Sokol. **ed**: Simon James. **m**: Paul Smyth. **p.d.**: Peta Lawson. **sd**: Toivo Lember. **line p**: Su Armstrong. **p.m.**: Lesley Parker. **a.d.**: David Wolfe-Barry. Fujicolor. 109 mins. 1990.

Garry McDonald (Ollie Rennie), Brian Vriends (Pat Cannizzaro), Catherine McClements (Jill McHugh), Brian M. Logan (Kevin), Henry Salter (Noel), Syd Brisbane (Spencer), Briony Williams (Gail), Denis Moore (Foster), Su Cruickshank (Chicquita), Maria Donato (Mama), Vittorio Andreacchio (Papa), Judith Stratford (Mrs Reschke), Dennis Olsen (David Barnabus), Daphne Grey (Margaret McMaster).

Pat Cannizzaro, a phys. ed. teacher, is fired from the Education Department and gets a job at Saltmarsh, a home for physically disabled adults which is managed by alcoholic Ollie Rennie, a self-pitying failure hopelessly in love with social worker Jill McHugh. Pat, whose own brother is disabled, trains a team of male and female 'retards' (as Ollie calls them) to play soccer, and in doing so gives them all, including Ollie, self-respect.

TILL THERE WAS YOU
p.c.: Ayer Productions. **p**: Jim McElroy. **d**: John Seale. **sc**: Michael Thomas. **ph**: Geoff Simpson. **ed**: Jill Bilcock. **p.d.**: George Liddle. **sd**: Gary Wilkins. **line p**: Tim Sanders. **p.m.**: Grant Hill. **a.d.**: Steve Andrews. Colour. 1990.

Mark Harmon (Frank Flynn), Jeroen Krabbe (Viv), Deborah Unger (Anna), Shane Briant (Rex).

Frank Flynn, an American musician, arrives in Vanuatu and has a love affair with Anna, a married woman.

WAITING
P.C.: Filmside Prods. **ex. p**: Penny Chapman.

p: Ross Matthews. **d, sc**: Jackie McKimmie. **ph**: Steve Mason. **ed**: Mike Honey. **p.d.**: Murray Picknett. **p.m.**: Carol Chirlian. Eastmancolour. Aust dist: Ronin. 1990.

Noni Hazlehurst (Clare), John Hargreaves (Michael), Deborra-Lee Furness (Sandy), Ray Barrett, Frank Whitten, Noga Bernstein, Helen Jones, Fiona Press, Denis Moore.

Clare is a surrogate mother-to-be on behalf of her best friend, Sandy. Friends congregate to the isolated farmhouse where she's about to give birth.

WEEKEND WITH KATE

p.c.: Phillip Emanuel Productions. **ex.p.**: Phillip Emanuel. **p**: David C. J. Douglas. **d**: Arch Nicholson. **sc**: Henry Tefay, Kee Young. **ph**: Dan Burstall. **ed**: Rose Evans. **m**: Peter Kaldor. **p.d.**: Larry Eastwood. **sd**: Tim Lloyd. **p.m.**: Sally Ayre-Smith. **a.d.**: Bob Donaldson. Colour. 1990.

Colin Friels (Richard), Catherine McClements (Kate), Jerome Ehlers (Jon Thorne), Helen Mutkins (Carla), Kate Sheil (Phoebe).

The marriage of Richard, a PR man, and Kate, is heading for the rocks, and Kate has planned an intimate weekend to improve things. But Richard, whose mistress, Carla, is getting possessive, comes home with Jon Thorne, a rock star, to whom the vulnerable Kate finds herself attracted.

WENDY CRACKED A WALNUT

p.c.: Classic Films, in association with the ABC. **ex.p**: Brian Rosen, Sandra Levy. **p**: John Edwards. **d**: Michael Pattinson. **sc**: Suzanne Hawley. **ph**: Jeffrey Malouf. **ed**: Michael Honey. **m**: Bruce Smeaton. **p.d.**: Leigh Tierney. **sd**: Nicholas Wood. **a.p.**: Ray Brown. **p.m.**: Susan Wild. **a.d.**: Scott Hartford-Davis. Colour. Aust dist: Hoyts. 1990.

Rosanna Arquette (Wendy), Bruce Spence (Ronnie), Hugo Weaving (Jake), Kerry Walker (Deirdre), Doreen Warburton (Elsie), Desiree Smith (Cynthia), Susan Lyons (Caroline), Barry Jenkins (Pierre), Betty Lucas (Mrs Taggart), Douglas Hedge (Mr Leveredge).

Wendy works in a shoe factory and is married to Ronnie, a good-natured, hard-working, predictable confectionery salesman. When she meets Jake in a supermarket there is an immediate attraction: but whom will she choose, Ronnie or handsome, romantic Jake?

• INDEX •

E ntries in italics are book or film titles. Italic page numbers indicate an illustration. Page numbers in bold type refer to the appendices, giving all credits for films included.